Transactions of ADIA Lab

Interdisciplinary Advances in Data and Computational Science

ANNUAL ADIA LAB TRANSACTIONS IN DATA SCIENCE AND FINANCE

Print ISSN: 3082-8406
Online ISSN: 3082-8392

Series Editor: Horst Simon *(ADIA Lab, United Arab Emirates)*

The Transactions of ADIA Lab is an interdisciplinary series capturing cutting-edge advances in computational and data science. Focusing on areas such as AI for medical applications, climate modeling, and infrastructure sustainability, it bridges academia and industry. This book series showcases peer-reviewed research, insights from global collaborations, and innovative methodologies that drive the forefront of data-intensive research.

Published

Vol. 1 *Transactions of ADIA Lab:*
Interdisciplinary Advances in Data and Computational Science
edited by Horst Simon

More information on this series can also be found at https://www.worldscientific.com/series/aaltdsf

Annual ADIA Lab Transactions in Data Science and Finance – Volume 1

Transactions of ADIA Lab

Interdisciplinary Advances in Data and Computational Science

Editor

Horst Simon

ADIA Lab, United Arab Emirates

World Scientific

NEW JERSEY • LONDON • SINGAPORE • BEIJING • SHANGHAI • TAIPEI • CHENNAI

Published by

ADIA Lab RSC Limited
Level 26, Al Khatem Tower, Abu Dhabi, U.A.E.

and

World Scientific Publishing Co. Pte. Ltd.

5 Toh Tuck Link, Singapore 596224

USA office: 27 Warren Street, Suite 401-402, Hackensack, NJ 07601

UK office: 57 Shelton Street, Covent Garden, London WC2H 9HE

British Library Cataloguing-in-Publication Data
A catalogue record for this book is available from the British Library.

Annual ADIA Lab Transactions in Data Science and Finance — Vol. 1
TRANSACTIONS OF ADIA LAB
Interdisciplinary Advances in Data and Computational Science

ISBN 978-981-98-1303-2 (hardcover)
ISBN 978-981-98-1304-9 (ebook for institutions)
ISBN 978-981-98-1305-6 (ebook for individuals)

For any available supplementary material, please visit
https://www.worldscientific.com/worldscibooks/10.1142/14310#t=suppl

Desk Editor: Jiang Yulin

Typeset by Diacritech Technologies Pvt. Ltd.
Chennai - 600106, India

https://doi.org/10.1142/9789819813049_fmatter

Contents

https://doi.org/10.1142/9789819813049_fmatter

About the Contributors

Vinicius V. L. Albani received the B Math degree from the Federal University of Rio de Janeiro, Rio de Janeiro, Brazil, in 2006, the MSc degree from the Institute for Pure and Applied Mathematics (IMPA), Rio de Janeiro, in 2008, and the DSc degree in mathematics also from IMPA, in 2012. He is currently an assistant professor in the mathematics department at the Federal University of Santa Catarina, Florianopolis, Brazil. He has also taught graduate courses, including the Professional Master's Program on Mathematical Methods in Quantitative Finance at IMPA. He has supervised 12 MSc students and has been an active member of the organizing committee for events in the field of Quantitative Finance and Inverse Problems in Brazil, such as the Research in Options conferences since 2021, the 2024 World Congress of the Bachelier Finance Society, and the Applied Inverse Problems conference in 2025. He has published 27 articles in refereed journals and serves as an editorial board member of the Springer journal *Computational and Applied Mathematics*.

Alexandre Antonov received his PhD degree from the Landau Institute for Theoretical Physics in 1997. He worked for Numerix during 1998–2017, Danske Bank, as the Chief Analyst in Copenhagen, and is currently the Quantitative Research and Development Lead at Abu Dhabi Investment Authority (ADIA). His activity is concentrated on modeling and numerical methods for the sell side (interest rates, cross currency, hybrid, credit, and CVA/FVA/MVA) and, recently, for the buy-side applications. Alexandre is a published author for multiple publications in mathematical finance and a frequent speaker at financial conferences. He received a Quant of the Year Award from *Risk Magazine* in 2016.

Koushik Balasubramanian is a Quantitative Research and Development Lead at Abu Dhabi Investment Authority (ADIA). He earned his PhD in theoretical physics from MIT and was a postdoctoral researcher at Stony Brook. He began his financial career with Goldman Sachs and was an associate director in the Systematic Investment Strategies (SIS) within the Alpha Strategies group at Loomis, Sayles (Boston) before moving to ADIA. His research interests include the application of optimal transport, network analysis, topological data analysis, synthetic data generation, and related machine learning techniques to finance. He has published numerous papers in finance, string theory, and fluid dynamics, accumulating over 2,000 citations.

Alexandru Calotoiu is a scientist at ETH Zurich. His main research interests are the optimization of high-performance computing programs and performance modeling. He received his PhD in Computer Science from TU Darmstadt.

Joshua Chung is currently a data scientist for CrowdStrike Holdings, Inc. His work has been presented at SSDBM and been published in SSRN. His research is currently centered around leveraging machine learning to improve cybersecurity systems.

Manuel Jesús Cobo received his MSc and PhD degrees in Computer Science from the University of Granada, Spain, in 2008 and 2011, respectively. He is an associate professor in the Department of Computer Science and Artificial Intelligence at the University of Granada.

He is the principal developer of SciMAT, an open-access software tool for science mapping, widely used in bibliometric analysis and research evaluation. His research focuses on bibliometrics, science mapping, artificial intelligence, and data-driven approaches to understanding scientific and technological knowledge. He has published extensively in high-impact journals on topics such as emerging research areas, citation context analysis, international collaboration, gender disparities in science, and translational biomedical research.

Juan Manuel Corchado is the director of the BISITE Research Group (Bioinformatics, Intelligent Systems and Educational Technology) and director of the IoT Digital Innovation Hub. He is also a visiting professor at the Osaka Institute of Technology and a visiting professor at the Universiti Malaysia Kelantan. Juan M. Corchado has been vice-rector for research from 2013 to 2017 and director of the Science Park of the University of Salamanca. He was elected twice as Dean of the Faculty of Science, has been president of the IEEE Systems, Man and Cybernetics association, and academic coordinator of the University Institute for Research in Art and Animation Technology of the University of Salamanca, as well as a researcher at the Universities of Paisley (UK), Vigo (Spain), and the Plymouth Marine Laboratory (UK). He has also been a member of the Advisory Group on Online Terrorist Propaganda of the European Counter Terrorism Centre (EUROPOL) and has been a visiting professor at the University of Technology Malaysia. J. M. Corchado mainly works on projects related to artificial intelligence, machine learning, fintech, blockchain, cybersecurity, IoT, fog computing, edge computing, smart cities, smart grids, bioinformatics, neuroscience and sentiment analysis.

Javier Del Ser received his first PhD in telecommunication engineering (Cum Laude) from the University of Navarra, Spain, in 2006, and a second PhD in computational intelligence (Summa Cum Laude, Extraordinary Prize) from the University of Alcala, Spain, in 2013. He is a research professor in applied artificial intelligence at TECNALIA (Spain) and a distinguished research professor at the University of the Basque Country (UPV/EHU). His research interests gravitate on the use of artificial intelligence for data modeling and optimization problems arising in a diversity of fields, such as energy, transportation, health, and industry, among others. In these fields he has authored more than 450 scientific articles, co-supervised 20 PhD theses, edited six books, co-authored nine patents, and participated/led more than 60 research projects. He has received several recognitions for his research activity, including the BRTA Award for Excellence in Research (2023) and the IJCNN 2024 Best Paper Award. He is a senior member of IEEE and serves as an associate editor in several journals, including *Information Fusion and Swarm* and *Evolutionary Computation.*

Anurag Dipankar is the director of Science for EXCLAIM. He has extensive experience in climate and weather modeling, large-eddy simulation, and convection research. He received his PhD in Turbulence from Pierre and Marie Curie University in Paris in 2010.

Javier Parra Domínguez is an associate professor in the Department of Business and Economics Administration at the University of Salamanca. Since 2009, Javier has been complementing his work as a professor with the management of different technology departments in private companies.

He is a computer technician from the University of Wales and has a master's in macroeconometrics and finance from the Menéndez Pelayo International University, the Institute of Fiscal Studies, and the Centre for Economic and Commercial Studies of Spain. Javier is a member of the BISITE Research Group, where he develops his research interests related to economics, technological finance, econometrics, and digital intelligence.

Currently, Javier combines research at BISITE with his work at IoT Digital Innovation Hub, which has been founded with the objective of developing innovation in the Internet of Things of small and medium enterprises.

Behzad Azadie Faraz finished his BA and master of mathematics at Ecole Normale Superieure (Paris) and Sorbonne University and is now a PhD student of financial mathematics at Sharif University of Technology and a quantitative researcher at RiskLab, University of Toronto.

Oliver Fuhrer is the head of numerical prediction with MeteoSwiss, 8058, Zurich, Switzerland. His research interests include high-resolution numerical weather prediction and HPC for weather and climate. Fuhrer received his PhD degree in physics from ETH Zurich.

Nadia Karina Gamboa-Rosales received a bachelor's degree in chemical engineering from the Universidad Autónoma de Zacatecas (Mexico, 2006). She completed her MSc and PhD degrees in chemical engineering at the Universidad del País Vasco (Spain, 2008 and 2014). She has been actively involved in cooperation, innovation, energy and advanced manufacturing projects. She is currently collaborating as a researcher at the CONAHCYT—Consejo Nacional de Humanidades, Ciencias y Tecnologías (Mexico) and Universidad Autónoma de Zacatecas (Mexico).

David Garvin is the Head of Applications, Quantum Finance at Rigetti Computing. David focuses on researching, developing, and implementing financial industry applications of quantum computing. Previously, he worked in the Quantum Computing Office at NEC and at QxBranch, a quantum applications company acquired by Rigetti in 2019.

David has over 20 years' experience as a front-office quant in the finance industry. Previously, he served as the Global Head of Quantitative Analysis at the Commonwealth Bank of Australia. Prior to that, he was a director at Deutsche Bank and a Quant Analyst at Morgan Grenfell. He has covered all asset classes and been involved in management, modeling, risk and analytics, derivatives and structured products, machine learning, and electronic trading.

David holds a PhD in artificial intelligence from Cambridge University and an MBA (Exec) from the Australian Graduate School of Management. He has authored articles in finance, physics, engineering, classical computing, and quantum computing.

Thomas Hardjono is the CTO of Connection Science and Engineering at MIT in Cambridge, Massachusetts. He is an early pioneer in the field of digital identities and trusted hardware, and was instrumental in the development and broad adoption of the MIT Kerberos authentication protocol. He is active in leading standardization efforts across several industry forums, including the IETF, the IEEE, Trusted Computing Group, and others. Thomas has published over 80 technical conference/journal papers, several books, and over 30 patents. Current areas of research interest include blockchain interoperability, tokenized assets, decentralized architecture, and cyber-resilient protocols.

Francisco Herrera is a professor in the Department of Computer Science and Artificial Intelligence at the University of Granada and director of the Andalusian Research Institute in Data Science and Computational Intelligence (DaSCI). He is also a member of the Royal Academy of Sciences (Spain).

Professor Herrera received his MSc in mathematics in 1988 and PhD in mathematics in 1991, both from the University of Granada, Spain. He is an academician of the Royal Academy of Engineering (Spain) and has published more than 600 journal papers, receiving more than 130,000 citations (Scholar Google, H-index 173), and acts as an editorial member of a dozen academic journals. Professor Herrera has been nominated as a highly cited researcher in the fields of Computer Science, Engineering, and Clarivate Analytics.

His current research interests include, among others, computational intelligence, information fusion and decision-making, explainable artificial intelligence, and data science (including data preprocessing, prediction, and big data).

Andrés Herrera-Poyatos received an MSc in Mathematics and Foundations of Computer Science in 2019 and a PhD in Computer Science in 2023, both from the University of Oxford, United Kingdom. He is currently a lecturer in the Department of Algebra at the University of Granada, Spain, and a researcher at the Andalusian Research Institute in Data Science (DASCI). His research interests include mathematical foundations of deep learning, AI safety, security of large language models, and computer vision applications.

Enrique Herrera-Viedma is a professor in the Department of Computer Science and Artificial Intelligence at the University of Granada, and he is currently serving as vice chancellor for research and knowledge transfer at the UGR. He is a fellow of IEEE, fellow of IFSA, member of the European Academy of Sciences, and Doctor Honoris Causa by Oradea University. He was Vice President (VP) for Publications in the IEEE System Man and Cybernetics Society, and currently he is VP for Cybernetics, one of the founders of the IEEE Trans. in Artificial Intelligence, and Highly Cited Researcher by Clarivate Analytics in Computer Science and Engineering in 2014–2023. He has published more than 350 papers in JCR journals, coordinated more than 25 research projects, and his h-index is 121 in Google Scholar (>65,000 citations) and 92 in WoS (>35,000 citations). He has also been a guest lecturer in plenary lectures and tutorials in multiple national and international conferences related to artificial intelligence, and he is also an associated editor in several international journals like IEEE TFS, IEEE ITS, IEEE TSMC-Syst, Knosys, and ASOC.

Torsten Hoefler is a professor at ETH Zurich. His research interests revolve around the central topic of "Performance-centric System Design" and include scalable networks, parallel programming techniques, and performance modeling. He received his PhD in Computer Science from Indiana University.

Dr. Oleksiy Kondratyev is an ADIA Lab research fellow and visiting professor at the Department of Mathematics, Imperial College London. Prior to joining ADIA in 2021 as Quantitative Research and Development Lead, Oleksiy was managing director and head of Data Science and Innovation at Standard Chartered Bank in London.

Oleksiy has over 20 years of quantitative finance experience in both risk management and front office roles and has been recognized as Quant of the Year (2019) by *Risk Magazine* for his research on the application of machine learning techniques to risk factor analysis and portfolio optimization.

Oleksiy holds an MSc in Theoretical Physics from Taras Shevchenko National University of Kyiv and a PhD in Mathematical Physics from the Institute for Mathematics, National Academy of Sciences of Ukraine. His research interests are in machine learning and quantum computing.

Xavier Lapillonne is a scientific developer at the Center for Climate System Modeling, which is a joint center between MeteoSwiss and ETH Zurich, Switzerland. His main research interests are high-performance computing, GPU computing, physical parametrizations, and turbulence modeling. He received a PhD in physics from EPF Lausanne in 2010.

Wuding Li is a PhD student in mathematics at the University of Montreal and a quantitative researcher at RiskLab, University of Toronto.

Alexander Lipton is global head, Research and Development at Abu Dhabi Investment Authority, professor of practice at Khalifa University, senior founding connection science fellow at MIT, and founding advisory board member at ADIA Lab. Alex is a co-founder of Sila and an advisory board member at several fintech companies, including Swiss-Singaporean bank Sygnum. From 2006 to 2016, Alex was co-head of the Global Quantitative Group and Quantitative Solutions Executive at Bank of America. Earlier, he was a senior manager at Citadel, Credit Suisse, Deutsche Bank, and Bankers Trust. In addition, Alex held visiting professorships at HUJI, EPFL, NYU, Oxford University, and Imperial College. Before becoming a quant, Alex was a full professor of mathematics at the University of Illinois and a consultant at the Los Alamos National Laboratory. *Risk Magazine* awarded him the Inaugural Quant of the Year Award in 2000 and the Buy-side Quant of the Year Award in 2021 (jointly with M. Lopez de Prado). Alex authored/edited 13 books and more than 100 scientific papers on nuclear fusion, astrophysics, applied mathematics, financial engineering, and distributed ledgers. He frequently gives keynote presentations at Quantitative Finance and FinTech conferences and forums worldwide. His latest book, *Hydrodynamics of Markets: Hidden Links Between Physics and Finance* was recently published by Cambridge University Press.

José Ricardo López-Robles received a bachelor's degree in industrial engineering from the Instituto Tecnológico y de Estudios Superiores de Monterrey (Mexico, 2007), a master's degree in project management from the Universidad del País Vasco (Spain, 2010), a master's degree in business administration from the ENEB Business School (Spain, 2017), and a PhD degree in engineering from the Universidad del País Vasco. He is the recipient of the Ibero-American Award “Veta de Plata 2016” in the category “Science and Technology.” Finally, he is a collaborating professor of the Unit Accounting and Management at the Universidad Autónoma de Zacatecas (Mexico).

Álvaro F. Macías holds a doctorate in applied mathematics from IMPA-Brazil and a bachelor’s degree in mathematical engineering from CMM-Chile, bringing over a decade of experience in multinational banks and research institutions. Currently serving as a model specialist at Banco Internacional in Chile, he focuses on financial risk management, quantitative analysis, and econometrics. Dr. Macías has spearheaded the development of advanced predictive models, contributed to academic research with published articles, and holds a patent related to robust static liquidation strategies. His expertise encompasses machine learning, financial modeling, and data analysis, further enhanced by teaching experience and proficiency in multiple programming languages.

Marco Paini is VP Quantum Finance Solutions at Rigetti Computing and focuses on the growth of Rigetti’s financial services practice, including the continued development of proprietary solutions, an expert team, and impactful partnerships with finance institutions. Marco has recently been managing the program to build the first commercial quantum computer in the UK, a collaboration led by Rigetti and sponsored by Innovate UK with Oxford Instruments, Phasecraft, the University of Edinburgh, and Standard Chartered.

Marco previously led quantum computing applications portfolio development of QxBranch, a quantum computing software company acquired by Rigetti in 2019. Prior to QxBranch, Marco spent more than 18 years with Accenture, where he held several roles in technology. In the last part of his career with Accenture, Marco oversaw the AI ecosystem and the development of the quantum computing offering for the Accenture UKI Financial Services Technology Advisory practice.

Marco studied physics at the University of Pavia, where he collaborated with the Quantum Information Theory Group of the University of Pavia.

Alex Pentland is HAI Fellow at Stanford and Toshiba Professor at MIT. He is a member of the US National Academy of Engineering and has won numerous awards and prizes, including the 40th Anniversary of the Internet from DARPA, the Brandeis Privacy Award, AI Influencer Lifetime Achievement Award, as well as many scientific awards.

Ana Paula Peron was born in 1970 in the city of Jundiaí, state of São Paulo, Brazil. She graduated in mathematics from the UNESP, Rio Claro campus, São Paulo, and holds a PhD from the USP, São Carlos campus, São Paulo. She was a professor at the UEM in Maringá, Paraná, between 1995 and 2006. Since 2006, she has been an associate professor in the Department of Mathematics at the USP, São Carlos campus.

Ana is a specialist in mathematical, complex, and harmonic analysis. She has crucially contributed to the theory of positive definite functions over manifolds, including hyperspheres and dynamical spatial domains. Her results have been published in top mathematical journals and widely used by the spatial statistics community for the construction of spatial and space-time correlation structures.

The orthogonal decomposition proved by Ana for isotropic kernels on (finite and Hilbert) complex spheres has opened a fertile statistical literature that is still rich in open problems.

Emilio Porcu received his PhD in statistics in 2005. He became a full professor in 2012, Chair of Statistics at Newcastle University, and then at Trinity College, Dublin, at the School of Computer Science and Statistics. He has been a professor of Statistics and Data Science at Khalifa University since August 2020 and a member of the *Biotechnology* as well as ENGEOS Research Centers. Emilio is a senior fellow at ADIA Lab.

His previous roles include senior scientist at the MIDAS Research Center on Data Complexity in Santiago, Chile, co-chair of Spatial Analytics in Newcastle, and adjoint professor at ADAPT Trinity College.

Emilio's main research interests lie within statistical and machine learning, data science, and spatial statistics. He has published over 160 peer-reviewed papers in top journals in statistics, machine learning, and mathematics. Applications of his research have involved climate change, natural and anthropogenic catastrophes, weather forecasts, genetics, as well as spatial criminology. His theoretical research has been published in the very top journals in his field, such as the Royal Statistical Society, Annals of Statistics, American Statistical Association, and Bernoulli, to mention a few.

Emilio has covered editorial roles in top journals in statistics and mathematics and has reviewed more than 300 papers in his career. He has supervised about 20 PhD students, all of them currently employed in academia around the planet.

Marcos López de Prado serves as global head of quantitative research and development at the Abu Dhabi Investment Authority and as a professor of practice at Cornell University. Over the past 25 years, he has helped modernize finance by pioneering machine learning and statistical inference methods that are now widely adopted at some of the largest investment corporations. The Social Science Research Network (SSRN) ranks him among the 10 most-read authors in economics, and the U.S. Congress has invited him to testify on AI policy. His contributions have earned him several scientific, state, and industry awards, including the National Award for Academic Excellence (1999) from the Kingdom of Spain, the Quant Researcher of the Year Award (2019) from Portfolio Management Research, the Buy-Side Quant of the Year Award (2021) from Risk.net, and the Bernstein Fabozzi/Jacobs Levy Award (2024) from *The Journal of Portfolio Management*. In 2024, His Majesty King Felipe VI and the Government of Spain appointed him Knight Officer of the Royal Order of Civil Merit (OMC), "*for distinguished services to science and the global investment industry.*"

Fabrizzio Sabelli is a master's student in mathematics at the University of Montreal and a quantitative researcher at RiskLab, University of Toronto.

Leonardo Sarmanho received the BEng degree from the Military Institute of Engineering, Rio de Janeiro, Brazil, in 2018, and the MSc degree from the Institute for Pure and Applied Mathematics, Rio de Janeiro, in 2022. Since 2018, he has been working as a quantitative researcher in hedge funds in Brazil. His research focuses on statistical modeling, machine learning, and derivatives pricing across multiple asset classes. He has contributed to the development of quantitative strategies and risk models in the financial industry.

Laura Sanz Martín is a student of the Master's in Advanced Multivariate Data Analysis and Big Data at the University of Salamanca, studies that she combines with her work in the BISITE Research Group (Bioinformatics, Intelligent Systems, and Educational Technology). Her work focuses on research into artificial intelligence applied to different fields, such as economics, sustainability, and accounting. With a degree in statistics from the University of Salamanca, she has experience in data analysis and the use of predictive models. Her interest in artificial intelligence and big data has led her to research into the optimization and improvement of processes using advanced data analysis techniques.

Thomas Schulthess is director of the Swiss National Supercomputing Center (CSCS). His research interests include High-Performance and Cloud Computing. Schulthess received his PhD in Physics from ETH Zurich.

Luis Seco is a professor of financial mathematics at the University of Toronto, director of RiskLab at the University of Toronto, and director of the master's of mathematical finance program at the University of Toronto.

Horst D. Simon, director of ADIA Lab, is an internationally recognized expert in parallel computational methods for large-scale scientific problems, with research spanning sparse matrix algorithms, large-scale eigenvalue problems, and domain decomposition. His recursive spectral bisection algorithm is a breakthrough in parallel computing. With 40 years of experience in high-performance computing and numerical algorithms, he has worked in industry (Boeing, SGI), research labs (NASA Ames, Berkeley Lab), and academia (Stony Brook University, UC Berkeley). Before joining ADIA Lab as its inaugural director in 2022, he spent over two decades at Berkeley Lab, serving as deputy director for research, associate laboratory director for computing sciences, and director of NERSC, where he played a key role in initiatives like Cyclotron Road and CalCharge. A two-time Gordon Bell Prize winner (1988, 2009), he has also received the ACM SC Test of Time Award and the SIAM CSE Career Award. He is a SIAM Fellow and a key contributor to the biannual TOP500 list of the world's most powerful supercomputers.

Alik Sokolov is a PhD candidate at the University of Toronto, and managing director of machine learning at RiskLab at the University of Toronto. Alik has a professional background in machine learning consulting and finance and also serves as the CEO of Sibli.

Kevin Webster is a visiting assistant professor at Imperial College London. He has held several industry positions, including at Deutsche Bank and Citadel. He received his PhD from Princeton University.

Nicholas Westray is currently a visiting researcher in financial machine learning at NYU. He has held several industry positions, including Head of Execution Research in the Multi Asset and Hedge Fund Solutions group at AllianceBernstein as well as senior execution researcher at Citadel. He received his PhD from Imperial College London.

Kesheng (John) Wu leads multiple R&D endeavors focused on advanced technologies and testbeds at the Scientific Networking Division of Lawrence Berkeley National Laboratory. These projects aim to expedite data transfer among DOE user facilities, implement in-network storage and computational resources for intricate scientific workflows, and explore algorithms, strategies, and practices to enhance the efficiency of network operations. Additionally, Dr. Wu's team is tasked with developing and managing networking testbeds, providing the broader research community with platforms to explore future generations of networking technologies and optimize their utilization. These testbeds encompass conventional optical networking alongside cutting-edge quantum communication capabilities.

Jorge P. Zubelli obtained his PhD in applied mathematics from the University of California at Berkeley (1989), his MSc from the National Institute for Pure and Applied Mathematics (IMPA—Brazil) in 1984, and his Electrical Engineering degree from IME-RJ in 1983 with a specialization in telecommunications engineering. He has previous experience as a professor of mathematics at IMPA and heading the Laboratory for Analysis and Mathematical Modeling in the Physical Sciences (LAMCA—IMPA). From 2002 till 2017, he coordinated the Mathematical Methods in Finance Professional MSc program at IMPA. His main research area is inverse problems and mathematical modeling with a focus on its applications to real-world problems where he published in highly selective journals such as *Science, PLOS One, SIAM Journal of Numerical Analysis, SIAM Journal on Applied Mathematics*, and *Physical Review B*. He supervised 13 PhD theses and over 30 MSc students. He coordinated a number of academic projects and research networks, such as a PROSUL Latin America network (2008–2011), a Math-AmSud France-Latin America network (2009–2010), and an ALFA European Union and Latin America network (2003–2007). He also coordinated a number of industrial projects in energy and finance with corporations such as Petrobras and the Brazilian stock exchange BMF-Bovespa (currently called B3). He is currently an ADIA Lab Visiting Fellow.

https://doi.org/10.1142/9789819813049_fmatter

Preface

As we reflect on the inaugural year of ADIA Lab, it is with great pride that we present this compilation of papers, which collectively showcase the significant strides we have made in the realms of computational finance, digital economy, advanced computational methods, and trustworthy artificial intelligence (AI). ADIA Lab was established with the ambitious vision of harnessing cutting-edge research to address some of the most pressing challenges of our time. This collection serves as a testament to our commitment to innovation, collaboration, and the pursuit of excellence in these critical fields.

In this first year, ADIA Lab has rapidly evolved into a hub of intellectual rigor and practical impact, bringing together a diverse group of researchers and thought leaders from around the world. The papers in this volume are a reflection of the depth and breadth of the work undertaken by our teams, and they underscore the lab's dedication to pushing the boundaries of knowledge and technology.

Section 1: Computational Finance highlights our contributions to the financial sector, where the application of advanced mathematical models and algorithms has led to new insights and tools for asset allocation, portfolio management, and risk mitigation. The work on geometric approaches to asset allocation, as well as comparisons between traditional and novel optimization techniques, exemplifies our focus on providing robust and practical solutions for financial professionals. These advancements are not just theoretical; they are designed with the real-world needs of investors and financial institutions in mind, ensuring that our research is both innovative and applicable.

Section 2: Digital Economy reflects our recognition of the transformative power of digital technologies and the critical need for robust, interoperable systems in the rapidly evolving global economy. The studies presented here explore the intersections of artificial intelligence, quantum computing, and blockchain, offering insights into the challenges and opportunities these technologies present. Through this work, ADIA Lab is contributing to the development of a more secure, efficient, and inclusive digital economy, aligning with global trends and addressing emerging needs in this space.

Section 3: Advanced Computational Methods showcases our efforts to pioneer new computational techniques that have far-reaching implications across various scientific domains. Whether through quantum-safe encryption methods, the integration of machine learning with causal inference, or the development of specialized supercomputers for climate science, the research in this section highlights the innovative approaches ADIA Lab is taking to solve complex problems. These contributions are paving the way for advancements that will impact industries and societies worldwide.

Section 4: Trustworthy Artificial Intelligence emphasizes the critical importance of developing artificial intelligence systems that are ethical, reliable, and transparent. This section delves into the frameworks and methodologies that ensure AI systems foster trust among users, regulators, and society at large. Topics include ethical and legal challenges, causal regularization to improve A/B testing, and methods to enhance the explainability of AI in high-stakes applications such as finance and healthcare. By addressing these challenges, ADIA Lab's research underscores the necessity of aligning AI technologies with societal values, creating a foundation for innovation that is not only impactful but also responsible.

As we move forward, the work presented in this publication lays a strong foundation for the future of ADIA Lab. It demonstrates our ability to foster cross-disciplinary collaborations, to bridge the gap between theory and practice, and to make meaningful contributions to both academia and industry. The first year of ADIA Lab has been marked by rapid growth and significant achievements, and we are excited about the future as we continue to build on this momentum.

We extend our deepest gratitude to ADIA for its visionary support, which has been instrumental in establishing ADIA Lab as a leading research institution. Without ADIA's foresight and commitment to fostering innovation, the accomplishments we celebrate today would not have been possible. We also wish to thank the ADIA Lab Scientific Advisory Board for its invaluable guidance and expertise, which has shaped our research direction and ensured the highest standards of excellence. Our heartfelt thanks go to the ADIA Lab Operations Board for providing the day-to-day support that has been crucial in turning our ambitious ideas into reality. Their dedication and hard work have enabled us to focus on our mission and achieve these remarkable milestones.

Additionally, our partnership with Spain has been particularly beneficial, resulting in several of the papers included in this volume. The collaboration and support of our colleagues in Spain have been invaluable, and we extend our sincere thanks to them for their contributions. This partnership exemplifies the spirit of international cooperation that is at the heart of ADIA Lab's mission, and we look forward to continuing and expanding these collaborations in the years to come.

As we look ahead, we are confident that the work initiated here will continue to drive innovation and create lasting impact, both within ADIA Lab and beyond.

Horst Simon
Director, ADIA Lab
August 2024

https://doi.org/10.1142/9789819813049_fmatter

Introduction

Section 1: Computational Finance

Financial markets and investment strategies have become increasingly sophisticated, driven by advancements in financial engineering and risk management techniques. In this section, we explore innovative approaches to asset allocation, portfolio management, and risk mitigation. The introduction of geometric methods to incorporate investor views into asset allocation marks a significant departure from traditional models, offering more flexible and accurate ways to manage investments. Additionally, the comparison of different portfolio optimization techniques, such as Markowitz and hierarchical risk parity (HRP), sheds light on how these models perform in varying market conditions. Furthermore, the development of advanced methodologies for managing liquidation and market risks provides critical insights for financial professionals navigating high-stress environments. This section provides a comprehensive overview of modern financial engineering practices aimed at optimizing portfolio performance and mitigating risks.

Authors and Titles:

1. **A Geometric Approach to Asset Allocation with Investor Views**
   Authors: Alexandre V. Antonov, Koushik Balasubramanian, Alexander Lipton, Marcos Lopez de Prado
2. **Static Liquidation and Risk Management**
   Authors: Álvaro F. Macías, Jorge P. Zubelli
3. **Overcoming Markowitz's Instability with the Help of the Hierarchical Risk Parity (HRP): Theoretical Evidence**
   Authors: Alexandre Antonov, Alexander Lipton, Marcos Lopez de Prado
4. **A Statistical Learning Approach to Local Volatility Calibration and Option Pricing**
   Authors: Vinicius V. L. Albani, Leonardo Sarmanho, Jorge P. Zubelli

Section 2: Digital Economy

The rapid evolution of digital technologies has dramatically reshaped the global economy, leading to what is now known as the digital economy. This transformation is characterized by the widespread adoption of advanced technologies such as artificial intelligence (AI), quantum computing, and blockchain. As these technologies become more ingrained in various sectors, they bring both significant opportunities and complex challenges. One of the critical areas of focus in this section is the interoperability of decentralized networks, particularly in tokenized asset ecosystems. Ensuring that these systems can seamlessly interact while maintaining security and regulatory compliance is vital for the sustainable growth of the digital economy. This section explores the transformative impact of these technologies, the challenges of interoperability, and the role of quantum computing and generative AI in shaping the future of digital economies.

Authors and Titles:

1. **Challenges of Artificial Intelligence and Quantum Potential in the Digital Economy: A Literature Review**
   Authors: Laura Sanz Martín, Javier Parra Domínguez, Guillermo Rivas, Alexander Lipton, Juan Manuel Corchado
2. **Exploring the Digital Economy: Current Research Trends, Challenges, and Opportunities**
   Authors: Manuel J. Cobo, Nadia Karina Gamboa-Rosales, José Ricardo López-Robles, Enrique Herrera-Viedma
3. **Interoperability Challenges in Tokenized Asset Networks**
   Authors: Thomas Hardjono, Alexander Lipton, Alex Pentland

Section 3: Advanced Computational Methods

The intersection of advanced computational methods and applied sciences has led to significant breakthroughs in fields ranging from finance to climate science. This section delves into the application of cutting-edge computational techniques such as quantum computing, machine learning, and stochastic processes. The use of parameterized quantum circuits for encryption highlights the growing importance of quantum-safe methods in securing communications. Meanwhile, integrating machine learning with causal inference represents a novel approach to understanding complex datasets, particularly in financial contexts. Hyperparameter optimization in machine learning is also explored, emphasizing the need for robust data-driven approaches in model development. Additionally, the computational demands of climate modeling underscore the need for specialized supercomputers to enhance the accuracy of high-resolution simulations. Finally, the application of geometric approaches in stochastic processes demonstrates the versatility of these methods in tackling challenges across various scientific domains. This section provides a glimpse into the future of computational science and its potential to drive innovation across multiple fields.

Authors and Titles:

1. **Symmetric Encryption on a Quantum Computer**
   Authors: David Garvin, Oleksiy Kondratyev, Alexander Lipton, Marco Paini
2. **Performance-Driven Dimensionality Reduction: A Data-Centric Approach to Feature Engineering in Machine Learning**
   Authors: Joshua Chung, Marcos Lopez de Prado, Horst D. Simon, Kesheng Wu
3. **Toward Specialized Supercomputers for Climate Sciences: Computational Requirements of the Icosahedral Nonhydrostatic Weather and Climate Model**
   Authors: Torsten Hoefler, Alexandru Calotoiu, Anurag Dipankar, Thomas Schulthess, Xavier Lapillonne, Oliver Fuhrer
4. **Dimension Walks on Generalized Spaces**
   Authors: Ana Paula Peron, Emilio Porcu

Section 4: Trustworthy Artificial Intelligence

Trustworthy artificial intelligence (TAI) ensures that AI systems are reliable, ethical, and transparent. The first paper explores the ethical, legal, and technical aspects of TAI, emphasizing the need for transparency and accountability to foster trust in AI systems. The second paper introduces causal regularization as a method to improve the reliability of AI-driven trading systems by reducing bias in A/B testing, thus enhancing explainability and decision-making. The third paper focuses on using causal modeling to increase the explainability of large language models, making them more interpretable and trustworthy, particularly in high-stakes applications. Together, these works highlight the importance of TAI in building AI systems that are transparent, reliable, and aligned with societal values.

Authors and Titles:

1. **Trustworthy Artificial Intelligence: Nature, Requirements, Regulation, and Emerging Discussions**
   Authors: Francisco Herrera, Andres Hererra, Javier Del Ser, Enrique Herrera-Viedma, Marcos López de Prado
2. **Getting More for Less: Better A/B Testing via Causal Regularization**
   Authors: Nicholas Webster, Kevin Westray
3. **Toward Automating Causal Discovery in Financial Markets and Beyond**
   Authors: Alik Sokolov, Fabrizzio Sabelli, Behzad Azadie Faraz, Wuding Li, Luis Seco

Section 1: Computational Finance

Marcos Lopez de Prado
Advisory Board at ADIA Lab
Global Head—Quantitative R&D at ADIA
Professor of Practice at Cornell University

Mathematical finance is the field of applied mathematics dedicated to the study of financial problems. It concerns itself with two main questions: investing and valuation. Both, investing and valuation, are important activities for the correct functioning of modern societies. Incorrect investing and valuation decisions result in suboptimal decision-making and policy designs, which can have a dramatic social impact, as evidenced by the 2008 Great Financial Crisis.

The central problem of investing consists in the optimal assignment of scarce resources in exchange for a contingent future gain. Investing is therefore an intrinsically speculative activity whereby investors make economic decisions under uncertainty. For centuries, investors made subjective investment decisions with the help of heuristics, such as so-called technical analysis or fundamental investing. In the second half of the 20th century, academics developed rigorous mathematical frameworks to model investment uncertainty. Mathematics provides the objectivity needed to make sophisticated and coherent data-driven decisions that can be improved over time. This section contains two prime examples of mathematical finance applied to investing.

Overcoming Markowitz's Instability with the Help of the Hierarchical Risk Parity (HRP): Theoretical Evidence, written by Antonov, Lipton, and Lopez de Prado, compares the classical Markowitz portfolio optimization method with the HRP approach, highlighting the limitations of Markowitz's method, which is highly sensitive to estimation errors in the covariance matrix, particularly as the size of the investment universe increases. The HRP approach, developed as a more robust alternative, is shown to reduce noise in portfolio allocation weights and provides more stable, less risky portfolios, particularly in out-of-sample scenarios. The authors derive analytical formulas to demonstrate HRP's superiority over the Markowitz method in minimizing portfolio variance and confirm these findings through extensive numerical experiments. The study also offers practical applications, including methods for fast estimation of optimization weights' confidence levels and criteria for constructing HRP portfolios that minimize analytical variance.

A Geometric Approach to Asset Allocation with Investor Views, written by Antonov, Balasubramanian, Lipton, and Lopez de Prado, introduces a geometric approach to asset allocation that incorporates investor views by utilizing the concept of the generalized Wasserstein barycenter (GWB). The proposed method improves upon the conventional Black–Litterman model by offering investors more flexibility in specifying their confidence in their views, allowing for a smoother interpolation between prior distributions and updated views. This approach not only provides more accurate updates to asset drifts and covariances but also rewards investors for making correct decisions. The authors present both empirical and theoretical justifications, demonstrating that the geometric method can yield more intuitive and reliable portfolio allocations compared to traditional methods.

Conversely, the central problem of valuation consists in estimating the intrinsic price of an investment as a function of its features or characteristics. For example, a company's share may be priced as a function of the discounted future cash flows. In the case of derivative products, their price can be derived as a function of their contingent payoffs, weighted by their respective probabilities. For the past fifty years, derivatives pricing has been a highly stylized mathematical problem, which has allowed investment firms to hedge and transfer unwanted risks. This section contains two prime examples of mathematical finance applied to valuation.

A Statistical Learning Approach to Local Volatility Calibration and Option Pricing, written by Albani, Sarmanho, and Zubelli, provides an in-depth analysis of a statistical learning approach to local volatility calibration and option pricing, focusing on European options. The study introduces a novel technique that combines Bayes' theorem with maximum entropy densities (MED) to enhance the calibration of local volatility models without relying on traditional methods like partial differential equations (PDEs) or Monte Carlo simulations. This approach offers computational efficiency and accuracy in pricing options, which is demonstrated through both synthetic and real-world data, such as SPX option data. The method is particularly useful for its applicability in pricing path-independent derivatives and for providing a streamlined, robust alternative to more complex calibration techniques.

Static Liquidation and Risk Management, written by Macías and Zubelli, presents a comprehensive approach to managing risk in portfolio liquidation scenarios, particularly in high-stress financial environments. The authors introduce a methodology that improves upon traditional models like variance and Conditional Value at Risk (CVaR) by incorporating a more robust framework for minimizing losses due to market and liquidity risks. This approach emphasizes the importance of evaluating the entire portfolio when calculating margins for collateral and aims to enhance stability and security in financial transactions. The study is particularly relevant for risk management professionals working with central counterparties and clearing houses, offering insights into optimizing liquidation strategies while addressing intraday price fluctuations and execution price impacts.

The above four papers propose advanced solutions to some of the most fundamental problems faced by investors. They demonstrate the power of mathematics to inform rational and coherent investment decisions and to help governments design better policies.

Section 2: Digital Economy

Alexander Lipton
Advisory Board at ADIA Lab
Global Head—Quantitative R&D at ADIA
Connection Science and Engineering Fellow at MIT

This section contains three chapters covering various topics pertinent to developing this rapidly evolving scientific discipline.

The digital economy is not just a collection of economic activities but a transformative force that results from the billions of online connections among people, businesses, devices, data, and processes. It significantly impacts numerous industries and economic activities, including e-commerce, digital finance, online services, and content creation. The digital economy both relies on and inspires cutting-edge technologies, including artificial intelligence (AI), blockchain, and the Internet of Things (IoT).

The digital economy is highly relevant to society's future because it transforms how businesses operate, how consumers interact with products and services, how economies grow, and how they compete globally. It drives innovation, increases efficiency, and opens up new markets and opportunities for economic participation. However, it also presents challenges such as the digital divide, cybersecurity threats, and shifts in the labor market, making it essential for businesses, governments, and societies to adapt and harness its potential for a more inclusive and sustainable future.

Let us briefly summarize the papers dedicated to the digital economy, which, taken together, cover a lot of ground. In **"Challenges of Artificial Intelligence and Quantum Potential in the Digital Economy: A Literature Review,"** Sanz Martín et al. explore the transformative impact of cutting-edge technologies, particularly quantum computing and generative AI, on organizations and the digital economy. They systematically reviewed 44 articles using the PRISMA methodology, which provides insights into these technologies' fundamentals, applications, and technical requirements. The authors make the following observations. AI and quantum technologies are significantly impacting economic and business practices, especially in data analytics for business and finance. Notable applications of these technologies impact various sectors, including mobile networks, education, medicine, cybersecurity, and astronomy. However, numerous ethical and legal issues, particularly concerning human–AI relationships, still exist and must be addressed. Generative AI is crucial in enhancing educational methods, particularly in higher education and professional training, with expectations for innovative content generation and potential metaverse integration. Yet, the increasing use of large language models like generative AI in research processes raises concerns about the scientific community's perception and the value of researchers' contributions. Overall, the study emphasizes these emerging technologies' profound and wide-reaching effects on society and the economy while highlighting the need to address challenges and ethical considerations.

In **"Exploring the Digital Economy: Current Research Trends, Challenges, and Opportunities,"** Cobo et al. claim that the global economy is undergoing a significant transformation driven by technological advancements, demographic shifts, and changing consumer behaviors. The digital economy, spanning various industries, including e-commerce, digital finance, online services, and content creation, is at the forefront of this transformation because it accelerates the exchange of information and integrates new and emerging technologies, including blockchain, AI, and the IoT.

The authors make several key observations. Digitization reshapes traditional business models, disrupts established industries, and offers challenges and opportunities. E-commerce revolutionizes consumer shopping, but the digital divide remains a challenge, exacerbating inequalities. Automation, AI, and the gig economy transform the labor market, raising concerns about job displacement and income inequality.

Addressing the above problems requires urgent education reimagining, enhancing social safety nets, and fostering collaboration. Cybersecurity and data privacy become critical issues as reliance on digital technologies grows, since protecting information and ensuring digital infrastructure security is vital for maintaining trust in the digital economy. Despite challenges, the digital economy offers opportunities for businesses to innovate and expand globally. Blockchain and AI enable secure transactions, automate tasks, and provide insights, while digital platforms connect businesses to global markets. The metaverse concept is gaining prominence, presenting new opportunities for businesses to create and monetize digital experiences. Ongoing research and analysis are needed to fully harness the digital economy's potential. The study uses bibliometric analysis to explore key research topics in the digital economy, identifying gaps and opportunities for future innovation.

In **"Interoperability Challenges in Tokenized Asset Networks,"** Hardjono et al. explain the need for interoperability to tokenize physical assets successfully. The tokenized asset industry received a significant boost with the approval of the EU Markets in Crypto-Assets Regulation (MiCA) in mid-2023. MiCA aims to establish a robust regulatory framework for asset-referenced tokens (ARTs), designed to maintain stable value by referencing another asset, unlike electronic money tokens (EMTs). While the regulation is a positive step forward, numerous challenges remain, particularly in ensuring interoperability across the various systems and networks that make up the token ecosystem.

Three critical requirements for the success of the new token ecosystem are highlighted: The system has to be interoperable since users must be able to legally own, trade, and transfer their tokenized assets across different blockchain networks without compromising the stability and integrity of the tokens. There must be a balance between user privacy and the need for verifiable digital identities to ensure accountability across decentralized asset networks and that the system is audible. Anonymity should be limited to prevent economic and legal issues. The origins of asset-referenced tokens must be traceable from the dematerialization of real-world assets to their on-chain tokenization. This requirement necessitates clear definitions of which assets can be tokenized and the development of tools and infrastructure that integrate seamlessly with existing financial industry systems.

The authors explore these challenges in detail and contribute to a roadmap for the digital assets industry to address them. By minimizing technical jargon, they keep the discussion accessible.

Section 3: Advanced Computational Methods

Horst Simon, ADIA Lab, Abu Dhabi

The paper titled **"Symmetric Encryption on a Quantum Computer"** by David Garvin, Oleksiy Kondratyev, Alexander Lipton, and Marco Paini proposes a novel symmetric encryption algorithm that leverages the power of parameterized quantum circuits (PQC). The algorithm is designed to ensure secure communication between trusted parties by utilizing quantum circuits that create entangled quantum states. These states, when measured using Pauli operators, generate expectation values that can be used to encode and decode messages securely. The approach addresses potential vulnerabilities posed by quantum attacks on classical encryption systems like RSA, offering a quantum-safe alternative. The document provides a detailed example of how the algorithm can be implemented and discusses the benefits of using adjustable quantum gates and randomized bitstring mappings to enhance security.

The report by Wu et al. discusses the lessons learned from hyperparameter optimization (HPO) in machine learning, particularly focusing on data-driven dimensionality reduction. It highlights the importance of understanding the data, selecting appropriate objective functions, and using robust parallelization strategies to optimize model performance. The authors emphasize that HPO success depends not only on the algorithms used but also on the careful selection of hyperparameters that align with the specific context and goals of the analysis. The document provides practical insights and recommendations for effectively implementing HPO, particularly in complex scenarios like dimensionality reduction, where the relationship between hyperparameters and model quality can be intricate and challenging to navigate.

The document titled **"Toward Specialized Supercomputers for Climate Sciences: Computational Requirements of the Icosahedral Nonhydrostatic Weather and Climate Model"** by Torsten Hoefler et al. discusses the computational demands of the ICON climate model, which is crucial for improving high-resolution climate predictions. The authors analyze the performance of this complex model, which requires significant computational power, particularly for high-resolution simulations necessary to capture detailed atmospheric phenomena like cloud formation. The study emphasizes the need for future supercomputers to achieve these high resolutions, requiring three to four orders of magnitude greater performance than currently available. The research also explores potential optimizations and the integration of machine learning to enhance the accuracy and speed of climate simulations, highlighting the challenges and opportunities in designing specialized computing systems for climate science.

The paper titled **"Dimension Walks on Generalized Spaces"** by Ana Paula Peron and Emilio Porcu explores the mathematical foundations for stochastic processes defined over generalized spaces, which are Cartesian products of Euclidean spaces and spheres of various dimensions. The authors introduce and rigorously define operators called "Monteé" and "Descente," which facilitate walks through different dimensions while maintaining positive definiteness in the associated functions. These concepts are essential for modeling complex processes in fields such as climate science, finance, and spatial statistics, where data can have both spatial and temporal dependencies. The paper's contributions provide significant theoretical tools that can be applied to a broad range of applied sciences.

Section 4: Trustworthy AI

Prof. Enrique Herrera Viedma
Vice-Rector for Research and Knowledge Transfer
University of Granada

Artificial Intelligence (AI) holds the promise of performing tasks that until now were reserved for skilled workers. In some cases, AI may enable the full or partial automation of some of these tasks, while in other cases AI may act as an advisor to a human who ultimately makes a decision. Both the automation and advisory use cases give rise to legal and ethical questions. Who is responsible for the mistakes made by the algorithm? Every activity that requires skill poses the risk of making mistakes; however, what mistakes are acceptable under the intrinsic risks posed by the activity in question? Put differently, what makes an AI trustworthy, in the sense that its field deployment is not considered reckless?

Trustworthy Artificial Intelligence: Nature, Requirements, Regulation, and Emerging Discussions, written by Herrera, Herrera, Del Ser, Herrera-Viedma, and López de Prado, discusses the framework and critical goal of developing and deploying reliable and ethical AI systems, which are essential for user confidence, societal acceptance, and responsible use. The authors explore Trustworthy Artificial Intelligence (TAI) from three perspectives: its importance, the requirements and characteristics proposed by the High-Level Expert Group on Artificial Intelligence and the American National Institute of Standards and Technology, and the role of TAI in AI regulation and governance discussions. They also highlight contributions that offer interesting reflections from theory to practice, aiming to provide a holistic vision of TAI.

A key aspect that makes an algorithm trustworthy is explainability. Roughly speaking, explainability comes in two forms: weak and strong. An AI algorithm is weakly explainable when we understand its output values in terms of the input values provided, even if the underlying function that transformed the inputs into outputs remains unknown. For example, an algorithm may use a radiological exam to predict whether a patient will develop a medical condition, albeit we do not know exactly what causes the condition to appear. Still, it may be possible to explain what features of the radiological exam are associated with a certain diagnosis. For instance, the algorithm may rely on a symptom or a highly correlated condition to predict another. This information, while useful in the sense that diagnostics are not entirely opaque, may not suffice to develop a treatment. In contrast, an AI algorithm is strongly explainable when the algorithm discovers or explicitly uses the causal structure that produced the data. Under strong explainability, it is possible to establish *why* the algorithm works, answer counterfactual questions, and extrapolate potential outcomes. In recent years, strong explainability has attracted the attention of researchers towards causal AI, that is, the application of AI to the discovery and exploit causal mechanisms.

Getting More for Less: Better A/B Testing via Causal Regularization, written by Webster and Westray, applies causal regularization to solving several practical problems in live trading applications, namely estimating price impact when alpha is unknown and estimating alpha when price impact is unknown. They show how causal regularization can increase the value of small A/B tests by drawing more robust conclusions from smaller live trading experiments than traditional econometric methods. Requiring less A/B test data, trading teams can run more live trading experiments and improve the performance of more trading algorithms. Using a realistic order simulator, the authors quantify these benefits for a canonical A/B trading experiment. This paper was awarded the First Prize at the ADIA Lab Competition on Causal Inference Applied to Investing.

Toward Automating Causal Discovery in Financial Markets and Beyond, written by Sokolov, Sabelli, Faraz, Li, and Seco, introduces a novel machine learning framework for causal discovery based on recent advances in large language models (LLMs), and discusses the applications of these causal discovery techniques to investment management. Unlike typical data-driven methods for data discovery, the framework using the implicit "world knowledge" in state-of-the-art LLMs to automate the expert judgment approach to causal discovery. A key application that is explored in detail is end-to-end causal factor analysis, where the authors demonstrate the utility of our method in specifying and analyzing detailed causal models for financial markets. This paper also conducts a comparative analysis, juxtaposing the new approach with conventional methods, to underscore the enhanced capability of the framework in revealing intricate causal dynamics in financial data.

https://doi.org/10.1142/9789819813049_fmatter

List of Figures

https://doi.org/10.1142/9789819813049_fmatter

List of Tables

SECTION

1

Computational Finance

https://doi.org/10.1142/9789819813049_0001

CHAPTER 1 A Geometric Approach to Asset Allocation with Investor Views

Alexandre V. Antonov[1], Koushik Balasubramanian[1,*], Alexander Lipton[1,2,3,4], and Marcos Lopez de Prado[1,2,3,5,6]

[1] *Strategy and Planning Department, ADIA, Abu Dhabi, UAE*
[2] *ADIA Lab, Abu Dhabi, UAE*
[3] *Khalifa University, Abu Dhabi, UAE*
[4] *MIT Connection Science, MIT Cambridge, MA, USA*
[5] *School of Engineering, Cornell University, Ithaca, NY, USA*
[6] *Lawrence Berkeley National Laboratory, Berkeley, CA, USA*
[*] *Corresponding author. E-mail: koushik.balasubramanian@adia.ae*

Herein, a geometric approach that incorporates investor views into portfolio construction is presented. In particular, the proposed approach utilizes the notion of *generalized Wasserstein barycenter* (GWB) to combine statistical information regarding asset returns with investor views to obtain an updated estimate of asset drifts and covariance as inputs to a mean–variance optimizer. Quantitative comparisons of the proposed geometric approach with the conventional Black–Litterman (BL) model (and a closely related variant) are presented. The proposed geometric approach provides investors with more flexibility in specifying their confidence in their views than conventional BL model-based approaches. Additionally, the geometric approach rewards investors more for making correct decisions than conventional BL model-based approaches. We provide empirical and theoretical justifications for our claim.

1.1. Introduction

The Black–Litterman (BL) asset allocation model uses a Bayesian approach to analyze the expected returns of an asset based on a prior along with investor-specific views [1]. Despite the extensive research conducted to date on this topic [2–10], the BL model continues to be an area of great interest. In this study, we present a geometric approach for incorporating investor views, rather than the conventional Bayesian approach used in the traditional BL model, and provide a means to incorporate the conviction levels of views. Before we proceed to a formal introduction of the geometric approach, we will discuss the need for an alternative approach for incorporating views.

To understand the need for an alternative approach, it is essential to recognize that an investor's personal confidence and the precision of their views are independent. Investors who wish to incorporate their views must provide expectations regarding asset returns, along with "error-bars" (or technically, "confidence" intervals) for their views. In fact, investors must provide complete information regarding the views distribution if views are non-Gaussian. The "confidence" intervals do not represent an investor's personal confidence. An investor can choose to use "confidence" intervals as a measure of personal confidence but may also choose to use other metrics (can be subjective) to specify their personal confidence. We provide a concrete example to highlight this remark— if an investor believes that the methodology used to determine the views is not technically reliable, the investor will have no confidence in the views irrespective of their precision (or "error-bars"). For instance, an investor will have no confidence in a set of views if they discover that the views were determined using look-ahead bias or corrupt data irrespective of the precision of those views.

Though extreme, this example demonstrates that the investor confidence and precision of the views are independent. To provide a less-extreme example, let us consider an investor who uses proprietary signals to generate views systematically and generate views based on analysts estimates. Let us assume that the investor chooses to use only the proprietary model to determine the views on expected returns. The precision (inverse covariance) of views can be derived from historical predictions generated by the proprietary model. The investor's confidence in the proprietary model-based views can be determined from the fraction of the observation period in which the proprietary model outperformed the model based on analysts' estimates. In this example, it is again clear that the investor's confidence is unrelated to the precision of the views.

The conventional BL model incorporates the precision of views into the allocation process while not incorporating the investor's subjective confidence. This claim will be demonstrated with the help of a *gedankenexperiment* in Section 1.2.3. For now, we will present some heuristic arguments to support this claim. An investor wishing to incorporate their views should have the flexibility to specify any degree of confidence for a given views distribution.[a] That is, if an investor has 100% confidence in their views, then it is desirable to have the posterior or updated distribution match with the views distribution; furthermore, if they have 0% confidence, then the desired update should match with the prior. For degrees of confidence strictly between 0% and 100%, then it is desirable to have the updated distribution smoothly interpolate between the prior and views. Figure 1.1 shows the "evolution" of the **desired** posterior distribution as a function of the degree of confidence, for a hypothetical example where the prior and views distributions are Gaussian distributions on $\mathbb{R}^2$. In the conventional BL approach, if the prior and views distribution are specified, then the prior and likelihood function for the Bayesian update rule are known, and the posterior is computed from the product of these two functions obtained from the views (see, e.g., Ref.

[a]We refrain from using the term confidence level here as this can be misinterpreted as the statistical confidence interval associated the views. The degree of confidence is the investor's subjective confidence on their views.

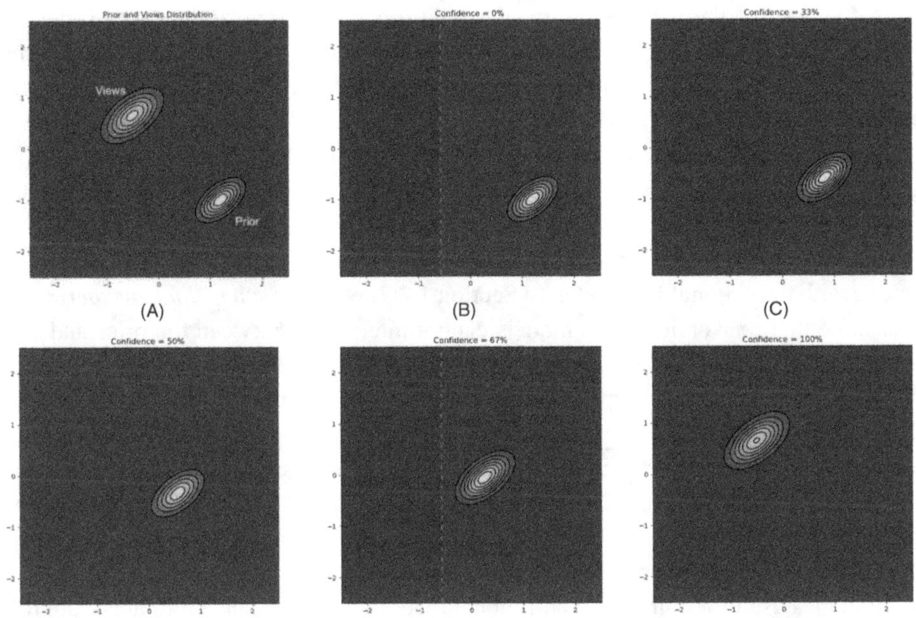

(A) (B) (C) (D) (E) (F)

Fig. 1.1 (a) Shows a contour plot of hypothetical prior and views distributions. In this hypothetical example, we assume there are only two assets and two views on assets. We also assume that the distributions are normal as in the Black–Litterman model. (b)–(f) Desired updated distribution for different levels of investors' "confidence." When an investor is 100% confident of their views, then it is desirable to have an updated distribution match with views distribution and when the confidence in the views is 0%, then it is desirable to have an updated distribution match with the prior.

[6]). Hence, it is not possible to tune the investor's confidence in the conventional BL framework as it does not even appear in the update rule. From the earlier discussion, because the precision of the views and investor confidence are independent, it is clear that tweaking the parameters that change the precision of the views is not equivalent to tuning the investor's confidence. Hence, it seems that an alternate approach is needed for incorporating the subjective confidence of an investor into the allocation model.

At first sight, a mathematical model that incorporates subjective confidence into an allocation model may seem infeasible. In this paper, we describe a rigorous geometric approach that incorporates the subjective confidence of an investor. As observed earlier in the hypothetical example, confidence is a parameter that allows us to smoothly interpolate between the prior and views distribution. Interpolating between probability distributions is a well-studied topic in the optimal transport theory. The optimal transport theory is a field of study that combines ideas from geometry and measure theory. In this paper, we propose an approach for incorporating investor's views by using the notion of generalized Wasserstein barycenter (GWB) introduced in Ref. [11]. In particular, we show that the GWB of the prior and views distribution satisfies the desired properties of a posterior discussed earlier. We derive a closed form expression for the GWB of the prior and views distribution, which is a generalization of the McCann interpolant [12]. This generalization is the primary result of our paper.

The rest of this article is organized as follows: In Section 1.2, we present a review of the original BL model and a closely related variant proposed by Meucci [4]. We notice that our alternative geometric approach based on a previous proposal in Ref. [4] has properties that are intuitive to an investor. Hence, it is worthwhile to review the proposal presented in Ref. [4] along with the original BL model. In Section 1.2.3, we present a *gedankenexperiment* to demonstrate that conventional BL models cannot interpolate between the prior and views distribution. In Section 1.3, we explain the utilization of GWB in our geometric approach. In Section 1.4, we present an optimization problem for determining the GWB of the prior and views distribution. We also explain how the geometric approach extends to the case when the views are degenerate in Section 1.4.2. The main result of the paper is presented in Section 1.5, where we present a closed form expression for the optimal update (or posterior) in our geometric approach. In Section 1.6, we show how the geometric updates can be used within the mean-variance optimization (MVO) framework. Section 1.7 describes methodologies used for comparing current approaches with the conventional BL approach (and its variant). Finally, we summarize our findings and present a brief outlook on future directions.

1.2. Review of Black–Litterman Model and a Variant

In this section, we present a lightning review of two versions of the BL model. The review of the BL model is in no way comprehensive, and readers might find more elaborate reviews in literature (see, e.g., Ref. [1–6]). In the first subsection, we will discuss the original proposal of Black and Litterman, and in the second subsection, we will discuss a variant proposed by Meucci. The two models differ in the way investors wish to incorporate their views. In the original BL model, the investors specify their views on the expected drift of a linear combination of assets (or drifts of certain portfolios). Subsequently, Meucci [4] proposed a minor modification of the model, where the prior beliefs and the investor views are directly specified on the asset returns instead of the drifts. In practice, these two approaches yield very different portfolios with different performance characteristics.

In this chapter, we will refer to the conventional BL model or the original model proposed by Black and Litterman as the BL Model-I and the variant discussed in Ref. [4] as the BL Model-II. We will now present a review of these two models.

1.2.1. *Original Black–Litterman model*

A detailed discussion of the BL Model-I will take us too far; however, it is worthwhile reviewing the assumptions of the BL Model-I and aspects of the model that are related to its underlying assumptions.

- **Assumption 1.2.1.** Observable asset returns ($\vec{R}$) are assumed to follow a Gaussian distribution centered around a mean value ($\vec{\mu}_R$) and the covariance of the returns is denoted by $\mathscr{C}_R$. Mathematically,

$$\vec{R} \sim \mathcal{N}(\vec{\mu}_R, \mathscr{C}_R), \qquad \vec{\mu}_R \in \mathbb{R}^{N_a}, \ \mathscr{C}_R \in \mathrm{Sym}^{++}_{N_a}(\mathbb{R}) \tag{1.1}$$

where $\vec{\mu}_R$ is the drift, $\mathscr{C}_R$ is the covariance of returns, and $\mathrm{Sym}^{++}_N(\mathbb{R})$ is the set of all symmetric, real $N \times N$ positive definite matrices. Though the assumption of the Gaussianity of asset returns does not completely corroborate with real-world data, this is mathematically convenient and is a relatively common assumption in mathematical finance. Note that $\vec{\mu}_R$ and $\mathscr{C}_R$ are unobserved quantities and need to be estimated. We will denote the estimate of $\vec{\mu}_R$ by $\hat{\vec{\mu}}_R$ and $\mathrm{Cov}(\vec{R}|\hat{\vec{\mu}}_R)$ by $\hat{\mathscr{C}}_R$. In the original BL model, the estimate of $\hat{\vec{\mu}}_R$ is assumed to be uncertain, and it is the next item in the list of assumptions.

- **Assumption 1.2.2.** The estimate of the drift $\hat{\vec{\mu}}_R$ is assumed to be normally distributed with covariance ($\mathscr{C}_d$):

$$\hat{\vec{\mu}}_R = \vec{\mu}_d + \vec{\epsilon}_d, \quad \text{where } \vec{\epsilon}_d \sim \mathcal{N}(\vec{0}_{N_a}, \mathscr{C}_d), \tag{1.2}$$

where $\vec{\mu}_d \in \mathbb{R}^{N_a}$ is the expected value of the estimated drift in returns, $\mathscr{C}_d \in \mathrm{Sym}^{++}_{N_a}(\mathbb{R})$ is the covariance of the estimated drift in returns, $\vec{0}_{N_a}$ denotes the zero-vector or the origin of $\mathbb{R}^{N_a}$ and $\vec{\epsilon}_d$ models the noise resulting from the uncertainty in the estimation of drift. Note that $\mathscr{C}_R \neq \hat{\mathscr{C}}_R \equiv \mathrm{Cov}(\vec{R}|\hat{\vec{\mu}}_R)$ as the uncertainties in $\hat{\vec{\mu}}_R$ contributes to $\mathscr{C}_R$, additionally, $\mathscr{C}_R = \hat{\mathscr{C}}_R + \mathscr{C}_d$ (see Ref. [6], for instance).

The following example provides a simple approach for obtaining $\vec{\mu}_d$ and $\mathscr{C}_d$ statistically. The historical sample mean is a simple *estimate* of the drift in the returns ($\hat{\vec{\mu}}_R$). Different estimates of the drift can be computed as the mean of multiple bootstrapped samples obtained by resampling the sample data. In this case, $\vec{\mu}_d$ is the bootstrap aggregated mean, and $\mathscr{C}_d$ is the bootstrap aggregation of the covariance of the drifts. However, this method of estimating the drift using historical returns cannot incorporate investor views and is often considered unsatisfactory to be used for determining the estimate for drift even in the absence of views [1]. Black and Litterman [1] provide an argument for estimating the drift $\vec{\mu}_d$ in the absence of investor-specific views (i.e., all investor views are identical). This argument will be discussed in the following assumption.

- **Assumption 1.2.3.** If all investors have identical views, then all investor positions align with the market (or a relevant benchmark portfolio) weights, $\vec{w}_{\mathrm{BM}}$. If all investors use an unconstrained MVO with an average risk aversion parameter γ_R to determine the weights, then the expected drift, $\vec{\mu}_d$ is obtained from the reference or benchmark weights ($\vec{w}_{\mathrm{BM}}$) by inverting the Markowitz optimality condition as shown below [3].

$$\vec{\mu}_d = r_f\vec{e} + \gamma_R\mathscr{C}_R\vec{w}_{\mathrm{BM}} = r_f\vec{e} + \gamma_R(\hat{\mathscr{C}}_R + \mathscr{C}_d)\vec{w}_{\mathrm{BM}} \tag{1.3}$$

where r_f is the risk-free rate. Eq. (1.3) is referred to as the "equilibrium" model because it explains the drift in asset returns when the market is in full-equilibrium where all participants have equal information and use the same methodology for allocation [1, 3]. In general, other estimates of the covariance matrix $\hat{\mathscr{C}}_R$ and the expected drift $\vec{\mu}_d$ can be obtained through a reverse optimization procedure [3], where utility functions are different from mean–variance-based utility functions. Furthermore, the covariance of $\hat{\vec{\mu}}_R$ is assumed to be proportional to the conditional covariance of $\vec{R}$. That is,

$$\mathscr{C}_d = \tau \hat{\mathscr{C}}_R \tag{1.4}$$

where τ is some scalar parameter, which has received a lot of attention from researchers [4]. The condition $0 \leq \tau \leq 1$ is necessary for $\vec{\mu}_d$ to be a reasonable estimate of $\hat{\vec{\mu}}_R$ or $\vec{\mu}_R$. This is because the mean of expectation returns can be more accurately estimated than the mean of returns. If the equilibrium-model drift is computed using the sample mean of an observation of length T, we will have $\tau = 1/T$ (assuming independence of observations). If τ is obtained based on a calibration procedure that compares the uncertainty of the equilibrium model with the sample estimator, then it seems reasonable to set $\tau \approx 1/T$ [4, 5].

- **Assumption 1.2.4.** Investors and experts may have views ($\mathcal{V}_d$) that are not aligned with the market (or the benchmark) and may wish to incorporate them in their allocation process. Note that the investor must also provide a level of uncertainty by specifying $\mathscr{C}_{\mathcal{V}_d}$. More generally, an investor specifies their views by specifying the distribution of expected returns, which could be non-normal. In the original BL model (BL Model-I), the views distribution is assumed to be Gaussian. That is, the investors specify their views on the expected drifts (expectation on expected returns) of assets as shown below:

$$\mathscr{P}.\hat{\vec{\mu}}_R = \vec{\nu}_{\mathcal{V}_d} + \vec{\eta}_{\mathcal{V}_d}, \quad \text{where } \vec{\eta}_{\mathcal{V}_d} \sim \mathcal{N}(\vec{0}_{N_v}, \mathscr{C}_{\mathcal{V}_d}) \tag{1.5}$$

where $\mathscr{P} \in \mathbb{R}^{N_v \times N_a}$ is the views matrix, which specifies the expected return on specific assets or some combinations of assets; $\vec{\nu}_{\mathcal{V}_d} \in \mathbb{R}^{N_v}$, $\mathscr{C}_{\mathcal{V}_d} \in \mathrm{Sym}^{++}_{N_v}(\mathbb{R})$, and N_v is the number of views. Note that each row (denoted by $\vec{p}_r$) of the views matrix $\mathscr{P}$ represents the weight of a portfolio Π_r, and the expectation of the expected return of this portfolio is $\nu_{\mathcal{V}_d,r}$ [2]. The portfolio Π_r could be a long-only portfolio (even possibly with only asset) or could be a long-short portfolio. Note that $\mathscr{P}$ could be degenerate (in principle) due to the presence of multiple views (could even be conflicting) on the same assets. If the views are independent, then the covariance matrix $\mathscr{C}_{\mathcal{V}_d}$ associated with the views is a diagonal matrix. In a general case, the views matrix $\mathscr{P}$ and the view drift $\vec{\nu}_{\mathcal{V}_d}$ can be transformed in such a way that $\mathscr{C}_{\mathcal{V}}$ is diagonal [2]. However, for the purpose of the current study, we do not make any assumptions regarding $\mathscr{C}_{\mathcal{V}_d}$ and allow it to be a symmetric non-diagonal matrix. We have used the suffix $\mathcal{V}_d$ for denoting the views covariance matrix, $\mathscr{C}_{\mathcal{V}_d}$, to emphasize that the views are specified on the drifts.

The BL model estimates the drift in the presence of views using a Bayesian approach where the prior distribution is given (1.2) with the drift parameter given by Eq. (1.3) and the posterior distribution is obtained by computing the distribution of the expected returns given the views $\mathcal{V}_d$ $\left(\text{denoted by } \mathbb{P}(\hat{\vec{\mu}}_R | \mathcal{V}_d) \text{ in this chapter}\right)$.

We now state the main result of the BL model: Given the views $\mathcal{V}_d$ on the drift in Eq. (1.5), the updated or posterior distribution of the estimated expected returns $\hat{\vec{\mu}}_R$ is given by

$$\mathbb{P}(\hat{\vec{\mu}}_R|\mathcal{V}_d) = \phi\left(\hat{\vec{\mu}}_R; \vec{\mu}_{BL}, \mathscr{C}_{BL}^{(\vec{\mu}_R)}\right) \tag{1.6}$$

where $\phi\left(\vec{Z}; \vec{\mu}, \mathscr{C}\right)$ is the probability distribution function (PDF) of a Gaussian random variable, $\vec{Z} \sim \mathcal{N}\left(\vec{\mu}, \mathscr{C}\right)$ and[b]

$$\vec{\mu}_{BL} = \left(\left(\tau\hat{\mathscr{C}}_R\right)^{-1} + \mathscr{P}^T\mathscr{C}_{\mathcal{V}_d}^{-1}\mathscr{P}\right)^{-1}\left(\left(\tau\hat{\mathscr{C}}_R\right)^{-1}\vec{\mu}_d + \mathscr{P}^T\mathscr{C}_{\mathcal{V}_d}^{-1}\vec{v}_{\mathcal{V}_d}\right). \tag{1.7}$$

$$\mathscr{C}_{BL}^{(\vec{\mu}_R)} = \left(\left(\tau\hat{\mathscr{C}}_R\right)^{-1} + \mathscr{P}^T\mathscr{C}_{\mathcal{V}_d}^{-1}\mathscr{P}\right)^{-1}. \tag{1.8}$$

The derivation of the above updated equations can be found in the literature [4, 6]. Note that the updated estimate for the distribution of asset returns is now given by

$$\mathbb{P}\left(\vec{R}|\mathcal{V}_d\right) = \phi\left(\vec{\mu}_{BL}, \hat{\mathscr{C}}_{\vec{R}|\mathcal{V}_d}\right), \quad \text{where } \hat{\mathscr{C}}_{\vec{R}|\mathcal{V}_d} = \hat{\mathscr{C}}_R + \mathscr{C}_{BL}^{(\vec{\mu}_R)}. \tag{1.9}$$

1.2.2. *Variant of the Black–Litterman model*

In a study [4], it was suggested that investor views can be directly expressed on the raw asset returns instead of the expected returns. Meucci argued that specifying the views on the estimated drifts, as done in the BL Model-I, is often "counterintuitive" in limiting situations (for instance, when $\tau \to 0$), even though the results are consistent with the assumptions of the model. For instance, the covariance of the posterior distribution has a nontrivial dependence on τ even in the limit when the views are completely uninformative as well as in the case when the views are completely correct. This dependence on τ stems from the fact that the estimated drift is uncertain, which is inherent in the model assumptions.

Meucci [4] proposed an alternate way to incorporate views that exhibit intuitive limiting behaviors. In this study, we develop geometric methods that are analogous to the BL Model-I and BL Model-II to verify if any geometric methods yield "counterintuitive" results. Hence, understanding the differences in the underlying assumptions of both approaches seems essential.

- **Assumption 1.2.1.** As in the original BL model, observable asset returns ($\vec{R}$) are assumed to follow a Gaussian distribution centered around a mean ($\vec{\mu}_R$) and the covariance of the returns is denoted by $\mathscr{C}_R$. Mathematically,

$$\vec{R} \sim \mathcal{N}(\vec{\mu}_R, \mathscr{C}_R), \qquad \vec{\mu}_R \in \mathbb{R}^{N_a}, \ \mathscr{C}_R \in \mathrm{Sym}_{N_a}^{++}(\mathbb{R}) \tag{1.10}$$

[b]Using Woodbury identity $\vec{\mu}_{BL}$ and $\mathscr{C}_{BL}^{(\vec{\mu}_R)}$ can be written in a form that does not require the inverses of $\mathscr{C}_R$ and $\mathscr{C}_{\mathcal{V}_d}$ separately.

Unlike the original BL model, it is assumed that $\vec{\mu}_R = r_f\vec{e}+\gamma_R\mathscr{C}_R\vec{w}_{\text{BM}}$. This eliminates the need for modeling it as a random variable.

- **Assumption 1.2.2.** Expert views are expressed on asset returns directly instead of expected returns as shown below:

$$\mathscr{P}.\vec{R} = \vec{\nu}_{\mathcal{V}} + \vec{\eta}_{\mathcal{V}_R}, \quad \text{where } \vec{\eta}_{\mathcal{V}} \sim \mathcal{N}(\vec{0}_{N_v}, \mathscr{C}_{\mathcal{V}_R}) \tag{1.11}$$

We use the suffix $\mathcal{V}_R$ to denote the view covariance matrix, $\mathscr{C}_{\mathcal{V}_R}$, to emphasize that views are specified on asset returns directly. In this variant of the BL model, the returns distribution is updated as shown below:

$$\mathbb{P}\left(\vec{R}|\mathcal{V}_R\right) = \phi\left(\vec{\mu}^{(\vec{R})}_{BL'}, \mathscr{C}^{(\vec{R})}_{BL'}\right) \tag{1.12}$$

where

$$\vec{\mu}^{(\vec{R})}_{BL'} = \left(\hat{\mathscr{C}}_R^{-1} + \mathscr{P}^T\mathscr{C}_{\mathcal{V}_R}^{-1}\mathscr{P}\right)^{-1}\left(\hat{\mathscr{C}}_R^{-1}\hat{\vec{\mu}}_R + \mathscr{P}^T\mathscr{C}_{\mathcal{V}_R}^{-1}\vec{\nu}_{\mathcal{V}}\right) \tag{1.13}$$

$$\mathscr{C}^{(\vec{R})}_{BL'} = \left(\hat{\mathscr{C}}_R^{-1} + \mathscr{P}^T\mathscr{C}_{\mathcal{V}_R}^{-1}\mathscr{P}\right)^{-1} \tag{1.14}$$

where $\hat{\mathscr{C}}_R$ is an estimate for the covariance of returns ($\mathscr{C}_R$) and $\hat{\vec{\mu}}_R$ is an estimate of the expected returns of assets prior to incorporating any views. The above results can be obtained in the same manner as that used for deriving updates in the original BL model. Note that the parameter τ does not appear in this model (as the update equations for the drift and covariance are independent of τ). The details of this derivation can be found in Ref. [4].

1.2.3. *A simple* gedankenexperiment

Let us imagine that there is only one asset in the entire investible universe, that is, $N_a = 1$ in Sections 1.2.1 and 1.2.2. Let us also assume that an investor has a view about this asset ($N_v = 1$), which could be a view on the expected returns of the asset (as in the BL Model-I) or the asset returns directly (as in the BL Model-II).

First, we present an analysis of the BL Model-I . We denote the estimate of variance of the asset return (R) by $\hat{\sigma}_R^2$ and the variance of the expected returns of the asset ($\hat{\mu}_R$) by σ_d^2. In notations presented in Section 1.2.1, we have $\hat{\mathscr{C}}_R = \hat{\sigma}_R^2 = \text{VAR}(R|\hat{\mu}_R)$ and $\mathscr{C}_d = \sigma_d^2 = \tau\hat{\sigma}_R^2$. The investor's view on the drift is denoted by $\nu_{\mathcal{V}}$, and the corresponding variance is denoted by $\sigma_{\mathcal{V}}^2$. After incorporating the investor's view using the BL Model-I, the updated expected return of assets is given by

$$\mu_{BL} = \left(\frac{\sigma_{\mathcal{V}_d}^2\hat{\mu}_R + \sigma_d^2\nu_{\mathcal{V}_d}}{\sigma_{\mathcal{V}_d}^2 + \sigma_d^2}\right) \equiv \left(\frac{\sigma_{\mathcal{V}_d}^2\hat{\mu}_R + \tau\hat{\sigma}_R^2\nu_{\mathcal{V}_d}}{\sigma_{\mathcal{V}_d}^2 + \tau\hat{\sigma}_R^2}\right). \tag{1.15}$$

The above result is a direct application of Eq. (1.9) for a single asset and a single view. Though the result presented in Eq. (1.15) is sufficient for this *gedankenexperiment*, we also present the updated variance of returns below (for the sake of completeness):

$$\hat{\sigma}^2_{\hat{R}|V_d} = \hat{\sigma}^2_R + \sigma^2_{BL}, \qquad \text{where } \sigma^2_{BL} = \tau\left(\frac{\hat{\sigma}^2_R \sigma^2_{V_d}}{\tau\hat{\sigma}^2_R + \sigma^2_{V_d}}\right). \tag{1.16}$$

Recall that $\mathcal{N}(\mu_{BL}, \sigma^2_{BL})$ is the updated distribution of the expected asset return (drift), while $\mathcal{N}(\mu_{BL}, \hat{\sigma}^2_{\hat{R}|V_d})$ is the updated distribution of the asset return. We now present the main findings of this *gedankenexperiment*.

If the investor is completely confident about their views, then the intuitive expectation is that the posterior distribution will match with the investor's views distribution. However, it is clear from Eqs. (1.15) to (1.16) that BL Model-I cannot produce the investor's views distribution as the updated distribution for any value of τ, as $\tau \in [0, 1]$. Therefore, aligning the updated distribution with the views distribution by choosing artificially high values of τ ($\tau \to \infty$) is illogical as it will imply $\sigma^2_d \gg \hat{\sigma}^2_R$, that is, the noise in the expected returns is much greater than the noise in the returns. Therefore, it is not possible to obtain the views distribution as the posterior by tuning τ, and hence τ is not a parameter that specifies an investor's personal confidence. It is, in fact, a parameter that specifies the "error-bars" for the estimates in estimates of expected return. Because investors provide views on the expected drift with a level of uncertainty, $\sigma^2_{V_d}$ is not tunable either. In some research articles, a τ-dependent scaling factor is introduced (sometimes implicitly) in the definition of $\sigma^2_{V_d}$. In this case, tuning τ also changes $\sigma^2_{V_d}$ and taking $\tau \to \infty$ turns the views distribution into a multivariate Dirac delta distribution. In summary, τ cannot be used to interpolate between the "equilibrium" distribution and the views distribution.

In the case of BL Model-II, it is clear from Eqs. (1.12) to (1.14) that there are no tunable parameters. Thus, it is not possible to obtain the investor's views distribution as the posterior without data dredging the views covariance matrix in the BL Model-II as well.

With the help of this simple *gedankenexperiment*, we have demonstrated that neither the BL Model-I nor the BL Model-II can reproduce the investor's views distribution as the posterior distribution without making illogical parameter choices or data dredging. We show that the geometric approach gives an investor flexibility to tune the degree of conviction so that the geometric posterior distribution will match with the investor's views distribution.

1.3. Distance between Distributions

In this note, we provide an alternate approach for incorporating investor views. In particular, we obtain the distribution of estimated drift (or returns) in the presence of views, as the GWB of the views and reference distribution. The focus of this section is to introduce the notion of GWB and discuss its relevance for asset allocation.

In the following, the prior distribution could refer to the distribution of estimated drift or that of asset returns. If the prior is assumed to be the estimated drift, then the views are expressed on the drift, and in the other model, the views are directly expressed on the asset returns. We can then derive geometric methods that are analogous to the BL Model-I and BL Model-II by a simple mapping and renaming of variables (discussed in Remarks 1.5.3 and 1.5.4 of Section 1.5).

We are interested in finding a target or updated distribution f_U that is as "close" as possible to the prior (or reference) distribution, f_P, while remaining in "proximity" to the views. "Proximity" between distributions can be defined by introducing the notion of dissimilarity between distributions. The goal of the current approach can then be restated mathematically as follows:

$$f_\star = \underset{f_U}{\operatorname{argmin}}\ \textsc{Diss}(f_U, f_P) \tag{1.17}$$

subject to

$$\textsc{Diss}(\mathscr{P}_\sharp[f_U], f_V) \leq d_0 \tag{1.18}$$

where $f_\star$ is the desired optimal update, $\textsc{Diss}(A, B)$ denotes a generic measure of dissimilarity between the distributions A and B and $\mathscr{P}_\sharp[f_U]$ denotes the *push-forward* of the "update" measure onto the views space along the map, $\mathscr{P}$. A formal definition of a push-forward measure can be found in Appendix C.

We can modify the optimization problem in the constrained form to a Lagrangian form as shown below:

$$f_\star = \underset{f_U}{\operatorname{argmin}} \left[\left(\textsc{Diss}(f_U, f_P) + \lambda \textsc{Diss}(\mathscr{P}_\sharp[f_U], f_V)\right)\right] \tag{1.19}$$

where λ is a Lagrange multiplier that serves as a tuning parameter that turns the constraint in Eq. (1.18) into a term in the cost function. Note that dissimilarity or distance-based approaches to BL models have appeared before in Refs. [8] and [10].

The optimization problem specified in Eq. (1.19) is in the Lagrangian form, while the problem in Eqs. (1.17) and (1.18) is a constrained optimization problem (COP). The equivalence between the optimization problem in the Lagrangian form and the COP form can be guaranteed by choosing a dissimilarity metric $\textsc{Diss}$ such that the Slater conditions are satisfied for all $d_0 > 0$ and $\textsc{Diss}(A, B) \geq 0$ for any distributions A and B for which the dissimilarity is defined. Proposition B.1 in Appendix B provides the precise details of this equivalence.

The problem in Eq. (1.19) is quite abstract as the dissimilarity measure is not yet specified. In this note, we consider the Fréchét or L_2-Wasserstein distance as the dissimilarity measure. The definition of the L_2-Wasserstein distance can be found in Appendix B. The L_2-Wasserstein distance induces a metric on the space of probability measures. Note that the problem in Eq. (1.19) can be written as the minimization of the following Lagrangian:

$$\mathscr{L}_{GWB} = \left(\mathcal{D}_{WD}(f_U, f_P) + \lambda \mathcal{D}_{WD}(\mathscr{P}_\sharp[f_U], f_V)\right) \tag{1.20}$$

The minimization problem Eq. (1.20) is the same as computing the GWB for two centers [11] after expressing $\lambda = t/(1-t)$ and multiplying $\mathscr{L}_{GWB}$ by $(1-t)$ for $t \in [0, 1)$. Fig. 1.2 is a pictorial representation of the space of prior distributions, the views distribution and the pushforward of f_U onto the space of views distribution.

In a previous study [11], the authors consider the problem of finding the GWB when there are more than two centers. An analytical expression can be obtained for the GWB of two Gaussian distributions, and we show that it is a generalization of McCann interpolant [12]. The problem in Eq. (1.23) can be generalized to other returns and views distributions. Additionally, views can be prescribed through an arbitrary map $\mathscr{P}$, which need not be linear. However, an analytical solution seems feasible only for the case when $\mathscr{P}$ is linear (even when the two distributions are Gaussian). In other cases, the problem needs a numerical approach.

In the next section, we present the problem specialized to Gaussian distributions.

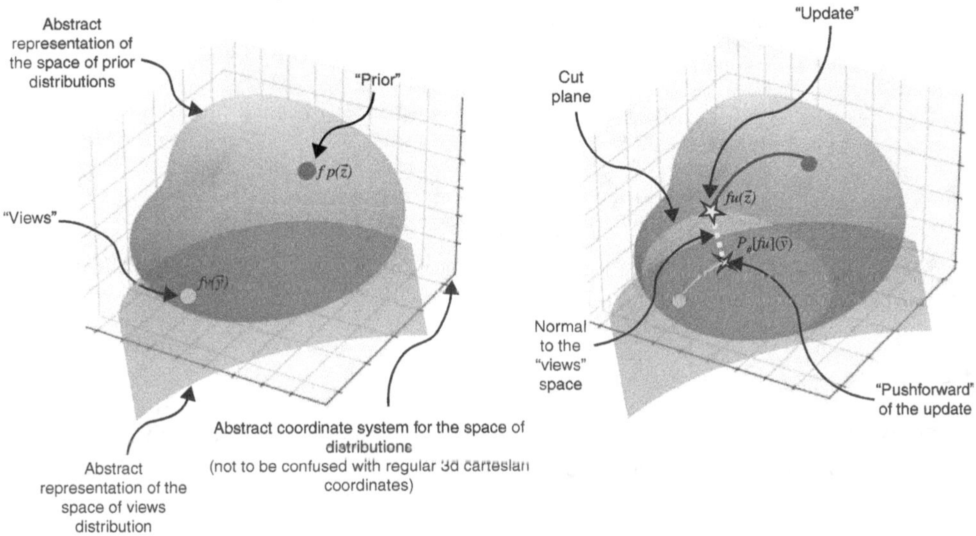

Fig. 1.2 (Left) Shows an abstract representation of the space of probability measures containing the prior distribution f_P and the space of measures containing the views distribution f_V. In the space of probability measures, distributions are points, with the point corresponding to f_P (in the space of prior distribution) is represented by ● (solid brown circle) and that corresponding to f_V (in the space of views distribution) is represented by ● (solid cyan-colored circle). **(Right)** The *push-forward* of f_U on to the views space is denoted by ✕ (orange cross) and the update distribution (f_U) is represented by ☆ (yellow star).

1.4. Generalized Wasserstein Barycenters for Gaussian Prior and Views

As mentioned earlier, the geometric method provides models that are analogous to the BL Model-I and BL Model-II, which will be discussed in Remarks 1.5.3 and 1.5.4 of Section

1.5. As in the BL model and its variants, we assume that the prior and views distributions are Gaussian and have the following PDFs:

$$f_P(\vec{z}) = \frac{1}{\sqrt{(2\pi)^{N_a} \det \mathscr{C}_P}} .e^{-\frac{1}{2}(\vec{z}-\vec{\mu}_P)^T \mathscr{C}_P^{-1}(\vec{z}-\vec{\mu}_P)}, \tag{1.21}$$

$$f_V(\vec{y}) = \frac{1}{\sqrt{(2\pi)^{N_v} \det \mathscr{C}_V}} .e^{-\frac{1}{2}(\vec{y}-\vec{\nu}_V)^T \mathscr{C}_V^{-1}(\vec{y}-\vec{\nu}_V)} \tag{1.22}$$

where $\vec{z}, \vec{\mu}_P \in \mathbb{R}^{N_a}$, $\vec{y}, \vec{\nu}_V \in \mathbb{R}^{N_v}$, $\mathscr{C}_P \in \text{Sym}_{N_a}^{++}(\mathbb{R})$ and $\mathscr{C}_V \in \text{Sym}_{N_v}^{++}(\mathbb{R})$. For convenience, we refer to the subspace in which $\vec{y}$ resides as the "views" subspace. Additionally, we assume that the target distribution f_U is Gaussian. Note that in the original BL model and in its variant, the updated distribution is Gaussian. Hence, we are justified in seeking a target or updated distribution that is also Gaussian.

$$f_U(\vec{z}) = \frac{1}{\sqrt{(2\pi)^{N} \det \mathscr{C}_U}} .e^{-\frac{1}{2}\left((\vec{z}-\vec{m}_U)^T \mathscr{C}_U^{-1}(\vec{z}-\vec{m}_U)\right)} \tag{1.23}$$

where $\vec{m}_U \in \mathbb{R}^{N_a}$ and $\mathscr{C}_U \in \text{Sym}_{N_a}^{++}(\mathbb{R})$. To define the proximity to the views distribution, it seems essential to define the distribution of $\mathscr{P}\vec{z}$ (which resides in the views subspace). However, the existence of such a distribution might be thwarted by the degeneracy of the views matrix $\mathscr{P}$ (for instance, identical rows in $\mathscr{P}$).

1.4.1. *Nondegenerate views matrix*

Before we proceed to handle degeneracies in the views matrix, we discuss the case where the distribution of $\mathscr{P}\vec{z}$ is well-defined, and it is given by

$$\mathscr{P}_\sharp [f_U](\vec{y}) = \frac{1}{\sqrt{(2\pi)^{V} \det(\mathscr{P}\mathscr{C}_U\mathscr{P}^T)}} .e^{-\frac{1}{2}(\vec{y}-\mathscr{P}\vec{m}_U)^T (\mathscr{P}\mathscr{C}_U\mathscr{P}^T)^{-1}(\vec{y}-\mathscr{P}\vec{m}_U)} \tag{1.24}$$

Push-forward of a Gaussian distribution along a linear map can be computed quite easily using the fact that $\mathscr{P}\vec{z}$ is itself a normal distribution. Hence, it is sufficient to compute $\mathbb{E}[\mathscr{P}\vec{z}]$ and $\text{VAR}[\mathscr{P}\vec{z}]$. Note that $\mathbb{E}[\mathscr{P}\vec{z}] = \mathscr{P}\vec{m}_U$ and $\text{VAR}[\mathscr{P}\vec{z}] = \mathscr{P}\mathscr{C}_P\mathscr{P}^T$. We also provide a longer derivation of the result in Eq. (1.22) using the formal definition of a push-forward measure in Appendix C. The computations in Appendix C can be extended to more general maps and distributions.

Note that when the views are degenerate, the determinant in the denominator could vanish, resulting in an ill-defined distribution. In this subsection we assume that $\mathscr{P}_\sharp[f_U](\vec{y})$ exists, in which case it is possible to introduce notions of "proximity" between distributions. In the next subsection, a method for handling degenerate views will be presented. As mentioned earlier, we only discuss the case of nondegenerate views in this subsection.

The L_2-Wasserstein distance between two Gaussian measures can be computed analytically (see for e.g., Refs. [13–15]). The details of the computation are presented in Appendix D. Using Eq. (D.13) in Appendix D, we obtain

$$\begin{aligned}\mathscr{L}_{GWB} &= \|\vec{m}_U - \vec{\mu}_P\|^2 + \operatorname{tr}\left(\mathscr{C}_P + \mathscr{C}_U - 2\left(\mathscr{C}_P^{\frac{1}{2}}\mathscr{C}_U\mathscr{C}_P^{\frac{1}{2}}\right)^{\frac{1}{2}}\right) \\ &+ \lambda\left(\|\mathscr{P}\vec{m}_U - \vec{v}\|^2 + \operatorname{tr}\left(\mathscr{C} + \mathscr{P}\mathscr{C}_U\mathscr{P}^T - 2\left(\mathscr{C}^{\frac{1}{2}}\mathscr{P}\mathscr{C}_U\mathscr{P}^T\mathscr{C}^{\frac{1}{2}}\right)^{\frac{1}{2}}\right)\right).\end{aligned} \tag{1.25}$$

The expression in Eq. (1.25) is well-defined even when the views matrix $\mathscr{P}$ is degenerate. Hence, the above cost function can be used for finding a target distribution that lies in the "proximity" of the prior and views, even when the views matrix is degenerate. The case of a degenerate distribution will be discussed in more details in a subsequent part of this note.

1.4.2. *Degenerate views matrix*

In this section, we demonstrate how the geometric approach extends to the degenerate case. We start with a formal definition of a multivariate normal (MVN) distribution and utilize this definition to generalize the geometric approach to include degenerate views.

Definition 1.4.1. *A random vector $\vec{\chi} = [\chi_1, \chi_2, \dots \chi_k]^T$ has an MVN if $\vec{a}^T\vec{\chi}$ is a univariate random distribution for any $\vec{a} \in \mathbb{R}^k$. Note that a univariate normal distribution with zero variance is a Dirac delta distribution located at the mean of the distribution.*

The above definition is applicable even when the "naive" probability of $\vec{\chi}$ is degenerate, that is, when the covariance of $\vec{\chi}$ is not invertible. Alternatively, we could define the MVN distribution in terms of its characteristic function, $\varphi_{\vec{\chi}}(\vec{v})$, of $\vec{\chi}$ as follows: A random vector $\vec{\chi} = [\chi_1, \chi_2, \dots \chi_k]^T$ has a MVN distribution if the characteristic function, $\varphi_{\vec{\chi}}(\vec{v})$, of $\vec{\chi}$

$$\varphi_{\vec{\chi}}(\vec{v}) \equiv \mathbb{E}_{\vec{\chi}}\left[e^{i\vec{v}^T\vec{\chi}}\right] = \exp\left(i\vec{v}^T\vec{\mu} - \frac{1}{2}\vec{v}^T\mathscr{C}\vec{v}\right), \qquad i \equiv \sqrt{-1} \tag{1.26}$$

for some $\vec{\mu} \in \mathbb{R}^k$ and $\mathscr{C} \in \mathrm{Sym}_k^+(\mathbb{R})$, where $\mathrm{Sym}_k^+(\mathbb{R})$ is the set of all symmetric and real $k \times k$ positive *semi-definite* matrices. The probability mass function or the PDF can be obtained as the Fourier transform of the aforementioned characteristic function as shown below:

$$\begin{aligned}&\int \lim \frac{d^N\vec{v}}{(2\pi)^N}\exp\left(-i\vec{v}^T\vec{\chi} + i\vec{v}^T\vec{\mu} - \frac{1}{2}\vec{v}^T\mathscr{C}\vec{v}\right) \\ &= \left(\frac{1}{(2\pi)^N\det\mathscr{C}}\right)^{\frac{1}{2}} \cdot \exp\left(-\frac{1}{2}(\vec{\chi} - \vec{\mu})^T\mathscr{C}^{-1}(\vec{\chi} - \vec{\mu})\right)\end{aligned} \tag{1.27}$$

To handle degenerate distributions, it is essential to define the pseudoinverse and pseudo-determinant of a matrix. We show that a degenerate Gaussian distribution can be defined by replacing $\mathscr{C}^{-1}$ in Eq. (1.25) with the pseudoinverse of $\mathscr{C}$ and $\det(\mathscr{C})$ with the pseudodeterminant of $\mathscr{C}$, when the covariance matrix $\mathscr{C}$ has zero eigenvalues. The Moore–Penrose pseudoinverse (denoted by the superscript +) and the pseudodeterminant (denoted by subscript +) of a matrix Z can be obtained using the following limiting procedure:

$$Z^{+} = \lim_{\delta \to 0} \left(Z^T Z + \delta^2 \mathbb{I}\right)^{-1} Z^T = \lim_{\delta \to 0} Z^T \left(Z Z^T + \delta^2 \mathbb{I}\right)^{-1} \tag{1.28}$$

$$\det{}_{+}(Z) = \lim_{\delta \to 0} \frac{1}{\delta^{2(N-\mathrm{rank}(A))}} \det\left(Z + \delta^2 \mathbb{I}\right) \tag{1.29}$$

By introducing a regularization parameter δ for the covariance in Eq. (1.25), a normal distribution with a degenerate covariance can then be defined as follows:

$$f_{\mathrm{Degen}}(\vec{\chi}) = \left(\frac{1}{(2\pi)^N \det_{+}(\mathscr{C})}\right)^{\frac{1}{2}} \cdot \exp\left(-\frac{1}{2}(\vec{\chi} - \vec{\mu})^T \mathscr{C}^{+} (\vec{\chi} - \vec{\mu})\right) \tag{1.30}$$

The characteristic function of a degenerate distribution is still given by Eq. (1.24), which is well-defined. In other words, the degenerate distribution can be defined as the inverse Fourier transform of the characteristic function (with appropriate regularization). Covariance can then be obtained by taking the second derivative of the characteristic function. To compute the Wasserstein distance between two Gaussian distributions, it is sufficient that the second derivatives of the characteristic functions of the two distributions are well-defined. In Appendix D, we show that the Wasserstein distance is well-defined even when the covariance matrices of interest are degenerate.

In the next section, we will present the optimal updates for $\vec{m}_U$ and $\mathscr{C}_U$.

1.5. Main Result: Optimal Update

Theorem 1.5.1. *$\mathscr{L}_{GWB}$ is minimized when,*

$$\vec{m}_U = \vec{m}_\star = W\left(\vec{\mu}_P + \lambda \mathscr{P}^T \vec{\nu}_V\right) \quad \textit{with} \;\; W = \left(\mathbb{I}_{N_a} + \lambda \mathscr{P}^T \mathscr{P}\right)^{-1} = W^T \tag{1.31}$$

$$\mathscr{C}_U = \mathscr{C}_\star = (W + \mathcal{B})\mathscr{C}_P (W + \mathcal{B}) \tag{1.32}$$

where $\mathcal{B} = \mathcal{B}^T$, which is given by

$$\mathcal{B} = \lambda W A^{-\frac{1}{2}} \left(A^{\frac{1}{2}} \mathscr{P}^T \mathscr{C}_V \mathscr{P} A^{\frac{1}{2}}\right)^{\frac{1}{2}} A^{-\frac{1}{2}} W, \qquad A = W \mathscr{C}_P W \tag{1.33}$$

Proof. A detailed proof of this theorem is presented in Appendix E. ∎

In Eq. (1.29), $A^{\frac{1}{2}}$ denotes the matrix square root as usual, and its existence is guaranteed by the spectral theorem. The result in Theorem 1.5.1 is a generalization of the McCann interpolant for two Gaussian distributions living on (sub)spaces of different dimensions. To our knowledge, the result in Theorem 1.5.1 and its proof in Appendix E have not been previously reported in the literature. Theorem 1.5.1 is the main result of this article, and in the following we present comments and some consistency checks for this result.

Remark 1.5.1. The optimal update for the drift does not depend on the prior or view covariance matrices.[c] In particular, if $N_v = N_a$ and $\mathscr{P} = \mathbb{I}_{N_a}$ (i.e., the investor has an absolute view regarding every single asset), then the update drift is simply a weighted average of $\vec{\mu}_P$ and $\vec{\nu}_{\mathcal{V}}$.

Remark 1.5.2. In the case when $\mathscr{P}^T\mathscr{C}_{\mathcal{V}}\mathscr{P}$ is invertible, using Lemma A.2 in Appendix A repeatedly, we obtain

$$\mathscr{C}_\star = (\lambda W + \Gamma)\mathscr{P}^T\mathscr{C}_{\mathcal{V}}\mathscr{P}(\lambda W + \Gamma),$$

$$\text{where } \Gamma = W\mathscr{C}_P^{\frac{1}{2}}\left(\mathscr{C}_P^{\frac{1}{2}}W\mathscr{P}^T\mathscr{C}_{\mathcal{V}}\mathscr{P}W\mathscr{C}_P^{\frac{1}{2}}\right)^{-\frac{1}{2}}\mathscr{C}_P^{\frac{1}{2}}W \tag{1.34}$$

$$= A + \lambda^2 W\mathscr{P}^T\mathscr{C}_{\mathcal{V}}\mathscr{P}W + \lambda(A\mathscr{P}^T\mathscr{C}_{\mathcal{V}}\mathscr{P})^{\frac{1}{2}}W + \lambda W(\mathscr{P}^T\mathscr{C}_{\mathcal{V}}\mathscr{P}A)^{\frac{1}{2}} \tag{1.35}$$

To obtain the expression in Eq. (1.30), we use the definition of Γ in Eq. (E.32) shown in Appendix E.2. When the views matrix $\mathscr{P} = \mathbb{I}$, Eq. (1.30) reduces to the McCann interpolant (refer to Example 1.7 of Ref. [12] or Lemma 2.3 in Ref. [17]), with the identification $t \to \frac{1}{1+\lambda}$. Similarly, Eq. (1.31) reduces to Eqs. (1.39) and (1.63) in Ref. [18] when $\mathscr{P} = \mathbb{I}$. This implies that $\mathscr{C}_\star$ is a point on the geodesic connecting the two points corresponding to $\mathscr{C}_P$ and $\mathscr{C}_{\mathcal{V}}$ on the Bures–Wasserstein manifold (when $\mathscr{P} = \mathbb{I}$). The parameter t controls the distance of $\mathscr{C}_\star$ from $\mathscr{C}_P$; meanwhile, in the financial context, the parameter λ is used to control the confidence in investor views. When an investor has complete confidence in their views, $\lambda \to \infty$; similarly, if an investor has very low confidence in the views then $\lambda \to 0$.

In the case when the matrices $\mathscr{C}_{\mathcal{V}}$ and $\mathscr{C}_P$ are diagonal matrices and the views matrix $\mathscr{P} = \mathbb{I}$, we get the following simple expression for the updated volatility:

$$\sigma_{\star,i} = \frac{\sigma_{P,i} + \lambda\sigma_{\mathcal{V},i}}{1+\lambda}, \quad \text{where } \mathscr{C}_\circ = \text{DIAG}\left(\sigma_{\circ,i}^2\right) \Rightarrow \sigma_{\circ,i}^2 = \left(\mathscr{C}_\circ\right)_{ii}, \quad \circ \in \{\star, P, \mathcal{V}\} \tag{1.36}$$

Remark 1.5.3. When an investor provides views on the expected returns, we set $\mathscr{C}_P = \mathscr{C}_d = \tau\hat{\mathscr{C}}_R$, $\mathscr{C}_{\mathcal{V}} = \mathscr{C}_{\mathcal{V}_d}$, $\vec{\mu}_P = \vec{\mu}_d$, and $\vec{\nu}_{\mathcal{V}} = \vec{\nu}_{\mathcal{V}_d}$. In this case, the updated distribution for the returns (using the geometric approach) is given by

$$\mathbb{P}_{\mathcal{V}_d,\star}(\vec{R}) = \phi(\vec{m}_{\text{GWBI}}, \mathscr{C}_{\text{GWBI}}) \tag{1.37}$$

[c]This expression for the drift update has a lot of resemblance to the drift update proposed by Doust [16]. However, there are many crucial differences and the resemblance might just be a coincidence.

where $\mathbb{P}_{V_d,\star}(\vec{R})$ denotes the distribution of returns obtained from the optimal updates for the expected returns, $\vec{m}_{\text{GWBI}}$ and $\mathscr{C}_{\text{GWBI}}$ are given by

$$\vec{m}_{\text{GWBI}} = W\left(\vec{\mu}_d + \lambda \mathscr{P}^T \vec{v}_{V_d}\right) \tag{1.38}$$

$$\mathscr{C}_{\text{GWBI}} = \hat{\mathscr{C}}_R + \tau\left(W + \mathcal{B}_{V_d}\right)\hat{\mathscr{C}}_R\left(W + \mathcal{B}_{V_d}\right) \tag{1.39}$$

$$\mathcal{B}_{V_d} = \lambda W A_d^{-\frac{1}{2}}\left(A_d^{\frac{1}{2}} \mathscr{P}^T \mathscr{C}_{V_d} \mathscr{P} A_d^{\frac{1}{2}}\right)^{\frac{1}{2}} A_d^{-\frac{1}{2}} W \tag{1.40}$$

$$A_d = W\mathscr{C}_d W = \tau W \hat{\mathscr{C}}_R W \tag{1.41}$$

Note that $\mathbb{P}_{V_d,\star}(\vec{R})$ is not a conditional distribution. We refer to the model that uses the geometric approach to incorporate views on the **expected returns** as the GWBMODEL-I.

Remark 1.5.4. When an investor provides views on the asset returns (as in BL Model-II), we set $\mathscr{C}_P = \hat{\mathscr{C}}_R$, $\mathscr{C}_V = \mathscr{C}_{V_R}$, $\vec{\mu}_P = \hat{\vec{\mu}}_R$, and $\vec{v}_V = \vec{v}_{V_R}$. In this case, the updated distribution for returns (in the geometric approach) is given by

$$\mathbb{P}_{V_R,\star}(\vec{R}) = \phi(\vec{m}_{\text{GWBII}}, \mathscr{C}_{\text{GWBII}}) \tag{1.42}$$

where $\mathbb{P}_{V_R,\star}(\vec{R})$ denotes the distribution of returns obtained from the optimal updates for the expected returns, $\vec{m}_{\text{GWBII}}$ and $\mathscr{C}_{\text{GWBII}}$ are given by,

$$\vec{m}_{\text{GWBII}} = W\left(\hat{\vec{\mu}}_R + \lambda \mathscr{P}^T \vec{v}_{V_R}\right) \tag{1.43}$$

$$\mathscr{C}_{\text{GWBII}} = \left(W + \mathcal{B}_{V_R}\right)\hat{\mathscr{C}}_R\left(W + \mathcal{B}_{V_R}\right) \tag{1.44}$$

$$\mathcal{B}_{V_R} = \lambda W A_R^{-\frac{1}{2}}\left(A_R^{\frac{1}{2}} \mathscr{P}^T \mathscr{C}_{V_R} \mathscr{P} A_R^{\frac{1}{2}}\right)^{\frac{1}{2}} A_R^{-\frac{1}{2}} W \tag{1.45}$$

$$A_R = W\hat{\mathscr{C}}_R W \tag{1.46}$$

We refer to the model that uses the geometric approach to incorporate views on the **asset returns** as the GWBMODEL-II.

Remark 1.5.5. When $\lambda = 0$, we have $(\vec{m}_\star, \mathscr{C}_\star) = (\vec{\mu}_P, \mathscr{C}_P)$ and when $\lambda \to \infty$, we have $\mathscr{P}\vec{m}_\star = \vec{v}_V$ and $\mathscr{P}\mathscr{C}_U\mathscr{P}^T = \mathscr{C}_V$. Hence, $t = 1/(1+\lambda)$ plays the role of investor confidence, as it allows us to interpolate smoothly between the prior and views distribution (as described in Section 1.1). The parameter λ has no counterpart in the conventional BL model. Note that in GWBMODEL-I, which is the geometric analog of BL Model-I, the updated drift of the returns aligns with the views drift when $\lambda \to \infty$; however, the updated covariance of returns is $\mathscr{C}_{\text{GWBI}} = \hat{\mathscr{C}}_R + \mathscr{P}^T \mathscr{C}_{V_d} \mathscr{P}$ which depends on $\hat{\mathscr{C}}_R$. This is counterintuitive as the updates $\vec{m}_\star$ and $\mathscr{C}_\star$ match the views distribution. This is an artifact of the model that stems from the views being specified on the expected returns and not on the returns themselves.

This is also a feature of the BL Model-I, which was pointed out by Meucci in Ref. [4]. The fact that the posterior drift of GWBMODEL-I matches the drift of views when investor confidence is 100% is a desirable feature, as it rewards an investor for having confidence in correct views. In GWBMODEL-II, which is the geometric analog of BL Model-II, the updated drift and covariance of the returns match the views distribution as the views are expressed directly on the returns. As explained in Section 1.2.3, neither BL Model-I nor BL Model-II can produce a posterior distribution that matches with the views distribution when the investor is 100% confident in their views.

A judicious method of hyperparameter tuning based on regime shift models can be used for determining the optimal λ. Though, tuning the values of λ dynamically is an interesting topic for further exploration, in this note, we assume λ is a constant for simplicity.

Remark 1.5.6. An additional point worth mentioning is that the inverse of the update covariance matrix does not involve inverting $\mathscr{C}_P$ and can also be written as follows:

$$\mathscr{C}_\star^{-1} = W^{-1}A^{\frac{1}{2}}\left(A^{\frac{1}{2}}W^{-1}A^{\frac{1}{2}} + \lambda\left(A^{\frac{1}{2}}\mathscr{P}^T\mathscr{C}_V\mathscr{P}A^{\frac{1}{2}}\right)^{\frac{1}{2}}\right)^{-2}A^{\frac{1}{2}}W^{-1} \tag{1.47}$$

It would be interesting to check if portfolios constructed using the above estimation for the covariance matrix and drift are less sensitive to estimation errors. This note will not address questions surrounding the sensitivity of portfolios constructed using the approach described here. We do, however, present an approach for comparing portfolios constructed using the approach described here and the traditional BL approach. In the next section, we briefly describe the portfolio construction methodology.

1.6. Incorporating Investor Views in Mean-Variance Portfolio

In this study, we are interested in comparing the efficacy of incorporating investor views in a simple allocation model where the weights are computed by solving the following MVO problem:

$$\text{MVO}[\vec{m}_E, \mathscr{C}_E; \gamma_R, r_f]:$$

$$\vec{w} = \underset{\vec{x}}{\operatorname{argmax}}\left[\left(\vec{m}_E - r_f\vec{e}\right)^T\vec{x} - \frac{\gamma_R}{2}\vec{x}^T\mathscr{C}_E\vec{x}\right] \tag{1.48}$$

subject to

$$\vec{e}^T\vec{x} = 1 \tag{1.49}$$

$$x_i \geq 0, \quad \forall\, i \in \{1, 2, \ldots, N_a\} \tag{1.50}$$

In the aforementioned optimization problem, r_f is the risk free rate, $\vec{e}^T = [1, 1, \ldots, 1]_{N_a} \equiv \vec{\mathbf{1}}_{N_a}$, N_a is the total number of assets, γ_R is a risk aversion parameter (positive), $\vec{m}_E$ is an estimate for the drift and $\mathscr{C}_E$ is an estimate of the covariance matrix. In the rest of this article, we assume $r_f = 0$. The optimization problem, $\mathrm{MVO}[\vec{m}_E, \mathscr{C}_E; \gamma_R] \equiv \mathrm{MVO}[\vec{m}_E, \mathscr{C}_E; \gamma_R, r_f = 0]$, is solved using CvxPy [19, 20].

We do not analyze the impacts of transaction costs, holding or borrowing costs, slippage, and so on, in our present analysis as the primary goal of this study is to compare the efficacy of the drift and covariance corrections. In realistic investment (or trading) processes, it is often essential to enforce constraints on factor exposures and other trading constraints. In Refs. [21, 22], the authors provide a formulation that incorporates realistic cost models, constraints that are convex and certain risk measures that are different from the risk metric considered in Markowitz's original proposal. The analysis in Refs. [21, 22] can be extended to incorporate investor views using the updated covariance and drift. However, we do not present such a study here as it will largely deviate from the objective of this paper.

We evaluate the efficacy of the traditional BL and the current geometric approaches by solving $\mathrm{MVO}[\vec{m}_E, \mathscr{C}_E; \gamma_R]$ for the following four methods of estimating the drift and covariance:

- $\mathrm{BL_I}$ **Allocation Methodology**: In this methodology, views are specified on the expected returns (or drift in returns). The reference or prior model specifies the distribution of expected drift, and the updates are computed using the BL Model-I. Drifts and covariance appearing in the updated distribution in Eq. (1.9) are used as inputs to the optimization problem MVO specified in Eqs. (1.44)–(1.46). A description of the methodology can be found in Appendix F.1.
- $\mathrm{BL_{II}}$ **Allocation Methodology**: In this methodology, views are specified directly on asset returns. The prior model specifies the distribution of asset returns and the updates are computed using BL Model-II. Drifts and covariance appearing in the updated distribution in Eq. (1.12) are used as inputs to the optimization problem MVO specified in Eqs. (1.44)–(1.46). A description of the methodology can be found in Appendix F.2.
- $\mathrm{GWB_I}$ **Allocation Methodology**: In this methodology, views are specified on the expected returns, similar to the approach used in the $\mathrm{BL_I}$ allocation model. The prior model specifies the distribution of asset returns, and the updates are computed using GWBModel-I. Drifts and covariance appearing in the updated distribution in Eqs. (1.34) and (1.35–1.37) are used as inputs to the optimization problem MVO specified in Eqs. (1.44)–(1.46). A description of the methodology can be found in Appendix F.3.
- $\mathrm{GWB_{II}}$ **Allocation Methodology**: This method is analogous to the $\mathrm{BL_{II}}$ allocation model. In this methodology, views are specified on asset returns directly. The prior model specifies the distribution of the asset returns, and the updates are computed using GWBModel-II. Drifts and covariance appearing in the updated distribution in Eqs. (1.39) and (1.40–1.42) are used as inputs to the optimization problem MVO specified in Eqs. (1.44)–(1.46). A description of the methodology is provided in Appendix F.4.

1.7. Testing and Evaluation Methodology

In this section, we present a methodology employed for comparing the efficacy of the aforementioned methods to incorporate views in asset allocation. The testing or evaluation methodology consists of the following two components:

(i) An evaluation where the inputs to the allocation methodologies can be controlled. We use simulated data (Gaussian) for this test to respect the assumptions of the allocation methodologies. This stage of testing will be called preliminary evaluation, as it is designed in such a way that the backtesting principles are violated. This violation is required at this stage to generate controlled views as inputs to the allocation methodologies. If a methodology fails at this stage of testing, it implies that the methodology does not work as expected. The precise details of the preliminary evaluation procedure will be discussed later in this section.

(ii) In the second stage, we use "walk-forward" backtesting to evaluate the allocation methodologies. At best, backtesting only estimates the efficacy of an investment strategy on the "single realization" of an unknown process that describes market dynamics. Making decisions purely based on the backtested results on a "single realization" leads to overfitted strategies [23]. Backtesting on synthetic paths that capture the stylized facts in historical market data is a reasonable alternative. However, the methodology for generating synthetic data and evaluating synthetic data quality must be developed with caution. Although the topic of generating realistic synthetic data is interesting in its own right, unfortunately a detailed discussion on this topic is beyond the scope of this paper. In this study, we present a simpler alternative to reducing the risks of backtest overfitting. This alternative approach will be discussed in Section 1.7.3.

We now present the details of the two stages of our testing methodology.

1.7.1. *Stage I testing: Simulated data*

The objective of this evaluation phase is to assess the effectiveness of the various allocation methodologies (outlined previously) across three scenarios: (i) when views are "correct," (ii) when views are "ambiguous," and (iii) when views are "incorrect." In the following, we provide a brief explanation of the three situations and the motivation to evaluate the methodologies across these situations:

(a) *Correct views*: A view is considered "correct" when it aligns with the future realization of returns or expected returns. In real trading, it is highly unlikely that there is an investor who is correct about his or her views consistently throughout history.[d] However, for preliminary evaluation, we are interested in testing if the proposed allocation

[d] In other words, we do not believe that any investor possesses a "clairvoyant crystal ball," nor do we believe such a thing exists. If it did, the authors would be searching for one rather than writing this paper.

methodology can outperform the conventional method if an investor uses "consistently correct" views with higher confidence. As emphasized earlier, an ideal allocation methodology should give an investor the flexibility to incorporate his or her views with the desired degree of subjective confidence. In addition, it is desirable to have a methodology that rewards the investor for choosing the right level of confidence for their correct views.

(b) *Ambiguous views*: An "ambiguous view" is a view that is uncorrelated with the future realization of the returns or expected returns. Though no investor intentionally picks "ambiguous views," the market can behave erratically making the views look ambiguous. An investor can make an informed decision regarding their confidence in a view, if an allocation methodology underperforms when the views are ambiguous in comparison with "correct views."[e]

(c) *Incorrect views*: A view is considered "incorrect" when the future realization of returns or expected returns negatively align with the view. Again, it is highly unlikely that an investor is incorrect consistently; however, it is desirable to have an allocation methodology that can penalize more for having more confidence in incorrect views. For instance, let us consider an investor who wishes to calibrate the confidence parameter (associated with a set of views) using backtested results on simulated or synthetic data. If the allocation methodology underperforms more often when confidence associated with incorrect views is high, the calibration (or "hyperparameter tuning") methodology is more likely to assign correspondingly lower confidence to incorrect views.

So far, we have not presented the procedure for generating views that can be classified as correct, ambiguous, or incorrect. The precise methodology for views generation used in our preliminary evaluation and other details of the testing procedure are described below:

- For preliminary evaluation, we use simulated returns data. In particular, we generate multiple ($N_{\wp}$) samples of the daily return time series of length T for N_a assets as follows: for each $\wp \in \{1, 2, \ldots, N_{\wp}\}$, we sample T independent identically distributed random variables from an MVN distribution $\mathcal{N}\left(\vec{\mu}_{\text{Sim},\wp},\ \mathscr{C}_{\text{Sim},\wp}\right)$, where $\vec{\mu}_{\text{Sim},\wp} \in \mathbb{R}^{N_a}$, and $\mathscr{C}_{\text{Sim},\wp} \in \text{Sym}_{N_a}(\mathbb{R})$. Note that for each $\wp$, the daily return series is in the form of a panel data with T rows and N_a columns. Furthermore, the $\wp^{th}$ return series can be represented as a path in N_a-dimensional space, and we refer to such a path as N_a-path. Hence, each simulated returns time series is a single sample from the space of all N_a-paths, and we generate $N_{\wp}$ samples. In our testing methodology, we choose T to be more than 10 years, the number of assets (N_a) to be 50 and $N_{\wp} \sim 250$.
- For each $\wp$, we use each of the allocation methodologies BL_{I}, BL_{II}, GWB_{I}, and GWB_{II} to construct portfolios of the N_a "simulated" assets. In the following we describe the inputs to the allocation methodologies and the rebalancing details:

[e]For example, if an investor makes more money from lottery winnings rather than their investment decisions, then he or she might be tempted to invest in lottery tickets rather than their investment ideas.

- Portfolio rebalancing occurs quarterly. We want to emphasize that the rebalancing method used in our preliminary evaluation is theoretical rather than practical, as the process for generating market views has been deliberately calibrated to either match or conflict with future actual returns.
- The covariance matrix of the prior distribution is estimated from the historical data using a look-back window of length ℓ_b (6 months) ending on the rebalance day. The drift of the prior distribution, $\vec{\mu}_P$, is computed using the reference model in Eq. (1.3) by assuming that the benchmark weights are all equal and sum up to 1. That is,

$$\vec{\mu}_P = \gamma_R \mathscr{C}_P \vec{w}_{\mathrm{BM}}, \qquad \text{where } \vec{w}_{\mathrm{BM}} = \frac{1}{N_a}\vec{\mathbf{e}} \tag{1.51}$$

In the above equations, $\vec{\mu}_P = \vec{\mu}_d$, $\mathscr{C}_P = \mathscr{C}_d$, $\vec{\nu}_V = \vec{\nu}_{V_d}$, and $\mathscr{C}_V = \mathscr{C}_{V_d}$ for the $\mathrm{BL_I}$ and $\mathrm{GWB_I}$ allocation methodologies, while for $\mathrm{BL_{II}}$ and $\mathrm{GWB_{II}}$ allocation methodologies $\vec{\mu}_P = \vec{\mu}_R$, $\mathscr{C}_P = \mathscr{C}_R$, $\vec{\nu}_V = \vec{\nu}_{V_R}$, and $\mathscr{C}_V = \mathscr{C}_{V_R}$.
- For testing, we choose $\mathscr{P} = \mathbb{I}_{N_a}$. Nevertheless, the discussions in the preceding sections (in particular, the main result in Section 1.5 and its proof in Appendix E) apply to any general views matrix $\mathscr{P}$.
- We now discuss the views generating process. In the preliminary evaluation, we use a *forward looking window* ($\mathbb{F}_W$) of length ℓ_f, starting from the date of rebalance. In this paper, we set ℓ_f to 3 years. For each method, we conduct experiments with the three views mentioned before:
  (a) *Correct (but "blurred") views*: As mentioned earlier, investor views are considered correct when they align with future returns. That is, the expected return and covariance of the views match with those of the returns in $\mathbb{F}_W$. We can get unreasonably good results if we assume that the views perfectly match with the future returns. Hence, we "blur" the views to make them align with the future returns only approximately by introducing some uncertainty. In particular, we sample $\mathscr{C}_V$ from a Wishart distribution and $\vec{\nu}_V$ from an MVN distribution as shown below:

$$\vec{\nu}_V \sim \mathcal{N}\left(\mathscr{P}\vec{\mu}_{P,\mathbb{F}_W}, \mathscr{C}_V\right), \tag{1.52}$$

$$\mathscr{C}_V = \ell_f^{-1}\mathfrak{S}, \quad \text{where } \mathfrak{S} \sim \mathcal{W}\left(\ell_f, \mathscr{P}\mathscr{C}_{P,\mathbb{F}_W}\mathscr{P}^T\right) \tag{1.53}$$

  where $\vec{\mu}_{P,\mathbb{F}_W}$ and $\mathscr{C}_{P,\mathbb{F}_W}$ are the drift and covariance of the prior distribution estimated from the forward-looking window. Note that the expected value of ν_V is $\mathscr{P}\vec{\mu}_{P,\mathbb{F}_W}$ and the expected covariance is $\mathscr{P}\mathscr{C}_{P,\mathbb{F}_W}\mathscr{P}^T$. This ensures that the views are approximately aligned with the future returns.
  (b) *Ambiguous view*: When the views are ambiguous, $\vec{\nu}_V$ has no positive or negative alignment with the future returns. Hence, we model ambiguous views as shown below:

$$\vec{\nu}_V \sim \mathcal{N}\left(\vec{0}_{N_v}, \mathscr{C}_V\right), \tag{1.54}$$

$$\mathscr{C}_V = \ell_f^{-1}\mathfrak{S}, \quad \text{where } \mathfrak{S} \sim \mathcal{W}\left(\ell_f, \mathscr{P}\mathscr{C}_{P,\mathbb{F}_W}\mathscr{P}^T\right) \tag{1.55}$$

(c) *Incorrect (but "blurred") views*: Incorrect views are modeled like correct views except that the drifts are drift of the views are negative, aligned with the future returns as shown below:

$$\vec{\nu}_V \sim \mathcal{N}\left(-\mathscr{P}\vec{\mu}_{P,\mathbb{F}_W}, \mathscr{C}_V\right), \tag{1.56}$$

$$\mathscr{C}_V = \ell_f^{-1}\mathfrak{S}, \quad \text{where } \mathfrak{S} \sim \mathcal{W}\left(\ell_f, \mathscr{P}\mathscr{C}_{P,\mathbb{F}_W}\mathscr{P}^T\right) \tag{1.57}$$

Note that the drift of the views is exactly the opposite of correct views.

- Using the above methodology for estimating prior and views and equations (F.3), (F.6), (F.9), and (F.15), we compute $\left(\vec{m}_E^{\mathrm{BL_I}}, \vec{m}_E^{\mathrm{BL_{II}}}, \vec{m}_E^{\mathrm{GWB_I}}, \vec{m}_E^{\mathrm{GWB_{II}}}\right)$. Similarly, we compute $\left(\mathscr{C}_E^{\mathrm{BL_I}}, \mathscr{C}_E^{\mathrm{BL_{II}}}, \mathscr{C}_E^{\mathrm{GWB_I}}, \mathscr{C}_E^{\mathrm{GWB_{II}}}\right)$ using equations (F.2), (F.5), (F.12), and (F.18) and the estimation for prior and views obtained using the methodology described in the earlier points.
- We define **back-validation** as the procedure for evaluating how a strategy would play out on historical data if the future information required for validating the strategy was made available.[f] For example, in our paper we are interested in playing out the strategy when we provide correct or incorrect views, and it is not possible to determine the correctness of a view without using future information. It is preferable to use the back-validation procedure on synthetic or simulated data that respects the assumptions of the model underlying the strategy.

  Using the weights allocation procedure described in Appendix F, we "back-validate" the four methodologies to compute the portfolios' returns and performance characteristics. We use a quarterly rebalancing schedule for all four allocation methodologies.

- For every path $\wp$, the Sharpe ratios $\mathscr{S}_{\mathrm{BL_I}}(\wp)$, $\mathscr{S}_{\mathrm{BL_I}}(\wp)$, $\mathscr{S}_{\mathrm{GWB_I}}(\wp)$, $\mathscr{S}_{\mathrm{GWB_{II}}}(\wp)$ are computed. We also compute the Sharpe ratio for the benchmark allocation methodology (specified by $\vec{\omega}_{\mathrm{BM}}$). The Sharpe ratio of the benchmark is denoted by $\mathscr{S}_{\mathrm{BM}}(\wp)$.[g]
- We measure two allocation methodologies using the Sharpe ratio as the evaluation metric. The outperformance metric $\Delta\mathscr{S}(A, B)$ is defined as the difference in the expected Sharpe ratios of methodology A and B. More precisely, the outperformance metric $\Delta\mathscr{S}(A, B)$ is

$$\Delta\mathscr{S}(A, B) = \mathbb{E}_{\wp}\left[\mathscr{S}_A(\wp) - \mathscr{S}_B(\wp)\right] \tag{1.58}$$

We can also evaluate outperformance by comparing other performance metrics, such as the Sortino ratio, Calmar ratio, Omega ratio, and so on; however, in this paper, we use the difference in Sharpe ratios as the chosen metric. If $\Delta\mathscr{S}(A, B)$ is statistically significant, we can infer that A outperforms B. The outperformance is considered statistically significant if the following test statistic is above a critical threshold t_c:

[f] The purpose of this definition is to distinguish the first stage of our testing methodology from regular backtesting.
[g] Recall that we have set the risk-free rate to zero.

$$t(A,B) = N_{\wp}^{\frac{1}{2}} \frac{\mathbb{E}_{\wp}\left[\mathcal{S}_A(\wp) - \mathcal{S}_B(\wp)\right]}{\sqrt{\mathrm{VAR}_{\wp}\left[\mathcal{S}_A(\wp) - \mathcal{S}_B(\wp)\right]}} \tag{1.59}$$

where $N_{\wp}$ is the number of paths.

1.7.2. *Results of stage I testing*

For the numerical study presented in this section, we chose $\gamma_R = 2.5$, $\ell_b = 125$, $\ell_f = 750$, $\tau = \ell_b^{-1}$, $N_a = 50$, $N_v = N_a$, $T = 4{,}000$, and $N_{\wp} = 250$.[h] We present the findings for two distinct values of the confidence parameter t defined as follows:

$$t = \frac{\lambda}{1+\lambda}$$

Note that $0 \leq t \leq 1$. In principle, t can be tuned dynamically or determined through a hyperparameter tuning methodology.

In our analysis, we examine the results of the methodology for two different values of the confidence parameter: $t = 95\%$ for high confidence and $t = 5\%$ for low confidence. We want to re-emphasize that t is the investor's subjective confidence, not the confidence interval determined by the covariance or precision. We denote the geometric allocation methodologies with $t = 95\%$ as $\mathrm{GWB_I}$ (High) and $\mathrm{GWB_{II}}$ (High) and those with $t = 5\%$ as $\mathrm{GWB_I}$ (Low) and $\mathrm{GWB_{II}}$ (Low).

In the following, we present our findings of the preliminary evaluation under the three scenarios: when views are (a) correct, (b) ambiguous, and (c) incorrect. The outperformance metric $\Delta\mathcal{S}$ (defined earlier) is used for comparing the $\mathrm{GWB_I}$ and $\mathrm{GWB_{II}}$ allocation methodologies (with confidence parameters $t = 95\%$ and $t = 5\%$) with the benchmark and $\mathrm{BL_I}$ and $\mathrm{BL_{II}}$ methodologies. We choose a threshold of $t_c = 3.125$ for the test statistic t. This t_c value corresponds to a significance level or $p-$value threshold of 0.001 with $N_{\wp} - 1$ as the degree of freedom.[i]

1.7.2.1. Performance with correct views

Figure 1.3 shows the distribution of Sharpe ratios for the different allocation methodologies when the investor views are correct. The location of the peaks of the histograms shows that the geometric approaches outperform the BL models. This can also be inferred quite directly from Table 1.1 (Top), which shows the outperformance metric $\Delta\mathcal{S}(A,B)$ for $A \in \{\mathrm{GWB_I}, \mathrm{GWB_{II}}\}$ and $B \in \{\mathrm{BM}, \mathrm{BL_I}, \mathrm{BL_{II}}, \mathrm{GWB_I}, \mathrm{GWB_{II}}\}$.

Clearly, both geometric approaches based on GWB outperform the benchmark and both BL models when the views are "correct" and the investor has *high* confidence in their views. The corresponding test static is shown in Table 1.1 (Bottom) and we conclude that the extent of outperformance is significant.

[h]Note that $T = 4{,}000$ corresponds to around 15 years of daily returns.

[i]We are only interested in one-sided tail.

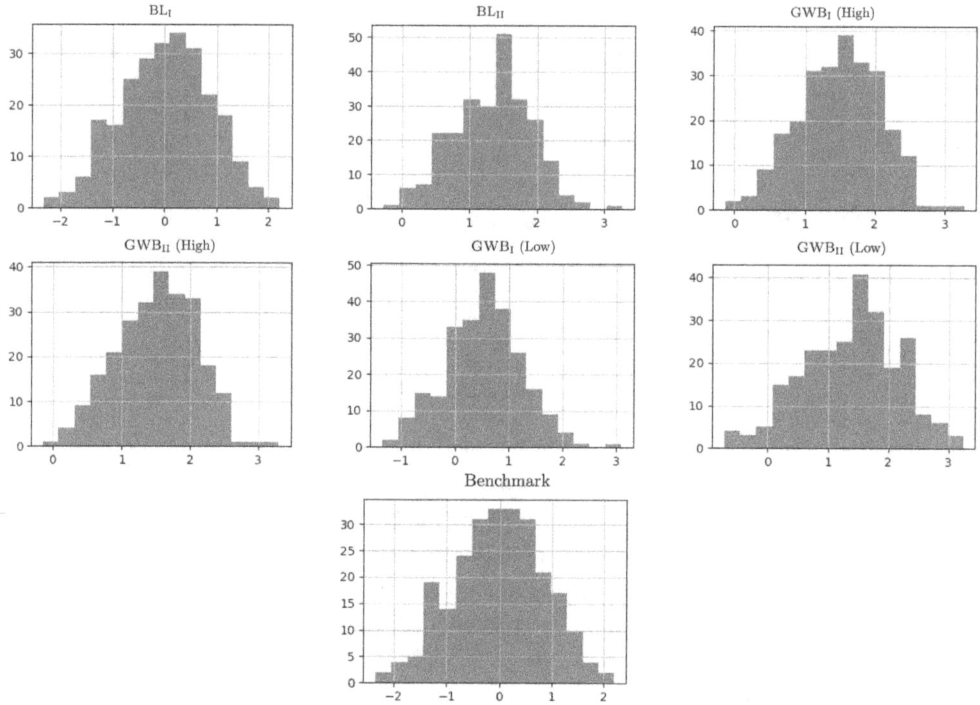

Fig. 1.3 Shows the distribution of Sharpe ratios for the benchmark, $\mathrm{BL_I}$, $\mathrm{BL_{II}}$, $\mathrm{GWB_I}$, and $\mathrm{GWB_{II}}$ (High and Low) allocation methodologies. All allocation methodologies use "correct" views to update the expected return and covariance.

However, if investors have *low* confidence in their "correct views" consistently, then they can only outperform the benchmark and $\mathrm{BL_I}$ model using the geometric approaches. The geometric approaches align closely with the benchmark allocation methodology when confidence is low. Since the $\mathrm{BL_{II}}$ methodology clearly outperforms the benchmark (see Fig. 1.3), it also outperforms the geometric approaches when the investor's degree of confidence is low. Interestingly, the $\mathrm{GWB_{II}}$ method consistently outperforms the $\mathrm{GWB_I}$ method, regardless of the degree of confidence.

Furthermore, geometric approaches incentivize investors for having greater confidence in their "correct" views. This seemingly "qualitative" statement is based on the empirical observation (from the top panel of Table 1.1) that $\mathrm{GWB_I}$(High) and $\mathrm{GWB_{II}}$(High) outperform $\mathrm{GWB_I}$(Low) and $\mathrm{GWB_{II}}$(Low). This outperformance is statistically significant, which is made clear in the bottom panel of Table 1.1. In particular, we note that the test statistic t satisfies

$$t\left(\mathrm{GWB_I(High)}, \mathrm{GWB_I(Low)}\right) > t_c$$

$$t\left(\mathrm{GWB_{II}(High)}, \mathrm{GWB_{II}(Low)}\right) > t_c$$

Table 1.1 (Top) Outperformance metric $\Delta\mathscr{S}(A,B)$ for $A \in$ {GWB_{I}(High), GWB_{II}(High), GWB_{I}(Low), GWB_{II}(Low)} and $B \in$ {BM, BL_{I}, BL_{II}, GWB_{I}(High), GWB_{II}(High), GWB_{I}(Low), GWB_{II}(Low)} when the views are "correct." **(Bottom)** The corresponding test statistic $t(A,B)$. If $t(A,B)$ is lower than t_c, the outperformance of A compared with B is statistically insignificant. If $t(B,A)$ is greater than t_c then the underperformance of A compared with B is statistically significant.

		A			
	Method	**GWB_{I} (High)**	**GWB_{II} (High)**	**GWB_{I} (Low)**	**GWB_{II} (Low)**
	Benchmark	1.51	1.52	0.54	1.39
	BL_{I}	1.48	1.49	0.51	1.36
B	BL_{II}	0.15	0.17	−0.81	0.04
	GWB_{I} (High)	0.00	0.02	−0.96	−0.11
	GWB_{II} (High)	−0.02	0.00	−0.98	−0.13
	GWB_{I} (Low)	0.96	0.98	0.00	0.85
	GWB_{II} (Low)	0.11	0.13	−0.85	0.00

		A			
	Method	**GWB_{I} (High)**	**GWB_{II} (High)**	**GWB_{I} (Low)**	**GWB_{II} (Low)**
	Benchmark	49.6	50.6	16.4	88.3
	BL_{I}	49.3	50.3	15.7	91.0
B	BL_{II}	16.9	18.5	−27.7	1.8
	GWB_{I} (High)	–	21.7	−31.6	−5.5
	GWB_{II} (High)	−21.7	–	−32.1	−6.4
	GWB_{I} (Low)	31.6	32.1	–	27.6
	GWB_{II} (Low)	5.5	6.4	−27.6	–

1.7.2.2. Ambiguous view

We now present the results for the case where the investor views are ambiguous. Table 1.2 shows that when the views are ambiguous and have no relation to the future returns, the outperformance metrics are not statistically significant. This conclusion is expected because there should be no material outperformance (or underperformance) when views have no material information. This conclusion is independent of the degree of confidence as well.

1.7.2.3. Incorrect views

Table 1.3 shows that when the investors provide consistently incorrect views with high confidence to the geometric approaches, they underperform the benchmark as well as the BL models. As explained at the beginning of this section, it is desirable to have a model that underperforms when the views are incorrect and when the confidence parameter is high. Recall that, if the confidence in the view is zero, then the geometric model coincides with

Table 1.2 (Top) Outperformance metric $\Delta\mathscr{S}(A,B)$ in the presence of "ambiguous" views for $A \in \{\text{GWB}_\text{I}, \text{GWB}_\text{II}\}$ and $B \in \{\text{BM}, \text{BL}_\text{I}, \text{BL}_\text{II}, \text{GWB}_\text{I}, \text{GWB}_\text{II}\}$ and for $t = 95\%$ (High) and $t = 5\%$ (Low). **(Bottom)** The corresponding test statistic. If the test statistic t is less than t_c, then the outperformance is statistically insignificant. It is clear from the values in the bottom table that the outperformance is statistically insignificant.

		A			
	Method	**GWB$_\text{I}$ (High)**	**GWB$_\text{II}$ (High)**	**GWB$_\text{I}$ (Low)**	**GWB$_\text{II}$ (Low)**
	Benchmark	−0.05	−0.05	−0.04	0.00
	BL$_\text{I}$	−0.05	−0.05	−0.04	0.00
B	BL$_\text{II}$	0.01	0.01	0.02	0.05
	GWB$_\text{I}$ (High)	0.00	0.00	0.01	0.05
	GWB$_\text{II}$ (High)	0.00	0.00	0.01	0.04
	GWB$_\text{I}$ (Low)	−0.01	−0.01	0.00	0.03
	GWB$_\text{II}$ (Low)	−0.05	−0.04	−0.03	0.00

		A			
	Method	**GWB$_\text{I}$ (High)**	**GWB$_\text{II}$ (High)**	**GWB$_\text{I}$ (Low)**	**GWB$_\text{II}$ (Low)**
	Benchmark	−2.0	−2.0	−1.2	−0.3
	BL$_\text{I}$	−2.0	−2.0	−1.2	−0.3
B	BL$_\text{II}$	0.8	1.1	0.8	2.8
	GWB$_\text{I}$ (High)	–	2.5	0.5	2.4
	GWB$_\text{II}$ (High)	−2.5	–	0.4	2.3
	GWB$_\text{I}$ (Low)	−0.5	−0.4	–	1.2
	GWB$_\text{II}$ (Low)	−2.4	−2.3	−1.2	–

the benchmark, and in the presence of negative views, it is desirable to have an allocation that is closer to the benchmark.

In the geometric approach, the investor is punished less for having lower confidence in "incorrect" views and, in fact, is not punished if they have zero confidence in incorrect views. This observation can be inferred from the two panels in Table 1.3) In particular, we note that

$$\Delta\mathscr{S}\left(\text{GWB}_\text{I}(\text{Low}), \text{GWB}_\text{I}(\text{High})\right) > 0, \qquad t\left(\text{GWB}_\text{I}(\text{Low}), \text{GWB}_\text{I}(\text{High})\right) > t_c$$

$$\Delta\mathscr{S}\left(\text{GWB}_\text{II}(\text{Low}), \text{GWB}_\text{II}(\text{High})\right) > 0, \qquad t\left(\text{GWB}_\text{II}(\text{Low}), \text{GWB}_\text{II}(\text{High})\right) > t_c$$

1.7.2.4. Inference

From the results of our preliminary evaluation, it is clear that the geometric approach behaves as desired in all three situations when the views are (a) correct, (b) ambiguous, and (c) incorrect. The confidence parameter, which is absent in the conventional BL models

Table 1.3 **(Top)** Outperformance metric $\Delta\mathscr{S}(A,B)$ in the presence of "incorrect" views for $A \in \{\text{GWB}_\text{I}, \text{GWB}_\text{II}\}$ and $B \in \{\text{BM}, \text{BL}_\text{I}, \text{BL}_\text{II}, \text{GWB}_\text{I}, \text{GWB}_\text{II}\}$ and for $t = 95\%$ (High) and $t = 5\%$ (Low). **(Bottom)** Shows the corresponding test statistic. If $t(B,A)$ is greater than t_c then the underperformance of A compared to B is statistically significant.

		A			
	Method	**GWB$_\text{I}$ (High)**	**GWB$_\text{II}$ (High)**	**GWB$_\text{I}$ (Low)**	**GWB$_\text{II}$ (Low)**
	Benchmark	−1.46	−1.51	−0.51	−1.39
	BL$_\text{I}$	−1.40	−1.50	−0.50	−1.31
B	BL$_\text{II}$	−0.11	−0.20	0.83	−0.12
	GWB$_\text{I}$ (High)	0.00	−0.01	0.88	0.09
	GWB$_\text{II}$ (High)	0.01	0.0	0.89	0.10
	GWB$_\text{I}$ (Low)	−0.88	−0.89	0.00	−0.80
	GWB$_\text{II}$ (Low)	−0.09	−0.10	0.80	0.00

		A			
	Method	**GWB$_\text{I}$ (High)**	**GWB$_\text{II}$ (High)**	**GWB$_\text{I}$ (Low)**	**GWB$_\text{II}$ (Low)**
	Benchmark	−48.2	−49.3	−15.6	−86.2
	BL$_\text{I}$	−48.1	−49.2	−14.8	−90.2
B	BL$_\text{II}$	−16.1	−17.8	28.2	−2.8
	GWB$_\text{I}$ (High)	–	−20.8	30.9	4.1
	GWB$_\text{II}$ (High)	20.8	–	31.4	5.0
	GWB$_\text{I}$ (Low)	−30.9	−31.4	–	−26.9
	GWB$_\text{II}$ (Low)	−4.1	−5.0	26.9	–

provide additional flexibility to the investors, who can take advantage of this parameter and can (in principle) outperform the benchmark consistently with suitable judicious tuning of the confidence parameter.

The preliminary evaluation was based on unrealistic assumptions and ideal conditions that do not occur in real trading. Hence, it is essential to test the different allocation methodologies on real-world data. The procedure for testing with real data will be described in Section 1.7.3.

1.7.3. *Stage II testing and results*

We now discuss the second stage of the testing methodology, which involves the use of real data. In particular, we utilize historical stock price data from Yahoo Finance to evaluate the performance of the different allocation methodologies discussed in earlier sections. However, unlike the previous stage of testing, we cannot generate multiple "paths" since real-world data represents only a "single realization" of the underlying process that describes the market dynamics. To address this, we propose an alternative approach to backtest on "multiple paths," which can reduce the risk of overfitting. The second stage of testing methodology is described below:

- To create multiple samples or "multiple paths" for backtesting, we choose N_a assets out of a larger universe (denoted by $\mathcal{U}$) with $N_{\mathcal{U}}$ (greater than N_a) assets. This can be done in $\binom{N_{\mathcal{U}}}{N_a}$ ways. For sufficiently large $N_{\mathcal{U}}$ we get a large number of choices, all of which represent paths in N_a-dimensional space. Since each choice leads to an N_a-path, we can label a random selection of N_a stocks by $\wp$ where $\wp \in \{1, 2, \ldots N_{\wp}\}$. Out of the $\binom{N_{\mathcal{U}}}{N_a}$ possible N_a-paths we choose $N_{\wp}$ paths and test our allocation methodologies using the $N_{\wp}$ samples obtained from real data. For each $\wp \in \{1, 2, \ldots N_{\wp}\}$, we use each of the allocation methodologies $\mathrm{BL_I}$, $\mathrm{BL_{II}}$, $\mathrm{GWB_I}$, and $\mathrm{GWB_{II}}$ to construct portfolios of the N_a chosen assets (labeled by $\wp$). In the following, we describe the inputs to the allocation methodologies and the rebalancing details.
- We assume that the prior or the reference distribution is determined using Eq. (1.47). That is, we assume that the benchmark weights are all equal. It is common practice to use weights determined from the market capitalization as the benchmark weights. However, in a random selection of stocks, using market capitalization-based weights could increase the risk of having concentrated benchmark weights. In this paper, we do not analyze whether capitalization-based weights are a better choice for benchmark weights than equal weights. Interesting discussions on this topic can be found in the literature (e.g., Ref. [24]). However, the precise nature of benchmark weights is not crucial for our discussion.

  Again, we use, $\vec{\mu}_P = \vec{\mu}_d$, $\mathscr{C}_P = \mathscr{C}_d$, $\vec{\nu}_V = \vec{\nu}_{V_d}$, and $\mathscr{C}_V = \mathscr{C}_{V_d}$ for the $\mathrm{BL_I}$ and $\mathrm{GWB_I}$ allocation methodologies, while for $\mathrm{BL_{II}}$ and $\mathrm{GWB_{II}}$ allocation methodologies $\vec{\mu}_P = \vec{\mu}_R$, $\mathscr{C}_P = \mathscr{C}_R$, $\vec{\nu}_V = \vec{\nu}_{V_R}$, and $\mathscr{C}_V = \mathscr{C}_{V_R}$.
- We use the weights of a minimum variance (or volatility) portfolio for generating views as shown below:

$$\vec{\mu}_V = \gamma_R \mathscr{C}_P \vec{w}_{\mathrm{MVOL}} \tag{1.60}$$

$$\vec{\nu}_V = \mathscr{P} \vec{\mu}_V \tag{1.61}$$

where $\vec{w}_{\mathrm{MVOL}} = \mathrm{MVO}[\vec{0}, \mathscr{C}_P; \gamma_R]$. Note that $\vec{w}_{\mathrm{MVOL}}$ is the weights of a long-only minimum volatility portfolio with weights adding up to 1. The views covariance matrix is obtained as described below:

$$\mathscr{C}_V = \mathscr{P} \mathscr{C}_P \mathscr{P}^T \tag{1.62}$$

Note that the above estimates of views drift and covariance are obtained using the **historical information only** and forward-looking information is not used here. The rationale behind using $\vec{w}_{\mathrm{MVOL}}$ for generating views is to specify views that reduce the risk of the final portfolio. In the geometric approach, choosing a very high confidence on the views will ensure that the final portfolio lies in the proximity of a minimum volatility portfolio. Hence, we can hope to get portfolios that interpolate between an equally weighted portfolio and a minimum volatility portfolio by tuning the confidence parameter.

- Using the above methodology for estimating prior and views and equations (F.3), (F.6), (F.9), and (F.15), we compute $\left(\vec{m}_E^{\,\mathrm{BL_I}}, \vec{m}_E^{\,\mathrm{BL_{II}}}, \vec{m}_E^{\,\mathrm{GWB_I}}, \vec{m}_E^{\,\mathrm{GWB_{II}}}\right)$. Similarly, we compute the covariances as we did in the preliminary evaluation methodology, using equations (F.2), (F.5), (F.12), and (F.18).
- Using the weights allocation procedure described in Appendix F, we backtest the four methodologies to compute the portfolios' returns and performance characteristics for every choice of N_a assets (i.e., for every $\wp \in \{1, 2, \ldots, N_{\wp}\}$). We use a quarterly rebalancing schedule for all four allocation methodologies. We want to emphasize that the "walk-forward" backtesting is used for this stage of the testing methodology, and only historical information is used.
- We then compute the outperformance metric (difference in Sharpe ratios) and the test statistic t using Eqs. (1.48) and (1.49) as done in the first stage of testing.

1.7.4. *Results of stage II testing*

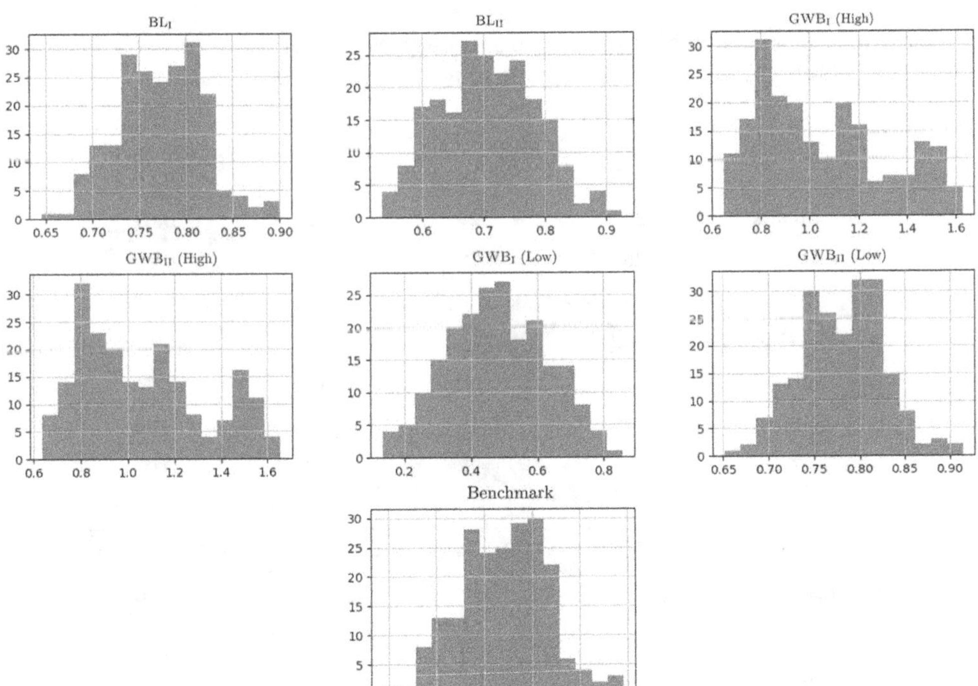

Fig. 1.4 The distribution of Sharpe ratios for the benchmark, $\mathrm{BL_I}$, $\mathrm{BL_{II}}$, $\mathrm{GWB_I}$, and $\mathrm{GWB_{II}}$ (high and low) allocation methodologies. Each distribution of Sharpe ratios shown in the figure is obtained by applying an allocation methodology to different selections of N_a real assets from the universe of stocks $\mathcal{U}$.

For this study, we select the stocks that are the current constituents of the S&P 500, having approximately 15 years of data as the universe $\mathcal{U}$. This has over 350 stocks, out of which we choose $N_a = 50$ stocks at random. By ensuring that the stocks have 15 years of data, we ensure that the universe size does not change with time. All model parameters are the same as those used in the preliminary evaluation. As done in the first stage of testing, we present the results for two confidence parameter values:(i) $t = 95\%$ and (ii) $t = 5\%$. All variables and methodology names are the same as those used in the preliminary evaluation. We now present the result of our testing.

Figure 1.4 shows the distribution of Sharpe ratios for the different allocation methodologies when used on a random selection of N_a real assets. It is quite evident from the histogram plots that the geometric approaches outperform the benchmark and the BL models when a high degree of confidence is specified for the views. It is also clear from Table 1.4 (top) that the GWB_{II} approach performs far better than the conventional BL models and even the GWB_{I} model. The GWB_{I} model underperforms all the methodologies

Table 1.4 (Top) Outperformance metric $\Delta\mathscr{S}(A, B)$ for $A \in \{\text{GWB}_{\text{I}}(\text{High}), \text{GWB}_{\text{II}}(\text{High}), \text{GWB}_{\text{I}}(\text{Low}), \text{GWB}_{\text{II}}(\text{Low})\}$ and $B \in \{\text{BM}, \text{BL}_{\text{I}}, \text{BL}_{\text{II}}, \text{GWB}_{\text{I}}(\text{High}), \text{GWB}_{\text{II}}(\text{High}), \text{GWB}_{\text{I}}(\text{Low}), \text{GWB}_{\text{II}}(\text{Low})\}$. **(Bottom)** The corresponding test statistic $t(A, B)$. If $t(A, B)$ is lower than t_c then the outperformance of A compared to B is statistically insignificant. If $t(B, A)$ is greater than t_c then the underperformance of A compared to B is statistically significant.

		A			
	Method	**GWB_{I} (High)**	**GWB_{II} (High)**	**GWB_{I} (Low)**	**GWB_{II} (Low)**
	Benchmark	0.28	0.29	−0.29	0.01
	BL_{I}	0.28	0.29	−0.29	0.01
B	BL_{II}	0.35	0.36	−0.23	0.07
	GWB_{I} (High)	0.00	0.01	−0.57	−0.27
	GWB_{II} (High)	−0.01	0.00	−0.58	−0.28
	GWB_{I} (Low)	0.57	0.58	0.00	0.30
	GWB_{II} (Low)	0.27	0.28	−0.30	0.00

		A			
	Method	**GWB_{I} (High)**	**GWB_{II} (High)**	**GWB_{I} (Low)**	**GWB_{II} (Low)**
	Benchmark	15.9	16.3	−28.5	30.6
	BL_{I}	15.8	16.2	−28.7	27.5
B	BL_{II}	23.0	23.1	−20.8	17.4
	GWB_{I} (High)	–	7.0	−28.0	−15.4
	GWB_{II} (High)	−7.0	–	−28.2	−15.8
	GWB_{I} (Low)	28.0	28.2	–	29.4
	GWB_{II} (Low)	15.4	15.8	−29.4	–

when a low confidence is specified. In our analysis, GWB_{II} method has outperformed all other approaches in both stages of testing, and it is also intuitive. Therefore, it is worthwhile to examine this allocation methodology in greater detail.

1.8. Conclusions and Outlook

In this study, we presented a geometric approach that incorporates investor views utilizing ideas from optimal transport theory. With the growing applications of optimal transport theory in fields such as machine learning, computer vision, physics, and so on, it is not surprising that optimal transport has utility in portfolio construction. The approach presented in this paper provides an investor with the flexibility to specify the confidence in the form of a parameter that does not exist in the conventional BL models. We provided empirical evidence and theoretical arguments to demonstrate that the geometric approach rewards skillful investors, who can adjust their confidence in their views judicially, more than the conventional BL models.

From a systematic investing perspective, it will be interesting to develop an allocation methodology that tunes the confidence parameter dynamically based on regime shift models that can identify if a view is correct, incorrect, or ambiguous. An investor who wishes to incorporate different views with different levels of confidence can do so by using the multicenter GWB [11], that is, by solving minimizing the following Lagrangian,

$$\mathscr{L}_{GWB} = \left(\mathcal{D}_{WD}(f_U, f_P) + \sum_{i=1}^{K} \lambda_i \mathcal{D}_{WD}(\mathscr{P}^{(i)}_{\sharp}[f_U], f_V) \right) \tag{1.63}$$

where $\mathscr{P}^{(i)}$ denotes the views matrix for the ith view and $t_i = \frac{\lambda_i}{1+\lambda_i}$ is the confidence associated with that view. The Lagrangian in Eq. (1.53) can in principle be minimized numerically; however, the authors are not aware of a closed form expression for the GWB when the number of centers $(K + 1)$ is more than two. Formally, the GWB problem in Eq. (1.53) can also be extended to non-Gaussian distributions.

Note that the main challenge in minimizing Eq. (1.53), when f_P and f_V are Gaussian, lies in deriving the covariance update. The covariance update rule can be applied to forecast covariance matrices and may incorporate various methods of estimating covariance as views. For instance, the covariance update rule (in Eq. 1.28) can be used to find the barycenter of a factor model covariance and historical covariance.

We believe that the geometric approach presented herein has many interesting applications in finance, and the proposed methodology will provide uncorrelated approaches for incorporating investor views.

Acknowledgments

We are grateful to our ADIA colleagues Majed Alromaithi, Dushyant Sharma, Adil Reghai, Oleksiy Kondratiev, Arthur Maghakian, Enzo Busetti, Thomas Schmelzer, Sebastien Lefort, Patrik Karlsson, and other Q-team colleagues, and we wish to thank them for their comments and encouragement.

APPENDIX

A. Some Useful Lemmas

We use the following lemmas in various parts of the papers. These are well-known results and proofs can be found in standard linear algebra text books.

Lemma A.1. $\forall\, Z \in \mathrm{Sym}(\mathbb{R})$,

$$\frac{d}{dZ}\mathrm{tr}\left(K_1 Z^2 K_2\right) = K_1^T K_2^T Z + Z K_1^T K_2^T \tag{A.1}$$

Lemma A.2. $\forall Z_1, Z_2 \in \mathrm{Sym}(\mathbb{R})$,

$$Z_1^{-\frac{1}{2}}\left(Z_1^{\frac{1}{2}} Z_2 Z_1^{\frac{1}{2}}\right)^{\frac{1}{2}} Z_1^{-\frac{1}{2}} = Z_1^{-1}(Z_1 Z_2)^{\frac{1}{2}} = (Z_2 Z_1)^{\frac{1}{2}} Z_1^{-1} \tag{A.2}$$

Lemma A.3. *(a) Solution of a special case of the Lyapunov equation: If A is a symmetric invertible matrix, then* $Z = \frac{\alpha}{2}\mathscr{A}^{-1}$ *is the unique solution* $\left(\text{for } Z \in \mathrm{Sym}_N(\mathbb{R})\right)$ *of the following equation:*

$$\mathscr{A} Z + Z \mathscr{A} = \alpha \mathbb{I} \tag{A.3}$$

That is, $\forall \mathscr{A} \in Sym_N(\mathbb{R})$

$$\mathscr{A} Z + Z \mathscr{A} = \alpha \mathbb{I}_N \Rightarrow Z = \frac{\alpha}{2}\mathscr{A}^{-1} \tag{A.4}$$

(b) If A is a symmetric matrix, then

$$\mathscr{A} Z + Z \mathscr{A} = \alpha \mathbb{I}_N \Rightarrow \mathscr{A} Z = \frac{\alpha}{2}\mathbb{I}_N = Z \mathscr{A} \tag{A.5}$$

Lemma A.4. $\forall Z \in \mathbb{R}^{N \times M}$

$$\mathrm{tr}\left[(Z Z^T)^{\frac{1}{2}}\right] = \mathrm{tr}\left[(Z^T Z)^{\frac{1}{2}}\right] \tag{A.6}$$

B. Lagrangian Form of the Constrained Optimization Problem

This appendix can be skipped by readers who are familiar with Slater conditions and its connection to the existence of Lagrange multipliers in a convex optimization problem.

Proposition B.1. *Let us consider the following optimization problems (with $\vec{\chi} \in \mathbb{R}^d$):*

- *COP:*

$$\min_{\vec{\chi}} \Psi(\vec{\chi}), \tag{B.1}$$

subject to,

$$\vartheta(\vec{\chi}) \leq \vartheta_0 \tag{B.2}$$

- *Lagrangian form (with $\lambda \geq 0$):*

$$\min_{\vec{\chi}} \left[\Psi(\vec{\chi}) + \lambda\vartheta(\vec{\chi})\right] \tag{B.3}$$

where Ψ and ϑ are convex. The above two formulations are equivalent if $\vartheta_0 = 0$ is the only value for which the constrain set (B.2) is feasible but not strictly feasible.

Proof. The statement and a sketch of the proof can be found in Ref. [25]. An equivalent form of the proposition can also be found in Ref. [26] (in particular, Proposition 12 of Ref. [26]). The following proof is a very minor modification of the proof in Ref. [26], and this proposition itself is reasonably well known in the literature on convex optimization. We present the proof here for the convenience of the readers not familiar with this topic.

(i) Let $\vec{\chi}^\star$ be the optimal solution of the COP with $\vartheta_0 \neq 0$. Since $\vartheta_0 = 0$ is the only value for which the constraint set (B.2) is feasible but not strictly feasible, the constraint set (B.2) is strictly feasible for $\vartheta_0 \neq 0$. This implies that the *Slater conditions* are satisfied and strong-duality holds good [27, 28] (Ψ and ϑ are convex functions). In this case, we have

$$\vec{\chi}^\star = \underset{\vec{\chi}}{\operatorname{argmin}} \left(\Psi(\vec{\chi}) + \gamma^\star(\vartheta(\vec{\chi}) - \vartheta_0)\right) \tag{B.4}$$

where $\gamma^\star$ is obtained as follows:

$$\gamma^\star = \underset{\gamma}{\operatorname{argmax}} \left[\min_{\vec{\chi}} \left(\Psi(\vec{\chi}) + \gamma(\vartheta(\vec{\chi}) - \vartheta_0)\right)\right] \tag{B.5}$$

Recall that the duality gap is zero when strong duality holds good, and hence solving (B.4–B.5) is equivalent to solving the original COP. Further, $\gamma^\star\vartheta_0$ is just a constant term while solving for $\vec{\chi}^\star$ in Eq. (B.4) and can be dropped. The problem in Eq. (B.4) is equivalent to solving Eq. (B.3) with $\lambda = \gamma^\star$. When $\vartheta_0 = 0$, the primal problem by itself is equivalent to Eq. (B.3). Hence, we have shown that if $\vec{\chi}^\star$ is an optimal solution of Eq. (B.2) for some ϑ_0, there exists a $\lambda \geq 0$ for which it is optimal in Eq. (B.3).
(ii) We now show that the reverse statement is also true, that is, if $\vec{\chi}^\star$ is an optimal solution of Eq. (B.3) for some $\lambda \geq 0$, there exists a ϑ_0 for which it is optimal in Eq. (B.2). By choosing $\vartheta_0 = \vartheta(\vec{\chi}^\star)$ we have $\vec{\chi}^\star$ to be optimal in Eq. (B.2) as well. This completes the proof of this proposition. ∎

C. Push-Forward of a Measure

Readers familiar with the notion of *push-forward* of a measure can skip this section of the paper.

This appendix provides a formal definition for the push-forward of a measure along a measurable map and a proposition that provides a method for computing the push-forward of a measure. We compute the distribution associated with the push-forward of a Gaussian measure along a linear map as an example application of the proposition. There are much simpler techniques to compute this push-forward (as discussed in the main text), but the method described below can be generalized to arbitrary maps and distributions and hence presented here. The advertised definition and proposition are presented below.

Definition C1.1. *Given a measure space (X_1, Ξ_1, ρ_1), a measurable space (X_2, Ξ_2) and a measurable map $\mathscr{F} : X_1 \mapsto X_2$, the push-forward of ρ_1, $\mathscr{F}_\sharp\, \rho_1$ is defined to be a measure on Ξ_2.*

The following proposition provides a practical definition of push-forward, which is useful for computations:

Proposition C1.1. *Let (X_1, Ξ_1, ρ_1) be a measure space, (X_2, Ξ_2) a measurable space, $\mathscr{F} : X_1 \mapsto X_2$ a measurable map, and a Ξ_2-measurable and integrable function on X_2, $\mathscr{F}_\sharp\, \rho_1$ satisfies the following:*

$$\int_{X_2} g(x_2) d(\mathscr{F}_\sharp\, \rho_1) = \int_{X_1} g(\mathscr{F}(x_1)) d\rho_1 \tag{C.1}$$

Proof. The proof of this proposition can be found in Ref. [29], and the proposition is sometimes known as the change-of-variables theorem [12]. ∎

As an example application, we compute the distribution associated with the push-forward of a Gaussian measure along a linear map $\mathscr{P}$, using Proposition C.1. The precise calculations are described below:

Let $\vec{\chi} \sim \mathcal{N}(\vec{\mu}, \mathscr{C}), f_\chi$ be the multivariate normal distribution associated with $\vec{\chi}$ and $\mathscr{P}$ be the linear map $\mathscr{P} : \vec{\chi} \mapsto \vec{\xi}$ such that $\vec{\xi} = \mathscr{P}\vec{\chi}$.[j] The push-forward $\mathscr{P}_\sharp\, [f_\chi](\vec{\xi})$ is computed by choosing $g(\vec{\xi}')$ as the indicator function $\mathbf{1}_{\vec{\xi}' < \vec{\xi}}$ and differentiating both sides of Eq. (C.1) with respect to $\vec{\xi}$ as shown below:

$$\mathscr{P}_\sharp\, [f_\chi](\vec{\xi}) = \int \frac{d^N \vec{\chi}}{\sqrt{(2\pi)^N \det \mathscr{C}}} \left(e^{-\frac{1}{2}(\vec{\chi}-\vec{\mu})^T \mathscr{C}^{-1}(\vec{\chi}-\vec{\mu})} \delta\left(\mathscr{P}\vec{\chi} - \vec{\xi}\right)\right) \tag{C.2}$$

[j] In Eq. (C.1), we set x_1 to $\vec{\chi}$, x_2 to $\vec{\xi}$, $\mathscr{F}$ to $\mathscr{P}$. The probability density associated with the measure ρ_1 is f_χ.

If $\mathscr{P}$ is a invertible matrix (hence a square matrix), the above integrand is straightforward and evaluates to the Gaussian distribution associated with $\mathcal{N}\left(\mathscr{P}\vec{\mu},\ \mathscr{P}\mathscr{C}\mathscr{P}^T\right)$. We now show that the distribution associated with the push-forward measure has the same form even when $\mathscr{P}$ is not a square matrix. This can be done by introducing the Fourier representation of the Dirac delta in Eq. (C.2) as shown below:

$$\mathscr{P}_\sharp\left[f_\chi\right](\vec{\xi}) = \int \frac{d^N\vec{v}}{(2\pi)^N} e^{-\iota\vec{v}^T(\vec{\xi}-\mathscr{P}\vec{\chi})} \int d^N\vec{\chi} \frac{\left(e^{-\frac{1}{2}(\vec{\chi}-\vec{\mu})^T\mathscr{C}^{-1}(\vec{\chi}-\vec{\mu})}\right)}{\sqrt{(2\pi)^N \det \mathscr{C}}} \tag{C.3}$$

Note that the integrand is still quadratic in $\vec{\chi}$. Hence the integral over $\vec{\chi}$ is a simple Gaussian integral and can be evaluated by reorganizing the integrand as shown below:

$$\begin{aligned}&\mathscr{P}_\sharp\left[f_\chi\right](\vec{\xi})\\ &= \int \frac{d^N\vec{v}}{(2\pi)^N} e^{-\iota\vec{v}^T(\vec{\xi}-\mathscr{P}\vec{\mu})-\frac{1}{2}\vec{v}^T\mathscr{P}\mathscr{C}\mathscr{P}^T\vec{v}} \int d^N\vec{\chi} \frac{\left(e^{-\frac{1}{2}(\vec{\chi}-(\vec{\mu}+\iota\mathscr{C}\mathscr{P}^T\vec{v}))^T\mathscr{C}^{-1}(\vec{\chi}-(\vec{\mu}+\iota\mathscr{C}\mathscr{P}^T\vec{v}))}\right)}{\sqrt{(2\pi)^N \det \mathscr{C}}}\end{aligned} \tag{C.4}$$

The integral over $\vec{\chi}$ is a straightforward Gaussian integral, and we get the following simplified expression for the push-forward distribution.

$$\mathscr{P}_\sharp\left[f_\chi\right](\vec{\xi}) = \int \frac{d^N\vec{v}}{(2\pi)^N} e^{-\iota\vec{v}^T(\vec{\xi}-\mathscr{P}\vec{\mu})-\frac{1}{2}\vec{v}^T\mathscr{P}\mathscr{C}\mathscr{P}^T\vec{v}} \tag{C.5}$$

The expression in Eq. (C.5) is the inverse Fourier transform of the characteristic function of $\mathcal{N}\left(\mathscr{P}\vec{\mu},\ \mathscr{P}\mathscr{C}\mathscr{P}^T\right)$. Note that the above derivation is applicable even when $\mathscr{P}\mathscr{C}\mathscr{P}^T$ is singular or when $\mathscr{P}$ is degenerate.

D. Wasserstein Distance between Two Gaussian Measures

The following details appear in Lemma 2 of Ref. [15], and we present it here again for the sake of clarity and also to emphasize that the Wasserstein distance is well defined even if the views matrix $\mathscr{P}$ is degenerate.

The L_2 Wasserstein distance $\mathscr{W}_2$ between two distributions g_1 and g_2, is defined as follows:

$$\mathscr{W}_2^2(g_1, g_2) = \min_{\gamma\in\mathscr{G}(g_1,g_2)} \mathbb{E}_{\vec{\chi},\vec{\xi}\sim\gamma}\left[\|\vec{\chi}-\vec{\xi}\|^2\right] \tag{D.1}$$

where $\mathscr{G}(g_1, g_2)$ denotes the set of all joint probability distributions whose marginals are g_1 and g_2. In the following, we assume that g_1 and g_2 are Gaussian distributions unless otherwise specified. We also assume that g_2 is non-degenerate while g_1 is allowed to be degenerate.[k]

Now, let us rewrite Eq. (D.1) as follows:

$$\mathbb{E}_\gamma\left[\|\vec{\chi}-\vec{\xi}\|^2\right] = \|\vec{\mu}_1-\vec{\mu}_2\|_2^2 + \mathbb{E}_\gamma\left[(\vec{\chi}-\vec{\mu}_1)^T(\vec{\chi}-\vec{\mu}_1) + (\vec{\xi}-\vec{\mu}_2)^T(\vec{\xi}-\vec{\mu}_2) - 2(\vec{\xi}-\vec{\mu}_2)^T(\vec{\chi}-\vec{\mu}_1)\right] \tag{D.2}$$

where $\vec{\mu}_i$ denotes the mean of the Gaussian distribution g_i. Further,

$$\mathbb{E}_\gamma\left[\|\vec{\chi}-\vec{\xi}\|^2\right] = \|\vec{\mu}_1-\vec{\mu}_2\|_2^2 + \mathrm{tr}(\mathscr{C}_1+\mathscr{C}_2-2K)$$

where $\mathscr{C}_i$ is the covariance matrix associated with the Gaussian g_i and $K = \mathbb{E}_\gamma[(\vec{\xi}-\vec{\mu}_2)^T(\vec{\chi}-\vec{\mu}_1)]$. From the assumption that g_2 is non-degenerate, it follows that $\mathscr{C}_2 \in \mathrm{Sym}_N^{++}(\mathbb{R})$ and is invertible. The covariance matrix can be obtained by evaluating the Hessian of the characteristic function, which is well defined even when the views matrix is degenerate.

Let us introduce the matrix $\mathfrak{C}$, which is defined as follows:

$$\mathfrak{C} = \begin{bmatrix} \mathbb{E}_\gamma[(\vec{\chi}-\vec{\mu}_1)(\vec{\chi}-\vec{\mu}_1)^T] & \mathbb{E}_\gamma[(\vec{\chi}-\vec{\mu}_1)(\vec{\xi}-\vec{\mu}_2)^T] \\ \mathbb{E}_\gamma[(\vec{\xi}-\vec{\mu}_2)(\vec{\chi}-\vec{\mu}_1)^T] & \mathbb{E}_\gamma[(\vec{\xi}-\vec{\mu}_2)(\vec{\xi}-\vec{\mu}_2)^T] \end{bmatrix} = \begin{bmatrix} \mathscr{C}_1 & K^T \\ K & \mathscr{C}_2 \end{bmatrix} \tag{D.3}$$

This matrix $\mathfrak{C}$ is clearly positive definite, and hence the Schur complement $\mathfrak{C}/\mathscr{C}_2$ is positive semi-definite. That is,

$$\mathscr{C}_1 - K^T\mathscr{C}_2^{-1}K \succeq 0 \tag{D.4}$$

Note that the matrix $\mathscr{C}_2$ needs to be invertible so that $\mathfrak{C}/\mathscr{C}_2$ is well-defined. This follows from our assumption that g_2 is non-degenerate. Let us denote $\mathscr{C}_1 - K^T\mathscr{C}_2^{-1}K$ by $\mathscr{S}$. Then we have

$$K^T\mathscr{C}_2^{-1}K = \mathscr{C}_1 - \mathscr{S} \tag{D.5}$$

Let us denote the diagonalization of $\mathscr{C}_1 - \mathscr{S}$ as follows:

$$[\mathscr{C}_1 - \mathscr{S}]_{ij} = \sum_{ik}\sum_{kj} U_{ik}\Lambda_{kk}^2 U_{jk} \text{ that is, } \mathscr{C}_1 - \mathscr{S} = U\Lambda^2 U^T \tag{D.6}$$

where Λ^2 denotes the diagonal matrix of eigenvalues and U denotes the matrix of the corresponding eigenvectors. If $\mathrm{rank}(\mathscr{C}_1 - \mathscr{S}) = r < N$, then $\Lambda^2 = \mathrm{diag}(\lambda_1^2, \lambda_2^2, \ldots \lambda_r^2) \oplus 0_{N-r}$ and $U = [U_r, U_{N-r}]$. Eq. (D.6) can now be written as follows:

$$\mathscr{C}_1 - \mathscr{S} = U_r\Lambda_r^2 U_r^T \tag{D.7}$$

[k]The proof can be modified to allow both g_1 and g_2 to be degenerate.

where $\Lambda_r^2 = \text{diag}(\lambda_1^2, \lambda_2^2, \ldots \lambda_r^2)$. Using Eq. (D.5) and (D.7), we get

$$K^T \mathscr{C}_2^{-1} K = U_r \Lambda_r^2 U_r^T \Rightarrow \left(\mathscr{C}_2^{-\frac{1}{2}} K \Lambda_r^{-1} U_r\right)^T \left(\mathscr{C}_2^{-\frac{1}{2}} K \Lambda_r^{-1} U_r\right) = \mathbb{I}_r \Rightarrow K = \mathscr{C}_2^{\frac{1}{2}} \mathscr{O}_r \Lambda_r U_r^T \tag{D.8}$$

for some $\mathscr{O}_r$ is an $N \times r$ matrix such that $\mathscr{O}_r^T \mathscr{O}_r = \mathbb{I}_r$. Note that this is an orthogonality condition on $\mathscr{O}_r$ in N dimensions. We can lift $\mathscr{O}_r$ to an N–dimensional orthogonal matrix $\mathscr{O}$ and obtain the following condition:

$$K = \mathscr{C}_2^{\frac{1}{2}} \mathscr{O} \Lambda U^T \tag{D.9}$$

We have used $\Lambda = \Lambda_r \oplus 0_{N-r}$ to obtain the above equation. Now we can work with $\mathscr{O}$ which is an $N \times N$ matrix such that $\mathscr{O}^T \mathscr{O} = \mathbb{I}_N$.

To find the minimum value of the objective defined in Eq. (D.1), we need to minimize $-2\text{Tr}(K)$ subject to the condition $\mathscr{O}\mathscr{O}^T = \mathbb{I}$. We introduce a matrix Lagrange multiplier $\mathscr{H}$ to enforce the orthogonality condition on the matrix $\mathscr{O}$. The modified objective function with the Lagrange multiplier is given by

$$\mathscr{L} = -2\text{Tr}[\mathscr{O}^T \mathscr{C}_2^{\frac{1}{2}} U \Lambda] + \text{Tr}[\mathscr{H}.(\mathscr{O}^T \mathscr{O} - \mathbb{I})] \tag{D.10}$$

After solving for $\mathscr{O}$ and the Lagrange multiplier $\mathscr{H}$ we obtain

$$\mathscr{O} = \mathscr{H}^{-1} \mathscr{C}_2^{\frac{1}{2}} U \Lambda, \quad \mathscr{H} = \left(\left(\mathscr{C}_2^{\frac{1}{2}} U \Lambda\right)\left(\mathscr{C}_2^{\frac{1}{2}} U \Lambda\right)^T\right)^{\frac{1}{2}} \tag{D.11}$$

Substituting for K in the definition of Wasserstein distance, we obtain

$$\mathscr{W}_2^2(g_1, g_2) = \min_{\mathscr{S}} \left[||\vec{\mu}_1 - \vec{\mu}_2||_2^2 + \text{tr}\left(\mathscr{C}_1 + \mathscr{C}_2 - 2\left(\mathscr{C}_2^{\frac{1}{2}} (\mathscr{C}_1 - \mathscr{S}) \mathscr{C}_2^{\frac{1}{2}} \right)^{\frac{1}{2}} \right) \right] \tag{D.12}$$

The minimum value is achieved when $\mathscr{S} = 0$ since $\mathscr{S}$ is a positive definite matrix. Therefore,

$$\mathscr{W}_2^2(g_1, g_2) = ||\vec{\mu}_1 - \vec{\mu}_2||_2^2 + \text{tr}\left(\mathscr{C}_1 + \mathscr{C}_2 - 2\left(\mathscr{C}_1^{\frac{1}{2}} \mathscr{C}_2 \mathscr{C}_1^{\frac{1}{2}} \right)^{\frac{1}{2}} \right) \tag{D.13}$$

We would like to emphasize that the above derivation is valid even when the distribution g_1 is degenerate. Hence, the above derivation is applicable even when the push-forward of the prior distribution is degenerate. It is possible to modify the above derivation to show that $\mathscr{W}_2^2(g_1, g_2)$ when both g_1 and g_2 are degenerate, by changing $\mathscr{C}_2 \to \mathscr{C}_2 + \delta^2\mathbb{I}$ and finally taking the limit as $\delta \to 0$. In the extreme case when $\mathscr{C}_1 = \mathscr{C}_2 = 0$, $\mathscr{W}_2^2(g_1, g_2)$ is equivalent to the distance between two point masses. However, for the analysis in the rest of the paper, we assume any form of degeneracy arises only from the degeneracy of covariance matrices of the form $\mathscr{P}\mathscr{C}\mathscr{P}^T$ for some $\mathscr{C} \in \mathrm{Sym}_{N_a}^{++}(\mathbb{R})$. This could arise from $\mathscr{P}$ having identical rows, for example.

E. Proof of Theorem 1.5.1: Main Result

In this section, we present the Proof of Theorem 1.5.1, which is the main result of this paper.

E.1. *Details of computing optimal updates*

Proof. The Wasserstein distance between Gaussian distributions can be written as sum of Euclidean distance between the drifts and the Bures distance between covariance matrices. Hence, the cost function in Eq. (1.23) can be written as:

$$\mathscr{L}_{GWB} = \mathscr{L}_{\text{DRIFT}}\left[\vec{m}_U; \vec{\mu}_P, \vec{\nu}_V, \mathscr{P}\right] + \mathscr{L}_{\text{COV}}\left[\mathscr{C}_U; \mathscr{C}_P, \mathscr{C}_V, \mathscr{P}\right] \tag{E.1}$$

where

$$\mathscr{L}_{\text{DRIFT}}\left[\vec{m}_U; \vec{\mu}_P, \vec{\nu}_V, \mathscr{P}\right] = ||\vec{m}_U - \vec{\mu}_P||^2 + \lambda||\mathscr{P}\vec{m}_U - \vec{\nu}_V||^2 \tag{E.2}$$

and

$$\mathscr{L}_{\text{COV}}\left[\mathscr{C}_U; \mathscr{C}_P, \mathscr{C}_V, \mathscr{P}\right] = \mathrm{tr}\left(\mathscr{C}_P + \mathscr{C}_U - 2\left(\mathscr{C}_P^{\frac{1}{2}}\mathscr{C}_U\mathscr{C}_P^{\frac{1}{2}}\right)^{\frac{1}{2}}\right) + \lambda\mathrm{tr}\left(\mathscr{C}_V + \mathscr{P}\mathscr{C}_U\mathscr{P}^T - 2\left(\mathscr{C}_V^{\frac{1}{2}}\mathscr{P}\mathscr{C}_U\mathscr{P}^T\mathscr{C}_V^{\frac{1}{2}}\right)^{\frac{1}{2}}\right) \tag{E.3}$$

Minimizing $\mathscr{L}_{GWB}$ with respect to $\vec{m}_U$ and $\mathscr{C}_U$ boils down to minimizing $\mathscr{L}_{\text{DRIFT}}$ with respect to $\vec{m}_U$ and $\mathscr{L}_{\text{COV}}$ with respect to $\mathscr{C}_U$. Minimizing $\mathscr{L}_{\text{DRIFT}}$ with respect to $\vec{m}_U$ is rather straightforward and yields the following equation:

$$(\vec{m}_U - \vec{\mu}_P) + \lambda\mathscr{P}^T(\mathscr{P}\vec{m}_U - \vec{\nu}_V) = 0 \tag{E.4}$$

Simple algebraic manipulation of the above equation yields the expression in Eq. (1.27). Minimization of $\mathscr{L}_{\text{COV}}$ is slightly more involved, and the rest of this appendix is dedicated to finding the optimal $\mathscr{C}_U$. To minimize $\mathscr{L}_{\text{Cov}}$, it seems convenient to employ the following change of variables:

$$X = \left(\mathscr{C}_P^{\frac{1}{2}}\mathscr{C}_U\mathscr{C}_P^{\frac{1}{2}}\right)^{\frac{1}{2}} \Rightarrow \mathscr{C}_U = \mathscr{C}_P^{-\frac{1}{2}}X^2\mathscr{C}_P^{-\frac{1}{2}} \tag{E.5}$$

$$Y = \left(\mathscr{C}_V^{\frac{1}{2}}\mathscr{P}\mathscr{C}_U\mathscr{P}^T\mathscr{C}_V^{\frac{1}{2}}\right)^{\frac{1}{2}} \Rightarrow \mathscr{P}\mathscr{C}_U\mathscr{P}^T = \mathscr{C}_V^{-\frac{1}{2}}Y^2\mathscr{C}_V^{-\frac{1}{2}} \tag{E.6}$$

where $X,\ Y \in \text{Sym}(\mathbb{R})$. After the change of variables, the minimization of $\mathscr{L}_{\text{Cov}}$ can then be recast into the COP:

$$(X_\star, Y_\star) = \underset{X,Y\in\text{Sym}(\mathbb{R})}{\text{argmin}}\left[\text{tr}\left(\mathscr{C}_P + \mathscr{C}_P^{-\frac{1}{2}}X^2\mathscr{C}_P^{-\frac{1}{2}} - 2X\right) + \lambda\text{tr}\left(\mathscr{C}_V + \mathscr{C}_V^{-\frac{1}{2}}Y^2\mathscr{C}_V^{-\frac{1}{2}} - 2Y\right)\right] \tag{E.7}$$

subject to

$$\mathscr{C}_V^{-\frac{1}{2}}Y^2\mathscr{C}_V^{-\frac{1}{2}} = \mathscr{P}\mathscr{C}_P^{-\frac{1}{2}}X^2\mathscr{C}_P^{-\frac{1}{2}}\mathscr{P}^T \tag{E.8}$$

To solve the constrained minimization problem, we introduce a matrix Lagrange multiplier $\mathscr{M}$ and minimize the following modified cost function:

$$\mathscr{L}[X, Y, \mathscr{M}] = \left[\text{tr}\left(\mathscr{C}_P + \mathscr{C}_P^{-\frac{1}{2}}X^2\mathscr{C}_P^{-\frac{1}{2}} - 2X\right) + \lambda\text{tr}\left(\mathscr{C}_V + \mathscr{C}_V^{-\frac{1}{2}}Y^2\mathscr{C}_V^{-\frac{1}{2}} - 2Y\right)\right] + \text{tr}\left[\mathscr{M}.\left(\mathscr{C}_V^{-\frac{1}{2}}Y^2\mathscr{C}_V^{-\frac{1}{2}} - \mathscr{P}\mathscr{C}_P^{-\frac{1}{2}}X^2\mathscr{C}_P^{-\frac{1}{2}}\mathscr{P}^T\right)\right] \tag{E.9}$$

The Lagrange multiplier matrix $\mathscr{M}$ is symmetric since $\mathscr{C}_V^{-\frac{1}{2}}Y^2\mathscr{C}_V^{-\frac{1}{2}} - \mathscr{P}\mathscr{C}_P^{-\frac{1}{2}}X^2\mathscr{C}_P^{-\frac{1}{2}}\mathscr{P}^T$ is symmetric. The modified cost function in Eq. (E.9) is minimized by setting the gradients with respect to X and Y to zero, and the Lagrange multiplier $\mathscr{M}$ is obtained by enforcing the constraint in Eq. (E.8). The gradient of $\mathscr{L}[X, Y, \mathscr{M}]$ with respect to X and Y is computed using the identity in Eq. (A.1). Setting these gradients to zero, we obtain

$$X\left(\mathscr{C}_P^{-1} - \mathscr{C}_P^{-\frac{1}{2}}\mathscr{P}^T\mathscr{M}\mathscr{P}\mathscr{C}_P^{-\frac{1}{2}}\right) + \left(\mathscr{C}_P^{-1} - \mathscr{C}_P^{-\frac{1}{2}}\mathscr{P}^T\mathscr{M}\mathscr{P}\mathscr{C}_P^{-\frac{1}{2}}\right)X = 2\mathbb{I}_{N_a} \tag{E.10}$$

$$Y\left(\lambda\mathscr{C}_\mathcal{V}^{-1} + \mathscr{C}_\mathcal{V}^{-\frac{1}{2}}\mathscr{M}\mathscr{C}_\mathcal{V}^{-\frac{1}{2}}\right) + \left(\lambda\mathscr{C}_\mathcal{V}^{-1} + \mathscr{C}_\mathcal{V}^{-\frac{1}{2}}\mathscr{M}\mathscr{C}_\mathcal{V}^{-\frac{1}{2}}\right)Y = 2\lambda\mathbb{I}_{N_v} \tag{E.11}$$

The above equations are special cases of the Lyapunov equation. If $(\mathbb{I}_{N_a} - \mathscr{P}^T\mathscr{M}\mathscr{P})$ is invertible, then the solution of Eq. (E.10) can be written as shown below:

$$X = \left(\mathscr{C}_P^{-1} - \mathscr{C}_P^{-\frac{1}{2}}\mathscr{P}^T\mathscr{M}\mathscr{P}\mathscr{C}_P^{-\frac{1}{2}}\right)^{-1} = \mathscr{C}_P^{\frac{1}{2}}(\mathbb{I}_{N_a} - \mathscr{P}^T\mathscr{M}\mathscr{P})^{-1}\mathscr{C}_P^{\frac{1}{2}} \tag{E.12}$$

We have used Eq. (A.4) or Lemma A.3(a) to obtain the above solution. It must be clear from the definition of X that $(\mathbb{I}_{N_a} - \mathscr{P}^T\mathscr{M}\mathscr{P})$ is invertible iff $\mathscr{C}_P$ and $\mathscr{C}_U$ are invertible. Hence, the validity of this assumption can be verified only after solving for $\mathscr{C}_U$. We show at the end of this section that $\mathscr{C}_U$ is indeed invertible, and hence the invertibility of $(\mathbb{I}_{N_a} - \mathscr{P}^T\mathscr{M}\mathscr{P})$ is justified. If $(\lambda\mathbb{I}_{N_v} + \mathscr{M})$ is invertible, then the Lyapunov equation (E.11) yields $Y = \lambda\mathscr{C}_\mathcal{V}^{\frac{1}{2}}(\lambda\mathbb{I}_{N_v} + \mathscr{M})^{-1}\mathscr{C}_\mathcal{V}^{\frac{1}{2}}$ as the unique solution; however, the invertibility of $(\lambda\mathbb{I}_{N_v} + \mathscr{M})$ is not justified if the views matrix $\mathscr{P}$ is degenerate. Fortunately, we can derive the optimal update for covariance $\mathscr{C}_U$ without inverting $(\lambda\mathbb{I}_{N_v} + \mathscr{M})$. Using Lemma A.3(b), we obtain

$$\mathscr{C}_\mathcal{V}^{-\frac{1}{2}}\left(\lambda\mathbb{I}_{N_v} + \mathscr{M}\right)\mathscr{C}_\mathcal{V}^{-\frac{1}{2}}Y = \lambda\mathbb{I}_{N_v} = Y\mathscr{C}_\mathcal{V}^{-\frac{1}{2}}\left(\lambda\mathbb{I}_{N_v} + \mathscr{M}\right)\mathscr{C}_\mathcal{V}^{-\frac{1}{2}} \tag{E.13}$$

Now, to determine the optimal values of X and Y we need to determine $\mathscr{M}$ in Eq. (E.12) and determine Y using the constraint in Eq. (E.8). In fact, $\mathscr{M}$, or rather $\mathscr{P}^T\mathscr{M}\mathscr{P}$ is determined by enforcing the constraint in Eq. (E.8). Using Eq. (E.13) we obtain

$$(\lambda\mathbb{I}_{N_v} + \mathscr{M})\mathscr{C}_\mathcal{V}^{-\frac{1}{2}}Y^2\mathscr{C}_\mathcal{V}^{-\frac{1}{2}}(\lambda\mathbb{I}_{N_v} + \mathscr{M}) = \lambda^2\mathscr{C}_\mathcal{V} \tag{E.14}$$

By making use of the constraint in (E.8), we first eliminate $\mathscr{C}_\mathcal{V}^{-\frac{1}{2}}Y^2\mathscr{C}_\mathcal{V}^{-\frac{1}{2}}$, and we then make use of Eq. (E.12) in the resulting expression to obtain

$$(\lambda\mathbb{I}_{N_v} + \mathscr{M})\mathscr{P}(\mathbb{I}_{N_a} - \mathscr{P}^T\mathscr{M}\mathscr{P})^{-1}\mathscr{C}_P(\mathbb{I}_{N_a} - \mathscr{P}^T\mathscr{M}\mathscr{P})^{-1}\mathscr{P}^T(\lambda\mathbb{I}_{N_v} + \mathscr{M}) = \lambda^2\mathscr{C}_\mathcal{V} \tag{E.15}$$

It is convenient to introduce a matrix $\mathscr{U}$ such that,

$$(\lambda\mathbb{I}_{N_v} + \mathscr{M})\mathscr{P}(\mathbb{I}_{N_a} - \mathscr{P}^T\mathscr{M}\mathscr{P})^{-1} = \lambda\mathscr{C}_\mathcal{V}^{\frac{1}{2}}\mathscr{U}\mathscr{C}_P^{-\frac{1}{2}} \tag{E.16}$$

The precise properties of the matrix $\mathscr{U}$ is not very important here as this will be eliminated in the following steps. Multiplying both sides of Eq. (E.16) by $\mathscr{P}^T$, we get the following result:

$$\left(\mathbb{I}_{N_a} + G\right) \mathscr{P}^T \mathscr{M} \mathscr{P} = (G - \lambda \mathscr{P}^T \mathscr{P}) \quad \Rightarrow \mathscr{P}^T \mathscr{M} \mathscr{P} = \left(\mathbb{I}_{N_a} + G\right)^{-1} (G - \lambda \mathscr{P}^T \mathscr{P}), \tag{E.17}$$

where G is defined as follows

$$G = \lambda \mathscr{P}^T \mathscr{C}_V^{\frac{1}{2}} \mathscr{U} \mathscr{C}_P^{-\frac{1}{2}} \tag{E.18}$$

Equation (E.17) provides an expression for $\mathscr{P}^T \mathscr{M} \mathscr{P}$ in terms of the matrix G. The matrix G contains an unknown unitary matrix, and we will now find an alternate expression for G by using Eq. (E.17) and the constraint $\mathscr{M} = \mathscr{M}^T$. Noting that $\mathscr{P}^T \mathscr{M} \mathscr{P} = (\mathscr{P}^T \mathscr{M} \mathscr{P})^T$ whenever $\mathscr{M} = \mathscr{M}^T$ in Eq. (E.17), we obtain

$$\left(\mathbb{I}_{N_a} + G\right)\left(G^T - \lambda \mathscr{P}^T \mathscr{P}\right) = \left(G - \lambda \mathscr{P}^T \mathscr{P}\right)\left(\mathbb{I}_{N_a} + G^T\right) \tag{E.19}$$

From the above condition, we can conclude that G can be written as

$$G = S.W, \qquad \text{where } S = S^T, \quad W = \left(\mathbb{I}_{N_a} + \lambda \mathscr{P}^T \mathscr{P}\right)^{-1} \tag{E.20}$$

We can compute X from Eq. (E.12) if $(\mathbb{I}_{N_a} - \mathscr{P}^T \mathscr{M} \mathscr{P})$ is known. Using Eqs. (E.17) and (E.20), we obtain

$$\mathbb{I}_{N_a} - \mathscr{P}^T \mathscr{M} \mathscr{P} = (\mathbb{I}_{N_a} + G)^{-1} \left(\mathbb{I}_{N_a} + \lambda \mathscr{P}^T \mathscr{P}\right) = (\mathbb{I} + S.W)^{-1} W^{-1} \tag{E.21}$$

We now describe the procedure to determine S in the above equation. By using the definition of G in Eqs. (E.18), (E.16), and (E.15), we obtain

$$G \mathscr{C}_P G^T = \lambda^2 \mathscr{P}^T \mathscr{C}_V \mathscr{P} \tag{E.22}$$

After defining $A = W \mathscr{C}_P W$, Eq. (E.22) can now be written as follows:

$$S.A.S = \lambda^2 \mathscr{P}^T \mathscr{C}_V \mathscr{P} \Rightarrow (A^{\frac{1}{2}} S A^{\frac{1}{2}})(A^{\frac{1}{2}} S A^{\frac{1}{2}}) = \lambda^2 A^{\frac{1}{2}} \mathscr{P}^T \mathscr{C}_V \mathscr{P} A^{\frac{1}{2}} \tag{E.23}$$

Hence S is given by,

$$S = s \lambda A^{-\frac{1}{2}} \left(A^{\frac{1}{2}} \mathscr{P}^T \mathscr{C}_V \mathscr{P} A^{\frac{1}{2}} \right)^{\frac{1}{2}} A^{-\frac{1}{2}} \tag{E.24}$$

where $s = \pm 1$. Using Eqs. (E.24), (E.21), (E.12), and (E.5) we obtain

$$\mathscr{C}(s) = \left(W + \mathcal{B}(s)\right) \mathscr{C}_P \left(W + \mathcal{B}(s)\right) \tag{E.25}$$

where $\mathcal{B}(s) = \mathcal{B}(s)^T$ and it is given by

$$\mathcal{B}(s) = s\lambda W A^{-\frac{1}{2}} \left(A^{\frac{1}{2}} \mathscr{P}^T \mathscr{C}_V \mathscr{P} A^{\frac{1}{2}} \right)^{\frac{1}{2}} A^{-\frac{1}{2}} W = W.S.W \tag{E.26}$$

In Appendix E.2, we show that $s = 1$ for $\mathscr{L}_{\text{Cov}}$ to be a minimum at $\mathscr{C}_U = \mathscr{C}(s)$. Hence,

$$\mathscr{C}_\star = (W + \mathcal{B}) \mathscr{C}_P (W + \mathcal{B}) \tag{E.27}$$

where $\mathcal{B} = \mathcal{B}^T$ and it is given by

$$\mathcal{B} = \lambda W A^{-\frac{1}{2}} \left(A^{\frac{1}{2}} \mathscr{P}^T \mathscr{C}_V \mathscr{P} A^{\frac{1}{2}} \right)^{\frac{1}{2}} A^{-\frac{1}{2}} W, \qquad A = W \mathscr{C}_P W \tag{E.28}$$

This completes the proof of the Theorem 1.5.1. ■

E.2. *Proof of* $s = 1$

We present a heuristic argument for the proof first to provide an intuition behind the proof, which requires tedious algebra. To fix s, we evaluate $\mathscr{L}_{\text{Cov}}$ at $\mathscr{C}_U = \mathscr{C}(s)$ and minimize with respect to s. We show that s should be $s = 1$ for $\mathscr{L}_{\text{Cov}}$ to be minimized. For the purpose of this heuristic argument, we assume $\mathscr{P} = \mathbb{I}_{N_a}$, $\mathscr{C}_{P,V} = \text{DIAG}(\sigma^2_{P,V})$. In this case, $\mathscr{L}_{\text{Cov}}$ can be written as follows:

$$\mathscr{L}_s = \left(\sigma_P - \frac{\sigma_P + \lambda s \sigma_V}{1 + \lambda} \right)^2 + \lambda \left(\sigma_V - \frac{\sigma_P + \lambda s \sigma_V}{1 + \lambda} \right)^2 \tag{E.29}$$

After a little bit of algebra, we can infer that $\mathscr{L}_s$ is minimized when $s = 1$. The same conclusion can be reached for a general $\mathscr{C}_{P,V}$ and $\mathscr{P}$, but the algebra is more tedious, and we present the proof for a general $\mathscr{C}_{P,V}$ and $\mathscr{P}$ below.

Proof. We prove this result for the case when the views matrix is not degenerate and $\mathscr{P}^T \mathscr{C}_V \mathscr{P}$ is not degenerate. The proof for a general views matrix can be modified by introducing a regulating parameter δ and then taking the limit $\delta \to 0$. Or alternatively, the proof can be modified by introducing the Moore-Penrose inverse wherever necessary.

We first prove that $W + \mathcal{B}(s)$ is positive definite. We know from that X is symmetric and positive definite by definition. Hence, X can be written as $\Upsilon \Upsilon^T$ for some Υ. Then, it follows from Eq. (E.12) that $\left(\mathbb{I}_{N_a} - \mathscr{P}^T \mathscr{M} \mathscr{P} \right)^{-1}$ is also positive definite. Using Eq. (E.21), we obtain

$$\left(\mathbb{I}_{N_a} - \mathscr{P}^T \mathscr{M} \mathscr{P} \right)^{-1} = W + \mathcal{B}(s) \quad \Rightarrow W + \mathcal{B}(s) \succ 0 \tag{E.30}$$

Let $Q = \mathscr{P}^T\mathscr{C}_V\mathscr{P}$ for convenience. Using Lemma A.2 repeatedly, S can be written as shown below

$$S = s\lambda A^{-\frac{1}{2}}\left(A^{\frac{1}{2}}QA^{\frac{1}{2}}\right)^{\frac{1}{2}}A^{-\frac{1}{2}} = s\lambda W^{-1}\mathscr{C}_P^{-\frac{1}{2}}\left(\mathscr{C}_P^{\frac{1}{2}}W.Q.W\mathscr{C}_P^{\frac{1}{2}}\right)^{\frac{1}{2}}\mathscr{C}_P^{-\frac{1}{2}}W^{-1} = s\lambda\Gamma^{-1} \tag{E.31}$$

$$\text{where}\quad \Gamma = W\mathscr{C}_P^{\frac{1}{2}}\left(\mathscr{C}_P^{\frac{1}{2}}W.Q.W\mathscr{C}_P^{\frac{1}{2}}\right)^{-\frac{1}{2}}\mathscr{C}_P^{\frac{1}{2}}W \tag{E.32}$$

Similarly, we know that Y is positive semi-definite. Then from Eq. (E.13), we can conclude that $\lambda\mathbb{I}_{N_v} + \mathscr{M}$ is also positive semi-definite.[l] Using Eq. (E.17), we obtain

$$\mathscr{P}^T\left(\lambda\mathbb{I}_{N_v} + \mathscr{M}\right)\mathscr{P} = \left(\mathbb{I}_{N_a} + G\right)^{-1}GW^{-1} \tag{E.34}$$

Now, from the definition of S in Eq. (E.20), (E.31), and (E.34), we obtain

$$\mathscr{P}^T\left(\lambda\mathbb{I}_{N_v} + \mathscr{M}\right)\mathscr{P} = \lambda(s\Gamma + \lambda W)^{-1} \Rightarrow (s\Gamma + \lambda W) \succeq 0 \tag{E.35}$$

That is, $(s\Gamma + \lambda W)$ is positive semi-definite.[m] Now, from Eqs. (E.25), (E.31), and (E.26), we obtain

$$\mathscr{C}(s) = (W + s\lambda W\Gamma^{-1}W)\mathscr{C}_P(W + s\lambda W\Gamma^{-1}W) = (s\Gamma + \lambda W)\mathscr{P}^T\mathscr{C}_V\mathscr{P}(s\Gamma + \lambda W) \tag{E.36}$$

We have used the fact that $s^2 = 1$ to obtain the above equation. From Eqs. (E.25) and (E.36), we obtain

$$\operatorname{tr}\left(\left(\mathscr{C}_P^{\frac{1}{2}}\mathscr{C}(s)\mathscr{C}_P^{\frac{1}{2}}\right)^{\frac{1}{2}}\right) = \operatorname{tr}\left(\mathscr{C}_P^{\frac{1}{2}}(W + \mathcal{B}(s))\mathscr{C}_P^{\frac{1}{2}}\right) \tag{E.37}$$

$$\operatorname{tr}\left(\left(\mathscr{C}_V^{\frac{1}{2}}\mathscr{P}\mathscr{C}(s)\mathscr{P}^T\mathscr{C}_V^{\frac{1}{2}}\right)^{\frac{1}{2}}\right) = \operatorname{tr}\left(\mathscr{C}_V^{\frac{1}{2}}\mathscr{P}(s\Gamma + \lambda W)\mathscr{P}^T\mathscr{C}_V^{\frac{1}{2}}\right) \tag{E.38}$$

---

[l]Eq. (E.13) implies

$$\vec{z}^T\left(\lambda\mathbb{I}_{N_v} + \mathscr{M}\right)\mathscr{C}_V^{-\frac{1}{2}}Y\mathscr{C}_V^{-\frac{1}{2}}\left(\lambda\mathbb{I}_{N_v} + \mathscr{M}\right)\vec{z} = \lambda\vec{z}^T\left(\lambda\mathbb{I}_{N_v} + \mathscr{M}\right)\vec{z}, \qquad \text{for any } \vec{z} \in \mathbb{R}^{N_v} \tag{E.33}$$

Note that LHS is greater than or equal to zero because Y is positive semi-definite. Hence $\left(\lambda\mathbb{I}_{N_v} + \mathscr{M}\right) \succeq 0$.

[m]Note that the positive semi-definiteness holds good even if the inverse is replaced by Moore–Penrose inverse in the degenerate case. In the non-degenerate case, $(s\Gamma + \lambda W) \succ 0$.

The positive definiteness of $W + \mathcal{B}(s)$ which was proved in Eq. (E.30) justifies the choice of using the positive square root of $\left(\mathscr{C}_P^{\frac{1}{2}}\mathscr{C}(s)\mathscr{C}_P^{\frac{1}{2}}\right)$. Similarly, the positive definiteness of $(s\Gamma + \lambda W)$, which was proved in Eq. (E.35), justifies the choice of using the positive square root of $\left(\mathscr{C}_\mathcal{V}^{\frac{1}{2}}\mathscr{P}\mathscr{C}(s)\mathscr{P}^T\mathscr{C}_\mathcal{V}^{\frac{1}{2}}\right)$ in Eq. (E.36).

By using Eqs. (E.37) and (E.38) in Eq. (E.3), we obtain the following simplified form of $\mathscr{L}_{\text{Cov}}$:[n]

$$\mathscr{L}_{\text{Cov}}\left[\mathscr{C}(s);\mathscr{C}_P,\mathscr{C}_\mathcal{V},\mathscr{P}\right] = \mathscr{L}_{\text{Cov}}^{(0)} - \text{str}\left(\mathscr{P}^T\mathscr{C}_\mathcal{V}\mathscr{P}W\right) = \mathscr{L}_{\text{Cov}}^{(0)} - \text{str}\left(\mathscr{C}_\mathcal{V}^{\frac{1}{2}}\mathscr{P}W\mathscr{P}^T\mathscr{C}_\mathcal{V}^{\frac{1}{2}}\right) \tag{E.39}$$

where $\mathscr{L}_{\text{Cov}}^{(0)}$ is a term independent of s and we have used $s^2 = 1$ to obtain the above expression. Since $\left(\mathscr{C}_\mathcal{V}^{\frac{1}{2}}\mathscr{P}W\mathscr{P}^T\mathscr{C}_\mathcal{V}^{\frac{1}{2}}\right)$ is positive definite,

$$\mathscr{L}_{\text{Cov}}\left[\mathscr{C}(s=1);\mathscr{C}_P,\mathscr{C}_\mathcal{V},\mathscr{P}\right] < \mathscr{L}_{\text{Cov}}\left[\mathscr{C}(s=-1);\mathscr{C}_P,\mathscr{C}_\mathcal{V},\mathscr{P}\right]$$

Hence $\mathscr{L}_{\text{Cov}}\left[\mathscr{C}(s);\mathscr{C}_P,\mathscr{C}_\mathcal{V},\mathscr{P}\right]$ is minimized at $s = 1$. ■

F. Allocation Methodologies Summary

In the following, we present the details of the four allocation methodologies BL_I BL_II, GWB_I, and GWB_II:

F.1. *BL$_I$ allocation method*

Algorithm: BL$_\text{I}$ Allocation Method

Input: $\vec{\mu}_d, \hat{\mathscr{C}}_R, \mathscr{P}, \nu_\mathcal{V}, \mathscr{C}_\mathcal{V}, \tau, \gamma_R$
Method:

- Using Eq. (1.8) we compute $\mathscr{C}_{BL}^{(\vec{\mu}_R)}$:

$$\mathscr{C}_{BL}^{(\vec{\mu}_R)} = \left(\left(\tau\hat{\mathscr{C}}_R\right)^{-1} + \mathscr{P}^T\mathscr{C}_\mathcal{V}^{-1}\mathscr{P}\right)^{-1} \tag{F.1}$$

[n]The algebra is slightly tedious, but if we only focus on the s dependent terms, the task of simplifying becomes less laborious. Lemma A.2 was used again.

- Covariance Update: Using Eq. (1.9) we set $\mathscr{C}_E^{(\mathrm{BLI})}$ to $\hat{\mathscr{C}}_{\vec{R}|\mathcal{V}}$:

$$\mathscr{C}_E^{(\mathrm{BL_I})} \leftarrow \hat{\mathscr{C}}_{\vec{R}|\mathcal{V}} = \hat{\mathscr{C}}_R + \mathscr{C}_{BL}^{(\vec{\mu}_R)} \tag{F.2}$$

- Drift Update: From Eqs. (1.7) and 1.9):

$$\vec{m}_E^{(\mathrm{BL_I})} \leftarrow \vec{\mu}_{BL} = \mathscr{C}_{BL}^{(\vec{\mu}_R)} \left(\left(\tau \hat{\mathscr{C}}_R \right)^{-1} \vec{\mu}_d + \mathscr{P}^T \mathscr{C}_{\mathcal{V}}^{-1} \vec{v}_{\mathcal{V}} \right) \tag{F.3}$$

- Optimal Weights: We compute optimal weights with the BL Model-I update as follows:

$$\vec{w}_{\mathrm{BL_I}} = \mathrm{MVO}\left[\vec{m}_E^{(\mathrm{BL_I})}, \mathscr{C}_E^{(\mathrm{BL_I})}; \gamma_R \right] \tag{F.4}$$

Result: Weights $\vec{w}_{\mathrm{BL_I}}$ computed in Eq. (F.4).

F.2. *BL$_{II}$ allocation method*

Algorithm: BL$_{\mathrm{II}}$ Allocation Method

Input: $\hat{\vec{\mu}}_R, \hat{\mathscr{C}}_R, \mathscr{P}, \nu_{\mathcal{V}_R}, \mathscr{C}_{\mathcal{V}_R}, \gamma_R$
Method:

- Covariance Update: Using Eq. (1.14), we compute $\mathscr{C}_E^{(\mathrm{BL_{II}})}$

$$\mathscr{C}_E^{(\mathrm{BL_{II}})} \leftarrow \mathscr{C}_{BL'}^{(\vec{R})} = \left(\hat{\mathscr{C}}_R^{-1} + \mathscr{P}^T \mathscr{C}_{\mathcal{V}_R}^{-1} \mathscr{P} \right)^{-1} \tag{F.5}$$

- Drift Update: Corrections to the drift are computed from Eq. (1.7):

$$\vec{m}_E^{(\mathrm{BL_{II}})} \leftarrow \vec{\mu}_{BL'}^{(\vec{R})} = \left(\hat{\mathscr{C}}_R^{-1} + \mathscr{P}^T \mathscr{C}_{\mathcal{V}_R}^{-1} \mathscr{P} \right)^{-1} \left(\hat{\mathscr{C}}_R^{-1} \hat{\vec{\mu}}_R + \mathscr{P}^T \mathscr{C}_{\mathcal{V}_R}^{-1} \vec{v}_{\mathcal{V}} \right) \tag{F.6}$$

- Optimal Weights: We compute optimal weights with the BL Model-II update as follows:

$$\vec{w}_{\mathrm{BL_{II}}} = \mathrm{MVO}\left[\vec{m}_E^{(\mathrm{BL_{II}})}, \mathscr{C}_E^{(\mathrm{BL_{II}})}; \gamma_R \right] \tag{F.7}$$

Result: Weights $\vec{w}_{\mathrm{BL_{II}}}$ computed in Eq. (F.7).

F.3. *GWB$_I$ allocation method*

Algorithm: GWB$_{\text{I}}$ Allocation Method

Input: $\vec{\mu}_d, \hat{\mathscr{C}}_R, \mathscr{P}, \nu_{\mathcal{V}_d}, \mathscr{C}_{\mathcal{V}_d}, \tau, \gamma_R, \lambda$
Method:

- Drift Update:

$$W = \left(\mathbb{I}_{N_a} + \mathscr{P}^T\mathscr{P}\right)^{-1} \tag{F.8}$$

$$\vec{m}_E^{(\text{GWBI})} \leftarrow \vec{m}_{\text{GWBI}} = W\left(\vec{\mu}_d + \lambda\mathscr{P}^T\vec{\nu}_{\mathcal{V}_d}\right) \tag{F.9}$$

- Covariance Update:

$$A_d = \tau W\hat{\mathscr{C}}_R W \tag{F.10}$$

$$\mathcal{B}_{\mathcal{V}_d} = \lambda W A_d^{-\frac{1}{2}}\left(A_d^{\frac{1}{2}}\mathscr{P}^T\mathscr{C}_{\mathcal{V}_d}\mathscr{P}A_d^{\frac{1}{2}}\right)^{\frac{1}{2}} A_d^{-\frac{1}{2}} W \tag{F.11}$$

$$\mathscr{C}_E^{(\text{GWBI})} \leftarrow \mathscr{C}_{\text{GWBI}} = \hat{\mathscr{C}}_R + \tau\left(W + \mathcal{B}_{\mathcal{V}_d}\right)\hat{\mathscr{C}}_R\left(W + \mathcal{B}_{\mathcal{V}_d}\right) \tag{F.12}$$

- Optimal Weights: We compute optimal weights with the GWBModel-I update as follows:

$$\vec{w}_{\text{GWB}_\text{I}} = \text{MVO}\left[\vec{m}_E^{(\text{GWBI})}, \mathscr{C}_E^{(\text{GWBI})}; \gamma_R\right] \tag{F.13}$$

Result: Weights $\vec{w}_{\text{GWB}_\text{I}}$ computed in Eq. (F.13).

F.4. *GWB$_{II}$ allocation method*

Algorithm: GWB$_{\text{II}}$ Allocation Method

Input: $\hat{\vec{\mu}}_R, \hat{\mathscr{C}}_R, \mathscr{P}, \nu_{\mathcal{V}_R}, \mathscr{C}_{\mathcal{V}_R}, \gamma_R, \lambda$
Method:

- Drift Update:

$$W = \left(\mathbb{I}_{N_a} + \mathscr{P}^T\mathscr{P}\right)^{-1} \tag{F.14}$$

$$\vec{m}_E^{(\text{GWBII})} \leftarrow \vec{m}_{\text{GWBII}} = W\left(\hat{\vec{\mu}}_R + \lambda\mathscr{P}^T\vec{\nu}_{\mathcal{V}_R}\right) \tag{F.15}$$

- Covariance Update:

$$A_R = W\hat{\mathscr{C}}_R W \tag{F.16}$$

$$\mathcal{B}_{\mathcal{V}_R} = \lambda W A_R^{-\frac{1}{2}} \left(A_R^{\frac{1}{2}} \mathscr{P}^T \mathscr{C}_R \mathscr{P} A_R^{\frac{1}{2}} \right)^{\frac{1}{2}} A_R^{-\frac{1}{2}} W \tag{F.17}$$

$$\mathscr{C}_E^{(\mathrm{GWBII})} \leftarrow \mathscr{C}_{\mathrm{GWBII}} = \left(W + \mathcal{B}_{\mathcal{V}_R}\right) \hat{\mathscr{C}}_R \left(W + \mathcal{B}_{\mathcal{V}_R}\right) \tag{F.18}$$

- Optimal Weights: We compute optimal weights with the GWBModel-I update as follows:

$$\vec{w}_{\mathrm{GWB}_{\mathrm{II}}} = \mathrm{MVO}\left[\vec{m}_E^{(\mathrm{GWBII})}, \mathscr{C}_E^{(\mathrm{GWBII})}; \gamma_R\right] \tag{F.19}$$

Result: Weights $\vec{w}_{\mathrm{GWB}_{\mathrm{II}}}$ computed in Eq. (F.19).

References

1. F. Black and R. Litterman, Asset allocation: Combining investor views with market equilibrium, *J. Fixed Income*. **1**(2), 7–18 (1991).
2. G. He and R. Litterman, The Intuition Behind Black–Litterman Model Portfolios (2022). Available at SSRN: https://ssrn.com/abstract=334304 or https://doi.org/10.2139/ssrn.334304.
3. D. Bertsimas, V. Gupta, and I. C. Paschalidis, A new perspective on the Black–Litterman model, *Oper. Res.* **60**(6), 1389–1403 (2012).
4. A. Meucci, The Black–Litterman Approach: Original Model and Extensions (2008). Available at SSRN: https://ssrn.com/abstract=1117574 or https://doi.org/10.2139/ssrn.1117574.
5. S. T. Rachev, J. S. J. Hsu, B. S. Bagasheva, and F. J. Fabozzi, *Bayesian Methods in Finance*. Wiley, Hoboken (2008). ISBN: 978-0-470-24924-6
6. P. Kolm and G. Ritter, On the Bayesian interpretation of Black–Litterman, *Eur. J. Oper. Res.* **252**(1), 378–385 (2016). https://doi.org/10.1016/j.ejor.2016.10.027.
7. A. Meucci, Fully flexible views: Theory and practice, *Risk*. **21**(10), 97–102 (2008).
8. A. Meucci, D. Ardia, and M. Colasante, Portfolio construction and systematic trading with factor entropy pooling, *Risk Mag.* **27**, 56–61 (2014).
9. F. J. Fabozzi, S. M. Focardi, and P. N. Kolm, Incorporating trading strategies in the Black–Litterman framework, *J. Trading*. **1**(2), 1021 (2006).
10. J. Duraj and C. Yu, Black–Litterman End-to-End (2023). Available at SSRN: https://ssrn.com/abstract=4532798
11. J. Delon, N. Gozlan, and A. Saint-Dizier, Generalized Wasserstein Barycenters Between Probability Measures Living on Different Subspaces (2021). arXiv:2105.09755v1.
12. R. J. McCann, A convexity principle for interacting gases, *Adv. Math.* **128**(1), 153–179 (1997).
13. I. Olkin and F. Pukelsheim, The distance between two random vectors with given dispersion matrices, *Linear Algebra its Appl.* **48**, 257–263 (1982).

14. D. C. Dowson and B. V. Landau, The Fréchet distance between multivariate normal distributions, *J. Multivar. Anal.* **12**(3), 450–455 (1982).
15. C. R. Givens and R. M. Shortt, A class of Wasserstein metrics for probability distributions, *Mich. Math J.* **31**(2), 231–240 (1984).
16. P. Doust, Geometric mean variance, *Risk.* **12**(2), 89–95 (2008).
17. A. Takatsu, Wasserstein geometry of Gaussian measures, *Osaka J. Math.* **48**(4), 1005–1026 (2011).
18. R. Bhatia, T. Jain, and Y. Lim, On the Bures–Wasserstein distance between positive definite matrices, *Expo. Math.* **37**(2), 165–191 (2019).
19. S. Diamond and S. Boyd, CVXPY: A Python-embedded modeling language for convex optimization, *J. Mach. Learn. Res.* **17**, 1–5 (2016).
20. A. Agarwal, R. Verschueren, S. Diamond, and S. Boyd, A rewriting system for convex optimization problems, *J. Control Decis.* **5**(1), 42–60 (2018).
21. E. Busseti, *Portfolio Management and Optimal Execution via Convex Optimization.* PhD thesis, Stanford University (2018).
22. S. Boyd, E. Busseti, S. Diamond, et al. Multi-Period Trading via Convex Optimization (2017). arXiv:1705.00109; CVXPortfolio: This website provides the code developed by the group for the above mentioned paper and thesis.
23. M. Lopez de Prado, *Advances in Financial Machine Learning*. John Wiley & Sons, Inc, Hoboken (2018).
24. A. Petajisto, *Underperformance of Concentrated Stock Positions.* (2023). Available at SSRN: https://doi.org/10.2139/ssrn.4541122.
25. R. Tibshirani, A general framework for fast stagewise algorithms, *J. Mach. Learn. Res.* **16**, 2543–2588 (2015); R. Tibshirani, "Convex Optimization," Lectures (CMU).
26. M. Kloft, U. Brefeld, S. Sonnenburg, and A. Zien, ℓ_p-Norm multiple kernel learning, *J. Mach. Learn. Res.* **12**, 953–997 (2011).
27. D. P. Bertsekas, *Convex Optimization Theory.* Athena Scientific (2009). ISBN 9781886529311.
28. S. Boyd and L. Vandenberghe, *Convex Optimization.* Cambridge University Press, Cambridge (2004).
29. V. I. Bogachev, *Measure Theory.* Springer Verlag, Berlin (2007). ISBN 9783540345138.

https://doi.org/10.1142/9789819813049_0002

CHAPTER 2 Static Liquidation and Risk Management

Álvaro F. Macías[1] and Jorge P. Zubelli[2,*]

[1]*AFMA Ingenieria Spa, Santiago, Chile*
[2]*Department of Mathematics, Khalifa University of Science and Technology, Abu Dhabi, UAE*
[*]*Corresponding author. E-mail: jorge.zubelli@ku.ac.ae*

During the last few years, it has become important to develop strategies to evaluate the necessary collateral to operate large portfolios efficiently. This is particularly important in situations where there is a lot of volatility and markets where new products are being introduced.

In this study, we introduce a groundbreaking approach to collateral management that emphasizes measuring haircuts for the entire portfolio. We achieve this by analyzing the liquidation process of portfolios within the context of static strategies, and presenting an innovative methodology for minimizing losses that accounts for both market and liquidity risks. These static strategies are typically employed in high-stress situations, such as fund collapses and liquidations. Our methodology offers an improvement over the classical variance and conditional value at risk (CVaR) models, which can lead to instabilities and exhibit a lack of robustness.

We propose an enhanced variance model that addresses market and liquidity risks, manifested as intraday changes and price impacts. Our model concurrently reduces CVaR and the variance associated with intraday fluctuations. This study holds particular interest for risk management professionals at central counterparties and clearing houses, as it assists in calculating margins for portfolio collateral, ensuring greater stability and security.

Keywords: Liquidation Strategies, Collateral, Monte-Carlo, Derivatives, Tikhonov Regularization, Price Impact, Intra-day Price.

2.1. Introduction

Collateral warranty is highly used in financial transactions to reduce credit and liquidity risk in case one of the parties involved does not fulfill their obligations. It does not necessarily have to be presented as cash. There are several financial instruments that can be used as collateral, such as bonds, shares of stock, derivatives, and so on. Therefore, it is essential to be able to determine the value and the risk of a portfolio as a whole in a situation that requires being liquidated in a short period, focusing on reducing capital loss.

Oftentimes, a third party, like a clearing house, takes the role of managing the risk for a trade. In order to do so, the participants have to deposit a collateral at the clearing house, which needs to monitor the margin levels to ensure they can cover losses in the case of a settlement failure. In this scenario, it is also essential to be able to understand the risk of a portfolio in the event one of the parties defaults.

This discussion, however, is not limited to clearing houses, but it also includes any financial institution that has to handle or place a collateral. For instance, suppose that the base currency of an investor that wants to operate with a bank is the USD. This investor holds a certificate of deposit for 1,000,000 EUR with a one-year duration that they want to leave as collateral in the bank to operate different products. The relevant market risk in this position is the exposure of the Foreign Exchange (FX) to the EUR currency. This product as a collateral would have a significant depreciation due to its FX risk. To hedge the FX exposition, the investor trades a forward, which buys USD and sells EUR for 1,000,000 for the same duration of the deposit. Now the full position only has rate risk in USD. Hence, if the bank includes this forward in the collateral, the latter will be less risky with a similar present value. Therefore, as the full collateral should be less risky, the investor would be able to trade more products or leave less amount of collateral to trade the same products. This illustrates how considering a full portfolio enhances the collateral risk evaluation.

The value of a portfolio can be determined by the market value (mark to market [MtM]) of the assets that could be calculated using market data, some available models, or historical data. Nevertheless, this might not be a good approximation to the real value because, after the liquidation process, there is a good chance of failing to obtain the full market value of the assets. This mismatch between the market value and the final price may be caused by intraday price variations, poor market, liquidity, and the size of the portfolio. Also, such liquidation procedures often occur during market stress events, and sizable transactions can negatively impact the market and produce further losses. Furthermore, the bigger the portfolio, the harder it is to find suitable buyers. We can also find different asset-dependent restrictions, such as the starting day of the liquidation process and other limitations.

Searching for efficient strategies to liquidate a portfolio is fundamental for determining its real value and its risk. In this report, we focus our interest in studying the risk of a portfolio under a liquidation strategy more than the strategy itself.

The standard practice in financial institutions, as far as margin calculations are concerned, is to consider static liquidation strategies; see Refs. [1–3]. For this reason, we shall concentrate on such strategies in this report.

The plan for this report goes as follows. In Section 2.2, we review basic definitions and concepts of portfolio management and risk measures. In Section 2.3, we discuss some liquidation strategy models and in Section 2.4, we compare such models. We provide in Section 2.5 some illustrative examples. In Section 2.6, we discuss the issue of the execution price during the liquidation. In Section 2.7, we propose the use of a Tikhonov-type regularization in order to incorporate the execution price risk to the optimization. Moreover, this approach improves the robustness of the liquidation process. Section 2.8 presents some illustrative examples and comparisons of the different results. Finally, in Section 2.9, we draw some conclusions and final comments.

An earlier version of this work was part of the unpublished PhD thesis of one of the authors (AFM) [4]. Several additions and examples have now been incorporated.

2.2. Definitions and Basic Concepts

2.2.1. *Definitions*

Let us consider a portfolio P with N_a assets that have m_i shares of an asset i, such that at the time $t = 0$, the portfolio has an MtM value of φ_i^0. This portfolio may include derivatives as an asset i, in which the value of φ_i depends on the price of the underlying asset S_i.

We want to find a strategy to liquidate this portfolio within T days starting at day $t = 1$. The value of the portfolio at the time $t = 0$ will be $P_0 := \sum_{i=1}^{N_a} m_i\varphi_i^0$.

We define the vector $q \in [0,1]^{N_a \times T}$, where q_i^t represents the fraction of the wealth invested on asset i that will be liquidated at the time t. Also, we define the set as:

$$I := \{(i,t) \in \{1, ..., N_a\} \times \{1, ..., T\}\}.$$

Assuming that we know the distributions of the underlying price vector of the assets $S_t = (S_1^t, \cdots, S_{N_u}^t)$ for all time $t \in \{1, \ldots, T\}$, we define $\psi_i^t(S^t) := m_i(\varphi_i^t(S^t)e^{-rt} - \varphi_i^0)$, where ψ_i^t is the present value of profit and loss (PnL) of the asset i at the time t. We are not making any assumptions of the random variables S^t other than being a real random variable and belongs to some probability space $\mathcal{L}^2(\Omega, \mathcal{F}, \mathbb{P})$.

Besides the restrictions of liquidating by the time T, we have other restrictions like the amount of the asset we can liquidate per day and the day we can start the liquidation.

Under these hypotheses, we define the set as:

$$Q := \left\{q \in [0,1]^{N_a \times T} \quad | \quad q_i^t \le k_i^t, \quad \forall (i,t) \in I, \quad \sum_{t=1}^{T} q_i^t = 1, \quad \forall i \in \{1, ..., N_a\}\right\},$$

where Q is a linear-bounded set and

$$\sum_{t=1}^{T} k_i^t \ge 1 \quad \forall i \in \{1, ..., N_a\}.$$

Observation 2.2.1. We use a matrix notation for the vectors ψ_i^t and q_i^t, where $(\cdot)_i^t$ is a reshaping of the vector $(\cdot)_{t+(i-1)T}$.

The PnL obtained by liquidating the portfolio using strategy q is represented by $\sum_{(i,t)\in I} q_i^t \psi_i^t$. So, given a multivariate random variable $S \in \Pi_{(i,t)\in I}\mathcal{L}^2(\Omega, \mathcal{F}, \mathbb{P})$, we define the functional:

$$Q \to \mathcal{L}^2(\Omega, \mathcal{F}, \mathbb{P}) \qquad q \to M_\psi(q) := \sum_{(i,t)\in I} q_i^t \psi_i^t(S^t) = \langle q, \psi \rangle, \tag{2.1}$$

where $M_{\psi}(q)$ represents the loss–gain value of the portfolio liquidated using strategy q.

Whenever we choose N_s samples of the multivariate random variable ψ, we shall write ψ_k or $\psi_i^t(k)$ for every $k \in \{1, \ldots, N_s\}$.

2.2.2. *The liquidation problem*

We wish to study the risk of a portfolio under a liquidation process. Every portfolio has its own risk derived from the combination of its assets; however, in the process of clearance of a portfolio, there are other risks involved. The fact that we cannot liquidate instantly at time zero will produce a temporal exposition of the portfolio. Also, buying and selling at the initial time can cause impacts on the prices, consequently increasing the cost. Moreover, if the portfolio has a derivative, it might include special rules for selling or buying. All of these factors may result in the selection of an unsuitable strategy for liquidation, causing unnecessary exposure and expenses.

The first action when choosing a strategy is to define what type of risk the holder wants to avoid. As it will be seen in the course of this report, there are different risk concepts, and each one can provide us with extremely different strategies. In the literature, there are several models that have been used to find an optimal allocation subject to reduce the defined risk [5]. These models can be easily reformulated to reflect strategies of liquidation instead of allocation. In this section, we will review two of the classical formulations applied to our particular problem: the Variance Model and the Expected Shortfall (ES) Model.

We concentrate on static strategies rather than dynamic strategies of liquidation as our focus is to understand the risk of the portfolio in the event of mandatory liquidation; see Refs. [1–3].

2.2.3. *Optimization problem*

There are many ways in which risk can be quantified [6], and we choose a class of definitions that are convenient for us. Our problem is to find how to liquidate our portfolio P optimally to be defined below. For that, we define an optimization functional F, which is not necessarily a risk measure. Since we know the distribution of S, and hence the distribution of ψ, we can define a stochastic control problem:

$$\min_{q \in Q} F(M_{\psi}(q)). \tag{2.2}$$

2.3. Liquidation Strategy Models

In this section, we present three models: the so-called Simpleminded Model, the Variance Model, and the Expected Shortfall of the Loss (ESL) Model. The first one is a naive model, and the other two have been used in allocation theory (see Ref. [6]). It will serve as a benchmark for the other ones. Notice that we are focusing on the risk of losing, not on increasing the expected returns, so we will not consider the expected returns in the objective function or the restrictions.

2.3.1. *Simpleminded model*

A simple, naive strategy is to try to liquidate all the assets independently and to think that the faster you sell or buy them, the better it is.

Let us write this strategy as an optimization problem:

$$\max_{q \in Q} \sum_{i=1}^{N_a} \sum_{t=1}^{T} (T + 1 - t) q_i^t \tag{2.3}$$

Note that for this strategy we do not consider the value of $M_\psi(q)$. This strategy is very elementary, and it does not need to be written as an optimization problem. This model is based on the principle that liquidating your asset faster would reduce the exposition and supposedly reduce the risk of the portfolio losing its market value. However, we are going to see that this idea is not necessarily a good one, especially if every asset has different rules for selling (starting day, the maximum amount per day) and there is hedging or correlation between them.

2.3.2. *Variance model*

The standard deviation is a deviation risk measure (see Ref. [7]). A commonly used model is the approach presented by Markovitz (1952) in Ref. [8] that consists of finding an optimal liquidation strategy for a portfolio minimizing the variance:

$$\min_{q \in Q} \sigma^2(M_\psi(q)) = \min_{q \in Q} \langle q, \Sigma q \rangle \tag{2.4}$$

Here Σ is the covariance matrix of ψ and as we said before, we eliminate the expected value constraint of the classical model. Equation (2.4) is a quadratic problem in a convex and compact setting, so the problem always has a solution, which is not necessarily unique. An advantage and feature of this model is that the calculus of the covariance matrix Σ can be very accurate, and the quantity of scenarios that we take to solve the Variance Model will not affect the performance of the optimization. In practice, we can simulate a considerable number of samples and calculate the covariance matrix with them (the calculus is just a process of matrix multiplication). This attribute of the model is advantageous for two reasons. The first is that, even if Eq. (2.4) defines a quadratic model, in practice it is a fast model to solve. The second reason is that this model is very stable and robust for small-scale problems.

One of the biggest disadvantages is that, since it reduces the variance in both directions, profit and loss are treated in the same way. Also, it does not handle extreme loss. Furthermore, if the problem becomes degenerate, several numerical issues may arise.

2.3.3. *ESL model*

The ES measure (also called the Conditional Value at Risk [CVaR], average value at risk, or expected tail loss) is a coherent risk measure (see Refs. [9–11]). It can be interpreted as the expected loss of a given α-quantile. A formal definition, given a random variable $X \in L^p$ and $\alpha \in (0, 1)$

$$ES_{\alpha}(X) := \int_0^{\alpha} VaR_{\gamma}(X)d\gamma,$$

where $VaR_{\gamma}(X)$ is the value at risk of X with confidence level γ.

The fact that the ES is a coherent measure implies that it is a convex function of $q \in Q$. Rockafellar and Uryasev [12] presented a linear formulation that seeks the optimal allocation that minimizes the CVaR and necessarily reduces the Value at Risk.

In Ref. [12], they introduced the functional

$$F_{\beta}(q, v) = v + \frac{1}{1-\beta}\int_{y \in \mathbb{R}^{TxN_a}} \left(-M_{\psi}(q) - v\right)^{+} p(y)dy,$$

where the solution (q^*, v^*) of

$$\min_{(q,v)\in Q\times\mathbb{R}} F_{\beta}(q, v) \tag{2.5}$$

is such that $v^* = VaR_{\beta}(-M(q^*, \psi))$ and $F_{\beta}(q^*, v^*) = ES_{\beta}(-M(q^*, \psi))$. Instead of solving Eq. (2.5), they take N_s sample of ψ and approximate F_{β} as

$$F_{\beta}(q, v) \approx \widehat{F}_{\beta}(q, v) := v + \frac{1}{N_s(1-\beta)} \sum_{k=1}^{N_s} \left(-M(q, \psi_k) - v\right)^{+}$$

and solve

$$\min_{(q,v)\in Q\times\mathbb{R}} \widehat{F}_{\beta}(q, v). \tag{2.6}$$

By using some auxiliary variables, they obtain the following linear problem:

$$\begin{aligned} \min_{(q,v,u)} \quad & v + \frac{1}{N_s(1-\beta)} \sum_{k=1}^{N_s} u_k \\ \text{s. t.} \quad & q \in Q, \quad v \in \mathbb{R}, \\ & -M_{\psi_k}(q) - v \le u_k, \qquad \forall k \in \{1, \ldots, N_s\}, \\ & u_k \ge 0, \qquad \forall k \in \{1, \ldots, N_s\}. \end{aligned} \tag{2.7}$$

As mentioned before, ideally, we are looking for strategies that reduce the risk of loss. In other words, just the risk of the negative part of $M_{\psi}(q)$. So, in Cont and He [13], a loss-based risk measure was introduced where they consider measures that focus only on the loss part. The conditional value of the loss is an example of this measure. Hence, we can easily extend the linear model in Ref. [12] for the ES to a model for the ESL. Remembering that $M_{\psi}(q)^{-} = \max\{-M_{\psi}(q), 0\}$,

$$\widehat{F}_{\beta}(q, v) := v + \frac{1}{N_s(1-\beta)} \sum_{k=1}^{N_s} \left(M_{\psi_k}(q)^{-} - v\right)^{+}.$$

The problem can be written as a linear program introducing a new auxiliary variable $\gamma \in \{1, \ldots, N_s\}$

$$
\begin{aligned}
\min_{(q,v,u,\gamma)} \quad & v + \frac{1}{N_s(1-\beta)} \sum_{k=1}^{N_s} u_k, & \\
\text{s. t.} \quad & q \in Q, \quad v \in \mathbb{R}, & \\
& \gamma_k - v \leq u_k, & \forall k \in \{1, \ldots, N_s\}, \\
& \gamma_k \geq -M_{\psi_k}(q), & \forall k \in \{1, \ldots, N_s\}, \\
& u_k \geq 0, \quad \gamma_k \geq 0, & \forall k \in \{1, \ldots, N_s\}.
\end{aligned}
\tag{2.8}
$$

Among the advantages, the ESL is a convenient representation of risks as it measures the downside risk. Also, it is applicable to nonsymmetric loss distribution. Other properties are that it is a convex model with respect to the portfolio position and that it is a loss-based risk measure, which can be used in a linear programming approach to solve the minimization. As for the disadvantages, we can cite, among others, the size of the Linear Programming problem, which increases when we increase the number of scenarios, focusing only on the tail of the loss, and fails to reduce more general risks.

2.4. Model Comparison

Choosing one model over the other will depend on the investor profile. However, it is important to make a comparison between them to have a better understanding of their properties. The first thing we are going to compare is the computational cost of each model. Second, since we are working with risk estimates to solve the optimization, we need to evaluate how robust these estimations are. So, we will define two measures that will help us study the stability of the models reviewed.

2.4.1. *Computational efficiency*

Let us write $R_q := N_a(1+2T)$. Table 2.1 shows the numbers of the constraints and variables for each model. A first observation is that the Simpleminded Model has the same number of constraints and variables as the Variance Model. Besides the fact that one is linear and the other quadratic, the difference arises from the fact that the Simpleminded Model does not have any information about the behavior of the portfolio. In the Variance Model, although the model is nonlinear, the fact that the optimization does not depend on the amount of scenarios (the input is just the covariance matrix) makes this model faster than the ESL Models when the number of simulations is large. Because the ESL Model depends on the number of scenarios, we need to choose an appropriate set of scenarios that are representative of the distribution ψ but not so big that the optimization algorithm could not converge in a reasonable time.

Table 2.1. Comparison of the models.

Model	Variables	Constraints	Problem type
Simpleminded	TN_a	R_q	Linear
Variance	TN_a	R_q	Quadratic convex
Ex. Sh. Loss	$TN_a + 1 + 2N_s$	$R_q + 2N_s$	Linear

Observation 2.4.1. We are going to refer to the order of the optimization problem as $O(n)$, which means that the computational time of the model depends linearly on n. There, we write $O(N_s)$ when the optimization problem depends linearly on the size of the sample, and we write $O(N_aT)$ when it depends on the number of assets and time step T. When it depends on the size of the sample N_s and the number of assets and time step N_aT independently, we write only $O(N_s)$ because in practice $N_s \gg N_aT$.

2.4.2. *Robustness*

In practice, we cannot work directly with the process ψ due to its complexity and since we do not want to make any assumption about it. Indeed, we are going to use Monte Carlo simulations to compute an approximation of the risk measures.

Consider that we have a risk functional F and $q^* \in Q$, which is the solution of Eq. (2.2), and suppose that Ω is a (large) finite set of all possible scenarios of ψ. To solve Eq. (2.2), we use the linear models, taking a sample with K scenarios of Ω and using an approximation $\widehat{F}$ of F to solve

$$\min_{q\in Q} \widehat{F}(\{M_{\psi_k}(q)\}_{k\in K}). \tag{2.9}$$

We are going to denote q^K as the solution to Eq. (2.9). We want to study how close $M_\psi(q^K)$ is to $M_\psi(q^*)$.

There is a trade-off between the computational time and the quality of the solution. If we increase the number of scenarios, we are going to have a better solution but with some efficiency cost. We need to study the size of a representative number of scenarios. For this reason, we are going to use two tests for robustness. They are going to be called a risk functional (RF) Robustness and cumulative distribution function (CDF) robustness. The RF robustness concerns how the risk value used in the optimization is behaving when the numbers of scenarios are increasing. The CDF studies the L^∞ norm of the cumulative function C_F of $M_\psi(q)$.

Definition 2.4.1. *The RF robustness is the study of the behavior of*

$$\frac{|F(M_\psi(q^K)) - F(M_\psi(q^{K'}))|}{F(M_\psi(q^K))}, \tag{2.10}$$

when $|K|, |K'| \to |\Omega|$.

Definition 2.4.2. *The CDF robustness is the study of the behavior of*

$$||C_F(M_\psi(q^K)) - C_F(M_\psi(q^{K'}))||_\infty, \tag{2.11}$$

when $|K|, |K'| \to |\Omega|$.

2.5. Illustrative Example

Let us consider a simple and fictional portfolio formed by a Share, a Forward, an Call Option, and a Put Option as in Table 2.2.

Table 2.2. Portfolio.

Asset	Product	Position	Exp day	Strike	Max p/ day	Initial day
1	Option Call	−4,000	60	1.2	2,000	5
2	Option Put	1,000	60	1.2	1,000	5
3	Forward	1,000	60	1.2	1,000	2
4	Share	1,000	N/A	N/A	1,000	1

We simulated 1,000,000 scenarios for the share S using a Brownian motion (see Ref. [14]) with an annual volatility of 0.25 and an annual drift of 9.00%. The annualized risk-free interest rate was 8.00%. The three derivatives are associated with the same share S of the first asset with initial value $S_0 = 1$, and the MtM values of the options were calculated using the Black–Scholes formula (see Ref. [15]). The initial value of the portfolio P_0 is 931.3.

The Simpleminded Model did not need the simulations. For the Variance Model, we used all the scenarios to calculate the covariance matrix. For the ESL Model, we choose 6,500 random scenarios from the 1,000,000 scenarios simulated. Finally, for the ESL Model, we used the confidence level $\beta = 0.05$.[a]

Table 2.3 shows the risk statistics of the solution of the different models.

Table 2.3. Statistics of $M_\psi(q)$.

Models	Std. des.	$CVaR_{0.05}$	$VaR_{0.05}$	$\mathbb{E}(X^-)$	Op. time (s)
Simpleminded	83.2	213.0	137.5	65.4	9.4
Variance	19.2	49.8	26.2	14.8	5.5
ESL	19.6	49.7	25.3	13.9	22.9

An important question is how the holder of the portfolio will value it in a liquidation condition. In this example, the initial value of the portfolio is 931.3; however, as we showed

[a]The optimization problems were run using Gurobi Optimizer; see Ref. [16]. We choose to use it due to its satisfactory handling of sparsity.

in Table 2.3, different strategies produce different risks. For example, if the strategy from the Simpleminded Model is used and the holder has a very adverse risk profile. He should consider the *CVaR* value, that is, price the warranty as 77.1% of the original value; however, if the holder does not have a very adverse risk aversion, he may use the percentage of the loss expectation, which is 93.0%; see Table 2.4. On the other hand, if the holder considers the strategy of the Variance Model or the ESL Model, and he has a very adverse risk profile, he is going to price the warranty with a higher value, 94.6% and 94.7%, respectively, than using the strategy from the Simpleminded Model and having a small adverse risk profile. Table 2.4 shows the advantage of using strategies that focus on reducing the risk; for example, the holder could ask for less collateral, or the owner will have more margin before the holder asks for more collateral.

Even more so, Figs. 2.1, 2.2, and 2.3 show the optimal strategies q and the histograms of $M_\psi(q)$, where they show that the Simpleminded Model is much riskier than the others. In Figs. 2.2 and 2.3, we can see that it does not matter if we can liquidate an asset at the initial time. It is more important to reduce the general risk. Also, in these figures, we can observe that although the solutions q are different for the Variance Model and the ESL Model, the risks are similar (see also Tables 2.3 and 2.4). We will see later that these risks will differ when we incorporate intraday variations.

Table 2.4. Percentage of the value of the initial portfolio that the holder will consider as warranty.

Models	$CVaR_{0.05}$	$VaR_{0.05}$	$\mathbb{E}(X^-)$
Simpleminded	77.1	85.2	93.0
Variance	94.6	97.2	98.4
ESL	94.7	97.3	98.5

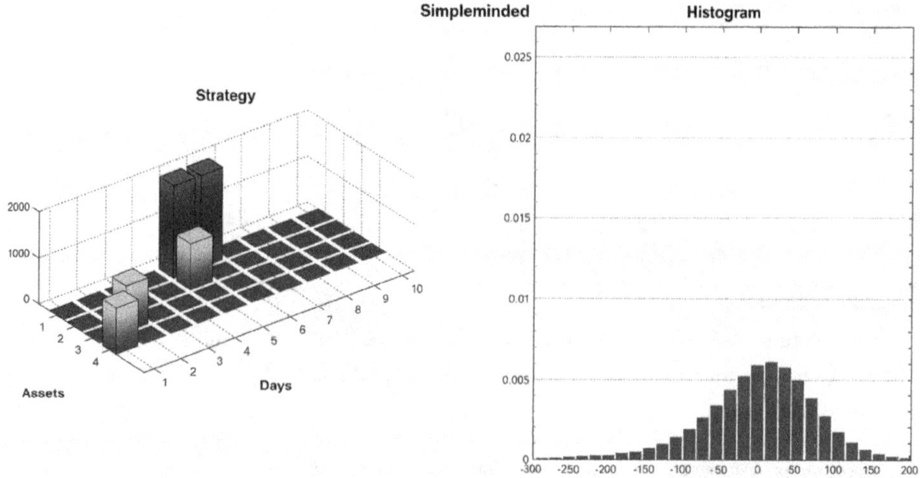

Fig. 2.1 Strategy q and distribution of $M_\psi(q)$ for the Simpleminded Model.

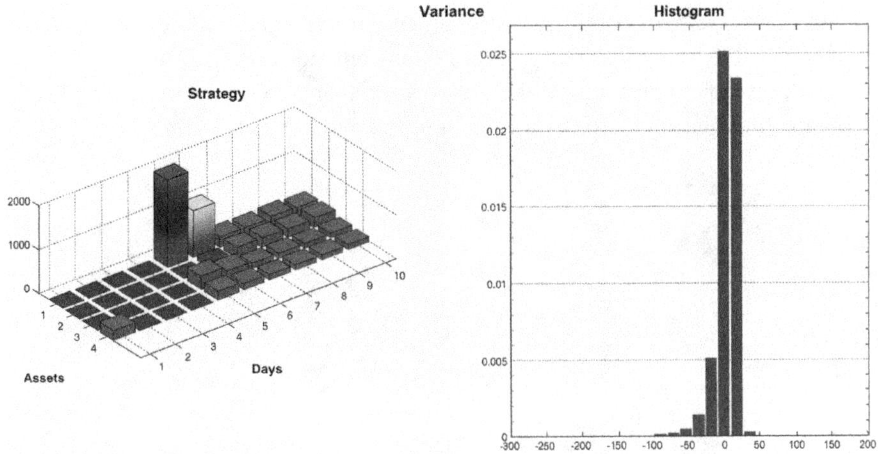

Fig. 2.2 Strategy q and distribution of $M_\psi(q)$ for the Variance Model.

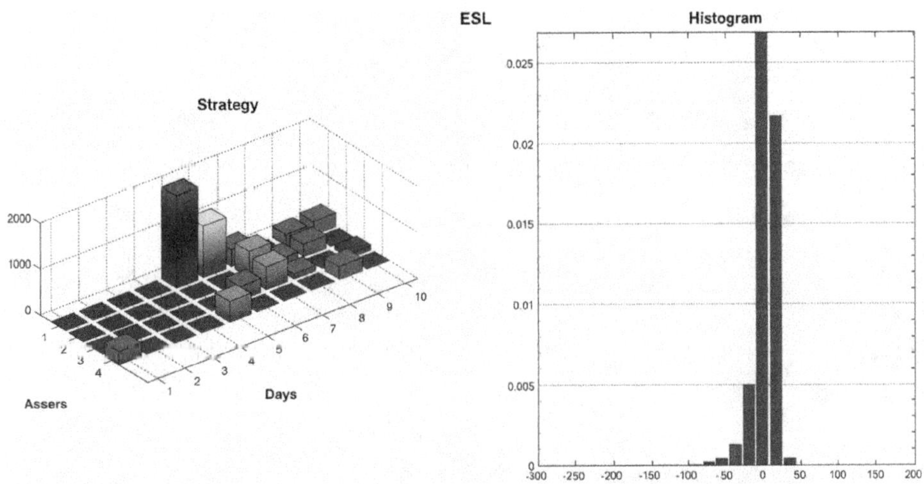

Fig. 2.3 Strategy q and distribution of $M_\psi(q)$ for the Expected Shortfall Model.

Remark 2.5.1. Notice that the histograms and the calculus of the statistics were made using all the scenarios. It does not matter whether we take a few scenarios to find q for the optimization problem, as we want to study the behavior of the random variable $M_\psi(q)$.

2.5.1. *Robustness of the ESL model*

We are going to study the behavior of the solution using the robustness defined above for the ESL model, which depends on the number of samples.

We ran the model with 1,000 scenarios, then with another 1,500 different scenarios, and so on until 6,500 scenarios. The graphics on the left side of Figs. 2.4 and 2.5 show that the ESL model is very robust, as it did not take more than 4,000 scenarios to become very stable. See the graphics on the right side of Figs. 2.4 and 2.5.

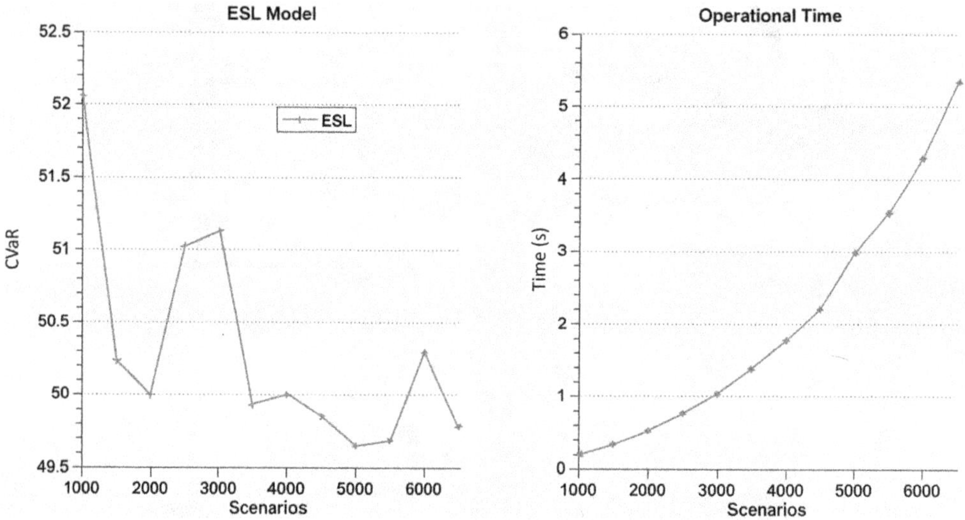

Fig. 2.4 CDF robustness.

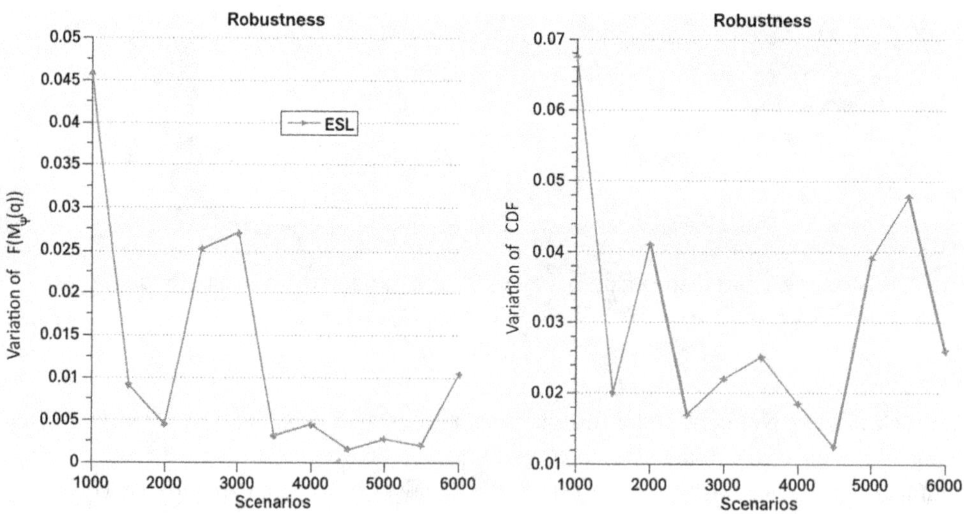

Fig. 2.5 RF robustness.

2.6. Execution Price

In almost every sale or purchase process of an asset, the final execution price will differ from the market value. This discrepancy is due to liquidation issues in the market, the alteration of the price caused by the transaction itself or transaction costs, the bid or offer price and the lack of market depth.

In the previous section, we reviewed some essential risk aversion models to find discrete strategies. However, the strategy q_t^i can be executed at any time during the interval $(t-1, t]$, not necessarily at a fixed time t. Thus, this discretization causes a loss of information about the price between periods (intraday price). In addition, these models do not consider the issues mentioned above. Motivated by these issues, different models have been introduced. Two models we should highlight are the articles by Bertsimas and Lo (see Ref. [17]) and Almgren and Chriss (see Ref. [18]).

We will briefly review the models in Refs. [17] and [18]. As a consequence of their work, we will present a simplified model where this simplification makes it easier to incorporate the perturbation effect in the liquidation models.

2.6.1. *Basic concepts and models' review*

2.6.1.1. *Intraday price*

The models we discussed in Section 2.2 lead to optimal discrete strategies of the amount that we should liquidate every day until day T. The problem with such an approach is that it assumes that the liquidation of the asset i will be at the end of the period or during an exact time. However, in practice, the execution takes place all along caused by the lack of liquidity of the market or by the trader's decision; thus, being exposed to intraday variations. In Fig. 2.6, we show the effect of time discretization, for each day and only one sample. It shows we may be subject to many possible prices.

2.6.1.2. *Price impact*

Bertsimas and Lo (see Ref. [17]) present optimal dynamic strategies to minimize the expected cost of trading a large block of equities over a fixed time horizon. Moreover, they present a model for the price of an asset affected by the impact of the amount of the asset. One such model is called "linear-percentage temporary" (LPT).

Another model is presented in Almgren and Chriss (see Ref. [18]); it is based on the idea of Ref. [17]. Nevertheless, it aims to find static strategies that minimize not only the expected cost but also the volatility risk. They suppose that they have a permanent impact on the price and a temporary impact on the price.

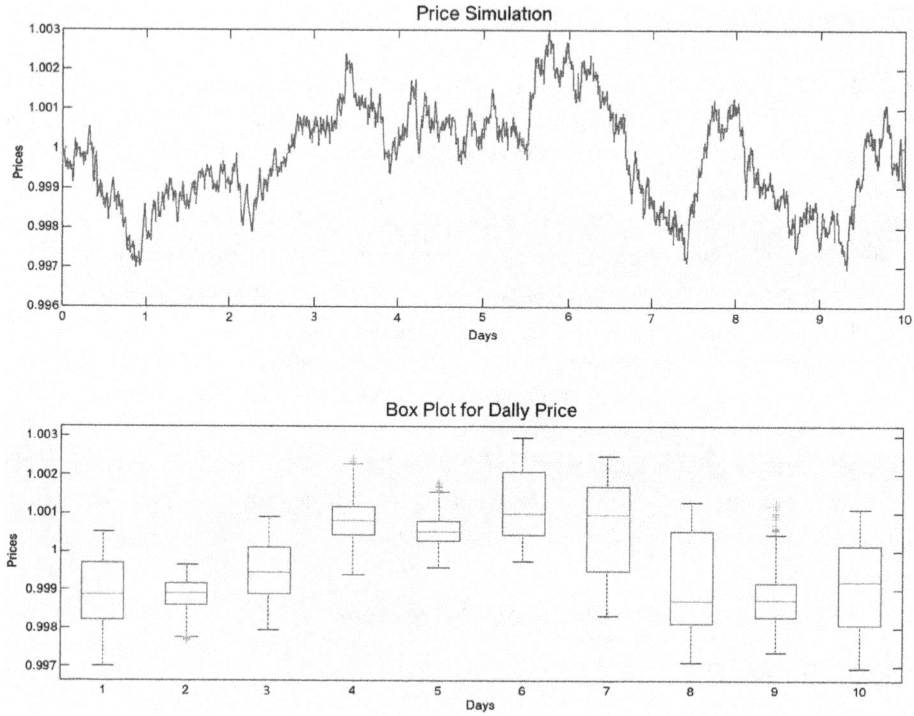

Fig. 2.6 Above: One sample for 10 days with time steps of 30 minutes. Below: The box plot for the daily price variation.

2.6.2. *Execution price model*

Recall that we are seeking strategies that minimize the risk of $M_\psi(q)$, where

$$M_\psi(q) = \sum_{(i,t)\in I} \psi_i^t q_i^t$$

and

$$\psi_i^t = m_i(\varphi_i^t e^{-rt} - \varphi_i^0).$$

Hence, if we consider that we have a permanent impact over φ that depends on $q \in Q$, M_ψ would lose the linearity concerning $q \in Q$. Thus, in the minimization problems, the objective function would lose the quadratic behavior in the Variance Model and the linearity in the ESL Model. Another difficulty is to find good estimations for the parameters of the models.

The issues presented above motivate us to simplify the model instead of supposing that we know the behavior of any impact function. We consider that the price for each asset i has only temporary perturbation δ. Considering this, we write,

$$\tilde{\varphi}_i^t := \varphi_i^t(1 + \delta_i^t), \tag{2.12}$$

where $\tilde{\varphi}_i^t$ is the execution price, φ_i^t is the expected price at the time t with no impact, and δ_i^t is the perturbation caused by the intraday variations and the price impact. Notice that Eq. (2.12) is a simplification of the LPT model presented in Ref. [17] with the difference that we do not make any a priori hypothesis from the behavior of the random variable δ. Also, δ could incorporate some transaction costs.

Observation 2.6.1. Hereafter, we will refer as intraday price to both the effect of the intraday price and the price impact.

Therefore, we define the execution loss or gain $\tilde{\psi}$ for the asset i at the time t:

$$\begin{aligned}\tilde{\psi}_i^t &= m_i(e^{-rt}\varphi_i^t(1+\delta_i^t) - \varphi_i^0) \\ &= \psi_i^t(1+\delta_i^t) + m_i\varphi_i^0\delta_i^t.\end{aligned} \tag{2.13}$$

And following the idea of Ref. [18], we are going to focus on reducing the variance of $M_{\tilde{\psi}}(q)$, changing ψ by $\tilde{\psi}$. We now introduce some hypothesis on $\{\delta_i^t\}_{(i,t)\in I}$,

(1) $\{\delta_i^t\}_{(i,t)\in I}$ is a set of independent random variables for all $(i,t) \in I$ and $\{\delta_i^t\}_{t=1}^T$ are identically distributed for all $i \in \{1,\ldots,N_a\}$.
(2) δ_j^s is independent of ψ_i^t for all $(j,s) \in I$ and $(i,t) \in I$.

We recall the following properties for two independently random variables X and Y:

(1) $cov(X,Y) = 0$,
(2) $\sigma^2(XY) = \sigma^2(X)\sigma^2(Y) + \mathbb{E}^2(Y)\sigma^2(X) + \mathbb{E}^2(X)\sigma^2(Y)$,
(3) $cov(X,XY) = \mathbb{E}(Y)\sigma^2(X)$.

With these, we calculate the variance of only ψ_i^t:

$$\begin{aligned}\sigma^2(\tilde{\psi}_i^t) &= \sigma^2(\psi_i^t(1+\delta_i^t)) + (m_i\varphi_i^0)^2\sigma^2(\delta_i^t) + 2m_i\varphi_i^0 cov(\psi_i^t(1+\delta_i^t),\delta_i^t) \\ &= \sigma^2(\psi_i^t) + \sigma^2(\psi_i^t\delta_i^t) + 2cov(\psi_i^t,\psi_i^t\delta_i^t) + (m_i\varphi_i^0)^2\sigma^2(\delta_i^t) \\ &\quad + 2m_i\varphi_i^0(cov(\psi_i^t,\delta_i^t) + cov(\psi_i^t\delta_i^t,\delta_i^t)) \\ &= \sigma^2(\psi_i^t) + \sigma^2(\psi_i^t)\sigma^2(\delta_i^t) + \mathbb{E}^2(\psi_i^t)\sigma^2(\delta_i^t) + \mathbb{E}^2(\delta_i^t)\sigma^2(\psi_i^t) \\ &\quad + 2\mathbb{E}(\delta_i^t)\sigma^2(\psi_i^t) + (m_i\varphi_i^0)^2\sigma^2(\delta_i^t) + 2m_i\varphi_i^0\sigma^2(\delta_i^t)\mathbb{E}(\psi_i^t) \\ &= \sigma^2(\psi_i^t)(1 + 2\mathbb{E}(\delta_i^t) + \mathbb{E}^2(\delta_i^t)) + \sigma^2(\delta_i^t)(\sigma^2(\psi_i^t) + (m_i\varphi_i^0)^2 \\ &\quad + \mathbb{E}^2(\psi_i^t) + 2\phi_i^0\mathbb{E}(\psi_i^t)) \\ &= \sigma^2(\psi_i^t)(1+\mathbb{E}(\delta_i^t))^2 + \sigma^2(\delta_i^t)(\sigma^2(\psi_i^t) + (m_i\varphi_i^0 + \mathbb{E}(\psi_i^t))^2).\end{aligned} \tag{2.14}$$

Using that the perturbations δ_i^t are independent, we conclude that the covariance of $\tilde{\psi}_i^t$ and $\tilde{\psi}_{i'}^{t'}$, where $(i,t) \neq (i',t')$ is

$$cov(\tilde{\psi}_i^t, \tilde{\psi}_{i'}^{t'}) = cov(\psi_i^t, \psi_{i'}^{t'}). \tag{2.15}$$

Hence, we can write the covariance matrix for $\tilde{\psi}$ as

$$\tilde{\Sigma} := \Sigma(\tilde{\psi}) = \Sigma(\psi) + \Delta(\psi, \delta), \tag{2.16}$$

where $\Delta(\psi, \delta)$ is a diagonal matrix with $\sigma^2(\psi_i^t)((1 + \mathbb{E}(\delta_i^t))^2 - 1) + \sigma^2(\delta_i^t)(\sigma^2(\psi_i^t) + (m_i\varphi_i^0 + \mathbb{E}(\psi_i^t))^2)$ in the diagonal.

Therefore, if we want to reduce the effect of the intraday price in the liquidation process, we can solve the Variance Model by considering the covariance matrix $\Sigma(\tilde{\psi})$ instead of $\Sigma(\psi)$.

$$\min_{q \in Q} \langle q, \tilde{\Sigma} q \rangle. \tag{2.17}$$

Observation 2.6.2. A simple idea to incorporate the perturbation in the ESL Model is to produce samples not only for S^t but also of δ_i^t and solve the optimization by adding these samples. However, this approach significantly affects the performance of the models because the linear problems depend directly on the amount of scenarios. In the next section, we will introduce a technique to treat the intraday price in the linear models without affecting their performances.

Proposition 2.6.1. *Assume that* $\mathbb{E}[\delta_i^t] = 0$ *and* $\sigma^2(\delta_i^t) = \sigma^2_{\delta_i}$, $\forall (i,t) \in I$, *and that the daily limitation for liquidation is* $k_i^t = 1$, $\forall (i,t) \in I$. *Then the solution of*

$$\min_{q \in Q} \frac{1}{2} \langle q, \Delta(\psi, \delta) q \rangle \tag{2.18}$$

is

$$(q_i^t)^* = \frac{1}{(d^t)^2} \left(\sum_{t=1}^{T} \frac{1}{(d^t)^2} \right)^{-1},$$

where $(d_i^t)^2 := \sigma^2(\psi_i^t) + (\phi_i^0 + \mathbb{E}(\psi_i^t))^2$ *independently of* $\sigma^2(\delta_i^t)$.

Proof. First, notice that $(d_i^t)^2 > 0$, because $\sigma^2(\psi_i^t) = 0$ and

$$m_i\varphi_i^0 + \mathbb{E}(\psi_i^t) = m_i\mathbb{E}(\varphi_i^t e^{-rt}) = m_i\varphi_i^t e^{-rt} = 0$$

means that certainly the asset i is going to lose everything at the time $t > 0$. Equation (2.18) is then equivalent to

$$\begin{aligned} \min_{q} \quad & \frac{1}{2} \sum_{(i,t) \in I} (q_i^t \sigma_{\delta_i}^2 d_i^t)^2, \\ \text{s. t.} \quad & \sum_{t=1}^{T} q_i^t = 1, \qquad \forall i \in \{1, \ldots, N_a\}, \\ & q_i^t \geq 0, \qquad \forall (i,t) \in I. \end{aligned} \tag{2.19}$$

Then, if $\sigma^2_{\delta_i}$ does not depend on t and Eq. (2.19) can be solved independently for each asset i, then without loss of generality we can write:

$$\begin{aligned} \min_{q} \quad & \frac{1}{2}\sum_{t=1}^{T}(q^t d^t)^2 \\ \text{s. t.} \quad & \sum_{t=1}^{T} q^t = 1, \quad q^t \geq 0, \qquad \forall t \in \{1, \ldots, T\}. \end{aligned} \tag{2.20}$$

The optimization problem in Eq. (2.20) has a strictly convex objective function in a compact space. Hence, it has a unique solution, and we can use the Karush–Kuhn–Tucker (KKT) conditions (see Ref. [19]) to find it. Therefore,

$$q^t_* = \frac{1}{(d^t)^2}\left(\sum_{t=1}^{T}\frac{1}{(d^t)^2}\right)^{-1}. \tag{2.21}$$

This concludes the proof. ■

Observation 2.6.3. The model presented in this section is not far away from the model in Ref. [18]. Despite not assuming a dependence on q of the price impact, we obtain that the variance of the intraday price in our model is

$$\sum_{t=1}^{T}(q^t)^2(d^t)^2.$$

Therefore, we also obtain a quadratic minimization over q in function of the variance.

2.7. A Tikhonov-Type Regularization to Reduce Both Risks Simultaneously

Reviewing Sections 2.2 and 2.6, we can find some relevant properties of the Variance Model. In Section 2.2, we showed that the Variance Model is a robust model, and it could be solved within a reasonable computational time. Furthermore, in Section 2.6, we showed that it can incorporate intraday risk without altering its efficiency. The idea consists in replacing the covariance matrix Σ by $\Sigma + \Delta$ and proceeding exactly as before.

On the other hand, the ESL Model seems to be more effective at controlling losses. However, as we studied in Section 2.5, these linear models present a trade-off between robustness and computational efficiency caused by the need of numerous scenarios for the estimation of the functional to represent uncertainty properly. Computational limitations preclude an arbitrary choice of the number of the sample. This is why we do not recommend simulating the intraday perturbations while generating the asset sample as we showed in Observation 2.6.2.

In this section, we shall present a formulation that takes the advantages of the VM and is used to increase the robustness of the ESL Model. Furthermore, we incorporate the intraday risk without increasing the numerical complexity. This technique will also help, on the one hand, to control the risk of large losses and, on the other hand, control a more global risk as is the variance.

2.7.1. *Preliminaries*

Consider the linear formulation $\tilde{F}$ of the ESL Model. As we remark in Observation 2.6.2, an idea is to incorporate the effect of the intraday price to minimize the linear models using $\tilde{\psi}$ instead of ψ, that is

$$\min_{q \in Q} \widetilde{F}(M_{\tilde{\psi}}(q)), \tag{2.22}$$

where $\tilde{\psi}_i^t$ depends on the underlying share S^t and the perturbation δ_i^t as in Eq. (2.13). Then, to solve Eq. (2.22), we need not only to simulate scenarios for all S^t but also for all δ_i^t. This means that for every simulation $k \in \{1, \ldots, N_s\}$, we will have N_δ simulations, where N_δ represent the number of simulations of δ_i^t. Hence, the linear problem becomes a model of order $O(N_s N_\delta)$, which leads us to conclude that this idea will bring operational issues because the runtime is going to be extremely high.

Another approach is to reduce the variance of $M_{\tilde{\psi}}(q)$. At the same time, we minimize $\tilde{F}(M_\psi(q))$. We do this by adding $\mathrm{Var}(M_{\tilde{\psi}}(q)) = \langle q, \tilde{\Sigma} q \rangle$ to the objective function as in Refs. [20, 21]. Thus, we now consider the problem

$$\min_{q \in Q} \gamma \widetilde{F}(M_\psi(q)) + (1 - \gamma)\langle q, \tilde{\Sigma} q \rangle, \tag{2.23}$$

where $\gamma \in (0, 1)$ is a parameter.

Recalling that $\tilde{\Sigma}$ is a covariance matrix, we can rewrite Eq. (2.23). Indeed, since $\tilde{\Sigma}$ is a covariance matrix, it is a symmetric, positive semidefinite matrix. Hence, we can use an eigenvector decomposition to write

$$\tilde{\Sigma} V = VD,$$

where V is an orthonormal matrix with the eigenvector of $\tilde{\Sigma}$ in the columns and D is diagonal with nonnegative eigenvalues. Let $W := VD^{\frac{1}{2}}$ and use it as a Cholesky decomposition for $\tilde{\Sigma}$,

$$\tilde{\Sigma} = VDV' = VD^{\frac{1}{2}}D^{\frac{1}{2}}V' = \left(VD^{\frac{1}{2}}\right)\left(VD^{\frac{1}{2}}\right)' = WW'.$$

Hence,

$$\langle q, \tilde{\Sigma} q \rangle = \langle q, WW'q \rangle = \langle W'q, W'q \rangle = \|W'q\|_2^2,$$

and Eq. (2.23) becomes

$$\min_{q\in Q} \gamma\widetilde{F}(M_\psi(q)) + (1-\gamma)||W'q||_2^2, \tag{2.24}$$

where the right-hand side of the term in Eq. (2.24) is a Tikhonov regularization with term W(see Ref. [22]) for the Linear Model using an L^2 semi-norm with respect to q. The benefits of adding the regularization terms are several. First, as we will show in the next examples, the model becomes more stable. Second, it is a simple tool for intraday risk control. On the other hand, one of the disadvantages of the quadratic regularization is that the models become harder to solve computationally. Table 2.1 shows that the ESL Model has $O(N_s)$ variables and $O(N_s)$ constraints. Hence, Eq. (2.23) is a quadratic problem with $O(N_s)$ variables and $O(N_s)$ constraints. Nevertheless, avoiding computational complexity is one of our goals. Thus, this approach will not help us keep the model simple and fast.

2.7.2. *The semi-norms Ws*

We remark that the regularization term is just the semi-norm computed according to the structure defined by W. Then, we are going to write $||\cdot||_{W^2}$ to refer to this semi-norm,

$$||q||_{W^2} := ||W'q||_2 = \left(\sum_{(j,s)\in I} \langle q, w_j^s\rangle^2\right)^{\frac{1}{2}}. \tag{2.25}$$

Remembering that $||\cdot||_W$ is a semi-norm if:

- $||aq||_W = |a|||q||_W, \forall a \in \mathbb{R}$.
- $||q+p||_W \leq ||q||_W + ||p||_W$.

Considering that the semi-norm $||\cdot||_{W2}^2$ is a quadratic regularization term and that we are also trying to avoid the issues of adding this term to a large-scale linear problem, it is natural to ask if we can replace the L^2 norm of $W'q$ for an L^1 norm in Eq. (2.24), that is,

$$\min_{q\in Q} \gamma\widetilde{F}(M_\psi(q)) + (1-\gamma)||W'q||_1. \tag{2.26}$$

Observation 2.7.1. The idea of changing the L^2 norm to the L^1 norm was motivated by the work in Ref. [23] applied to an inverse problem. The objective of this change in the norm is different from our case. However, it inspired us to take this direction.

To study the implications of this change, let us first define

$$||q||_{W^1} := ||W'q||_1 = \sum_{(j,s)\in I} |\langle q, w_j^s\rangle|. \tag{2.27}$$

And recall the following relationship between the norms L^1 and L^2,

$$||q||_{L^2} \leq ||q||_{L^1} \leq (N_a T)^{\frac{1}{2}} ||q||_{L^2}. \tag{2.28}$$

This property is easy to check using the definition of the norm, and it will help us prove Proposition 2.7.1, which is a result that assures us that the semi-norm W^1 will keep q close to the optimal variance. In practice, the optimal variance could not be zero, so if we minimize the term $||q||_{W^1}$, we cannot be sure that we are close to minimum variance. To avoid this problem, we first solve

$$q_a := argmin_{q \in Q} \langle q, \tilde{\Sigma} q \rangle. \tag{2.29}$$

And we use this as a priori term in Eq. (2.26). Therefore, we solve

$$\min_{q \in Q} \left\{ \gamma \widetilde{F}(M_{\psi}(q)) + (1-\gamma) ||(q - q_a)||_{W^1} \right\}. \tag{2.30}$$

Proposition 2.7.1. *If* $q_a \in Q$ *solves Eq. (2.29) and* $\{q_n\} \subseteq Q$ *is such that* $||q_n - q_a||_{W^1} \xrightarrow{n \to \infty} 0$*, then* $\mathrm{Var}(M_{\tilde{\psi}}(q_n)) \xrightarrow{n \to \infty} \mathrm{Var}(M_{\tilde{\psi}}(q_a))$.

Proof. Take $q_a \in Q$ solution of Eq. (2.29) and $q_n \in Q$, then

$$\mathrm{Var}(M_{\tilde{\psi}}(q_a)) \leq \mathrm{Var}(M_{\tilde{\psi}}(q_n)) \Rightarrow ||W' q_a||_2^2 \leq ||W' q_n||_2^2,$$

then

$$||q_a||_{W^2} \leq ||q_n||_{W^2},$$

by the definition of semi-norm,

$$||q_n||_{W^2} \leq ||q_n - q_a||_{W^2} + ||q_a||_{W^2}$$

and using the inequality for the norms in Eq. (2.28)

$$||q_n - q_a||_{W^2} \leq ||q_n - q_a||_{W^1}.$$

Therefore,

$$||q_a||_{W^2} \leq ||q_n||_{W^2} \leq ||q_n - q_a||_{W^1} + ||q_a||_{W^2}. \tag{2.31}$$

Letting $||q_n - q_a||_{W^1} \xrightarrow{n \to \infty} 0$ in Eq. (2.31), then $||q_n||_{W^2} \xrightarrow{n \to \infty} ||q_a||_{W^2}$. Finally, remembering that $||q||_{W^2}^2 = \langle q, \tilde{\Sigma} q \rangle = \mathrm{Var}(M_{\tilde{\psi}}(q))$, we can conclude the result. ∎

Remark 2.7.1. The last result shows the importance of using the a priori q_a. Without it, we could not be close to the optimal variance whenever we add the semi-norm W^1 to the linear model.

Remark 2.7.2. The use of an L^1 norm is not to obtain a spare solution of q. In fact, because we are using an a priori solution q_a that comes from a quadratic minimization, we cannot guarantee a spare solution. The change of norm is to write the minimization problem as a linear programming problem as we will show in Lemma 2.7.1.

2.7.3. *Linearization of W1 semi-norm*

Proposition 2.7.1 shows that if we seek strategies $q \in Q$ close in the semi-norm $\|\cdot\|_{W1}$ to a solution q_a of Eq. (2.29), the variance of $M_{\tilde{\psi}}(q)$ will be near the optimal. Moreover, the change of the norm leads us to an equivalent linear model for Eq. (2.30), as we prove in the following lemma.

Lemma 2.7.1. *Consider $q_a \in Q$ a solution of Eq. (2.29) and $\gamma \in (0,1)$. The minimization problem*

$$\min_{q\in Q}\left\{\gamma\widetilde{F}(M_{\psi}(q)) + (1-\gamma)\|q-q_a\|_{W^1}\right\} \tag{2.32}$$

is equivalent to the linear problem

$$\begin{aligned}
\min_{(q,\mu,\eta)} \quad & \gamma\tilde{F}(M_{\psi}(q)) + (1-\gamma)\sum_{(j,s)\in I}(\mu_j^s + \eta_j^s) \\
\text{s. t.} \quad & q \in Q, \\
& \mu_j^s - \langle q, \omega_j^s\rangle \geq -\langle q_a, \omega_j^s\rangle, \qquad \forall (j,s) \in I, \\
& \eta_j^s + \langle q, \omega_j^s\rangle \geq \langle q_a, \omega_j^s\rangle, \qquad \forall (j,s) \in I, \\
& \mu_j^s \geq 0, \quad \eta_j^s \geq 0, \qquad \forall (j,s) \in I.
\end{aligned} \tag{2.33}$$

Proof. Let $(\hat{q}, \hat{\mu}, \hat{\eta})$ be a solution of Eq. (2.33). So, $\hat{\mu}$ must satisfy

$$\hat{\mu}_j^s = \max\{\langle \hat{q} - q_a, \omega_j^s\rangle, 0\}, \quad \forall (j,s) \in I,$$

because if we fix $\hat{q}$, we are minimizing μ_j^s with the constraints $\mu_j^s \geq 0$ and $\mu_j^s \geq \langle \hat{q}-q_a, \omega_j^s\rangle$. The same argument leads to

$$\hat{\eta}_j^s = \max\{-\langle \hat{q} - q_a, \omega_j^s\rangle, 0\}, \quad \forall (j,s) \in I.$$

Now, suppose that q^* is a solution of Eq. (2.32) but not a solution of Eq. (2.33). Then,

$$\begin{aligned}
\min_{q}\left\{\gamma F(M_{\psi}(q)) + (1-\gamma)\|q-q_a\|_{W^1}\right\} &= \gamma F(M_{\psi}(q^*)) + (1-\gamma)\|q^*-q_a\|_{W^1} \\
&= \gamma F(M_{\psi}(q^*)) + (1-\gamma)\sum_{(j,s)\in I}|\langle \hat{q}^* - q_a, \omega_j^s\rangle| \\
&= \gamma F(M_{\psi}(q^*)) + (1-\gamma)\sum_{(j,s)\in I}\left(\langle q^* - q_a, \omega_j^s\rangle^+ + \langle q^* - q_a, \omega_j^s\rangle^-\right).
\end{aligned}$$

If we define (μ^*, η^*) as

$$(\mu^*)_j^s := \max\{\langle q^* - q_a, \omega_j^s\rangle, 0\}, \quad \forall (j,s) \in I$$

and

$$(\eta^*)_j^s := \max\{-\langle q^* - q_a, \omega_j^s\rangle, 0\}, \quad \forall (j,s) \in I,$$

we have that (q^*, μ^*, η^*) satisfies the constraints of Eq. (2.33). Hence, we can write

$$\begin{aligned}
&\min_q \left\{\gamma F(M_\psi(q)) + (1-\gamma)\|q - q_a\|_{W^1}\right\} \\
&\quad = \gamma F(M_\psi(q^*)) + (1-\gamma) \sum_{(j,s)\in I} \left((\mu^*)_j^s + (\eta^*)_j^s\right) \\
&\quad > \gamma F(M_\psi(\hat{q})) + (1-\gamma) \sum_{(j,s)\in I} \left(\hat{\mu}_j^s + \hat{\eta}_j^s\right) \\
&\quad = \gamma F(M_\psi(\hat{q})) + (1-\gamma) \sum_{(j,s)\in I} \left(\langle \hat{q} - q_a, \omega_j^s\rangle^+ + \langle \hat{q} - q_a, \omega_j^s\rangle^-\right) \\
&\quad = \gamma F(M_\psi(\hat{q})) + (1-\gamma)\|\hat{q} - q_a\|_{W^1}.
\end{aligned}$$

This is a contradiction. A very similar argument proves that if $(\hat{q}, \widehat{\mu}, \hat{\eta})$ is a solution of Eq.(2.33), $\hat{q}$ must be a solution of Eq. (2.32). ■

Remark 2.7.3. Instead of $\tilde{\Sigma}$, we can use a different covariance matrix. For example, if we do not have information on the intraday price, we can just use the covariance matrix of ψ. Nevertheless, it is recommended to use the covariance matrix $\tilde{\Sigma} = \Sigma(\psi) + \Delta(\psi, \delta)$, because $\tilde{\Sigma}$ is a positive definite matrix, that is, $\langle q, \tilde{\Sigma} q\rangle > 0$ for all $q \in Q$.

Thus, we are led to the following algorithm.

Algorithm 2.7.1.

---

1. Solve

$$\min_{q\in Q} \langle q, \tilde{\Sigma} q\rangle$$

   and choose a solution q_a.
2. Perform a Cholesky decomposition of $\tilde{\Sigma} = WW'$.
3. Solve

$$\min_{q\in Q} \left\{\gamma \widetilde{F}(M_\psi(q)) + (1-\gamma)\|q - q_a\|_{W^1}\right\}.$$

2.7.4. *Numerical issues*

In practice, solving this two-step problem does not add a significant complexity to the problem of minimizing $\tilde{F}(M_\psi(q))$. We confirm in Table 2.1 that the ESL Model has $O(N_s)$ variables and $O(N_s)$ constraints. Equation (2.26) is a linear programming problem with N_aT more variables and $4N_aT$ more constraints. However, $N_s \gg TN_a$, and thus, the operational time of the optimization with regularization will be of the same order as the optimization without it. Additionally, despite the fact that we are solving a quadratic model before Eq. (2.26), the operational time of the whole model will not be affected because this time for the Variance Model is significantly less than that of the ESL Model.

2.7.5. *Regularization in optimal allocation*

In Section 2.3, we reformulated the allocation models to use them to reflect liquidation strategies. Now, we reformulate the liquidation strategy with the regularization term to use it in the allocation context. There are several alternatives to deal with allocation when we have a multiobjective optimization problem; see Refs. [6, 8, 20, 21]. Although it will depend on the investor profile to define which one is the best for their purposes.

The approach that we are going to present takes into account our principle of controlling the operational costs. Thus, consider a linear formulation $\tilde{F}$ of the ESL Model. We assume that we have an initial investment of I_0 and that we want to put together a portfolio with the restriction of having an expected value of at least ε of the maximum value. At the same time, we minimize the risk $\tilde{F}$ and the variance. To simplify, we are going to suppose that $T = 1$. Therefore, we present a formulation that proceeds as follows.

Algorithm 2.7.2.

---

1. Solve

$$
\begin{aligned}
\max_{q} \quad & \langle \mathbb{E}(\psi), q \rangle \\
\text{s. t.} \quad & q \geq 0, \\
& \sum_{i=1}^{N_a} q_i m_i \varphi_i^0 = I_0.
\end{aligned}
\tag{2.34}
$$

and choose a solution q_e.

2. Solve

$$\begin{aligned} \min_{q} \quad & \langle q, \tilde{\Sigma} q \rangle \\ \text{s. t.} \quad & q \geq 0, \\ & \langle \mathbb{E}(\psi), q \rangle \geq \varepsilon \langle \mathbb{E}(\psi), q_e \rangle, \\ & \sum_{i=1}^{N_a} q_i m_i \varphi_i^0 = I_0. \end{aligned} \tag{2.35}$$

and choose a solution q_a.

3. Perform a Cholesky decomposition of $\tilde{\Sigma} = WW'$.

4. Solve

$$\begin{aligned} \min_{q} \quad & \left\{ \gamma \tilde{F}(M_\psi(q)) + (1-\gamma) \| q - q_a \|_{W^1} \right\} \\ \text{s. t.} \quad & q \geq 0, \\ & \langle \mathbb{E}(\psi), q \rangle \geq \varepsilon \langle \mathbb{E}(\psi), q_e \rangle, \\ & \sum_{i=1}^{N_a} q_i m_i \varphi_i^0 = I_0. \end{aligned} \tag{2.36}$$

In conclusion, there are several applications that can be given to $\| \cdot \|_{W^1}$, depending on the focus of the problem. For example, we can use it as a constraint if we want to impose a maximum value of variance. Also, we can use it in the context of allocation problems.

2.8. Illustrative Examples

This section presents a few examples that illustrate the claims of Section 2.7. The first one in Section 2.8.1 concerns the same portfolio used in Section 2.5 but using real data from the underlying asset. We are going to study the effect of using $\| \cdot \|_{W^1}$ indifferent covariance matrices. The second one in Section 2.8.2, wherein in a new portfolio, we will remove the restriction of sales by day and also consider the operational implications of using the $\| \cdot \|_{W^2}$ semi-norm instead of $\| \cdot \|_{W^1}$.

The upshot is that the use of regularization in the objective function can help improve the robustness of the liquidation strategies without a significant increase in the complexity. Furthermore, this is done while still keeping the financial interpretation and relevance of the model.

2.8.1. *Changing the covariance matrix*

Consider the same portfolio like the one illustrated in Section 2.5. However, instead of using a fictitious asset, we shall use the SolarCity Corp (SCTY)[b] share as the underlying asset.

[b]Prices were provided by the TradeStation Academic Program through the TradeStation platform.

Hence, we fit an ARMA-GARCH model (see Ref. [24]) to the log returns of the historical data. Figure 2.7 shows the historical prices of SCTY, and Fig. 2.8 shows the histogram of the log-return. Then, we simulate 5000,000 scenarios.

Fig. 2.7 Daily prices for SCTY.

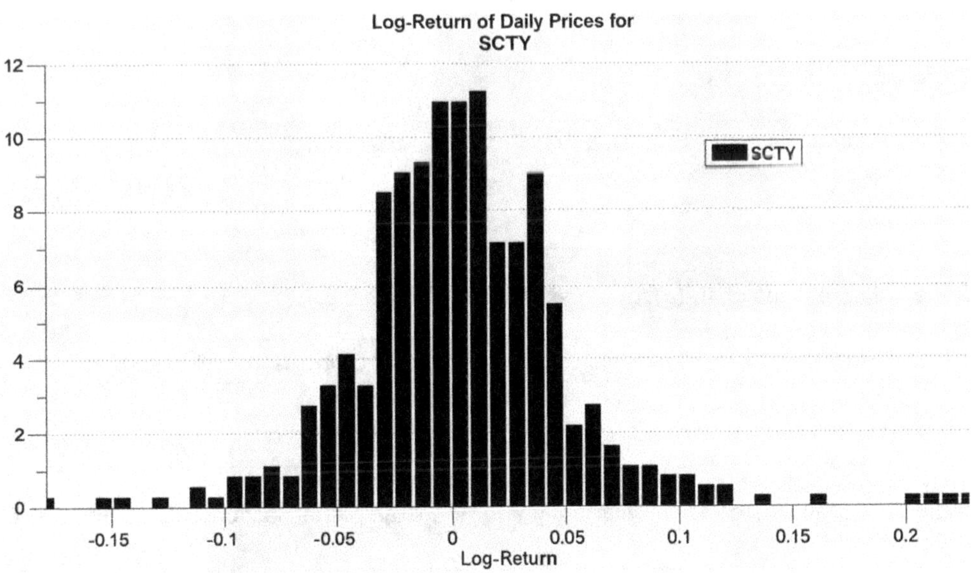

Fig. 2.8 Log returns for SCTY.

To simplify the analysis, in this example, we will not run the Simpleminded Model. For the Variance Model, we use all the scenarios to calculate the covariance matrix. Also, motivated by the robustness of the example in Section 2.5, we use 7,000 scenarios in the ESL Model. Finally, in the ESL Model, we use the confidence level of $\beta = 0.05$.[c]

Table 2.5 shows the statistics for $M_{\psi}(q)$. There we can see that the results are similar to the results of the example in Section 2.5. In fact, the Variance and ESL models have the best results in general.

Moreover, let us add a perturbation of φ as in Section 2.6, that is, instead of using ψ, we used $\widetilde{\psi}^t = \psi^t(1+\delta^t) + m\varphi^0\delta^t$ and simulated the perturbation δ using the intraday information of SCTY. The intraday prices were taken with intervals of 1 minute during 60 days, and we fitted a nonparametric distribution (see Ref. [6]). So, Table 2.6 shows the statistics of $M_{\widetilde{\psi}}(q)$ for the different models. Although the risks do not change significantly, they become worse when we compare them with the results of the same model in Table 2.5.

Furthermore, we ran the ESL model by adding the regularization term $\|\cdot\|_{W^1}$ as in Eq. (2.32) using a Cholesky decomposition. We do this for two covariance matrices $\Sigma(\psi)$, $\Sigma(\psi) + \Delta(\psi, \delta)$. The results are displayed in Tables 2.7 and 2.8, respectively. We can infer that $\Sigma(\psi)+\Delta(\psi,\delta)$ is the appropriate covariance matrix to use because it reduces almost all the risk factors as compared with Table 2.6. Indeed, when we use Σ, but we are not adding any information to the intraday risk, we are just controlling the variance.

In the case of the ESL Model, as we saw in Section 2.2, it seems to be very stable. Nevertheless, adding the regularization, especially $\Sigma + \Delta$, helps improve the robustness and reduce the risk (CVaR) without increasing the operational time, as we show in Figs. 2.9 and 2.10.

Table 2.5. Statistics of $M_{\psi}(q)$ for the example in Section 2.8.1.

Models	Std. Des.	Min	$CVaR_{0.05}$	$VaR_{0.05}$
Variance	1,379	42,240	5,710	3,879
ESL	1,526	44,290	5,639	3,874

Table 2.6. Statistics of $M_{\widetilde{\psi}}(q)$ for the example in Section 2.8.1.

Models	Std. Des.	Min	$CVaR_{0.05}$	$VaR_{0.05}$
Variance	1,407	45,540	5,744	3,914
ESL	1,562	47,690	5,698	3,903

Table 2.7. Statistics of $M_{\widetilde{\psi}}(q)$ with $\|\cdot\|_{W1}$ for the example in Section 2.8.1, with W s. t. $\Sigma = WW'$.

Models	Std. Des.	Min	$CVaR_{0.05}$	$VaR_{0.05}$
ESL $\gamma = 0.90$	1,612	47,800	5,953	3,997

[c]The optimization problems were run using Gurobi Optimizer; see Ref. [16].

Table 2.8. Statistics of $M_{\tilde{\psi}}(q)$ with $\|\cdot\|_{W1}$ for the example in Section 2.8.1, with W s. t. $\Sigma + \Delta = WW'$.

Models	Std. Des.	Min	$CVaR_{0.05}$	$VaR_{0.05}$
ESL $\gamma = 0.90$	1,412	46,900	5,674	3,881

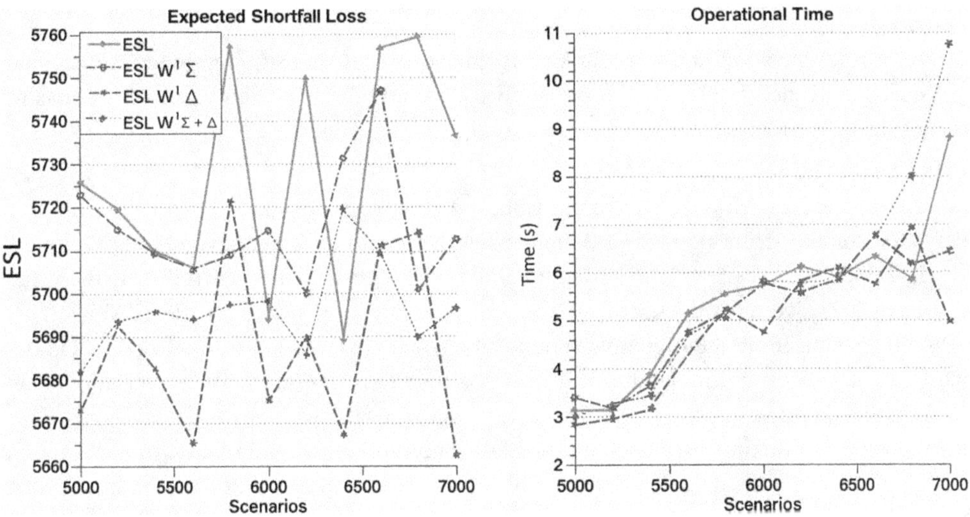

Fig. 2.9 ESL Model for the example in Section 2.8.1. Left: CVaR of the loss of $M_{\tilde{\psi}}(q)$. Right: Operational time.

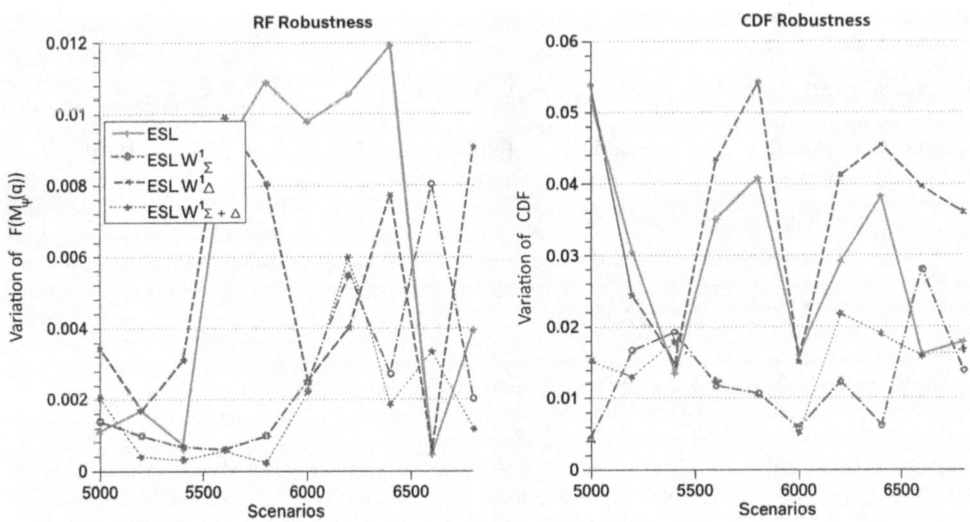

Fig. 2.10 Robustness of ESL Model for the example in Section 2.8.1. Left: RF Robustness. Right: CDF Robustness.

2.8.2. *An example without daily limitation*

Now we have a simpler portfolio using the same underlying asset as STCY in the example in Section 2.8.1, but removing the restrictions for the maximum we can sell or buy per day. See Table 2.9. The purpose of this example is to see the effect of the regularization when we did not use a daily limit on the sale or purchase of the assets. Also, we will analyze the problem of adding the quadratic term as regularization as in Eq. (2.31) instead of linear regularization.

As a reference, we show in Table 2.10 the results of the Simpleminded Model and the Variance Model. For an additional analysis, we add the expected value of the loss of $M_{\tilde{\psi}}(q)$, $\hat{\mathbb{E}}(M^{-}_{\tilde{\psi}}(q))$, in all statistical tables. Also, from now on, we are going to use only the regularization term in $\tilde{\Sigma} = \Sigma + \Delta$.

We ran the ESL Model for different values of γ between 0.9 and 1.0, with a sample size of 7,000. Remembering that $\gamma = 1.0$ means that the model does not have regularization.

In Table 2.11, we observe the effect of adding the regularization. By reducing the value of γ until 0.97, we reduce four of the five risk measures, including the ES (CVaR). This reduction is caused by the objective function $\gamma F_{ESL}(M_{\psi}(q)) + (1-\gamma)\|q - q_a\|_{W1}$. On the one hand, it seeks to minimize the ESL of $\langle \psi, q \rangle$ that does not see intraday variations. On the other hand, the term on the right-hand side minimizes the variance of $\langle \tilde{\psi}, q \rangle$, hence controlling (not minimizing) its expected shortfall. Therefore, the combination of minimizing the ES of $M_{\psi}(q)$ and controlling the ES of $M_{\tilde{\psi}}(q)$ produces a strategy that is better than only minimizing the ES.

Figures 2.11 and 2.12 show the difference in using the regularization term. We can see that when we only use $\gamma = 0.98$, the solution is better distributed over time, providing some improvement of the risk measure.

Table 2.9. Portfolio for the example in Section 2.8.2.

Asset	Product	Position	Exp day	Strike	Max p/ Day	Initial Day
1	Option call	−2,200	60	70	N/A	5
2	Option put	2,000	60	70	N/A	5
3	Forward	2,000	60	70	N/A	2

Table 2.10. Statistics of $M_{\tilde{\psi}}(q)$ for the example in Section 2.8.2.

Models	Std. Des.	Min	$CVaR_{0.05}$	$VaR_{0.05}$	$\hat{\mathbb{E}}(X^{-})$
Simpleminded	15,938	262,680	39,686	29,453	13,674
Variance	1,182	25,550	3,515	2,522	1,098

Table 2.11. ESL Model. Statistics of $M_{\bar{\psi}}(q)$ for ESL with $\|\cdot\|_{W1}$ for the example in Section 2.8.2.

Models	Std. Des.	Min	$CVaR_{0.05}$	$VaR_{0.05}$	$\hat{\mathbb{E}}(X^-)$
ESL $\gamma = 1.00$	1,618	39,181	3,493	2,462	1,214
ESL $\gamma = 0.99$	1,559	34,945	3,420	2,437	1,211
ESL $\gamma = 0.98$	1,514	39,659	3,476	2,424	1,168
ESL $\gamma = 0.97$	1,491	36,373	3,426	2,392	1,125
ESL $\gamma = 0.96$	1,245	30,786	3,459	2,460	1,048
ESL $\gamma = 0.95$	1,224	29,744	3,470	2,466	1,053
ESL $\gamma = 0.94$	1,258	31,595	3,464	2,447	1,037
ESL $\gamma = 0.93$	1,229	29,193	3,477	2,468	1,048
ESL $\gamma = 0.92$	1,193	28,301	3,497	2,483	1,078
ESL $\gamma = 0.91$	1,183	25,612	3,506	2,525	1,096
ESL $\gamma = 0.90$	1,182	25,692	3,513	2,516	1,095

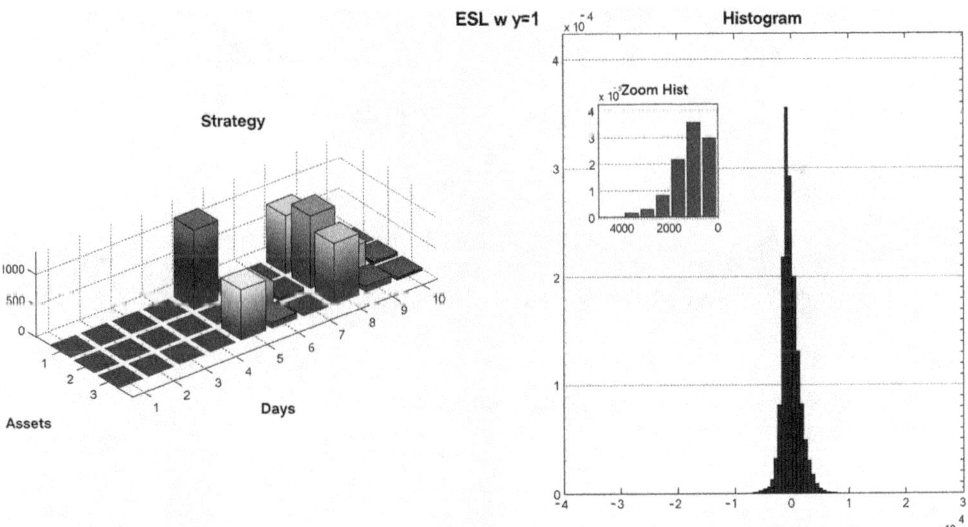

Fig. 2.11 Strategy q and distribution of $M_{\bar{\psi}}(q)$ for the ESL Model for the example in Section 2.8.2.

To study the robustness, we will also consider the model with the quadratic regularization, that is,

$$\gamma F_{ESL}(M_{\psi}(q)) + (1-\gamma)\|q - q_a\|^2_{W2}.$$

Thus, we run the three ESL models, without regularization, with $\|\cdot\|_{W1}$ regularization, and with $\|\cdot\|_{W2}$ regularization for 5,000 to 7,000 scenarios increasing by 200. In all of those, we set $\gamma = 0.9$.

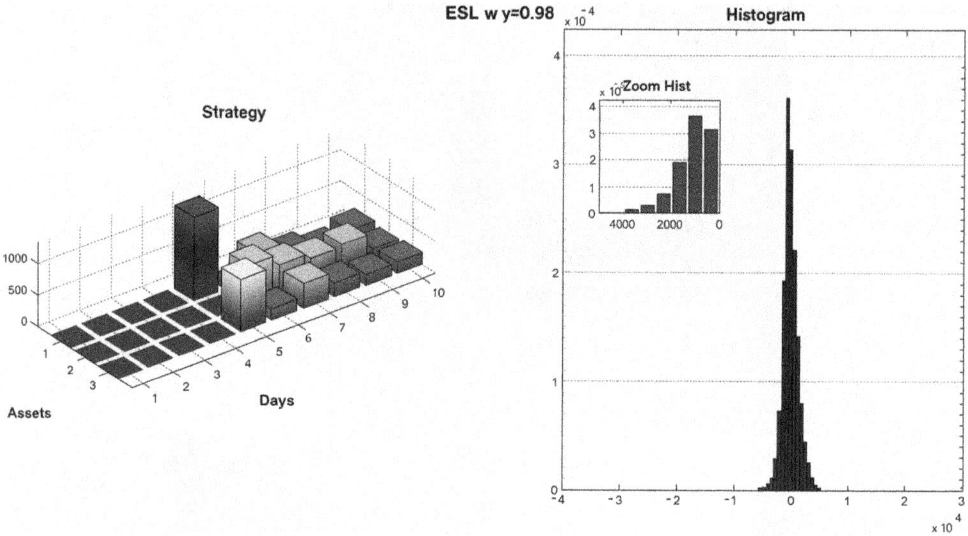

Fig. 2.12 Strategy q and distribution of $M_{\bar{\psi}}(q)$ for the ESL Model with $\gamma = 0.8$ for the example in Section 2.8.2.

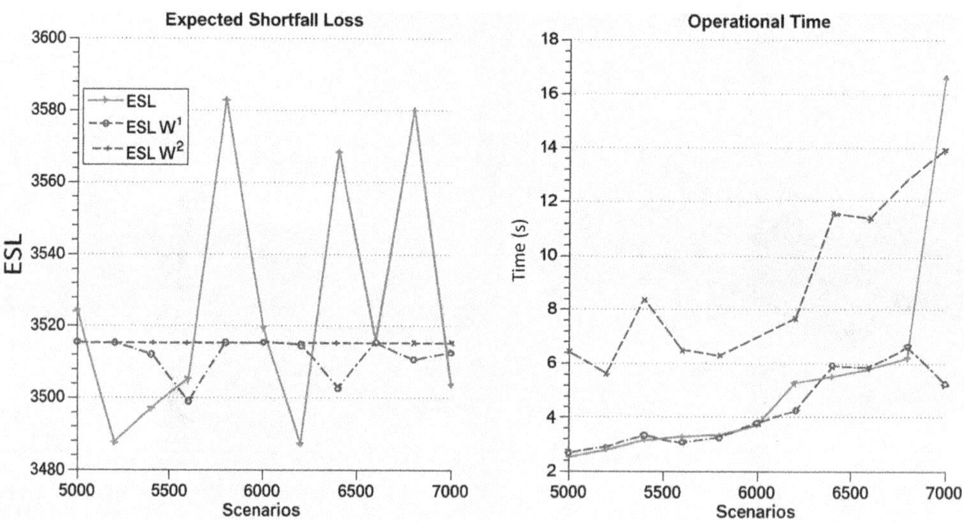

Fig. 2.13 ESL Model for the example in Section 2.8.2. Left: CVaR of the loss of $M_{\bar{\psi}}(q)$. Right: Operational time.

In Figs. 2.13 and 2.14, it seems that by using the linear term, we can reduce the ESL and improve the stability without affecting the runtime. On the other hand, the fact that with $\|\cdot\|^2_{W^2}$, the model is extremely stable because the quadratic norm weighs too much compared to ESL. Hence, the optimization leads to the use of only the variance. Moreover,

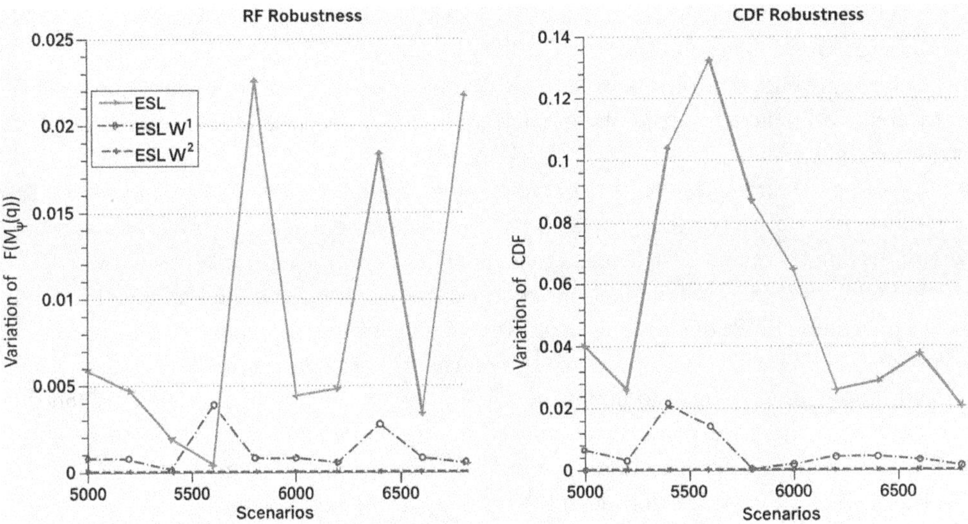

Fig. 2.14 Robustness of ESL Model for the example in Section 2.8.2. Left: RF robustness. Right: CDF robustness.

Table 2.12. ESL Model. Statistics of $M_{\bar{\psi}}(q)$ for ESL in the example in Section 2.8.2.

Models	Std. Des.	Min	$CVaR_{0.05}$	$VaR_{0.05}$	$\hat{\mathbb{F}}(X^-)$
ESL	1,634	44,638	3,579	2,482	1,212
ESL w $W^1, \gamma = 0.9$	1,182	25,830	3,510	2,514	1,095
ESL w $W^2, \gamma = 0.9$	1,182	25,571	3,515	2,521	1,097

using the quadratic term takes significantly longer than not using the regularization or using it with $\|\cdot\|_{W^1}$. Consequently, the results in Table 2.12 confirm our conclusions, namely, that by using $\|\cdot\|^2_{W^2}$, the solution is almost exactly the solution for variance (see Table 2.10). However, using $\|\cdot\|_{W^1}$ keeps the standard deviation close to the minimum value but also reduces the conditional VaR.

2.9. Conclusions

Due to the complexity of evaluating and liquidating collateral assets, the guarantee holder of such assets accepts only highly liquid assets (such as cash and bonds) and may impose a severe haircut on them. This may generate serious costs to investors that need to deposit such collateral, since the investor usually has positions in various assets, that, due to their own riskier characteristics, are not accepted as collateral.

The strategy presented in this article succeeds in incorporating the different assets evaluating the overall risk in the portfolio. The classical ES model correctly captures the loss risk, but it fails to capture the liquidity risk and selling delay from such assets. On the other hand, our models conjoin the ES and the Variance Models in an efficient way to incorporate their joint contributions and offsets.

Taking advantage of offsets between different securities is an important approach in many areas of finance; for example, in pairs trading. See for instance Ref. [25] and references therein.

By using the strategies presented herein, we increase competitiveness since they generate lower counterparties costs. Indeed, the counterparty can leave its assets as warranty without having to liquidate such assets to generate cash for the collateral.

We introduced a technique that incorporates the advantages of the Variance Model to the ES linear model. We did this by performing a Cholesky decomposition of the covariance matrix and adding a Tikhonov regularization term. This regularization term is used as an L^1 semi-norm, which, added to the linear model, has several practical properties. Indeed, we can control the price perturbation caused by the impact on the price as the result of the liquidation process or the intraday variations, improve the robustness, and control the variance. All of these were achieved without further computational cost.

Acknowledgments

This research was partially supported by LAMCA, IMPA, Rio de Janeiro, Brazil.

This work was supported by CNPq, FAPERJ, the Pensa-Rio program of FAPERJ, and FSU-Grant 2020-09. JPZ thanks Khalifa University, the Government of Abu Dhabi, and *Fundação Carlos Chagas Filho de Amparo à Pesquisa do Estado do Rio de Janeiro* (FAPERJ) through the grant E-26/202.927/2017 for the support during the course of this research. The final part of this research was supported by ADIA Lab, Abu Dhabi, UAE.

An earlier version of this work was part of the unpublished PhD thesis of one of the authors (AFM) [4]. Several additions and examples have now been incorporated.

We thank Claudia Sagastizabal for a number of very fruitful discussions and suggestions.

We dedicate this article to the memory of our dear colleague Marco Avellaneda.

References

1. L. Vicente, F. Cerezetti, S. De Faria, T. Iwashita, and O. Pereira, Managing risk in multi-asset class, multimarket central counterparties: The CORE approach, *J. Bank. Finance*. **51**, 119–130 (2015). https://doi.org/10.1016/j.jbankfin.2014.08.016. https://www.sciencedirect.com/science/article/pii/S0378426614002830.
2. M. Avellaneda and R. Cont, Close-Out Risk Evaluation (CORE): A New Risk Management Approach for Central Counterparties (Apr 9, 2013). Available at SSRN: https://ssrn.com/abstract=2247493 or http://dx.doi.org/10.2139/ssrn.2247493.
3. C. Group, CME Core: Clearing Online Risk Engine (2022). Available at: http://www.cmegroup.com/clearing/risk-management/ (accessed October 10, 2022).
4. A. F. Macías, Numerical methods and models for portfolio liquidation, risk quantification and project evaluation. PhD thesis, Instituto Nacional de Matemática Pura e Aplicada, IMPA, Rio de Janeiro, Brazil (Dec, 2014).

5. R. Cont, R. Deguest, and G. Scandolo, Robustness and sensitivity analysis of risk measurement procedures, *Quant. Finance.* **10**(6), 593–606 (2010).
6. A. Meucci, *Risk and asset allocation*. Springer Finance, Springer-Verlag, Berlin (2005).
7. R. T. Rockafellar, S. Uryasev, and M. Zabarankin, Deviation Measures in Risk Analysis and Optimization (Dec 22, 2002). University of Florida, Department of Industrial & Systems Engineering Working Paper No. 2002-7, Available at SSRN: https://ssrn.com/abstract=365640 or http://dx.doi.org/10.2139/ssrn.365640.
8. H. Markowitz, Portfolio selection, *J. Finance.* **7**, 77–91 (1952).
9. C. Acerbi, Spectral measures of risk: A coherent representation of subjective risk aversion, *J. Bank. Finance.* **26**, 1505–1518 (2002).
10. M. Frittelli and G. Scandolo, Risk measures and capital requirements for processes, *Math. Finance.* **16**(4), 589–612 (2006).
11. P. Artzner, F. Delbaen, J.-M. Eber, and D. Heath, Coherent measures of risk, *Math. Finance.* **9**(3), 203–228 (1999).
12. R. T. Rockafellar and S. Uryasev, Optimization of conditional value-at-risk, *J. Risk.* **2**, 21–41 (2000).
13. R. D. R. Cont and X. D. He, Loss-based risk measures, *Stat. Risk Model.* **30**, 133–167 (2013).
14. I. Karatzas and S. E. Shreve, *Brownian motion and stochastic calculus*, vol. 113, 2nd edn, Springer-Verlag, New York (1991).
15. F. Black and M. Scholes, The pricing of options and corporate liabilities, *J. Polit. Econ.* **81**, 637–659 (1973).
16. L. Gurobi Optimization. Gurobi optimizer reference manual (2022). http://www.gurobi.com.
17. D. Bertsimas and A. W. Lo, Optimal control of execution costs, *J. Financ. Mark.* **1**, 1–50 (1998).
18. R. Almgren and N. Chriss, Optimal execution of portfolio transactions, *J. Risk.* **3**, 5–39 (2000).
19. A. Izmailov and M. Solodov, *Otimização, Vol. 1: Condições de otimalidade, elementos de análise convexa e de dualidade*, 3rd edn. Instituto Nacional de Matemática Pura e Aplicada (IMPA), Rio de Janeiro (2014).
20. R. E. R. Aboulaich and S. E. Moumen, The mean-variance-CVaR model for portfolio optimization modeling using a multi-objective approach based on a hybrid method, *Math. Model. Nat. Phenom.* **5**(7), 103–108 (2010). https://doi.org/10.1051/mmnp/20105717.
21. Y. Elahi and M. I. A. Aziz, Mean-variance-CVaR model of multiportfolio optimization via linear weighted sum method, *Math. Probl. Eng.* **2014**, 104064 (2014). https://doi.org/10.1155/2014/104064.
22. V. S. A. Tikhonov, A. Goncharsky, and A. Yagola, *Numerical Methods for the Solution of Ill-Posed Problems, Mathematics and Its Applications*. Springer Science+Business Media Dordrecht, Moscow, Russia (1995).
23. K. van den Doel, U. Ascher, and E. Haber, The lost honour of ℓ_2 based regularization, In eds. M. Cullen, M. Freitag, S. Kindermann, and R. Scheichl, *Large Scale Inverse Problems: Computational Methods and Applications in the Earth Sciences*, pp. 181–203. De Gruyter, Berlin (2013).
24. T. C. Millis, *The Econometric Modelling of Financial Time Series*. Cambridge University Press, New York, USA (2012).
25. C. E. de Moura, A. Pizzinga, and J. Zubelli, A pairs trading strategy based on linear state space models and the Kalman filter, *Quant. Finance.* **16**(10), 1559–1573 (2016). https://doi.org/10.1080/14697688.2016.116. https://ideas.repec.org/a/taf/quantf/v16y2016i10p1559-1573.html.

https://doi.org/10.1142/9789819813049_0003

CHAPTER 3 Overcoming Markowitz's Instability with the Help of the Hierarchical Risk Parity (HRP): Theoretical Evidence

Alexandre Antonov*, Alexander Lipton, and Marcos Lopez de Prado

ADIA, ADIA Lab, Khalifa University, Abu Dhabi, UAE
**Corresponding author. E-mail: Alexandre.Antonov@adia.ae*

In this paper, we compare two methods of portfolio allocation: the classical Markowitz one and the hierarchical risk parity (HRP) approach. We derive analytical values for the noise of allocation weights coming from the estimated covariance. We demonstrate that the HRP is indeed less noisy (and thus more robust) w.r.t. the classical Markowitz. The second part of the paper is devoted to a detailed analysis of the optimal portfolio variance for which we derive analytical formulas and theoretically demonstrate the superiority of the HRP w.r.t. to the Markowitz optimization.

We also address practical outcomes of our analytics. The first one is a fast estimation of the confidence level of the optimization weights calculated for a single (real-life) scenario. The second practical usefulness of analytics is an HRP portfolio construction criterion that selects assets and clusters, minimizing the analytical portfolio variance. We confirm our theoretical results with numerous numerical experiments.

Our calculation technique can also be used in other areas of portfolio optimization.

3.1. Introduction

One of the most important questions in all economics concerns the development of systems that optimally allocate scarce resources. These systems are not unique, and their characteristics adapt to the peculiarity of each scarcity problem. For example, in the crude oil market, buyers arrive at an equilibrium price based on the volumes announced by producers. In contrast, a carmaker determines the amount and price of cars that maximizes its net profit. Investors face a similar question: What is the optimal allocation to various investments, in terms of minimizing the risk of achieving a predefined return? Like with the aforementioned examples, there is not a unique system capable of answering this question in a logical way. In fact, different investors may answer the same question using different methods, in reflection of their informational sets, biases, or objectives.

In the year 1954, Harry Markowitz proposed a celebrated framework for answering the question of assigning funds to an investable universe [1]. In this framework, investors know the parameters of the multivariate normal distribution of returns for that investment universe: the true vector of (future) mean returns and the true (future) covariance matrix of returns. With that information, Markowitz proved that an investor could derive the optimal allocation that would maximize the expected return for a given level of risk or that it would minimize the level of risk for a given expected return.

It is important to mention that another pioneer of the minimum variance approach, an Italian mathematician, de Finetti, has published his results 14 years before Markowitz in 1940 [2]. Moreover, de Finetti has studied a *constrained* minimization of the variance for positive weights (and given expected returns); see Pressacco and Serafini [3] describing de Finetti's findings under an angle of modern mathematical programming methods.

Needless to say, investors do not know the true vector of future means and the true future covariance matrix of returns. They do not know the sign of the expected means, much less the rounded percentage value. The problem is, Markowitz solutions are notoriously sensitive to even small changes in these parameters, and this instability increases with the size of the investment universe. Out of the two necessary parameters, the most uncertain is the vector of future means. For this reason, early on, many investors opted for estimating the minimum variance portfolio, that is, the optimal portfolio with minimum risk. This portfolio is convenient because it can be computed without any knowledge of the expected mean returns.

Unfortunately, minimum variance solutions have been met with strong criticism by practitioners. The reason is, it is very difficult to predict the future values of the off-diagonal elements of the covariance matrix. For example, the correlation between stocks and bonds may flip unpredictably from negative to positive; however, the volatility of stocks is relatively stable over time. Markowitz's minimum variance portfolios are very sensitive to changes in correlations, which makes its solutions not robust. To address this concern, in the 1990s, practitioners proposed so-called risk parity approaches. The general idea is, within the covariance matrix, investors are more confident about the main diagonal than about the off-diagonal elements, hence the allocation should be informed by variances rather than covariances.

One criticism of this risk parity approach is that it entirely throws out all correlation information. Surely, we may not be able to predict the correlation between stocks and bonds, but we may be able to predict the correlation between two stocks in the same sector, or in the same region, or stocks in the same supply chain, and so on. In 2016, Lopez de Prado proposed the hierarchical risk parity (HRP) approach [4] as a compromise between the two radical approaches of Markowitz's minimum variance portfolio (which assumes perfect knowledge of the future covariance matrix) and risk parity (which assumes perfect ignorance of all correlations). In his seminal paper, Lopez de Prado showed vis Monte Carlo experiments that "HRP delivers lower out-of-sample variance than [Markowitz's minimum variance portfolio], even though minimum-variance is Markowitz's optimization objective.

HRP also produces less risky portfolios out-of-sample compared to traditional risk parity methods." In this paper, we reach the same conclusions through analytical methods.

Namely, under Gaussian assumptions of the asset time series, we derive an analytical approximation of the noise of the allocation weights coming from the estimated covariance.

Our method, based on an expansion of the *noise* of the covariance matrix, is applicable when the number of assets is *moderate* w.r.t. the sample size used to estimate the covariance. This is in contrast with the Marchenko–Pastur criterion [5], where the number of assets is supposed to be *comparable* with the sample size.

Natural noise measures—such as the expected variance of the allocation weights, its trace, as well as the optimal portfolio risk variance—can be calculated analytically for the Markowitz optimization. The resulting formulas are quite compact and can be easily implemented.

To treat the HRP case, we assume that the asset clusters are already detected (see, e.g., Ref. [6]) and that the intra-cluster correlations are relatively low. This permits to derive the noise measures for the HRP case: the formulas are only slightly more complicated than these for the Markowitz optimization. We demonstrate that the HRP is indeed less noisy (and thus more robust) w.r.t. the classical Markowitz.

Another important part of the paper is devoted to a detailed analysis of the optimal *portfolio variance* for both Markowitz and HRP methods. We derive the portfolio variance analytical formulas and theoretically demonstrate that the out-of-sample HRP is indeed less noisy and more robust than the Markowitz optimization.

The first *practical* outcome of our analytics can be a fast estimation of the *confidence level* of the optimization weights calculated for a single (real-life) scenario. The second practical usefulness of the noise analytics can be a portfolio selection that minimizes the analytical HRP portfolio variance.

We confirm the theoretical results using multiple numerical experiments based on Monte Carlo simulations. The focus is made on the weights noise and the optimal portfolio statistics for in- and out-of-sample cases.

Finally, notice that we derive the formulas for the min-variance optimization, Gaussian assets, and low cross-correlations. However, our results can be generalized for other (analytical) portfolio optimization utility functions, arbitrary cross-correlations, and potentially non-Gaussian processes.

The paper is organized as follows. In the main body of the paper, we announce the main results with brief descriptions of the derivation logic, so that all (relatively tedious) calculations are put in the appendixes. In Section 3.2, we calculate the Markowitz optimization noise measures and comment on the formula's applicability criterion. In Section 3.3, we remind the HRP method work-flow, derive the noise measures, and compare the results with the Markowitz baseline. Next, in Section 3.4, we provide a detailed analysis of the optimal portfolio variance statistics for the Markowitz and the HRP for both in- and out-of-sample cases. We present numerical experiments in Section 3.5.

3.2. The Markowitz Optimization and Its Noise

Our optimization universe contains different assets with returns $X_i(t)$ and weights $w_i(t)$ where i is an asset index. The portfolio return is a weighted sum of the asset returns, that is, $\sum_i w_i(t)\, X_i(t)$. To calculate the weights on the next time period, we proceed with optimizing different utility functions of the distribution parameters of the portfolio increment: the simplest procedure is the **min-var** optimization.

The min-var optimization. The min-var optimization looks for weights w that will minimize the portfolio variance subjected to one constraint, that is, in vector/matrix notations:

$$\text{minimize}\ \sigma^2(w) = w^T V w \quad \text{s.t} \quad w^T a = 1 \tag{3.1}$$

The assets *covariance matrix* V elements are often estimated from returns time series.

$$V_{ij} = \frac{1}{N_T} \sum_{n=1}^{N_T} X_{i,n}\, X_{j,n} \tag{3.2}$$

where the summation runs over (business-daily) dates $\{t_n\}_{n=1}^{N_T}$ and $X_{i,n} = X_i(t_n)$. The asset indices i, j go from 1 to N_A.

Using a constrained Lagrangian, we obtain the following optimal weights

$$w^* = \frac{V^{-1}\, a}{a^T\, V^{-1}\, a} \tag{3.3}$$

with the corresponding optimal variance

$$\sigma^2(w^*) = \frac{1}{a^T\, V^{-1}\, a} \tag{3.4}$$

Of course, the covariance matrix is not necessarily positively defined: either by nature (some assets are linearly dependent) or by calculation errors (Monte Carlo estimation noise, etc.). However, for our calculations we suppose that, thanks to its clustered structure, the covariance matrix is invertible.

The sample size N_T can be rarely above 5 years of the daily data, otherwise, the estimated covariance matrix will be "stalled." In general, the number of *assets* N_A can be either small w.r.t. N_T or comparable to it. In both cases, the exact values are blurred by the noise from their *exact* positions corresponding to $N_T \to \infty$. In this paper, we concentrate on a **moderate number of assets**. Theoretically, it means that $N_A/N_T \ll 1$, but, in practice, this coefficient can be large enough, say, start with 1/2 or 1/3, to attain a reasonable accuracy. At the end of this section, we address the applicability criterion in more detail.

Monte Carlo noise for the allocation weights. Let us proceed with our main goal: estimation of the "Monte Carlo noise" coming from the covariance matrix summation (3.2) and penetrating into the optimal weights.

Let us decompose the estimated matrix in the exact value (denoted with "bar") and the finite-sample noise.

$$V = \bar{V} + \Delta V$$

where the noise has a Gaussian distribution for large N_T

$$\Delta V_{ij} = \frac{1}{N_T}\sum_{n=1}^{N_T}(X_{i,n}\, X_{j,n} - \mathbb{E}[X_i\, X_j])$$

Here X_i is a theoretical return *stochastic variable.*

Our first calculation tool is the matrix expansion for small ΔV. For example, let us apply it to the noise of the inverse of the matrix.

$$\Delta\left(V^{-1}\right) \equiv V^{-1} - \bar{V}^{-1}$$

Ignoring the square of ΔV in the following reasoning

$$\left(\bar{V}^{-1} + \Delta\left(V^{-1}\right)\right)\left(\bar{V} + \Delta V\right) = 1 \;\Rightarrow\; \Delta\left(V^{-1}\right)\bar{V} + \bar{V}^{-1}\,\Delta V \approx 0 \tag{3.5}$$

we obtain the noise of the inverse covariance matrix

$$\Delta\left(V^{-1}\right) \approx -\bar{V}^{-1}\,\Delta V\,\bar{V}^{-1} \tag{3.6}$$

As we will see below, the answer for the small sample size (say, corresponding to 1 year of daily data) can be sensitive to the second order of ΔV, but this dependence will radically decrease for three- or four-year intervals.

Inserting this approximation into the Markowitz formula, we obtain[a]

$$w \approx \frac{\left(\bar{V}^{-1} + \Delta\left(V^{-1}\right)\right) a}{a^T\left(\bar{V}^{-1} + \Delta\left(V^{-1}\right)\right) a}$$

Expanding it

$$w \approx \bar{w} + \Delta w$$

around the *exact weights*

$$\bar{w} = \frac{\bar{V}^{-1}\, a}{a^T\,\bar{V}^{-1}\, a} \tag{3.7}$$

we get the noise of the weights

$$\Delta w \approx -(I - \bar{w}\, a^T)\, V^{-1}\,\Delta V\,\bar{w} \tag{3.8}$$

The most natural noise measure is the covariance

$$\mathbb{E}\left[\Delta w\,\Delta w^T\right]$$

[a]We have removed the star from the weights for brevity.

with elements $\mathbb{E}\left[\Delta w_i \Delta w_j\right]$. To estimate it we notice that the expectations in hand depend on a quadratic expression of ΔV, namely, on $\mathbb{E}\left[\Delta V \bar{w}\, \bar{w}^T \Delta V\right]$. In Appendix A, we prove a general result for an arbitrary matrix M

$$\mathbb{E}\left[\Delta V M \Delta V\right] = \frac{1}{N_T}\left(\mathbb{E}\left[X X^T (X^T M X)\right] - \bar{V} M \bar{V}\right)$$

which gives the desired expectation for $M = \bar{w}\, \bar{w}^T$. This expression depends on the 4-point average of X's, that is, $\mathbb{E}\left[X_n X_m X_i X_j\right]$. We can exactly evaluate them, assuming that the normalized returns X are Gaussian which leads to the following general relationship

$$\mathbb{E}\left[\Delta V M \Delta V\right] = \frac{1}{N_T}\left(\bar{V}\,\mathrm{Tr}(\bar{V} M) + \bar{V} M^T \bar{V}\right) \tag{3.9}$$

which permits us to obtain an elegant expression for the noise matrix

$$\mathbb{E}\left[\Delta w\, \Delta w^T\right] \approx \frac{1}{N_T}\left(\frac{\bar{V}^{-1}}{a^T \bar{V}^{-1} a} - \bar{w}\, \bar{w}^T\right) \tag{3.10}$$

The trace of the noise matrix expectation can be considered as a *one-number measure* of the Markowitz noise such that

$$\mathcal{N}_M \equiv \mathbb{E}\left[\Delta w^T \Delta w\right] = \mathrm{Tr}\left(\mathbb{E}\left[\Delta w\, \Delta w^T\right]\right) \approx \frac{1}{N_T}\left(\frac{\mathrm{Tr}\; \bar{V}^{-1}}{a^T \bar{V}^{-1} a} - \frac{a^T \bar{V}^{-2} a}{\left(a^T \bar{V}^{-1} a\right)^2}\right) \tag{3.11}$$

Its slight generalization for some matrix M will be used below for the portfolio variance studies.

$$\mathbb{E}\left[\Delta w^T M \Delta w\right] \approx \frac{1}{N_T}\left(\frac{\mathrm{Tr}\;(\bar{V}^{-1} M)}{a^T \bar{V}^{-1} a} - \bar{w}^T M \bar{w}\right) \tag{3.12}$$

Of course, in practice, we use the *estimated* matrix V instead of its theoretical value in our formulas (3.10–3.11).

Noise inequality. To demonstrate a non-negativity of the noise expectation (3.11), we proceed as follows. Denote the eigenvalue decomposition of the exact covariance matrix as

$$\bar{V} = \bar{U} \bar{\Lambda} \bar{U}^T$$

with eigenvalues $\bar{\Lambda}_{ij} = \delta_{ij} \bar{\lambda}^{(i)}$ and eigenvectors matrix $\bar{U} = \left\{\bar{u}^{(1)}, \cdots, \bar{u}^{(N_A)}\right\}$,

$$\bar{V} \bar{u}^{(i)} = \bar{\lambda}^{(i)}\, \bar{u}^{(i)}$$

Thus, we rewrite the components of (3.11) as

$$\mathrm{Tr}\; \bar{V}^{-1} = \sum_n \bar{\lambda}_n^{-1} \quad \text{and} \quad a^T \bar{V}^{-k} a = \sum_n \bar{b}_n^2 \bar{\lambda}_n^{-k}$$

for $\bar{b} = \bar{U}a$. Clearly,

$$\mathrm{Tr}\,\bar{V}^{-1}\,a^T\,\bar{V}^{-1}\,a \geq a^T\,\bar{V}^{-2}\,a \tag{3.13}$$

due to

$$\sum_m \bar{\lambda}_m^{-1} \sum_n \bar{b}_n^2\,\bar{\lambda}_n^{-1} \geq \sum_n \bar{b}_n^2\,\lambda_n^{-2}$$

because

$$\sum_m \bar{\lambda}_m^{-1} \sum_n \bar{b}_n^2\,\bar{\lambda}_n^{-1} - \sum_k \bar{b}_k^2\,\bar{\lambda}_k^{-2} = \sum_{m\neq n} \bar{\lambda}_m^{-1}\bar{b}_n^2\,\bar{\lambda}_n^{-1} \geq 0$$

Indeed, all the elements in the last summation are positive. Thus, after the diagonalization, the Markowitz noise (3.11) looks as follows:

$$\mathcal{N}_M \approx \frac{1}{N_T}\frac{\sum_{m\neq n}\bar{\lambda}_n^{-1}\,\bar{\lambda}_m^{-1}\bar{b}_n^2}{\left(\sum_n \bar{b}_n^2\,\bar{\lambda}_n^{-1}\right)^2}$$

Applicability criterion. To assess the validity of our noise formula, we return to the inverse covariance matrix noise calculation in (3.5) and notice that in the approximation we ignored the following quadratic term.

$$\Delta\left(V^{-1}\right)\Delta V \approx -\bar{V}^{-1}\,\Delta V\,\bar{V}^{-1}\,\Delta V$$

If this quadratic term is small *in average*, our first-order expansion is valid. Using the general expectation formula (3.9), we readily obtain

$$\mathbb{E}\left[\Delta\left(V^{-1}\right)\Delta V\right] = -\frac{N_A+1}{N_T}I$$

which gives us *the criterion of a moderate number of assets*

$$\frac{N_A}{N_T} \ll 1.$$

Note that below, while studying the portfolio variance, we will also go *beyond* the leading order in N_A/N_T and reach a superior approximation quality.

3.3. HRP or Clustered Optimization

In Ref. [4], it was demonstrated that clusterization can help with noise reduction. Consider our assets (their returns) forming several *quasi-independent* groups or clusters.

$$X = \left\{Y^{(1)}, \cdots, Y^{(H)}\right\}$$

We denote the number of assets inside cluster h as N_h (they sum up into the total number of assets $\sum_{h=1}^{H} N_h = N_A$).

Inside each cluster, the correlation is large, while intra-cluster correlations are close to zero. The clustered optimization procedure starts with applying the Markowitz optimization *independently* for each cluster. This determines an optimal sub-portfolio allocation inside each cluster. The next step is to form a portfolio consisting of cluster sub-portfolios as assets. Finally, using the Markowitz optimization for this portfolio of the sub-portfolios, we come up with the final allocation: the resulting asset weights are the optimal sub-portfolio weights times the asset weight inside each sub-portfolio.

The formal steps are:

1. Calculate the Markowitz weights $w^{(h)}$ independently for each cluster $h = 1, \cdots, H$ using Eq. (3.3)

$$w^{(h)} = \frac{{V^{(h)}}^{-1} a^{(h)}}{{a^{(h)}}^T {V^{(h)}}^{-1} a^{(h)}} \tag{3.14}$$

where the cluster covariance matrix is estimated as

$$V_{ij}^{(h)} = \frac{1}{N_T} \sum_{n=1}^{N_T} Y_{i,n}^{(h)} Y_{j,n}^{(h)} \tag{3.15}$$

with the corresponding normalizers $a^{(h)}$ taken from the initial ones $a = \left(a^{(1)}, \cdots, a^{(H)}\right)$. We also denote the theoretical (infinite sample) covariance matrix as

$$\bar{V}^{(h)} = \mathbb{E}\left[Y^{(h)} {Y^{(h)}}^T\right] \tag{3.16}$$

2. Calculate a covariance matrix $K(H$ by $H)$ for *clustered* variables (cluster sub-portfolios)

$$C^{(h)} = {w^{(h)}}^T Y^{(h)} \quad \text{for} \quad h = 1, \cdots, H$$

defined as

$$K_{hq} = \frac{1}{N_T} \sum_{n,m,p} w_n^{(h)} Y_{n,p}^{(h)} Y_{m,p}^{(q)} w_m^{(q)}.$$

It has simplified diagonal elements due to (3.4)

$$K_{hh} = {w^{(h)}}^T V^{(h)} w^{(h)} = \frac{1}{\Omega_h}$$

where we have denoted the inverse cluster risk as Ω_h. Using Eq. (3.14), it can be shown that

$$\Omega_h = {a^{(h)}}^T {V^{(h)}}^{-1} a^{(h)} \tag{3.17}$$

3. Calculate the cluster weights ξ_h for the cluster variables $C^{(h)}$

$$\Pi = \xi_1 \, C^{(1)} + \cdots + \xi_H \, C^{(H)}$$

For this, we minimize the portfolio Π variance

$$\sigma^2(\xi) = \mathbb{E}\,[\Pi] = \xi^T K \, \xi$$

provided that

$$\left(\xi_1 \, w^{(1)}, \cdots, \xi_H \, w^{(H)}\right) \cdot \left(a^{(1)}, \cdots, a^{(H)}\right) = 1.$$

Note that this normalization condition is simply equivalent to

$$\xi_1 + \cdots + \xi_H = \xi \cdot \iota = 1$$

where $\iota = (1, \cdots, 1)$ because $w^{(h)} \cdot a^{(h)} = 1$. The optimal values of the clusters weights are given by the Markowitz formula (3.3).

$$\xi = \frac{K^{-1} \, \iota}{\iota^T \, K^{-1} \, \iota}$$

4. Determine the final portfolio full weights, $u^{(h)} = \xi_h \, w^{(h)}$,

$$\left(u^{(1)} | \cdots | u^{(H)}\right) = \left(\xi_1 \, w_1^{(1)} \cdots \xi_1 w_{N_1}^{(1)} | \cdots | \xi_H w_1^{(H)}, \cdots, \xi_H w_{N_H}^{(H)}\right). \tag{3.18}$$

As in the Markowitz case, we denote the *theoretical* HRP components with the bar symbol, for example, $\bar{u}$.

The total portfolio weights noise comes from the cluster weights ξ_h as well as from the asset weights inside the clusters $w^{(h)}$. To simplify calculations, we separate the noise coming from the diagonal blocks of the covariance matrix $V^{(h)}$ and the *off-diagonal* ones.

$$\delta V_{ij}^{(h,q)} = \frac{1}{N_T} \sum_n Y_{i,n}^{(h)} \, Y_{j,n}^{(q)} \quad \text{for} \quad h \neq q$$

We put a small delta in front of the off-diagonal covariance matrix because its average value is zero (or small enough) by the assumption. The second reason for the small delta notation is to distinguish the off-diagonal noise from the block-diagonal noise.

$$\Delta V_{ij}^{(h)} = \frac{1}{N_T} \sum_n \left(Y_{i,n}^{(h)} \, Y_{j,n}^{(h)} - \mathbb{E}\left[Y_i^{(h)} \, Y_j^{(h)} \right] \right)$$

denoted with a *capital* delta. These noises can be separated because their product expectations are zero.

$$\mathbb{E}\left[\delta V_{ij}^{(h,q)} \, \Delta V_{i'j'}^{(h')} \right] = 0$$

for all cluster/element indexes due to zero correlations between different cluster elements $\mathbb{E}\left[Y_i^{(h)} \, Y_{i'}^{(h')} \right] = 0$.

As we will see below, *the optimal weights for the Markowitz and HRP methods are identical if the covariance matrix is a block-diagonal one, that is, cross-cluster correlations are strictly zero*. This means that the noise difference between the Markowitz and the HRP comes from *cross-cluster correlations*. In Appendix B, we prove the following analytical formula for the HRP expected noise,

$$\begin{aligned} \mathcal{N}_C = \mathbb{E}\left[\Delta u^T \Delta u\right] &= \sum_h \mathbb{E}\left[\Delta u^{(h)^T} \Delta u^{(h)}\right] \\ &\simeq \frac{1}{N_T}\frac{1}{\bar{\Omega}}\left(\sum_h \mathrm{tr}\left(\bar{V}^{(h)^{-1}}\right)\frac{\bar{\Omega}_h}{\bar{\Omega}} + \sum_h \frac{a^{(h)^T}\,\bar{V}^{(h)^{-2}}\,a^{(h)}}{\bar{\Omega}_h}\left(1-2\frac{\bar{\Omega}_h}{\bar{\Omega}}\right)\right) \end{aligned} \tag{3.19}$$

where $\bar{V}^{(h)}$ is an *exact* covariance matrix of h-th cluster (3.16). Also, we have defined the exact inverse cluster covariance as $\bar{\Omega}_h$ and $\bar{\Omega} = \sum_h \bar{\Omega}_h$. As we have mentioned in Section 3.2, for practical noise calculation we use the estimated matrix instead of its theoretical value. This introduces an error of the order $O(N_T^{-2})$, which we can ignore.

A more general formula that we will use in the portfolio risk calculation is a simple modification of the formula (3.19).

$$\begin{aligned} \mathbb{E}\left[\Delta u^T M_B\, \Delta u\right] &= \sum_h \mathbb{E}\left[\Delta u^{(h)^T} M^{(h)}\, \Delta u^{(h)}\right] \\ &\simeq \frac{1}{N_T}\frac{1}{\bar{\Omega}}\left(\sum_h \mathrm{tr}\left(\bar{V}^{(h)^{-1}} M^{(h)}\right)\frac{\bar{\Omega}_h}{\bar{\Omega}} + \sum_h \frac{a^{(h)^T}\,\bar{V}^{(h)^{-1}}\,M^{(h)}\,\bar{V}^{(h)^{-1}}\,a^{(h)}}{\bar{\Omega}_h}\left(1-2\frac{\bar{\Omega}_h}{\bar{\Omega}}\right)\right) \end{aligned} \tag{3.20}$$

where M_B is a block matrix with the same dimensions as the block variance matrix.

One can easily demonstrate that the HRP noise (3.19) is always less than the direct Markowitz one (3.11) using arguments similar to the previous section ones. Indeed, under our assumption of zero intra-cluster correlations, the exact covariance matrix $\bar{V}$ is a block-one, such that its inversion simply consists of inversions of the cluster covariance matrices $\bar{V}^{(h)}$. It is easy to see that the Markowitz expected noise (3.11) can be written as

$$\mathcal{N}_M \simeq \frac{1}{N_T}\frac{1}{\bar{\Omega}}\left(\sum_h \mathrm{Tr}\,\bar{V}^{(h)^{-1}} - \frac{\sum_h a^{(h)^T}\,\bar{V}^{(h)^{-2}}\,a^{(h)}}{\bar{\Omega}}\right) \tag{3.21}$$

This permits us to prove that the difference $N_M - N_C$ is always non-negative

$$\mathcal{N}_M - \mathcal{N}_C \geq \frac{1}{N_T}\frac{1}{\bar{\Omega}^2}\sum_h\left(\mathrm{Tr}\,\bar{V}^{(h)^{-1}} - \frac{a^{(h)^T}\,\bar{V}^{(h)^{-2}}\,a^{(h)}}{\bar{\Omega}_h}\right)(\bar{\Omega} - \bar{\Omega}_h)$$

Indeed, the non-negativity of the first multiplier was proved in Eq. (3.13) and $\bar{\Omega} = \sum_q \bar{\Omega}_q \geq \bar{\Omega}_h$ because all inverse cluster risks are non-negative ($\bar{\Omega}_h \geq 0$) due to Eq. (3.17).

In the next section, we address the main practical application of our theory: the Markowitz and the HRP portfolio risk calculations.

3.4. Portfolio Variance Statistics

In this section, we will evaluate the portfolio variance (risk) statistics: its expectation and standard deviation with respect to movements of the covariance matrix. We will consider two important cases: in-sample (IS) and out-of-sample (OOS).

The IS portfolio variance is simply

$$\sigma^2 = w^T V w \tag{3.22}$$

where the weights are constructed using the *portfolio* covariance matrix V as in Eq. (3.3).

The OOS case risk

$$\tilde{\sigma}^2 = w^T \tilde{V} w \tag{3.23}$$

is when the *portfolio* covariance matrix $\tilde{V}$ is independent of the *weights* covariance matrix V. This is obviously the real-life case when we apply historically calculated weights to future returns that form a future covariance matrix. Indeed, the estimated variance reads

$$\widehat{\sigma}^2 = \frac{1}{N_T} \sum_{n=1}^{N_T} \left(\sum_i w_i X_{i,n} \right)^2$$

where the optimal weights w are calculated at t_0 by the Markowitz formula (3.3) with the covariance matrix estimated by Eq. (3.2) with returns $X_{i,-N_T}, \cdots, X_{i,-1}$. Thus, the OOS variance can be rewritten in the form of (3.23) where the weights covariance matrix is

$$V_{ij} = \frac{1}{N_T} \sum_{n=-N_T}^{-1} X_{i,n} X_{j,n}$$

while the portfolio covariance matrix is

$$\tilde{V}_{ij} = \frac{1}{N_T} \sum_{n=1}^{N_T} X_{i,n} X_{j,n}$$

Obviously, the weights matrix increment ΔV is independent of the portfolio one $\Delta \tilde{V}$.

While working with the portfolio variance, it is important to go *beyond* the leading order in the number of samples, $1/N_T$. Indeed, as we will see below, the IS and OOS portfolio risks coincide in a limit of a large number of samples, but the second-order effect is quite sizeable for standard portfolios.

Let us pass now to the IS and OSS portfolio variances.

Portfolio variances. An optimal portfolio IS variance is given by Eq. (3.22). For the Markowitz weights (3.3), the risk is minimal (3.4). To estimate its statistics, we can proceed directly using perturbation of the variance in its denominator, but instead, we will take another way that is more intuitive and explanatory. Indeed, the noise of the risk comes through the optimal w and V, that is,

$$\begin{aligned}\sigma^2 &= (\bar{w} + \Delta w)^T (\bar{V} + \Delta V)(\bar{w} + \Delta w) \\ &= \bar{w}^T \bar{V} \bar{w} + \underbrace{\bar{w}^T \Delta V \bar{w} + 2\bar{w}^T \bar{V} \Delta w}_{\text{1st order}} + \underbrace{2\bar{w}^T \Delta V \Delta w + \Delta w^T \bar{V} \Delta w}_{\text{2nd order}} + \underbrace{\Delta w^T \Delta V \Delta w}_{\text{3rd order}}\end{aligned}$$

The contribution of the weights noise in the first order $\bar{w}^T \bar{V} \Delta w$ cancels out. Due to the normalization constraint for both exact and realized weight, $a^T \bar{w} = 1$ and $a^T w = 1$, the weights noise is perpendicular to a, that is, $a^T \Delta w = 0$. As far as $\bar{w}^T \bar{V}$ is proportional to a, $\bar{w}^T \bar{V} \Delta w = 0$, giving

$$\sigma^2 = \bar{\sigma}^2 + \bar{w}^T \Delta V \bar{w} + 2\bar{w}^T \Delta V \Delta w + \Delta w^T \bar{V} \Delta w + \Delta w^T \Delta V \Delta w \tag{3.24}$$

where we have denoted the theoretical (infinite number of samples) risk as

$$\bar{\sigma}^2 = \bar{w}^T \bar{V} \bar{w} \tag{3.25}$$

Similarly, the OOS risk (3.23) can be expanded as

$$\tilde{\sigma}^2 = \bar{\sigma}^2 + \bar{w}^T \Delta \tilde{V} \bar{w} + 2\bar{w}^T \Delta \tilde{V} \Delta w + \Delta w^T \bar{V} \Delta w + \Delta w^T \Delta \tilde{V} \Delta w \tag{3.26}$$

Now let us start with the risk expectation calculations followed by the risk standard deviation.

The risk expectation. In these studies, we go beyond the leading order in $1/N_T$ to explain the effect of the risk noise increase when we switch from the IS to the OOS portfolio. Taking expectation of Eq. (3.24)

$$\mathbb{E}\left[\sigma^2\right] = \bar{\sigma}^2 + 2\mathbb{E}\left[\bar{w}^T \Delta V \Delta w\right] + \mathbb{E}\left[\Delta w^T \bar{V} \Delta w\right] + O\left(\frac{1}{N_T^2}\right)$$

we obtain

$$\mathbb{E}\left[\sigma^2\right] = \bar{\sigma}^2 - \mathbb{E}\left[\Delta w^T \bar{V} \Delta w\right] + O\left(\frac{1}{N_T^2}\right) \tag{3.27}$$

Here we have used the identity[b]

$$\mathbb{E}\left[\bar{w}^T \Delta V \Delta w\right] = -\mathbb{E}\left[\Delta w^T \bar{V} \Delta w\right] + O\left(\frac{1}{N_T^2}\right)$$

[b]It follows from

$$\mathbb{E}\left[\bar{w}^T \Delta V \Delta w\right] + \mathbb{E}\left[\Delta w^T \bar{V} \Delta w\right] = \mathbb{E}\left[\Delta (w^T V) \Delta w\right] + O\left(\frac{1}{N_T^2}\right) = O\left(\frac{1}{N_T^2}\right)$$

valid due to the proportionality of $\Delta(w^T V)$ to the normalization vector a and the constrain $a^T \Delta w = 0$.

In the OOS case, the risk expectation is simpler due to the independence of the weights and portfolio noises, ΔV and $\Delta\tilde{V}$, resulting in $\mathbb{E}\left[\bar{w}^T\Delta\tilde{V}\Delta w\right] = 0$. This leads to

$$\mathbb{E}\left[\tilde{\sigma}^2\right] = \bar{\sigma}^2 + \mathbb{E}\left[\Delta w^T\bar{V}\Delta w\right] + O\left(\frac{1}{N_T^2}\right) \tag{3.28}$$

We see that the IS risk expectation is always *smaller* than the OSS one by $2\mathbb{E}\left[\Delta w^T\bar{V}\Delta w\right]$. The reason is obvious: the risk is *explicitly* minimized in the IS case while the OOS risk is not.

Now we will evaluate the IS and OOS risk expectations for the Markowitz and the HRP methods. Thanks to the simplified expressions (3.27–28), this calculation can be easily performed.

For the Markowitz case, we use the expected noise formula (3.12) for the underlying expectation

$$\mathbb{E}\left[\Delta w^T\bar{V}\Delta w\right] = \frac{N_A - 1}{N_T}\bar{\sigma}^2 + O\left(\frac{1}{N_T^2}\right) \tag{3.29}$$

to obtain

$$\begin{aligned} \mathbb{E}\left[\sigma_M^2\right] &= \bar{\sigma}^2\left(1 - \frac{N_A - 1}{N_T}\right) + O\left(\frac{1}{N_T^2}\right) \\ \mathbb{E}\left[\tilde{\sigma}_M^2\right] &= \bar{\sigma}^2\left(1 + \frac{N_A - 1}{N_T}\right) + O\left(\frac{1}{N_T^2}\right) \end{aligned} \tag{3.30}$$

where we have put a subscript M to emphasize that the risk belongs to the Markowitz portfolio.

For the HRP case, we proceed in a similar manner, calculating the risk expectations for the pure block case such that the theoretical matrix $\bar{V}$ is the block one, that is, $\bar{V} = \bar{V}_B$. The expectation underlying the formulas (3.27–3.28) can be calculated using the generalized noise (3.20)

$$\mathbb{E}\left[\Delta u^T\bar{V}_B\Delta u\right] = \frac{1}{N_T}\frac{1}{\bar{\Omega}}\left(\sum_h N_h\frac{\bar{\Omega}_h}{\bar{\Omega}} + \sum_h\left(1 - 2\frac{\bar{\Omega}_h}{\bar{\Omega}}\right)\right) \tag{3.31}$$

where N_h is the number of assets in a cluster h. This leads to the final HRP answer for both IS and OSS cases

$$\begin{aligned} \mathbb{E}\left[\sigma_C^2\right] &= \bar{\sigma}^2\left(1 - \frac{H - 1 + \sum_h (N_h - 1)\frac{\bar{\Omega}_h}{\bar{\Omega}}}{N_T}\right) + O\left(\frac{1}{N_T^2}\right) \\ \mathbb{E}\left[\tilde{\sigma}_C^2\right] &= \bar{\sigma}^2\left(1 + \frac{H - 1 + \sum_h (N_h - 1)\frac{\bar{\Omega}_h}{\bar{\Omega}}}{N_T}\right) + O\left(\frac{1}{N_T^2}\right) \end{aligned} \tag{3.32}$$

where we put the subscript C to address the *clustered* (HRP) risk.

It is easy to see that the HRP risk expectation first-order correction (denoted as δ_C) is always less than the Markowitz one δ_M, that is,

$$\delta_C = \frac{H - 1 + \sum_h (N_h - 1)\frac{\bar{\Omega}_h}{\bar{\Omega}}}{N_T} \leq \frac{N_A - 1}{N_T} = \delta_M$$

Indeed, this inequality is equivalent to an obvious inequality.

$$\sum_h (N_h - 1)\left(1 - \frac{\bar{\Omega}_h}{\bar{\Omega}}\right) \geq 0$$

Having the analytical expression of the HRP correction, we can choose the portfolio/cluster composition to minimize the risk. For example, if the clusters contain the same number of elements, the minimal HRP correction corresponds to the number of clusters around $\sqrt{N_A}$, so that its minimal value

$$\min \delta_C \simeq 2\frac{\sqrt{N_A}}{N_T} \tag{3.33}$$

can be much less than the Markowitz one

$$\delta_M \simeq \frac{N_A}{N_T}. \tag{3.34}$$

We see that the expected risk for our four cases: IS/OOS and Markowitz/HRP satisfies the following inequality:

$$\mathbb{E}\left[\sigma_M^2\right] \leq \mathbb{E}\left[\sigma_C^2\right] \leq \bar{\sigma}^2 \leq \mathbb{E}\left[\tilde{\sigma}_C^2\right] \leq \mathbb{E}\left[\tilde{\sigma}_M^2\right]. \tag{3.35}$$

The IS Markowitz risk is less than the IS HRP because the former directly minimizes the risk. On the other hand, for the OOS cases, the HRP risk expectation is smaller than the Markowitz one because the HRP weights are less noisy than the Markowitz ones. This is also important for other aspects of the portfolio *robustness*: smaller weight noise leads to a lower turnover and transaction costs and makes the optimization less sensitive to sudden market changes.

The risk variance. The IS portfolio variance (risk) variance can be easily evaluated in the leading order.

$$\mathbb{V}\left[\sigma^2\right] = \frac{2}{N_T}\bar{\sigma}^4 + O\left(\frac{1}{N_T^2}\right) \tag{3.36}$$

For this we have selected the first-order term $\bar{w}^T \Delta V \bar{w}$ from the risk expansion (3.24) and calculated its square expectation using the general formula (3.11).

The same formula is valid for the OOS case.

$$\mathbb{V}\left[\bar{\sigma}^2\right] = \frac{2}{N_T}\bar{\sigma}^4 + O\left(\frac{1}{N_T^2}\right) \tag{3.37}$$

As far as the *theoretical* risks for the Markowitz and the HRP are identical (due to $\bar{u} = \bar{w}$), their *numerical* risk values coincide in the leading order. Going beyond the first order is *much* more complicated because the expectations in hand contain averages of the fourth order in ΔV. That is why we can repeat the qualitative arguments of the previous paragraph and come up with the following inequality *in the higher order.*

$$\mathbb{V}\left[\sigma_M^2\right] \leq \mathbb{V}\left[\sigma_C^2\right] \leq \frac{2}{N_T}\bar{\sigma}^4 \leq \mathbb{V}\left[\tilde{\sigma}_C^2\right] \leq \mathbb{V}\left[\tilde{\sigma}_M^2\right] \tag{3.38}$$

We will observe this equality in the next section of numerical experiments.

Finally, let us notice that for the Markowitz case, going beyond the leading order in the *risk variance* is less important for practical applications than for the *risk expectation.* Indeed, comparing corrections to the risk expectations (3.34) with its normalized theoretical standard deviation, that is,

$$\frac{N_A}{N_T} \text{ vs. } \sqrt{\frac{2}{N_T}}.$$

We conclude that the expectation corrections will dominate the risk standard deviation if the number of assets is more than a square root of the number of samples. This means that the difference between the Markowitz portfolio risk and the HRP one for **a single scenario** is mostly described by a difference between their **expected** values rather than by **standard deviations** of the risk.

3.5. Numerical Experiments

For numerical experiments, we set up a clustered correlation matrix with the following clusters on the block diagonal (Table 3.1).

Table 3.1 Correlation matrix cluster composition.

Cluster	0	1	2	3	4	5	6	7	8	9
Sizes	10	17	5	17	7	9	15	9	11	3
Corrs	0.9	0.8	0.8	0.9	0.8	0.8	0.7	0.8	0.7	0.7

The corresponding number of assets is $N_A = 103$. The matrix can be visualized below (Fig. 3.1).

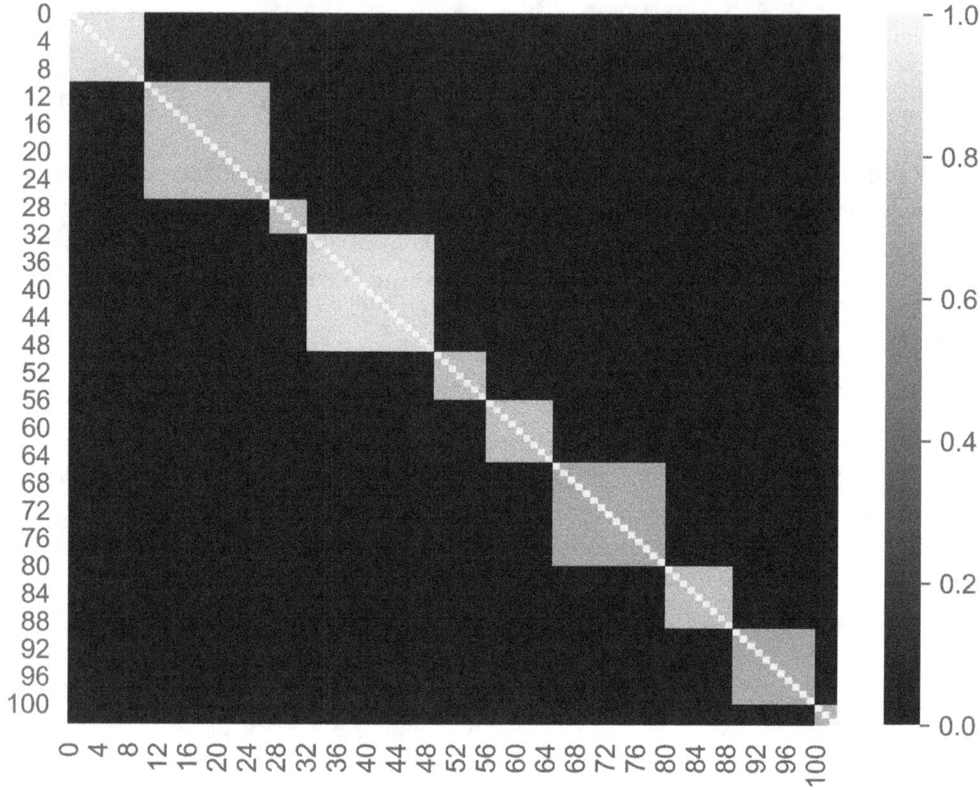

Fig. 3.1 Clustered (block) correlation matrix.

In our experiments we perturb the initial correlation matrix with *off-cluster* (or off-block) values, which we vary from 0 (unperturbed) till 60%. Then, we simulate N_A Gaussians with these correlation matrices[c] over a variable number of samples N_T: we try 250, 500, 750, and 1,000 time-steps corresponding approximately to 1, 2, 3, and 4 years of daily data. We produce 10,000 of such Monte Carlo trajectories—N_A assets over N_T samples ()—to ensure the Monte Carlo convergence. In the first group of experiments, we demonstrate the analytics validity and quantify the noise reduction of the HRP w.r.t. the Markowitz.

Noise measurements. We start with experiments for 500 timesteps (2 years of daily data) and zero off-block correlation. We output analytical (exact) values $\bar{w}$ as well as these for a typical simulation scenario for both Markowitz and HRP cases (See Fig 3.2).

[c]The volatility is set to one for simplicity.

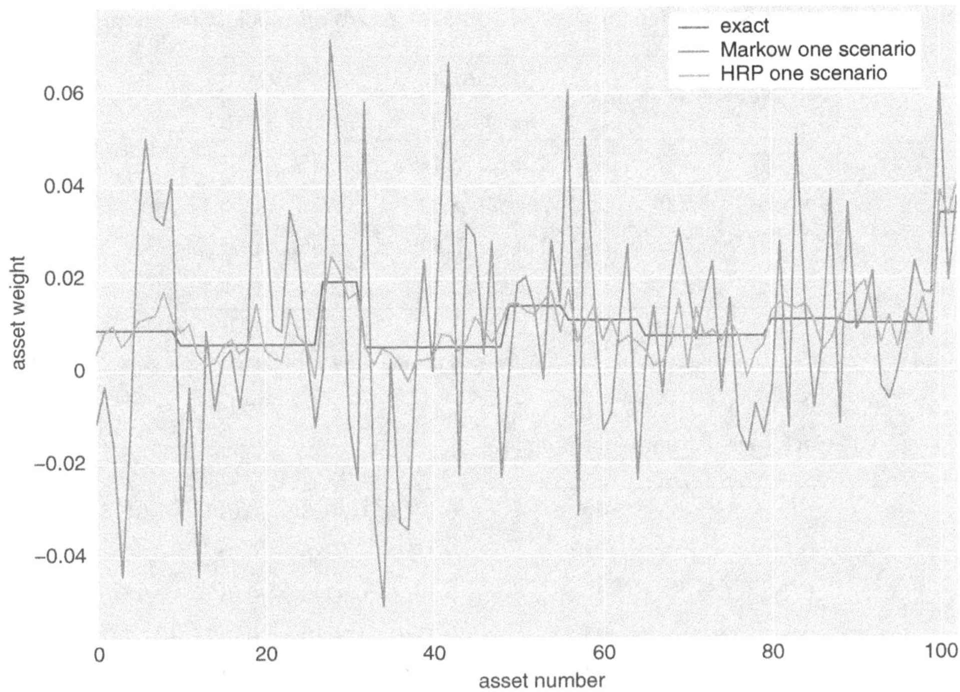

Fig. 3.2 Allocation weights.

For this single scenario, we clearly observe a large noise of the Markowitz optimization and a much lower HRP one. To analyze this noise more systematically, we will present the following standard deviation per asset, that is,

$$\sqrt{\frac{\mathbb{E}\left[\Delta w^T \Delta w\right]}{N_A}} \quad \text{and} \quad \sqrt{\frac{\mathbb{E}\left[\Delta u^T \Delta u\right]}{N_A}}$$

for the direct Markowitz and for the HRP, respectively (as stated above, this statistics is estimated for 10,000 Monte Carlo scenarios). This measure can also be thought as an *asset weight confidence interval* for one scenario (e.g., real-life one) estimation.

In Table 3.2, we will see that the obtained confidence intervals for the Markowitz optimization are (much) larger than the average asset weight $\sim$ 1%. On the other hand, the HRP gives much smaller confidence intervals.

Table 3.3 contains a full range of theoretical and Monte Carlo expectations:

$$\mathbb{E}\left[\Delta w^T \Delta w\right] \quad \text{and} \quad \mathbb{E}\left[\Delta u^T \Delta u\right]$$

for the direct Markowitz and for the HRP, respectively.

Table 3.2 Confidence intervals for asset weights for a zero off-block correlation.

Number of samples	Markowitz		HRP	
	Analyt	MC	Analyt	MC
250	4.16%	5.42%	1.31%	1.39%
500	2.94%	3.30%	0.93%	0.95%
750	2.40%	2.59%	0.76%	0.77%
1,000	2.08%	2.20%	0.66%	0.66%

Table 3.3 Analytical and estimated noise for the Markowitz and HRP optimizations.

Off-block corr	Number of samples	Markowitz		HRP	
		Analyt	MC	Analyt	MC
0	250	0.1785	0.3028	0.0177	0.0198
0.1	250	0.3759	0.6380	0.0177	0.0218
0.2	250	0.5733	0.9740	0.0177	0.0246
0.3	250	0.7710	1.3110	0.0177	0.0287
0.4	250	0.9692	1.6490	0.0177	0.0349
0.5	250	1.1683	1.9890	0.0177	0.0455
0.6	250	1.3695	2.3332	0.0177	0.0671
0	500	0.0893	0.1122	0.0089	0.0093
0.1	500	0.1879	0.2363	0.0089	0.0099
0.2	500	0.2867	0.3606	0.0089	0.0108
0.3	500	0.3855	0.4852	0.0089	0.0120
0.4	500	0.4846	0.6103	0.0089	0.0138
0.5	500	0.5841	0.7362	0.0089	0.0170
0.6	500	0.6848	0.8638	0.0089	0.0238
0	750	0.0595	0.0689	0.0059	0.0061
0.1	750	0.1253	0.1451	0.0059	0.0065
0.2	750	0.1911	0.2214	0.0059	0.0069
0.3	750	0.2570	0.2980	0.0059	0.0075
0.4	750	0.3231	0.3748	0.0059	0.0085
0.5	750	0.3894	0.4520	0.0059	0.0102
0.6	750	0.4565	0.5302	0.0059	0.0139

0	1,000	0.0446	0.0497	0.0044	0.0045
0.1	1,000	0.0940	0.1047	0.0044	0.0048
0.2	1,000	0.1433	0.1597	0.0044	0.0050
0.3	1,000	0.1928	0.2149	0.0044	0.0055
0.4	1,000	0.2423	0.2702	0.0044	0.0061
0.5	1,000	0.2921	0.3259	0.0044	0.0072
0.6	1,000	0.3424	0.3822	0.0044	0.0097

For better visualization, we also plot a *normalize* noise

$$N_T \mathbb{E}\left[\Delta w^T \Delta w\right] \quad \text{and} \quad N_T \mathbb{E}\left[\Delta u^T \Delta u\right]$$

for the direct Markowitz and for the HRP, respectively (See Fig 3.3).

We observe a gap between Monte Carlo noise calculation and the analytics for the Markowitz optimization. Its origin is due to nonlinear effects. Indeed, in the analytics we have ignored the second order of the covariance matrix noise. Increasing the number of time-steps reduces this gap.

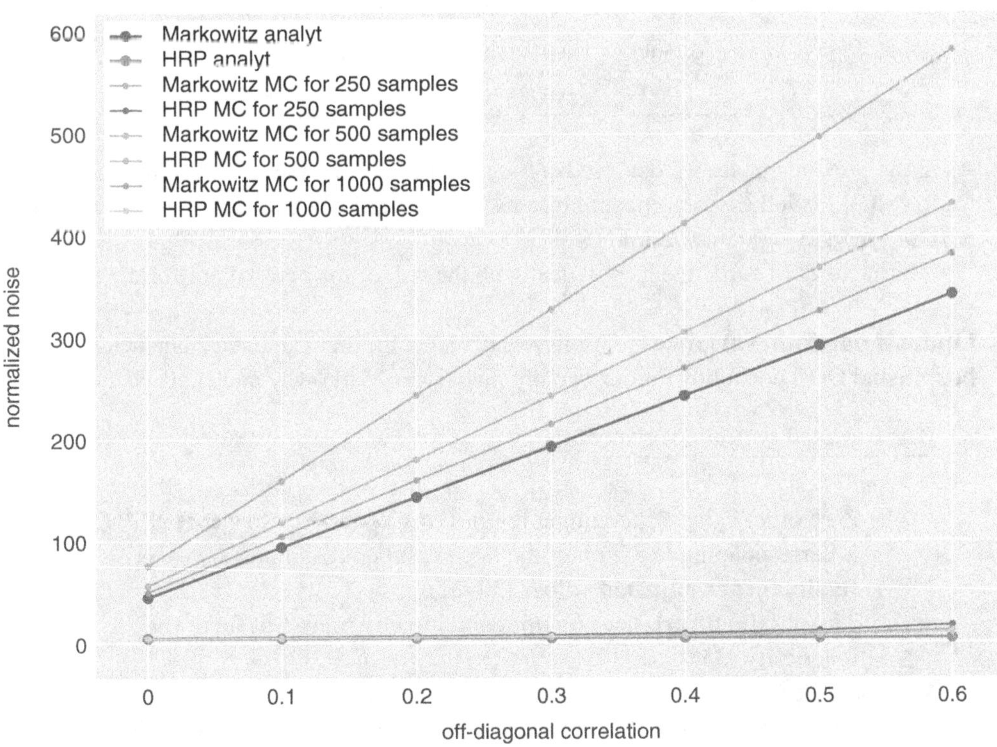

Fig. 3.3 Analytical and estimated relative noise for the Markowitz and HRP optimizations.

Similarly, a gap between the HRP Monte Carlo noise calculation and the analytics is due to the non-linearity *but also* the fact that the analytics ignores the off-block elements.

Importantly, we see that *the impact of the HRP on the noise reduction is very significant*: 10 times for a pure block structure and 30 for more significant off-block correlations!

To finalize this subsection, we address another noise measure introduced in Ref. [7]: a *variance error*

$$\mathbb{E}\left[\Delta w^T \bar{V} \Delta w\right] \quad \text{and} \quad \mathbb{E}\left[\Delta u^T \bar{V} \Delta u\right]$$

for Markowitz and HRP methods, respectively. As explained in the previous section, this expression participates in the optimal portfolio expected variance with different signs for the IS and OOS setups; see Eqs. (3.27) and (3.32). The expectations in hand are calculated analytically and numerically. For compactness, we provide errors corresponding to zero off-block correlation (Table 3.4).

Table 3.4 Variance error for a zero off-block correlation.

Number of samples	Markowitz		HRP	
	Analyt	MC	Analyt	MC
250	0.033	0.056	0.006	0.006
500	0.017	0.021	0.003	0.003
750	0.011	0.013	0.002	0.002
1,000	0.008	0.009	0.001	0.001

As in the previous table, we observe here a good fit between the analytics and the Monte Carlo (MC), as well as a significant noise reduction—as large as 5-10 times—of the HRP w.r.t. the Markowitz optimization.

Our next set of experiments will deal with the risk of the optimal portfolio.

Optimal portfolio variance. We have calculated different statistical characteristics of both IS and OOS portfolios for our two optimizations, Markowitz and HRP. Namely:

- The expected portfolio variance
  - Analytics
    - → Zero order value $\bar{\sigma}^2$ (common for all IS/OOS and Markowitz/HRP) is corresponding to a limit of the large number of samples $N_T \to \infty$.
    - → **Its first order adjusted values (30–32).** **The obtained variances do not coincide any more but form the inequality (35).**
  - Monte Carlo

    We calculate the numerical expectation over 10,000 simulation scenarios.

- The standard deviation of the portfolio variance
  - Analytics leading order value $\sqrt{2/N_T}\bar{\sigma}^2$.
    It is common for all IS/OOS and Markowitz/HRP due to (3.36–37).
  - Monte Carlo
    We calculate the numerical standard deviation over 10,000 simulation scenarios.

Let us start with the **expected portfolio variance** and summarize the results in Table 3.5.

Table 3.5 Portfolio variance expectation.

Off block corr	Number of samples	Analyt 0 order	In-sample				Out-of-sample			
			Markowitz		HRP		Markowitz		HRP	
			Analyt	MC	Analyt	MC	Analyt	MC	Analyt	MC
0	250	0.081	0.048	0.048	0.075	0.075	0.115	0.137	0.087	0.088
0.1	250	0.171	0.101	0.101	0.159	0.156	0.241	0.289	0.184	0.181
0.2	250	0.261	0.155	0.155	0.242	0.236	0.368	0.440	0.280	0.274
0.3	250	0.351	0.208	0.208	0.325	0.316	0.494	0.592	0.377	0.367
0.4	250	0.441	0.261	0.261	0.409	0.395	0.621	0.744	0.473	0.461
0.5	250	0.531	0.314	0.314	0.492	0.474	0.747	0.895	0.570	0.556
0.6	250	0.620	0.367	0.367	0.575	0.551	0.873	1.046	0.665	0.652
0	500	0.081	0.065	0.065	0.078	0.078	0.098	0.102	0.084	0.084
0.1	500	0.171	0.136	0.136	0.165	0.163	0.206	0.215	0.178	0.176
0.2	500	0.261	0.208	0.208	0.252	0.248	0.315	0.328	0.271	0.267
0.3	500	0.351	0.280	0.280	0.338	0.333	0.423	0.440	0.364	0.359
0.4	500	0.441	0.351	0.351	0.425	0.418	0.531	0.553	0.457	0.450
0.5	500	0.531	0.422	0.423	0.511	0.503	0.639	0.665	0.550	0.542
0.6	500	0.620	0.494	0.494	0.597	0.586	0.747	0.777	0.643	0.634
0	750	0.081	0.070	0.070	0.079	0.079	0.093	0.094	0.083	0.083
0.1	750	0.171	0.148	0.148	0.167	0.166	0.195	0.198	0.176	0.174
0.2	750	0.261	0.226	0.226	0.255	0.253	0.297	0.302	0.268	0.265
0.3	750	0.351	0.303	0.303	0.343	0.339	0.399	0.406	0.360	0.356
0.4	750	0.441	0.381	0.381	0.430	0.426	0.501	0.510	0.452	0.447
0.5	750	0.531	0.459	0.459	0.518	0.512	0.603	0.614	0.544	0.538
0.6	750	0.620	0.536	0.536	0.605	0.598	0.704	0.717	0.635	0.629

(Continued)

Table 3.5 Portfolio variance expectation. (*Continued*)

Off block corr	Number of samples	Analyt 0 order	In-sample				Out-of-sample			
			Markowitz		HRP		Markowitz		HRP	
			Analyt	MC	Analyt	MC	Analyt	MC	Analyt	MC
0	1,000	0.081	0.073	0.073	0.080	0.080	0.090	0.091	0.083	0.083
0.1	1,000	0.171	0.154	0.154	0.168	0.167	0.189	0.191	0.175	0.174
0.2	1,000	0.261	0.235	0.235	0.257	0.255	0.288	0.291	0.266	0.264
0.3	1,000	0.351	0.315	0.315	0.345	0.342	0.387	0.391	0.358	0.355
0.4	1,000	0.441	0.396	0.396	0.433	0.430	0.486	0.491	0.449	0.446
0.5	1,000	0.531	0.477	0.477	0.521	0.517	0.585	0.591	0.540	0.536
0.6	1,000	0.620	0.557	0.557	0.609	0.603	0.683	0.690	0.631	0.627

We observe the following:

- The expected variances do obey the inequality (3.35) for both analytical and Monte Carlo (MC) answers. Namely, the smallest value has the IS Markowitz portfolio followed by the IS HRP. Both are less than the theoretical variance. On the other side of the theoretical variance, there are the HRP OOS and the Markowitz OOS.
- The HRP values are much closer to the theoretical variance than the Markowitz ones.
- The OOS portfolio variance reduction of the HRP w.r.t. the Markowitz starts with 50% for 250 timesteps (one-year interval) and ends at 10% for 1,000 timesteps.
- The analytics quality is excellent due to its higher order in the number of samples.
- Off-diagonal correlations that pull us out of our assumptions do not break the picture: the HRP is much more efficient than the Markowitz method.

Below, for a better visualization of the above effects, we present a plot of the expected variance as a function of timesteps for all the portfolios for a zero off-block correlation (see Fig 3.4) as well as the expected variance as a function of different off-block correlations for 500 timesteps (see Fig 3.5).

Now we pass to the **standard deviation of the portfolio variance**, which we calculate analytically in the leading order and numerically over 10,000 simulations (Table 3.6).

As in the case of the expected variance, we observe that the portfolio variance noise (standard deviation) satisfies the similar inequality (3.38) and that the OOS noise of the Markowitz can be substantially lower than the Markowitz one, especially for low 200 or 500 samples.

We also see that the difference between the expected Markowitz portfolio risk and the HRP one is significantly larger than their standard deviations. This confirms our theoretical conclusion that the difference between the Markowitz portfolio risk and the HRP one for **a single scenario** is mostly due to a difference between their expected values rather than to a standard deviation of the risks.

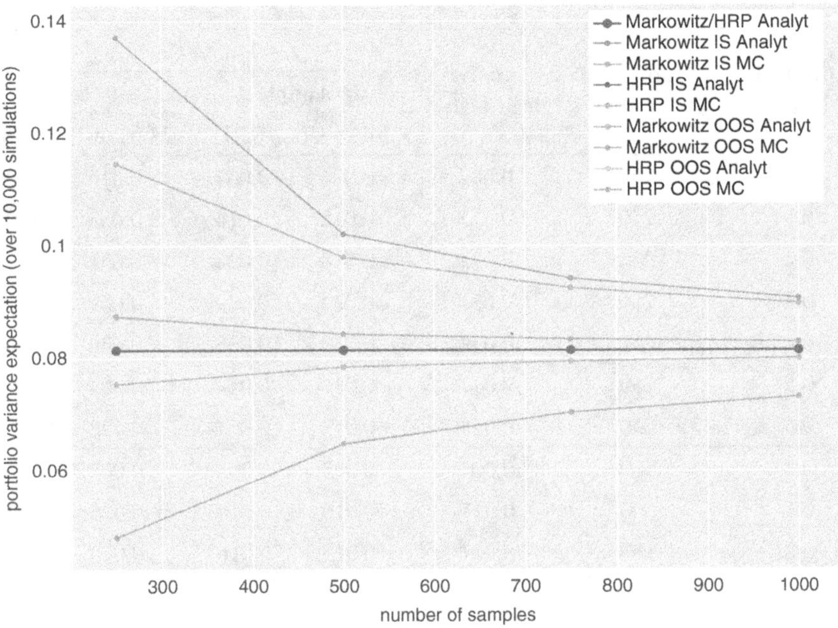

Fig. 3.4 Portfolio variance expectations for zero off-block correlation.

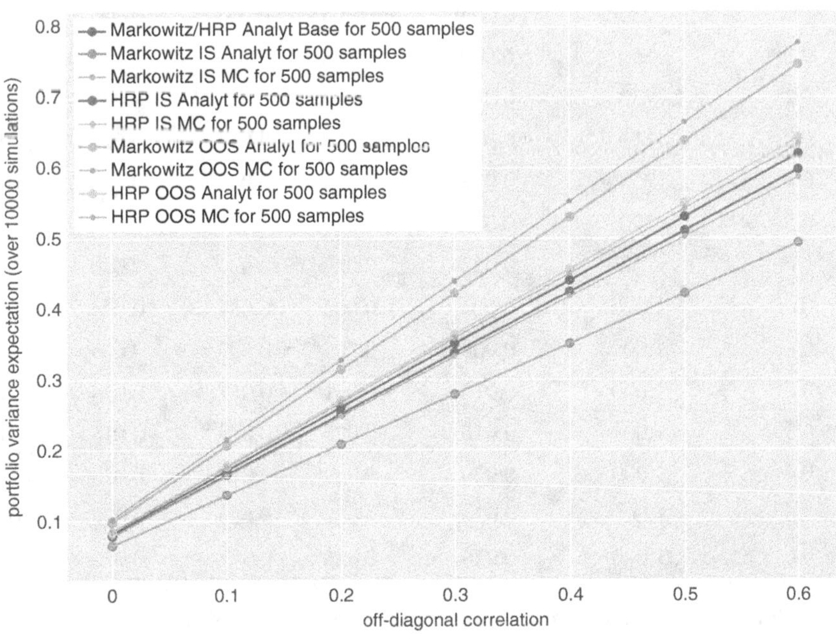

Fig. 3.5 Portfolio variance expectations for 500 samples.

Table 3.6 Portfolio variance standard deviation.

Off-block corr	Number of samples	Analyt lead-order	Monte Carlo			
			In-sample		Out-of-sample	
			Markowitz	HRP	Markowitz	HRP
0	250	0.007	0.006	0.007	0.016	0.008
0.1	250	0.015	0.012	0.014	0.033	0.016
0.2	250	0.023	0.018	0.022	0.051	0.025
0.3	250	0.031	0.024	0.029	0.069	0.034
0.4	250	0.039	0.030	0.036	0.086	0.042
0.5	250	0.047	0.036	0.044	0.104	0.051
0.6	250	0.055	0.042	0.051	0.122	0.061
0	500	0.005	0.005	0.005	0.007	0.005
0.1	500	0.011	0.010	0.010	0.015	0.011
0.2	500	0.017	0.015	0.016	0.023	0.017
0.3	500	0.022	0.020	0.021	0.031	0.023
0.4	500	0.028	0.025	0.027	0.039	0.029
0.5	500	0.034	0.030	0.032	0.047	0.035
0.6	500	0.039	0.035	0.038	0.055	0.041
0	750	0.004	0.004	0.004	0.005	0.004
0.1	750	0.009	0.008	0.009	0.011	0.009
0.2	750	0.013	0.012	0.013	0.017	0.014
0.3	750	0.018	0.017	0.017	0.023	0.019
0.4	750	0.023	0.021	0.022	0.028	0.023
0.5	750	0.027	0.025	0.026	0.034	0.028
0.6	750	0.032	0.029	0.031	0.040	0.033
0	1,000	0.004	0.003	0.004	0.004	0.004
0.1	1,000	0.008	0.007	0.007	0.009	0.008
0.2	1,000	0.012	0.011	0.011	0.014	0.012
0.3	1,000	0.016	0.015	0.015	0.018	0.016
0.4	1,000	0.020	0.019	0.019	0.023	0.020
0.5	1,000	0.024	0.022	0.023	0.028	0.024
0.6	1,000	0.028	0.026	0.027	0.032	0.028

Below, for a better visualization of the above effects, we present a plot of the standard deviation of the variance as a function of samples for all the portfolios for a zero off-block correlation (see Fig 3.6) as well as the standard deviation of the variance as a function of different off-block correlations for 500 samples (see Fig 3.7).

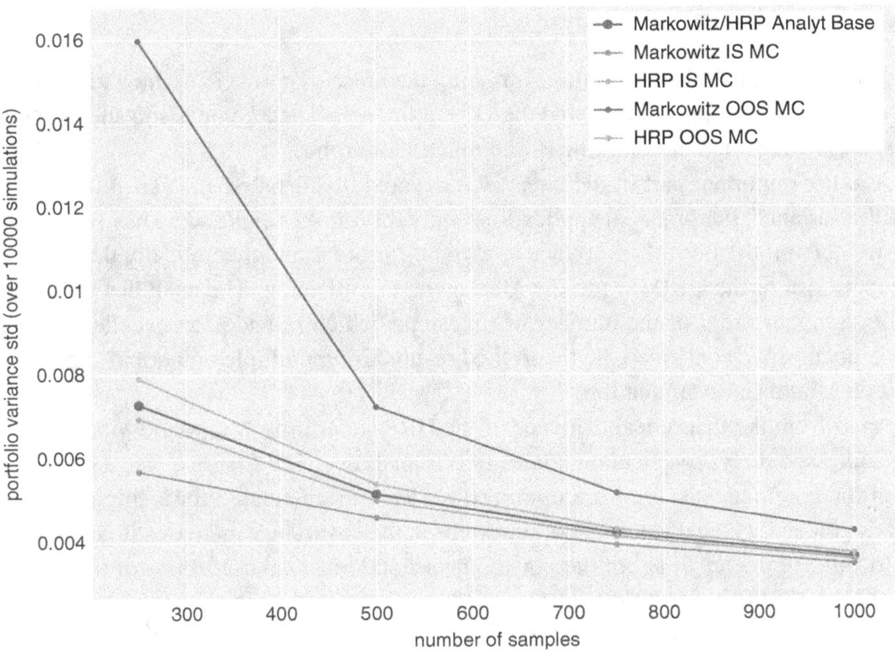

Fig. 3.6 Portfolio variance standard deviation for zero off-block correlation.

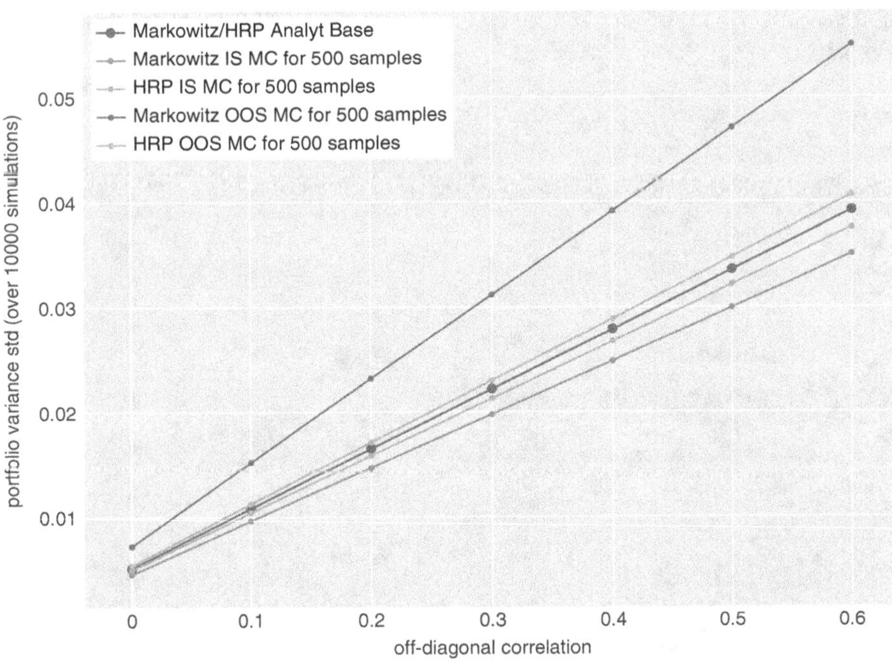

Fig. 3.7 Portfolio variance standard deviation for 500 time-steps.

3.6. Conclusions

We have derived analytical formulas estimating the noise of portfolio optimization weights for both Markowitz optimization and the HRP approach. Their comparison shows that the HRP is less noisy than the Markowitz and much more robust.

Another important part of the paper was devoted to a detailed analysis of the optimal portfolio variance. For practical applications, only the *out-of-sample* setup has value. In this way, we derived the portfolio variance analytical formulas and theoretically demonstrated the superiority of the HRP w.r.t to the Markowitz optimization. The analytics were calculated in a higher order of the number of timesteps, which provided an excellent approximation quality. We confirmed the theoretical results using multiple numerical experiments based on Monte Carlo simulations.

Apart from the theoretical evidence of the HRP superiority w.r.t to the Markowitz, we have addressed direct practical outcomes of our analytics. The first one was a fast estimation of the *confidence level* of the optimization weights calculated for a single (real-life) scenario. Indeed, given the number of timesteps in the covariance matrix estimation, we are able to validate the result out of the noise. The second practical usefulness of the analytics was an HRP portfolio construction criterion that selects assets and clusters minimizing the analytical portfolio variance.

We are grateful to our ADIA colleagues, especially to Adil Reghai, for stimulating discussions.

APPENDIX

A. Expected noise for the Markowitz weights.

As shown in the main body of the paper (3.8), the noise of the weights is

$$\Delta w \approx (1 - \bar{w}\, a^T)\, V^{-1}\, \Delta V\, \bar{w}$$

Below we will calculate the covariance $\mathbb{E}\left[\Delta w\, \Delta w^T\right]$, which depends on the following expectation

$$\mathbb{E}\left[\Delta V\, \bar{w}\, \bar{w}^T\, \Delta V\right].$$

For this we will use a general formula for an arbitrary matrix M

$$\mathbb{E}\left[\Delta V M \Delta V\right] = \frac{1}{N_T}\left(\mathbb{E}\left[X X^T (X^T M X)\right] - \bar{V} M \bar{V}\right)$$

which can be proven as follows

$$\begin{aligned}
\sum_{k,n} \mathbb{E}\left[\Delta V_{ik}\, M_{kn}\, \Delta V_{nj}\right] &= \frac{1}{N_T^2} \sum_{k,n,p,p'} \mathbb{E}\left[(X_{ip}\, X_{kp} - \mathbb{E}\left[X_i\, X_k\right])\, M_{kn}\, (X_{np'}\, X_{jp'} - \mathbb{E}\left[X_n\, X_j\right])\right] \\
&= \frac{1}{N_T^2} \sum_{k,n,p} \mathbb{E}\left[(X_{ip}\, X_{kp} - \mathbb{E}\left[X_i\, X_k\right])\, M_{kn}\, (X_{np}\, X_{jp} - \mathbb{E}\left[X_n\, X_j\right])\right] \\
&= \frac{1}{N_T} \sum_{k,n} \mathbb{E}\left[(X_i\, X_k - \mathbb{E}\left[X_i\, X_k\right])\, M_{kn}\, (X_n\, X_j - \mathbb{E}\left[X_n\, X_j\right])\right] \\
&= \frac{1}{N_T} \sum_{k,n} \mathbb{E}\left[X_i\, X_k\, M_{kn}\, X_n\, X_j\right] - \frac{1}{N_T} \sum_{k,n} \mathbb{E}\left[X_i\, X_k\right]\, M_{kn}\, \mathbb{E}\left[X_n\, X_j\right] \\
&= \frac{1}{N_T}\left(\mathbb{E}\left[X_i\, X_j\, (X^T M X)\right] - (\bar{V} M \bar{V})_{ij}\right)
\end{aligned}$$

For our concrete case of $M = \bar{w}\, \bar{w}^T$ we obtain

$$\mathbb{E}\left[\Delta V\, \bar{w}\, \bar{w}^T\, \Delta V\right] = \frac{1}{N_T}\left(\mathbb{E}\left[X X^T (\bar{w}^T\, X)^2\right] - \frac{1}{N_T}\, \bar{V}\, \bar{w}\, \bar{w}^T\, \bar{V}\right)$$

which gives the covariance of the weights noise

$$\begin{aligned}
\mathbb{E}\left[\Delta w\, \Delta w^T\right] &\approx \frac{1}{N_T}(1 - \bar{w}\, a^T)\left(\mathbb{E}\left[\bar{V}^{-1}\, X X^T\, \bar{V}^{-1}\, (\bar{w}^T X)^2\right] - \bar{w}\, \bar{w}^T\right)(1 - a\, \bar{w}^T) \\
&= \frac{1}{N_T}(1 - \bar{w}\, a^T)\, \mathbb{E}\left[\bar{V}^{-1}\, X X^T\, \bar{V}^{-1}\, (\bar{w}^T X)^2\right](1 - a\, \bar{w}^T)
\end{aligned} \qquad \text{(A.1)}$$

where the second equality is based on the weights constraint $a^T\, \bar{w} = 1$.

The noise covariance depends on *4-points averages* $\mathbb{E}\left[X_n\, X_m\, X_i\, X_j\right]$. Let us diagonalize the covariance matrix

$$\bar{V} = A\, A^T$$

so that each return

$$X_n = \sum_{n'} A_{nn'}\, Z_{n'}$$

for normalized Z's, $I = \mathbb{E}\left[ZZ^T\right]$. Their 4-points averages are simply

$$\mathbb{E}\left[Z_n Z_m Z_i Z_j\right] = \delta_{nm}\,\delta_{ij} + \delta_{ni}\,\delta_{mj} + \delta_{nj}\,\delta_{mi} + (\mathbb{E}\left[Z_n^4\right] - 3)\,\delta_{nm}\,\delta_{mi}\,\delta_{ij}$$

Coming back to our correlated X's 4-points, we have

$$\mathbb{E}\left[X_n X_m X_i X_j\right] = \bar{V}_{nm}\,\bar{V}_{ij} + \bar{V}_{ni}\,\bar{V}_{mj} + \bar{V}_{nj}\,\bar{V}_{mi} + (\mathbb{E}\left[Z_n^4\right] - 3)\sum_{n'} A_{nn'}\,A_{mn'}\,A_{in'}\,A_{jn'} \quad \text{(A.2)}$$

where the last (smaller) term contains much less summations than the main first three ones. Now, let us come to our main average (A.1), which can be expressed as

$$\begin{aligned}\mathbb{E}\left[\bar{V}^{-1}\,XX^T\,\bar{V}^{-1}\,(\bar{w}^T X)^2\right]_{nm} &= \sum_{'} \bar{V}^{-1}_{nm'}\,\bar{V}^{-1}_{k'm}\,\bar{w}_{j'}\,\bar{w}_{q'}\,\mathbb{E}\left[X_{m'}\,X_{k'}\,X_{j'}\,X_{q'}\right]\\ &= \bar{V}^{-1}_{nm}\,(\bar{w}^T\,\bar{V}\,\bar{w}) + 2\,\bar{w}_n\,\bar{w}_m\\ &\quad + (\mathbb{E}\left[Z_n^4\right] - 3)\sum_{n'}(\bar{V}^{-1}A)_{nn'}\,(\bar{V}^{-1}A)_{mn'}\,(a^T\,\bar{V}^{-1}A)^2_{n'}\end{aligned}$$

In what follows we will assume the Gaussian nature of the returns, which permits us to ignore the last term: it is exactly zero for Gaussian Z's. Given the above, we can easily derive a compact expression for the noise matrix[d]

$$\mathbb{E}\left[\Delta w\,\Delta w^T\right] \approx \frac{1}{N_T}(1 - \bar{w}\,a^T)\left(\frac{\bar{V}^{-1}}{\Omega} + 2\bar{w}\,\bar{w}^T\right)(1 - a\,\bar{w}^T) = \frac{1}{N_T}\left(\frac{\bar{V}^{-1}}{\Omega} - w\,w^T\right) \quad \text{(A.3)}$$

where Ω is the following quadratic form

$$\Omega = a^T\,\overline{V}^{-1}\,a = \frac{1}{\overline{w}^T\,\overline{V}\,\overline{w}}.$$

Similarly, we can derive a useful general formula

$$\mathbb{E}\left[\Delta V M \Delta V\right] = \frac{1}{N_T}\left(\bar{V}\,\mathrm{Tr}(\bar{V}M) + \bar{V}M^T\,\bar{V}\right)$$

valid for the Gaussian case which we will use in the main body of the paper.

B. The total noise for the HRP.

In this appendix, we derive the expected noise formula for the HRP. Let us start with its off-block part.

Off-block noise for the HRP. Denote diagonal block quantities with a subscript B : K_B is the diagonal part of the clusters' covariance matrix

$$\left(K_B^{-1}\right)_{hq} = \delta_{hq}\,\Omega_h$$

[d]We have used again $a^T\,\bar{w} = 1$.

The corresponding cluster weights read

$$\left(\xi_B\right)_h = \frac{\left(K_B^{-1}\,\iota\right)_h}{\iota^T K_B^{-1}\,\iota} = \frac{\Omega_h}{\Omega} \tag{B.1}$$

where $\Omega = \sum_h \Omega_h$. The off-diagonal noise in the ξ-weights, which we denote as

$$\delta\xi \equiv \xi - \xi_B,$$

corresponds to "Monte Carlo movements" of the clusters' covariance matrix out of its block diagonal

$$\delta K \equiv K - K_B$$

Applying the formula (3.8) to the optimal cluster weights ξ_B gives the noise

$$\delta\xi \approx -\left(I - \xi_B\,\iota^T\right) K_B{}^{-1}\delta K\,\xi_B$$

which comes from the Monte Carlo noise of the covariance matrix

$$\delta K_{hq} = 1_{h\neq q} w^{(h)^T}\,\delta V^{(h,q)} w^{(q)} \tag{B.2}$$

where

$$\left(\delta V^{(h,q)}\right)_{nm} = \frac{1}{N_T}\sum_{p=1}^{N_T} Y_{n,p}^{(h)}\,Y_{m,p}^{(q)}$$

Thus, the off-diagonal noise of the final weights $u^{(h)} = \xi_h\,w^{(h)}$ is only due to that inside ξ's

$$\delta u^{(h)} = w^{(h)}\,\delta\xi_h = -w^{(h)}\sum_{rq}\left(\delta_{hr} - \frac{\Omega_h}{\Omega}\right)\Omega_r\,\delta K_{rq}\,\frac{\Omega_q}{\Omega} \tag{B.3}$$

$$= -w^{(h)}\sum_{r\neq q}\left(\delta_{hr} - \frac{\Omega_h}{\Omega}\right)\frac{\Omega_r\,\Omega_q}{\Omega}\,w^{(r)^T}\,\delta V^{(r,q)} w^{(q)} \tag{B.4}$$

The cluster optimization noise[e] depends on a quadratic form expectation of the matrix δV

$$\begin{aligned}\mathcal{N}'_C &\equiv \sum_h \mathbb{E}\left[\delta u^{(h)^T}\,\delta u^{(h)}\right]\\ &\approx \sum_h w^{(h)^T}\,w^{(h)}\sum_{r\neq q}\sum_{r'\neq q'}\left(\delta_{hr} - \frac{\Omega_h}{\Omega}\right)\left(\delta_{hr'} - \frac{\Omega_h}{\Omega}\right)\frac{\Omega_r\,\Omega_q}{\Omega}\,\frac{\Omega_{r'}\,\Omega_{q'}}{\Omega}\\ &\times\, w^{(r)^T}\,\mathbb{E}\left[\delta V^{(r,q)}\,w^{(q)}\,w^{(r')^T}\,\delta V^{(r',q')}\right] w^{(q')}\end{aligned}$$

[e]The prime symbol in the notations corresponds to the off-block part.

The underlying expectation can be rewritten as

$$
\begin{aligned}
&\mathbb{E}\left[w^{(r)^T}\,\delta V^{(r,q)}\,w^{(q)}\,w^{(r')^T}\,\delta V^{(r',q')}w^{(q')}\right]\delta_{r\neq q}\,\delta_{r'\neq q'}\\
&=\frac{1}{N_T}\mathbb{E}\left[w^{(r)^T}\,Y^{(r)}\,Y^{(q)^T}\,w^{(q)}\,w^{(r')^T}\,Y^{(r')}\,Y^{(q')^T}\,w^{(q')}\right]\delta_{r\neq q}\,\delta_{r'\neq q'}\\
&=\frac{1}{N_T}\mathbb{E}\left[w^{(r)^T}\,Y^{(r)}\,Y^{(r')^T}\,w^{(r')}\right]\mathbb{E}\left[w^{(q)^T}\,Y^{(q)}\,Y^{(q')^T}\,w^{(q')}\right]\delta_{r=r'}\,\delta_{q=q'}\,\delta_{r\neq q}\,\delta_{r'\neq q'}\\
&\quad+\frac{1}{N_T}\mathbb{E}\left[w^{(r)^T}\,Y^{(r)}\,Y^{(q')^T}\,w^{(q')}\right]\mathbb{E}\left[w^{(q)^T}\,Y^{(q)}\,Y^{(r')^T}\,w^{(r')}\right]\delta_{r=q'}\,\delta_{q=r'}\,\delta_{r\neq q}\,\delta_{r'\neq q'}\\
&=\frac{1}{N_T}\mathbb{E}\left[w^{(r)^T}\,Y^{(r)}\,Y^{(r)^T}\,w^{(r)}\right]\mathbb{E}\left[w^{(q)^T}\,Y^{(q)}\,Y^{(q)^T}\,w^{(q)}\right]\left(\delta_{r=r'}\,\delta_{q=q'}+\delta_{r=q'}\,\delta_{q=r'}\right)\delta_{r\neq q}\,\delta_{r'\neq q'}\\
&\simeq\frac{1}{N_T}\Omega_r^{-1}\,\Omega_q^{-1}\left(\delta_{r=r'}\,\delta_{q=q'}+\delta_{r=q'}\,\delta_{q=r'}\right)\delta_{r\neq q}\,\delta_{r'\neq q'}
\end{aligned}
$$

where we have used

$$
\mathbb{E}\left[w^{(r)^T}\,Y^{(r)}\,Y^{(r)^T}\,w^{(r)}\right]=\mathbb{E}\left[w^{(r)^T}\,\bar{V}^{(r)}\,w^{(r)}\right]\simeq\Omega_r^{-1}
$$

and approximated $\bar{V}^{(r)}$ with $V^{(r)}+O(N_T^{-1})$. Inserting it into the formula for N'_C we obtain

$$
\begin{aligned}
\mathcal{N}'_C&\approx\frac{1}{N_T}\sum_h w^{(h)^T}\,w^{(h)}\sum_{r\neq q}\sum_{r'\neq q'}\left(\delta_{hr}-\frac{\Omega_h}{\Omega}\right)\left(\delta_{hr'}-\frac{\Omega_h}{\Omega}\right)\frac{\Omega_r\,\Omega_q}{\Omega}\,\frac{\Omega_{r'}\,\Omega_{q'}}{\Omega}\\
&\quad\times\Omega_r^{-1}\,\Omega_q^{-1}\left(\delta_{r=r'}\,\delta_{q=q'}+\delta_{r=q'}\,\delta_{q=r'}\right)\\
&=\frac{1}{N_T}\sum_h w^{(h)^T}\,w^{(h)}\sum_{r\neq q}\left(\delta_{hr}-\frac{\Omega_h}{\Omega}\right)^2\frac{\Omega_r\,\Omega_q}{\Omega}\,\frac{\Omega_r\,\Omega_q}{\Omega}\Omega_r^{-1}\,\Omega_q^{-1}\\
&\quad+\frac{1}{N_T}\sum_h w^{(h)^T}\,w^{(h)}\sum_{r\neq q}\left(\delta_{hr}-\frac{\Omega_h}{\Omega}\right)\left(\delta_{hq}-\frac{\Omega_h}{\Omega}\right)\frac{\Omega_r\,\Omega_q}{\Omega}\,\frac{\Omega_q\,\Omega_r}{\Omega}\Omega_r^{-1}\,\Omega_q^{-1}\\
&=\frac{1}{N_T}\sum_h w^{(h)^T}\,w^{(h)}\sum_{r\neq q}\left(\delta_{hr}-\frac{\Omega_h}{\Omega}\right)\left(\delta_{hq}+\delta_{hr}-2\frac{\Omega_h}{\Omega}\right)\frac{\Omega_r\,\Omega_q}{\Omega^2}\\
&=\frac{1}{N_T}\sum_h w^{(h)^T}\,w^{(h)}\sum_{r\neq q}\left(\delta_{hr}-\frac{\Omega_h}{\Omega}\left(3\delta_{hr}+\delta_{hq}\right)+2\left(\frac{\Omega_h}{\Omega}\right)^2\right)\frac{\Omega_r\,\Omega_q}{\Omega^2}\\
&=\frac{1}{N_T}\sum_h w^{(h)^T}\,w^{(h)}\sum_{r,q}\left(\delta_{hr}-\frac{\Omega_h}{\Omega}\left(3\delta_{hr}+\delta_{hq}\right)+2\left(\frac{\Omega_h}{\Omega}\right)^2\right)\frac{\Omega_r\,\Omega_q}{\Omega^2}\\
&\quad-\frac{1}{N_T}\sum_h w^{(h)^T}\,w^{(h)}\sum_r\left(\delta_{hr}-4\frac{\Omega_h}{\Omega}\,\delta_{hr}+2\left(\frac{\Omega_h}{\Omega}\right)^2\right)\frac{\Omega_r^2}{\Omega^2}
\end{aligned}
$$

$$= \frac{1}{N_T} \sum_h w^{(h)^T} w^{(h)} \left(\frac{\Omega_h}{\Omega} - 4\left(\frac{\Omega_h}{\Omega}\right)^2 + 2\left(\frac{\Omega_h}{\Omega}\right)^2 \right)$$

$$- \frac{1}{N_T} \sum_h w^{(h)^T} w^{(h)} \left(\frac{\Omega_h^2}{\Omega^2} - 4\frac{\Omega_h^3}{\Omega^3} + 2\left(\frac{\Omega_h}{\Omega}\right)^2 \sum_r \frac{\Omega_r^2}{\Omega^2} \right)$$

$$= \frac{1}{N_T} \sum_h w^{(h)^T} w^{(h)} \left(\frac{\Omega_h}{\Omega} - 3\left(\frac{\Omega_h}{\Omega}\right)^2 + 4\frac{\Omega_h^3}{\Omega^3} - 2\left(\frac{\Omega_h}{\Omega}\right)^2 \sum_r \frac{\Omega_r^2}{\Omega^2} \right)$$

Finally, using $\Omega_h^2 \, w^{(h)^T} w^{(h)} = a^{(h)^T} \, V^{(h)^{-2}} \, a^{(h)}$ we obtain the off-block clustered optimization noise

$$\mathcal{N}'_C \simeq \frac{1}{N_T} \frac{1}{\Omega} \sum_h \frac{a^{(h)^T} \, V^{(h)^{-2}} \, a^{(h)}}{\Omega_h} \left(1 - 3\frac{\Omega_h}{\Omega} + 4\frac{\Omega_h^2}{\Omega^2} - 2\frac{\Omega_h}{\Omega} \sum_r \frac{\Omega_r^2}{\Omega^2} \right) \tag{B.5}$$

Next, if order to prove that the HRP is less noisy than the classical Markowitz, we pass to the off-block noise calculations for the latter.

Off-block noise for the Markowitz optimization. To get the Markowitz *off-block* noise, we proceed as follows: instead of expanding around the exact covariance matrix $\bar{V}$ (as in Section 3.2) we will expand around the *block* matrix V_B. To do it, we simply replace everywhere $\bar{V}$ by V_B and $\bar{w}$ by w_B defined by Eq. (3.3)

$$w_B = \frac{V_B^{-1} \, a}{a^T \, V_B^{-1} \, a} \tag{B.6}$$

It is easy to see that these "block" weights coincide with the cluster-optimization weights with the block ξ's (B.1)

$$\left(\xi_{B1} \, w_1^{(1)} \cdots \xi_{B1} w_{N_1}^{(1)} \mid \cdots \mid \xi_{BH} w_1^{(H)}, \cdots, \xi_{BH} w_{N_H}^{(H)} \right)$$

so that

$$w_B^{(h)} = w^{(h)} \, \frac{\Omega_h}{\Omega}$$

The noise of the Markowitz weights over w_B can be calculated as in Eq. (3.8)

$$w - w_B \equiv \delta w_B \approx -(I - w_B \, a^T) \, V_B^{-1} \, \delta V_B \, w_B \tag{B.7}$$

For a cluster h we have

$$\delta w_B^{(h)} \approx \sum_{r' \neq q'} - \left(\delta_{hr'} - w^{(h)} \, a^{(r')^T} \frac{\Omega_h}{\Omega} \right) \, V^{(r')^{-1}} \, \delta V^{(r',q')} \, w^{(q')} \frac{\Omega_{q'}}{\Omega}$$

Then, to calculate the expectation $\mathbb{E}\left[\delta w_B^{(h)^T}\delta w_B^{(h)}\right]$ we notice that

$$\mathbb{E}\left[\delta V^{(r,q)^T} M\,\delta V^{(r',q')}\right]_{nm}\delta_{r\neq q}\,\delta_{r'\neq q'} = \frac{1}{N_T}\mathbb{E}\left[\left(Y^{(r)}\,Y^{(q)^T}\right)^T M\,Y^{(r')}\,Y^{(q')^T}\right]_{nm}\delta_{r\neq q}\,\delta_{r'\neq q'}$$
$$= \frac{1}{N_T}\sum_{n',m'}\mathbb{E}\left[Y_{n'}^{(r)}\,Y_n^{(q)}\,M_{n',m'}\,Y_{m'}^{(r')}\,Y_m^{(q')}\right]\delta_{r\neq q}\,\delta_{r'\neq q'}$$
$$= \frac{1}{N_T}\sum_{n',m'}\mathbb{E}\left[Y_{n'}^{(r)}\,Y_{m'}^{(r')}\right]M_{n',m'}\,\mathbb{E}\left[Y_n^{(q)}\,Y_m^{(q')}\right]\delta_{r=r'}\,\delta_{q=q'}\,\delta_{r\neq q}\,\delta_{r'\neq q'}$$
$$+\frac{1}{N_T}\sum_{n',m'}\mathbb{E}\left[Y_{n'}^{(r)}\,Y_m^{(q')}\right]M_{n',m'}\,\mathbb{E}\left[Y_{m'}^{(r')}Y_n^{(q)}\right]\delta_{r=q'}\,\delta_{q=r'}\,\delta_{r\neq q}\,\delta_{r'\neq q'}$$
$$= \frac{1}{N_T}\sum_{n',m'}\mathbb{E}\left[Y_{n'}^{(r)}\,Y_{m'}^{(r)}\right]M_{n',m'}\,\mathbb{E}\left[Y_n^{(q)}\,Y_m^{(q)}\right]\delta_{r=r'}\,\delta_{q=q'}\,\delta_{r\neq q}\,\delta_{r'\neq q'}$$
$$+\frac{1}{N_T}\sum_{n',m'}\mathbb{E}\left[Y_{n'}^{(r)}\,Y_m^{(r)}\right]M_{n',m'}\,\mathbb{E}\left[Y_{m'}^{(q)}Y_n^{(q)}\right]\delta_{r=q'}\,\delta_{q=r'}\,\delta_{r\neq q}\,\delta_{r'\neq q'}$$
$$\simeq \frac{1}{N_T}\sum_{n',m'}V_{n',m'}^{(r)}\,M_{n',m'}\,V_{n,m}^{(q)}\delta_{r=r'}\,\delta_{q=q'}\,\delta_{r\neq q}\,\delta_{r'\neq q'} + \frac{1}{N_T}\sum_{n',m'}V_{n'm}^{(r)}\,M_{n',m'}\,V_{m',n}^{(q)}\delta_{r=q'}\,\delta_{q=r'}$$
$$\delta_{r\neq q}\,\delta_{r'\neq q'}$$
$$= \frac{1}{N_T}\mathrm{tr}\left(MV^{(r)}\right)V_{n,m}^{(q)}\,\delta_{r=r'}\,\delta_{q=q'}\,\delta_{r\neq q}\,\delta_{r'\neq q'} + \frac{1}{N_T}\left(V^{(q)}M^T\,V^{(r)}\right)_{n,m}\delta_{r=q'}\,\delta_{q=r'}\,\delta_{r\neq q}\,\delta_{r'\neq q'}$$

It follows that

$$\mathcal{N}'_M = \sum_h \mathbb{E}\left[\delta w_B^{(h)^T}\,\delta w_B^{(h)}\right] = \sum_h\sum_{r\neq q}\sum_{r'\neq q'}\frac{\Omega_q\Omega_{q'}}{\Omega^2}$$
$$\times w^{(q)^T}\mathbb{E}\left[\delta V^{(r,q)^T}\,V^{(r)^{-1}}\left(\delta_{hr} - a^{(r)}w^{(h)^T}\frac{\Omega_h}{\Omega}\right)\left(\delta_{hr'} - w^{(h)}\,a^{(r')^T}\frac{\Omega_h}{\Omega}\right)\right.$$
$$\left.V^{(r')^{-1}}\,\delta V^{(r',q')}\right]w^{(q')}$$
$$= \sum_h\sum_{r\neq q}\sum_{r'\neq q'}\frac{\Omega_q\Omega_{q'}}{\Omega^2}w^{(q)^T}\mathbb{E}\left[\delta V^{(r,q)^T}\,M^{(h,r,r')}\,\delta V^{(r',q')}\right]w^{(q')}$$

where we have denoted the matrix M as

$$M^{(h,r,q)} = V^{(r)^{-1}}\left(\delta_{hr} - a^{(r)}w^{(h)^T}\frac{\Omega_h}{\Omega}\right)\left(\delta_{hq} - w^{(h)}\,a^{(q)^T}\frac{\Omega_h}{\Omega}\right)V^{(q)^{-1}}$$

Next, we have

$$\mathcal{N}'_M \simeq \frac{1}{N_T}\sum_h\sum_{r\neq q}\sum_{r'\neq q'}\frac{\Omega_q\Omega_{q'}}{\Omega^2}w^{(q)^T}\left(\mathrm{tr}\left(M^{(h,r,r')}V^{(r)}\right)V^{(q)}\,\delta_{r=r'}\,\delta_{q=q'}\right.$$
$$\left.+\left(V^{(q)}M^{(h,r,r')^T}\,V^{(r)}\right)\delta_{r=q'}\;\delta_{q=r'}\right)w^{(q')}$$
$$= \frac{1}{N_T}\sum_h\sum_{r\neq q}\sum_{r'\neq q'}\frac{\Omega_q\Omega_{q'}}{\Omega^2}w^{(q)^T}\mathrm{tr}\left(M^{(h,r,r')}V^{(r)}\right)V^{(q)}\,\delta_{r=r'}\,\delta_{q=q'}w^{(q')}$$
$$+\frac{1}{N_T}\sum_h\sum_{r\neq q}\sum_{r'\neq q'}\frac{\Omega_q\Omega_{q'}}{\Omega^2}w^{(q)^T}\left(V^{(q)}M^{(h,r,r')^T}\,V^{(r)}\right)\delta_{r=q'}\,\delta_{q=r'}w^{(q')}$$

$$
\begin{aligned}
&= \frac{1}{N_T}\sum_h \sum_{r\neq q} \frac{\Omega_q^2}{\Omega^2}\mathrm{tr}\left(M^{(h,r,r)}V^{(r)}\right) w^{(q)^T} V^{(q)}\, w^{(q)} \\
&+ \frac{1}{N_T}\sum_h \sum_{r\neq q} \frac{\Omega_q\Omega_r}{\Omega^2} w^{(q)^T}\left(V^{(q)}M^{(h,r,q)^T}\, V^{(r)}\right) w^{(r)} \\
&= \frac{1}{N_T}\sum_h \sum_{r\neq q} \frac{\Omega_q^2}{\Omega^2}\mathrm{tr}\left(V^{(r)^{-1}}\left(\delta_{hr} - a^{(r)}w^{(h)^T}\frac{\Omega_h}{\Omega}\right)\left(\delta_{hr} - w^{(h)}\, a^{(r)^T}\frac{\Omega_h}{\Omega}\right)\right)\frac{1}{\Omega_q} \\
&+ \frac{1}{N_T}\sum_h \sum_{r\neq q} \frac{\Omega_q\Omega_r}{\Omega^2} w^{(r)^T}\left(V^{(r)}M^{(h,r,q)}\, V^{(q)}\right) w^{(q)}
\end{aligned}
$$

Finally, expanding the product we obtain

$$
\begin{aligned}
\mathcal{N}'_M &\simeq \frac{1}{N_T}\sum_h \sum_{r\neq q} \frac{\Omega_q}{\Omega^2}\mathrm{tr}\left(V^{(r)^{-1}}\left(\delta_{hr} - \delta_{hr}a^{(r)}w^{(h)^T}\frac{\Omega_h}{\Omega} - \delta_{hr}w^{(h)}\, a^{(r)^T}\frac{\Omega_h}{\Omega}\right.\right. \\
&\quad \left.\left. + a^{(r)}w^{(h)^T}\, w^{(h)}\, a^{(r)^T}\frac{\Omega_h^2}{\Omega^2}\right)\right) \\
&+ \frac{1}{N_T}\sum_h \sum_{r\neq q} \frac{\Omega_q\Omega_r}{\Omega^2} w^{(r)^T}\left(\delta_{hr} - a^{(r)}w^{(h)^T}\frac{\Omega_h}{\Omega}\right)\left(\delta_{hq} - w^{(h)}\, a^{(q)^T}\frac{\Omega_h}{\Omega}\right) w^{(q)} \\
&= \frac{1}{N_T}\sum_h \sum_{r\neq q} \frac{\Omega_q}{\Omega^2}\left(\delta_{hr}\left(\mathrm{tr}\left(V^{(r)^{-1}}\right) - 2\frac{a^{(h)^T}\, V^{(h)^{-2}}\, a^{(h)}}{\Omega}\right) + \frac{a^{(h)^T}\, V^{(h)^{-2}}\, a^{(h)}}{\Omega}\frac{\Omega_r}{\Omega}\right) \\
&+ \frac{1}{N_T}\sum_h \sum_{r\neq q} \frac{\Omega_q\Omega_r}{\Omega^2}\left(-\delta_{hr} - \delta_{hq} + \frac{\Omega_h}{\Omega}\right)\frac{a^{(h)^T}\, V^{(h)^{-2}}\, a^{(h)}}{\Omega}\frac{1}{\Omega_h} \\
&= \frac{1}{N_T}\sum_h \sum_{r\neq q} \frac{\Omega_q}{\Omega^2}\left(\delta_{hr}\mathrm{tr}\left(V^{(h)^{-1}}\right) + \left(-2\delta_{hr} + \frac{\Omega_r}{\Omega}\right)\frac{a^{(h)^T}\, V^{(h)^{-2}}\, a^{(h)}}{\Omega}\right) \\
&+ \frac{1}{N_T}\sum_h \frac{a^{(h)^T}\, V^{(h)^{-2}}\, a^{(h)}}{\Omega}\sum_{r\neq q} \frac{\Omega_q\Omega_r}{\Omega^2}\left(\ 2\delta_{hr} + \frac{\Omega_h}{\Omega}\right)\frac{a^{(h)^T}\, V^{(h)^{-2}}\, a^{(h)}}{\Omega}\frac{1}{\Omega_h}
\end{aligned}
$$

$$
\begin{aligned}
&= \frac{1}{N_T}\sum_h \sum_{q\neq h} \frac{\Omega_q}{\Omega^2}\mathrm{tr}\left(V^{(h)^{-1}}\right) + \frac{1}{N_T}\sum_h \frac{a^{(h)^T}\, V^{(h)^{-2}}\, a^{(h)}}{\Omega}\sum_{r\neq q}\left(-4\delta_{hr}\frac{\Omega_q}{\Omega^2} + 2\frac{\Omega_q\Omega_r}{\Omega^3}\right) \\
&= \frac{1}{N_T}\frac{1}{\Omega}\sum_h \mathrm{tr}\left(V^{(h)^{-1}}\right)\left(1 - \frac{\Omega_h}{\Omega}\right) - 2\frac{1}{N_T}\frac{1}{\Omega}\sum_h \frac{a^{(h)^T}\, V^{(h)^{-2}}\, a^{(h)}}{\Omega}\left(1 - 2\frac{\Omega_h}{\Omega} + 2\sum_q \frac{\Omega_q^2}{\Omega^2}\right)
\end{aligned}
\tag{B.8}
$$

The total noise for the HRP optimization. The total noise inside the clustered optimization weights

$$
u^{(h)} = \xi_h\, w^{(h)}
$$

can be decomposed (in the first order) as follows

$$\begin{aligned}\Delta u^{(h)} &= u^{(h)} - \bar{u}^{(h)} = \left((\xi_B)_h + \delta\xi_h\right) w^{(h)} - \bar{u}^{(h)} \simeq \left((\xi_B)_h\, w^{(h)} - \bar{u}^{(h)}\right) + \delta\xi_h\, \bar{w}^{\,(h)} \\ &= \Delta\left((\xi_B)_h\, w^{(h)}\right) + \delta\xi_h\, \bar{w}^{\,(h)}\end{aligned}$$

where $\Delta\left((\xi_B)_h\, w^{(h)}\right)$ is the block-diagonal noise.

Using the theoretical values of the weights (denoted with the bar symbol)

$$\left(\bar{\xi}_B\right)_h = \frac{\bar{\Omega}_h}{\bar{\Omega}} \quad \text{and} \quad \bar{w}^{(h)} = \frac{\bar{V}^{(h)^{-1}}\, a^{(h)}}{a^{(h)^T}\, \bar{V}^{(h)^{-1}}\, a^{(h)}}$$

permits us to calculate the *full* theoretical clustered optimization weights

$$\bar{u}^{(h)} = \frac{\bar{V}^{(h)^{-1}}\, a^{(h)}}{\bar{\Omega}}$$

We immediately see that they coincide with the Markowitz ones (3.7), that is,

$$\overline{u} = \overline{w}.$$

As we have seen above, the off-block and diagonal-block noises are independent, so that their expectations can be summed up

$$\mathbb{E}\left[\Delta u^{(h)^T}\, \Delta u^{(h)}\right] = \mathbb{E}\left[\delta\xi_h\, \bar{w}^{\,(h)^T}\, \bar{w}^{\,(h)}\, \delta\xi_h\right] + \mathbb{E}\left[\Delta\left((\xi_B)_h\, w^{(h)}\right)^T \Delta\left((\xi_B)_h\, w^{(h)}\right)\right]$$

Although we can calculate directly the diagonal-block expectation

$$\mathbb{E}\left[\Delta\left((\xi_B)_h\, w^{(h)}\right)^T \Delta\left((\xi_B)_h\, w^{(h)}\right)\right] \tag{B.9}$$

it will be simpler to derive it from the similar block/off-block decomposition for the standard Markowitz optimization. Namely, we decompose the Markowitz noise into two parts.

$$\Delta w = w - \bar{w} = w - w_B + w_B - \bar{w} = \delta w_B + \Delta w_B$$

As in the clustered case, these noises are independent, and their variances can be treated separately. Indeed, we have already calculated the off-block noise $\mathbb{E}\left[\delta w_B^T\, \delta w_B\right]$ in Eq. (B.8) as well as the total noise (3.11). Thus, the diagonal-block noise can be obtained by subtraction of Eq. (B.8) from Eq. (3.21).

$$\mathbb{E}\left[\Delta w_B^T\, \Delta w_B\right] \approx \frac{1}{N_T}\frac{1}{\Omega}\left(\sum_h \operatorname{tr}\left(V^{(h)^{-1}}\right)\frac{\Omega_h}{\Omega} + \sum_h \frac{a^{(h)^T}\, V^{(h)^{-2}}\, a^{(h)}}{\Omega}\left(1 - 4\frac{\Omega_h}{\Omega} + 2\sum_q \frac{\Omega_q^2}{\Omega^2}\right)\right)$$

As we mentioned, it coincides with the HRP diagonal-block noise (B.9), such that the final formula for the total HRP noise (3.19) can be obtained by summing up the diagonal-block noise and the off-diagonal one (B.5).

References

1. H. Markowitz, Portfolio selection, *J. Finance*. **7**, 77–91 (1952).
2. B. de Finetti, Il problema dei "Pieni", *Giorn. Ist. Ital. Attuar*. **11**, 1–88 (1940); (translation " L. Barone, The problem of full-risk insurances. Chapter I. The risk within a single accounting period, *J. Invest. Manag*. **4**(3), 19–43 (2006)).
3. F. Pressacco and P. Serafini, The origins of the mean-variance approach in finance: Revisiting de Finetti 65 years later, *Decis. Econ. Finance*. **30**, 19–49 (2007).
4. M. L. de Prado, Building diversified portfolios that outperform out of sample, *J. Portf. Manag*. **42**(4) 59–69 (2016).
5. V. Marchenko and L. Pastur, Distribution of eigenvalues for some sets of random matrices, *Mat. Sb*. **114**(4), 507–536 (1967).
6. M. L. de Prado, *Machine Learning for Asset Managers: Cambridge Elements in Quantitative Finance*. Cambridge University Press (2020).
7. M. L. de Prado, A Robust Estimator of the Efficient Frontier (2016). Available at SSRN: https://ssrn.com/abstract=3469961

https://doi.org/10.1142/9789819813049_0004

CHAPTER 4 A Statistical Learning Approach to Local Volatility Calibration and Option Pricing

Vinicius V. L. Albani[1], Leonardo Sarmanho[2], and Jorge P. Zubelli[3,4,*]

[1] *Department of Mathematics, Federal University of Santa Catarina, Florianopolis, Brazil*
[2] *SPX Capital, Rio de Janeiro, Brazil*
[3] *Department of Mathematics, Khalifa University, Abu Dhabi, UAE*
[4] *ADIA Lab, Abu Dhabi, UAE*
[*] *Corresponding author. E-mail: jorge.zubelli@ku.ac.ae*

By combining Bayes' theorem and maximum entropy densities (MED), we propose an accurate and computationally efficient technique for European option pricing and local volatility calibration. The resulting data-driven technique avoids the solution of partial differential equations and the use of Monte Carlo methods. We also show that, under the proposed setting, the price of European options can be expressed as the average Black–Scholes option prices. Numerical examples with synthetic and real data illustrate the effectiveness of the pricing and estimation tools.

Keywords: Bayes Theorem, Maximum Entropy Density, Option Pricing, Local Volatility Model, Calibration.

4.1. Introduction

The local volatility model (LVM), introduced by Dupire [1], Derman and Kani [2], represents one of the most well-known generalizations of the Black–Scholes model [3] to price European vanilla options. The LVM assumes that the volatility of the asset price is a deterministic function of time and the asset itself, which allows the calibrated model to fit the so-called implied volatility smile of quoted call and put options.

One of the main difficulties of the LVM is its calibration from option prices. As pointed out in the literature, this is an ill-posed inverse problem, and many different regularization techniques were used in its solution [4–20]. Many of them rely on the numerical solution of a partial differential equation (PDE) combined with some estimation technique.

For example, in Refs. [4, 5], the authors proposed a multilevel approach for faster calibration. The generalized Black–Scholes PDE is solved by a least-squares finite-element formulation, and the inverse problem solution is given by Tikhonov-type regularization. In articles [6–10], different aspects of the calibration problem by Tikhonov-type regularization were investigated, such as finding a term structure for the local volatility surface, the data-driven simultaneous choice of the regularization parameter and the discretization level used in the PDE solution, the effect of including data by interpolation in the estimation, as well as sufficient conditions for the uniqueness of estimated local volatility surfaces.

The literature on stochastic models for asset prices is vast. It includes models under discrete-time and continuous-time settings, as well as continuous diffusion and jump-diffusion models. See Refs. [21, 22] and references therein. The bottleneck of sophisticated models is their calibration from observed data since the more terms to be estimated, the closer to under-determination the estimation becomes. Thus, although its ill-posedness, local volatility calibration still maintains a good compromise between model sophistication and model identifiability.

Since its introduction in the seminal works of Dupire and Derman, and Kani, local volatility calibration is still an important inverse problem in quantitative finance, and the search for a simple way to implement an accurate estimation procedure is still active (see, e.g., Refs. [23–26]). References [23] and [24] used deep learning techniques to address the estimation. References [17] and [19] studied the simultaneous calibration of local volatility and other parameters.

Some generalizations of the LVM and their calibration have received considerable attention, especially in recent years. For example, the jump-diffusion models with a local volatility term were studied in Refs. [27–31]. Stochastic LVMs, which add a stochastic component to the LVM, were considered, for example, in Refs. [32–35].

The aim of this work is to introduce a framework to calibrate the LVM using a simplified setup that is accurate and computationally efficient. It does not rely on the numerical solution of PDEs nor on Monte Carlo methods. The continuous-time asset price dynamics is approximated by a Markov chain using the Euler–Maruyama scheme [36], and the transition density is defined by the Bayes theorem. The marginal distributions of the states in the Markov chain are defined by the maximum entropy probability densities introduced in Neri and Schneider [37], which in turn is based on a deep circle of ideas that can be traced to Csiszar [38]. The resulting pricing formula is the weighted mean of Black–Scholes prices, with local volatility values in place of the constant Black–Scholes volatility. The estimation is performed by Tikhonov-type regularization [39], with the data misfit term measuring the discrepancy between quoted European option prices and the prices evaluated by the proposed model.

It is worth mentioning that in Cont [40], the Bayes theorem was used to account for model uncertainty in the calibration and in the pricing of derivatives. This is different from the proposed model, where the Bayes theorem is used to design the derivative pricing formula.

Furthermore, seminal contributions were introduced in the works of A. Itkin, A. Lipton, and A. Sepp [41-45], although with substantially different techniques from what we are considering here. More precisely, Lipton [41] discussed how the liquidity of both vanilla and exotic options in major Forex markets provides a valuable setting for testing volatility smile models. He also explored various models in this context and identified the ones that perform the best. Finally, he obtained an equation to calibrate the local volatility to the market which can be used after suitable numerical techniques to avoid instabilities. The work of Lipton and Sepp [43] described a robust and precise algorithm designed to calibrate a tiled local volatility model using sparse market data. The effectiveness of this algorithm was demonstrated through its application to a specific set of sparse market data. The result is a non-arbitrageable and well-behaved implied volatility surface for options on the SX5E index. An extension of the approach proposed by Lipton and Sepp [43] was developed in the work of Itkin and Lipton [44] by (i) replacing a piecewise constant local variance construction with a piecewise linear one, and (ii) allowing non-zero interest rates and dividend yields. See also the work of some the current authors [27,46] and references therein. The techniques are distinct from the ones employed herein.

The article is organized as follows: Section 4.2 presents the proposed derivative pricing technique. The maximum entropy density (MEP) approach from Ref. [37] is recalled in Section 4.3. In Section 4.4, we present the local volatility calibration tool. Section 4.5 presents a numerical illustration of the method. Concluding remarks are drawn in Section 4.6.

4.2. The Pricing Formulas

The present section is devoted to the development of a derivative pricing technique. For simplicity, the analysis is performed for European call options; however, it can be extended to any path-independent derivative with European exercise. To do that we use the classical stochastic process formalism [47] for financial assets.

Consider a filtered probability space $\left(\Omega, \mathcal{F}, \mathscr{F}, \widetilde{\mathbb{P}}\right)$, where $\mathscr{F} = \{\mathscr{F}\}_{t\geq 0}$ is a filtration and $\widetilde{\mathbb{P}}$ is the risk neutral probability measure. In this model, the stock price follows the stochastic differential equation (SDE):

$$dS_t = rS_t dt + \sigma(t, S_t)S_t d\widetilde{W}_t, \text{ with } t \in [0, T] \text{ and } S_0 \text{ known.} \tag{4.1}$$

with $\widetilde{W}$ a Brownian motion under $\widetilde{\mathbb{P}}$, r a constant risk-free interest rate, and $\sigma(t, S_t)$ the local volatility, a deterministic function of t and S_t. We assume that $\sigma(t, S_t)$ is bounded and sufficiently smooth, so the SDE problem in Eq. (4.1) has a unique strong solution [47].

For every $0 \leq s < t \leq T$, Eq. (4.1) can be rewritten as

$$S_t = S_s + r\int_s^t S_u du + \int_s^t \sigma(u, S_u)S_u \, d\widetilde{W}_u. \tag{4.2}$$

Assuming that t is "sufficiently close" to s, we consider the Euler–Maruyama approximation for the SDE solution:

$$\int_s^t \sigma(u, S_u)S_u d\widetilde{W}_u \approx \sigma(s, S_s)\int_s^t S_u \, d\widetilde{W}_u.$$

Hence, S_t can be approximated by

$$S_t \approx S_s \cdot \exp\left[\left(r - \frac{1}{2}\sigma(s, S_s)^2\right)(t-s) + \sigma(s, S_s)\left(\widetilde{W}_t - \widetilde{W}_s\right)\right].$$

Thus, given a partition of the interval $[0, T]$ into N sub-intervals of length $\Delta t := T/N$ and defining $t_n := n \cdot \Delta t$, $S_n := S_{t_n}$, $\sigma_n = \sigma(t_n, S_n)$, and $\widetilde{W}_n := \widetilde{W}_{t_n}$, we have

$$S_{n+1} = S_n \cdot \exp\left[\left(r - \frac{1}{2}\sigma_n^2\right)\Delta t + \sigma_n\left(\widetilde{W}_{n+1} - \widetilde{W}_n\right)\right]. \tag{4.3}$$

for $n = 0, 1, \ldots, N-1$. Thus, $\{(S_n)\}_{n=0}^N$ is a Markov chain.

The distribution of S_{n+1}, given S_n, is log-normal, that is,

$$\Pi(s_{n+1}|s_n) = \frac{1}{\sqrt{2\pi\Delta t}} \cdot \exp\left[-\frac{1}{2}\frac{\left(\log\left(\frac{s_{n+1}}{s_n}\right) - \left(r - \frac{1}{2}\sigma_n^2\right)\Delta t\right)^2}{\sigma_n^2 \Delta t}\right]. \tag{4.4}$$

The density $\Pi(s_{n+1}|s_n)$ denotes the passage density of the Markov chain $\{S_n\}_{n=0}^N$ from the nth step to the $(n+1)$th step.

Given an initial step s_0 for the chain, for each $n = 1, \ldots, N$, we denote the density of S_n by $\Pi(s_n, \sigma_n) = \Pi(s_n, |s_0)$. Then, by the Bayes formula [48, Section 3.1], the density of S_{n+1} can be obtained from $\Pi(s_n)$ and $\Pi(s_{n+1}|s_n)$ through the equation

$$\Pi(s_{n+1}) = \int_0^\infty \Pi(s_{n+1}|s_n)\Pi(s_n)ds_n, \tag{4.5}$$

where $s_n \geq 0$ for every n.

Let $C(t_{n+1}, K)$ denote the price of a European option with time to maturity $t_{n+1} = (n+1)\,\Delta t$ and strike K. Then, it is given by

$$C(t_{n+1}, K) = \mathrm{e}^{-r t_{n+1}} \int_0^\infty \max(0, s_{n+1} - K)\Pi(s_{n+1})\, ds_{n+1}. \tag{4.6}$$

From Eqs. (4.4) and (4.5) and Fubini's theorem, we have the following identities:

$$\begin{aligned} &C(t_{n+1}, K) \\ &= \mathrm{e}^{-r t_{n+1}} \int_0^\infty \max(0, s_{n+1} - K) \int_0^\infty \Pi(s_{n+1}|s_n)\Pi(s_n)\, ds_n\, ds_{n+1} \\ &= \mathrm{e}^{-r t_n} \int_0^\infty \Pi(s_n) \int_0^\infty \mathrm{e}^{-r\Delta t} \max(0, s_{n+1} - K)\Pi(s_{n+1}|s_n)\, ds_{n+1} ds_n \\ &= \mathrm{e}^{-r t_n} \int_0^\infty \Pi(s_n)\, C_{BS}(s_n, K, r, \Delta t, \sigma_n)\, ds_n, \end{aligned} \tag{4.7}$$

where $C_{BS}(s_n, K, r, \Delta t, \sigma(t_n, s_n))$ represents the Black–Scholes price of a European call option with stock price s_n, strike K, interest rate r, time to maturity Δt, and volatility σ_n. In other words, the proposed pricing method implies that a European call is the average of Black–Scholes call prices. It is worth mentioning that different payoffs can be used in Eqs. (4.6) and (4.7), giving similar pricing formulas.

4.3. Maximum Entropy Densities

When the stock price model in Eq. (4.1) is the LVM of Dupire [1], the call option price can be approximated as in Eq. (4.7). In this case, the density Π can be approximated in different ways. The most natural is by Monte Carlo, where different samples for S_n are generated, and the integral is approximated as follows:

$$\int_0^{\infty} \Pi(s_n)\, C_{BS}(s_n, K, r, \Delta t, \sigma(t_n, s_n))\, ds_n \approx \frac{1}{M} \sum_{m=1}^{M} C_{BS}(S_n^{(m)}, K, r, \Delta t, \sigma(t_n, S_n^{(m)})), \quad (4.8)$$

where $S_n^{(m)}$ represents the mth sample of S_n. In general, to achieve accurate results, M must be large, and the time step Δt must be small. This may turn the present pricing technique computationally intensive, especially for model calibration.

As an alternative to Monte Carlo integration, the integral in Eq. (4.7) can be solved by some quadrature rule when $\Pi(s_n)$ is approximated by a MED [37, 49]. In what follows, we give a brief review of the technique proposed in [37].

To address the possible numerical instability in the optimization problem proposed in Buchen and Kelly [49] to obtain MED, in Neri and Schneider [37], the authors turn the n-dimensional problem into n one-dimensional problems by making use of synthetic digital option prices and the Newton–Raphson method. By a digital option, we mean the cash-or-nothing option, which pays a fixed amount or nothing in the maturity.

Thus, let $\tilde{C}_i$ and $\tilde{D}_i$ $(i = 1, \ldots, n)$ denote, respectively, the undiscounted prices of call and digital options. In Neri and Schneider [37], it is shown that there exists a unique density g that maximizes an entropy functional and matches the prices of the call and the digital options. The undiscounted prices of the call and the digital options are given by:

$$\int_{K_i}^{\infty} (x - K_i) g(x) dx = \tilde{C}_i \quad \text{and} \quad \int_{K_i}^{\infty} g(x) dx = \tilde{D}_i \quad (i = 1, \ldots, n). \quad (4.9)$$

The density g maximizes the entropy functional:

$$H(g) = -\int_0^{\infty} g(x) \log g(x) dx \quad (4.10)$$

subject to the restrictions in Eq. (4.9) if, and only if, it maximizes $H(g)$ in the intervals $[K_i, K_{i+1})$, subject to the following restrictions:

$$\int_{K_i}^{K_{i+1}} x g(x) dx = (\tilde{C}_{i+1} + K_{i+1}\tilde{D}_{i+1}) - (\tilde{C}_i + K_i \tilde{D}_i) \quad (i = 1, \ldots, n) \quad (4.11)$$

$$\int_{K_i}^{K_{i+1}} g(x) dx = \tilde{D}_{i+1} - \tilde{D}_i \quad (i = 1, \ldots, n). \quad (4.12)$$

For each $i = 1, \ldots, n$, define $\bar{K}_i$ as

$$\bar{K}_i := \frac{(\widetilde{C}_i + K_i\widetilde{D}_i) - (\widetilde{C}_{i+1} + K_{i+1}\widetilde{D}_{i+1})}{\widetilde{D}_i - \widetilde{D}_{i+1}} \quad (i = 1, \ldots, n). \tag{4.13}$$

Thus, inside each interval $[K_i, K_{i+1})$, the MED admits the following expression,

$$g(x) = \alpha_i e^{\beta_i x} \tag{4.14}$$

with

$$\alpha_i = p_i e^{c_i(\beta_i)} \quad \text{and} \quad c'(\beta_i) = \bar{K}_i, \tag{4.15}$$

and

$$c_i(\beta) = \begin{cases} c\log\left(\dfrac{e^{\beta K_{i+1}} - e^{\beta K_i}}{\beta}\right) & \text{for } i < n \text{ and } \beta \neq 0, \\ \log\left(K_{i+1} - K_i\right) & \text{for } i < n \text{ and } \beta = 0, \\ \log\left(-\dfrac{e^{\beta K_i}}{\beta}\right) & \text{for } i = n \text{ and } \beta < 0, \end{cases} \tag{4.16}$$

$$c_i'(\beta) = \begin{cases} \dfrac{K_{i+1}e^{\beta K_{i+1}} - K_i e^{\beta K_i}}{e^{\beta K_{i+1}} - e^{\beta K_i}} - \dfrac{1}{\beta} & \text{for } i < n \text{ and } \beta \neq 0, \\ \dfrac{K_{i+1} + K_i}{2} & \text{for } i < n \text{ and } \beta = 0, \\ K_i - \dfrac{1}{\beta} & \text{for } i = n \text{ and } \beta < 0, \end{cases} \tag{4.17}$$

$$c_i''(\beta) = \begin{cases} -(K_{i+1} - K_i)^2 \dfrac{e^{\beta(K_{i+1}+K_i)}}{\left(e^{\beta K_{i+1}} - e^{\beta K_i}\right)^2} + \dfrac{1}{\beta^2} & \text{for } i < n \text{ e } \beta \neq 0, \\ \dfrac{(K_{i+1} - K_i)^2}{12} & \text{for } i < n \text{ e } \beta = 0, \\ \dfrac{1}{\beta^2} & \text{for } i = n \text{ e } \beta < 0, \end{cases} \tag{4.18}$$

Thus, the optimization problem is written in terms of α_i and β_i for each interval $[K_i, K_{i+1})$. The optimization can be performed such that the resulting MED is continuously differentiable for every $x > 0$.

4.4. Local Volatility Calibration

Another important problem is the local volatility calibration, which can be solved using the pricing formula in Eq. (4.7) and the MED of the previous subsection. In what follows, we present a calibration strategy that is an alternative to the one that uses the Dupire PDE [1, 6–10, 46].

The Direct Operator For simplicity, we restrict the analysis to the interval $[0, \bar{K}]$, with $\bar{K}$ large, instead of $\mathbb{R}_+$. We assume that, for each t_n,

$$\sigma(t_n, \cdot) \in (C) := \{\sigma \in \sigma_0 + H^1\left([0, \bar{K}]\right) : \underline{\sigma} \leq \sigma \leq \overline{\sigma}\},$$

where $0 < \underline{\sigma} \leq \overline{\sigma} < +\infty$ are constants and $\sigma_0 \in L^\infty\left([0, \bar{K}]\right)$ is nonnegative and $\|\sigma_0\|_\infty \leq \overline{\sigma}$.

Then, the forward operator

$$C : \mathcal{D}(C) \subset H^1\left([0,\bar{K}]\right) \to L^2\left([0,\bar{K}]\right),$$

for a fixed time t_{n+1} and strike K in $[0, \bar{K}]$, is defined as

$$C(t_n, K; \sigma(t_n; \cdot)) = \mathrm{e}^{-r\, t_n} \int_0^{\bar{K}} \Pi(s_n)\, C_{BS}(s_n, K, r, \Delta t, \sigma(t_n, s_n))\, ds_n\,. \tag{4.19}$$

Proposition 4.4.1. *The forward operator is continuous. Moreover, if $\sigma, \tilde{\sigma}$ are in $\mathcal{D}(C)$, then C satisfies*

$$\| C(\sigma) - C(\widetilde{\sigma}) \|_{L^2([0,\bar{K}])} \leq \rho \,\| \sigma - \widetilde{\sigma} \|_{H^1([0,\bar{K}])}, \tag{4.20}$$

where ρ is a positive constant independent of σ and $\tilde{\sigma}$.

Proof. Let $\sigma, \tilde{\sigma}$ be in $\mathcal{D}(C)$. By the definition of C, we have:

$$\| C(\sigma) - C(\widetilde{\sigma}) \|^2_{L^2([0,\, \bar{K}]} = \int_0^{\bar{K}} \left(\int_0^{\bar{K}} \Pi(s)(C_{BS}(s, K, \sigma(s)) - C_{BS}(s, K, \widetilde{\sigma}(s)))ds \right)^2 dK.$$

Applying Jensen's inequality and Fubini's theorem, we have:

$$\| C(\sigma) - C(\widetilde{\sigma}) \|^2_{L^2([0,\, \bar{K}]} \leq \int_0^{\bar{K}} \Pi(s) \int_0^{\bar{K}} (C_{BS}(s, K, \sigma(s)) - C_{BS}(s, K, \widetilde{\sigma}(s)))^2 dK\, ds.$$

Since C_{BS} is differentiable with respect to σ, it follows that

$$\| C(\sigma) - C(\widetilde{\sigma}) \|^2_{L^2([0,\, \bar{K}]} \leq \int_0^{\bar{K}} \Pi(s) \int_0^{\bar{K}} \max_{l \subset [\underline{\sigma},\, \overline{\sigma}]} \left| \frac{\partial C_{BS}}{\partial \sigma}(s, K, l) \right|^2 |\sigma(s) - \widetilde{\sigma}(s)|^2 dK\, ds.$$

Since all the integrands are bounded, the result follows. ∎

Proposition 4.4.2. *The forward operator is compact.*

Proof. Let $\{\sigma_n\}_{n \in \mathbb{N}}$ be a weakly convergent sequence in $H^1([0,\bar{K}])$, with limit σ. By the Sobolev compact embedding, the sequence converges strongly to σ in $L^2([0,\bar{K}])$. Using the estimates of the proof of the previous proposition and applying the L^2-convergence of the sequence, the result follows. ∎

Proposition 4.4.3. *For each $\sigma \in \mathcal{D}(C)$, the forward operator has a directional derivative. More precisely, the directional derivative of C at σ in the direction h, denoted by $C'(\sigma)h$, is given by:*

$$[C'(\sigma)h](t_{n+1}, K) = \mathrm{e}^{-r\,t_n} \int_0^{\overline{K}} \Pi(s_n) \frac{\partial C_{BS}}{\partial \sigma}(s_n, K, r, \Delta t, \sigma(t_n, s_n)) h(t_n, s_n)\, ds_n. \qquad (4.21)$$

Proof. Let σ and h be such that $\sigma, \sigma \pm h \in \mathcal{D}(C)$. Assume that $0 < |\varepsilon| < 1$, then, dropping the dependence on t_n, K, and the term e^{-rt_n}, we have,

$$C(\sigma + \varepsilon h) - C(\sigma) = \int_0^{\overline{K}} \Pi(s)(C_{BS}(s, K, \sigma + \varepsilon h) - C_{BS}(s, K, \sigma))ds.$$

For each $s > 0$, we have

$$\begin{aligned} |C_{BS}(s, K, \sigma + \varepsilon h) - C_{BS}(s, K, \sigma)| &= \left| \int_{\sigma}^{\sigma+\varepsilon h} \frac{\partial C_{BS}}{\partial \sigma}(s, K, l)\, dl \right| \\ &\leq |\varepsilon| \max_{l \in [\underline{\sigma}, \overline{\sigma}]} \left| \frac{\partial C_{BS}}{\partial \sigma}(s, K, l) \right| |h(s)|. \end{aligned}$$

The derivative in the last inequality is bounded with respect to s and K. Then, by the dominated convergence theorem, the limit holds:

$$\lim_{\varepsilon \to 0} \frac{C(\sigma + \varepsilon h) - C(\sigma)}{\varepsilon} = \int_0^{\overline{K}} \Pi(s) \frac{\partial C_{BS}}{\partial \sigma}(s, K, \sigma)\, h(s)\, ds.$$ ∎

The Calibration Problem We assume that, for each n, the risk-neutral probability density $\Pi(s_n)$ is known. It is obtained by the approach introduced in Neri and Schneider [37]. We are concerned with the calibration of the local volatility function $s_n \mapsto \sigma(t_n, s_n)$, given a set of European call option prices $K \mapsto C(t_{n+1}, K)$.

More precisely, we want to find a minimizer for the functional

$$F(\sigma) = \int_0^{\overline{K}} \frac{1}{2} |C_{MKT}(t_{n+1}, K) - C(t_{n+1}, K; \sigma)|^2\, dK + \alpha f(\sigma), \qquad (4.22)$$

within the set $\mathcal{D}(C)$, where $C_{MKT}(t_n, K)$ is a market price of a European call and $C(t_{n+1}, K; \sigma)$ is given by Eq. (4.19). We assume that the functional f is convex, weakly lower semi-continuous, and coercive. Then, by the compactness of the forward operator, for each $\zeta > 0$, the level set

$$L(\zeta) := \{\sigma \in (C) \;:\; F(\sigma) \leq \zeta\}$$

is weakly pre-compact and weakly closed. In Ref. [39, Theorem 3.22], the Tikhonov functional (4.22) has a minimizer, whenever the regularization parameter satisfies $\alpha > 0$. We also have that the minimizers are stable. See Ref. [39, Theorem 3.23].

We use a gradient-based method to minimize Eq. (4.22). Thus, defining

$$J(\sigma) = \frac{1}{2}||C_{MKT} - C(\sigma)||^2,$$

we have to find $\nabla J(\sigma)$. Given $h \in H^1([0,\overline{K}])$ such that $\sigma \pm h \in \mathcal{D}(C)$, we consider the directional derivative $C'(\sigma)h$, defined in Eq. (4.21). Thus, by Fubini's theorem, we have

$$\langle \nabla J(\sigma), h\rangle = \langle C_{MKT} - C(\sigma), C'(\sigma)h\rangle = \langle C'(\sigma)^*(C_{MKT} - C(\sigma)), h\rangle,$$

where, for each t_{n+1} and K,

$$[C'(\sigma)^* g](t_{n+1}, s) = \Pi(s) \int_0^{\overline{K}} \frac{\partial C_{BS}}{\partial \sigma}(s, K, r, \Delta t, \sigma(t_n, s))g(K)dK.$$

In other words, the directional derivative is the average of the Vega, which is given by the derivative of the Black–Scholes pricing formula with respect to the volatility.

The resulting local volatility calibration technique is computationally efficient since it reduces the dimension of the calibration problem and does not depend on the numerical solution of PDEs or Monte Carlo integration.

4.5. Numerical Results

4.5.1. *Synthetic data*

To generate the synthetic data, we use Dupire's PDE in the time-to-maturity × log moneyness variables (τ, y) with the local volatility surface given as follows,

$$\sigma(\tau, y) = \begin{cases} \frac{2}{5} - \frac{4}{25}e^{-\tau/2}\cos\left(\frac{4\pi y}{5}\right), & \text{if } -2/5 \le y \le 2/5 \\ 2/5, & \text{otherwise.} \end{cases} \qquad (4.23)$$

We numerically solve Dupire's PDE by a Crank–Nicolson-type scheme [6, 8, 9, 46] with the mesh time step $\Delta\tau = 0.001$ and log-moneyness step $\Delta y = 0.05$. The interest rate is taken as $r = 0.03$. The domain (time to maturity × log-moneyness) used was $D = [0, 1] \times [-5, 5]$. The dataset used in the calibration is the set of Dupire's call prices for the maturity times $\tau = 0.5 + \Delta\tau, 0.5 + 2\Delta\tau$, and the log-moneyness strikes $-0.5 : \Delta y : 0.5$.

We extract the MED $\Pi(s)$ for the maturities τ and $\tau + \Delta\tau$ following the techniques from Section 4.3. The integral in Eq. (4.6) is solved by Simpson's rule, and the call prices obtained with the MED are called MED's call prices. The comparison between Dupire's and MED's call prices, as well as the relative error between MED's prices with respect to Dupire's prices, can be found in Fig. 4.1.

The local volatility is then calibrated from Dupire's prices, using the pricing formula in Eq. (4.7) by minimizing the Tikhonov-type function in Eq. (4.22). The regularization parameter used in the calibration was $\alpha = 0.0025$ and the minimization was performed using MATLAB's function "LSQNONLIN."

The comparison between the calibrated local volatility and the original one can be seen in Fig. 4.2. They look quite similar. Such a figure also presents the relative error

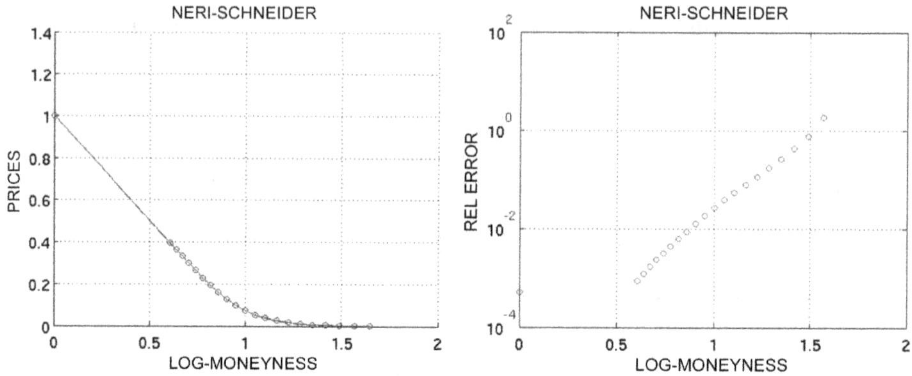

Fig. 4.1 Left: Comparison between Dupire's and MED's call prices. Right: Relative error of the MED's prices with respect to Dupire's prices.

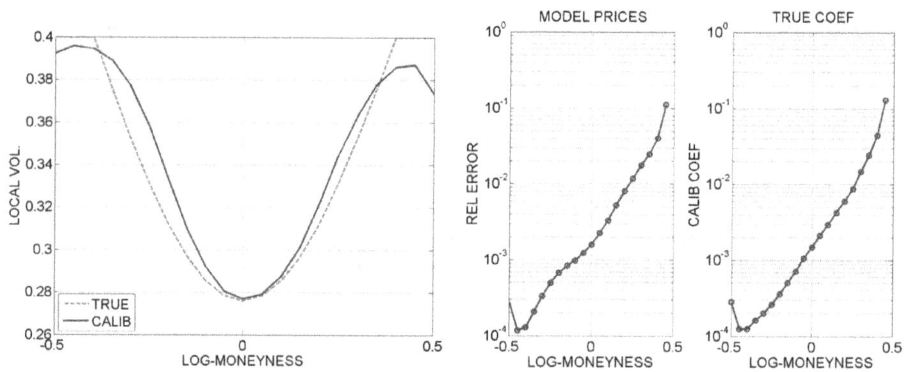

Fig. 4.2 Left: Comparison between the calibrated local volatility (continuous) and the ground-truth local volatility (dashed). Right: Relative error of the call prices given by the calibrated local volatility with respect to Dupire's call prices.

between the prices obtained using the calibrated local volatility with respect to Dupire's call prices.

4.5.2. *SPX option data*

In this section, we present calibration results using real data. We extract the local volatility surface from S&P 500 end-of-the-day call options, quoted in November 2022. To validate our results, we compare the market-implied volatility data with the implied volatility curves of the model prices. This comparison is presented for all the considered maturities in Fig. 4.3. The calibrated local volatility curves for both models at different maturities are depicted in Fig. 4.4.

As Fig. 4.3 shows, adherence to the quoted SPX implied volatilities was rather satisfactory. This illustrates the ability of the proposed calibration tool to fit the market data. Moreover, the estimated SPX local volatility curves, depicted in Fig. 4.4, presented a smooth shape, as expected in general. With the proposed estimation model, we achieved accurate results, especially with larger maturities, with smaller computational efforts if compared to calibrating LVM by solving Dupire's PDE.

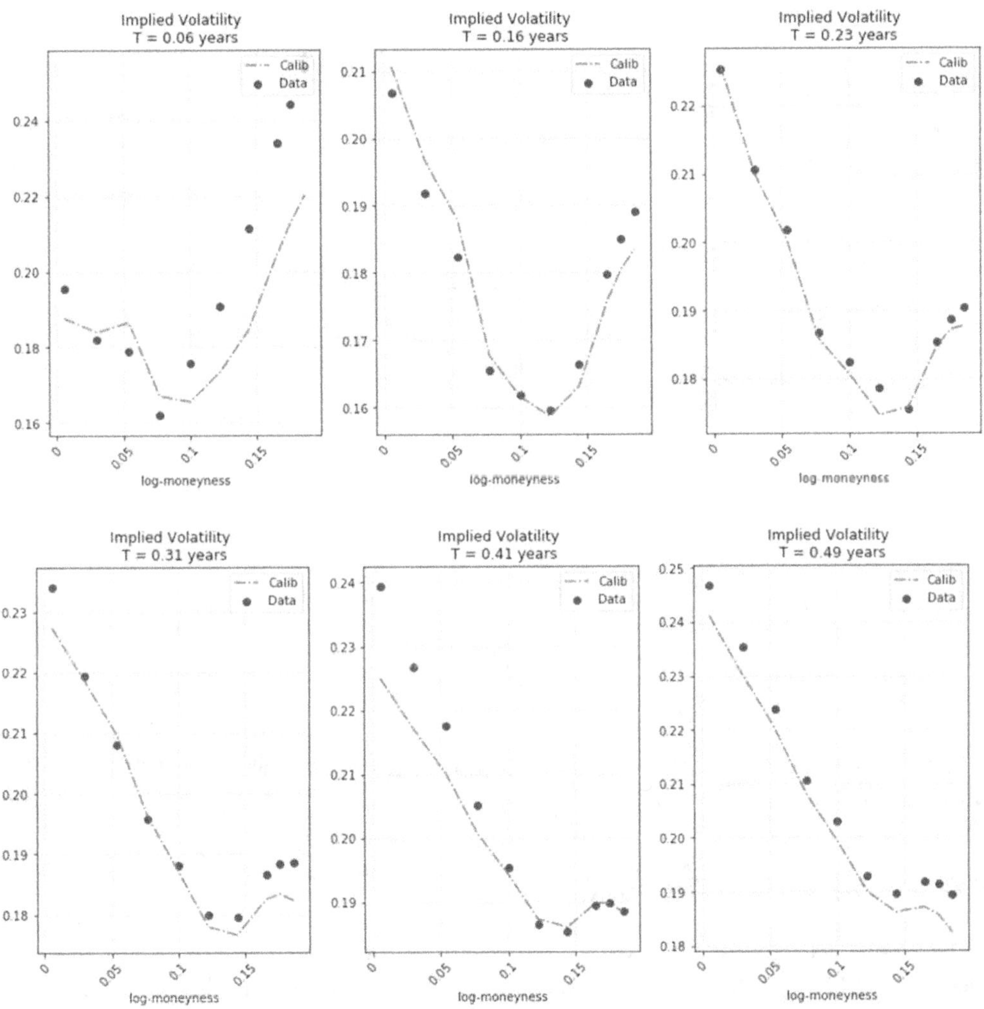

Fig. 4.3 Comparison between the implied volatility of the prices given by the calibrated local volatility surface, as well as the S&P 500 call prices quoted in November 2022.

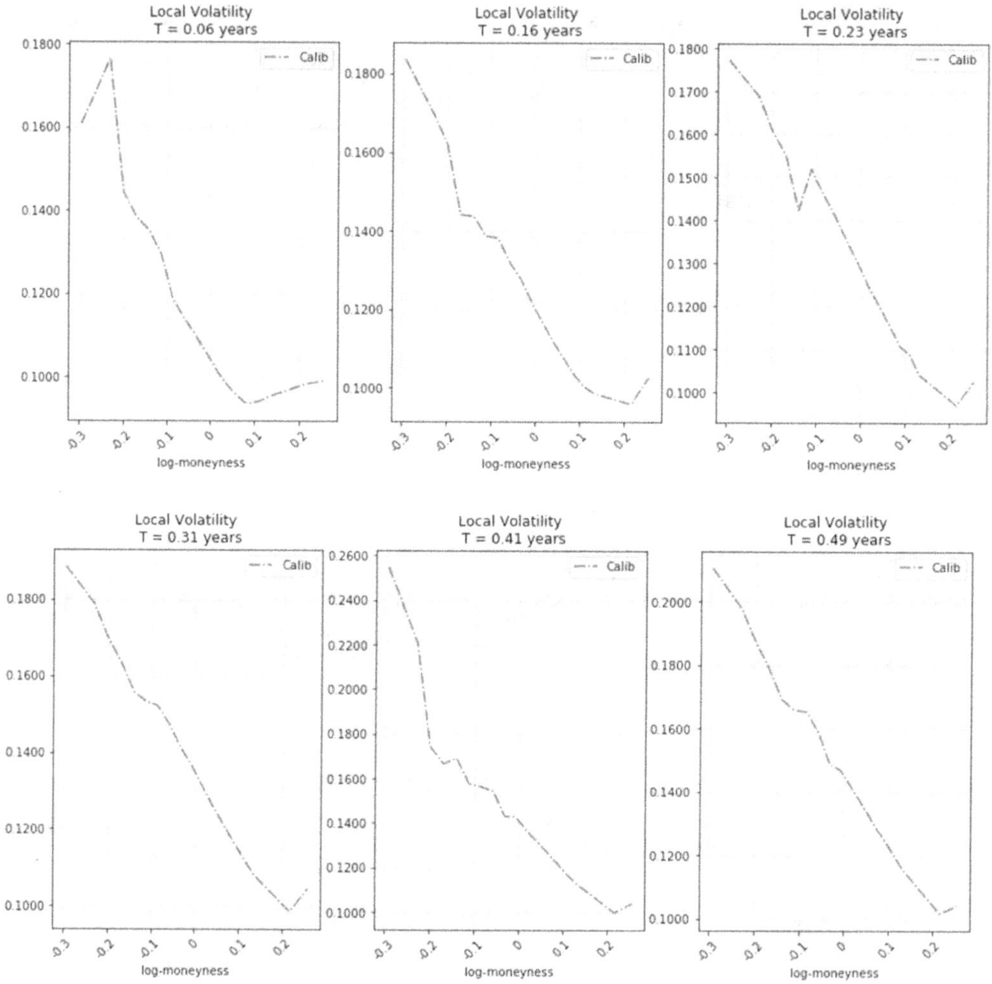

Fig. 4.4 The calibrated local volatility of the proposed model (Calib) from S&P 500 call prices quoted in November 2022.

4.6. Concluding Remarks

In this work, we proposed a new method to calibrate the local volatility using Bayes' theorem and MEDs. This method allows parallel calculations and avoids the use of PDE numerical solutions, improving considerably the computational efficiency of local volatility calibration. Moreover, the pricing formulas and the gradient used in the optimization employ the Black–Scholes formulas for the calculation of vanilla option prices and the Greek Vega. Both formulas are inexpensive to evaluate. The MED estimation is also based on an efficient and robust technique that was proposed in Neri and Schneider [37].

Numerical examples with synthetic and quoted SPX option data illustrated the referred advantages of the proposed methodology. Moreover, estimating the local volatility, instead of only the MEDs, is useful to evaluate path-dependent derivatives, such as Asian options, barrier options, lookback options, and calendar spread options, among others. The calibrated surface can be used in the LVM directly. Under the risk-neutral framework, it is also relatively simple to adapt the proposed technique to vanilla options on commodity futures, following the guidelines proposed in the article [46].

It is worth mentioning that the proposed calibration tool has some limitations. Extending it to more than one asset or to more general models is not obvious. Moreover, since it is a discrete-time approximation of the LVM, its accuracy is limited by the chosen time discretization.

Local volatility is yet one of the most accurate models in quantitative finance, which means that it is still quite useful, not only as a baseline model but also for pricing derivatives. Thus, it is important to provide a computationally efficient local volatility calibration tool that can compete with new methodologies, such as deep learning, that can also be included in computational libraries or in market tracking/trading software.

Acknowledgments

VA thanks the financial support from the Fundação Butantan and Fundação de Amparo à Pesquisa e Inovação do Estado de Santa Catarina through the grants 01/2020 and 00002847/2021, respectively. JPZ thanks Khalifa University, the Government of Abu Dhabi, and *Fundação Carlos Chagas Filho de Amparo à Pesquisa do Estado do Rio de Janeiro* (FAPERJ) through the grant E-26/202.927/2017 for the support during the course of this research.

References

1. B. Dupire, Pricing with a smile, *Risk.* **7**, 18–20 (1994). http://www.cmap.polytechnique.fr/~rama/dea/dupire.pdf.
2. E. Derman and I. Kani, Riding on a smile, *Risk.* **7**, 32–39 (1994). http://www.math.ku.dk/kurser/2005-1/finmathtowork/DermanKaniRISK.PDF.
3. F. Black and M. Scholes, The pricing of options and corporate liabilities, *J. Polit. Econ.* **81**(3), 637–654 (1973). https://doi.org/10.1086/260062.
4. Y. Achdou and O. Pironneau, Volatility smile by Multilevel least square, *Int. J. Theor. Appl. Finance.* **5**(6), 619–643 (2002). https://doi.org/10.1142/S0219024902001602.
5. Y. Achdou and O. Pironneau, *Computational Methods for Option Pricing*. Frontiers in Applied Mathematics, SIAM, Philadelphia (2005).
6. V. Albani, U. Ascher, X. Yang, and J. Zubelli, Data driven recovery of local volatility surfaces, *Inverse Probl. Imaging.* **11**(5), 799–823 (2017). https://doi.org/10.3934/ipi.2017038. http://arxiv.org/abs/1512.07660.

7. V. Albani and A. De Cezaro, A connection between uniqueness of minimizers and Morozov-like discrepancy principles in Tikhonov-type regularization, *Inverse Probl. Imaging*. **13**(1), 211–229 (2019). https://doi.org/10.3934/ipi.2019012.
8. V. Albani, A. De Cezaro, and J. Zubelli, On the choice of the Tikhonov regularization parameter and the discretization level: A discrepancy-based strategy, *Inverse Probl. Imaging*. **10**(1), 1–25 (2016). https://doi.org/10.3934/ipi.2016.10.1. https://aimsciences.org/journals/displayArticlesnew.jsp?paperID=12262.
9. V. Albani, A. De Cezaro, and J. P. Zubelli, Convex regularization of local volatility estimation, *Int. J. Theor. Appl. Finan*. **20**(1), 1750006 (2017). https://doi.org/10.1142/S0219024917500066.
10. V. Albani and J. P. Zubelli, Online local volatility calibration by convex regularization, *Appl. Anal. Discrete Math*. **8**(2), 243–268 (2014). https://doi.org/10.2298/AADM140811012A.
11. M. Avellaneda, C. Friedman, R. Holmes, and D. Samperi, calibrating volatility surfaces via relative-entropy minimization, *Appl. Math. Finance*. **4**(1), 37–64 (1997). https://doi.org/10.1080/135048697334827.
12. S. Crepey, Calibration of the local volatility in a generalized Black–Scholes model using Tikhonov regularization, *SIAM J. Math. Anal*. **34**(5), 1183–1206 (2003). https://doi.org/10.1137/S0036141001400202.
13. A. De Cezaro, O. Scherzer, and J. Zubelli, Convex regularization of local volatility models from option prices: Convergence analysis and rates, *Nonlinear Anal. Theory Methods Appl*. **75**(4), 2398–2415 (2012). https://doi.org/10.1016/j.na.2011.10.037.
14. B. Düring, A. Jüngel, and S. Volkwein, Sequential quadratic programming method for volatility estimation in option pricing, *J. Optim. Theory Appl*. **139**(3), 515–540 (2008). https://doi.org/10.1007/s10957-008-9404-4.
15. H. Egger and H. W. Engl, Tikhonov regularization applied to the inverse problem of option pricing: Convergence analysis and rates, *Inverse Probl*. **21**, 1027–1045 (2005). https://doi.org/10.1088/0266-5611/21/3/014.
16. G. Callegaro, M. Grasselli, and L. Fiorin, Quantized calibration in local volatility, *Risk Magazine* (May 04, 2015).
17. S. Georgiev and L. Vulkov, Fast reconstruction of time-dependent market volatility for European options, *Comput. Appl. Math*. **40**(30), 1–19 (2021). https://doi.org/s10.1007/s40314-021-01422-9.
18. T. Hein and B. Hoffman, On the nature of ill-posedness of an inverse problem arising in option pricing, *Inverse Probl*. **19**(6), 1319–1338 (2003). https://doi.org/10.1088/0266-5611/19/6/006.
19. C. Hofmann, B. Hofmann, and A. Pichler, Simultaneous identification of volatility and interest rate functions: A two-parameter regularization approach, *Electronic Transactions on Numerical Analysis*. **51**, 99–117 (2019). https://doi.org/10.1553/etna_vol51s99.
20. N. Jackson, E. Süli, and S. Howinson, Computation of deterministic volatility surfaces, *J. Comput. Finance*. **2**, 5–32 (1998). http://eprints.maths.ox.ac.uk/1308/1/NA-98-01.pdf.
21. P. Vassiliou, *Discrete-Time Asset Pricing Models in Applied Stochastic Finance*. Wiley, US (03, 2013). https://doi.org/10.1002/9781118557860.
22. R. Craine, L. A. Lochstoer, and K. Syrtveit, Estimation of a stochasticvolatility jump-diffusion model, *Economic Analysis Review*. **15**(1), 61–87 (1, 2000).
23. M. Chataigner, S. Crépey, and M. Dixon, Deep local volatility, *Risks*. **8**(3), 82 (2020). https://doi.org/10.3390/risks8030082.

24. M. Chataigner, A. Cousin, S. Crépey, M. Dixon, and D. Gueye, Beyond surrogate modeling: Learning the local volatility via shape constraints, *SIAM J. Financ. Math.* **12**(3), SC58–SC69 (2021).

25. X.-J. He and S.-P. Zhu, On full calibration of hybrid local volatility and regime-switching models, *J. Futures Mark.* **38**(5), 586–606 (2018).

26. S. Kim, H. Han, H. Jang, D. Jeong, C. Lee, W. Lee, and J. Kim, Reconstruction of the local volatility function using the Black–Scholes model, *J. Comput. Sci.* **51**, 101341 (2021).

27. V. Albani and J. Zubelli, A splitting strategy for the calibration of jump-diffusion models, *Finan. Stoch.* **24**, 677–722 (2020). https://doi.org/10.1007/s00780-020-00425-4.

28. L. Andersen and J. Andreasen, Jump-diffusion processes: Volatility smile fitting and numerical methods for option pricing, *Rev. Deriv. Res.* **4**, 231–262 (2000).

29. P. Carr, H. Geman, D. B. Madan, and M. Yor. From local volatility to local Lévy models, *Quantitative Finance.* **4**(5), 581–588 (2004). https://doi.org/10.1080/14697680400024921. https://www.tandfonline.com/doi/abs/10.1080/14697680400024921.

30. P. Carr and D. B. Madan, Local volatility enhanced by a jump to default, *SIAM J. Financ. Math.* **1**(1), 2–15 (2010). https://doi.org/10.1137/090750731.

31. S. Kindermann and P. Mayer, On the calibration of local jump-diffusion asset price models, *Finan. Stoch.* **15**(4), 685–724 (2011). https://doi.org/10.1007/s00780-011-0159-7.

32. B. Engelmann, F. Koster, and D. Oeltz, Calibration of the Heston stochastic local volatility model: A finite volume scheme, *Int. J. Financ. Eng.* **8**(01), 2050048 (2021). http://dx.doi.org/10.2139/ssrn.1823769.

33. Z. Cui, J. L. Kirkby, and D. Nguyen, A general valuation framework for SABR and stochastic local volatility models, *SIAM J. Financ. Math.* **9**(2), 520–563 (2018). https://doi.org/10.1137/16M1106572.

34. Y. F. Saporito, X. Yang, and J. P. Zubelli, The calibration of stochastic local-volatility models: An inverse problem perspective, *Comput. Math. Appl.* **77**(12), 3054–3067 (2019). https://doi.org/10.1016/j.camwa.2019.01.029.

35. Y. Tian, Z. Zhu, G. Lee, F. Klebaner, and K. Hamza, Calibrating and pricing with a stochastic-local volatility model, *J. Deriv.* **22**(3), 21–39 (2015). https://doi.org/10.3905/jod.2015.22.3.021.

36. D. J. Higham, An algorithmic introduction to numerical simulation of stochastic differential equations, *SIAM Rev.* **43**(3), 525–546 (2001). https://doi.org/10.1137/S0036144500378302.

37. C. Neri and L. Schneider, Maximum entropy distributions inferred from option portfolios on an asset, *Financ. Stoch.* **16**(2), 293–318 (2012). ISSN 0949-2984. https://dx.doi.org/10.1007/s00780-011-0167-7.

38. I. Csiszar, *I*-divergence geometry of probability distributions and minimization problems, *Ann. Probab.* **3**(1), 146–158 (1975). ISSN 0091-1798. https://doi.org/10.1214/aop/1176996454.

39. O. Scherzer, M. Grasmair, H. Grossauer, M. Haltmeier, and F. Lenzen, *Variational Methods in Imaging*, vol. 167, *Applied Mathematical Sciences*, Springer, New York (2008).

40. R. Cont, Model uncertainty and its impact on the pricing of derivative instruments, *Math. Financ.* **16**(3), 519–547 (2006).

41. A. Lipton, The vol smile problem, *Risk Magazine.* **15**, 61–65 (2002).

42. A. Lipton, Assets with jumps, *Risk Magazine.* pp. 149–153 (2002).

43. A. Lipton and A. Sepp, Filling the gaps, *Risk Magazine.* pp. 66–71 (2011).

44. A. Itkin and A. Lipton, Filling the gaps smoothly, *Journal of Computational Science.* **24**, 195–208 (2018).

45. A. Lipton, *Financial Engineering: Selected Works of Alexander Lipton*. World Scientific (2018). ISBN 978-9813209152.

46. V. Albani, U. Ascher, and J. Zubelli, Local volatility models in commodity markets and online calibration, *J. Comput. Finance*. **21**(5), 63–95 (2018). https://doi.org/10.21314/JCF.2018.345. http://arxiv.org/abs/1602.04372.

47. B. Øksendal, *Stochastic Differential Equations*. Springer, New York (2003).

48. E. Somersalo and J. Kapio, *Statistical and Computational Inverse Problems*, vol. 160, *Applied Mathematical Sciences*, Springer, New York (2004).

49. P. W. Buchen and M. Kelly, The maximum entropy distribution of an asset inferred from option prices, *J. Financ. Quant. Anal.* **31**(1), 143–159 (3, 1996). ISSN 1756-6916. https://doi.org/10.2307/2331391. http://journals.cambridge.org/article_S002210900000048X.

SECTION

2

Digital Economy

https://doi.org/10.1142/9789819813049_0005

CHAPTER 5

Challenges of Artificial Intelligence and Quantum Potential in the Digital Economy: A Literature Review

Laura Sanz Martín[1], Javier Parra Domínguez[1], Guillermo Rivas[1], Alexander Lipton[2], and Juan Manuel Corchado[1,*]

[1] *University of Salamanca, Edificio I+D+i - C, C. Espejo, s/n, Salamanca, Spain*
[2] *ADIA Lab, Al Khatem Tower, Abu Dhabi Global Market Square, Al Maryah Island, Abu Dhabi, UAE*
[*] *Corresponding author. E-mail: jm@corchado.net*

The latest technologies, driven by advances such as quantum computing or generative artificial intelligence (AI), are transforming organizations of all kinds, including businesses. Navigating through emerging technologies is key for the digital economy. Thus, the motivation behind this study is to provide a better insight into the role of AI and quantum technology in the digital economy. With this aim, a systematic review has been conducted of 44 articles, following the PRISMA methodology. The latest technologies have been extensively analyzed, from their fundamentals and theory to diverse applications. The technical requirements of the reviewed technologies have been explored as well as their impact on economic and business practices, particularly in revolutionizing business and finance data analytics. Special attention has been paid to the ethical and legal challenges, especially concerning human–AI relationships. Significant applications in sectors such as mobile networks, education, medicine, cybersecurity, and astronomy have been identified. Moreover, the article addresses the unique challenges associated with generative adversarial networks based on game theory. The importance of generative AI in improving educational methods, especially in higher education and professional training, is evidenced. It has been observed that innovative content generation applications are expected to emerge, and that scientific advancements may bring about metaverse integration. Lastly, the growing trend of delegating research processes to large language models, such as generative AI, has raised concerns about the perception of the scientific and academic community and the value of researchers' work.

Keywords: Digital Economy, Artificial Intelligence, Quantum, Generative Artificial Intelligence.

5.1. Introduction

The digital economy is an intrinsic part of the modern world. Technologies are transforming economies and offering businesses opportunities for global scale-up while removing the need for physical migration. This rapidly growing phenomenon broadens the labor market and gives rise to new professions [1]. In the context of globalization, the digitization of the national economy promotes economic integration among developed countries by providing a global platform through digital networks and communication infrastructures, facilitating business development, economic communication, and collaboration [2]. The concept of the digital economy was first proposed by Tapscott [3] and has evolved into new related concepts [4]. Currently, the main technological trends of the digital economy are artificial intelligence (AI), blockchain, Internet of Things (IoT), and quantum computing (QC) [5].

AI is now considered the driving force of today's digital economy, and many companies have already invested in it [6]. Recent advances in AI enable machines to learn, adapt, and perform tasks. Such capabilities bring great potential to businesses and organizations, helping transform their operations by leveraging knowledge, and increasing productivity and innovation [7]. The rapid progression of science and technology has precipitated the widespread integration of technologies such as AI, big data, or blockchain, across numerous sectors [8]. Today, it is clear how companies improve their cooperation through the integration of individual technologies; however, given the context of the digital economy, many areas of business will change significantly thanks to AI [9].

On the other hand, QC implies a revolutionary technological paradigm shift that will radically transform the capabilities of computing systems [10]. In recent decades, quantum information science has emerged to explore whether it can gain advantages by storing, transmitting, and processing information encoded in systems with distinctive quantum properties [11]. Early progress is now being made in asserting quantum supremacy in a wide variety of innovative devices, which refers to the ability of a quantum computer to perform computations that a conventional computer cannot, representing a significant milestone in the history of science [12]. The transition to a circular economy is a necessity, and QC can play a crucial role in this transition by enabling real-time data analysis [13].

Quantum technology, AI, and generative AI are becoming increasingly intertwined, which is reflected in research and development. The integration of those technologies marks a significant shift in computational capabilities and applications [14]. QC allows for complex calculations at never-before-seen speeds, thereby significantly enhancing the processing power of AI algorithms.

The application of quantum technologies to generative AI, a subset of AI designed to create new data that resembles training data, results in transformative advancements. This enables generative AI models to process and learn from vast datasets with unprecedented efficiency, improving their ability to generate realistic and complex outputs. Additionally, the exploration of quantum algorithms has led to increasingly feasible solutions to complex optimization problems and to large dataset processing, facilitating advances in fields such as cryptography, drug discovery, and materials science [15].

Quantum-enhanced algorithms in machine learning promise accelerated learning processes and improved model performance with less data, potentially revolutionizing areas such as personalized medicine or autonomous systems. This groundbreaking intersection signifies a shift toward utilizing quantum mechanics to tackle complex scientific and technological challenges, expanding computational possibilities and leading to innovative applications [16].

This new paradigm holds significant implications for the technology sector within the digital economy. The enhanced computational power and efficiency of quantum technology are essential for driving innovation, competitiveness, and growth in the digital economy [17]. By enabling more complex data analyzes, faster problem-solving, and innovative product development, quantum technology, AI, and generative AI are at the forefront of transforming industries and reshaping the global economic landscape, underlining the critical importance of these advancements in the digital age [18].

This article presents a PRISMA-protocol-based systematic review, which sheds light on the involvement of technologies such as AI, generative AI, and QC in the digital economy and to appraise their evolution over the years.

The article is structured as follows. Section 5.2 presents the methodology. Section 5.3 covers the findings of the review, such as the evolution of technologies and their importance in the concept of the digital economy. Finally, Section 5.4 draws conclusions from the conducted review.

5.2. Methodology

Systematic reviews have become widespread in all fields of research, as they provide a comprehensive and up-to-date assessment of the state of the art, using methods that are transparent and that minimize bias. In fact, systematic reviews have become a powerful tool that assists professionals from diverse sectors in making decisions and optimizing their professional practice on an ongoing basis [19].

Scopus and Web of Science were chosen because they are the most widespread and recognized databases in the scientific community. The search equation for the Scopus search was (ALL ("DIGITAL ECONOMY") AND ALL ("ARTIFICIAL INTELLIGENCE") AND ALL ("QUANTUM")). The search was conducted on March 7, 2024, and resulted in 494 documents in Scopus. The results were limited to articles in English, and the chosen keywords were "digital economy," "artificial intelligence," and "quantum computing," resulting in 44 articles. In the Web of Science, the search equation was ((TS=(ARTIFICIAL INTELLIGENCE)) AND TS=(digital economy)) AND TS=(quantum); limiting document search to articles in English gave us eight articles. After analyzing these 52 articles, five articles were eliminated due to duplicates and three due to titles.

5.3. Results

5.3.1. *Evolution*

It can be seen in Fig. 5.1 that the first article that is part of our research was published in 2018. This date evidences the recency of the topic under study. In addition, the number of articles that make up our review is relatively low. In 2019, the production of articles grew to five, dropping in 2020 to two. In 2021, production rose, reaching nine articles, and peaked in 2022 and 2023, with 10 articles each year. We can see that in 2024, four articles have already been published on this topic, which not only suggests that the 10 articles published in 2022 and 2023 will be surpassed this year, but also that the importance of technologies such as AI and quantum in the digital economy is booming.

Figure 5.2 shows a map of the scientific production per country. Not surprisingly, China is the country that has published the most articles on this subject. The number of articles published in this country is double that of those published by the next country, the United States. Germany follows this with nine articles and the United Kingdom with six.

Figure 5.3 shows the network of keyword co-occurrences. The original dataset contained a total of 422 different keywords. It was imported through the VOSviewer program using the co-occurrence criterion for all keywords (according to the author's data and the database provided), and a minimum threshold of three occurrences was set. This process resulted in identifying nine keywords organized into three groups with four, four, and two keywords each. The LinLog/Modularity method was used to normalize the analysis. In the visualization network of keyword co-occurrences, the interconnection between concepts of great importance within technology and computer science is highlighted. It is observed that the terms "digital economy" and "big data" are closely related, indicating the growing importance of big data in driving and transforming digital economies.

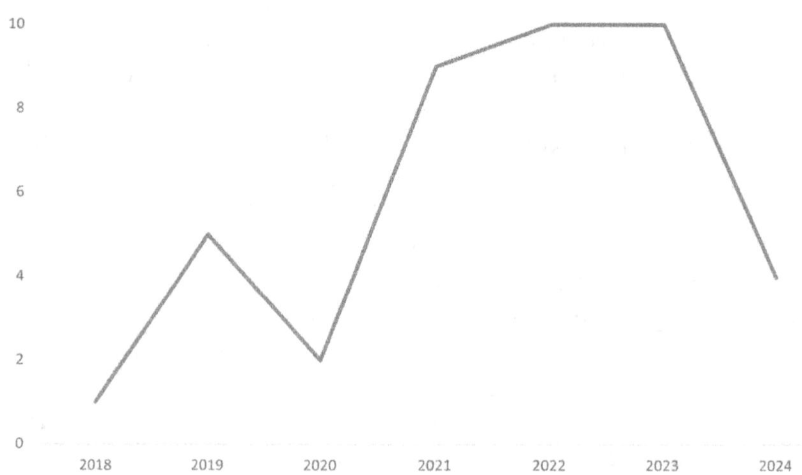

Fig. 5.1 Article production over the years.

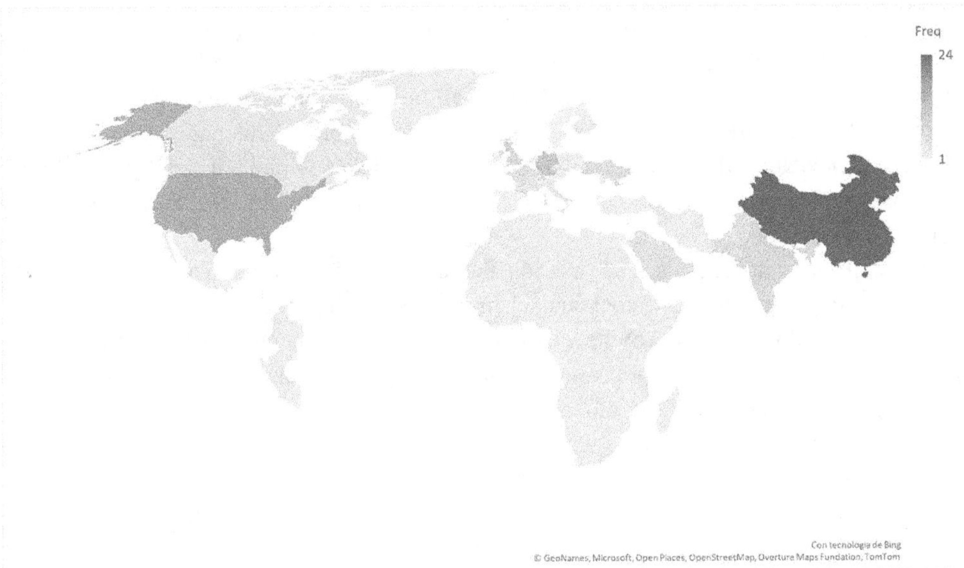

Fig. 5.2 Scientific production per country.

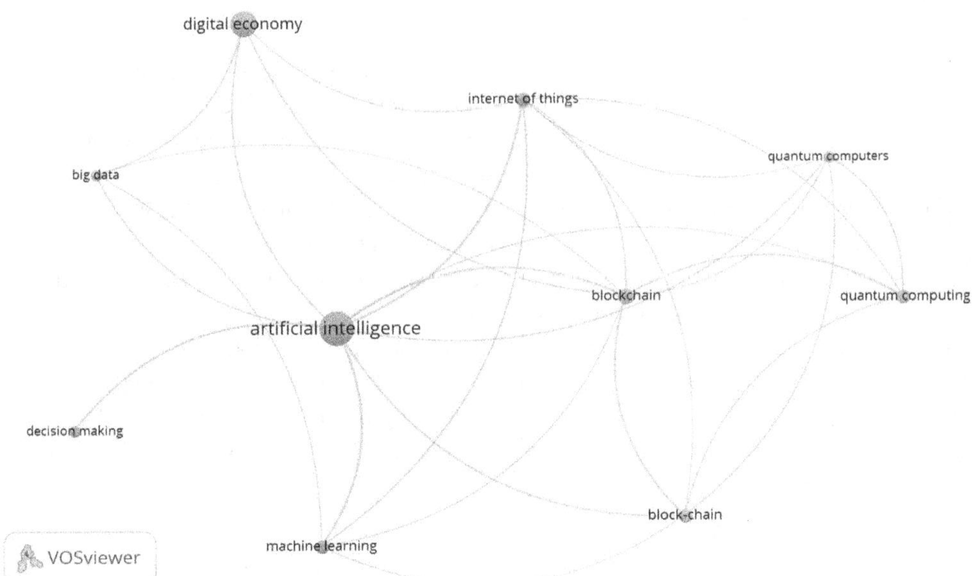

Fig. 5.3 Keyword co-occurrence network.

On the other hand, the keywords "quantum computing" and "quantum computers" are linked to "blockchain," suggesting possible applications in security or cryptography. Finally, "artificial intelligence" shows significant connections with "Internet of Things," "decision-making," and "machine learning," indicating the recent integration of AI in various areas and its role in process automation and optimization, as well as in data-driven decision-making. The only term that relates to all others in our study is "artificial intelligence," with 25 occurrences in the 44 articles in our database. This analysis reflects the interdependence and synergy between these emerging fields, which are rapidly transforming how we interact with technology and how current and future societal challenges are addressed.

In addition to the expected keywords, such as "artificial intelligence," "digital economy," "quantum computing," "blockchain," "machine learning," or "big data," Fig. 5.4 also reveals additional terms that provide valuable insights into the central themes addressed in the articles. For example, the inclusion of words such as "sustainability," "digital transformation," "supply chain," or "digitalization" suggests a broader approach to sustainability, digital transformation, and supply chain management in the context of the digital economy. These findings reflect the diversity and complexity of the topics covered in the articles and the growing awareness of the importance of sustainability and adaptation to technological changes in the business and socioeconomic environment.

5.3.2. *The importance of technology in the concept of the digital economy*

Digital transformation is considered to be a primary strategy for promoting transitions in various fields [20]. Digital transformation involves incorporating the latest technologies into all aspects of a business organization [21]. Emerging digital technologies are transforming modern society and the economy, increasing demand in technology-intensive sectors, and reshaping the current and future labor market [22]. The changes associated with these technologies will not only augment tasks associated with the production, sale, and scale-up of ideas but will also replace some tasks and create new forms of work. Thus, the implications of these changes should be considered in the organizational design of entrepreneurial firms [23]. Scholz et al. [24] presented a European Expert Roundtable on the effects of the digital transition, highlighting the importance of addressing ownership, economic value, access to data, and algorithmic decision-making processes. The authors also highlighted how digital transformation redefines the economy, work, democracy, and humanity.

Fig. 5.4 WordCloud of author keywords.

Information technology is fundamental to modern business. However, improvements must be backed by increased computing power or productivity of systems, and algorithm advancement, as this is what can foster competitive advantage [25]. These technological transformations can also have drawbacks, such as information explosion, which can hinder decision-making, or lead to misinformation, damaging the economy and society [26]. Effective privacy management is crucial for users, service providers, and the government in today's digital economy, which is why regulatory policies have been implemented to control the processing of personal data by digital service providers [27].

The growth of AI technology is closely linked to the progressive development of the Information and Communications Technology (ICT) sector. In recent decades, there has been a sharp increase in information processing capacity, a reduction in the size of computing devices, and increased versatility [28]. AI has advanced from a field of research to reality, as reflected in the implementation of this technology in businesses, where it has contributed to increased revenue, reduced costs, and expanded organizational performance [29]. Nevertheless, the practical implementation of AI poses technological challenges, as ensuring the reliability of its applications is key, especially its ability to process data effectively and contribute to decision-making. In addition, consideration should be given to how AI can be integrated with other emerging technologies to enhance technological innovation and its own evolution [30]. The use of machine learning and deep learning, as well as AI systems, augmented automation, natural language processing, and decision optimization, are necessary to maximize the effectiveness of AI [31].

The aforementioned technological advances, such as QC, AI, cognitive systems, and the expansion of IoT, are transforming security practices, rendering current methodologies obsolete. In fact, QC has the potential to provide much better security, surpassing today's capabilities by far [32]. Moreover, QC holds the promise of dramatically increasing the speed of computation and solving problems that currently take a long time to solve [33]. The domain name system (DNS), initially designed for speed and scalability, has become a vital asset of the digital economy. However, it is also a prime target for cybercriminals, putting users' privacy at risk. In fact, there is a growing number of DNS, and attackers have learned to evade traditional security systems. To address these issues, a review of DNS has been published with an examination of its features and an effort has been made to update its design and implementation [34]. Yin et al. [35] proposed a quantum signature protocol closely linked to the digital economy by offering an advanced and secure method for the authentication and security of digital transactions. Using asymmetric quantum keys acquired through secret sharing, universal one-time hashing, and a one-time pad, this protocol guarantees data integrity and authenticity. With these advances, it is anticipated that a new network architecture will be needed to meet the diverse demands of the hyper-connected society of 2030, which will require adopting new enabling technologies for 6G wireless services [36]. The growth of the mobile economy will be driven by multimedia applications in the 6G era, while the integration of AI and machine learning in telecommunications will be critical to optimize IoT performance [37].

Metaverse technology has also gained importance in recent times. There is a need to establish meaningful relationships between real-world assets and the digital world as the world becomes digitized. The metaverse is a novel and promising digital technology that combines several cutting-edge technologies, such as AI, virtual reality, augmented reality, the IoT, robotics, blockchain, and even QC [38]. Generative AI is one of the most recent digital technologies and has experienced exponential growth. These models, trained on large datasets, can generate creative content in response to a specific input, and this generalization capability allows them to respond accurately even to inputs not seen during their training [39]. To maximize the economic and transformative benefits of generative AI, ethical, legal, and environmental concerns must be addressed, equitable access ensured, and comprehensive support provided to developing countries [40].

Digitizing financial processes can improve the efficiency of banking [41]. Digitization has the potential to simplify traditional operations, prevent fraud, and create new and more personalized offers according to customer needs while changing the way they interact with them. Reut et al. [42] discussed the challenge of the controlled scaling of information systems. The authors used a hierarchical data matrix, which reflected the different lifeworlds within an industrial enterprise. It was proposed to divide the control into independent subsystems, each with its own big data processing, and to use integration algorithms for greater efficiency and data storage in larger objects such as regions or countries. Lu et al. [34] investigated the effects of the digital economy on women's employment in China. The authors found evidence that the digital economy boosts women's employment by creating gender perspectives, increasing labor demand in some areas, and encouraging the use of technology. However, it does not improve the quality of women's employment and may increase the number of working hours for underemployed women. Liu [43] proposed the use of particle swarm optimization (PSO) to improve the traditional back propagation neural network (BPNN), thus developing an intelligent financial disaster risk prevention model in the digital economy. Joshi et al. [44] presented QBeep, a blockchain quantum exchange protocol that enables secure digital asset transactions between multiple parties in decentralized networks, which use QC and homomorphic encryption to guarantee security and transparency, addressing challenges in traditional cryptography. Shang and Asif [45] proposed an innovative economic management model based on a composite neural network that uses the Bi-LSTM as the primary predictive analysis tool and is complemented by the Markov chain model. The conducted experiments showed an accuracy of 87.66% and an error evaluation index R2 close to 1, demonstrating high accuracy and reliability in economic prediction.

5.4. Conclusions

Digital transformation has become a crucial strategy for businesses and other sectors, enabling them to leverage technological advances to enhance performance and increase revenues. By optimizing the production and sale of goods and services, digital transformation drives growth and innovation. However, these changes also introduce new work paradigms and necessitate a reconsideration of organizational design.

Emerging technologies like AI and quantum computing are reshaping society and the economy, particularly in technology-intensive sectors. As these technologies become more prevalent, they are transforming the labor market and creating new opportunities and challenges. For instance, AI's ability to process large amounts of data can significantly enhance decision-making, but it also requires sophisticated systems to ensure accuracy and reliability. Quantum computing, when combined with AI and other technologies like the Internet of Things (IoT), holds promise for overcoming these challenges by revolutionizing security practices.

The expansion of the digital economy has made cybersecurity a cornerstone of global commerce and communication. As businesses increasingly rely on digital platforms to manage assets and exchange information, ensuring the security and integrity of these systems has become critical. Quantum technologies offer groundbreaking solutions to these security challenges. For example, quantum communication protocols, such as quantum key distribution (QKD), provide unparalleled security by leveraging the principles of quantum mechanics. These protocols ensure that any attempt to intercept or copy information will be detected, making them ideal for securing sensitive transactions and data.

Beyond secure communication, quantum technologies could revolutionize digital finance through the concept of quantum money. This involves creating unique, unforgeable digital tokens that rely on quantum states, potentially eliminating counterfeiting and enhancing trust in financial transactions. However, significant technical challenges, such as the stability of quantum bits (qubits) and the development of reliable quantum memories, must be addressed before these technologies can be widely implemented.

Meanwhile, metaverse technology, which integrates AI, virtual reality, and blockchain, is gaining importance by enabling meaningful interactions between real-world and digital assets. As these technologies evolve, they will further transform the digital economy, fostering innovation and new opportunities.

In conclusion, while the potential of emerging technologies like AI, quantum computing, and the metaverse is vast, their successful integration requires overcoming significant challenges. Ongoing research and development are essential to unlocking their full potential and addressing the complexities of the ever-changing digital landscape.

Acknowledgments

This activity is conducted as part of the Strategic Project Cybersecure platform for the exchange of digital tokens based on low-power distributed registration technologies (CSDT) (C075/23), established through a collaboration agreement between the National Institute of Cybersecurity (INCIBE) and the University of Salamanca. It falls within the framework of the Recovery, Transformation, and Resilience Plan, funded by the European Union (Next Generation). This Spanish government initiative serves as a roadmap for modernizing the economy, fostering economic growth, and creating jobs, ensuring a robust, inclusive, and resilient recovery from the COVID-19 crisis while addressing the challenges of the coming decade.

References

1. V. Amuso, G. Poletti, and D. Montibello, The digital economy: Opportunities and challenges, *Glob. Policy*. **11**(1), 124–127 (2020). https://doi.org/10.1111/1758-5899.12745.
2. M. B. Bulturbayevich and M. B. Jurayevich, The impact of the digital economy on economic growth, *Int. J. Bus. Law Educ.* **1**(1), 4–7 (2020). https://doi.org/10.56442/IJBLE.V1I1.2.
3. D. Tapscott, *The Digital Economy: Promise and Peril in the Age of Networked Intelligence*, McGraw-Hill, New York (1996).
4. D. Ma and Q. Zhu, Innovation in emerging economies: Research on the digital economy driving high-quality green development, *J. Bus. Res.* **145**, 801–813 (2022). https://doi.org/10.1016/j.jbusres.2022.03.041.
5. M. Kamil, J. Shodiev, and R. Zarina, Technological trends in the digital economy, *Am. J. Lang. Literacy Learn. STEM Educ. (2993-2769)*. **2**(1), 406–408 (2024). https://grnjournal.us/index.php/STEM/article/view/2797.
6. H. Hang and Z. Chen, How to realize the full potentials of artificial intelligence (AI) in digital economy? A literature review. *J. Decis. Econ.* **59**(4), 555–578 (2022). https://doi.org/10.1016/j.jdec.2022.11.003.
7. G. Ben-Ishai, J. Dean, J. Manyika, et al. *AI and the Opportunity for Shared Prosperity: Lessons from the History of Technology and the Economy*. (2024). arXiv preprint arXiv:2401.09718.
8. Z. Zhang, The impact of the artificial intelligence industry on the number and structure of employments in the digital economy environment, *Technol. Forecast. Soc. Change*. **197**, 40–1625 (2023). https://doi.org/10.1016/j.techfore.2023.122881.
9. O. I. Maslak, M. V. Maslak, N. Y. Grishko, et al. Artificial intelligence as a key driver of business operations transformation in the conditions of the digital economy. In *Proc. 20th IEEE Int. Mod. Electr. Energy Syst., MEES 2021*, pp. 1–6, Kremenchuk, Ukraine (2021). https://doi.org/10.1109/MEES52427.2021.9598744.
10. X. Li and W. Chen, Economic impacts of quantum computing: Strategies for integrating quantum technologies into business models, *Eigenpub Rev. Sci. Technol.* **7**(1), 277–290 (2023). https://studies.eigenpub.com/index.php/erst/article/view/46.
11. T. D. Ladd, F. Jelezko, R. Laflamme, et al. Quantum computers, *Nature*. **464**(7285), 45–53 (2010). https://doi.org/10.1038/nature08812.
12. F. Bova, A. Goldfarb, and R. G. Melko, Quantum economic advantage, *Manag. Sci.* **69**(2), 1116–1126 (2023). https://doi.org/10.1287/MNSC.2022.4578/ASSET/IMAGES/LARGE/MNSC.2022.4578F2.JPEG.
13. M. Aljaafari and S. Alotaibi, Importance of quantum technology in economy paradigm shift, *Soft Comput.* **27**(8), 3271–3281 (2023). https://doi.org/10.1007/s00500-023-08514-0.
14. M.-L. How and S.-M. Cheah, Forging the future: Strategic approaches to quantum AI integration for industry transformation, *AI*, **5**(1), 290–323 (2024). https://doi.org/10.3390/ai5010015.
15. T. Haug, C. N. Self, and M. S. Kim, Quantum machine learning of large datasets using randomized measurements, *Mach. Learn. Sci. Technol.* **4**(1), 015005 (2023). https://doi.org/10.1088/2632-2153/acb0b4.

16. V. Dunjko, J. M. Taylor, and H. J. Briegel, Quantum-enhanced machine learning, *Phys. Rev. Lett.* **117**(13), 130501 (2016). https://doi.org/10.1103/PhysRevLett.117.130501.

17. OECD. Stimulating digital innovation for growth and inclusiveness: The role of policies for the successful diffusion of ICT. OECD Digital Economy Papers, No. 256, OECD Publishing, Paris (2016). https://doi.org/10.1787/5jlwqvhg3l31-en.

18. I. Jackson, D. Ivanov, A. Dolgui, and J. Namdar, Generative artificial intelligence in supply chain and operations management: A capability-based framework for analysis and implementation, *Int. J. Prod. Res.* **62**(17), 1–26 (2024). https://doi.org/10.1080/00207543.2024.2309309.

19. I. G. Needleman, A guide to systematic reviews Needleman IG: A guide to systematic reviews. *J. Clin. Periodontol.* **29**, 6–9 (2002). https://doi.org/10.1034/j.1600-051X.29.s3.15.x.

20. W. Wang, Y. Chen, Y. Wang, et al. Unveiling the implementation barriers to the digital transformation in the energy sector using the Fermatean cubic fuzzy method, *Appl. Energy.* **360**, 122756 (2024). https://doi.org/10.1016/j.apenergy.2024.122756.

21. R. F. Reier Forradellas and L. M. Garay Gallastegui, Digital transformation and artificial intelligence applied to business: Legal regulations, economic impact, and perspective, *Laws.* **10**(3), 70 (2021). https://doi.org/10.3390/laws10030070.

22. W. Lyu and J. Liu, Artificial intelligence and emerging digital technologies in the energy sector, *Appl. Energy.* **289**, 117615 (2021). https://doi.org/10.1016/j.apenergy.2021.117615.

23. D. Chalmers, N. G. MacKenzie and S. Carter, Artificial Intelligence and Entrepreneurship: Implications for Venture Creation in the Fourth Industrial Revolution, *Entrepreneurship Theory and Practice.* **45**(5), 1028–1053 (2021). https://doi.org/10.1177/1042258720934581.

24. W. R. Scholz, E. J. Bartelsman, S. Diefenbach, et al. Unintended side effects of the digital transition: European scientists' messages from a proposition-based expert round table, *Sustainability.* **10**(6), 2001 (2018). https://doi.org/10.3390/su10062001.

25. N. C. Thompson, S. Ge, and Y. M. Sherry, Building the algorithm commons: Who discovered the algorithms that underpin computing in the modern enterprise? *Glob. Strateg. J.* **11**(1), 17–33 (2021). https://doi.org/10.1002/gsj.1393.

26. Q. Tang, F. R. Yu, R. Xie, et al. Internet of intelligence: A survey on the enabling technologies, applications, and challenges, *IEEE Commun. Surv. Tutor.* **24**(2), 1043–1070 (2022). https://doi.org/10.1109/COMST.2022.3175453.

27. C. Wang, N. Zhang, and C. Wang, Managing privacy in the digital economy, *Fundam. Res.* **1**(5), 543–551 (2021). https://doi.org/10.1016/j.fmre.2021.08.009.

28. Y. Xu, P. Ahokangas, M. Turunen, M. Mäntymäki, and J. Heikkilä, Platform-based business models: Insights from an emerging AI-enabled smart building ecosystem, *Electronics (Switzerland).* **8**(10), 1150 (2019). https://doi.org/10.3390/electronics8101150.

29. T. M. H. Nguyen, V. P. Nguyen, and D. T. Nguyen, A new hybrid Pythagorean fuzzy AHP and COCOSO MCDM based approach by adopting artificial intelligence technologies, *J. Exp. Theor. Artif. Intell.* **34**(4), 859–880 (2022). https://doi.org/10.1080/0952813X.2022.2143908.

30. C. Bjola, AI for development: Implications for theory and practice, *Oxf. Dev. Stud.* **50**(1), 78–90 (2022). https://doi.org/10.1080/13600818.2021.1960960.

31. S. Yablonsky, AI-driven platform enterprise maturity: From human led to machine governed, *Kybernetes.* **50**(10), 2753–2789 (2021). https://doi.org/10.1108/K-06-2020-0384.

32. A. Jurcut, T. Niculcea, P. Ranaweera, and N.-A. Le-Khac, Security considerations for Internet of Things: A survey, *SN Comput. Sci.* **1**, 193 (2020). https://doi.org/10.1007/s42979-020-00201-3.

33. O. Dupouët, Y. Pitarch, M. Ferru, and B. Bernela, Community dynamics and knowledge production: Forty years of research in quantum computing, *J. Knowl. Manag.* **27**(8), 1991–2010. (2023). https://doi.org/10.1108/JKM-01-2023-0083.

34. J. Lu, Q. Xiao, and T. Wang, Does the digital economy generate a gender dividend for female employment? Evidence from China, *Telecommun. Policy.* **47**(6), 102545 (2023). https://doi.org/10.1016/j.telpol.2023.102545.

35. H.-L. Yin, Y. Fu, C.-L. Li, et al. Experimental quantum secure network with digital signatures and encryption, *Nat. Sci. Rev.* **10**(4), nwac228 (2023). https://doi.org/10.1093/nsr/nwac228.

36. R. Dhinesh Kumar and S. Chavhan, Shift to 6G: Exploration on trends, vision, requirements, technologies, research, and standardization efforts, *Sustain. Energy Technol. Assess.* **54**, 102666 (2022). https://doi.org/10.1016/j.seta.2022.102666.

37. J. Yang, Y. Zhao, C. Han, Y. Liu, and M. Yang, Big data, big challenges: Risk management of financial market in the digital economy, *J. Enterp. Inf. Manag.* **35**(4), 1288–1304 (2022). https://doi.org/10.1108/JEIM-01-2021-0057.

38. M. Jamshidi, A. Dehghaniyan Serej, A. Jamshidi, and O. Moztarzadeh, The meta-metaverse: Ideation and future directions, *Futur. Internet.* **15**(8), 252 (2023). https://doi.org/10.3390/fi15080252.

39. T. Orchard and L. Tasiemski, The rise of generative AI and possible effects on the economy, *Econ. Bus. Rev.* **9**(2), 2023 (2023). https://doi.org/10.18559/ebr.2023.2.732.

40. N. R. Mannuru, S. Shahriar, Z. A. Teel, et al. Artificial intelligence in developing countries: The impact of generative artificial intelligence (AI) technologies for development, *Inf. Dev.* **39**(4), 531–548 (2023). https://doi.org/10.1177/02666669231200628.

41. D. A. Artemenko and S. V. Zenchenko, Digital technologies in the financial sector: Evolution and major development trends in Russia and Abroad, *Financ. Theory Pract.* **25**(3), 90–101 (2021). https://doi.org/10.26794/2587-5671-2021-25-3-90-101.

42. D. Reut, S. Falko, and E. Postnikova, About scaling of controlling information system of industrial complex by streamlining of big data arrays in compliance with hierarchy of the present life-worlds. *Int. J. Math. Eng. Manag. Sci.* **4**(5), 1127–1139 (2019). https://doi.org/10.33889/IJMEMS.2019.4.5-089.

43. L. Liu, Research on digital economy of intelligent emergency risk avoidance in sudden financial disasters based on PSO-BPNN algorithm, *Comput. Intell. Neurosci.* **2021**, 7708422 (2021). https://doi.org/10.1155/2021/7708422.

44. S. Joshi, A. Choudhury, and R. I. Minu, Quantum blockchain-enabled exchange protocol model for decentralized systems, *Quant. Inf. Process.* **22**(11), 404 (2023). https://doi.org/10.1007/s11128-023-04156-1.

45. K. Shang and M. Asif, The design of a compound neural network-based economic management model for advancing the digital economy, *J. Organ. End User Comput.* **35**(1), 1–16 (2023). https://doi.org/10.4018/JOEUC.330678.

https://doi.org/10.1142/9789819813049_0006

CHAPTER 6

Exploring the Digital Economy: Current Research Trends, Challenges, and Opportunities

Manuel J. Cobo[1,*], Nadia Karina Gamboa-Rosales[2], José Ricardo López-Robles[3], and Enrique Herrera-Viedma[1]

[1] *Department of Computer Science and Artificial Intelligence, Andalusian Research Institute in Data Science and Computational Intelligence (DaSCI), University of Granada, Granada, Spain*

[2] *CONAHCYT, Centro de Investigación e Innovación Automotriz, Universidad Autónoma de Zacatecas, Zacatecas, Mexico*

[3] *Doctorado en Administración, Unidad Académica de Contaduría y Administración, Universidad Autónoma de Zacatecas, Zacatecas, Mexico*

**Corresponding author. E-mail: mjcobo@decsai.ugr.es*

The digital economy is transforming global markets, industries, and labor structures through the integration of advanced digital technologies such as artificial intelligence, blockchain, and the Internet of Things. This chapter explores the current research trends, challenges, and opportunities in the digital economy using a bibliometric and science mapping approach. By analyzing 3,226 publications from 2019 to 2023 using SciMAT, we identify the conceptual structure of digital economy research, highlighting key themes such as innovation management, digital transformation, artificial intelligence, and blockchain technology. The findings indicate that while digitalization fosters economic growth and business model innovation, it also presents challenges, including cybersecurity threats, digital divides, and labor market disruptions. Our analysis provides a strategic framework for understanding the evolution of digital economy research and offers insights into future research directions, emphasizing the need for inclusive digital policies and interdisciplinary collaboration. This study contributes to the ongoing discourse on the digital economy, aiding policymakers, researchers, and industry stakeholders in navigating the digital transformation landscape.

6.1. Introduction

The global economy transformation is being fueled by factors such as technological advancements, demographic shifts, and evolving consumer behaviors. Central to this transformation is the emergence and proliferation of the digital economy, encompassing a broad spectrum of industries and activities. From e-commerce platforms and digital finance to online services and content creation, the digital economy is characterized by the rapid exchange of information, digitization of goods and services, and integration of cutting-edge digital technologies, such as artificial intelligence, blockchain, and the Internet of Things [1, 2].

This digital revolution has fundamentally reshaped traditional business models and disrupted established industries, presenting challenges and opportunities for businesses and policymakers. On the one hand, e-commerce platforms have revolutionized how consumers shop, offering unparalleled convenience, choice, and accessibility. On the other hand, the digital divide remains a persistent challenge, exacerbating existing inequalities between regions, industries, and individuals. Bridging this gap requires concerted efforts to expand the internet infrastructure, improve digital literacy, and promote inclusive policies, ensuring equitable access to digital technologies and opportunities for economic participation [3, 4].

In addition to the digital divide, the changing nature of work poses notable challenges in the digital era. Automation, artificial intelligence, and the gig economy are transforming the labor market, raising concerns about job displacement, income inequality, and the erosion of traditional employment structures. Addressing these challenges requires proactive measures to reimagine education and training programs; enhance social safety nets; and foster collaboration among governments, businesses, and labor unions for a smooth transition to the future digital workforce [5, 6].

The digital economy presents unique cybersecurity and data privacy challenges. As businesses and individuals increasingly rely on digital technologies and online platforms for daily activities, they become vulnerable to cyberattacks, data breaches, and privacy violations. Protecting sensitive information and ensuring digital infrastructure security are paramount to maintaining trust and confidence in the digital economy [7, 8].

Despite these challenges, the digital economy offers many opportunities for businesses to innovate, expand, and thrive in a globalized marketplace. Digital technologies such as blockchain, artificial intelligence, and the Internet of Things offer new ways to streamline operations, improve efficiency, and create value across industries. For example, blockchain technology enables secure and transparent transactions, while artificial intelligence automates routine tasks and provides valuable insights into data [9, 10].

Furthermore, the increasing interconnectedness of the global economy facilitates collaboration, knowledge sharing, and innovation on unprecedented scales. Digital platforms and online marketplaces connect businesses with customers, suppliers, and partners worldwide, enabling them to access new markets, customers, and resources. Moreover, the metaverse concept is gaining prominence, offering new opportunities for businesses to create and monetize digital experiences in virtual worlds [11, 12].

In summary, the digital economy is reshaping the global economic landscape, presenting challenges and opportunities for businesses, governments, and societies worldwide. Embracing digital transformation, addressing inequalities, and fostering collaboration are key to unlocking the full potential of the digital economy and building an inclusive and sustainable future for all. By leveraging digital technologies, investing in digital infrastructure, and promoting digital literacy, we can navigate the complexities of the digital age and harness its transformative power to drive innovation, efficiency, and prosperity in the global economy [13, 14].

The digital economy continues to evolve, necessitating, identifying, and understanding the main applications and research around this concept in academics, science, and technology to consolidate its adoption. Therefore, an analysis of performance and bibliometric conceptual networks [15, 16] was proposed as a suitable framework for a thorough, comparative, and objective examination of the primary research topics in the digital economy research field and to evaluate their progression. This approach will enable prospective insights into identifying opportunities and addressing gaps in research, development, and innovation, aiding future decision-making by stakeholders in this field [17].

This study aims to visualize and understand the digital economy and identify its conceptual structure. Using the SciMAT bibliometric software tool, this study evaluates the leading indicators of bibliometric performance (e.g., publications, citations received, authors, and geographic distribution) [18–23].

6.2. Methods

Bibliometric methods are widely recognized as one of the most common and accepted strategies for analyzing basic and applied research output. They are increasingly valued for assessing scientific and academic quality, impact, productivity, and evolution [16].

Herein, a consolidated method [16] has been employed to uncover the themes of the digital economy using a conceptual framework and thematic relationship, focusing on the most influential publications and their impact. Additionally, this approach evaluates performance by analyzing key bibliometric indicators.

The method comprises two main components—bibliometric performance and science mapping analysis. Performance analysis relies on bibliometric indicators to gauge author productivity and impact, drawing on methodologies established in the literature [24]. Additionally, a conceptual science mapping analysis is conducted using a cowords network approach [25, 26], facilitated by the SciMAT software tool developed by Cobo et al. [27].

Although several software tools are available for conducting science mapping analysis [25], SciMAT was chosen because of its versatility in supporting various analytical approaches, including bibliometric performance analysis, strategic diagram creation, thematic network visualization, and thematic area identification [16]. The bibliometric employed methodology identified three phases of analysis in the research field during the research period:

- In the first phase, research themes are identified by applying a clustering algorithm to a normalized cowords network for each period under analysis.
- Visualization of research themes and the thematic network involves determining the identified research themes based on their centrality and density rank values, utilizing two specific tools—the strategic diagram and the thematic network. Centrality assesses

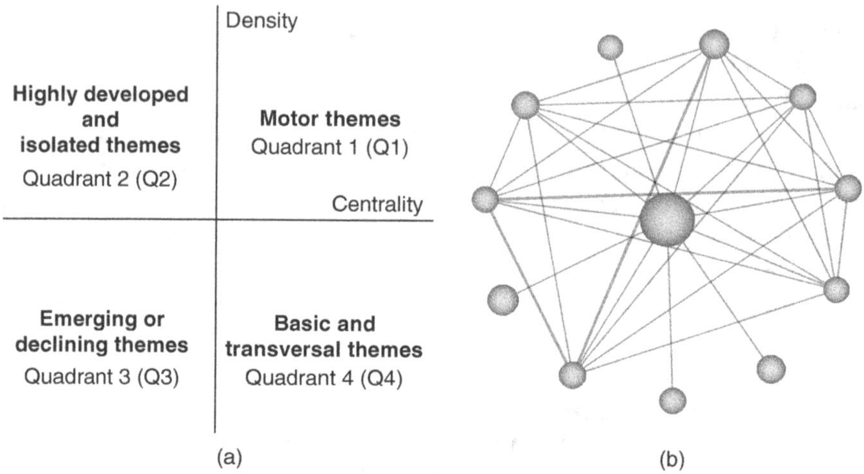

Fig. 6.1 (a) Strategic diagram and (b) thematic network.

the interaction level of a network with others, whereas density measures its internal strength. Considering both measures, the field of research can be visualized as a collection of research themes plotted on a two-dimensional strategic diagram (Fig. 6.1). Consequently, the following four research themes can be categorized [16]:

(i) Motor themes (Quadrant 1 [Q1]): Themes are pivotal for developing and structuring the research, denoted as the driving forces behind its advancement because of their high centrality and density.

(ii) Highly developed and isolated themes (Quadrant 2 [Q2]): Themes exhibit strong interrelations and specialization but remain peripheral to the field, lacking the necessary background or significance.

(iii) Emerging or declining themes (Quadrant 3 [Q3]): Representing relatively weak connections with low density and centrality, themes typically signify emerging trends or fading topics in the field.

(iv) Basic and transversal themes (Quadrant 4 [Q4]): Themes are relevant to the research field but are yet to be extensively developed. This quadrant encompasses broad and fundamental themes with cross-disciplinary implications.

Performance analysis quantitatively and qualitatively measures the relative contributions of research themes and thematic areas to the overall research field. This analysis is instrumental in identifying the most productive and pertinent areas.

6.3. Dataset

The Web of Science Core Collection database was employed to collect raw data on the digital economy. The following advanced query was used: TS = ("DIGITAL ECONOMY")

AND 2023 OR 2022 OR 2021 OR 2020 OR 2019 (PUBLICATION YEARS) AND ARTICLE (DOCUMENT TYPES) AND ENGLISH (LANGUAGES). This query retrieved 3,226 publications (articles and reviews) from 2019 to 2023. Furthermore, citations of these publications were analyzed and counted up to February 14, 2024.

The digital economy publications were procured in plain text format in this framework and subsequently imported into SciMAT to establish the foundation for science mapping analysis. All bibliographic details stored in the Web of Science Core Collection, including authorship, affiliations, abstracts, keywords, publication dates, citations, and references, were retained for each publication. This comprehensive dataset enables data analysis and identification of relationships, yielding robust outcomes during the science mapping analysis. Furthermore, a meticulous revision process was employed to ensure and enhance the quality of the raw data. This process entails analyzing, correcting, and amalgamating concepts that share the same meaning or represent identical ideas; for instance, terms such as "Artificial-Intelligence," "AI-Artificial-Intelligence," and "Artificial-Intelligence-(AI)," were unified under a single category called "Artificial-Intelligence."

As a next step, the SciMAT software tool was used to map the research period. Considering the results, a future research line can be considered to develop year-by-year analyses to recognize singular factors.

6.4. Productivity and Impact Analysis

The bibliometric performance of the digital economy field was assessed based on publications, citations, and impact. The analysis was divided into three sections: (i) an overview of the overall production and impact of published documents; (ii) an examination of the contributions made by authors, countries, and organizations; and (iii) an analysis of the primary sources of publication.

Thus, Fig. 6.2 depicts the distribution of publications and cites per year in the digital economy from 2019 to 2023. Notably, the evolution of both indicators has been positive, positioning this knowledge field among the most relevant subjects for academic, scientific, business, political, and social communities.

Concerning publications, the trend is positive. Since 2020, despite the pandemic, a new historical maximum has been recorded every year, which will potentially remain as it is in 2024. The advanced search used in this study retrieved 3,226 publications from 2019 to 2023, concentrated on 25,973 citations (19,520 without self-citation) in the research period (Fig. 6.2).

The sustained and positive evolution observed in both cases implies that the digital economy will remain a subject of considerable interest in the years ahead. Thus, identifying the key stakeholders, including the most productive and cited authors, as well as their geographical distribution, affiliations, and related research areas, is essential.

Tables 6.1 and 6.2 present the most productive and cited authors from 2019 to 2023. Some positions are tied among multiple authors; hence, they are presented alphabetically. Notably, only three of the most productive authors feature among the most cited

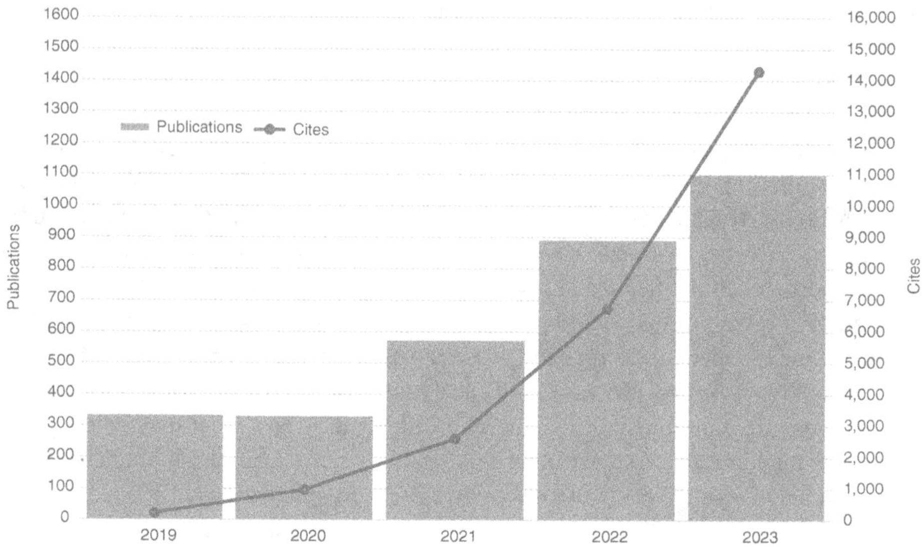

Fig. 6.2 Distribution of publications and cites by year from 2019 to 2023.

authors—H. T. Wu (12 publications, 1,254 citations), Y. Hao (10 publications, 859 citations), and W. Zhang (7 publications, 297 citations). This dual scenario highlights the importance of productivity and citation impact in fostering the growth and advancement of the research field.

Table 6.1 Most productive authors (2019–2023).

Publications	Author(s)
25	J. Wang
21	Y. Wang; Y. Zhang
15	Y. Liu
13	H. Zhang; J. Zhang; X. Zhang
12	K. Y. Dong; Y. Li; H. T. Wu; L. Zhang
11	Y. Yang
10	L. Chen; Y. Hao; J. Li; X. Zhao
9	X. H. Chen; Y. Chen; H. Wang; J. D. Wang; L. Wang; Q. Wang; X. Y. Wang; H. W. Wen; J. Wu; C. Zhang
8	A. V. Bogoviz; J. Chen; N. Li; Y. Wu
7	W. Chen; J. Huang; C. C. Lee; F. Li; J. Y. Li; S. L. Li; B. Liu; H. J. Liu; L. Liu; Q. Liu; Y. J. Liu; X. Y. Ma; E. G. Popkova; X. Wang; X. M. Wang; Z. Wang; Z. Y. Wang; C. Watanabe; W. Zhang; Y. Zhao

Table 6.2 Most cited authors.

Citations	Author(s)
1,254	H. T. Wu
859	Y. Hao
610	S. Y. Ren
501	M. Irfan
430	Q. Y. Ran; X. D. Yang
409	X. Han; X. C. Ni; L. W. Ouyang; F. Y. Wang; S. Wang; Y. Yuan
389	F. Li
371	M. Ahmad
344	N. Ba; L. Xu
297	W. Zhang

Regarding the involvement of countries and organizations in digital economy research (Tables 6.3 and 6.4), 105 countries spanning five continents are engaged. There is a balanced representation among European, Asian, and American countries concerning productivity. This balance is reflected in the performance of the most productive organizations as well. In 2019–2023, China emerged as the foremost productive country, with 1,375 publications, followed by Russia and the United States of America, contributing 465 and 232 publications, respectively. Similarly, the most prolific organizations include the Ministry of Education and Science of Ukraine, State University of Management (Russia), Financial University under the Government of the Russian Federation (Russia), Plekhanov Russian University of Economics (Russia), and University of London (England).

Table 6.3 Most productive countries (2019–2023).

Publications	Countries
1,375	People's Republic of China
465	Russia
232	United States of America
201	England
173	Ukraine
114	Australia
89	Germany
85	Spain
74	Poland
66	Italy

Table 6.4 Most productive organizations (2019–2023).

Publications	Organization
147	Ministry of Education Science of Ukraine
64	State University of Management
53	Financial University under the Government of the Russian Federation
44	Plekhanov Russian University of Economics; University of London
36	Russian Academy of Sciences
35	Chinese Academy of Sciences; Xinjiang University
32	Southwestern University of Finance Economics China
31	Renmin University of China
30	Wuhan University
28	Beijing Institute of Technology

According to the Web of Science Core Collection, the indexes with the most remarkable number of publications related to the digital economy are the Social Sciences Citation Index (1,392 publications), Emerging Sources Citation Index (1,103 publications), and Science Citation Index Expanded (1,077 publications). Table 6.3 presents the most productive journals identified in the research period.

Regarding the publication sources (Table 6.5), various journals host digital economy papers, covering knowledge areas from business management to engineering. Further, this research field covers an excellent variety of Web of Science categories, such as environmental sciences (559), economics (465), environmental studies (371), green sustainable science technology (357), business (335), management (290), law (229), social sciences interdisciplinary (187), computer science information systems (171), and multidisciplinary sciences (151).

Table 6.5 Most productive sources related to the digital economy.

Publications	Sources	2022 Impact factor
299	Sustainability	3.9
67	Environmental Science and Pollution Research	5.8
61	Studies in Systems Decision and Control (Book series)	–
57	Socio-Economic Systems Vol 2 (Book)	–
45	International Journal of Environmental Research and Public Health	4.614
44	Frontiers in Environmental Science	4.6
44	Frontiers in Psychology	3.8

37	Technological Forecasting and Social Change	12.0
35	PLOS One	3.7
28	Studies in Computational Intelligence (Book series)	–
28	Ubiquitous Computing and the Internet of Things Prerequisites for the development of ICT (Book)	–
26	Financial and Credit Activity: Problems of Theory and Practice	11.1
26	Journal of Cleaner Production	

6.5. Conceptual Analysis of the Research Period (2019–2023)

This section overviews the conceptual structure of the digital economy through science mapping analysis, complemented by performance analysis. This overview covers two complementary approaches: thematic and thematic network analyses.

Digital economy research themes are presented in Fig. 6.3, in which the core themes from 2019 to 2023 are identified and visualized. The digital economy literature has focused on 20 research themes. Considering their performance measures (Table 6.6), the most productive themes (>125 publications) were basic and transversal, such as innovation management (426), strategic management (301), big data technology (274), artificial intelligence (270), social media strategy (257), greenhouse gas emissions (204), and spatial spillover effect (174), as well as motor themes, such as digital transformation (263), sustainable development (168), and blockchain technology (129). The most cited themes (>1,900 cites) are basic and transversal, such as innovation management (4,846), greenhouse gas emissions (4,010), strategic management (3,680), big data technology (3,222), spatial spillover effect (2,747), social media strategy (2,310), and artificial intelligence (1,842); motor themes, such as sustainable development (1,997); highly developed and isolated themes, such as pollution control (2,093); and emerging or declining themes, such as digital transformation (2, 523).

The main research themes identified in the digital economy field in recent years coincide in terms of relevance and impact, representing coherence in the development of the research field. The following is a description of the thematic networks and their relationship with the development of intellectual structure:

Innovation management (Fig. 6.4) and strategic management (Fig. 6.5) are the basic and transversal themes with the highest impact and number of publications, respectively. As these themes are intertwined, they foster growth and competitiveness through various avenues. On the one hand, the innovation management theme plays a vital role in the digital economy, shaping the way businesses adapt, compete, and thrive in dynamic environments. It drives the exploration and implementation of new business models, leveraging emerging technologies and market trends to create value and sustain competitive advantage. Moreover, this theme operates within innovation systems, fostering collaboration among stakeholders, institutions, and policies to facilitate knowledge exchange and resource allocation. Finally, it fosters entrepreneurship by providing resources and support

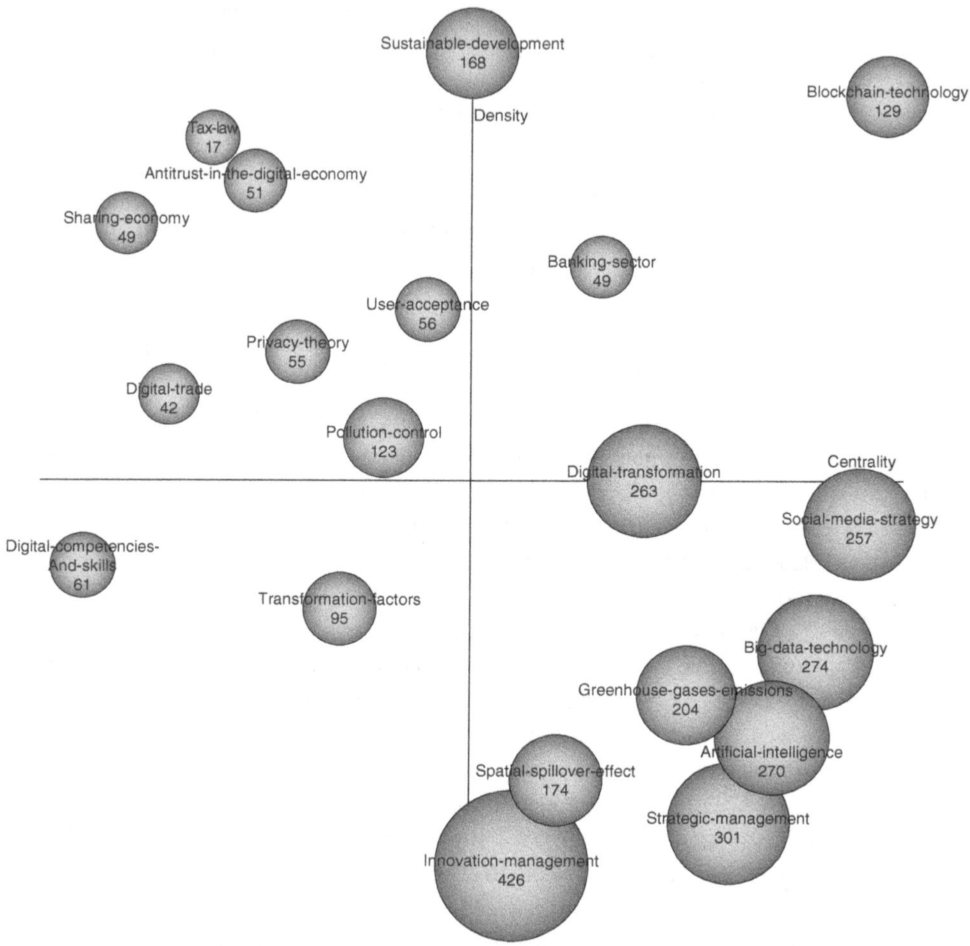

Fig. 6.3 Strategic diagram of the digital economy.

for new ventures and promotes crowdsourcing, tapping into diverse perspectives to collaboratively generate innovative solutions. On the other hand, the strategic management theme is linked to digital innovation, value creation systems, open innovation, knowledge management, organizational performance, and business ecosystems. Aligning digital economy initiatives is required with strategic goals for creating value by adopting the emerging technologies and novel business models. Additionally, this theme is crucial to driving innovation, competitiveness, and organizational adaptability in a dynamic and evolving environment.

Concerning the basic and transversal themes, the big data technology theme is third-ranked concerning the number of documents and impact (Fig. 6.6). This theme intersects with various themes to drive efficiency and innovation, such as big data analytics, supply

Table 6.6 Performance of themes (2019–2023).

Theme	Quadrant	Publications	h-index	Cites	Average citations
INNOVATION MANAGEMENT					11.38
STRATEGIC MANAGEMENT	Q 4	426	34	4,846	12.23
BIG-DATA TECHNOLOGY	Q 4	301	32	3,680	12.23
ARTIFICIAL INTELLIGENCE	Q 4	274	31	3,222	11.76
DIGITAL TRANSFORMATION	Q 1	263	20	1,842	6.82
SOCIAL MEDIA STRATEGY	Q 4	257	23	2,523	9.59
GREENHOUSE GAS EMISSIONS	Q 4	204	25	2,310	8.99
SPATIAL SPILLOVER EFFECT	Q 4	174	32	4,010	19.66
SUSTAINABLE DEVELOPMENT	Q 1	168	26	2,747	15.79
BLOCKCHAIN TECHNOLOGY	Q 1	129	23	1,997	11.89
POLLUTION CONTROL	Q 2	123	19	1,668	12.93
TRANSFORMATION FACTORS	Q 3	95	23	2,093	17.02
DIGITAL COMPETENCIES AND SKILLS	Q 3	61	16	1,104	11.62
USER ACCEPTANCE	Q 2	56	12	468	7.67
PRIVACY THEORY	Q 2	55	14	611	10.91
ANTITRUST IN THE DIGITAL ECONOMY	Q 2	51	11	545	9.91
BANKING SECTOR	Q 1	49	6	141	2.76
SHARING ECONOMY	Q 2	49	11	320	6.53
DIGITAL TRADE	Q 2	42	9	259	5.29
TAX LAW	Q 2	17	10	305	7.6

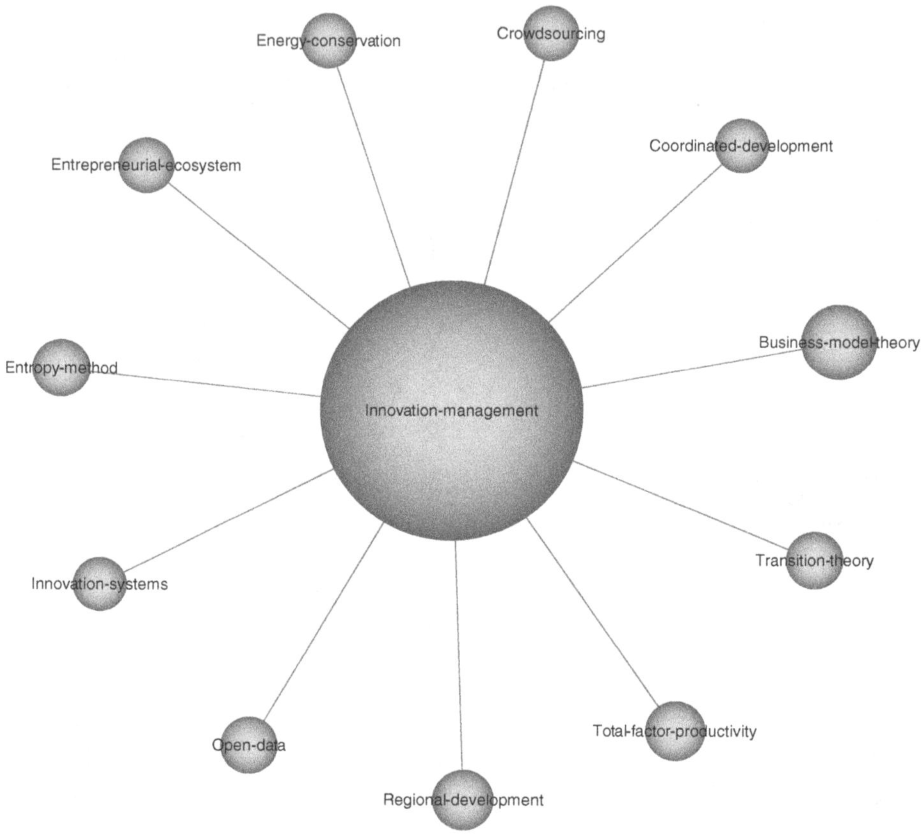

Fig. 6.4 Theme: Innovation management.

chain management, machine learning, information systems, and the Internet of Things. It holds immense importance for the digital economy because it enables the analysis of vast amounts of information, facilitating informed decision-making, personalized experiences, and targeted strategies. By harnessing big data analytics, businesses can gain valuable insights, enhance operational efficiency, and drive innovation, ultimately fostering growth and competitiveness in the digital landscape.

Following closely the previous theme, artificial intelligence (Fig. 6.7) is in the basic and transversal quadrant, ranked among the most productive themes and mainly focusing on digital platforms, smart technologies, cybersecurity, neural networks, and sustainable strategies. This theme is relevant because of its current evolution and potential role in the future, considering its transformative potential in revolutionizing industries, enhancing efficiency, and driving innovation across various sectors worldwide.

Fig. 6.5 Theme: Strategic management.

Along with the previous theme, digital transformation is the first theme ranked in the motor themes quadrant (Fig. 6.8), which mainly delves into business strategy, regional economy, the latest technology advances, and digital maturity. This theme is crucial for businesses to stay competitive and relevant in this fast-paced world. Embracing digital transformation enables organizations to adapt to changing market demands, improve efficiency, and unlock new growth opportunities. Furthermore, it fosters agility and flexibility, allowing businesses to quickly respond to market shifts and emerging trends. Ultimately, it empowers organizations to optimize processes, leverage data-driven insights, and create value in an increasingly digitalized economy, ensuring long-term success and sustainability in the digital age.

The social media strategy is another core theme in the basic and transversal quadrant. It acts as a powerful tool for engaging with customers, creating brand awareness, and

Fig. 6.6 Theme: Big data technology.

boosting sales (Fig. 6.9). This theme primarily covers entrepreneurship strategies, digital engagement, social network sites, and e-commerce, among others. Social media strategy is a driving force for entrepreneurship and e-commerce, making it a vital component of the digital economy. Moreover, based on the abovementioned issues, it offers valuable market insights, enabling businesses to tailor their offerings and marketing strategies effectively. With its ability to facilitate direct communication and engagement with customers, social media fosters customer trust and loyalty, which are crucial for e-commerce successes.

The greenhouse gas emissions theme is intricately linked with various aspects of energy systems and socioeconomic structures and is a part of basic and transversal themes (Fig. 6.10). Understanding this theme will support the optimization of energy infrastructure,

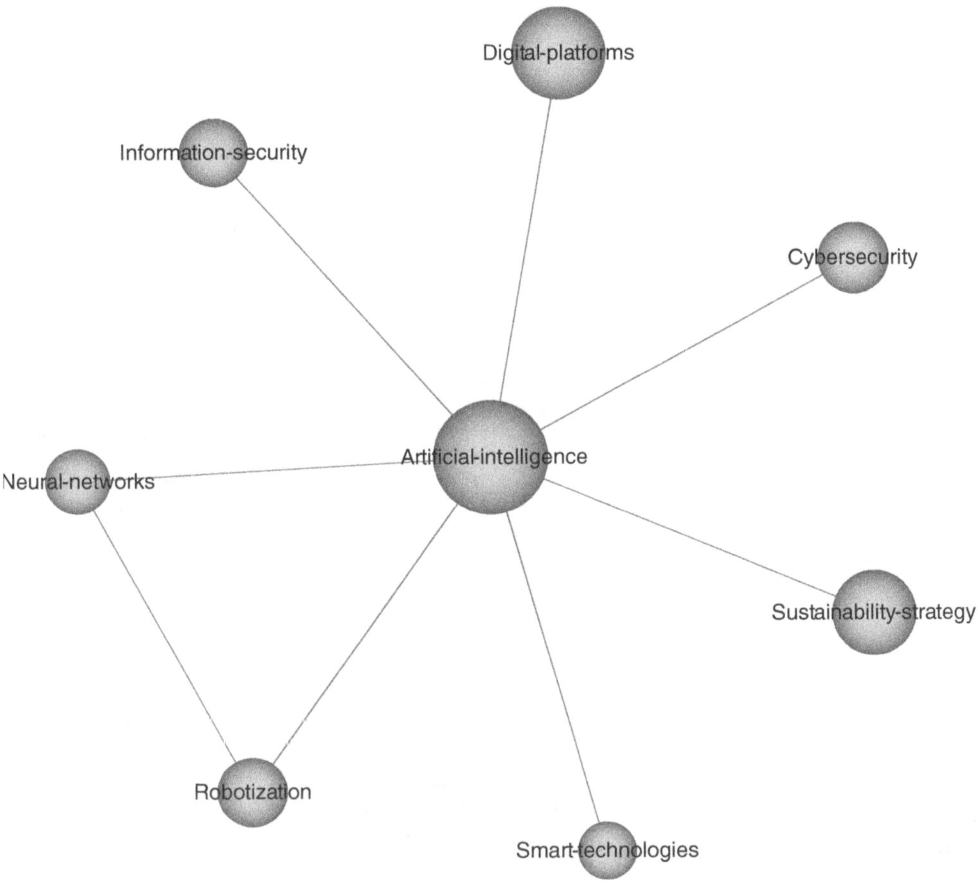

Fig. 6.7 Theme: Artificial intelligence.

transitioning toward cleaner sources, and enhancing industrial processes for reduced carbon footprints, which mitigates environmental impact and drives innovation in low-carbon technologies, promoting economic growth and resilience. Integrating sustainability principles into energy and industrial sectors creates opportunities for digitalization, such as smart grids, the Internet of Things in energy management, and digital optimization of industrial processes, fostering efficiency, competitiveness, and sustainable development in the digital era. The pollution control theme (Fig. 6.11), a widely cited theme that covers subjects related to air quality, urbanization, and public policies, is similar.

Synergistically, there is the motor theme—sustainable development (Fig. 6.12)—which has a significant number of publications and citations that are expected to continually grow in the coming years. Sustainable development covers subjects such as economic security, environmental protection, land resource management, renewable energy sources,

Fig. 6.8 Theme: Digital transformation.

and sustainable development goals. Promoting responsible conduct, reducing the environmental footprint, and ensuring lasting inclusivity and viability is crucial in the digital economy.

Furthermore, the spatial spillover effect is one of the most cited themes in the basic and transversal quadrants, covering topics related to environmental regulation, energy efficiency, green productivity, and the difference-in-differences model (Fig. 6.13). This theme plays an important role in supporting the development of the digital economy by fostering innovation, collaboration, and economic growth across geographical boundaries. In the digital era, this theme is especially prominent as digital tools allow effortless communication, collaboration, and knowledge exchange, regardless of physical distance. A prime example of this is a tech startup in Silicon Valley, where its pioneering software can spread its knowledge, technology, and successful practices to other tech hubs.

Fig. 6.9 Theme: Social media strategy.

Finally, blockchain technology is a major theme with a relevant number of publications and citations. This theme is predominantly related to cryptocurrencies, smart contracts, transactions, and the metaverse (Fig. 6.14). Blockchain technology influences the growth of the digital economy via its revolutionary impact on transaction and contract systems. However, it is rapidly transforming the sectors in which it is applied, emerging as a burgeoning field. It will continue to revolutionize financial systems, with cryptocurrencies such as Bitcoin and Ethereum, further facilitating secure and decentralized transactions, reducing reliance on traditional banking systems, and enabling financial inclusion for underserved populations. Additionally, its potential extends beyond finance into supply chain management, in which it enhances value, transparency, traceability, and efficiency by securely recording and verifying transactions across the supply chain. Moreover, this theme promises to revolutionize digital identity management, offering a secure and immutable way to store and verify personal information, leading to enhanced privacy

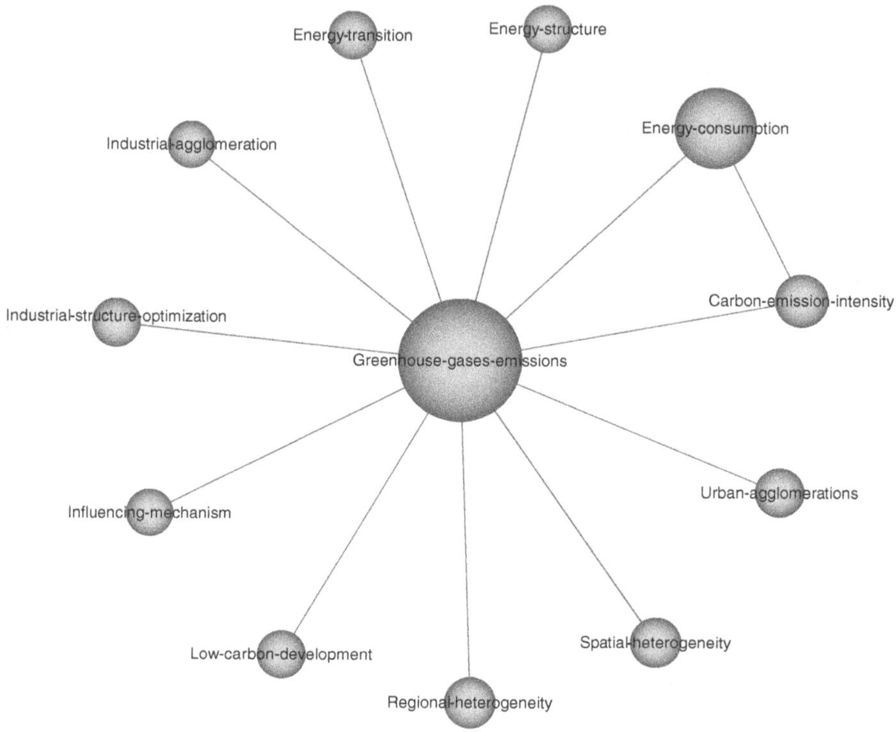

Fig. 6.10 Theme: Greenhouse gas emissions.

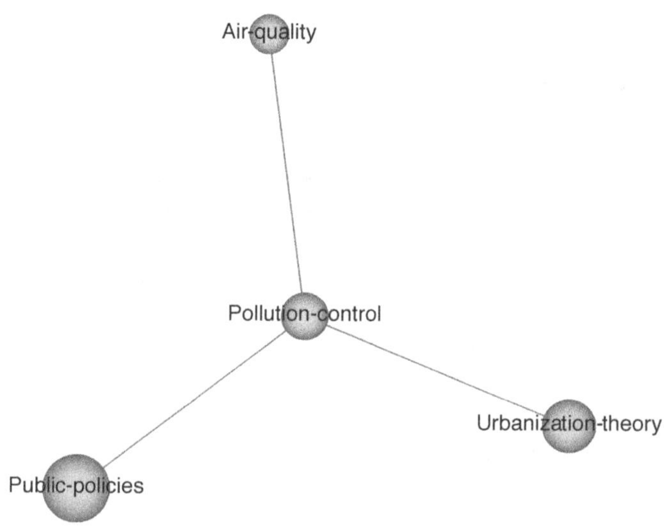

Fig. 6.11 Theme: Pollution control.

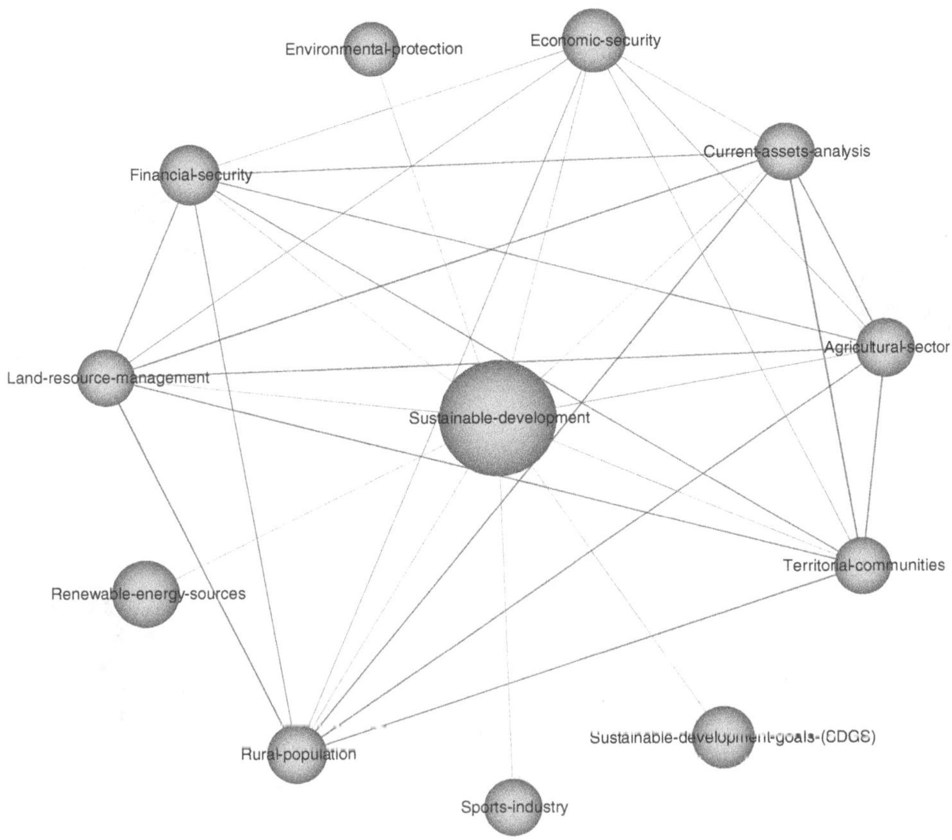

Fig. 6.12 Theme: Sustainable development.

and security on the internet. Finally, as the new concept of the metaverse gains prominence, blockchain technology will play a crucial role in managing digital assets and virtual economies in virtual worlds, enabling secure ownership, trading, and monetization of digital assets.

Although they are not the most productive or have the highest impact, the themes in the third quadrant (emerging or declining themes) are important because they complementarily clarify the digital economy development. Transformation factors and digital competencies and skills are the emerging or declining themes (Figs. 6.15 and 6.16). Transformation factors are related to the circular economy and organizational readiness; this is justified because organizations embrace circular principles; they are prompted to integrate digital technologies for enhanced resource management, supply chain optimization, and value creation in a digitally driven circular economy. Digital competencies and skills support the transformation factors to analyze the digital inequality and higher education system as drivers of digital economy development, considering that

Fig. 6.13 Theme: Spatial spillover effect.

effective policies targeting digital inequality and education accessibility are essential for leveraging the potential of digital technologies and driving economic growth in the digital era.

In summary, the strategic diagram (Fig. 6.3) and thematic networks (Figs. 6.4–6.16) and their performance measures (Table 6.4) reveal that the digital economy is a growing research field, driven by relevant knowledge areas such as computer science, finance, and business management.

Finally, according to the results obtained and considering the main topics covered in the most cited themes, the following subjects will drive the development of the digital economy: big data technologies, blockchain technology, artificial intelligence, sustainable development, new business models, and innovation management.

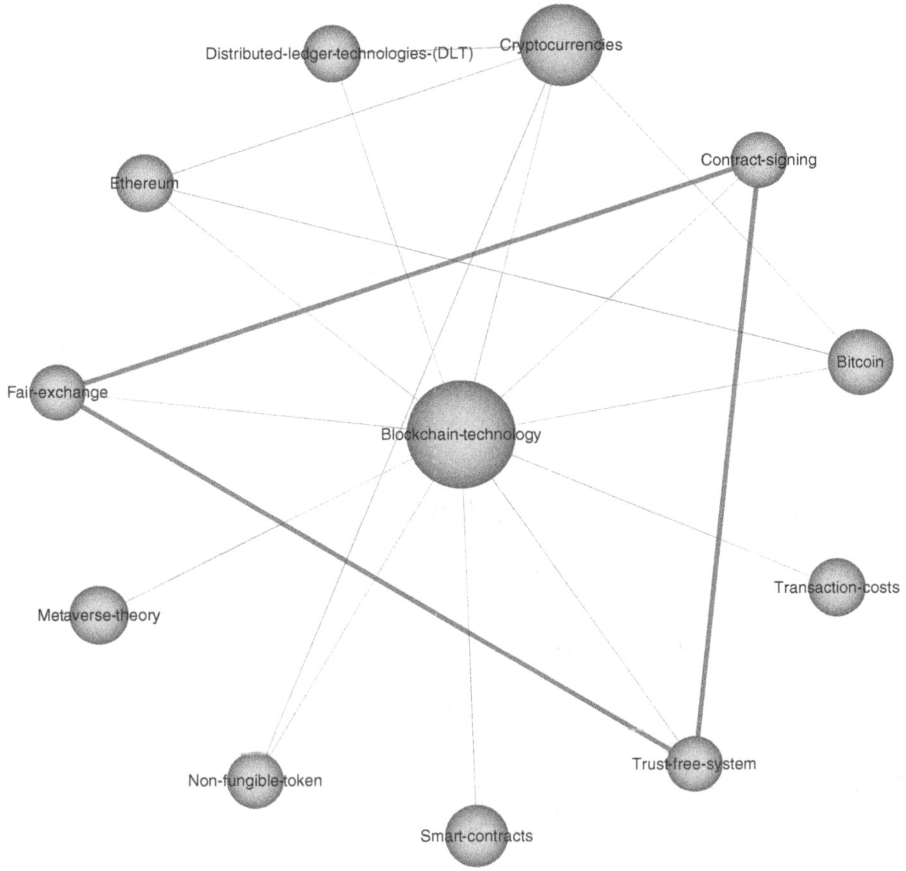

Fig. 6.14 Theme: Blockchain technology.

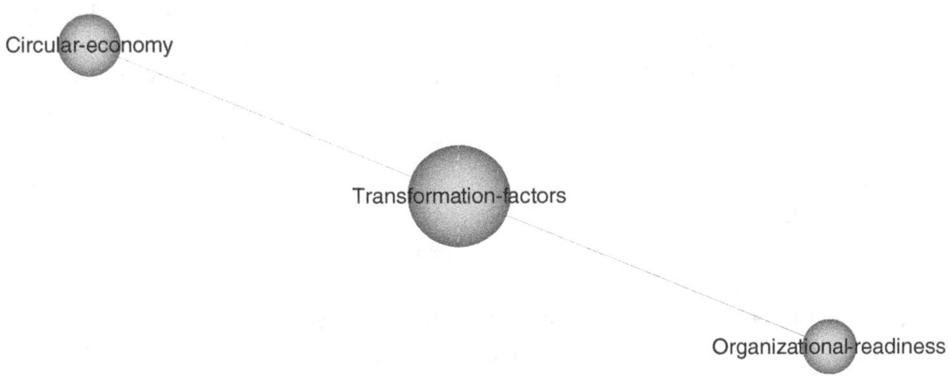

Fig. 6.15 Theme: Transformation factors.

Fig. 6.16 Theme: Digital competencies and skills.

6.6. Discussion and Conclusions

Consistent with the objectives of this article, over 9,000 research themes have been identified, analyzing their impact, interrelation, and evolution. These findings enable the establishment of a comprehensive framework for understanding the digital economy from various approaches, including academic, scientific, technological, entrepreneurial, social, and political perspectives. Specific themes have emerged for their pivotal, fundamental, and cross-cutting significance, including innovation management, strategic management, big data technology, social media strategy, greenhouse gas emissions, spatial spillover effect, blockchain technology, digital transformation, artificial intelligence, pollution control, and sustainable development.

The digital economy is poised as a continuous process of transformation driven by technological innovation and global interconnectedness. The increasing relevance of the digital economy is reflected in its ability to generate growth and development opportunities across various domains, from business and science to social and political spheres. With rising access to digital technology and the expansion of communication networks, the digital economy will potentially, continually expand, encompassing new sectors and facilitating technology integration into virtually every aspect of modern life. However, this growth poses significant challenges, such as the need to address the issues of data privacy, cybersecurity, and the digital divide. Contextually, ongoing research and adopting robust policies are essential to harnessing the full potential of the opportunities and overcoming the challenges associated with the constantly evolving digital economy.

Regarding relevant bibliometric measures, the digital economy field had an h-index of 67 from 2019 to 2023, reflecting the high impact of such publications and their use by the communities. This group of publications had 25,973 citations (including self-citations) and an average citation count of 8.05 per item. Considering the performance and thematic analysis obtained in SciMAT, this field may experience substantial growth in the coming years, becoming a cross-cutting knowledge area.

Thus, considering the approaches included in the quadrant of emerging themes—which include the circular economy, education, and other key aspects of the digitization of organizations—is necessary. The transition toward a circular economy fosters resource efficiency and sustainability, driving organizations to adapt and innovate, catalyzing the advancement of digital economy solutions. The shift toward a digital economy necessitates a population with enhanced digital skills capable of adapting to the evolving demands of the job market. Additionally, organizations must align their strategies with these transformations by implementing policies and strategies that foster innovation, agility, and the adoption of digital technologies to maintain competitiveness in an increasingly digitized business environment.

The evolution of the digital economy is poised to profoundly impact various facets of society, economics, and science in the future. With technological advancements such as artificial intelligence, the blockchain, and big data analytics driving innovation, the digital economy will potentially undergo rapid transformation. This evolution will lead to increased connectivity, automation, and data-driven decision-making processes, reshaping traditional business models and creating new opportunities for growth and efficiency.

In economics, the digital economy evolution is critical for fostering sustainable development and competitiveness. By leveraging technologies such as big data analytics, businesses can gain deeper insights into consumer behavior, market trends, and industry dynamics, allowing informed strategic decision-making. Moreover, the digital economy enables the emergence of new business models, such as platform-based ecosystems and digital marketplaces, which potentially drive economic growth, job creation, and innovation.

The evolution of the digital economy has significant implications for society and science. Enhanced connectivity and access to information fostered by digital technologies can facilitate social inclusion, knowledge sharing, and collaboration across geographical boundaries. Moreover, digital platforms and tools can empower individuals and communities to address societal challenges, such as healthcare disparities and environmental sustainability, through innovative solutions. Moreover, the digital economy provides researchers and scientists with unprecedented access to data and computational resources, accelerating scientific discovery and enabling interdisciplinary collaboration to tackle complex global issues.

Overall, the evolution of the digital economy represents a transformative force with far-reaching implications for economic development, societal progress, and scientific advancement. Embracing and harnessing the opportunities presented by this evolution crucially drive sustainable growth, foster social inclusion, and address pressing challenges in the 21st century.

In conclusion, the digital economy has emerged as a rapidly expanding field of interdisciplinary research, projected to solidify in the future, particularly in highly developed regions. The potential for growth and sustainability hinges on the integration of diverse areas of knowledge and the depth of analyzes conducted across major global regions. Furthermore, future research endeavors may entail a comprehensive global analysis, spanning annual intervals, to discern the evolution of each theme in its respective thematic network.

Our study has some limitations. First, we should remark that we have used the Web of Science to retrieve our corpus. Although the Web of Science is an important and widely used database, it is restricted and biased toward science and English. Therefore, documents not indexed in this database are not taken into account. Moreover, we should stand that this study is limited to the last 5 years, so we cannot see the global evolution of this research field.

Acknowledgments

This contribution is supported by the grants PID2019-105381GA-I00 (iScience) and PID2022-139297OB-I00 funded by MCIN/AEI/10.13039/501100011033. Additionally, it is part of the project C-ING-165UGR23, cofunded by the Regional Ministry of University, Research and Innovation and by the European Union under the Andalusia ERDF Programme 2021–2027. Moreover, the authors want to acknowledge the support of Universidad Autónoma de Zacatecas, Consejo Nacional de Humanidades, Ciencias y Tecnologías, Consejo Zacatecano de Ciencia Tecnología e Innovación (COZCYT), and Cuerpo Académico Gestión, Evaluación y Procesos de Formación de Políticas Públicas de México (CA-206) to carry out this piece of research.

References

1. M. B. Bulturbayevich and M. B. Jurayevich, The impact of the digital economy on economic growth, *Int. J. Bus. Law Educ.* **1**(1), 4–7 (2020).
2. X. Jiang, Digital economy in the post-pandemic era, *J. Chin. Econ. Bus. Stud.* **18**(4), 333–339 (2020).
3. D. Ma and Q. Zhu, Innovation in emerging economies: Research on the digital economy driving high-quality green development, *J. Bus. Res.* **145**, 801–813 (2022).
4. T. J. Sturgeon, Upgrading strategies for the digital economy, *GSJ.* **11**, 34–57 (2021).
5. C. Ding, C. Liu, C. Zheng, and F. Li, Digital economy, technological innovation and high-quality economic development: Based on spatial effect and mediation effect, *Sustainability.* **14**(1), 216 (2021).
6. W. Pan, T. Xie, Z. Wang, and L. Ma, Digital economy: An innovation driver for total factor productivity, *J. Bus. Res.* **139**, 303–311 (2022).
7. K. A. Barmuta, E. M. Akhmetshin, I. Y. Andryushchenko, et al. Problems of business processes transformation in the context of building digital economy, *Entrep. Sustain. Issues.* **8**(1), 945–959 (2020).

8. A. Rainnie and M. Dean, Industry 4.0 and the future of quality work in the global digital economy, *Labour Ind.* **30**, 16–33 (2020).
9. F. Almeida, J. Duarte Santos, and J. Augusto Monteiro, The challenges and opportunities in the digitalization of companies in a post-Covid-19 world, *IEEE Eng. Manag. Rev.* **48**(3), 97–103 (2020).
10. Y. Chen, Improving market performance in the digital economy, *China Econ. Rev.* **62**, 101482 (2020).
11. I. Mancuso, A. M. Messeni Petruzzelli, and U. Panniello, Digital business model innovation in metaverse: How to approach virtual economy opportunities, *Inf. Process. Manag.* **60**(5), 103457 (2023).
12. S. Sahay, N. Mahajan, S. Malik, and J. Kaur, Metaverse: Research based analysis and impact on economy and business. In *Proc. 2022 2nd Asian Conference on Innovation in Technology (ASIANCON)*, pp. 1–8, IEEE (2022).
13. S. Luo, N. Yimamu, Y. Li, et al. Digitalization and sustainable development: How could digital economy development improve green innovation in china? *Bus. Strat. Env.* **32**(4), 1847–1871 (2023).
14. J. Zhang, Y. Lyu, Y. Li and Y. Geng, Digital economy: An innovation driving factor for low-carbon development, *Environ. Impact Assess. Rev.* **96**, 106821 (2022).
15. V. Batagelj and M. Cerinšek, On bibliographic networks, *Scientometrics.* **96**(3), 845–864 (2013).
16. M. J. Cobo, A. G. López-Herrera, E. Herrera-Viedma, and F. Herrera, An approach for detecting, quantifying, and visualizing the evolution of a research field: A practical application to the fuzzy sets theory field, *J. Informetr.* **5**(1), 146–166 (2011).
17. A. Purnomo, T. Susanti, E. Rosyidah, N. Firdausi, and M. Idhom, Digital economy research: Thirty-five years insights of retrospective review, *Procedia Comput. Sci.* **197**, 68–75 (2022).
18. V. C. Burbano, M. A. Delmas, and M. J. Cobo, The past and future of Corporate Sustainability Research, *Organ. Environ.* **37**(2), 133–158 (2023).
19. E. Herrera-Viedma, J.-R. López-Robles, J. Guallar, and M.-J. Cobo, Global trends in coronavirus research at the time of Covid-19: A general bibliometric approach and content analysis using SciMAT, *El Prof. Inf.* **29**(3), 22 (2020).
20. J. R. López-Robles, J. R. Otegi-Olaso, I. P. Porto Gómez, and M. J. Cobo, 30 years of intelligence models in management and business: A bibliometric review, *Int. J. Inf. Manag.* **48**, 22–38 (2019).
21. M. K. Sott, L. B. Furstenau, L. M. Kipper, et al. Process modeling for smart factories: Using science mapping to understand the strategic themes, main challenges and future trends, *BPMJ.* **27**(5), 1391–1417 (2021).
22. A. Velez-Estevez, P. García-Sánchez, J. A. Moral-Munoz, and M. J. Cobo, Why do papers from international collaborations get more citations? A bibliometric analysis of library and information science papers, *Scientometrics.* **127**(12), 7517–7555 (2022).
23. A. Velez-Estevez, I. J. Perez, P. García-Sánchez, J. A. Moral-Munoz, and M. J. Cobo, New trends in bibliometric apis: A comparative analysis, *Inf. Process. Manag.* **60**(4), 103385 (2023).
24. J. A. Moral-Muñoz, E. Herrera-Viedma, A. Santisteban-Espejo, and M. J. Cobo, Software tools for conducting bibliometric analysis in science: An up-to-date review, *El Prof. Inf.* **29**(1) (2020).

25. M. Callon, J. P. Courtial, and F. Laville, Co-word analysis as a tool for describing the network of interactions between basic and technological research: The case of polymer chemistry, *Scientometrics*. **22**(1), 155–205 (1991).

26. N. Coulter, I. Monarch, and S. Konda, Software engineering as seen through its research literature: A study in co-word analysis, *J. Am. Soc. Inf. Sci.* **49**(13), 1206–1223 (1998).

27. M. J. Cobo, A. G. López-Herrera, E. Herrera-Viedma, and F. Herrera, SciMAT: A new science mapping analysis software tool, *JASIST, J. Am. Soc. Inf. Sci. Tec.* **63**(8), 1609–1630 (2012).

https://doi.org/10.1142/9789819813049_0007

CHAPTER 7 Interoperability Challenges in Tokenized Asset Networks

Thomas Hardjono[1,2,*], Alexander Lipton[1,2], and Alex Pentland[1]

[1] *MIT Connection Science & Engineering, Cambridge, MA, USA*
[2] *ADIA Lab, Level 26, Al Khatem Tower, Abu Dhabi Global Market Square, Al Maryah Island, Abu Dhabi, UAE*
[*] *Corresponding author. E-mail: hardjono@mit.edu*

The recent recognition of digital assets by the EU Markets in Crypto-Assets (MiCA) regulation is a landmark event in that it opens new horizons for opportunities in tokenizing real-world assets. However, numerous challenges await the development of the Web3 tokenized asset networks that may utilize decentralized ledger technology. A major challenge concerns the interoperability of token networks, both at the network technology layer and at the asset definition layer. A new generation of decentralized computing infrastructures will be required to support the issuance and management of asset-referenced tokens. This paper touches on several of these multilayer challenges and discusses the use of standardized service interfaces (application programming interfaces [APIs]). Standardized APIs have been the foundation stone for the success of the Web2 internet, and several lessons can be learned from its evolutionary development.

7.1. Introduction

The nascent tokenized asset industry received a positive boost with the approval of the EU Markets in Crypto-Assets (MiCA) regulation in mid-2023. This regulation aims to establish a robust regulatory framework for asset-referenced tokens (ARTs), which are distinct from electronic money tokens. ARTs are designed to maintain stable value by referencing another valuable asset, potentially off-chain.

We believe this new MiCA regulation is a step in the right direction, emphasizing the urgent need for decentralized computing infrastructures and services to support the token ecosystem. However, several challenges remain in building decentralized token networks, particularly the need for interoperability across the various systems, networks, and data structures that constitute the token ecosystem.

We approach the interoperability issue from an asset-centric perspective, focusing on the user's (token holder's) point of view. Users want to legally own, trade, and transfer their tokenized assets independent of the underlying blockchain's technical capabilities. Therefore, one general requirement is that ARTs must be easily transferable across different blockchain-based networks. This cross-network transfer must occur without compromising the stability and integrity of the token's value.

A second requirement of the new token ecosystem is ensuring that all actors and their actions are accountable and auditable. While there are concerns about potential privacy infringements on public blockchain networks, user anonymity must be supported only to a limited extent. Otherwise, anonymity could become a source of economic and legal problems for token networks. Verifiable digital identities and their attribute data are essential for achieving accountable actors across decentralized asset networks. Without identifiability and accountability, the average person may be reluctant to engage with the new token ecosystem.

A third requirement is the ability to trace the origins of an ART, from the dematerialization of its real-world assets to the digitization of certificates and receipts, and ultimately to its on-chain tokenization. A clear definition of tokenizable assets is needed, potentially based on existing asset class definitions in securities trading. New tools and infrastructures are also required to make these asset-related artifacts easily accessible and verifiable. This requires seamless integration with the existing financial industry IT infrastructure, including traditional payment, clearing, and settlement networks. Standardized service interfaces or application programming interfaces (APIs) are essential for achieving this integration.

The purpose of this work is to discuss in detail the various challenges in these three areas of interoperability, with the broader goal of helping the digital assets industry develop a coherent roadmap to address these challenges. A concerted effort is needed to tackle these three interconnected problem areas.

We have aimed to make this work accessible to a broad audience and have minimized the use of overly technical terminology wherever possible.

7.2. Areas of Interoperability

Several areas within the Web3 Internet of Value require a high degree of technical, semantic, and legal interoperability to achieve the Web3 vision. For simplicity, we have grouped these challenges into three broad categories, based on fundamental economic activities: people (digital identity), value (digitized assets), and transactions (networks and digital systems). This is summarized in Fig. 7.1:

- Asset schemas and profiles: The rise of digital tokens as representations of value within asset networks utilizing distributed ledger technology (DLT) raises the question of how to universally define which assets (e.g., real-world assets) can be represented digitally via tokens [1, 2], and who has the legal authority to do so within a jurisdiction [3]. The topic of compatible tokens, based on standardized asset schemas and industry-specific profiles, will be discussed in Section 7.3.

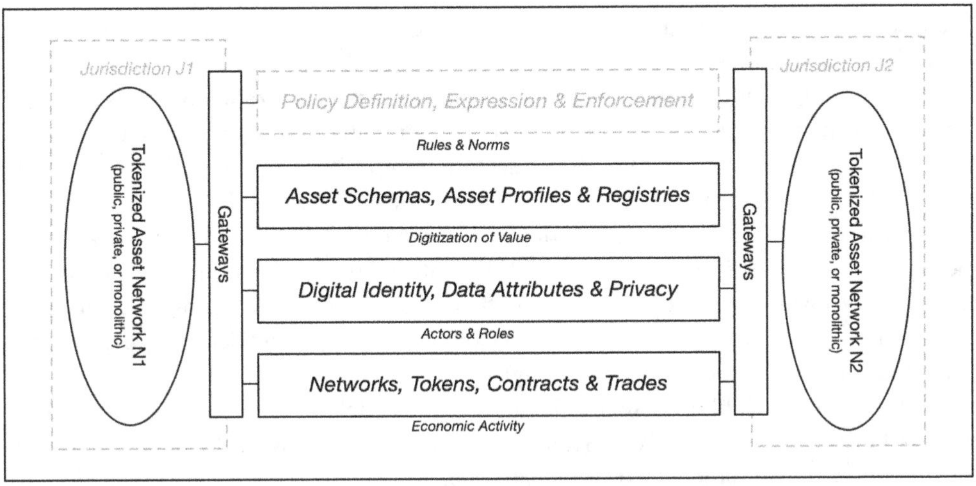

Fig. 7.1 Layers of identity, assets, and networks.

- Digital identity and attribute data: The concept of digital identity has been a topic of interest since the advent of public-key cryptographic systems in the mid-1970s [4, 5]. The primary question then, as it is today, is how to prove that an entity (individual or organization) is the legitimate owner of a public–private key pair [6]. This question also extends to various data attributes relevant to the entity, such as credit score data in the context of a loan application [7]. Digital identity, data attributes, and privacy within token networks are the subjects of Section 7.4.
- Standard service interfaces for token networks and systems: The proliferation of blockchain solutions today raises numerous technical and legal challenges in connecting these blockchain-based networks [8]. Many Layer 1 blockchains are not interoperable, and the addition of new off-chain layers (Layer 2 networks) further complicates matters. We believe interoperability across autonomous networks can be achieved through standardized service interfaces, specifically APIs. This will be discussed in Section 7.5.

It is important to note that the fourth and topmost layer in Fig. 7.1 is policy expression compatibility and enforcement. This topic is extensive, involving machine-interpretable languages and enforcement mechanisms within the tokenized asset network. Therefore, the policy layer will be addressed in future work.

7.3. Asset Definition Schemas and Profiles

The full scope of the challenges facing decentralized finance (DeFi) would have been clearer much earlier if not for the confusing language and hype generated by blockchain DeFi proponents. In reality, these challenges are broad, ranging from the dematerialization of paper-based securities to the issuance of new on-chain tokens, something that has never been done on a large scale.

Historically, the move toward immobilization and dematerialization of assets began in the 1960s with the introduction of electronic computer systems, many of which used punch cards. Over time, physical certificates for securities deposits were gradually "dematerialized," replaced by electronic book-entry records in the databases of these systems. Examples of institutions that handle the immobilization and dematerialization of physical assets include the DTCC and its subsidiaries (e.g., Depository Trust & Clearing Corporation) and Euroclear. Many of these depository institutions are centralized, meaning the functions related to deposits of physical assets, issuance of paper receipts, and dematerialization into book-entry records are performed by a single entity.

While the goals of blockchain DeFi may be commendable, it falls short by overlooking the core functions of traditional depository and clearing institutions and by failing to provide a well-designed, well-architected technical roadmap to connect these traditional systems with blockchain and DLT-based networks [9, 10].

One key aspect of this technical roadmap for decentralized networks of asset-referencing tokens is the development of asset definition schemas and profiles, enabling on-chain tokens to correctly reference the off-chain data stored in these traditional depository and clearing systems.

It is also worth noting the significant progress in smart contract specifications. Solutions such as the digital asset modeling language (DAML) language in the Canton Network [11] and other syntaxes like Lexon [12] are promising because they allow for a "mid-level" syntax to be compiled into ledger-specific smart contracts [13]. However, even these contract specification languages and templates must still rely on data schemas that define the real-world assets being acted upon by the smart contracts.

7.3.1. *Schemas and profiles: An asset-centric approach*

Currently, no standard asset schemas define which real-world assets can be tokenized in a given jurisdiction. The recent EU MiCA regulation [14] recognizes ART but does not identify which real-world asset classes or types can be tokenized. Regardless of who decides the eligible asset classes or types, there remains the challenge of defining a general *asset definition schemas* that can be digitized, be machine-readable, and then be "profiled" (i.e., narrowed in scope) for specific industry verticals. Each industry must take responsibility for creating its own industry-specific profiles derived from the common asset definition schema.[a]

[a]We use the term profile in the technical sense, where a profile is a subset of the broader schema structure definition. Many technical specifications use this term to narrow-down implementation options for specific use-cases, message flows, devices and so on. For example, the SAML Profile for browser-based single-sign on (SSO) [101] narrows down message-flow patterns for browsers versus full clients. The certificate profile for cable modem devices (Section 7 of the CableLabs specifications [123]) narrows down parameter options for device certificates versus human identity certificates.

For asset networks (e.g., blockchain-based), a standard asset profile for a given industry or asset class is beneficial because it provides consistent semantic expression across different asset networks. End-users who purchase and trade tokenized assets view these assets from an economic perspective. For example, consider an asset profile defined for a 1-kg gold bar with a standard fineness of content between 0.995% and 0.9999%. When a user sees that an asset token on network N1 is based on this gold bar schema profile, and network N2 has tokens minted using the same schema profile, the user will expect both tokens to be equivalent, though they represent different physical gold bars. Currently, such standard definitions for real-world assets do not exist in a smart contract-accessible manner. Therefore, standardized schema profiles are needed to capture semantic expressions like "fineness of content between 0.995% and 0.9999%" in a machine-readable format.

At least three kinds of data structures may be required off-chain to support the tokenization of real-world assets. The first is the asset definition schema data structure, the second is the schema profiles derived from the definition in machine-readable format (e.g., JavaScript Object Notation [JSON] [15] or Concise Binary Object Representation [CBOR] [16]), and the third is the tokenized representation of the profile in a smart contract-readable form. This is illustrated in Fig. 7.2(a). Once an asset profile has been derived from a given asset definition schema and the profile is expressed in a machine-readable format, an on-chain version of the same profile must be created. This is referred to as the "asset profile token" (or simply profile "data-token") in Fig. 7.2(b). This on-chain version is essential because the profile-specific smart contract is required to read and parse the on-chain profile token to mint ART asset tokens that comply with the profile. The current smart contract stack architecture in the major blockchains today (e.g., Ethereum) is limited to reading data that resides on the same ledger as the smart contract code. Smart contracts are blind to the external world. In order to make a piece of data (bytes) accessible to the smart contract code, the data must be purposely recorded onto the same shared ledger by special types of programs referred to commonly as "Oracles."

In the case of an asset profile file (e.g., in JSON format), a tokenized version of the JSON profile must be written onto the ledger of the blockchain by an Oracle that is controlled by the legal issuer (publisher) of the asset profile. The format of the tokenized version of the profile is dependent on the specific blockchain implementation syntax. It is this tokenized version of the profile that will be read by the smart contract logic. In other words, the smart contract must be "guided" when minting an ART (based on the on-chain tokenized profile), ensuring that the links and contents of the ART will reference (link to) the correct off-chain JSON schema profile (e.g., a 1-kg gold bar ART must reference the 1-kg gold bar schema profile, not the 1-kg wheat commodity schema profile).

The following explains the elements shown in Fig. 7.2 in more detail:

- Asset definition schema (off-chain file): This is the data organization framework that defines various aspects of asset digitization (e.g., real-world assets). The asset definition schema provides the generic data structure in a given computer syntax notation for defining tokenizable assets in a legal manner for a given jurisdiction. The logical design of an asset definition schema should be specified both on paper and in digital

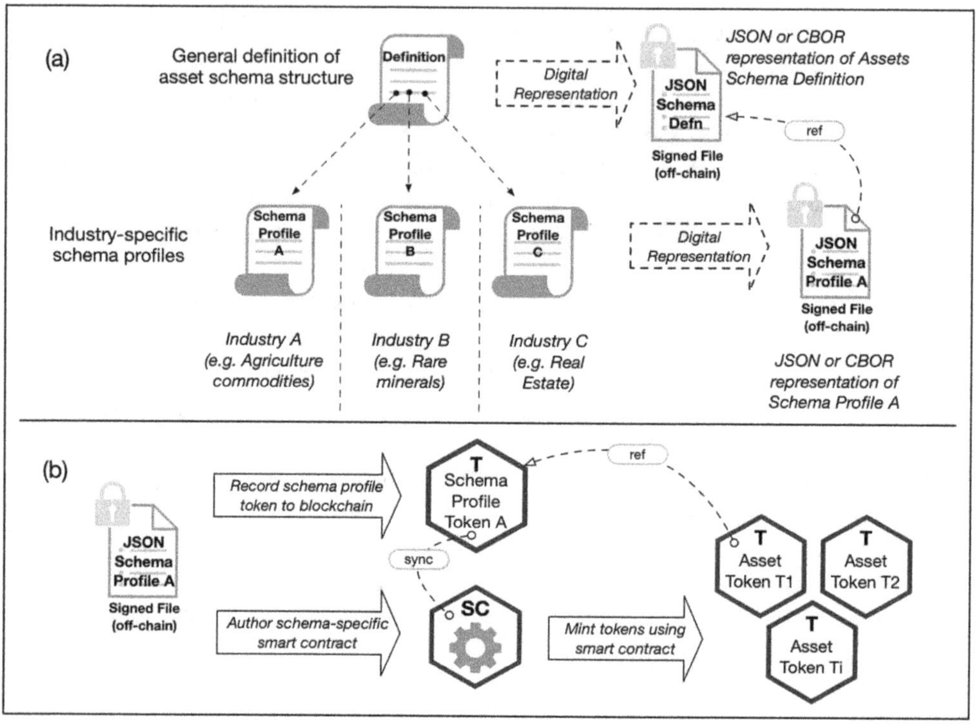

Fig. 7.2 Overview of (a) the asset schema structure and schema profiles and (b) on-chain token representation of these schema profiles.

format (e.g., JSON). The entity responsible for publishing and signing the asset definition schema is referred to as the *asset definition authority*, as shown in part (a) of Fig. 7.2.

- Industry-specific schema profiles (off-chain file): A schema profile narrows (constrains) the options available in the asset definition schema, making them relevant for a specific industry, sector vertical, asset class, or trading community. Certain industries may use their own schema profiles, enabling markets in different countries and jurisdictions to interoperate based on a shared understanding of tokenizable asset classes and types. The profile should be available in a machine-readable standard format (e.g., JSON) and should be a standalone signed file (independent of any blockchain implementation). The entity responsible for publishing and signing an industry-specific schema profile is referred to as the *asset profile authority*. The off-chain signed JSON file should be available in publicly accessible repositories, enabling anyone to verify that an asset token complies with the JSON profile representation.
- Tokenized schema profile (on-chain): Based on the published JSON profile, a "tokenized" version of the profile must be made available on the blockchain to allow the relevant smart contract to access the on-chain version. We refer to this version of the

profile as a "profile data-token" (or simply "data-token") to signify that it is data only (i.e., not an executable code). The author of the smart contract must design the contract code to read the profile data-token on the same blockchain and mint the ART based on the information fields in the data-token. Ideally, the entity who published (signed) the off-chain JSON profile should be the same entity that records the data-token on the blockchain. Any programmer should be able to make a comparison between an issued ART on-chain (referencing the profile data-token) with the contents of the data-token to ensure the ART complies with the profile. The same programmer should even be able to fetch the signed JSON file located off-chain and make a similar comparison.

The process of minting tokens on a given blockchain is illustrated in Fig. 7.2(b). First, the JSON schema profile must be recorded on the target blockchain as a static profile "data-token." This is a data-token that merely records information (corresponding to the JSON profile) onto the shared ledger, timestamped, and is not transferrable. The need for this arises because smart contracts can only access information and data present on the blocks of the same ledger as the smart contract code. Thus, a smart contract must be able to read the schema profile data-token on the same ledger to execute its function. Updates to an existing profile data-token can be made by the same issuing authority publishing a new data-token, using the same public key (address). The new profile data-token must include a hash or pointer to the old data-token.

To mint actual value-bearing asset tokens (e.g., ARTs), a profile-specific smart contract must be authored and deployed on the blockchain. The actual code of the smart contract should be manually verified by human authorities to ensure it is functionally correct and relatively bug-free. By verifying the smart contract code prior to its publication onto the blockchain, we obtain a high degree of assurance that any minted ART will comply with the schema profile (data-token) that is accessed by the smart contract. The resulting token is shown as the *asset token* (i.e., ART) in Fig. 7.2(b). An asset token should reference the schema-profile token (i.e., data-token) on the same blockchain, enabling potential buyers to verify the token's compliance with the schema profile. The digital signature on the profile enables the identity verification of the entity who issued/published the asset profile. Since a profile derived from an asset definition schema carries a link to its "parent" schema (signed file located off-chain), the identity of the issuer/publisher of the top-level schema can also be verified.

An asset definition schema and profiles derived from the schema should meet the following general requirements:

- Publisher identifier: An asset schema must carry the identity of its publisher (asset definition authority), using a globally unique entity identifier recognized in multiple jurisdictions. Examples include the Legal Entity Identifier (LEI) number [17].
- Schema identifier and profile identifier: Each published asset definition schema and the profiles (derived from that definition schema) must have a unique identifier (e.g.,

serial number) to distinguish it from other schemas and profiles. Combining the publisher identifier with the schema/profile identifiers should eliminate any identification ambiguity.
- Digitally representable off-chain and on-chain: Asset definition schemas and profiles must be written in a syntax that allows them to be stored both as standalone files (signed by the author) and as data on the ledger. The JSON and CBOR formats are established industry standards, and digital signatures can be applied to either a JSON file [18] or a CBOR file [19]. As shown in Fig. 7.2(b), there must be a 1-to-1 correspondence between an on-chain schema profile (data-token) and the off-chain schema profile (JSON file) upon which the token is based.
- Support for a range of assets: The schema syntax and semantics must support a wide variety of real-world assets to be represented as on-chain tokens (e.g., ART-compliant tokens).
- Support for rule/policy expression and policy inheritance: Rules to be observed by smart contracts handling tokens should be expressible within the schema and the profiles. Depending on the policy expression syntax, these policies could be automatically inherited by profiles derived from an existing asset definition schema. This is similar to inheritance and polymorphism in object-oriented programming. For example, if a schema specifies that the asset definition is valid only within a given jurisdiction (e.g., EU jurisdiction), this expression should be inherited automatically by any profile derived from the schema. Any asset token (i.e., ART) issued based on the profile must automatically include markings or information fields indicating that the token is valid in the designated jurisdiction.
- Expression of asset-specific capabilities: The asset definition schema must support the declaration of the set of operations (capabilities) applicable to the ART that implements the profile derived from the asset schema. These capabilities include the transferability of the ART, the jurisdiction-based tradability of the ART, their collateralization, and others [20].

It is worth noting that the list of the applicable operations and capabilities of a tokenized asset could be defined at the schema and profile levels. This capabilities list will be helpful for a gateway fronting an asset network (i.e., blockchain-based) in determining whether an incoming tokenized asset can be accommodated by the asset network.

7.3.2. *Asset schemas in the token lifecycle management*

Similar to paper-based assets (e.g., securities) and related instruments, tokenized assets in decentralized networks require a well-defined and universally understood lifecycle model. This lifecycle must account for (i) the asset's value prior to digitization (pre-network), (ii) the commissioning of the token representing the asset into a network or system, and (iii) the decommissioning of the token from the network or system when required (e.g., due to the destruction of the physical asset).

7.3.2.1. Overview of token lifecycle: Commissioning

Figure 7.3 outlines the commissioning phase of a token within the broader lifecycle of tokenized assets. The general steps involved in commissioning tokenized assets are as follows:

(1) Publication of a schema profile based on a common asset definition schema: The profile must exist before the real-world asset fitting that profile can be tokenized (i.e., before the asset token can be created). This is shown as Item 1 in Fig. 7.3.

(2) Issuance of a depository receipt certificate (off-chain): Before issuing asset tokens, the provider must surrender the real-world asset to a custodian/depository entity for safekeeping (immobilization). The custodian/depository entity then publishes an off-chain depository receipt certificate file as evidence of the asset's immobilization. This is shown as Item 2 in Fig. 7.3. The certificate must be a standalone file, integrity-protected via digital signatures [21], and can be created using standards like X.509 Attribute Certificates [22, 23] or JSON/JWT [18]. Notably, the certificate does not carry ownership information.[b]

(3) Issuance of a depository receipt token corresponding to the depository certificate: This token, shown as Item 3 in Fig. 7.3, serves as an on-chain equivalent of the off-chain depository receipt certificate. It is a static "data-token" recording data on the

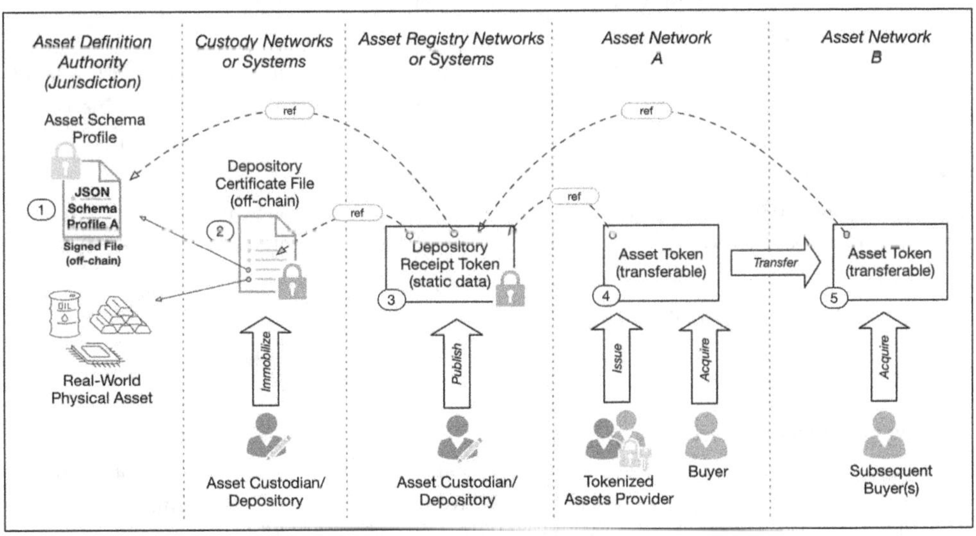

Fig. 7.3 Overview of the commissioning phase within an asset-referenced token [14], with pointers or references to metadata and other data structures.

[b]Note the historical similarities in the evolutionary way in which traditional physical assets were converted into paper certificates, which then became electronic book-entry forms in accounts at the central securities depositories (CSD).

ledger but is non-transferrable.[c] The issuer of the token should be the same custodian/depository entity that published the off-chain certificate. The token must reference both the certificate (Item 2) and the schema profile (Item 1), ensuring a clear connection between the on-chain token and the off-chain asset.

(4) Issuance of an asset token and subsequent acquisitions: The asset token (Item 4 in Fig. 7.3) represents the ownership of the real-world asset. The chain of custody—from the asset token (Item 4 and Item 5), to the depository receipt token (Item 3), and to the depository receipt certificate (Item 2)—must be traceable by any potential buyers. The asset token can then be sold across different asset networks (e.g., Asset Network B, shown as Item 5).

Key points to highlight in the asset lifecycle:

(1) Real-world actors guaranteeing asset states: The custodian/depository entity serves as the critical link between physical assets and their digital representations. By issuing the depository receipt certificate (Item 2) and depository receipt token (Item 3), the custodian assumes legal and financial liabilities.

(2) Separation of asset states: The real-world asset's physical state (being under the custodian's control) is distinct from the ownership state of the asset token. The physical asset's condition is long-term information, while ownership can change as the asset token is transferred to new owners.

(3) Independence of asset token movement: An asset token and the value it represents can move across different asset networks without changing the state or value of the real-world asset (referenced by the depository receipt certificate and token).

(4) Chain of custody as a basis for insurance: The traceable chain of custody from the on-chain asset token to the off-chain depository receipt certificate is essential for insurance providers. This highlights the need for publicly accessible networks of registries that store schema profiles (Item 1), depository receipt certificates (Item 2), and depository receipt tokens (Item 3).

7.3.2.2. Decommissioning of tokens

A lifecycle model must also address the end-of-life aspects of tokenized assets. Since tokens are digital representations of real-world assets that predate the token creation, any significant changes to these off-chain assets must be reflected in the corresponding tokens. The term "decommissioning" is used to describe this process. Examples of significant changes to real-world assets that affect tokens include unintended destruction of the asset (e.g., artwork, real estate), consumption of assets (e.g., commodities like wheat and oil), intentional removal of assets from circulation by the owner or a legal authority, and other similar cases.

---

[c]The notion of a *static data-token* is similar in the non-transferable tokens (NTT) in Ethereum, where additional rules are applied to ERC721 tokens [124] to prevent further modifications or transfers.

One of the key benefits of shared ledger systems with immutable, append-only capabilities is that token traces remain available even after decommissioning. This allows the history of a given digital asset to be verified (by authorized entities) by tracing from the decommissioned ownership token back to the depository receipt tokens and ultimately to the revoked depository receipt certificate.

The stages in the decommissioning process of asset tokens are summarized in Fig. 7.4:

- Revocation of the depository receipt certificate (off-chain): The revocation or cancelation of the off-chain depository receipt certificate indicates that the integrity of the underlying physical asset can no longer be guaranteed. Regardless of the reason, the custodian/depository entity that originally created the depository receipt certificate must be the one to revoke it. This is shown as Item 1 in Fig. 7.4.
- Revocation of the depository receipt token: The revocation of the depository receipt certificate (off-chain) triggers a corresponding revocation of the depository receipt token (on-chain). This is shown as Item 2 in Fig. 7.4. Several mechanisms can achieve this, depending on the DLT network technology used by the registry. One approach is for the custodian/depository entity to mint a special revocation token (Item 2) on the same ledger as the original depository receipt token. This signals to all participants in the ecosystem that the asset token is also about to be decommissioned. The revoked depository receipt token must include a hash of the original depository receipt token and a hash of the revoked depository receipt certificate file (off-chain).
- Decommissioning of the asset token: The issuance of the revoked depository receipt token (Item 2 in Fig. 7.4) is authoritative. From this point onward, the corresponding asset token, which represents the legal ownership of the real-world asset, is no longer

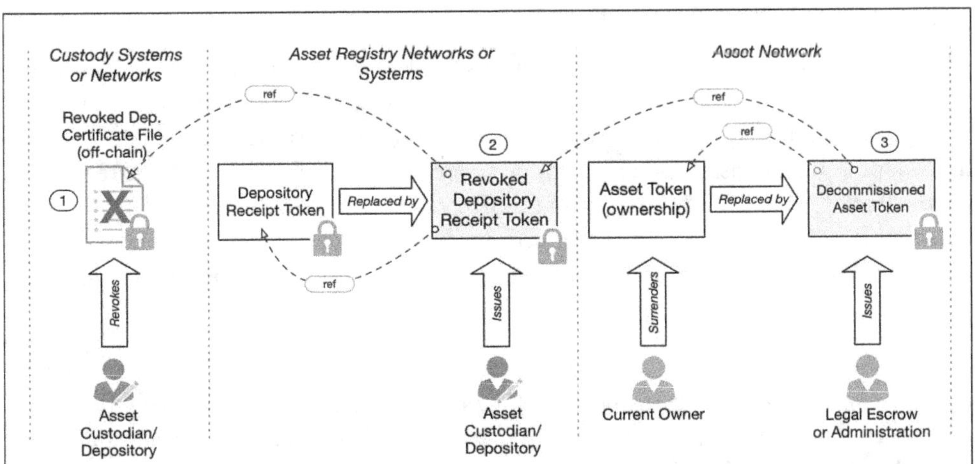

Fig. 7.4 Overview of the decommissioning process for registry tokens and ownership-tokens.

valid. It cannot be sold or transferred to another entity. This process is represented by the decommissioned asset token (Item 3) in Fig. 7.4.

- The decommissioned asset token must include a reference to the hash of (i) the last valid asset token and (ii) the revoked depository receipt token in the publicly readable registry. The presence of both tokens on-chain ensures a ledger-based history for future audit requirements.

7.3.3. *Toward a global network of artifacts registries*

In addition to challenges related to the semantic compatibility of schema profiles and their digital representations—both off-chain (e.g., signed JSON/CBOR) and on-chain (e.g., schema profile data-tokens)—there is also the question of accessibility, availability, and persistence of these artifacts that support the functioning of asset tokens across various asset networks.

To ensure accessibility to these asset-related artifacts, multiple registries will need to be implemented based on a common asset artifact management architecture [20] that exposes standardized service interfaces. These registries could include

- Registry of asset definition schemas: A repository of signed asset definition schemas, along with copies of the issuer's identity public key and certificates.
- Registry of schema profiles: Industries or sectors may opt to make copies of signed schema profiles available within a shared registry.
- Repository of smart contract code: This registry could store verified smart contract code (for specific blockchain EVMs), which implements the off-chain schema profile into equivalent on-chain profile data-tokens. For example, the DAML/Canton architecture [24] includes smart contract libraries as part of its platform.

There are various architectural approaches for artifact registries, such as blockchain-based, databases, or cloud services (see Figure 7.5). Regardless of the chosen technology, registries must utilize a standardized service interface (API), discussed in Section 7.5. This network of artifact registries aligns with the concept of ARTs in the EU MiCA regulation and the Bank for International Settlements (BIS) vision of the "unified ledger" [25], which aims for high interoperability across ledgers and legacy systems.

The following is a short list of the fundamental requirements for the network of asset-related artifact registries:

- Persistence of registry information: Some data artifacts recorded in the registry network may need to be accessible over long periods (e.g., years or decades). Given the nascent state of blockchain and DLT, it remains to be seen whether the current iteration of blockchains will evolve to provide data persistence guarantees that meet business requirements.
- Identifier mapping for private registries: Depending on the jurisdiction and type of asset, there may be scenarios where the registry network must be private or closed (i.e., permissioned). This raises the challenge of how to reference (hash) depository receipt

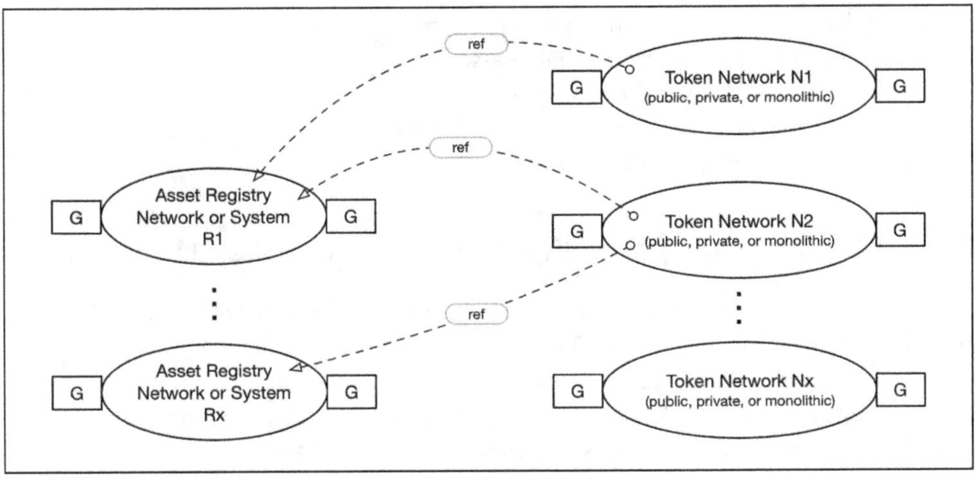

Fig. 7.5 Overview of a global network of registries with artifacts referenceable from token networks.

certificates, tokens, and other asset artifacts when these are inaccessible from outside the private registry network. One proposed solution [8] suggests using transaction processing gateways to perform mediated referencing and de-referencing of identifiers.[d] If further information is needed from a private registry network, the gateways could also provide cryptographic proof of the data artifacts, offering a limited "view" of the information from the network's ledger [26].

- Identification of registry networks and subnetworks: Currently, there is no common standard for the network-level identification of blockchains and DLT networks. Local transactions within a given blockchain may include identifiers for "subnetworks" (e.g., different blockchains running the same consensus protocol, such as testnets and mainnets). However, these subnet identifiers can become problematic when forks occur, as seen in the Ethereum fork caused by the infamous DAO hack [27, 28]. The core issue is that, without a clear identifier/numbering scheme for networks, cross-chain transactions from other blockchain networks may be processed (added to the blocks) on the wrong fork of the destination network. An informal list of blockchain network names can be found in Ref. [29].

Efforts are underway in the Ethereum community to standardize blockchain subnetwork identifiers to ensure correct cross-chain transactions (IEP-3220) [30], while broader initiatives have begun within the Internet Engineering Task Force (IETF) [31], which is home to the majority of Web2 standards. Network-level identification is also relevant for

[d]This mediated identifier mapping strategy is similar in function to classic network-address translators (NAT) for private IP domains in TCP/IP routing.

blockchain-based registry networks. Here, the correct blockchain identifier and the relevant block number (of the block containing asset artifact data) must be fully referenceable by remote tokenized asset networks. Therefore, a unique identifier resolution path must be unambiguously provided between the asset blockchain (i.e., a smart contract or oracle service) and the relevant block of data in the registry network.

7.4. Identity Interoperability Challenges in Token Networks

One of the main requirements of the emerging token ecosystem is that all actors and actions must be accountable and auditable. This need arises from both economic stability requirements and the reality that an ecosystem with too many unpredictable variables—due to unaccountable actors—cannot endure for long. While market behavior is inherently unpredictable, the presence of rogue actors undermines the utility of a tokenized asset ecosystem for society.

Although there is legitimate concern about potential user privacy infringements in public (permissionless) blockchain networks, user anonymity should be supported only to a limited extent. If taken too far, anonymity can lead to economic and legal problems for token networks. Thus, verifiable digital identities and their attribute data are crucial for ensuring accountability among actors within decentralized asset networks. Without the identifiability and accountability of network actors, ordinary citizens may be reluctant to participate in the new token ecosystem.

This section discusses two seemingly conflicting requirements arising from the application of Travel Rule policies to tokenized assets[e] and the basic data privacy requirements of users (holders) of these tokens. The discussion consists of three interrelated threads. First, we address the need for attesters of attribute data regarding the user (the originator and beneficiary) in a token transaction under the Travel Rule. Second, we explore the potential use of a simple blinding mechanism to temporarily withhold these attributes by an identity provider (IdP), aided by legal services that afford attorney–client privilege (ACP). Lastly, we discuss the necessity of an identity legal trust framework specifically designed for entities covered under the Travel Rule.

7.4.1. *Travel Rules and tokenized assets*

Identifying users, actors, and service providers poses a significant challenge in transactions conducted on public blockchain-based peer-to-peer networks.

In traditional correspondent banking, identity information for the originator and beneficiary is required for wire transfers between banks. This information is necessary on both sides of the wire transfer to comply with anti-money laundering (AML) and counterterrorism financing (CFT) regulations. In short, the identity information must "travel"

[e]Tokenized assets are referred to as *virtual assets* in the FATF Recommendations documents [34].

alongside the funds during the transfer. This requirement is known as the Funds Travel Rule or simply the "Travel Rule." The Travel Rule originates from the US Bank Secrecy Act (BSA—31 USC 5311–5330), which mandates that financial institutions deliver specific information to the next financial institution involved in a funds transmittal event when more than one institution is involved. This requirement is essentially crucial for international wire transfers. The ISO20022 standard used by the SWIFT network includes these fields in messages related to correspondent banking (see Ref. [32]).

In response to the emergence of various crypto exchanges—many of which initially claimed exemption from banking regulations for currency transmitters—the Financial Action Task Force (FATF) [33], the primary global organization for AML regulations, published several new requirements toward the end of 2018, notably FATF Recommendation No. 15 [34, 35]. These new requirements emphasize the need for user identification to be available and validated before asset transmittal.

FATF Recommendation No. 15 defines a virtual asset as a digital representation of value that can be digitally traded or transferred and can be used for payment or investment purposes. It defines a virtual asset service provider (VASP)—exemplified today by crypto exchanges—as a business that conducts one or more of the following activities for or on behalf of another natural or legal person or business: (i) exchange between virtual assets and fiat currencies; (ii) exchange between one or more forms of virtual assets; (iii) transfer of virtual assets; (iv) safekeeping and/or administration of virtual assets or instruments enabling control over virtual assets; and (v) participation in and provision of financial services related to an issuer's offer and/or sale of a virtual asset.

The implication of Recommendation 15, among others, is that crypto exchanges and other types of VASPs must be able to obtain and securely share customer information (originator and beneficiary) in the same manner that banks and financial institutions have done over the past 30 years. This customer information includes (i) the originator's name; (ii) originator's account number (e.g., at the originator's VASP); (iii) originator's geographical address, or national identity number, or customer identification number (or date and place of birth); (iv) beneficiary's name; (v) beneficiary account number (e.g., at the Beneficiary-VASP).

One critical issue with the FATF regulations for crypto assets is enforcing these regulations alongside other data privacy regulations (e.g., GDPR [36, 37]) across different jurisdictions worldwide. Users who provide their personal information to a local VASP (e.g., crypto exchanges) may trust that their VASP will not leak their account data. However, once this personal data is sent to a remote VASP in another jurisdiction, users have little control over how their personal data will be treated.

What is lacking in the tokenized asset industry is a framework akin to the SWIFT arrangement, where members must adhere to the bylaws and general terms and conditions [38], as well as the SWIFT personal data protection policy [39]. Unlike correspondent banking based on interbank messaging, token networks involve an actual change of control over tokens through public-key cryptography and an append-only ledger. This creates a greater need for identity verification before transactions are transmitted to the underlying blockchain propagation network, particularly because reversing a token transfer is cumbersome. In the digital identity industry, such a "trust network" arrangement is referred to as an identity legal trust framework [40].

7.4.2. *Identifiers, attribute data, and attribute attesters*

For tokenized asset networks, the three minimal elements of digital identity required for any functional system are as follows: (i) an identifier string that represents an individual (subject) online; (ii) a public key (key pair) bound to the subject's identifier; and (iii) a sufficient number of data attributes regarding the subject to enable the counterparty (or other external entities) to verify that the subject is a real person (e.g., not a fictitious entity with a fake account) and has legal status in the relevant jurisdiction.

The first two elements—namely, how to prove that an entity (individual or organization) is the true owner of a public–private key pair—have been of interest since the mid-1970s [4–6]. The third aspect—user attributes and citizen privacy—remains an ongoing challenge, especially in cross-jurisdiction token transactions.

The work of Hardjono and Pentland [41] introduced the notion of core identity as the collective set of characteristics or attributes (represented by personal data) that uniquely identify a person. Thus, personal data (i.e., data about the individual) plays a crucial role in this context. Much of a person's attributes and history consists of static attributes, which are fixed personal facts such as birth date, country of birth, and eye color.

Other historical data about a person are accumulative; while older data remains unchanged, additional data can accumulate over time. We refer to this type of personal data as dynamic attributes [42]. Examples of dynamic attributes include a person's creditworthiness score, based on historical financial transaction data (e.g., credit card payment history), and vehicle driving history [43].

The basic model for sharing attribute information about a person is illustrated in Fig. 7.6. In this model, the attribute attester issues a signed attestation regarding an attribute of the data subject[f] or user (flow-1). When the user seeks a service from a risk-bearing entity, they must provide a copy of this attestation to the entity, such as a counterparty (flow-2). This entity is referred to as the relying party (RP) because it relies on the attester to verify the accuracy of the attribute-related claims in the attestation (flow-3). Variations of this interaction may include an intermediary[g] entity that assists with scaling up the validation process (flows 4(a) and 4(b)).

It is important to note that the attribute attester assumes legal and financial liabilities when signing attestations about the data subject. This responsibility requires the attester to

[f]We use the term *data subject* following the terminology of the EU GDPR data privacy regulations [36]

[g]It is worthwhile highlighting the similarity of the attribute attester model in Fig. 7.6 with the classic four corners model [125] used in the card payments industry. In the four corners model, the card issuing bank (Issuer) provides the user (Cardholder subject) with a credit card (i.e., an assertion or claim about creditworthiness up to a limit). The user utilizes the card at the point-of-sale (Merchant), who is able to verify the current balance on the card via an intermediary bank (Acquirer).

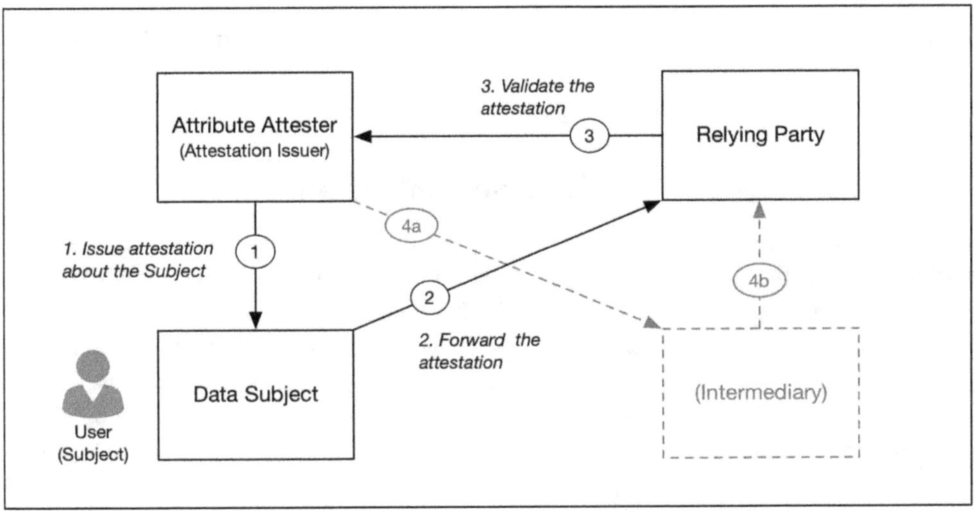

Fig. 7.6 Overview of the attribute attester that issues attestations regarding the subject.

gather accurate information from various data sources, making it a complex process that can only be viable if the attester is compensated.

A digital identifier for a subject (e.g., a person) is a "transactional" fixed-length string used as a reference in specific contexts, such as online payments or memberships (e.g., golf club, university, airline mileage points) [44, 45]. A useful analogy is a credit card number, which acts as a transactional identifier. It can be used at point-of-sale locations without requiring the user to provide additional personal data. The issuer (e.g., a bank) has already verified the static and dynamic attributes of the person holding the card. Since the credit card number is transactional, it can be replaced (e.g., in case of loss or theft) without impacting the user's core identity. In financial transactions, entities at risk (e.g., insurance providers) are typically more concerned with the dynamic attributes of the individuals involved, rather than with the digital identifiers, which can be changed at any time.

Similarly, in blockchain systems, a public key pair functions as the key holder's (owner's) address. Like transactional identifiers, public key pairs can be replaced when tokens or cryptocurrencies are transferred to a new key pair held by the same owner. Given that cryptocurrencies are increasingly used for transferring monetary value, regulators are concerned about these transactions from an AML perspective. Governments and regulators focus on the attributes of the parties involved in on-chain transactions rather than the key pairs, which are considered temporary.

There has been significant discussion recently around decentralized identity, where identity management is aided by blockchain technology. However, many proposed solutions (e.g., self-sovereign identity) confuse the issue of user-managed control over personal data with the challenge of verifying claims derived from that data. A "self-sovereign, self-asserted" claim has limited value in financial transactions with a counterparty [46]. Even when a subject stores a signed claim on a blockchain, its value lies in the signature of the attribute attester, not in the blockchain itself. The decentralized identifier (DID) construct [47] on a blockchain is a useful tool for enabling the RP to locate off-chain endpoints storing signed claims issued by the attester [48].

7.4.3. *Challenges of interoperable attribute attesters*

The central challenge for digital identity interoperability in token networks is ensuring that attribute attesters (attestation issuers) are trusted across legal jurisdictions on a global scale. A legal framework must exist that allows an RP in one jurisdiction to trust attestations issued by an attester in another jurisdiction, and vice versa. This requires a common legal trust framework to govern the sharing of subject information within signed attestations as they are exchanged internationally. This concept is similar to the "system rules" used by multi-member financial consortiums to regulate member behavior and define their obligations and benefits (e.g., Visa Rules [49]).

Figure 7.7 illustrates cross-jurisdiction sharing of attested attributes. In this example, an originator in jurisdiction J1 requests the beneficiary in jurisdiction J2 to provide attestations (e.g., as a condition for transferring tokenized assets). The beneficiary delivers signed attestations to the originator (flow-2). The originator then becomes the RP, depending on the attester in J2 to verify the attestations (flows 3 and 4). Figure 7.7 only shows a unidirectional flow, but a mirrored process may be required where the originator must also deliver attestations to the beneficiary (see Fig. 7.8).

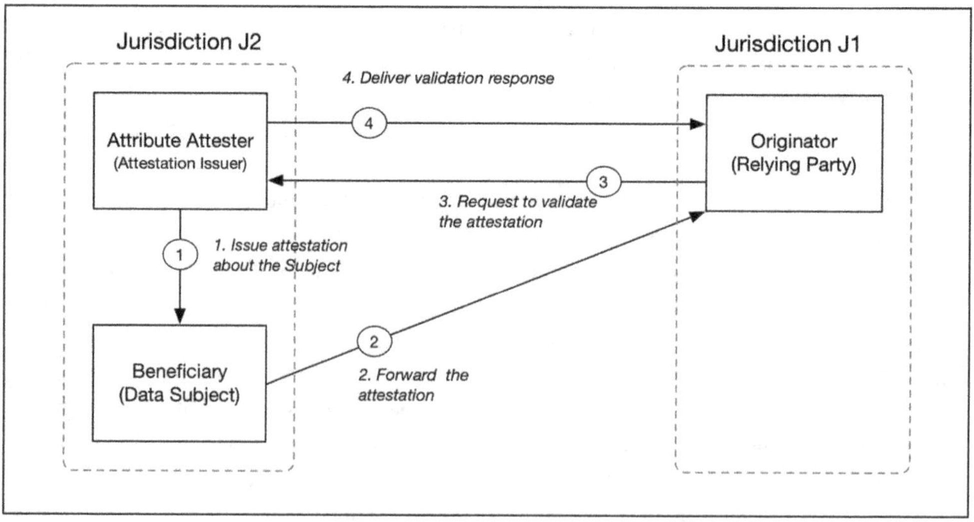

Fig. 7.7 Overview of the unidirectional validation of an attestation in the case where the subject (beneficiary) and relying party (originator) are located in different jurisdictions.

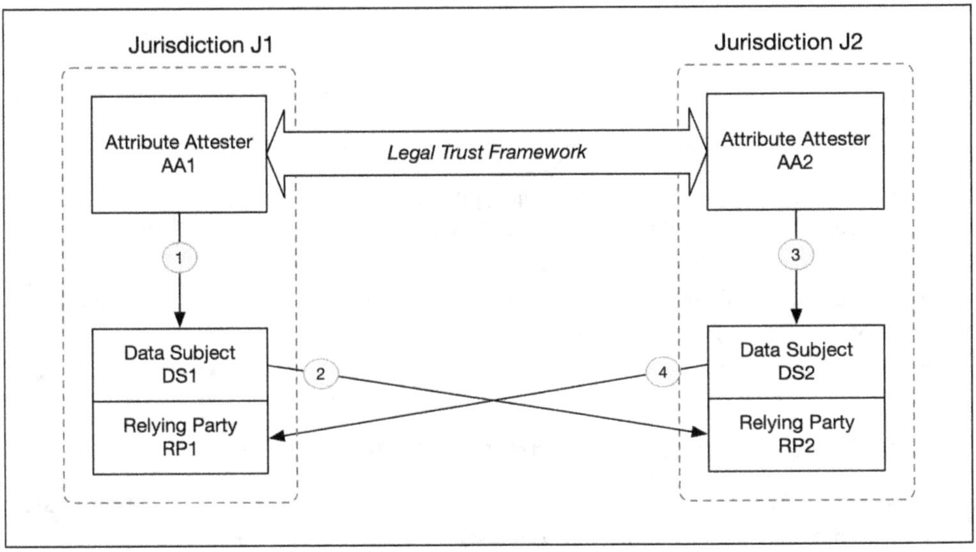

Fig. 7.8 Overview of a bidirectional attestation validation across jurisdictions based on an identity trust framework.

The interoperability of systems handling identity attributes across jurisdictions J1 and J2 (Fig. 7.8) requires agreed-upon protocols and rules, often referred to as an identity trust framework.

7.4.4. *Digital identity trust frameworks*

A digital identity trust framework is a set of rules based on technical standards that organizations and individuals follow to comply with data-related regulations [40]. The framework's goals are to: (i) build a well-designed digital identity system with clear technical specifications, and (ii) ensure users (citizens) trust and participate in the system. Achieving these goals requires both sound engineering and robust operational rules. A useful analogy is air travel: people trust airplanes because of strong engineering and regulatory oversight (e.g., by the Federal Aviation Administration [FAA]) over both the operators (airlines) and manufacturers. The risks and accountability mechanisms must be clearly defined upfront [50]. Similar trust frameworks exist in the financial industry (e.g., card payments and automated clearing house [ACH] electronic funds).

For digital identity systems, risks are managed by communities handling personal data, through the creation of a trust framework adhered to by all members. A digital identity trust framework consists of two core elements [40, 51]:

(1) Technical and operational specifications: These are detailed technical requirements for the proper operation of an identity system. They must define roles, responsibilities, and mechanisms to ensure data accuracy, integrity, security, and user privacy.

(2) Legal rules: A set of legal rules and contracts regulate the technical and operational specifications, making them legally binding and enforceable. These rules must define participants' legal rights, obligations, and liabilities and outline avenues for resolving disputes.

In many jurisdictions, public laws underpin the legal rules in a trust framework. In private industry consortiums, the framework may be enforced contractually, based on prevailing contract law in the jurisdiction. Legally binding obligations (e.g., financial penalties) deter participants from disregarding agreed rules. Examples of legal trust frameworks include those by SAFE Biopharma [52] and the UK Government for digital services for its citizens [53].

7.4.5. *Toward a trust framework for the Travel Rule*

Many identity trust frameworks today are designed for complex scenarios, often related to access control for specific online resources. For example, the UK Government's trust framework (called UK.Gov) [53] enables citizens to access government services such as healthcare and finance. In some cases, citizens can log in and modify personal data entries.

In contrast, the Travel Rule focuses on sharing subject attributes—many of which are considered personal data—between VASPs in different jurisdictions. The Travel Rule mandates that a fixed set of originator and beneficiary attributes be shared among registered entities covered by FATF regulations and that these attributes are logged for future AML compliance.

To create a trust framework for sharing subject data attributes among VASPs, the framework must address several key aspects:

- Limited scope of static attributes: The attributes shared (e.g., name, account number, address) are limited and static, as used in banking for customer wire transfers [34].
- Attested by a trusted third party: A trusted third party, covered under FATF regulations, must verify the static attributes. The framework must govern the actions and obligations of these third parties across jurisdictions.
- Distinct from access control systems: Sharing attributes for the Travel Rule should not grant VASPs or other parties extended access to private data in another jurisdiction's identity system. However, VASPs may still choose to enter more complex trust frameworks, such as those involving shared databases or data cooperatives [54, 55].

A major challenge remains in ensuring that a VASP in one jurisdiction handles the personal data of a subject from another jurisdiction properly. Preventing data mishandling or leaks after a cross-jurisdiction transfer is highly difficult. The next section discusses potential short-term solutions to this cross-jurisdiction privacy dilemma.

7.4.6. *The privacy identity provider model*

User privacy has been a contentious issue in the rise of cryptocurrency networks, starting with Bitcoin. These networks generally operate using public keys (addresses) as user identifiers, making these keys the primary mechanism to identify users on the network. In some cases, user anonymity is highly valued in these cryptocurrency networks.

Historically, interest in cryptographic anonymity pre-dates blockchains and cryptocurrencies, with researchers exploring various identity anonymity schemes for over three decades [56–59]. Yet, most of these schemes have not undergone rigorous technical standardization or extensive real-world deployment, which usually reveals flaws. However, in many practical scenarios on token networks, unconditional anonymity—such as cryptographic *untraceability* and *unlinkability* [58]—is not always necessary. Instead, what is often required is a temporary hold on disclosing identity attributes, pending a legal demand. In other words, most honest users don't seek perfect cryptographic anonymity but want to disclose their identity only when relevant (e.g., to law enforcement bodies).

This "temporary hold" paradigm is a promising short-term solution to the conflict between the Travel Rule and user data privacy. One method for achieving this involves blinding certain attributes and using a local legal representative (such as a law firm) as the point of contact for unblinding these hidden attributes. For simplicity, this solution is referred to as *attestation blinding*.[h] The attribute attester entity, discussed in Fig. 7.9, handles the blinding process.

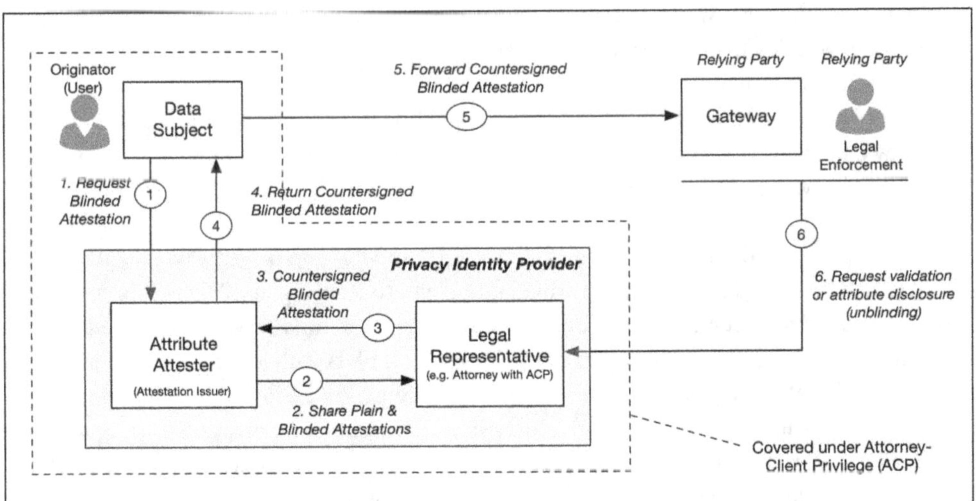

Fig. 7.9 Overview of the privacy identity provider (Privacy-IdP) for the Travel Rule, combining the attribute attester and a legal service provider with attorney–client privilege.

[h]We borrow the term "blinding" from the classic work of Chaum on blinded electronic cash [126].

The process involves combining (i) the attribute attester with attribute-blinding capabilities and (ii) a third-party legal service provider (e.g., law firm), providing *attorney–client privilege* (ACP) [60], under a legal trust framework. The basic steps are as follows:

(1) Attestation Blinding: The attribute attester hides (blinds) the relevant data until disclosure is necessary. When the data subject (e.g., originator) initiates a transaction, they request a blinded attestation from the attester (Flow-1 in Fig. 7.9). The attester generates two attestations: one plaintext (non-blinded) and one blinded. Both are sent to the legal service provider (Flow-2).

(2) Legal Representative with ACP: The legal service provider archives both the plaintext and blinded attestations. The firm then countersigns the blinded attestation and returns it to the attester (Flow-3), who forwards it to the data subject (e.g., the originator). The originator includes this countersigned attestation in their transaction to the remote VASP or gateway in the beneficiary's jurisdiction (Flow-5).

(3) First Point of Contact: The legal service provider acts as the first point of contact if the remote VASP or gateway (or legal enforcement) requests validation of the blinded attestation. Two types of queries are possible:
- A validation request without disclosing the attributes, where the legal service provider confirms the validity of the attestation.
- A request to unblind the attestation, in which case the legal service provider releases the plaintext attestation obtained in Flow-2.

(4) Trust Framework Membership as Selection Criteria: The legal service provider prioritizes queries from VASPs or gateways that are members of a common trust framework. Non-members will not receive the plaintext attestation and may only receive confirmation that the blinded attestation is valid. If a VASP is unsatisfied with this, they can drop the transaction, leaving it to be processed by compliant VASPs or gateways (Flow-6 in Fig. 7.9).

In the privacy identity provider (Privacy-IdP) model in Fig. 7.9, the legal service provider acts as the data subject's formal representative, using its ACP. This approach strikes a balance between users who demand on-chain anonymity (due to state surveillance concerns) and law enforcement agencies (e.g., FinCEN, FBI) with legitimate concerns over certain questionable transactions. For small transactions, the countersigned blinded attestation from a trusted legal representative may be sufficient for remote VASPs or gateways.

In Fig. 7.9, for simplicity, the Privacy-IdP) refers to the combination of the attribute attester and the legal service provider. Although the notion of an IdP is used historically in various technical communities [61, 62], modern IdPs do not directly confer identities. For brevity, the attribute provider (data source)—which holds authoritative attributes such as age, residence, credit score, or income—is omitted from the figure. A discussion on data providers and privacy is available in Ref. [63]. The user consent management phase, where users give explicit consent for attribute release to the IdP, is also not shown. For further reading on consent management, see works on User Managed Access (UMA) [64–66] based on the OAuth2.0 framework [67]. For similar attribute credential systems, see Refs. [68, 69].

7.4.7. *Attestation blinding and ZKP schemes*

As mentioned before, in Step 1 of Fig. 7.9, the user, as the data subject (originator), requests the Privacy-IdP (i.e., the attribute attester in the IdP) to issue a blinded attestation that displays only the user's attributes, without any personal identification. The attribute attester creates two versions of the attestation: one plaintext (unblinded) and one blinded, which contains a cryptographic hash of the plaintext attestation. Both are digitally signed by the attribute attester (as the issuer) and delivered to the legal representative (e.g., law firm) under ACP, as shown in Step 2.

The legal representative compares the plaintext and blinded attestations to ensure consistency (i.e., matching attributes, valid hash, timestamp, etc.). It then countersigns (appends its signature to) the blinded attestation and returns it to the issuer (Step 3). The firm also archives copies of the plaintext attestation, blinded attestation, and countersigned blinded attestation. The attribute attester provides the data subject with a copy of the countersigned blinded attestation (Step 4). Current industry standards for digital signatures support both enveloping and countersigning [18, 70–72], and these standards have been broadly deployed for over two decades.

When the data subject (originator) wishes to perform a cross-network tokenized asset transfer, they must include the countersigned blinded attestation in their transfer (Step 5). This attestation can be delivered to the RP (shown as the gateway and legal enforcement party in Fig. 7.9) via on-chain or off-chain methods. The RP retains the attestation for FATF compliance and may request full disclosure of the originator's identity from the Privacy-IdP (Step 6).

The introduction of the legal representative under an attorney–client relationship with the Privacy-IdP and its customer (the originator) serves several purposes, as illustrated in Fig. 7.10:

- Blinded Attestation (inner part): The blinded attestation hides the user's identity and is signed by the attribute attester, signifying the attester's confidence in the accuracy of the user's attribute (Fig. 7.10(a)).
- Countersignature (outer envelope): The legal representative countersigns the blinded attestation to confirm that it has verified the existence of both a plaintext attestation and a matching blinded attestation, both signed by the attribute attester. The countersignature also indicates that the legal representative is authorized to act as the first point of contact for any legal inquiries (Fig. 7.10(b)).

Since the legal representative archives copies of the attestations, it can respond to future queries about the user's identity. It is important to emphasize that the legal representative

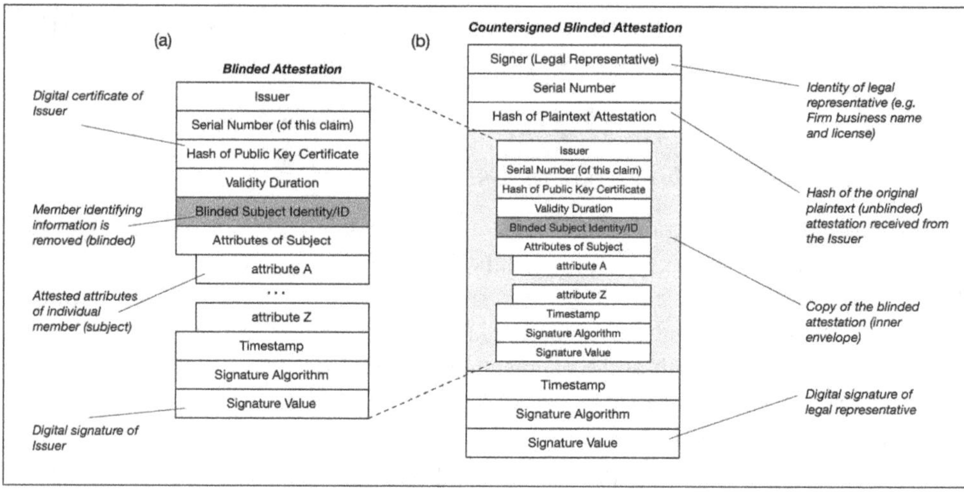

Fig. 7.10 Summary of (a) the blinded attestation issued by the Privacy-IdP as the attestation issuer, and (b) the countersigned by the legal representative of the Privacy-IdP (shown using the standard X. 509 and CMS syntax [71, 73, 74]).

does not attest to the accuracy of the attribute attester's claims but merely verifies the existence of both attestations.

The approach summarized in Fig. 7.9 may also be used for delivering parameters related to zero-knowledge proof (ZKP) schemes. For instance, Step 6 in Fig. 7.9 could in fact be a run of a ZKP protocol between the relying party and the legal representative. The goal of the ZKP in this case is for the legal representative to prove knowledge of the contents of the blinded attestations, without immediately disclosing it to the relying party.

ZKP protocols, first introduced in the mid-1980s [75], enable one party (the prover) to prove knowledge of information to another party (the verifier) without revealing the information itself. Some ZKP schemes are interactive, requiring multiple rounds of communication between the prover and verifier, while others are noninteractive. The promising use of ZKP schemes in the context of blockchains was first made evident in the *Zcash* system [76]. New ZKP techniques, such as SNARKs (succinct noninteractive arguments of knowledge) and STARKs (succinct transparent arguments of knowledge), are continually being developed.

In the context of tokenized assets with economic value, long-term retention of data for regulatory compliance (e.g., 7 years in the United States for tax purposes) is crucial. Both parties in the transaction must retain verifiable data for third-party review (e.g., tax authorities). This requirement may complicate the deployment of some ZKP schemes, especially those involving interactive proofs, as it may not be feasible to recreate the interactive proof cycles at a later time.

Moreover, some jurisdictions may mandate the retention of plaintext data about the originator and beneficiary, making cryptographic parameters or proof structures (e.g., ZKP circuit parameters) insufficient for Travel Rule compliance.

7.4.8. *Identity gateways: Toward auditable networks*

The construction of the Privacy-IdP (Fig. 7.9) can also be applied to the gateway nodes that verify and process incoming (outgoing) assets in a given token network. The notion of gateways for blockchains or DLT-based networks was first proposed in Hardjono et al. [8], following the fundamental design of gateway routers that demarcate the boundary of ISP routing networks [77]. The design principles put forward in Hardjono et al. [8] are consistent with the design principles of the internet architecture [78–80], where each network is seen as an autonomous network that must be able to operate without any dependence on other networks. This means that specific nodes in a tokenized asset network must be designated as gateways to ensure the safe transfer of tokenized assets to a different network. Thus, we say that gateways must "peer" with each other to ensure this safe transfer, based on a peering agreement by the gateway operators or owners.

Gateways for cross-network asset transfers must be multifunctional in the sense that it needs to validate at least three categories of information related to a transfer event [81]:

- Verification of the identity of originators, beneficiaries, and related entities: When network N1 seeks to transfer assets (i.e., token on the ledger of N1) to another user located in network N2, their respective gateways must perform identity validation of both the originator (located in N1) and beneficiary (located in N2). A gateway as an ingress point must reject the transfer request if it is unable to validate the relevant identities.
- Verification of asset types and classes: Similarly, a gateway as an ingress point must check if its network is technically capable and legally permitted to intake tokenized assets of a given class or type. This is the importance of standard asset schemas and profiles that are meaningful across different token networks. Asset schemas and schema profiles were discussed in Section 7.3.
- Verification of gateway service operators/owners: Gateways must not be anonymous. All nodes and gateways (and all commercial computer systems worldwide) in reality are owned and operated by individuals, organizations, or governments. As such, there must be a means for peer gateways to verify the identity of their respective owners. Examples of mechanisms used to validate a VASP legal status include LEI numbers [17], VASP directories [82], Extended Validation (EV) X.509 certificates for VASPs [83, 84], and others.
- Validation of owner legal status: There must be a means for peer gateways to verify the legal status of the VASPs who own the gateways. In some jurisdictions, limitations may be placed for regulated VASPs to transact only with other similarly regulated VASPs [85]. Examples of ownership verification mechanisms include the chaining of

the gateway-device X.509 certificate up to a business entity certificate, directories of gateways and exchanges (e.g. TRISA [84]), and other approaches.

Other types of validations include mutual gateway device hardware verification, mutual remote attestations of the software stack of the peer gateways, and others [86].

An overview of the message flows for attestation verifications is shown in Fig. 7.11, based on gateways as the checkpoints of assets coming into token networks. The IETF asset gateways paradigm is based on the assumption that one or both of the token networks N1 and N2 may be private/closed [81]. This means that cross-network (cross-chain) transfers of assets (flow-1) must be performed with the assistance of one of the trusted gateways in each network. The gateways also become the relying party (RP) as illustrated previously in Figs. 7.6 and 7.9, because the gateway is dependent on one or more of the Privacy-IdP entities for attribute verifications. Also noteworthy is that the gateway operator is covered under the VASP definition[i] even though the gateway does not function as a crypto exchange.

Looking at Fig. 7.11, when the originator transmits a transaction in network N1 intended for a beneficiary in network N2 (i.e., a cross-network transaction), the originator must attach the blinded attestation previously issued by Privacy-IdP1. The originator and Privacy-IdP1 are both located in jurisdiction J1. Since the transaction involves a cross-network (or cross-chain) transfer to a beneficiary outside the local network, gateway G2 initiates a transfer session with its peer, gateway G3, in network N2. As part of this session, G2 sends a copy of the blinded attestation to G3 in network N2, shown as flow-2.

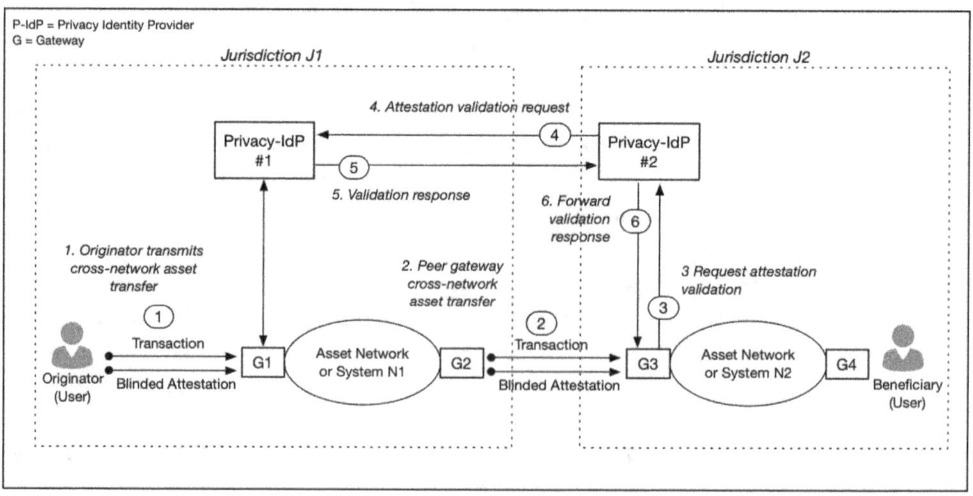

Fig. 7.11 Overview of the role of the privacy identity provider (Privacy-IdP) in attestation validation across jurisdictions for the Travel Rule compliance.

[i]See the definitions on p. 137 of Ref. [127] regarding entities and functions covered under the Travel Rule.

Gateway G3 can request validation of the blinded attestation (flow-3) and, optionally, a full identity disclosure of the originator by consulting its Privacy-IdP2 in jurisdiction J2. Since Privacy-IdP2 was not the original issuer, it forwards the validation request to Privacy-IdP1 in jurisdiction J1 (flow-4). The identity disclosure response from Privacy-IdP1 is sent to Privacy-IdP2 (flow-5) and finally to gateway G3 (flow-6).

The nascent tokenized assets industry needs to develop standard service interfaces (APIs) to enable secure, rapid, and consistent verification processes. This topic will be discussed further in Section 7.5.

7.5. Standardized Service Interfaces for Interoperability

The growing number of blockchain networks (Layer-1) indicates a maturing technology where multiple blockchains offer similar or identical functions. The diminishing returns from new blockchain entrants further signal this maturity [87, 88]. At the same time, the design limitations of many blockchains, such as slow settlement times, high processing costs, and increasing storage requirements for nodes, have become apparent [89]. These limitations have led to the creation of Layer-2 networks to address inherent issues in Layer-1 networks.[j] Many Layer-2 network implementers view them as an opportunity to differentiate themselves from the increasingly "plain vanilla" Layer-1 offerings.

Today, businesses looking to adopt blockchain functions may hesitate due to fears of "vendor lock-in" with a specific blockchain [90]. Many blockchains are accessible only through ledger-specific smart contracts, and a smart contract written for one blockchain (e.g., one Ethereum Virtual Machine [EVM]) may not be deployable on another without significant code rewriting.

From an asset-centric perspective, most businesses seek functional guarantees about the state of tokenized assets (e.g., no double-spending, no unauthorized duplicate tokens across blockchains). For many business use cases, the specific underlying technology (e.g., linked blocks, hash graphs) is of secondary concern, as long as it can provide these guarantees.

Additionally, most financial institutions still operate legacy IT systems, representing significant capital investments over decades. These systems manage data constructs (e.g., depository receipts) relevant to the tokenized Web3 world. New technologies like blockchains must integrate seamlessly with these existing systems while offering substantial functional improvements.

Thus, *standardized service interfaces* (APIs) are needed to provide businesses with access to new blockchain capabilities without disrupting their current services. These APIs are essential for various segments of transaction flows, including application-to-network

[j]Layer-2 networks are essentially a collection of computer systems that off-load certain computationally expensive operations from the main Layer-1 blockchain. When the off-chain computation has been completed, the results are said to be rolled-up to the Layer-1 blockchain.

interactions, network-to-network (blockchain-to-blockchain) transactions, and interactions with off-chain resources (e.g., asset metadata registries) (see Fig. 7.12).

Written specification standards are crucial to ensure that blockchain providers and related service providers (e.g., gateways, oracles, registries) can implement stable APIs, regardless of their systems' technical implementations. Businesses' IT divisions need these specifications to make informed decisions between the choice of blockchain networks (Layer-1 and Layer-2) and related services.

7.5.1. *Web2 service interfaces: Scalable services*

One of the achievements of Web2 systems was their use of microservices to delineate function-specific backend systems. Two important aspects of scalable web services today are: (i) the use of standard service interfaces like RESTful APIs (Representational State Transfer or REST) [91, 92] and (ii) the elimination of "backdoors" (direct links bypassing the APIs) to access backend systems.

RESTful service interfaces ensure that clients and servers share the same expectations regarding the "stateless" behavior of servers, simplifying client–server interactions and reducing the scope for errors.

The second feature, exemplified by today's microservices architecture, ensures the independence of backend systems by preventing direct links to data and functions from external systems [93]. Such direct links create interdependencies across systems, where changes in one system can lead to unpredictable behavior in others. This approach requires

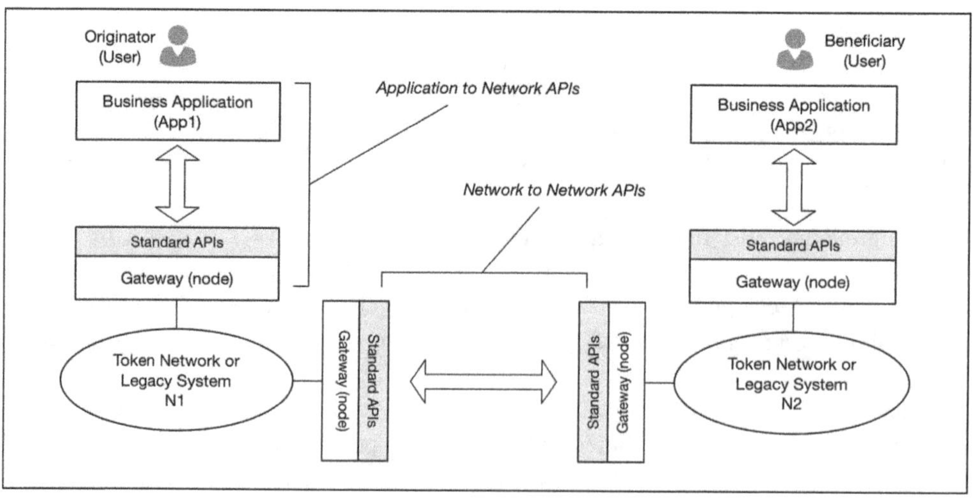

Fig. 7.12 High-level illustration of the standardized APIs between the application and the network and between networks.

each system (e.g., microservice) to implement the same front-facing APIs while allowing freedom in the choice of internal technologies without affecting adjacent systems.

A clear example of the benefits of using service interfaces in Web2 can be seen in online commerce, where many merchants use standardized shopping carts and payment APIs. In many merchants' backend systems, the shopping cart microservice and the payments (card payments) microservice are handled by separate systems, allowing each microservice to support a broad range of use cases [94]. This separation of functions, defined by service interfaces, also enables smaller web-based merchants to outsource shopping cart payments to specialized companies, such as Shopify. This creates a rich ecosystem of both large and small players, fostering market competition based on meaningful services to consumers.

7.5.2. *Benefits of standardized service interfaces*

The economic benefits of standardized APIs are well-established and are often the deciding factor in enterprise purchase decisions:

- Stable services: A well-defined interface ensures service stability because other systems using that interface are unaffected by changes behind the interface. Well-defined APIs rarely need updates or modifications.
- Consistent API behavior: API users, such as client systems, gateways, and networks, can expect consistent behavior from APIs, providing the same response for the same input parameters. This consistency is often referred to as a "contract" (agreement) between the client (caller) and the server (callee) in object-oriented computing [95, 96]. The API's function is defined by this agreement.
- Integration with existing IT infrastructure: Standardized APIs provide a clear integration path with existing IT systems or networks, preserving the value of past investments. Existing services can be "wrapped" with a new API that maps the new structure to the old one, a common practice in IT.
- Reduction in IT costs: Writing business software against a standard API allows companies to "code once, deploy multiple times." If most blockchain networks expose the same standard APIs for functions (e.g., minting tokens), businesses need to implement the client software only once. This reduces the need for specialized client software and lowers costs related to fixing bugs or development errors.

7.5.3. *Model for families of APIs for token networks*

The concept of standardized service interfaces (APIs) is illustrated in Fig. 7.13, where these APIs are implemented at multi-modal gateways [8]. A gateway is "multi-modal" when it interacts with two sides and supports interactions across different layers. In the transaction layer, gateways peer with others to transfer assets between networks. At the application layer, API gateways interact with various business applications. The architecture of API gateways is well-known in IT [97–99]. In the jurisdictional layer, gateway nodes serve

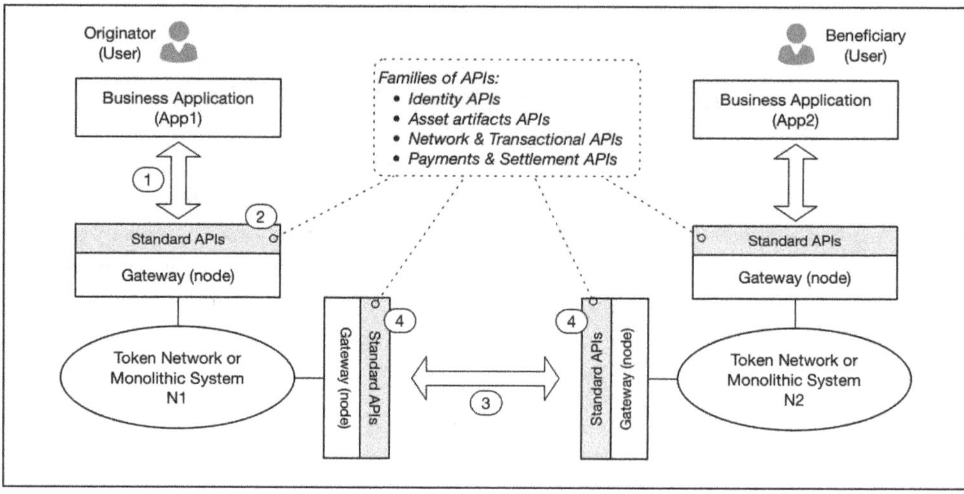

Fig. 7.13 Summary of the basic model for the family of service interfaces (APIs) for tokenized asset networks.

as the physical landing points for token networks in national regions or economic zones (see Section 7.5.8 on asset landing points).

At least three main classes of APIs are needed, with each class comprising a family of functionally relevant APIs (Fig. 7.13):

- Application-to-Network APIs: These are the interfaces that a blockchain-based asset network must expose to applications seeking to perform tasks (e.g., transferring asset tokens from Alice to Bob). This includes APIs for pre-transaction validation, such as "pre-flight" checks, shown as items (1) and (2) in Fig. 7.13. This will be discussed further in Section 7.5.5.
- Network-to-Network interoperability APIs: These APIs enable blockchains to connect via gateway nodes. This includes APIs for checking network-level information (e.g., blockchain identifier) and for cross-network asset transfers, shown as item (4) in Fig. 7.13. This will be explored further in Section 7.5.6.
- Common APIs for validating off-chain asset-related artifacts: These APIs connect to off-chain services to validate artifacts related to the tokenized asset. For example, an ART-compliant token could reference an off-chain real-world asset. Asset definition schemas and industry-specific profiles may also be stored off-chain. Similarly, a depository receipt for the asset could be housed in an off-chain database or registry. These need standardized APIs.

In addition to these classes, APIs are also needed for existing services such as payments and clearing systems. For certain transactions, like delivery vs. payment (DvP), where the on-chain transfer of a token is matched with off-chain fiat payment, access to these services via standard APIs will be necessary.

As the discussion will show, the complexity of Web3 lies not only in blockchain network interoperability but also in integrating with the existing financial IT infrastructure, which is already highly complex.

7.5.4. *Basic elements of a transaction data structure*

To understand the types of required APIs, it helps to examine the elements of a typical blockchain transaction data structure. Many of these data elements need to be validated before the transaction is transmitted across the blockchain's underlying network. These validation requirements can guide the development of APIs for validation services.

Key elements of a typical transaction include:

- Actor identification elements: These parts of the transaction data relate to the originator (sender) and beneficiary (recipient), whether on the same or different networks.
  - Originator and beneficiary identifiers: These are the digital identities of the sender and recipient of a token ownership transfer. Although many blockchains operate solely on public keys or on-chain addresses, higher-layer services will likely use digital identifiers (e.g., email, account number). These identifiers are typically associated with data attributes (e.g., country of residence, passport number), which will need to be verifiable through standardized APIs.
  - Originator and beneficiary addresses: These are the network-level addresses (i.e., public keys) on the token network. A mechanism is needed to bind a user's digital identifier with their blockchain address. Various cryptographic binding mechanisms exist (e.g., X.509 certificates, W3C Verifiable Credentials), each requiring distinct verification APIs.
- Network identification elements: This is the blockchain network identifier used to distinguish between networks in cross-network transactions. In most blockchains, a "local" transaction does not require a network identifier, since it is assumed to be on the local blockchain. However, for cross-chain transactions, the absence of a clear destination network identifier may cause assets to be lost at the destination.
  - Origin network identifier: This identifies the network where the tokenized asset currently resides, associated with the asset owner's address.
  - Destination network identifier: In cross-network transfers, this identifies the destination network where the beneficiary's address is located.

  Standardized APIs may be needed to query whether a network identifier corresponds to an operational network and to obtain other relevant network information (e.g., type of network, public or private).

- Asset-related elements:
  - Asset-related references: These are the references contained within a token. For example, an ART compliant with the EU MiCA Regulations may include several references (e.g., URLs, hash values) pointing to off-chain data or resources. These

references must be validated before accepting the ART as a compliant on-chain representation of a financial instrument.

- Operation (action) type: This refers to the asset state modification operation being executed on the token on-chain, such as ownership transfer (locally or cross-chain), token locking/unlocking, or escrowing. In cross-network transactions, it may be necessary to verify whether specific operations (e.g., lock or escrow) are interpreted the same way across the networks. This indicates the need for verification APIs, allowing callers to query such details in advance. Additionally, the tokenized assets industry should work toward enumerating and classifying operation types in each network (syntax) and describing their effects (semantics).
- Transaction integrity elements: This includes the digital signature applied to the proposed transaction, allowing it to be processed by blockchain nodes. Typically, a timestamp is also included. Beyond verifying that the transaction is syntactically correct, there may be a need to ensure that the signature was created using the keys of the same entity that owns the token on-chain (i.e., the same public-private key pair).

Information and metadata about actors: Metadata on actors participating in the token network will also be necessary. This includes business identities of VASPs, gateway and node owner/operators, smart contract authors and deployers, escrow entities, temporary token holders, and others.

7.5.5. *APIs for the validation of proposed transactions*

Based on the key elements of a transaction, at least four families of service interfaces (APIs) correspond to the types of information that need validation in relation to the transaction's data elements. These are denoted as API-A to API-D in Fig. 7.14. For clarity, the business logic handling calls to these APIs is collectively referred to as the local validation service, which has its own client logic (Item-2 in Fig. 7.14) that interacts with various validation services (Items-3(a) to 3(d)). The entire system (server system) can be part of a business application within an enterprise or function as a separate enterprise gateway system interacting with business applications. It could also be deployed by a gateway service provider (GSP).

The families of service interfaces (APIs) are described below (see Item-1 in Fig. 7.14):

- API-A: Actors Identity-Related Service Interfaces.

  This family of APIs verifies the digital identities of actors involved in a proposed transaction, including the originator/beneficiary user identifiers, digital identity attributes, on-chain addresses, etc. API-A corresponds to the remote validation APIs shown as Item-3(a) in Fig. 7.14. The validation service logic (Item-2) uses parameters from API-A to interact with remote identity services fronted by trusted third parties, based on an agreed identity legal trust framework [40]. Examples include traditional

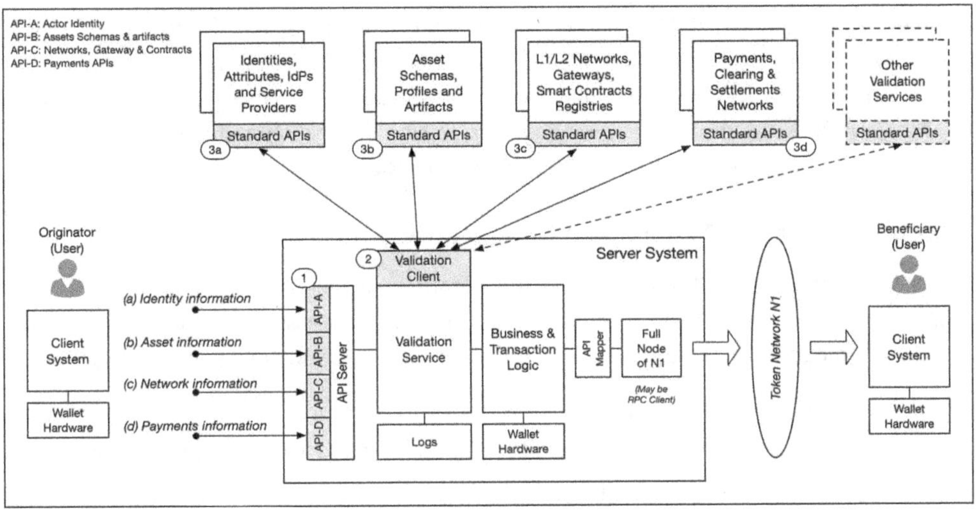

Fig. 7.14 Summary of the four types of services interfaces (APIs) for transaction related data validation.

IdP, attribute-data providers (AtPs), and existing data sources (e.g., banks, motor vehicle registries). Established APIs for querying user identity information, such as the ID-token validation endpoint in the OpenID-Connect (OIDC) standard [62], already exist.

- API-B: Asset Artifacts Service Interfaces.

  This family of APIs verifies the off-chain artifacts behind the tokenized asset. It ensures the existence and legal ownership of real-world assets (e.g., goods) underlying the token. Similar to verifying property deeds before purchasing real estate, decentralized infrastructures will be needed to verify off-chain artifacts. This creates opportunities for new service providers and revenue streams.
- API-C: Networks, Gateways, and Smart-Contracts Service Interfaces.

  A new family of APIs and services is required for the validation of network-level information in Web3 token networks. This includes verifying network identifiers, on-chain addresses, ledger state information, smart contract authors, etc. Many current blockchains use node-level interaction via Remote Procedure Calls[k] (RPC) connections [30], which lack security guarantees. Key validations include (i) verifying the correct destination blockchain network identifier in the transaction, (ii) verifying gateways' identifiers and status, and (iii) verifying smart-contract identifiers and their authors' status.

[k]The Remote Procedure Calls (RPC) construct has been around for at least four decades [128], and became incorporated into the Unix operating system [129]. It consists of two major parts, namely (i) the request/response messaging protocol between the client and the node (server), and (ii) the programming language and stub compiler that can pack the parameters (arguments) into a request message on the client-side and unpack them on the server-side (and vice versa).

- API-D: Interfaces with Existing Payments & Settlement Networks.
  ART transactions may involve fiat payments through traditional mechanisms (e.g., DvP model [100]). API-D handles payment proof validation, ensuring the proof is valid before processing the transaction (e.g., transferring the token on-chain). Payments and settlement networks are well-established, so this topic is not covered further.

7.5.5.1. Standard APIs for identities and attributes verification

Within the family of APIs for verifying digital identity and attributes, there are several types of actors involved in a token network. Clarifying these roles is essential, as there is currently no standard mechanism to validate actor legitimacy across public and private blockchains:

- Originator and Beneficiary Identity Verification.
  There is a gap between what is required under the Travel Rule [34] and what IdP offers. IdPs do not currently provide attestations for the accuracy of user identifier attributes, which is key for compliance.
- Operator Identity Verification.
  In some cases, operator service providers may participate in transaction flows (e.g., crypto exchanges or gateway operators). The legal status of these operators is relevant to token holders.
- Smart Contract Source/Author Verification.
  Similar to the originators and beneficiaries' addresses, smart contracts deployed on blockchains are linked to their authors' public key pairs. In some jurisdictions, the identity of smart contract authors may need verification, given that these contracts facilitate value transfers.

Many IdP protocols today do not support API-based verification of originator and beneficiary identities. Most IdPs only support Single-Sign-On (SSO) or managed authorization for resource access. For example, the SAML2.0 standard handles user access to online services [101], while the OAuth 2.0 framework allows a resource owner to grant access to specific resources [67]. OIDC extends OAuth 2.0 by introducing the OpenID Provider to support limited attributes (e.g., email, name) [62]. Similarly, UMA adds user consent management to OAuth 2.0 [65].

The key point is distinguishing between user authentication/authorization protocols and systems for attesting to the truthfulness and freshness of user attributes, which the IdP industry lacks today [102].

7.5.5.2. Standard APIs for asset schema and profile registries

As discussed in Section 7.3.3, globally accessible, persistent registries are needed to manage asset schemas and schema profiles across industries, communities, and jurisdictions (see Section 7.3.1 on schemas and profiles). These asset-related artifacts are critical to regulated token networks.

Future token networks will require new types of shared artifact registries, offering consistent and stable standard interfaces for managing schemas and profiles. These APIs will be necessary regardless of how the registry is technically implemented (e.g., databases, private/public blockchains). Some of the APIs that will require standardization include

- APIs for Publishing Asset-Related Artifacts:
  Schema-definition issuers and schema-profile authors (e.g., industry groups, decentralized trading communities, governments) will need APIs to publish schema/profile files into the registry. These APIs must support the lifecycle management of artifacts, such as publishing, updating, and deprecating artifacts. Decentralized replication technologies (e.g., IPFS [103]) can make artifacts available across multiple registries.
- APIs for Subscribing Asset-Related Artifacts:
  Standard APIs will allow users to subscribe to or fetch asset-related artifacts. A publish-subscribe (pub-sub) model can notify users when updated schema profiles are available.
- APIs for Authorization to Use Schema Profiles:
  In some jurisdictions, token issuance based on a schema profile may require authorization. This information must be publicly accessible for token buyers to verify that the token issuer is authorized. Standard APIs will be needed for token issuers to request and for other entities to verify authorization. The authorization grant may be stored in the same registry that houses the asset schema/profile or as a static data-token (non-transferable) on a public ledger.

Figure 7.15 illustrates the potential use of the gateway model as API endpoints for accessing the artifacts registries. These registries could be blockchain-based, referred to as an artifacts registry network (R1), or implemented as a monolithic system, shown in Fig. 7.15 as the artifacts and depository systems (D1). The key aspect illustrated in Fig. 7.15 is that the caller to the API does not need to know how an artifacts registry is implemented behind the API. For instance, if a user in a token network N1 seeks to transfer an asset token to a different network N2, the gateway G2 at network N2 can validate the schema profile's correctness before accepting the transfer from N1. Gateway G2 can query the registry blockchain R1 regarding the profile (see line 4 in Fig. 7.15) through API gateway G7. Similarly, gateway G2 may query the depository service by contacting API gateway G10 (see line 5).

In all these interaction flows, the APIs implemented at the gateways conceal the complexities of the registry implementations.

7.5.6. *Service interfaces at peer gateways*

Standard service interfaces are essential for gateways that interconnect private (closed) token networks to public token networks, as well as those connecting private token networks to each other. A significant challenge with private/closed networks is the limited visibility into the internal ledger and resources, including user addresses. The opaqueness of a private

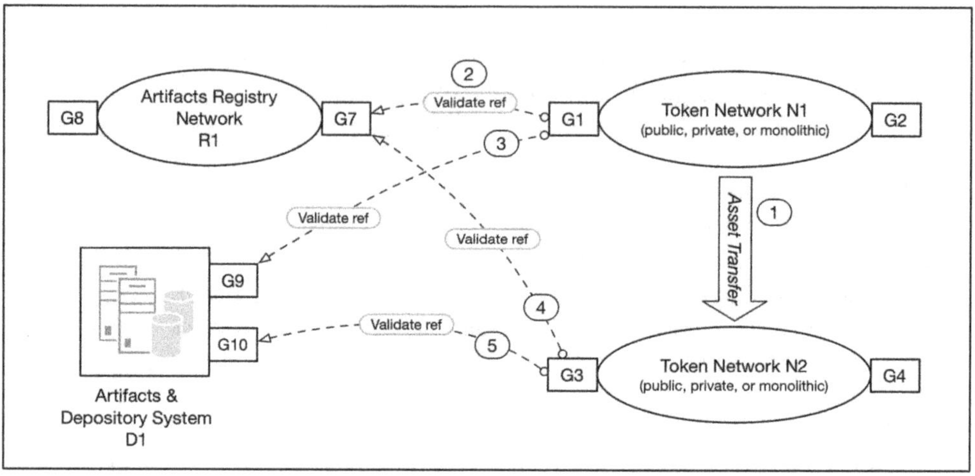

Fig. 7.15 Illustration of API gateways to publish and verify asset-related artifacts.

blockchain network has been a foundational design assumption of the IETF SATP protocol [104], which facilitates transferring assets from one private network to another through peer gateways. This protocol supports various systems behind the gateway, including public and private blockchains, as well as monolithic systems (e.g., RTGS systems).

The emergence of private tokenized asset networks is a natural development within the decentralized ledger technology paradigm, where public blockchain technology is utilized internally within an enterprise or among collaborating organizations. Enterprises have been developing open-source systems in-house for the past three decades. As of this writing, several private networks have been announced (e.g., DTCC [105], Goldman [106], SWIFT [107]).

Private asset networks (i.e., private blockchains) introduce new technical challenges. First, interaction with private token networks will likely occur only through designated endpoints, referred to here as "gateways." Second, functions or capabilities commonly available in public/permissionless token networks (e.g., looking up an address and reading ledger blocks) are inaccessible to external entities in private networks. Third, this necessitates deploying standardized APIs at these gateways to enable high interoperability between private and public networks (and between private networks). These APIs must address not only asset-related functions (e.g., transferring tokens across networks) but also mundane tasks related to network management (e.g., network address lookup, beneficiary address lookup, etc.).

Several types of standard APIs are required at gateways to facilitate peer-to-peer interactions with minimal human intervention. Some APIs may be designed to allow information retrieval from a gateway (representing a private network) using a simple request/response protocol. Other, more complex APIs will be necessary at gateways to confirm an asset's state on a ledger within a private network. Here, the gateway must produce a signed claim (assertion) regarding the asset's status in the private network (e.g., whether settlement/finalization occurred on the ledger for a given address/transaction) [26, 108].

Several families and types of service interfaces could be made available at gateways; we highlight a few below (e.g., see Fig. 7.16):

- Discovery APIs for Networks, Gateways, and Configuration: Although lists of public asset networks are currently maintained by third parties (e.g., ChainList [29]), these lists need to be formalized and guaranteed to persist over decades. Importantly, private/closed token networks may not be publicly listed. Currently, there are no worldwide standards for network and subnetwork identifiers across all blockchain networks[1]. A standardized and global blockchain network identifier assignment scheme offers business advantages, such as reducing human errors in transaction preparation (e.g., users mistakenly inputting the wrong blockchain network identifier). It also aids in logging cross-network (cross-jurisdiction) transactions for post-event auditing and analysis, which requires all network identifiers to be known and fixed. A unique network identifier is necessary within the transaction construct to distinguish the beneficiary address and the blockchain where that address is utilized. This poses challenges today, as a user may employ the same address (public key) across multiple blockchain networks. The originator (and the application) must uniquely identify both the beneficiary address and the target blockchain intended by the beneficiary. Standardizing this pair of identifiers (user address and network identifier) is essential for scalable Web3 token networks. Efforts are underway [30, 31] to standardize network-layer identifiers for

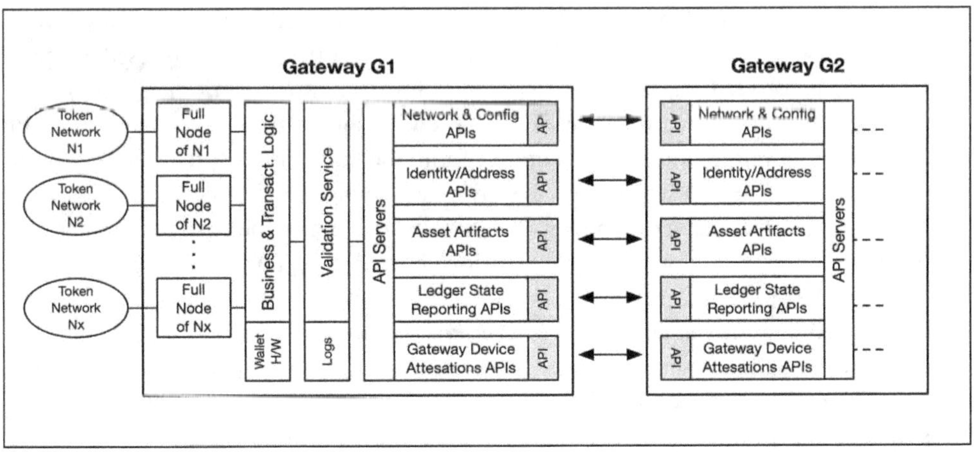

Fig. 7.16 High-level illustration of the standard APIs at gateways.

[1]The TCP/IP internet utilizes a standard *Autonomous System* (AS) number for each ISP network (i.e., routing domain). The list is maintained by ARIN [130], and any ISP can register their AS number to ARIN.

various blockchain types and to connect blockchains with traditional monolithic systems (e.g., existing payment IT infrastructure).

- User Address Validation APIs: When the originator of a cross-network (cross-chain) transaction inputs the beneficiary address into a proposed transaction, a mechanism must exist to verify if the beneficiary address exists within the destination network. This address validation function should be accessible as an authenticated call to a protected API at a gateway.
- Cross-Chain Asset Transfer APIs: The degree of interoperability between token networks is determined by the ease, security, and reliability with which tokenized assets can be transferred across networks. As stated elsewhere, users (asset owners) prioritize the safety and integrity of their tokenized assets over the specific technical features of individual blockchains.
- Ledger State Reporting APIs: Interacting with external entities from private token networks can be challenging without sharing some state information regarding a specific token within the private network. New types of protected APIs are necessary to allow external entities to query the state of a tokenized asset within a private network [26, 108]. This state information is valuable in various scenarios, including shipping (e.g., bills of lading and letters of credit) and requesting loans based on asset tokens as collateral (see Ref. [109] for a summary of these use cases). If a gateway implements the protected API, it must digitally sign the ledger-state report or assertion, introducing legal and financial liabilities for the gateway's operator/owner and discouraging dishonest assertions.
- Gateway Owner Verification APIs: In certain situations, gateways in private networks may only be permitted to peer with other gateways owned or operated by known entities (e.g., organizations within the same business consortium). This necessitates protected APIs for verifying gateway ownership. Since gateways act as the public-facing interface of a private network, any external entity should be able to query the API for ownership information. In its simplest form, the verification API could return the X.509 EV Certificate used by the gateway's underlying SSL server or load balancer. The specific information returned by this API will depend on the legal requirements in the gateway's jurisdiction (see the discussion about landing points in Section 7.5.8).
- APIs for Device-Stack Remote Attestations: Recent implementations of "bridges" have raised concerns about the cybersecurity of nodes and gateways [110]. For gateways managing high-value cross-network transactions, mutual device attestations may provide an attractive feature for these nodes and gateways [111, 112]. Each node or gateway must provide hardware-based attestation evidence regarding its hardware and software stack composition and configuration. The root of trust for the gateway device would be the tamper-resistant hardware used (e.g., TPM chip, SGX-type hardware [113], etc.). A gateway may assume the role of a verifier (appraiser) of the attestation evidence provided by a peer gateway. Alternatively, if this task places too much demand on the gateway function, it may rely on a trusted third-party verifier service [114]. The interactions between gateways related to attestations must utilize standard

APIs designed for delivering attestation evidence, validating endorsements, and providing Software Bill of Materials from manufacturers, along with appraisal reports. For gateways implemented on cloud infrastructure, device attestations introduce additional complexity because the gateway itself may operate as a process that can migrate rapidly across different hardware platforms [115, 116].

Readers seeking more information on device attestations for nodes and wallets are directed to [117–119].

7.5.7. *Service interface deployment models*

A significant value proposition of the standardized APIs approach is to preserve IT infrastructure investments for enterprise organizations, such as financial institutions. Many existing IT infrastructures must continue operating in the future for business survival while simultaneously extending to address new opportunities presented by tokenized assets and currencies (e.g., CBDCs) [100, 120]. Standardized APIs are crucial for integrating new token-related services into existing financial IT infrastructures and legacy systems.

The need to interconnect token networks—particularly private networks—introduces a potential new category of service providers, referred to here as GSP for lack of a better term. These GSP entities can offer various services to individual consumers, institutional customers, and VASPs. These services range from actor validation (e.g., beneficiary address validation) to global network discovery services and executing cross-network token transactions.

- API-based Integration with Enterprise IT Systems: One potential model for API-based integration of existing IT infrastructures is illustrated in Fig. 7.17, where a new enterprise gateway is added as another internal service/resource. The existing systems and applications continue to utilize their existing asset database (item 2) and directory services (item 3), following the same access control and privilege regime defined in the employee directory services [42]. Certain employees may be authorized to conduct token-based transactions (e.g., up to a specified dollar value or specific classes of assets). Figure 7.17 presents at least two modes for the enterprise gateway's connection to the token network. One method involves using an RPC client (item 4), while the other allows the enterprise to operate a full node (item 5) connecting to the blockchain's propagation network.
- Gateway Service Providers (GSP): Standardized APIs can be implemented by GSP entities, enabling them to connect with other gateways that use the same APIs. Customers with existing IT systems who may not wish to implement their own enterprise gateway can obtain interoperability services through a GSP. A core requirement for GSPs is validating the various parameters inputted into their APIs (in a proposed transaction) from customers or peer gateways. This involves establishing multiple business relationships with other entities and services in the ecosystem, such as IdPs, attribute

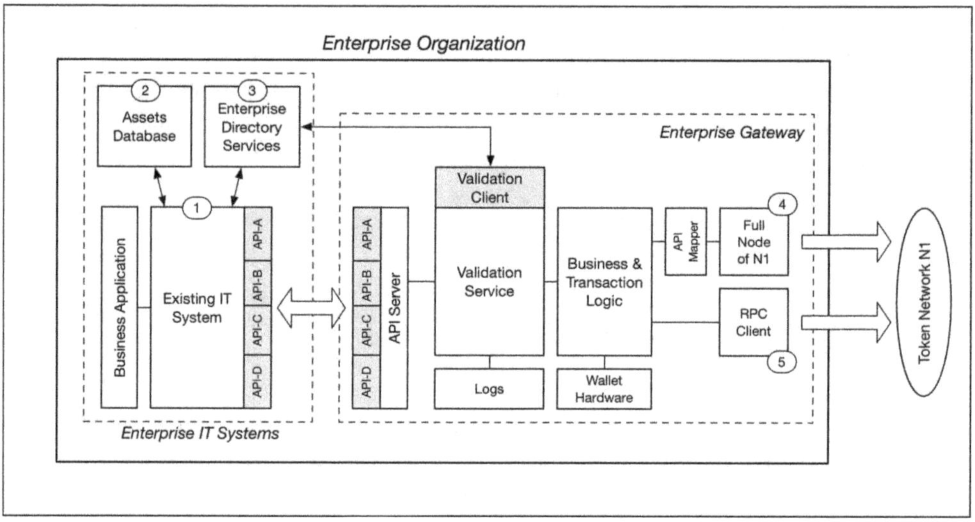

Fig. 7.17 Overview of an enterprise-operated gateway utilizing standardized APIs, following the pattern in Fig. 7.14.

attesters, asset artifacts registries, and payment/settlement networks. Depending on the range of services offered, a given GSP may provide interoperability and connectivity services to multiple DLT-based token networks (item 3). This may require the GSP to operate full nodes for each distinct token network it serves, similar to how a traditional internet service provider (ISP) connects with multiple other ISPs on the internet.

7.5.8. *Landing points: Gateways as network boundaries*

Much has been discussed regarding the globally distributed nodes of many blockchain networks, particularly those involved in public/permissionless blockchains. These networks often assume that if a participating node (computer system) physically resides in a specific nation or jurisdiction, that jurisdiction implicitly approves of the tokenized assets represented on the blockchain. However, these assumptions are untested and may be untenable.

This scenario brings to mind the analogy of landing points used in undersea submarine telecommunications and power cables. A landing point is a geographic location where a submarine or underwater cable makes landfall [121]. The underwater cable may traverse parts of the ocean floor that are legally recognized as belonging to a nation without actually making landfall there. The same logic applies to nodes within a blockchain network. Some nations may be attractive for business reasons (e.g., cheaper or greener electricity), where data centers provide cost-effective solutions for running nodes in a global asset network.

However, if a jurisdiction does not legally recognize the asset token as an economic instrument, those nodes do not constitute asset landing points from a jurisdictional perspective. In other words, the token network does not achieve asset landfall within that jurisdiction.

Gateways serve as suitable means to define both the technical entry (and exit) points of assets into a token network and the asset landing points in a jurisdiction from a legal/economic perspective. This is illustrated in Fig. 7.18, which depicts a blockchain-based asset network with three landing points denoted by the gray squares labeled "G." The other nodes (circles labeled "n") are physically located in various countries but are simply data processing facilities without any asset landfalls. Encrypted blockchains (e.g., SCRT network [122]) on confidential computing hardware (e.g., SGX [113]) may provide a solution for running nodes in a foreign jurisdiction without achieving an asset landfall (i.e., no decryption gateways) in that jurisdiction.

One benefit of this demarcation using gateways is that it allows a national jurisdiction to decide whether to participate in a given tokenized asset network by legally permitting a gateway to operate within that jurisdiction. Such a gateway may be managed by a business registered in that jurisdiction, such as a bank, licensed money transmitter, crypto-exchange, or even the government itself.

A second, more challenging aspect is the need for business applications (i.e., software clients) and their users to be authenticated by the API endpoint at the gateway, regardless of the user's physical location. Given the global nature of internet communications, a user or client in one jurisdiction may connect to a gateway (i.e., API endpoint) located in another

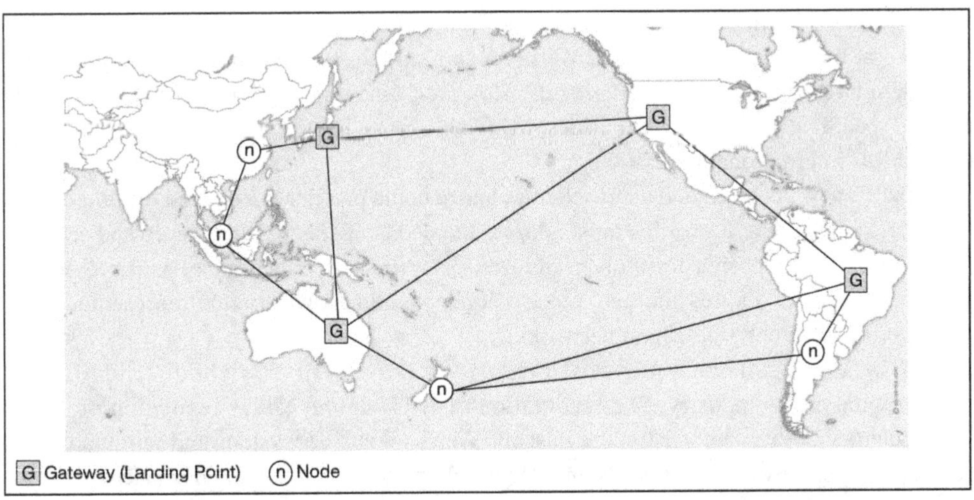

Fig. 7.18 Illustration of the notion of gateways as asset landing points into jurisdictions.

jurisdiction.[m] This necessitates that both the user (individual or organization) and the client system be authenticated by the API endpoint at the gateway, with their access privileges (authorization level) verified.

7.6. Conclusions

This work has addressed three interrelated areas relevant to the interoperability challenge in the future tokenized assets ecosystem.

First, ARTs—such as those recognized by the EU MiCA Regulations—must be transferable across different blockchain-based token networks without any degradation in the stability and integrity of the value they represent. This requires a high degree of interoperability at the Layer-1 network level. Consequently, new standardized service interfaces (APIs) must be developed, tested, and deployed by various actors and service providers in the emerging Web3 tokens ecosystem. A well-defined service interface ensures service stability and consistent API behavior, which is vital for any scalable ecosystem. Additionally, a well-designed service interface enables existing IT infrastructures to integrate more readily and seamlessly into the emerging tokenized assets ecosystem, thereby preserving the value of those existing IT investments.

Second, interoperability among token networks relates to the identifiability and accountability of actors within these networks. The Travel Rule for tokenized assets mandates the identification of originators and beneficiaries as the key holders on the networks. For cross-jurisdiction (cross-network) transfers of tokenized assets, data privacy becomes a significant concern, as the data attributes of originators and beneficiaries may be leaked or stolen at their respective VASPs. We propose a middle-ground short-term solution for this dilemma in the form of a Privacy-IdP. However, a new legal identity trust framework must be specifically designed for entities involved in cross-jurisdiction asset transfers under FATF AML international regulations.

Finally, new standardized asset schemas and schema profiles are needed for tokenizing real-world assets. These profiles must address the needs of specific industries and sectors. A standard schema profile for a given industry or asset class is beneficial as it provides a consistent semantic expression and a shared understanding of the value represented by a token across different blockchain networks.

We believe that the new EU MiCA regulation is a step in the right direction for the global digital assets industry. The recognition of ARTs in the MiCA regulation provides the regulatory clarity needed for the nascent Web3 tokens ecosystem and stimulates the development of new asset networks and decentralized infrastructures and services.

[m] This is akin to a user watching content online (e.g., movie) that is located at a content server in a different country. In some cases, the copyright associated with the content may prohibit the content from being consumed from a different jurisdiction or country. Hence, the popularity today of consumer-grade VPN services to circumvent these geolocation-based licensing regimes.

References

1. A. Lipton, A. Sardon, F. Schär, and C. Schüpbach, Stablecoins, digital currency, and the future of money. In eds. A. Pentland, A. Lipton, and T. Hardjono, *Building the New Economy: Data as Capital*, MIT Press, Cambridge (2021).
2. A. Sardon, T. Hardjono, and B. Schuppli, *Asset Profile Definitions for DLT Interoperability: Internet-draft-sardon-blockchain-interop-asset-profile-00*, IETF (2021). Available at: https://datatracker.ietf.org/doc/draft-sardon-blockchain-interop-asset-profile/.
3. D. Avrilionis and T. Hardjono, *The Legal Ramifications of Digital Tokenization*. Research Gate (2023). https://doi.org/10.36227/techrxiv.22776560.v1.
4. R. Rivest, A. Shamir, and L. Adleman, A method for obtaining digital signatures and public-key cryptosystems, *Commun. ACM*. **21**, 120126 (1978).
5. W. Diffie and M. Hellman, New directions in cryptography, *IEEE Trans. Inf. Theor.* **22**(6), 644–654 (1976).
6. L. Kohnfelder, Towards a practical public-key cryptosystem. BS thesis. MIT, Cambridge (1978). Available at: http://hdl.handle.net/1721.1/15993.
7. T. Hardjono, ed., *The Impact of Blockchain for Government: Insights on Identity, Payments, and Supply Chains*. Report from the Congressional Blockchain Caucus (2018). Available at: http://www.businessofgovernment.org/report/impact-blockchain-government-insights-identity-payments-and-supply-chain.
8. T. Hardjono, A. Lipton, and A. Pentland, Towards an interoperability architecture blockchain autonomous systems, *IEEE Trans. Eng. Manag.* **67**(4), 1298–1309 (2019).
9. DTCC. *Project Whitney: Case Study, DTCC Report*. Depository Trust and Clearing Corporation (2020). Available at: https://www.dtcc.com/~/media/Files/Downloads/settlement-asset-services/user-documentation/Project-Whitney-Paper.pdf.
10. DTCC. *Project Ion: Case Study, DTCC Report*. Depository Trust and Clearing Corporation (2020). Available at: https://www.dtcc.com/~/media/Files/Downloads/settlement-asset-services/user-documentation/project-ION-paper-2020.pdf.
11. Digital Asset Inc, *Canton Network: A Network of Networks for Smart Contract Applications* (2023). Available at: https://www.digitalasset.com/hubfs/Canton/Canton%20Network%20-%20White%20Paper.pdf.
12. H. Diedrich, *Lexon: Digital Contracts*. Lexon Foundation (2019).
13. J. Hazard and T. Hardjono, CommonAccord: Towards a foundation for smart contracts in future blockchains. In *W3C Workshop on Distributed Ledgers on the Web*, W3C, Cambridge, MA, USA (2016). Available at: https://www.w3.org/2016/04/blockchain-workshop.
14. European Commission, Regulation (EU) 22023/1114 of the European Parliament and of the Council of 27 April 2016 on markets in crypto-assets, and amending Regulations (EU) No 1093/2010 and (EU) No 1095/2010 and Directives 2013/36/EU and (EU) 2019/1937, *Off. J. Eur. Union*. **L150**, 1–166 (2023).
15. T. Bray, *The JavaScript Object Notation (JSON) Data Interchange Format*. IETF (2017). Standard RFC8259. Available at: https://datatracker.ietf.org/doc/html/rfc8259.
16. C. Bormann and P. Hoffman, *Concise Binary Object Representation (CBOR)*. IETF (2020). Standard RFC8949. Available at: https://datatracker.ietf.org/doc/html/rfc8949.
17. GLEIF. *LEI in KYC: A New Future for Legal Entity Identification*. GLEIF Research Report—a New Future for Legal Entity Identification, Global Legal Entity Identifier Foundation (GLEIF)

(2018). Available at: https://www.gleif.org/en/lei-solutions/lei-in-kyc-a-new-future-for-legal-entity-identification.

18. M. Jones, J. Bradley, and N. Sakimura, *JSON Web Signature (JWS).* IETF (2017). Standard RFC7515. Available at: https://tools.ietf.org/html/rfc7515.

19. J. Schaad, *CBOR Object Signing and Encryption (COSE)*, IETF (2017). Standard RFC8152. Available at: http://datatracker.ietf.org/doc/html/rfc8152.

20. D. Avrilionis and T. Hardjono, *SATP Asset Schema Management Architecture, Draft Specifications.* IETF (2023).

21. Esign, United States Congress, Electronic signatures in global and national commerce act (ESIGN), In *Public Law United States of America Congress*, pp. 106–229, Authenticated U.S. Government Information (2000).

22. R. Housley, W. Ford, W. Polk, and D. Solo, Internet, *X, 509 Public Key Infrastructure Certificate and CRL Profile.* (1999). IETF Standard RFC2459. Available at: http://tools.ietf.org/rfc/rfc2459.txt.

23. S. Farrell and R. Housley, *An Internet Attribute Certificate Profile for Authorization.* IETF (2002). Standard RFC3281. Available at: http://tools.ietf.org/rfc/rfc3281.txt.

24. Digital Asset Inc, *The Digital Asset Platform: Non-Technical White Paper.* Digital Asset Inc (2016).

25. BIS. *Blueprint for the Future Monetary System: Improving the Old, Enabling the New, Bis Annual Economic Report.* Bank for International Settlements (2023). Available at: https://www.bis.org/publ/arpdf/ar2023e.pdf.

26. V. Ramakrishna, V. Pandit, E. Abebe, S. Nishad, and K. Narayanam, *Views and View Addresses for Secure Asset Transfer, Draft Specifications, Internet Engineering Task Force (IETF), Draft-ramakrishna-satp-views-addresses-01* (2023).

27. D. Siegel, *Understanding the DAO Attack.* Coindesk (2016). Available at: http://coindesk.com/understanding-dao-hack-journalists.

28. M. del Castillo, *Blockchain Hard Fork to Return DAO Funds.* Coindesk (2016). Available at: https://www.coindesk.com/ethereum-executes-blockchain-hard-fork-return-dao-investor-funds.

29. Chainlist, *Chainlist List of EVM Networks* (2023). Available at: https://chainlist.org (accessed November 9, 2023).

30. W. Zhang and P. Robinson, *EIP-3220: Crosschain Identifier Specification, Ethereum Improvement Proposals.* Ethereum.org (2020). Available at: https://eips.ethereum.org/EIPS/eip-3220.

31. W. Zhang and T. Hardjono, *SATP Network Identification, Draft Specifications*, IETF (2023). Available at: https://datatracker.ietf.org/doc/draft-zhang-satp-network-identification/.

32. ISO, *Financial Services—Universal Financial Industry Message Scheme Part 1: Metamodel, ISO/IEC.* International Organization for Standardization (2013). p. 20022-1.

33. FATF, FATF recommendations. In *International Standards on Combating Money Laundering and the Financing of Terrorism and Proliferation*, FATF Revision of Recommendation 16; vol *2012*, FATF (2023). Available at: https://www.fatf-gafi.org/en/publications/Fatfrecommendations/Fatf-recommendations.html.

34. FATF. *International Standards on Combating Money Laundering and the Financing of Terrorism and Proliferation, FATF Revision of Recommendation 15.* FATF (2018). Available at: http://www.fatfgafi.org/publications/fatfrecommendations/documents/fatfrecommendations.html.

35. FATF, *Guidance for a Risk-Based Approach to Virtual Assets and Virtual Asset Service Providers, FATF Guidance*. FATF (2019). Available at: http://www.fatfgafi.org/publications/fatfrecommendations/documents/Guidance-RBAvirtual-assets.html.
36. European Commission, Regulation (EU) 2016/679 of the European Parliament and of the Council of 27 April 2016 on the protection of natural persons with regard to the processing of personal data and on the free movement of such data (General Data Protection Regulation), *Off. J. Eur. Union*. **L119**, 1–88 (2016).
37. OAIC, *Australian entities and the EU General Data Protection Regulation (GDPR) [Tech Rep]*. Australian Government Office of the Australian Information Commissioner (2018). Available at: https://www.oaic.gov.au/privacy/guidance-and-advice/australian-entities-and-the-eu-general-dataprotection-regulation/. (accessed August 23, 2021).
38. SWIFT, *SWIFT General Terms and Conditions [Tech Rep*]. SWIFT (2020). Available at: https://www2.swift.com/knowledgecentre/publications/sgtc.
39. SWIFT. *SWIFT Personal Data Protection Policy [Tech Rep*]. SWIFT (2022). Available at: https://www2.swift.com/go/book/book85008.
40. American Bar Association, *An Overview of Identity Management: Submission for UNCITRAL Commission 45th Session*. ABA Identity Management Legal Task Force (2012). Available at: https://docs.un.org/en/A/CN.9/WG.IV/WP.120.
41. T. Hardjono and A. Pentland, Core identities for future transaction systems. In eds. T. Hardjono, A. Pentland, D. Shrier, and T. Data, *A New Framework for Identity and Data Sharing*, pp. 41–81. MIT Press, Cambridge (2019).
42. T. Hardjono, Federated authorization over access to personal data for decentralized identity management, *IEEE Comm. Stand. Mag*. **3**(4), 32–38 (2019). https://doi.org/10.1109/MCOMSTD.001.1900019.
43. A. Pentland, *Social Physics: How Social Networks Can Make Us Smarter*. Penguin Books, London (2015).
44. The Jericho Forum, *Identity Commandments*. Open Group (2011). Available at: http://www.opengroup.org.
45. K. Cameron, The Laws of Identity. (2004). Available at: https://www.identityblog.com/stories/2005/05/13/TheLawsOfIdentity.pdf.
46. A. Pentland and T. Hardjono, Digital identity is broken: Here is a way to fix it, *Wall St. J*. (2018). https://www.wsj.com/articles/digital-identity-is-broken-heres-a-way-to-fix-it-1522782822.
47. W3C, *Decentralized Identifiers v1.0 W3C Proposed Recommendation*, W3C (2021). Available at: https://www.w3.org/TR/did-core/ (accessed August 3, 2021).
48. W3C, *Decentralized identifiers, Resolution. v0.2, W3C Draft Community Group Report*, W3C (2022). Available at: https://www.w3.org/TR/did-resolution/ (accessed March 24, 2022).
49. Visa, *Visa Core Rules and Visa Product and Service Rules, Specification*. Visa (2017).
50. The White House, *National Strategy for Trusted Identities in Cyberspace: Enhancing Online Choice, Efficiency, Security, and Privacy*. White House (2011). Available at: https://obamawhitehouse.archives.gov/sites/default/files/rss_viewer/NSTICstrategy_041511.pdf.
51. E. Makaay, T. Smedinghoff, and D. Thibeau, *OpenID Exchange: Trust Frameworks for Identity Systems* (2017). Available at: http://www.openidentityexchange.org..
52. SAFE, BioPharma Association, *Trust Framework Provider Services* (2014). Available at: https://oixnet.org/registry/safe-biopharma-global-tfp/.

53. United Kingdom Government, *UK Digital Identity and Attributes Trust Framework—Beta Version.* GOV.UK (2023). Available at: https://www.gov.uk/government/publications/uk-digital-identity-and-attributes-trust-framework-beta-version.

54. A. Pentland and T. Hardjono, Building data cooperatives. In eds. A. Pentland, A. Lipton, and T. Hardjono, *Building the New Economy: Data as Capital*, pp. 19–33. MIT Press, Cambridge (2021).

55. M. M. Buhler, I. Calzada, I. Cane, et al. Unlocking the power of digital commons: Data cooperatives as a pathway for data sovereign, Innovative and Equitable Digital Communities, *Digital.* **3**, 146–171 (2023).

56. D. L. Chaum, Untraceable electronic mail, return addresses, and digital pseudonyms, *Commun. ACM.* **24**(2), 84–90 (1981).

57. S. Brands, Untraceable off-line cash in wallets with observers. In *CRYPTO1993 Proc. 13th Annu. Int. Cryptol*, pp. 302–318, Springer-Verlag (1993).

58. J. Camenisch and E. Van Herreweghen, Design and implementation of the Idemix anonymous credential system. In *Proc. 9th ACM Conf. Comput. Commun, Security (ACM)*, pp. 21–30 (2002).

59. E. Brickell and J. Li, Enhanced privacy ID: A direct anonymous attestation scheme with enhanced revocation capabilities, *IEEE Trans. Depend. Sec. Comput.* **9**(3), 345–360 (2012).

60. American Bar Association, *Rules of Professional Conduct Rule 1.6: Confidentiality of information.* American Bar Association (1983). Available at: https://www.americanbar.org/groups/professional_responsibility/publications/model_rules_of_professional_conduct/.

61. OASIS, *Assertions and Protocols for the OASIS Security Assertion Markup Language (SAML).* (2005). V2.0. Available at: http://docs.oasisopen.org/security/saml/v2.0/saml-core-2.0-os.pdf.

62. N. Sakimura, J. Bradley, M. Jones, B. de Medeiros, and C. Mortimore, *OpenID Connect Core 1.0, Technical Specification v1.0—Errata Set 1.* OpenID Foundation (2014). Available at: http://openid.net/specs/openid-connect-core1_0.html.

63. T. Hardjono and A. Pentland, MIT open algorithms. In eds. T. Hardjono, A. Pentland, D. Shrier, and T. Data, *A New Framework for Identity and Data Sharing*, pp. 83–107. MIT Press, Cambridge, (2019).

64. T. Hardjono, E. Maler, M. Machulak, and D. Catalano, *User-Managed Access (UMA) Profile of OAuth2.0—Specification.* Kantara Initiative (2015). Available at: https://docs.kantarainitiative.org/uma/rec-uma-core.html. (version 1.0, Kantara published specification).

65. E. Maler, M. Machulak, and J. Richer, *User-Managed Access (UMA) 2.0, Kantara published specification.* Kantara Initiative (2017). Available at: https://docs.kantarainitiative.org/uma/ed/uma-core-2.0-10.html.

66. E. Maler and T. Hardjono, *Binding Obligations on User Managed Access (UMA) Participants, draft-maler-oauth-umatrust-03.* Internet Engineering Task Force (2015). Available at: https://tools.ietf.org/html/draft-maler-oauth-umatrust.

67. D. Hardt, *The OAuth 2.0 Authorization Framework.* IETF (2012). Standard RFC6749. Available at: https://tools.ietf.org/html/rfc6749.

68. ABC4Trust, *ABC4Trust: Attribute-Based Credentials for Trust.* ABC4Trust (2012). Available at: https://abc4trust.eu.

69. A. Sabouri, I. Krontiris, and K. Rannenberg, Attribute-based credentials for trust (ABC4Trust). In eds. S. Fischer-Hubner, S. Katsikas, and G. Quirchmayr, *Proc. 9th International Conference on Trust, Privacy and Security in Digital Business (TrustBus 2012)*, pp. 218–219, Springer International Publishing, Vienna (2012). https://doi.org/10.1007/978-3-642-32287-7_21.

70. National Institute of Standards and Technology, *Digital Signature Standard (DSS), NIST FIPS*; vols 186–5. NIST (2023). https://doi.org/10.6028/NIST.FIPS.186-5.

71. R. Housley, *Cryptographic Message Syntax (CMS),* IETF (2009). Standard RFC5652. Available at: https://datatracker.ietf.org/doc/html/rfc5652.

72. M. Jones, *JSON Web Key (JWK).* IETF (2015). Standard RFC7517. Available at: https://www.rfc-editor.org/rfc/rfc7517.

73. S. Farrell, R. Housley, and S. Turner, *An Internet Attribute Certificate Profile for Authorization.* IETF (2010). Standard RFC5755. Available at: https://datatracker.ietf.org/doc/html/rfc5755.

74. D. Cooper, S. Santesson, S. Farrell, et al. Internet, *X, 509 Public Key Infrastructure Certificate and Certificate Revocation List (CRL) Profile.* (2008). IETF Standard RFC5280. Available at: http://tools.ietf.org/rfc/rfc5280.txt.

75. S. Goldwasser, S. Micali, and C. Rackoff, The knowledge complexity of interactive proof systems. In *Proc. Seventeenth Annu. ACM Symp. Theor. Comput. (STOC85),* pp. 291–304, Association for Computing Machinery (1985).

76. E. Ben Sasson, A. Chiesa, C. Garman, et al. Zerocash: Decentralized anonymous payments from bitcoin. In *2014 IEEE Symp. Secur. Priv.* pp. 459–474, Berkeley, CA, USA (2014).

77. Y. Richter, T. Li, and S. Hares, *A Border Gateway Protocol 4 (BGP-4),* IETF (2006). Standard RFC4271. Available at: https://datatracker.ietf.org/doc/html/rfc4271.

78. D. Clark, The design philosophy of the DARPA internet protocols, *ACM Sigcomm Comput. Commun. Rev.* **18**, 106114 (1988).

79. D. D. Clark, *Designing an Internet.* MIT Press, Cambridge (2018).

80. J. H. Saltzer, Protection and the control of information sharing in MULTICS, *Commun. ACM.* **17**(7), 388–402 (1974).

81. T. Hardjono, M. Hargreaves, N. Smith, and V. Ramakrishna, *Secure Asset Transfer Interoperability Architecture, Draft specifications*, IETF (2023a). Available at: https://datatracker.ietf.org/doc/draft-hardjono-sat-architecture/.

82. S. Sinclair, *Crypto Exchange Group Eyes "Bulletin Board" System for FATF Compliance.* Coindesk (2020). Available at: https://www.coindesk.com/crypto-exchange-group-eyes-bulletin-board-system-for-fatf-compliance-coinbase-exec.

83. T. Hardjono, Development of trust infrastructures for virtual asset service providers. In eds. I. Boureanu, C. C. Dragan, M. Manulis, et al. *Lecture Notes in Computer Science*, pp. 74–91. Springer, Berlin, Germany (2020). Available at: https://arxiv.org/abs/2008.05048. 12580 Interdisciplinary Workshop on Trust, Identity, Privacy and Security in the Digital Economy; vol 2020.

84. D. Jevans, T. Hardjono, J. Vink, et al. *Travel Rule Information Sharing Architecture for Virtual Asset Service Providers.* TRISA (2020). Available at: https://trisa.io/wp-content/uploads/2020/06/TRISAEnablingFATFTravelRuleWhitePaperV7.pdf. (version 7).

85. FINMA. *FINMA Guidance: Payments on the Blockchain, Finma Guidance Report, Swiss Financial Market Supervisory Authority (FINMA)* (2019). Available at: https://www.finma.ch/en/media/finma/dokumente/dokumentencenter/myfinma/4dokumentation/finma-aufsichtsmitteilungen/20190826-finma-aufsichtsmitteilung-02-2019.pdf.

86. T. Hardjono, *Blockchain Gateways, Bridges and Delegated Hash-Locks* (2021). Available at: https://arxiv.org/abs/2102.03933.

87. R. Belchior, A. Vasconcelos, S. Guerreiro, and M. Correia, A survey on blockchain interoperability: Past, present, and future trends, *ACM. Comput. Surv.* **54**, 1–41 (2021).

88. R. Belchior, L. Riley, T. Hardjono, A. Vasconcelos, and M. Correia, Do you need a distributed ledger technology interoperability solution? *Distrib. Ledger Technol.* **2**(1), 1–37 (2023).

89. A. Lipton and A. Treccani, *Blockchain and Distributed Ledgers: Mathematics, Technology and Economics*. World Scientific Publishing, Singapore (2021).

90. The Geneva Association. *Assessing the Potential of Decentralized Finance and Blockchain Technology [Tech Rep]*. Geneva Association (2023). Available at: https://www.genevaassociation.org/publication/new-technologies-and-data/assessing-potential-decentralised-finance-and-blockchain.

91. R. T. Fielding, Architectural Styles and the Design of Network-Based Software Architectures. Doctoral thesis, University of California at Irvine (2000). Available at: https://www.ics.uci.edu/fielding/pubs/dissertation/fielding_dissertation.pdf.

92. T. Berners-Lee, R. Fielding, and H. Frystyk, *Hypertext Transfer Protocol-HTTP1.0*. IETF (1996). Standard RFC1945. Available at: https://datatracker.ietf.org/doc/html/rfc1945.

93. S. Yegge, Jeff Bezos Mandate (Stevey's Google Platforms Rant). (2002). Available at: https://gist.github.com/chitchcock/1281611.

94. W. Vogels, Amazon CTO Werner Vogels on innovating with APIs, *Wall St. J.* (2018). Available at: https://deloitte.wsj.com/cio/amazon-cto-werner-vogels-on-innovating-with-apis-1524196930.

95. E. Gamma, R. Helm, R. Johnson, and J. Vlissides, *Design Patterns: Elements of Reusable Object-Oriented Software*. Addison-Wesley Professional, Reading (1994).

96. B. Meyer, *Object-Oriented Software Construction*. Prentice Hall International, New York, NY (1994).

97. G. Piccinelli, W. Jin, P. Dumas, and N. Carter, Market guide for API gateways, *Res. Rep.* Gartner, G00777062 (2022).

98. Amazon AWS, *Amazon API Gateway: Create, Maintain, and Secure APIs at Any Scale*. Amazon AWS (2023). Available at: https://aws.amazon.com/api-gateway/.

99. Microsoft Azure, Use API Gateways in Microservices (2023). Available at: https://learn.microsoft.com/en-us/azure/architecture/microservices/design/gateway.

100. M. L. Bech, J. Hancock, T. Rice, and A. Wadsworth, On the future of securities settlement, *BIS Quarterly Review*. (2020). Bank for International Settlements. Available at: https://www.bis.org/publ/qtrpdf/r_qt2003i.htm.

101. OASIS, *Profiles for the OASIS Security Assertion Markup Language (SAML)*. (2005). V2.0. Available at: https://docs.oasis-open.org/security/saml/v2.0/saml-profiles-2.0-os.pdf.

102. T. Hardjono, Owner-centric access to IoT data. In eds. H. Shrobe, D. Shrier, and A. Pentland, *New Solutions for Cybersecurity*, pp. 405–422. MIT Press, Cambridge (2017).

103. Protocol Labs, Inter Planetary File System (IPFS). (2019). Available at: https://docs.ipfs.io. (accessed September 23, 2019).

104. M. Hargreaves, T. Hardjono, and R. Belchior, *Secure Asset Transfer Protocol, Draft Specifications*, IETF (2023). Available at: https://datatracker.ietf.org/doc/draft-hargreaves-sat-core/.

105. O. Knight, *Wall Street Giant DTCC Launches Private Blockchain in Big Crypto-Milestone for TradFi*. CoinDesk (2022). Available at: https://www.coindesk.com/business/2022/08/22/wall-streets-dtcc-launches-private-blockchain-platform-to-settle-trades/.

106. G. Kaloudis, *Goldman Sachs Is Trying to Make Blockchain Bonds Happen*. CoinDesk (2022). Available at: https://www.coindesk.com/business/2022/12/11/goldman-sachs-is-trying-to-make-blockchain-bonds-happen/.

107. SWIFT, Swift Unlocks Potential of Tokenisation with Successful Blockchain Experiments (2023). Available at: https://www.swift.com/news-events/press-releases/swift-unlocks-potential-tokenisation-successful-blockchain-experiments.

108. D. Behl, P. Kodeswaran, V. Ramakrishna, S. Sen, and D. Vinayagamurthy, Trusted data notifications from private blockchains. In *Proc. 2020 IEEE International Conference Blockchain*, pp. 53–61, Cornell University (2000).

109. V. Ramakrishna, *Secure Asset Transfer (SAT) Use Cases, Draft Specifications*, IETF (2023). Available at: https://datatracker.ietf.org/doc/draft-ietf-satp-usecases/.

110. R. Browne and M. Sigalos, *Hackers Have Stolen $1.4 Billion This Year Using Crypto Bridges*, CNBC. HTML (2022). Available at: https://www.cnbc.com/2022/08/10/hackers-have-stolen-1point4-billion-this-year-using-crypto-bridges.

111. TCG, *DICE Layering Architecture*. Trusted Computing Group (2020). Available at: https://trustedcomputinggroup.org/wp-content/uploads/DICE-Layering-Architecture-r19_pub.pdf. (version 1.0, TCG published specifications).

112. IETF, *Remote ATtestation ProcedureS (RATS) working group*. Approved Charter, Internet Engineering Task Force (2019). Available at: https://datatracker.ietf.org/wg/rats/about/.

113. F. McKeen, I. Alexandrovich, I. Anati, et al. Intel software guard extensions (intel SGX) support for dynamic memory management inside an enclave. In *Proc. Workshop on Hardware and Architectural Support for Security and Privacy (HASP)*, Seoul, South Korea (2016). Available at: http://caslab.csl.yale.edu/workshops/hasp2016/program.html.

114. J. Zic and T. Hardjono, Towards a cloud-based integrity measurement service, *J. Cloud Comput. Adv. Syst. Appl.* **2**(1), 4 (2013).

115. TCG. *Attestations Working Group*. Trusted Computing Group (2020). Available at: https://members.trustedcomputinggroup.org.

116. T. Hardjono and N. Smith, Towards an attestation architecture for blockchain networks, *World Wide Web*. **24**(5), 1587–1615 (2021).

117. G. Fedorkow, J. Fitzgerald-McKay, and T. Hardjono, Overview of TCG Technologies for device identification and attestation. In *TCG Published Specifications*, Trusted Computing Group, (2023). Available at: https://trustedcomputinggroup.org/specifications-public-review/. (version 1.0, p r1.33).

118. T. Hardjono and N. Smith, Decentralized trusted computing base for blockchain infrastructure security, *Front. Blockchains*. **2** (2019).

119. T. Hardjono, A. Lipton, and A. Pentland, Towards attestable wallets for tokenized assets, RG. **1**, 24716136 (2023). http://dx.doi.org/10.36227/techrxiv.24716136.v1. (*Manuscript* under review).

120. I. Aldasoro, S. Doerr, L. Gambacorta, R. Garratt, and P. K. Wilkens, The tokenisation continuum, *Bis Bull*. **72**, (2023). Bank for International Settlements. Available at: https://www.bis.org/publ/bisbull72.htm.

121. Wikipedia, *Cable Landing Point*, Wikipedia (2023), Available at: https://en.wikipedia.org/wiki/Cable_landing_point.

122. SCRT, *How Secret Network's Privacy as a Service Unlocks Web3 for the Next Billion Users.* CoinDesk (2023). Available at: https://www.coindesk.com/sponsored-content/how-secret-networks-privacy-as-a-service-unlocks-web3-for-the-next-billion-users/.

123. Cable Labs, *CableLabs PKI Certification Practice Statement.* Cable Television Laboratories Inc. (2019). Available at: https://www-res.cablelabs.com/wp-content/uploads/2019/09/13124937/CableLabs-New-PKI-CP-V3.0-Public.pdf. (version 3 issued).

124. W. Entriken, D. Shirley, J. Evans, and N. Sachs, *ERC-721 Non-Fungible Token Standard (EIP 721), Ethereum Improvement Proposals*. Ethereum.org (2018). Available at: https://eips.ethereum.org/EIPS/eip-721.

125. IBM, Four-party credit/debit payment protocol (EU Patent EP1017030A2) (1999). Available at: https://patentimages.storage.googleapis.com/68/7d/68/51b6337757ed7a/EP1017030A2.pdf.

126. D. Chaum, A. Fiat, and M. Naor, Untraceable electronic cash. In *Proc. Adv. Cryptol. Cryptogr.*, vol 1988, pp. 319–327, Springer-Verlag New York Inc, New York, NY, (1990).

127. FATF. *Oman's Measures to Combat Money Laundering and Terrorist Financing*. FATF (2023). Available at: http://www.fatf-gafi.org.

128. B. J. Nelson, Remote Procedure Call (Report CSL-81-9). Doctoral thesis, Xerox-PARC and Carnegie-Mellon University (1981).

129. B. W. Kernighan and R. Pike, *The Unix Programming Environment.* Prentice Hall, Englewood Cliffs (1983).

130. American Registry for Internet Numbers, *Autonomous System Numbers (ARIN)*, American Registry for Internet Numbers, (2023). Available at: https://www.arin.net/resources/guide/asn/.

SECTION

3

Advanced Computational Methods

https://doi.org/10.1142/9789819813049_0008

CHAPTER 8 Symmetric Encryption on a Quantum Computer

David Garvin[1], Oleksiy Kondratyev[2,*], Alexander Lipton[3], and Marco Paini[1]

[1]*Rigetti Computing, USA*
[2]*Imperial College London, UK*
[3]*Abu Dhabi Investment Authority (ADIA), UAE*
[*]*Corresponding author. E-mail: a.kondratyev@imperial.ac.uk*

In this article, we propose a symmetric encryption algorithm based on the utilization of the expressive power of parameterized quantum circuits.

8.1. Introduction

Quantum computing and cryptography are often mentioned together. To a large extent, this is due to the fame of Shor's algorithm, designed to factor integer numbers with an exponential speedup with respect to the best-known classical algorithms (see, e.g., Ref. [1]). Integer number factoring is a hard computational problem for classical computers that, due to its hardness, lies at the heart of the RSA protocol, an asymmetric public–private key cryptosystem.

The basic idea behind RSA is very simple. There is a public key based on two large prime numbers and some auxiliary value that can be freely shared with external parties and used for encryption. Only the owner of the private key, who has knowledge of the two prime numbers used to create the public key, can perform decryption. This asymmetry supports this secure and convenient communication protocol.

However, as the invention of Shor's algorithm shows, asymmetric encryption in the spirit of the RSA protocol may be vulnerable to a quantum attack. This prompts us to have another look at the much older (probably, as old as writing itself) symmetric encryption. In a symmetric encryption protocol, the same key is used to encrypt and decrypt the message, which means that the key can only be shared with trusted parties. This significantly reduces the protocol's utility as a communication tool between arbitrary external parties, but at the same time allows us to make communications between trusted parties almost perfectly secure as long as the key remains unknown to the potential adversary.

In this article, we propose a symmetric encryption algorithm executable on a quantum computer. Although we are not analyzing the proposed encryption protocol from the computational theory point of view, some general considerations suggest that it can be made as

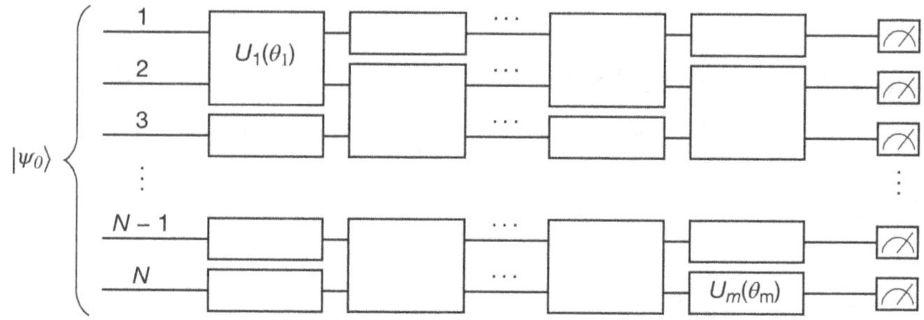

Fig. 8.1 Schematic representation of an N-qubit PQC.

secure as a one-time pad system, which is the only theoretically secure classical cipher [2]. The algorithm is based on utilizing the expressive power of parameterized quantum circuits (PQC) [3, 4].

Figure 8.1 shows a schematic representation of a PQC composed of single-qubit and multi-qubit quantum gates. Quantum gates are unitary linear operators that transform the quantum state (represented by a complex unit vector in a high-dimensional Hilbert space), thus implementing the computational protocol. Multi-qubit gates are used to create entanglement—the key source of the expressive power of PQCs. The final quantum state, $|\psi_f\rangle$, is obtained after the application of the quantum circuit—a sequence of quantum gates controlled by adjustable parameters $\theta_1, \ldots, \theta_m$—to the initial quantum state, $|\psi_0\rangle$:

$$|\psi_f\rangle = U_m(\theta_m)\ldots U_2(\theta_2)U_1(\theta_1)|\psi_0\rangle.$$

The final state can be measured. The measurement produces a classical bitstring, which is a sample from one of the probability distributions encoded in the final quantum state. The computational basis is the z-basis (unless explicitly specified otherwise), and the measurement of the qubit state in the z-basis gives us either "0" (corresponding to the $+1$ eigenvalue of the Pauli Z operator) or "1" (corresponding to the -1 eigenvalue of the Pauli Z operator). The outcome is probabilistic, but running the same quantum circuit multiple times allows us to calculate the expectation value of Pauli Z on the corresponding qubit. Changing the z-basis to the x-basis or the y-basis allows us to calculate the expectation values of, respectively, Pauli X and Pauli Y operators.

The proposed symmetric encryption algorithm relies on the fact that the knowledge of which Pauli operators have been measured reveals nothing about their expectation values unless the quantum state in which they have been measured is also known.

8.2. Stylized Example

Alice and Bob, two trusted parties, would like to communicate securely via unsecure channels. They meet at Alice's office, which is a secure place, where Alice generates a random quantum circuit in the form of Python code on her laptop. The circuit looks like the one shown in Fig. 8.2.

In this stylized example, the randomly generated quantum circuit consists of five quantum registers and six layers of one-qubit and two-qubit gates. The one-qubit gates are

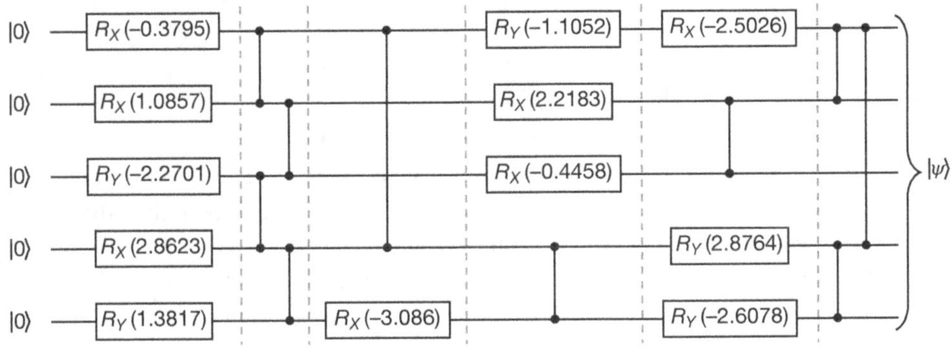

Fig. 8.2 Randomly generated quantum circuit.

random rotations around the x and y axes and the two-qubit gates are CZ (controlled Z) gates that create entanglement:

$$R_x(\theta) = \begin{bmatrix} \cos\left(\frac{\theta}{2}\right) & -i\sin\left(\frac{\theta}{2}\right) \\ -i\sin\left(\frac{\theta}{2}\right) & \cos\left(\frac{\theta}{2}\right) \end{bmatrix}, \quad R_y(\theta) = \begin{bmatrix} \cos\left(\frac{\theta}{2}\right) & -\sin\left(\frac{\theta}{2}\right) \\ \sin\left(\frac{\theta}{2}\right) & \cos\left(\frac{\theta}{2}\right) \end{bmatrix},$$

$$CZ = \begin{bmatrix} 1 & 0 & 0 & 0 \\ 0 & 1 & 0 & 0 \\ 0 & 0 & 1 & 0 \\ 0 & 0 & 0 & -1 \end{bmatrix}.$$

Alice shares this circuit with Bob via a secure in-house communication channel. Now both Alice and Bob have the same quantum circuit on their laptops in the form of Python code—completely hardware agnostic. Running this quantum circuit would transform the initial quantum state $|0\rangle^{\otimes n}$ into a unique entangled quantum state $|\psi\rangle$ that can only be fully described by specifying 2^n probability amplitudes, where n is the number of qubits.

The next day, Alice wants to communicate with Bob. She decides to send him an encrypted message consisting of the letter "K" in the ASCII binary format:

Letter	Radio signal	ASCII	ICS meaning
K	Kilo	1001011	"I wish to communicate with you"

Therefore, Alice needs to encrypt the bitstring [1001011].

Alice starts with generating a random string of Pauli operators X, Y, and Z—the same length as the width of the quantum circuit she shared with Bob:

$$[X, Z, Y, Y, X],$$

where

$$X = \begin{bmatrix} 0 & 1 \\ 1 & 0 \end{bmatrix}, \quad Y = \begin{bmatrix} 0 & -i \\ i & 0 \end{bmatrix}, \quad Z = \begin{bmatrix} 1 & 0 \\ 0 & -1 \end{bmatrix}.$$

This determines the bases in which qubits should be measured: the first and fifth qubits in the x-basis, the second qubit in the z-basis, the third and fourth qubits in the y-basis. The objective is to calculate the expectation values of the Pauli operators on various quantum registers. In this stylized example, we have the following possibilities for measuring the expectation value of a tensor product of two Pauli operators P_k and P_l on quantum registers k and l, $\langle P_k \otimes P_l \rangle$:

$$\langle X_1 \otimes Z_2 \rangle, \langle X_1 \otimes Y_3 \rangle, \langle X_1 \otimes Y_4 \rangle, \langle X_1 \otimes X_5 \rangle, \langle Z_2 \otimes Y_3 \rangle,$$

$$\langle Z_2 \otimes Y_4 \rangle, \langle Z_2 \otimes X_5 \rangle, \langle Y_3 \otimes Y_4 \rangle, \langle Y_3 \otimes X_5 \rangle, \langle Y_4 \otimes X_5 \rangle.$$

To measure these expectation values, Alice has to add "change of basis" gates to the quantum circuit before measurement (see, e.g., Ref. [5]) as shown in Fig. 8.3:

- Add nothing (or identity gate I) to the second quantum register as the computational basis is the z-basis.
- Add H gates to the first and fifth quantum registers to transform the z-basis into the x-basis.
- Add $HS^\dagger$ gates to the third and fourth quantum registers to transform the z-basis into the y-basis (the $S^\dagger$ gate should be applied first).

The change of basis gates are as follows:

$$I = \begin{bmatrix} 1 & 0 \\ 0 & 1 \end{bmatrix}, \quad H = \frac{1}{\sqrt{2}} \begin{bmatrix} 1 & 1 \\ 1 & -1 \end{bmatrix}, \quad S^\dagger = \begin{bmatrix} 1 & 0 \\ 0 & -i \end{bmatrix}.$$

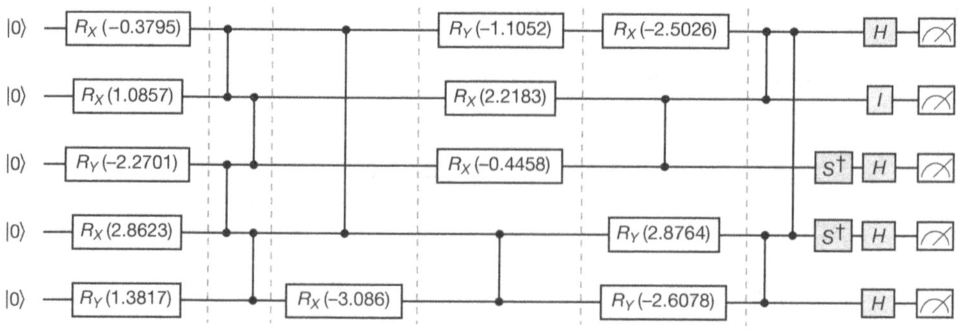

Fig. 8.3 Measurement in different bases.

Next, Alice runs this quantum circuit 100,000 times and saves the measurement results in a 100,000 × 5 array. If "0" is measured, the eigenvalue of the corresponding Pauli operator is +1. If "1" is measured, the eigenvalue of the corresponding Pauli operator is −1. Therefore, the array entries are either +1 or −1. The number of rows is equal to the number of quantum circuit runs and the number of columns is equal to the number of quantum registers.

Then Alice computes the expectation values for the pairs of Pauli operators (tensor products of two Pauli operators). The expectation value $\langle P_k \otimes P_l \rangle \equiv \langle P_k P_l \rangle$ is the dot product of columns k and l, normalized by the number of rows. She gets:

$$
\begin{aligned}
\langle X_1 Z_2 \rangle &= -0.76160 \\
\langle X_1 Y_3 \rangle &= 0.22724 \\
\langle X_1 Y_4 \rangle &= -0.00574 \\
\langle X_1 X_5 \rangle &= 0.13070 \\
\langle Z_2 Y_3 \rangle &= 0.81316 \\
\langle Z_2 Y_4 \rangle &= 0.02814 \\
\langle Z_2 X_5 \rangle &= -0.09922 \\
\langle Y_3 Y_4 \rangle &= -0.01034 \\
\langle Y_3 X_5 \rangle &= 0.12158 \\
\langle Y_4 X_5 \rangle &= 0.00368.
\end{aligned}
$$

If the expectation value $\langle P_k P_l \rangle$ is larger than the chosen threshold value ϵ, the pair $P_k P_l$ can be used to encode "1."

If the expectation value $\langle P_k P_l \rangle$ is smaller than $-\epsilon$, the pair $P_k P_l$ can be used to encode "0."

The value of ϵ depends on the circuit configuration and the number of runs. Alice sets it at $\epsilon = 0.01$.

Therefore, Alice can use the following pairs of Pauli operators for encrypting her message:

$$
\begin{aligned}
&\langle X_1 Z_2 \rangle \Rightarrow 0 \\
&\langle X_1 Y_3 \rangle \Rightarrow 1 \\
&\langle X_1 Y_4 \rangle \Rightarrow - \qquad \text{(expectation value falls with in the } [-\epsilon, \epsilon] \text{ interval)} \\
&\langle X_1 X_5 \rangle \Rightarrow 1 \\
&\langle Z_2 Y_3 \rangle \Rightarrow 1 \\
&\langle Z_2 Y_4 \rangle \Rightarrow 1 \\
&\langle Z_2 X_5 \rangle \Rightarrow 0
\end{aligned}
$$

$$\langle Y_3 Y_4 \rangle \Rightarrow 0$$
$$\langle Y_3 X_5 \rangle \Rightarrow 1$$
$$\langle Y_4 X_5 \rangle \Rightarrow - \qquad \text{(expectation value falls with in the } [-\epsilon, \epsilon] \text{ interval)}$$

Alice sends Bob a text message that reads: XZYYX.

Then Alice sends Bob an email that reads: (1,3) (1,2) (2,5) (1,5) (3,4) (2,3) (2,4).

After Bob receives the text message, he knows that he must change the basis on quantum registers 1, 3, 4, and 5 (add H to the first and fifth quantum registers and add $HS^\dagger$ to the third and fourth quantum registers).

After Bob receives the email, he knows what expectation values he needs to calculate and in what order.

Bob runs the quantum circuit (the same as Alice's) and gets the following expectation values (they would differ slightly from Alice's values due to the finite number of quantum circuit runs and some hardware noise):

$$\langle X_1 Y_3 \rangle = 0.22762 \Rightarrow 1$$
$$\langle X_1 Z_2 \rangle = -0.76166 \Rightarrow 0$$
$$\langle Z_2 X_5 \rangle = -0.09430 \Rightarrow 0$$
$$\langle X_1 X_5 \rangle = 0.12724 \Rightarrow 1$$
$$\langle Y_3 Y_4 \rangle = -0.00986 \Rightarrow 0$$
$$\langle Z_2 Y_3 \rangle = 0.81240 \Rightarrow 1$$
$$\langle Z_2 Y_4 \rangle = 0.03230 \Rightarrow 1.$$

Bob correctly decrypts the message, reads the bitstring [1001011], and learns that Alice would like to get in touch with him.

Two unsecure channels (text and email) were used to transmit the message. Even if both channels are compromised, it is impossible to decipher the message without the knowledge of the quantum circuit that creates the quantum state in which the Pauli operators are measured. In other words, the quantum circuit plays the role of a symmetric key used to encrypt and decrypt messages between two trusted parties.

In this stylized example, there are two additional important elements of the security protocol that provide additional protection:

- No Pauli pairs are repeated.
- Only some of the possible Pauli pairs are used.

In practice, if encrypting a large amount of data rather than a single ASCII symbol, we would face additional challenges. This means that the general encryption protocol based on measuring the expectation values of second-order Pauli operators should provide additional degrees of security.

In fact, we cannot use ASCII encoding for plain text symbols. To see why, let us have a look at how ASCII encodes letters. First, we notice that all uppercase letters (from "A" to "Z") start with "10" as leading digits in the seven-digit binary encoding, while all lowercase letters (from "a" to "z") start with "11" as the two leading digits. Secondly, letter encodings have unequal numbers of "0"s and "1"s. For example, uppercase "A" is encoded as five "0"s and two "1"s: 1000001. This means that a relatively simple frequency analysis can help break the encryption, given a sufficiently large amount of text. Therefore, we need to generate a random mapping of the plaintext symbols to the bitstrings of fixed length simultaneously with the generation of the quantum circuit. The key condition is that the number of "0"s and "1"s in each randomly generated bitstring should be the same to prevent any possible attempt at frequency analysis. A sample random mapping that illustrates this principle is shown in Table A.1 in Appendix A. There, each plain text symbol is represented by a 12-bit bitstring with six "0"s and six "1"s. The table is shared with the trusted parties together with the generated quantum circuit.

Another consideration concerns the architecture of the quantum circuit. Security can be dramatically improved if the quantum circuit is modified by making the one-qubit gates in the first layer adjustable as shown in Fig. 8.4.

Making the first layer adjustable turns the generated quantum circuit into a de facto family of quantum circuits, where the configuration of adjustable parameters plays the role of a "seed" that can be set according to some rules. For example, it can be derived from the time stamp of some process as explained below. Without this functionality, we will be limited in how much text we can encode before we start reusing the same pairs of Pauli operators with the same expectation values. With this functionality, assuming that we perform a regular reset of the seed, the same pairs of Pauli operators will have different expectation values for different seeds. This should prevent any meaningful attempt at analysis of large amounts of intercepted encrypted text as long as the seed is changed before the Pauli pairs are repeated.

In Fig. 8.4, the one-qubit gates in the first layer are rotations around the x, y, and z axes by angle $\alpha_i\theta$, where i indicates the quantum register number. Coefficients $\alpha_i \in [-1, 1]$ are fixed. Parameter θ is a function of the time stamp of the generated vector of Pauli operators. For example, we can adopt the following scheme for setting the value of θ.

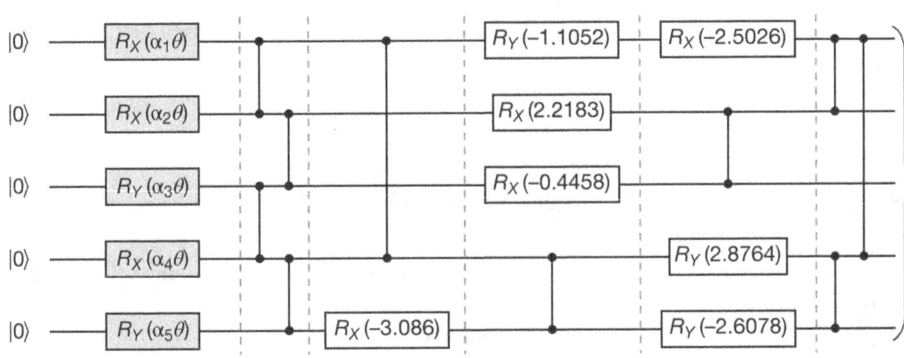

Fig. 8.4 Quantum circuit with adjustable gates in the first layer.

Let us write down the time stamp in the format: YYMMDDhhmmss. For example, 13:03:46 on November 27, 2023, would be represented by the following integer number: 231127130346. Then the value of parameter θ is set equal to the YYMMDDhhmmss modulo 2π. In our example, it would be $\theta = 1.32392129$. The value of θ is unique for each time stamp. At the same time, the knowledge of θ will be of no use unless the whole quantum circuit is known. It means that the time stamp can also be shared between the trusted parties using the unsecure channel—the same channel that is used for communicating the vector of Pauli operators.

Making the parameters of the first layer's gates depend on the time stamp ensures that it is fruitless to try to establish the mapping between the pairs of Pauli operators and their binary values: each random vector of Pauli operators that are used to encode the message will be accompanied by a unique quantum circuit given by the unique time stamp. This would allow us to reuse the same quantum circuit multiple times, since every configuration of adjustable parameters in the first layer will lead to the corresponding unique quantum state in which Pauli operators are measured.

8.3. General Algorithm

We can now formulate the general symmetric encryption or decryption Algorithm 8.3.1.

Algorithm 8.3.1 (Symmetric Encryption).

---

1. Generation of a random quantum circuit on N quantum registers with M layers of one-qubit and two-qubit gates (e.g., $M = \text{int}(2\sqrt{N})$). The one-qubit gates are random rotations around the x, y, and z axes; the two-qubit gates are suitable native gates (e.g., CZ or $iSWAP$). The first layer of the quantum circuit consists of one-qubit gates with parameters (rotation angles) of the form $\alpha_i\theta$, where all $\alpha_i \in [-1, 1]$, $i = 1, \ldots, N$, are randomly generated coefficients and the parameter θ is the same for all one-qubit gates in the first layer.
2. Generation of a random mapping scheme that would provide a one-to-one mapping between any desired plain text symbol and a $2n$-digit bitstring with exactly n 0s and exactly n 1s.
3. Sharing of the generated quantum circuit and the plain text symbol mapping scheme with the trusted party. The quantum circuit is a symmetric key that can be used by trusted parties to encrypt and decrypt data in binary format.
4. When one trusted party (Alice) wants to communicate with another trusted party (Bob), the protocol is as follows:
   - **(a)** Alice converts the plain text she wants to encrypt into a bitstring using the generated mapping scheme.
   - **(b)** Alice generates a random vector of Pauli operators $\{X, Y, Z\}$. The length of the vector should be equal to the width of the quantum circuit, with one-to-one mapping

between the elements of the vector of Pauli operators and the quantum registers (e.g., $[Z_1, Y_2, X_3, \ldots, Y_N]$).

(c) Alice saves the time stamp of the generated random vector of Pauli operators as an integer number in the format YYMMDDhhmmss. This number modulo 2π (double precision) is the value of parameter θ in the first layer of the generated quantum circuit.

(d) Alice adds "change of basis" gates to each quantum register in accordance with the Pauli operator that is assigned to the quantum register:
- nothing to quantum registers with Pauli Z (z-basis);
- H to quantum registers with Pauli X (transformation from the z-basis to the x-basis);
- $HS^\dagger$ to quantum registers with Pauli Y (transformation from the z-basis to the y-basis).

(e) Alice executes L runs of the quantum circuit and saves the measurement results in a $L \times N$ array:
- **if** "0" is measured
  then the eigenvalue of the corresponding Pauli operator is $+1$;
- **if** "1" is measured
  then the eigenvalue of the corresponding Pauli operator is -1.

Therefore, the array entries are either $+1$ or -1. The number of rows is equal to the number of quantum circuit runs and the number of columns is equal to the number of quantum registers.

(f) Alice randomly selects two quantum registers i and j (without replacement). She calculates the expectation value of Pauli operators $\langle P_i P_j \rangle$ as the dot product of columns i and j, normalized by the number of rows:
- **if** the value of $\langle P_i P_j \rangle$ is larger than ϵ
  then this pair of quantum registers can be used to encode "1";
- **if** the value of $\langle P_i P_j \rangle$ is smaller than $-\epsilon$
  then this pair of quantum registers can be used to encode "0".

The value of ϵ is one of the algorithm's parameters. The broad condition is $\epsilon \geq m\sigma$, where σ is the estimated average standard deviation of expectation values. The value of m can be chosen from some general considerations.

(g) Alice takes the first bit from the bitstring she wants to encrypt:
if the bit value is "1" and $\langle P_i P_j \rangle > \epsilon$ **or** the bit value is "0" and $\langle P_i P_j \rangle < -\epsilon$
then Alice encrypts this bit with the pair (i,j)
else the pair (i,j) is either discarded (if $-\epsilon \leq \langle P_i P_j \rangle \leq \epsilon$) or put on hold (for the next suitable bit), and Alice tries another random pair of Pauli operators (without replacement).

(h) This process continues (steps (f) and (g) are repeated) until Alice encrypts the first K bits with the pairs of quantum register indices. The broad condition is $K < N(N-1)/2$.

(i) After that, Alice generates a new random vector of Pauli operators, saves its time stamp as an integer number in the format YYMMDDhhmmss, and repeats the above procedure for the next K bits.

(j) This process continues until Alyce encrypts the whole bitstring (the whole dataset in binary format). If the bitstring length is B, then we end up with D vectors of Pauli operators, D time stamps, and D cycles of quantum circuit runs: $(D-1)K < B \leq DK$.

5. The encrypted dataset consists of three arrays:
   (a) $D \times N$ array of Pauli operators (D rows, N columns), where each kth row is the vector of Pauli operators used to encrypt the $[(k-1)K+1, kK]$ section of the bitstring.
   (b) $D \times 1$ array of time stamps (a time stamp for each vector of Pauli operators).
   (c) $D \times K$ array of pairs of quantum register indices (D rows, K columns), where each kth row is the vector of quantum register index pairs used to encrypt the $[(k-1)K+1, kK]$ section of the bitstring.

   Alice sends the first and second arrays to Bob via a preferred unsecure communication channel (e.g., email). Then Alice sends the third array to Bob via the same or different unsecure channel (e.g., second email).
6. After receiving the arrays from Alice:
   (a) Bob takes the first value from the time stamp array as an integer number in the format YYMMDDhhmmss. This number modulo 2π is the value that should be assigned to the parameter θ in the first layer of the quantum circuit.
   (b) Bob takes the first row from the Pauli operator array and adds the corresponding basis transformation gates to the quantum circuit—exactly the same procedure as done by Alice. Bob runs the quantum circuit L times and saves the measurement results $(+1, -1)$ in an $L \times N$ array.
   (c) Bob takes the first element (i,j) from the index pairs array and calculates the dot product of columns i and j from the $L \times N$ array:
   if the value of the dot product of columns i and j is positive
   then Bob decrypts (i,j) as "1"
   else Bob decrypts (i,j) as "0."
   Bob continues this procedure until he reaches the end of the first row of the index pairs array (i.e., until he decrypts first K bits).
   (d) Bob switches to the second row of the Pauli operators array and repeats steps (a) and (b). He continues until the whole bitstring is decrypted.
   (e) Bob translates the decrypted bitstring into plain text using the same mapping scheme as Alice.

Components of the algorithm are illustrated in Fig. 8.5.

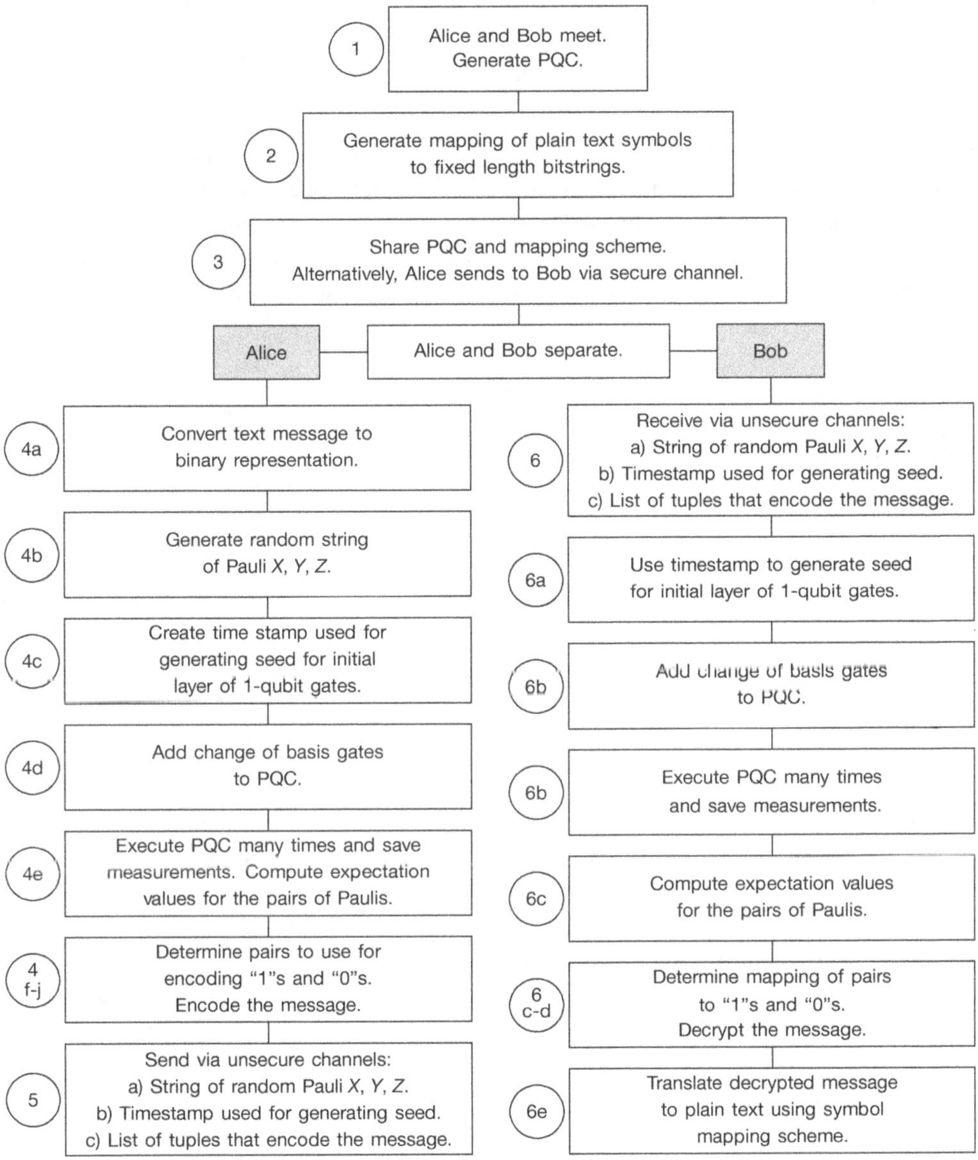

Fig. 8.5 Components of the symmetric encryption algorithm. Detailed explanations of the blocks are provided in Section 8.3.

Remark 8.3.1. With $N = 2{,}500$, $M = 100$, $L = 500{,}000$, $K = 1{,}000{,}000$, $\epsilon = 0.01$, $m = 6$, and $n = 6$, Algorithm 8.3.1 would allow encryption of 26 full pages of dense normal text per single vector of Pauli operators (40 lines × 80 symbols per line × 12 bits per symbol). The six-sigma threshold is equivalent to one typo per about 26,000 pages of dense normal text.

Remark 8.3.2. It is possible to transform the proposed algorithm into a multiple key encryption protocol. For example, Alice splits the quantum circuit into two parts: the first M_1 layers and the second M_2 layers ($M_1 + M_2 = M$). Then Alice shares the first M_1 layers with Bob and the second M_2 layers with Charlie. It would only be possible to perform decryption if both Bob and Charlie combine their quantum sub-circuits into a single complete quantum circuit.

APPENDIX

A. Plain Text Symbol to Bitstring Encoding Scheme

Table A8.1 Sample encoding scheme (randomly generated).

Symbol	Encoding	Symbol	Encoding	Symbol	Encoding
A	111100100010	a	100110001011	0	101010110100
B	111101010000	b	100001100111	1	001001101011
C	011101101000	c	100000101111	2	001010110101
D	011011001010	d	101100101010	3	100010101101
E	110001110010	e	101000001111	4	101000110011
F	110100010101	f	011110101000	5	010100011011
G	110100111000	g	100111101000	6	011010001110
H	010010101101	h	001011000111	7	011111000010
I	001110011010	i	000100101111	8	011100001011
J	011110010100	j	001110001101	9	110100001101
K	001011010101	k	100101010011	+	010101100101
L	100001110110	l	110010011010	–	011001011010
M	110101010010	m	100010101011	*	001011110001
N	011011000110	n	010101101100	/	011001001110
O	001110001011	o	011101011000	=	001101000111
P	101011000011	p	101011010100	(	110000110011
Q	011110010001	q	101000011101	)	010100111001
R	100100011101	r	101101010100	.	001110101001
S	101111100000	s	010101010011	,	101001110010
T	001111011000	t	011001101001	:	010011000111
U	101100010101	u	111000010101	;	110010101010
V	110100011010	v	111101001000	?	001101100011
W	111110000100	w	110111010000	!	110010110100
X	111011000001	x	001101001011	"	100110110100
Y	101101001001	y	000111001011	'	101010011010
Z	100001101101	z	101110110000	*space*	000110010111

References

1. R. Sutor, *Dancing with Qubits*. Packt, Birmingham (2019).
2. A. Lipton and A. Treccani, *Blockchain and Distributed Ledgers: Mathematics, Technology, and Economics*. World Scientific, Singapore (2022).
3. M. Benedetti, E. Lloyd, S. Sack, and M. Fiorentini, Parameterized quantum circuits as machine learning models, *Quantum Sci. Technol.* **4**(4), 043001 (2019). https://doi.org/10.1088/2058-9565/ab4eb5.
4. Y. Du, M.-H. Hsieh, T. Liu, and D. Tao. Expressive power of parameterized quantum circuits. *Phys. Rev. Res.* **2**, 033125 (2020).
5. A. Jacquier and O. Kondratyev, *Quantum Machine Learning and Optimisation in Finance: On the Road to Quantum Advantage*. Packt, Birmingham (2022).

https://doi.org/10.1142/9789819813049_0009

CHAPTER 9 Performance-Driven Dimensionality Reduction: A Data-Centric Approach to Feature Engineering in Machine Learning

Joshua Chung[1], Marcos Lopez de Prado[2,†], Horst D. Simon[3,‡], and Kesheng Wu[1,*]

[1] *Lawrence Berkeley National Lab and UC Berkeley, Berkeley, CA, United States*
[2] *ADIA, Abu Dhabi, UAE*
[3] *ADIA Lab, Abu Dhabi, UAE*
**Corresponding author. E-mail: KWu@lbl.gov*

In a number of applications, data may be anonymized, obfuscated, and highly noisy. In such cases, it is difficult to use domain knowledge and low-dimensional visualizations to engineer the features for tasks such as machine learning. In this work, we explore a variety of dimensionality reduction (DR) techniques in the form of feature extraction and feature selection to decrease multicollinearity and improve the predictive power of our modeling tasks. These techniques include principal component analysis (PCA), locally linear embedding (LLE), Isomap, Kernel principal component analysis (KPCA), uniform manifold approximation and projection (UMAP), mean decrease accuracy, Shapley Values, and feature clustering. Due to the data-driven nature of our methodology, all forms of DR algorithm selection, hyperparameter tuning, and model tuning are done purely based on performance on our models, rather than a priori knowledge. This method will show which technique will increase the predictive power of our random forest model. Due to the generality of our method, this approach offers flexibility for regression or classification with any machine learning model and any unsupervised DR technique.

9.1. Introduction

Dimensionality reduction (DR) methods are essential for a data scientist to build models and to lower the variance and bias of these models [1, 2]. Oftentimes, DR is conducted

†The work was initiated prior to joining ADIA.
‡The work was initiated prior to joining ADIA Lab.

by first consulting and applying domain knowledge, then by visualizing the data, and then through experimentation, since the search space for experimentation is usually reduced by the first two steps. Without these two steps, the search space for the experimentation stage becomes infeasible computation-wise for a lone data scientist using standard tuning and testing algorithms.

Typically, a data scientist might be able to reduce this exploration by using domain knowledge to select which models and features to use [3]. However, there are many cases where the domain expertise is not available or could not be easily applied, or is even intentionally hidden for various considerations, for example, to preserve privacy. In these cases, it would be necessary to select DR algorithms purely based on the available data, without utilizing any domain knowledge.

Redundant features are a major cause of poor model performance as they introduce multicollinearity and noise to the data. Domain expertise can provide important information to remove these redundant features [4].

However, we are motivated to consider these purely data-driven scenarios because they could be considered more challenging for selecting and tuning these data processing algorithms. We are unable to apply any domain knowledge to obfuscated data, as the feature names are removed and the original distribution of the features is nonlinearly transformed and scaled. The DR algorithms that work well in these scenarios could be considered more effective in extracting useful features without domain knowledge, a common objective in automated data cleaning [5].

Another common method of determining the quality of DR is by visualizing the lower-dimensional embedding. This is commonly done on artificial datasets, which include the helix, swiss-roll, and double-peaks datasets, in order to validate the efficacy of the algorithm on various data topologies [6]. Again, this is another method that cannot work with the data we are using, as the obfuscation/quantization process removes all continuity from the data needed to validate through visualization.

Therefore, the only methodology that we can utilize for DR is through a purely experimental approach. We measure the success of an experiment through modeling performance rather than metrics on the DR algorithm itself. We also tune the hyperparameters of the DR algorithms using the same model metrics. In this way, measuring our DR quality is purely data-driven.

Reducing the variance of our model is vital in making useful predictions of unseen data, as applying modeling effectively to a problem relies on consistent real-world performance. This is especially pertinent when considering scenarios where a model's poor performance can lead to dire consequences, such as disease classification or securities portfolio optimization. Given its importance in the data science life cycle, many algorithms have been developed; however, this diversity only benefits us if we can choose the optimal one.

Our systematic framework is considerably computationally intensive, given our data-driven approach. The idea is to first tune a model on the data without any DR in order to get the minimum baseline that the DR should be greater than. Then for each DR technique, the hyperparameters are tuned based on the baseline model performance for that DR technique's output. Once the DR hyperparameters are tuned, the model's hyperparameters are tuned again using the lower-dimensional data for the final validation score. In order to reduce overfitting on certain parts of the data, each hyperparameter combination for either the model or DR technique is validated through a k-fold cross-validation (or a variant). Given the large search space for these hyperparameters and DR techniques, this leads to a large number of computations necessary.

Therefore, we focus on making the framework computationally feasible by using more efficient hyperparameter tuning algorithms and building certain DR algorithms to work with parallel processing. We have adapted all the algorithms necessary for our data-driven framework to utilize Dask, a Python-based parallel computation solution that connects to a remote computation cluster. While our own computation utilizes the Cori computer from National Energy Research Scientific Computing (NERSC), the software released should be compatible with distributed clusters from any cloud service provider.

We validated our framework on an obfuscated financial data set released by the hedge fund Numer.ai and on our own obfuscated Weather/HVAC usage dataset from Lawrence Berkeley National Laboratory. The Numer.ai dataset was the original motivation for developing the said framework and is a suitable case study on the efficacy of our system. However, due to the obfuscation of the data set, we cannot fully validate if our methodology is consistent with our prior/domain knowledge. Therefore, we chose to also validate our framework on a dataset aimed to predict kiloWatt-Hour (kWh) used for the heating, ventilation, and air conditioning (HVAC) system based on four weather features. We obfuscate the data in a similar fashion in order to emulate the Numer.ai data but with a stronger understanding of the correlations and origins of this data. This will allow us to validate our framework based on what we would have done given the knowledge we have about the data.

The main contributions of this work:

- A systematic framework for evaluating DR techniques that is parallelized by Dask.
- Implemented both Latin hypercube sampling and hyperband using Dask and adapted them to tune DR techniques.
- Improved the hyperband algorithm using Latin hypercube sampling rather than random sampling and cross-validation scoring metrics.
- Validated said framework using two different obfuscated datasets.

The remainder of this paper is organized as follows. Section 9.2 describes background and related works and initial motivations for developing the framework. Section 9.3 reviews the different types of DR techniques available and the explanation of why DR hyperparameter tuning is important to the framework. Section 9.4 goes over the technical details of the modeling, scoring, validating, tuning, and parallelizing within the framework. Section 9.5 pertains to constructing the HVAC/Weather dataset for our framework, the results of the framework, and the effect quantization/obfuscation had on the framework. Section 9.6 discusses using the framework on the Numer.ai data set, specifically its challenges, solutions, and results. Section 9.7 summarizes the work and discusses the observations of the work done.

9.2. Background and Related Work

9.2.1. *Privacy and other reasons for obfuscation*

Considering the growth in sensitive data collection and the Internet's availability of public data, we see an imperative to obfuscate any personally identifiable information (PII) intended for public use, such as data science competitions or education purposes [7, 8]. Data collection methods have become so advanced and nuanced that even omitted details can be inferred with statistical methods. An example of this danger is showcased in Narayanan and Shmatikov's paper using the Netflix Prize dataset [9].

We also consider situations where data is sensitive to release for other reasons, such as to protect company trade secrets, to profit from a company's costly data collection, or to maintain the security of a company's data system. In these cases, data is most likely analyzed and modeled in-house; however, there is no question that companies have taken the data science competition route as well, especially for problems that have stumped their own employees.

Not only would obfuscating the data ensure greater security for the data subject, but this would also allow public analysis of the data to be possible without concerns for said data subject's privacy. The public data science competition, such as Kaggle or Numer.ai, has become a popular method to develop accurate models for difficult data science problems, as it takes advantage of both a growing data science community and the diverse and novel approaches each data scientist may take. By showing that strong obfuscation does not prevent imperative data modeling steps, we aim to show that data that requires stronger obfuscation methods to protect privacy can still be used by the public in data science competitions.

9.2.2. *Data-driven dimensionality reduction*

Given the obfuscation of the names and distributions of the features in the dataset, traditional feature engineering methods would not be possible, such as using domain expertise. Therefore, any method must be utilized without any prior assumptions about the features themselves. Such methods tend to rely on either maximizing variance between components (such as principal component analysis [PCA]), increasing predictive power of a baseline model (such as mean decrease accuracy), or by optimizing a metric that measures how faithful a lower-dimensional embedding represents a higher-dimensional space (such as uniform manifold approximation and projection [UMAP]). Because we do not have a priori knowledge on which of these algorithms work best with Numer.ai data, or any obfuscated data for that matter, we must determine which algorithm to use based on our model's performance on the transformed data. This is the basis for data-driven feature engineering, where we choose algorithms and their hyperparameters solely on how the model performs, making no assumptions on how the data is structured or which features have the most predictive value. Not only does this allow data scientists to improve models based on a series of scientific tests, rather than intuition, but it also decreases inherent biases that a data scientist may impart on the modeling process, which could lead to poorer prediction quality.

9.2.3. *Numer.ai and obfuscated data*

Numer.ai is a decentralized hedge fund, in which portfolio optimization and allocation are decided by a metamodel that aggregates predictions of participants' models in a weekly data science competition. Participants are able to make predictions with the stock data, which contains 310 columns of features that are released by Numer.ai. Because these data sets are expensive to procure and normally only provide competitive value if kept in-house, Numer.ai obfuscates and quantizes these financial datasets before releasing them to participants. Feature names are anonymized, the features are quantized and obfuscated into five bins such that feature origins cannot be inferred by the distribution of the data, and target variables represent abstract rank values that only Numer.ai's metamodel is able to interpret. This way, Numer.ai can provide its participants with data vital to financial modeling without allowing competitors to use the same data.

The participants in the Numer.ai competition stake money on their predictions, essentially placing bets on their model's accuracy. This staked prediction can either earn more money or lose a portion of the original stake, so improving predictive performance and lowering the variance of the model are vital for a successful strategy. However, due to the obfuscation of data, it is somewhat difficult to improve models through conventional DR techniques, such as utilizing domain expertise for feature selection, visualizing data to determine lower dimensional embedding quality, or using common feature extraction methods. Therefore, we have come up with a data-driven strategy in order to reduce the dimensionality of our data, which would improve predictive performance, shorten training times, and decrease the variance of our models. By demonstrating our strategy, we hope to improve the viability of public data science competitions that contain highly sensitive information and require obfuscation.

9.3. Review of Dimensionality Reduction Algorithms

9.3.1. *Taxonomy of DR algorithms*

There are two different families of DR algorithms: feature selection and feature extraction. Feature selection algorithms select a subset of features from the original feature set. Three main feature selection algorithms exist: wrappers, filters, and embedded methods [10]. In this paper, we focus on two different wrapper methods, mean decrease accuracy (MDA) and a short-hand for Shapley (SHAP) Values, since wrapper methods tend to perform the best in improving predictive performance. Wrapper methods use a predictive model by training on feature subsets and scoring said subsets based on the model's performance on a hold-out set.

Feature clustering selection could be argued as a hybrid of a wrapper method and a filter method, as the clusters are formed through a proxy measure, but the clusters (or subsets) are selected through a wrapper method (MDA to be specific).

We also tested a diverse group of feature extraction methods. Feature extraction algorithms create new features in a lower dimension to attempt to reduce the dimensionality of the data set. In order to select from a comprehensive selection of feature extraction

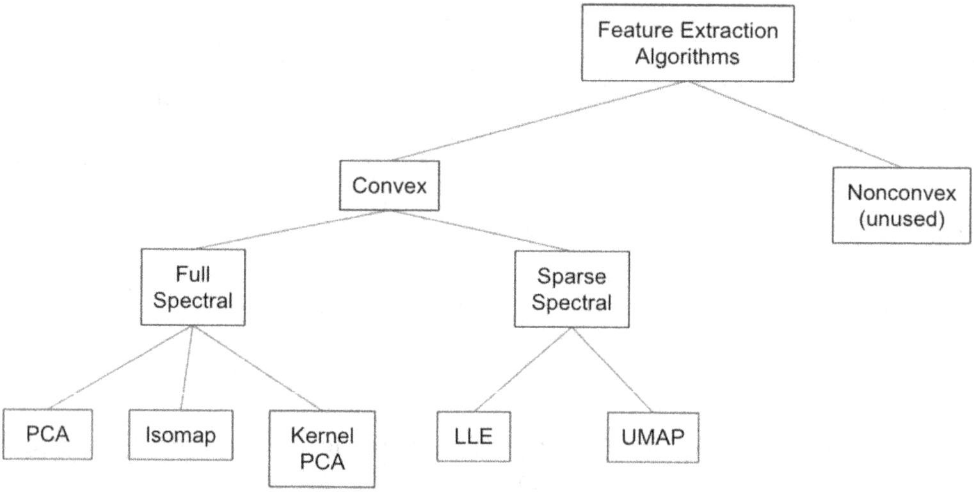

Fig. 9.1 A simplified taxonomy tree of the different DR algorithms reviewed by Van der Maaten et al.

algorithms, we referenced Van der Maaten et al.'s taxonomy of DR techniques [6]. A simplified version of their taxonomy tree is shown in Fig. 9.1. We chose these methods due to their popularity and effectiveness in previous studies.

9.3.2. *DR hyperparameter optimization*

9.3.2.1. Necessity of hyperparameter tuning

All DR algorithms' hyperparameters are tuned such that the model's performance is optimized on the lower-dimensional dataset post-DR transformation/selection. Because many of these DR algorithms vary in their quality based on the hyperparameter selection, where quality is model performance on the transformed data, hyperparameter optimization is vital to accurately measure the efficacy of each DR algorithm. Certain hyperparameters drastically change the structure of the outcome matrix, such as deciding between various kernels or the number of nearest neighbors.

For example, when optimizing Kernel PCA hyperparameters, the Spearman Rank Correlation values vary between 0.0017 and 0.0404, a significant range considering 0.05 Spearman Rank Correlation is considered as a high-quality model and 0.001 is considered to be an extremely poor model and would lead to a loss of the money staked on Numer.ai's weekly competition [11]. Looking at Table 9.1, we see that the key difference between the most optimal sets of hyperparameters versus the weakest performing sets of hyperparameters is the kernel function used, where the radial basis function (RBF) kernel performs much better in combination with any other variation in hyperparameters when compared to the sigmoid kernel. This is quite a common occurrence with DR techniques and hyperparameter tuning, as certain hyperparameters are extremely influential on the outcome of the transformation.

Table 9.1 A table showing the sorted Spearman Rank Correlations scoring different hyperparameter combinations for Kernel PCA.

Alpha	Coef0	Degree	Eigen_solver	Kernel	n_components	n_jobs	Spearman Rank Corr.
1	2	3	arpack	rbf	182	−1	0.0409
5	8	6	arpack	rbf	162	−1	0.0404
3	4	6	arpack	rbf	162	−1	0.0404
2	7	3	arpack	rbf	72	−1	0.0396
...	...	...	...	...	...	...	...
5	8	3	arpack	sigmoid	182	−1	0.0039
8	8	3	arpack	sigmoid	92	−1	0.0034
6	8	2	arpack	sigmoid	72	−1	0.0018

9.3.2.2. Hyperparameter tuning algorithms

In order to tune our DR algorithms, we use three different approaches that are suitable for certain data sizes, algorithms, and number of hyperparameters to search through. For both of the tuning algorithms used for feature extraction methods, we adapted two previously mentioned model hyperparameter tuning techniques, Latin hypercube sampling and hyperband. For feature selection methods, we use a wrapper method of recursive selection for the number of features, which we consider to be a hyperparameter in this case, to be selected from the ranked features.

For each algorithm used, every configuration is tested through the Numer.ai adapted randomized k-fold cross-validation process. The transformated data is split into k-folds, and then the metric of the model is the average of the performance of a model on all folds. For each of these algorithms, we also utilize Dask to parallelize the fitting/transformation of the DR algorithms and the training of the models post-transformation. Without this parallelization, the computation would be fundamentally intractable and not realistic as tuning methods for DR techniques.

9.4. Technical Details

9.4.1. *Model selection, metrics, and evaluation*

In the methodology we discuss further in the paper, it is intended that any form of models, metrics, and evaluation algorithms can be substituted in for the specific ones we use in our latter examples. Our solution also extends to both classification and regression problems as well. This option is available with the function in our software package we are releasing concurrently with the paper.

9.4.1.1. Random forest regressors

With our particular usage of methodology, we use a random forest regressor model to make predictions and act as a metric in our wrapper algorithms. We use this model for several reasons. In our discussions with Numer.ai's team, they noted that ensemble and gradient-boosted models tend to work the best with their data and metamodel. Random forests and gradient-boosted decision trees (GBDTs) are both utilized for this reason, however, random forest models can far more effectively take advantage of the parallel computation power, as the ensemble can be trained all at once, rather than sequentially like GBDTs. This sequential training would be a major bottleneck in a majority of our tuning and testing methodologies and make our solutions intractable. The only downsides that we observed with this choice are that GBDTs are deterministic in training and predicting, as well as GBDTs perform slightly better than Random Forests in a majority of post-DR datasets, both of which are favorable behaviors in model selection.

We also use a regression model even though our Y data is in five quantized bins due to Numer.ai's recommendation. The Numer.ai team stated that although both regression and classification have its merits when approaching this problem in their own research they have found that modeling through regression leads to less overfitting of historical data and thereby reducing variance of our models. In our own testing, we found that classification models were unable to differentiate or improve as the area under curve (AUC)-receiver operating characteristic (ROC) of our models never improved beyond what would be considered random guesses.

9.4.1.2. Spearman rank correlation and quartic mean error

For metrics, we use two metrics to judge modeling performance: Spearman Rank Correlation and Quartic Mean Error. We use Spearman Rank Correlation as recommended by Numer.ai, as this metric correlates positively with the performance of the metamodel Numer.ai uses to make their final portfolio allocation in their weekly contest [11]. However, Spearman Rank Correlation does not monotonically decrease with the RMSE loss of the Random Forest model. Because of this, we also use Quartic Mean Error as a way to reflect the RMSE loss of our models, while also magnifying the error of more extreme errors of our models. These extreme errors may have a greater impact on the quality of our model's submission, given the nature of modeling-based portfolio optimization and that extreme errors could lead to greater losses. When optimizing based on metrics, we use the Spearman Rank Correlation in every scenario, but the Quartic Mean Error does become useful in indicating anomalies, as most of the time the Quartic Mean Error does monotonically increase with Spearman Rank Correlation.

9.4.1.3. Adapted k-fold cross-validation

To more accurately evaluate our models and DR algorithms, we would like to use a k-fold cross-validation schema that reduces the variance of our metrics and models for future submissions of our predictions to the weekly contest. Numer.ai provides an additional feature, called eras, in the training data, which indicates the time period, which the historical data came from Ref. [11]. This is especially important when considering how we randomize our rows for k-fold cross-validation. Rows that belong in the same era imply certain base economic and political conditions, which allow for consistency of feature correlations with each other and our target variable. In order to still randomize our training data for k-fold cross-validation, which is vital in reducing variability of our metrics and evaluation, we choose to randomize the rows by era rather than index. This gives us the desired behavior of randomized cross-validation that we use for every scenario that requires model evaluation, including judging DR algorithm quality, hyperparameter tuning, and wrapper methodologies.

9.4.2. *Model hyperparameter tuning*

Random forest models require a high degree of hyperparameter tuning, as there are eight hyperparameters that we set at object instantiation. Even if we only chose to search through three different options per hyperparameter, an extremely modest amount, this would give 3^8 configurations, and if we chose to do fivefold cross-validated grid search, this would take at least 9,000 compute hours, since each model takes anywhere from 180 to 800 seconds to train per CV fold. Since our methodology is primarily meant for data scientists who wish to individually participate in the Numer.ai contest, we need to make sure that we efficiently utilize the limited computational resources that an individual would hypothetically have access to, such as Google Cloud Platform or AWS. That is why we utilize algorithms that explore the hyperparameter grid without redundant computation and more diverse configurations.

We utilize two hyperparameter tuning algorithms: Latin hypercube sampling (LHS) grid search and hyperband. LHS works similarly to random grid search, but with each hyperparameter configuration being sampled from stratifications of each dimension of the hyperparameter grid [12]. This way we avoid having two samples with extremely similar hyperparameters, which would be inefficient. For larger datasets, such as Numer.ai's, we use an improved version of hyperband in order to avoid extremely long computational time. This is because hyperband only devotes full computational resources on configurations that perform the best in each round of tuning [13]. While this means that we avoid extra computation on poor performing configurations, we also risk not exploring configurations that perform the best with full computational resources given to training said model. That is why LHS Grid Search is preferred if computation is not an issue for the data scientist. We have improved the original Hyperband by evaluating each configuration using k-fold cross-validation and by sampling each configuration using LHS.

9.4.3. *Utilizing Dask parallel computation*

Given the computationally intensive DR algorithms' and random forest model's training, we need to utilize parallel computation. Although other platforms exist to utilize parallel computation, such as Spark, we wanted to use software that worked with interactive computation and Jupyter notebooks, both of which allow for real-time computation. Jupyter notebooks are fast becoming a standard for data scientists as their flexibility for performing analysis and tuning models are far more suited for common data science tasks [14]. Because of this, we decided to use Dask, a software package that can connect local or remote compute clusters as a Python object which can be used interactively in Jupyter notebooks [15]. Our algorithms have many "embarrassingly parallel" operations, which can be easily adapted into parallel operations due to Dask's interface. Dask also builds DAGs for parallel operations that require computation done in a particular order as well, allowing for further flexibility if necessary. The pseudo code of our algorithm is given in Algorithm1 in Appendix B. An alternate version for the limited memory case is given in Algorithm 2. The symbols used in these algorithms are given in Tables B9.1 and B9.2.

9.5. Downsampling DR Algorithms with Independent Data Sources

Because we are testing 16 different DR algorithms with heavy compute cost, we attempted to down-sample the number of DR algorithms that we test with the Numer.ai data. By testing each algorithm on a smaller, time-series dataset that is quantized in the same fashion, we can attempt to exclude algorithms that do not improve modeling performance using less computation. We use the Lawrence Berkeley National Lab's HVAC/Weather dataset, which contains four different climate measurements (temperature, humidity, dew point, and solar radiation) and the HVAC usage measured in kWh, all of which were recorded every half-hour between January 1, 2018, and December 31, 2019. We know from domain knowledge and intuition that these weather features are highly correlated with each other and with total HVAC usage. Because of this knowledge, we construct the prediction problem such that the model uses one day's 48 recordings of the four weather features as individual columns, giving us a total of 192 features. We make our target of prediction to be the total HVAC kWh usage of one day. We then quantize the real values similarly to Numer.ai data in order to effectively downsample the DR algorithms we have at our disposal (Table A9.1).

9.5.1. *How the HVAC/weather dataset relates to Numer.ai*

Although it may seem that this HVAC/weather dataset is unrelated to Numer.ai's financial dataset, there are key similarities in how the data is constructed, its quantization procedure, and how we model the data. On how the data is constructed, both the Numer.ai and HVAC/Weather data are derived from time series data but are turned stationary through the framing of the problem. Numer.ai's feature set represents quantitative attributes of a stock at a single point in time, removing the time dimension from said data. As seen in Fig. 9.2, a day's 48 half-hour timesteps of each weather feature are pivoted into a single row. By constructing our HVAC/weather data such that each row represents a single day with all-weather attributes of that day as features, we similarly remove the time dependency between each row. For the y-target variable, we total the HVAC usage for a specific day such that our model will predict the total kWh use of a single day of the HVAC system based on the weather features of that day.

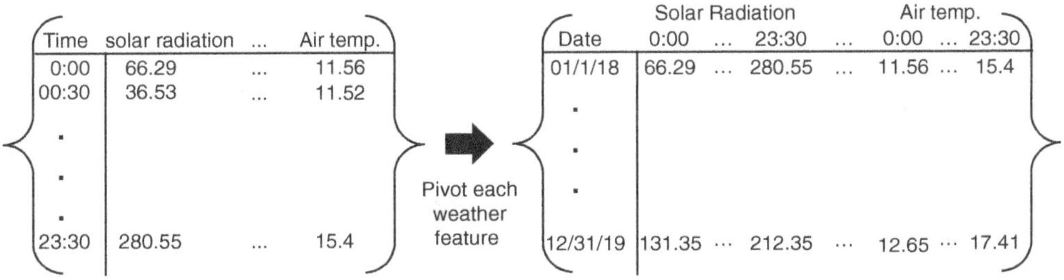

Fig. 9.2 The pivoting procedure for the HVAC/weather dataset illustrated.

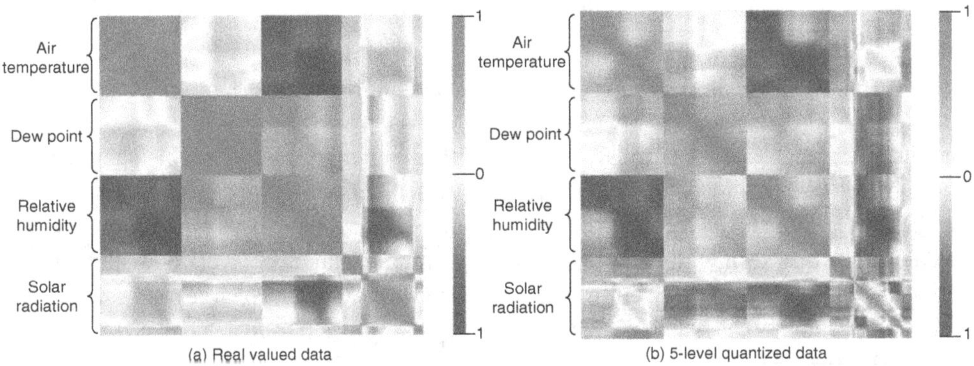

Fig. 9.3 Correlation heatmaps of both real-valued and quantized HVAC/weather data.

Because of the data construction process, the HVAC/weather dataset shows high multicollinearity since groups of features are derived from each weather feature, as apparent in Fig. 9.3(a). Just as we will see later with the Numer.ai data, the modeling of the HVAC/Weather dataset would benefit from DR, since reducing multicollinearity leads to a decrease in the variance of our models. However, since the HVAC/weather dataset has much greater multicollinearity than the Numer.ai data, we expect to see greater improvements from our baseline model with the HVAC/weather dataset. If a specific DR algorithm has no success in statistically significantly improving the performance of our model, this gives us good reason to think that said DR algorithm would not be able to improve the Numer.ai model either.

Because our data is originally real-valued, we need to quantize the HVAC/weather data in a similar fashion as Numer.ai's quantization process. Although the exact obfuscation/quantization procedure Numer.ai uses is a trade secret, we consulted with their team on designing an alike procedure for the HVAC/weather data. First, like Numer.ai, we split up our dataset by each month, which we refer to as an era. In Fig. 9.4, we see that each weather feature (such as air temperature) of an era is flattened into a 1-D array and numerically ranked, then quantized into five equally sized bins. Each era is then reshaped such that each row represents a day's worth of measurements, horizontally appended to the

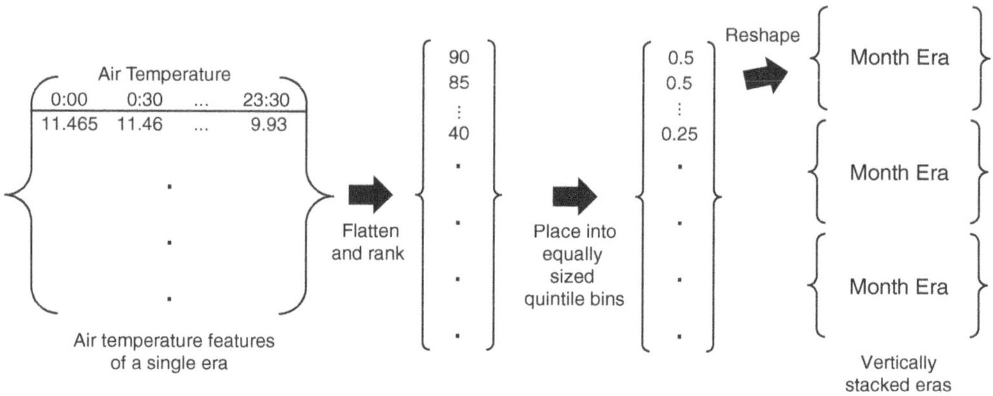

Fig. 9.4 The quantization procedure for the HVAC/weather dataset illustrated.

other weather features, then vertically stacked with all other eras. Because this quantization procedure removes a high degree of information from the features, we can see in Fig. 9.3 (b) that the multicollinearity is reduced between features and a degree of noise is introduced to the data as well, as seen with certain features becoming negatively correlated with features they were originally positively correlated with, or vice versa. The y-target variable is also quantized by ranking the values per era, quantizing the values into five evenly sized bins of $[0, 0.25, 0.5, 0.75, 1]$.

Just like how we model the Numer.ai data, we model the HVAC/Weather data using a regressive Random Forest model, even though the y-target variable is discretized. For that reason, we also use Spearman Rank Correlation as the metric of choice as well. In the next section, we can see that the modeling will be easier to achieve a higher Spearman Rank Correlation than the Numer.ai modeling due to the strong correlations between our features and the y-target variable.

9.5.2. *Why HVAC/weather data modeling is simple*

One of the justifications for using the HVAC/weather dataset is that modeling the quantized data is considerably easier when compared to the Numer.ai data, so any DR technique that fails to improve the baseline model is reasonably omitted from the Numer.ai testing. The HVAC/Weather dataset is considerably smaller (529 rows and 192 columns vs. 500,000 rows and 310 columns), so training, tuning, and testing are much faster with the HVAC/Weather dataset. Because we only have 529 rows total of data and 192 features, the testing of different hyperparameters and DR techniques is unstable due to the cross-validation technique we use involving the random sampling of different eras for the train and validation sets. To account for this, we repeat cross-validation sampling multiple times to account for the variation that random cross-validation leads to. Having low data depth allows us to test more configurations of hyperparameters for each DR technique and have a more precise result of each DR algorithm's performance. We also know that the weather features and their quantized counterparts are highly correlated with the HVAC kWh daily

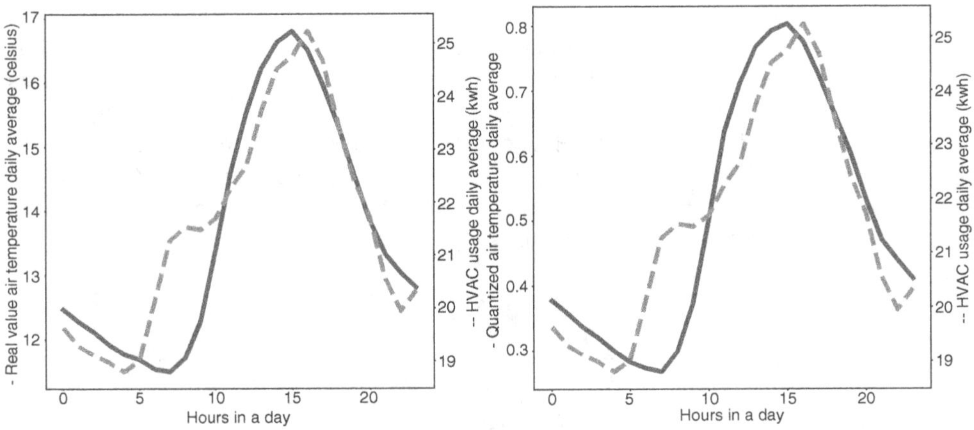

Fig. 9.5 Hourly daily averages of real-valued and quantized air temperature and HVAC usage (kWh).

usage, which is apparent in Fig. 9.5. Considering this, we know a priori that there is a strong non-linear relationship between our feature space and our target variable.

9.5.3. *Results of data-driven DR selection for HVAC/weather dataset*

Using the methodology described in Section 9.4, we tested and recorded the performance of each DR algorithm on the HVAC/weather dataset for the purposes of downsampling the number of DR techniques to be used on the Numer.ai data. The results can be seen in Table 9.2. We use the 25% and 75% quantiles in order to show the variance in the model performance after each DR technique. Although half of the DR techniques end up having considerably worse average performance compared to our baseline of no DR algorithm, we see in Fig. 9.6 that none of the DR algorithms have a larger quantile range than our baseline. This is inline with our expectation that DR reduces the variance in our model's performance, creating more consistent metrics using unseen data.

None of the feature extraction methods end up performing better than the baseline score, which is unsurprising given that the data is nonparametric (since our transformations are rank based). This outlines the weakness of feature extraction methods for our obfuscated data problem. We also see that feature selection and feature clustering methods perform better as these methods do not depend on parametric relationships of the feature space.

One interesting observation is that even though the obfuscated data problem is a less-than-ideal application of feature extraction methods, our data-driven approach to selecting hyperparameters gave us the same configuration if we had used the typical hyperparameter tuning method used for PCA. For PCA, one common way to select the number of principal components is to graph the singular values of each principal component on a log scale as we do in Fig. 9.7. Since these singular values signify the importance of each principal component, we choose the number of principal components where an additional principal component explains much less variance of the feature space. For PCA, the rule of thumb

Table 9.2 The results of testing each DR technique on the HVAC/weather dataset are where the x and y datasets are quantized into five quantiles. The DR algorithms are grouped by type and then ordered in descending value of Spearman Rank Correlation mean. SRC refers to Spearman Rank Correlation, and QME refers to Quartic Mean Error. Runtime is measured in seconds and refers to the DR algorithm fitting and transformation time. Feature clustering includes feature distance calculations, clustering algorithm, and MDA computation. The number following the long dash in the DR technique column is the number of features/components post-transformation.

DR technique	SRC mean	SRC [25% 75%] quantile	QME mean	QME [25% 75%] quantile	Runtime
None	0.556	[0.136, 0.906]	0.02	[0.003, 0.039]	0
Feature Selection					
MDA—15	0.561	[0.146, 0.906]	0.019	[0.004, 0.037]	29.504
SHAP—26	0.546	[0.175, 0.914]	0.018	[0.002, 0.031]	10.043
Feature Extraction					
KPCA—32	0.567	[0.237, 0.825]	0.018	[0.007, 0.036]	3.904
Isomap—35	0.565	[0.204, 0.831]	0.017	[0.008, 0.028]	12.261
UMAP—65	0.501	[0.152, 0.878]	0.024	[0.005, 0.043]	10.659
LLE—93	0.558	[0.175, 0.883]	0.02	[0.004, 0.04]	1.654
PCA—15	0.501	[0.104, 0.789]	0.02	[0.007, 0.037]	16.318
Feature Clustering					
Dist. Correlation K-Medoids—78	0.569	[0.227, 0.883]	0.02	[0.003, 0.037]	21.946
Var. of Info. Hier—144	0.564	[0.198, 0.871]	0.02	[0.003, 0.037]	31.145
Var. of Info. K-Medoids—108	0.552	[0.136, 0.85]	0.02	[0.004, 0.04]	38.038
Dist. Correlation HDBSCAN—98	0.552	[0.156, 0.908]	0.017	[0.006, 0.032]	22.185
Max Correlation HDBSCAN—185	0.549	[0.136, 0.868]	0.02	[0.003, 0.041]	349.174
Max Correlation K-Medoids—149	0.545	[0.175, 0.831]	0.02	[0.004, 0.043]	344.869
Max Correlation Hier—175	0.544	[0.185, 0.85]	0.019	[0.004, 0.038]	345.044
Dist. Correlation Hier—191	0.544	[0.123, 0.868]	0.02	[0.003, 0.041]	52.908
Var. of Info. HDBSCAN—84	0.538	[0.159, 0.775]	0.017	[0.007, 0.031]	36.781

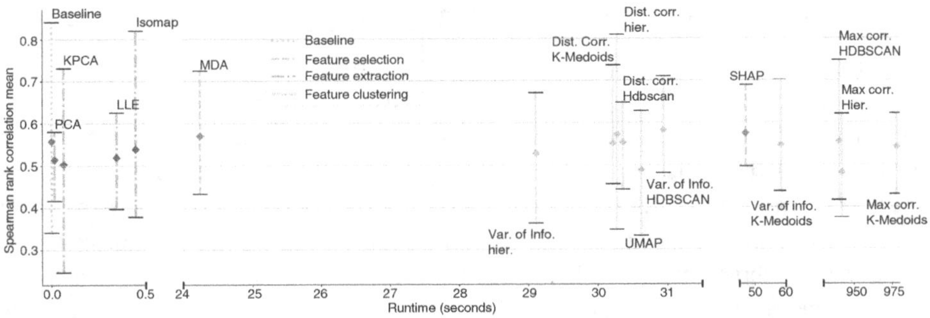

Fig. 9.6 Spearman Rank Correlation mean and quantiles of each HVAC/weather DR technique and their respective runtimes. Tick marks are 25% and 75% quantiles.

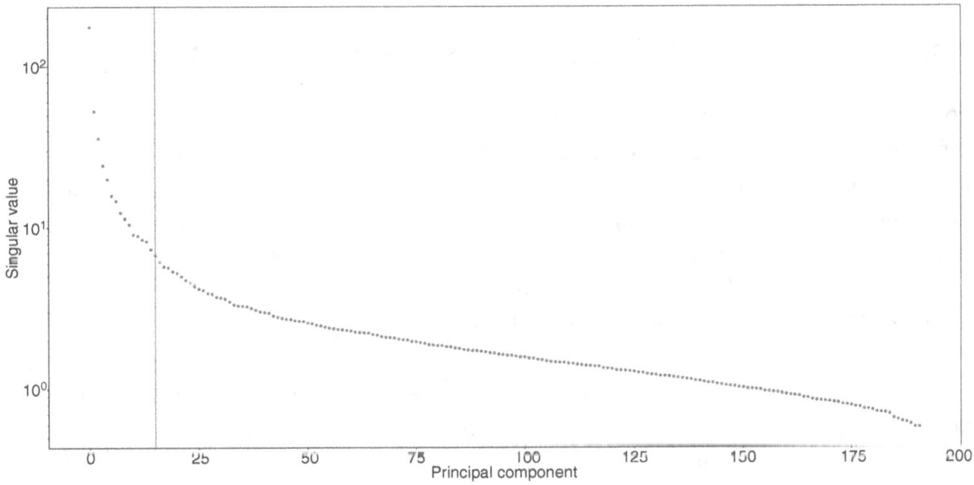

Fig. 9.7 Singular values for each principal component of the quantized HVAC/weather dataset.

is to use the "elbow method," where we select the number of singular values where there is an elbow bend (the red line in Fig. 9.7). This "elbow method" tells us to use the same number of principal components as we found through data-driven hyperparameter tuning (16 components).

Given the results of our HVAC/weather DR algorithm selection, we choose to discard UMAP and maximal correlation hierarchical single linkage from the Numer.ai DR algorithm selection. This is a somewhat arbitrary decision, based on the DR algorithms' SRC performance and runtime, since the downsampling is done out of practicality. We see that both of these algorithms are outliers in runtime and SRC performance for their respective categories of DR algorithms.

9.5.4. *The effects of data quantization on model performance*

By quantizing the weather data, we notice that the correlation between features changed as well as the correlation between the features and the target variable, as seen in Fig. 9.3. With quantization, there is a loss in precision in the data, thus reducing the signal latent in the data. We hypothesize that modeling performance and DR techniques suffer due to this reduction in precision, thus lowering the probability of finding DR transformation, which improves performance over the baseline. To demonstrate this, we evaluated the DR techniques using three different X datasets (50 quantiles, 500 quantiles, and untransformed data) using the same y dataset. The same y dataset is used in order to be able to keep the Spearman Rank Correlations comparable, as increasing the cardinality of the y data will affect the calculation of the score. We carried out different tests and three sets of results are shown in Tables 9.3, 9.4, and 9.5.

9.6. Testing the DR Framework on the Numer.ai Dataset

Now that we have a deeper understanding of which DR algorithms tend to succeed with obfuscated data, we now test our DR testing framework with a considerably more difficult dataset to model. The Numer.ai dataset is a strong example of why obfuscated data can add great value to the data science community. Numer.ai, like other organizations that wish to utilize a public data competition format, is first and foremost concerned with the risks of releasing their data to the public. By heavily obfuscating their data, organizations can protect the privacy of the data, prevent users from imparting their own bias to their models, and prevent competing firms from utilizing their data as well. If our framework can quell concerns about the problems with modeling obfuscated data, other industries that rely on data science and modeling but are concerned about risks regarding public data science competitions may be able to adopt a similar tactic when trying to adapt a format for their own data competitions, spurring growth in domains that were previously deemed impractical for such applications.

9.6.1. *How does the Numer.ai dataset pose new challenges?*

The Numer.ai dataset is a more difficult DR testing problem than our HVAC/weather dataset because of the size of the data, weaker signals between features and the target variable, and lower multicollinearity between features. Because of these challenges, DR algorithms will take considerably longer to tune hyperparameters, models will perform worse using the same metrics used with our HVAC/weather dataset, and the DR algorithms will be less effective at filtering out redundant features and information.

9.6.1.1. Size of Numer.ai dataset

As mentioned previously, the Numer.ai dataset is significantly larger than the HVAC/Weather dataset, which affects how thorough we can be with our hyperparameter

Table 9.3 The results of testing each DR technique on the HVAC/weather dataset, where the x data is quantized into 50 quantiles and the y data is quantized to five quantiles.

DR technique	SRC mean	SRC [25% 75%] quantile	QME mean	QME [25% 75%] quantile	Runtime
None	0.566	[0.191, 0.887]	0.019	[0.003, 0.035]	0
Feature Selection					
SHAP—31	0.558	[0.214, 0.897]	0.021	[0.003, 0.031]	16.774
MDA—18	0.495	[0.081, 0.862]	0.024	[0.005, 0.042]	25.255
Feature Extraction					
KPCA—32	0.567	[0.292, 0.766]	0.018	[0.007, 0.034]	6.694
LLE—43	0.527	[0.201, 0.756]	0.023	[0.005, 0.042]	3.138
Isomap—23	0.516	[0.123, 0.833]	0.018	[0.007, 0.034]	6.979
PCA—21	0.506	[0.107, 0.811]	0.02	[0.007, 0.034]	4.04
UMAP—5	0.502	[0.269, 0.812]	0.025	[0.006, 0.043]	12.386
Feature Clustering					
Dist. Correlation K-Medoids—86	0.592	[0.25, 0.914]	0.021	[0.004, 0.043]	27.005
Var. of Info. K-Medoids—79	0.57	[0.23, 0.903]	0.02	[0.003, 0.032]	30.935
Max Correlation HDBSCAN—141	0.567	[0.273, 0.831]	0.024	[0.003, 0.044]	123.726
Max Correlation K-Medoids—159	0.558	[0.195, 0.859]	0.018	[0.003, 0.037]	111.397
Max Correlation Hier—144	0.556	[0.237, 0.812]	0.023	[0.003, 0.044]	111.073
Dist. Correlation HDBSCAN—97	0.543	[0.058, 0.883]	0.018	[0.008, 0.032]	28.809
Var. of Info. Hier—144	0.541	[0.195, 0.84]	0.02	[0.003, 0.034]	32.941
Dist. Correlation Hier—172	0.538	[0.169, 0.821]	0.019	[0.003, 0.039]	29.586
Var. of Info. HDBSCAN—132	0.536	[0.165, 0.84]	0.02	[0.003, 0.035]	34.315

tuning for both our model and DR algorithms. The HVAC/Weather feature set is 0.7750 MB, while the Numer.ai feature set is 1,186 MB, raising both runtime and memory usage concerns. Although we attempt to alleviate these issues by utilizing parallel computation with distributed compute nodes, we still need to adapt our methodology slightly for practicality. Because of these adaptations, we are not utilizing the most optimal format of our

Table 9.4 The results of testing each DR technique on the HVAC/weather dataset, where the x data is quantized with 500 quantiles and the y data is quantized with five quantiles.

DR technique	SRC mean	SRC [25% 75%] quantile	QME mean	QME [25% 75%] quantile	Runtime
None	0.554	[0.14, 0.85]	0.019	[0.003, 0.036]	0
Feature Selection					
SHAP—29	0.563	[0.23, 0.88]	0.018	[0.003, 0.03]	7.007
MDA—24	0.558	[0.23, 0.821]	0.022	[0.004, 0.041]	19.433
Feature Extraction					
KPCA—32	0.551	[0.273, 0.781]	0.019	[0.008, 0.033]	2.147
LLE—33	0.548	[0.178, 0.796]	0.02	[0.005, 0.037]	1.21
UMAP—15	0.541	[0.237, 0.9]	0.02	[0.006, 0.033]	9.093
Isomap—7	0.529	[0.101, 0.85]	0.021	[0.004, 0.044]	5.363
PCA—20	0.487	[0.058, 0.752]	0.023	[0.008, 0.041]	3.83
Feature Clustering					
Max Correlation HDBSCAN—99	0.585	[0.178, 0.874]	0.02	[0.004, 0.038]	109.607
Var. of Info. HDBSCAN—139	0.565	[0.201, 0.887]	0.018	[0.003, 0.033]	23.793
Max Correlation K-Medoids—95	0.565	[0.175, 0.871]	0.019	[0.004, 0.036]	108.776
Dist. Correlation Hier—172	0.562	[0.214, 0.84]	0.018	[0.003, 0.036]	30.204
Max Correlation Hier—144	0.552	[0.214, 0.812]	0.022	[0.003, 0.044]	111.554
Var. of Info. Hier—144	0.55	[0.162, 0.9]	0.019	[0.003, 0.036]	23.16
Var. of Info. K-Medoids—54	0.542	[0.211, 0.793]	0.021	[0.004, 0.036]	23.627
Dist. Correlation HDBSCAN—97	0.54	[0.065, 0.88]	0.018	[0.008, 0.031]	30.354
Dist. Correlation K-Medoids—91	0.54	[0.188, 0.821]	0.02	[0.003, 0.04]	28.953

data-driven framework; however, as we see later, we do still achieve substantial improvements in our modeling metrics.

We use hyperband instead of LHS, which trains model configurations with a portion of the data, giving less accurate scores of each hyperparameter configuration compared to training the model on the entire dataset. This saves computation from being used on

Table 9.5 The results of testing each DR technique on the HVAC/weather dataset, where the x data is not quantized and the y data is quantized to five quantiles.

DR technique	SRC mean	SRC [25% 75%] quantile	QME mean	QME [25% 75%] quantile	Runtime
None	0.502	[0.357, 0.862]	0.030	[0.024, 0.038]	0.000
		Feature Selection			
MDA—26	0.527	[0.38, 0.868]	0.031	[0.03, 0.037]	18.879
SHAP—5	0.503	[0.279, 0.868]	0.030	[0.025, 0.035]	1.464
		Feature Extraction			
LLE—38	0.546	[0.431, 0.742]	0.022	[0.019, 0.027]	5.258
KPCA—72	0.344	[0.071, 0.553]	0.028	[0.016, 0.036]	7.613
PCA—78	0.341	[0.019, 0.575]	0.029	[0.015, 0.039]	5.906
Isomap—45	0.335	[0.196, 0.685]	0.025	[0.015, 0.029]	5.708
UMAP—35	0.302	[−0.23, 0.682]	0.026	[0.02, 0.038]	14.359
		Feature Clustering			
Dist. Correlation K-Medoids—76	0.566	[0.344, 0.877]	0.028	[0.028, 0.031]	32.478
Max Correlation HDBSCAN—138	0.566	[0.393, 0.85]	0.028	[0.025, 0.029]	135.342
Dist. Correlation Hier—79	0.561	[0.337, 0.878]	0.028	[0.028, 0.031]	35.353
Dist. Correlation HDBSCAN—78	0.558	[0.354, 0.878]	0.027	[0.028, 0.03]	28.550
Max Correlation Hier—78	0.550	[0.357, 0.821]	0.026	[0.027, 0.029]	135.694
Var. of Info. HDBSCAN—88	0.540	[0.417, 0.891]	0.029	[0.024, 0.03]	30.517
Var. of Info. K-Medoids—48	0.520	[0.24, 0.85]	0.031	[0.032, 0.036]	29.285
Var. of Info. Hier—99	0.513	[0.376, 0.84]	0.031	[0.023, 0.039]	29.128
Max Correlation K-Medoids—157	0.512	[0.369, 0.891]	0.029	[0.025, 0.034]	134.807

configurations that seem less promising initially with a small portion of the data. However, this also means that configurations that only perform better than others when the model is training on the full dataset may be discarded erroneously.

When fitting our feature extraction methods, either with full spectral methods such as PCA and Isomap or with sparse spectral methods like locally linear embedding (LLE), we use only a sample of the Numer.ai data. One reason is that for certain DR methods, a matrix is decomposed into eigenvectors, which can lead to memory issues with too many samples to calculate from. The other reason is that some methods form a nearest neighbors graph of each data point, which would be computationally intractable for the size of the full Numer.ai dataset. We use around $18,000$ data points for the fitting of the feature extraction algorithms, which can lead to less accurate reconstructions of the feature space in lower dimensional embeddings.

For feature clustering methods, we need to calculate a distance matrix for each feature corresponding to each other feature, leading to $(310^2)/2 - 310$ separate distance calculations. These distance calculations are also computationally intractable to compute, so we need to compute the distances using a sample of the Numer.ai data. We use around 2,000 data points to compute our distances, which can lead to less accurate calculations and less accurate clusterings.

9.6.1.2. Weaker signals within features

The Numer.ai dataset represents features traditionally used in quantitative finance to predict various metrics for the stock market and individual securities. These features are known to be weak predictors of securities performance due to the weak Efficient Market Hypothesis, where the price of the security reflects the information available to rational actors in the market, and therefore the information would not give an edge to any single actor [16]. Because the stock market is not completely efficient, information can still be valuable to profiting from securities; however, the information and inference become marginally more difficult to obtain and use effectively for modeling. Thus, Numer.ai democratizes its modeling approach to gain a greater edge on its data and why participants' models require rigorous and copious amounts of back-testing, feature selection, and hyperparameter tuning to perform well with Numer.ai data.

9.7. Summary and Observations

Our work demonstrates the effectiveness of data-driven dimensionality reduction approaches, even when domain knowledge is limited. We evaluated various Feature Extraction, Feature Selection, and Feature Clustering methods on two distinct problems with different types of data obfuscation. In the building energy dataset with known key features, our data-driven approach successfully identified the expected features. Feature Clustering methods showed superior modeling performance across both datasets. Future work will include testing with additional datasets and exploring different obfuscation techniques to further validate our approach and investigate feature clustering design options.

APPENDIX A

A.1. Summary of DR Techniques

Table A9.1 DR techniques and packages

DR technique	Description	Package used
PCA [17]	A technique that projects data onto the first n-principal components, which are formed to maximize the variance between each principal component.	Sci-kit Learn
KPCA [18]	An extension of PCA, which uses a kernel to transform and project the data onto the principal components.	Sci-kit Learn
Locally Linear Embedding [19]	A projection of the data based on preserving neighborhood embeddings by mapping inputs to a single global coordinate system in a lower dimension.	Sci-kit Learn
Isomap [20]	Finds a lower-dimensional embedding of the underlying global geometry of the data set by using local metric information.	Sci-kit Learn
UMAP [21]	A stochastic neighbor embedding method which assumes that the data is uniformly distributed on a locally connected Riemannian manifold.	UMAP Learn
Mean Decrease Accuracy [22]	A feature importance algorithm that ranks each feature based on the difference in score modeling out-of-sample (OOS) data and the same OOS data with the permuted feature.	Code inspired by: MLFin Lab
Shapely Values [23]	A feature importance algorithm that uses a game theoretic approach and explanation model to estimate the effect a feature has on the output of the original model.	SHAP Values
Feature Clustering [24]	An extension of Mean Decrease Accuracy, but could feasibly be extended to other feature importance algorithms, in which correlated features are clustered and ranked by cluster importance.	MLFin Lab + Custom Code

APPENDIX B

B.1. Modified DR Hyperband

Algorithm B9.1 Modified DR Hyperband

function ModifiedDRHyperband(η, $num_{samples}$, k, $ratio_{max}$, num_{fit_rows}, f_{DR}, f_{model}, f_{score}, X_{train}, y_{train}, num_{folds}, $Low\ Memory$)
    $S_{max} = \left\lfloor \frac{\log_2 ratio_{max}}{log_2 \eta} \right\rfloor$, $B = (S_{max} + 1) * ratio_{max}$, $score_{opt} \leftarrow -1e^8$, $parameter_{opt} \leftarrow Null$,
    $X_{folds}, y_{folds} \leftarrow k\text{-}FoldCV(X_{train}, y_{train}, num_{folds})$, $X_{folds\_fut}, y_{folds\_fut} \leftarrow scatter(X_{folds}, y_{folds})$
    for $S \in \{S_{max}, S_{max} - 1, \ldots, 0\}$ **do**
        $n = \left\lceil \frac{\eta B}{R(S+1)} \right\rceil$
        $T \leftarrow Latin\ Hypercube\ Sample(Hyper\text{-}Parameter\ Grid, num_{samples})$
        for $i \in \{0, 1, \ldots, S\}$ **do**
            $num_{config} = \lfloor n * \eta^i \rfloor$
            $ratio = r * \eta^i$
            $fit\_rows = \lfloor num_{fit\_rows} * \frac{ratio}{100} \rceil$
            $folds_{array} \leftarrow [\,]$
            for $t \in T$ **do**
                for $X_{train}, X_{val} \in X_{folds\_fut}$ **do**
                    if $Low\ Memory == True$ **then**
                        Use Algorithm 2
                    else
                        Submit as parallel future tasks:
                        $f'_{DR} \leftarrow$ Train f_{DR} using $X_{train}[: fit\_rows]$ and hyperparameters t
                        $X'_{train} \leftarrow f'_{DR}(X_{train})$
                        $X'_{val} \leftarrow f'_{DR}(X_{val})$
                        $X'_{folds} \leftarrow (X'_{train}, X'_{val})$
                    Append X'_{folds} to $folds_{array}$
                    $folds_{array} \leftarrow Gather\ Tasks(folds_{array})$
                    $\overline{folds\_fut}_{array} \leftarrow Scatter(folds_{array})$
                    $\overline{scores\_fut}_{array} \leftarrow [\,]$
                for $X'_{folds} \in folds\_fut_{array}$ **do**
                    $scores_{array} \leftarrow [\,]$
                    for $X'_{train}, X'_{val} \in X'_{folds}$ and $y_{train}, y_{val} \in y_{folds\_fut}$ **do**
                        Submit as parallel future tasks:
                        $f'_{model} \leftarrow f_{model}$ and fit using X'_{train} and y_{train}
                        $y_{pred} \leftarrow f'_{model}(X'_{val})$
                        $score \leftarrow f_{score}(y_{val}, y_{pred})$
                        Append $score$ to $scores_{array}$
                    $\overline{score} = mean(scores_{array})$
                    Append $\overline{score}$ to $\overline{scores\_fut}_{array}$
                $\overline{scores}_{array} \leftarrow Gather\ Tasks(\overline{scores\_fut}_{array})$
                $parameter_{curr} \leftarrow T[argmax(\overline{scores}_{array})]$
                $score_{curr} \leftarrow max(\overline{scores}_{array})$
                $T \leftarrow T[argsort(\overline{scores}_{array})]$
                $T \leftarrow T[-\lfloor num_{config}/eta \rceil :]$
                if $score_{opt} < score_{curr}$ **then**
                    $score_{opt} \leftarrow score_{curr}$
                    $parameter_{opt} \leftarrow parameter_{curr}$
    return $score_{opt}$ and $parameter_{opt}$
    end function

B.2. Low-Memory Hyperband Sub-Routine

Algorithm B9.2 Low-Memory Hyperband Sub-Routine

function LOW-MEMORY HYPERBAND SUB-ROUTINE(X_{fold_fut}, y_{fold_fut}, f_{DR}, f_{model}, $num_{workers}$, $memory\_limit$, $\overline{scores}_{array}$)
    $num_{futures} \leftarrow 0$
    for $X_{train}, X_{val} \in X_{folds\_fut}$ **do**
        Submit as parallel future tasks:
            Copy f_{DR} and fit using $X_{train}[: fit\_rows]$ and hyperparameters t
            $X'_{train} \leftarrow f_{DR}(X_{train})$
            $X'_{val} \leftarrow f_{DR}(X_{val})$
            $num_{futures} = num_{futures} + 1$
        $X'_{folds} \leftarrow (X'_{train}, X'_{val})$
        Append X'_{folds} to $folds_{array}$
        if $num_{futures} == num_{workers}$ **then**
            $folds_{array} \leftarrow Gather\ Tasks(folds_{array})$
            if $check\_mem\_usage() \geq memory\_limit$ **then**
                $folds\_fut_{array} \leftarrow Scatter(folds_{array})$
                $\overline{scores\_fut}_{array} \leftarrow [\,]$
                for $X'_{folds} \subset folds_{array}$ **do**
                    $scores_{array} \leftarrow [\,]$
                    for $X'_{train}, X'_{val} \in X'_{folds}$ *and* $y_{train}, y_{val} \in y_{folds\_fut}$ **do**
                        Submit as parallel future tasks:
                            $f_{DR} \leftarrow$ Train f_{model} using X'_{train} and y_{train}
                            $y_{pred} \leftarrow f_{model}(X'_{val})$
                            $score \leftarrow f_{score}(y_{val}, y_{pred})$
                        Append $score$ to $scores\_fut_{array}$
                    $\overline{score} = mean(scores_{array})$
                    Append $\overline{scores}$ to $\overline{scores\_fut}_{array}$
                $\bar{s}_{array} \leftarrow Gather\ Tasks(\overline{scores\_fut}_{array})$
                Append $\bar{s}_{array}$ to $\overline{scores}_{array}$
    return $\overline{scores}_{array}$
    end function

B.3. Legend of Symbols

Table B9.1 Symbols legend

Variable	Definition	Required/Suggested values
η	Branching factor for hyperband	$\eta \geq 1$, suggested between 3 and 4
$num_{samples}$	Number of hyperparameter configurations to be sampled from the hyperparameter grid	$num_{samples} > 1$
$ratio_{max}$	The maximum ratio of num_{fit_rows} to be used when fitting f_{DR}	$0 < ratio_{max} < 100$
num_{fit_rows}	The maximum number of rows to be used when fitting f_{DR}	$0 < num_{fit\_rows} \leq N$, where N is the number of rows in X_{train}
num_{folds}	The number of folds for k-fold cross-validation	\$0 $< num_{folds}$, suggested 5 to 10, depending on data size

B.4. Functions Legend

Table B9.2 Functions legend

Function	Purpose
f_{DR}	Dimensionality reduction function
f_{model}	Classification or regression model
f_{score}	Scoring function for f_{model}
k-FoldCV	Function which splits up both X and y datasets into k train and validation folds
Scatter	Data to workers through the scheduler to persist data on a cluster and be used in future calculations (called Futures)
Gather Tasks	Block later code from running until Futures are finished, then collect all Futures from workers into local processor memory
Latin Hypercube Sample	Takes in a hyperparameter grid, samples from the grid using the Latin hypercube sampling method. Implementation in Python can be found here: https://github.com/sahilm89/lhsmdu
argsort	Sort arguments of array and return indices
check_mem_usage	Check current percentage memory usage on the local processor

APPENDIX C

C.1. HVAC/Weather DR Algorithm Hyperparameters

DR algorithm	Hyperparameter name	Hyperparameter value
MDA	n_features	27
SHAP	n_features	5
Isomap	n_components	8
	n_neighbors	45
	metric	correlation
LLE	n_components	3
	n_neighbors	53
	reg	0.002
	method	standard
PCA	n_components	16
	whiten	False
KPCA	n_components	42
	kernel	poly
	degree	5
	coef	1
	alpha	4
	eigen_solver	arpack
UMAP	n_components	95
	n_neighbors	82
	metric	hamming
	n_epochs	200
	a	1.9
	b	2.6
	init	spectral
	local_connectivity	1
	low_memory	True
Var. of Info. HDBSCAN	n_features	105
Dist. Corr. Hier.	n_features	191

(*Continued*)

(*Continued*)

DR algorithm	Hyperparameter name	Hyperparameter value
Max Corr. HDBSCAN	n_features	163
Dist. Corr. HDBSCAN	n_features	97
Dist. Corr. K-Medoids	n_features	91
Var. of Info. K-Medoids	n_features	70
Max Corr. K-Medoids	n_features	82
Var. of Info. Hier.	n_features	144
Max Corr. Hier.	n_features	187

C.2. HVAC/Weather Random Forest Hyperparameters

DR algorithm	n estimator	min samples_ split	max leaf_node	max depth	min samples_ leaf	max samples	max features
None	500	12	660	43	7	0.6	45
MDA	240	8	420	33	5	0.7	12
SHAP	250	2	640	33	39	0.7	4
Isomap	1,500	8	420	53	39	0.5	4
LLE	750	5	620	3	5	0.8	2
PCA	750	6	500	23	11	0.6	4
KPCA	250	8	740	43	13	0.5	30
UMAP	750	8	420	23	13	0.6	51
Var of Info. HDBSCAN	1,500	4	680	43	5	0.8	9
Dist. Corr. Hier.	500	4	560	13	7	0.5	35
Max Corr. HDBSCAN	1,000	4	460	43	5	0.9	10
Dist. Corr. HDBSCAN	250	2	560	43	31	0.7	4
Dist. Corr. K-Medoids	1,250	6	720	23	5	0.8	20
Var. of Info K-Medoids	500	8	480	33	7	0.5	32
Max Corr. K-Medoids	250	8	660	13	7	0.5	8
Var of Info. Hier.	1,500	4	440	3	27	0.9	115
Max Corr. Hier.	1,250	4	640	33	5	0.7	15

References

1. X. Huang, L. Wu, and Y. Ye, A review on dimensionality reduction techniques, *Int. J. Pattern Recognit. Artif. Intell.* **33**(10), 1950017 (2019).
2. R. Zebari, A. Abdulazeez, D. Zeebaree, D. Zebari, and J. Saeed, A comprehensive review of dimensionality reduction techniques for feature selection and feature extraction, *J. Appl. Sci. Technol. Trends.* **1**(2), 56–70 (2020).
3. L. H. Nguyen and S. Holmes, Ten quick tips for effective dimensionality reduction, *PLoS Comput. Biol.* **15**(6), e1006907 (2019).
4. T. Yu, S. Simoff, and T. Jan, VQSVm: A case study for incorporating prior domain knowledge into inductive machine learning, *Neurocomputing.* **73**(13), 2614–2623 (2010). Pattern Recognition in Bioinformatics Advances in Neural Control.
5. N. Polyzotis, S. Roy, S. E. Whang, and M. Zinkevich, Data management challenges in production machine learning. *In Proc. 2017 ACM International Conference on Management of Data (SIGMOD '17)*, pp. 1723–1726, New York, NY, USA (2017). Association for Computing Machinery.
6. L. Van Der Maaten, E. Postma, J. Van den Herik, et al., Dimensionality reduction: A comparative, *J. Mach. Learn. Res.* **10**(66-71), 13 (2009).
7. A. Khanan, S. Abdullah, A. H. M. Mohamed, A. Mehmood, and K. A. Z. Ariffin, Big data security and privacy concerns: A review. In eds. A. Al-Masri and K. Curran, *Smart Technol. Innov. Sustain. Future.* pp. 55–61. Springer, Cham (2019).
8. W. N. Price and I. G. Cohen, Privacy in the age of medical big data, *Nat. Med.* **25**(1), 37–43 (2019).
9. A. Narayanan and V. Shmatikov, How to break anonymity of the Netflix Prize dataset (2006). http://arxiv.org/abs/cs/0610105.
10. I. Guyon and A. Elisseeff, An introduction to variable and feature selection, *J. Mach. Learn. Res.* **3**(Mar), 1157–1182 (2003).
11. Numerai, *Numerai Tournament Overview* (n.d.). Available at: https://docs.numer.ai/tournament/learn
12. J. L. Deutsch and C. V. Deutsch, Latin hypercube sampling with multidimensional uniformity, *J. Stat. Plan. Inference.* **142**(3), 763–772 (2012).
13. L. Li, K. Jamieson, G. DeSalvo, A. Rostamizadeh, and A. Talwalkar, Hyperband: A novel bandit-based approach to hyperparameter optimization, *J. Mach. Learn. Res.* **18**(1), 6765–6816 (2017).
14. F. Perez and B. E. Granger, IPython: A system for interactive scientific computing, *Comput. Sci. Eng.* **9**(3), 21–29 (2007).
15. M. Rocklin, Dask: Parallel computation with blocked algorithms and task scheduling. In *Proc. 14th Python in Science Conference, Vol. 130*, p. 136, Citeseer (2015).
16. E. F. Fama, Random walks in stock market prices, *Fin. Anal. J.* **51**(1), 75–80 (1995).
17. A. Mackiewicz and W. Ratajczak, Principal components analysis (FPCA), *Comput. Geosci.* **19**, 303–342 (1993).
18. B. Schölkopf, A. Smola, and K.-R. Müller, Kernel principal component analysis. In *Proceedings of the International Conference on Artificial Neural Networks (ICANN-1997)*, pp. 583–588, BibSonomy (1997).
19. S. T. Roweis and L. K. Saul, Nonlinear dimensionality reduction by locally linear embedding, *Science.* **290**(5500), 2323–2326 (2000).

20. J. B. Tenenbaum, V. de Silva, and J. C. Langford, A global geometric framework for nonlinear dimensionality reduction, *Science.* **290**(5500), 2319–2323 (2000).

21. L. McInnes, J. Melville, and J. H. Healy, UMAP: Uniform manifold approximation and projection for dimension reduction, arXiv, (2020).

22. H. Han, X. Guo, and H. Yu, Variable selection using mean decrease accuracy and mean decrease Gini based on random forest. In *Proc. 7th IEEE International Conference on Software Engineering and Service Science (ICSESS),* pp. 219–224, Beijing (2016).

23. S. M. Lundberg and S.-I. Lee, A unified approach to interpreting model predictions. In eds. I. Guyon, U. V. Luxburg, S. Bengio, et al. *Advances in Neural Information Processing Systems 30,* pp. 4765–4774. Curran Associates, Inc., (2017).

24. M. López de Prado, Clustered feature importance (presentation slides) (2020). https://papers.ssrn.com/sol3/Delivery.cfm?abstractid=3517595.

https://doi.org/10.1142/9789819813049_0010

CHAPTER 10

Toward Specialized Supercomputers for Climate Sciences: Computational Requirements of the Icosahedral Nonhydrostatic Weather and Climate Model

Torsten Hoefler[1,*], Alexandru Calotoiu[1], Anurag Dipankar[1], Thomas Schulthess[1], Xavier Lapillonne[2], and Oliver Fuhrer[2]

[1]ETH Zürich, Andreasstrasse 5. 8050, Zurich, Switzerland
[2]The Federal Office of Meteorology and Climatology, MeteoSwiss, Operation Center 1, P.O. Box, 8058 Zurich Airport, Zurich, Switzerland
[*]Corresponding author. E-mail: htor@ethz.ch

We discuss the computational challenges and requirements for high-resolution climate simulations using the Icosahedral Nonhydrostatic Weather and Climate Model (ICON). We define a detailed requirements model for ICON which emphasizes the need for specialized supercomputers to accurately predict climate change impacts and extreme weather events. Based on the requirements model, we outline computational demands for km-scale simulations, and suggests machine learning techniques to enhance model accuracy and efficiency. Our findings aim to guide the design of future supercomputers for advanced climate science.

Keywords: Climate Prediction, Supercomputing, Large-Scale Climate Simulations, Weather Forecasting

While the impact of climate change is clearly visible in our daily experiences, news, and short-term predictions, we are not yet equipped to predict the long-term effects at accurate spatial and temporal resolution, like months, years, or decades in the future. For example, while all simulations agree that the global mean temperature is increasing, they are starkly disagreeing on the exact dynamics of this increase. One or two degrees may make the difference, especially near points that may fundamentally change ecosystems [1]. An important simulation scenario is the Equilibrium Climate Sensitivity (ECS), which estimates the global average temperature increase given that the CO_2 concentration doubled. Predictions for ECS range from 2°C to 5°C and the uncertainty is mainly caused by different representations of clouds [2]. This global average prediction is likely the simplest important metric of CO_2's impact and acts as a good litmus test to see where the quality of climate models stands. If we cannot predict average global temperature change with high confidence, we will surely not be able to predict the frequency or likelihood of localized events.

Yet, such localized predictions of the likelihood of future extreme events are crucial to drive prevention as well as adaptation. The most promising avenue to improve this prediction is to increase the model's resolution to capture the physics of clouds and global circulation using first principles. This also enables *more accurate predictions of future climate scenarios in specific regions, which can guide our decisions where to invest in local infrastructure to mitigate extreme events*. Today's simulations operate at resolutions of tens of kilometers and are mainly limited by our available compute infrastructure. Large thunderstorm clouds are resolved at a single-digit kilometer scale, while smaller cloud formations need a resolution of hundreds of meters. Clouds have a large impact on the Earth's climate, not only through precipitation events but also reflection or absorption of radiation originating from the sun or reflected by the surface. Thus, to enable accurate predictions, we need to push climate simulations to higher resolution. Unfortunately, each doubling in the horizontal resolution of a climate simulation increases the computational requirements between eight and 16 times. Given where we stand today, *we require three to four orders of magnitude higher performance to achieve this goal*.

To achieve these orders of magnitude, we need to *push future computer architecture and software design to their limits to achieve higher performance*. In this work, we progress toward this goal: *we analyze the performance of a leading complex climate simulation code with more than 630k lines of Fortran code in detail*. This model will not only help us understand the compute and storage requirements of a candidate high-resolution simulation in detail but may also uncover scaling issues in the components themselves and guide code optimization efforts to "where the puck is going." Furthermore, our requirements models return the exact number of floating-point operations as well as information about data movement. Thus, *our requirements models can guide the design of next-generation supercomputers to optimally execute kilometer-scale climate simulations*.

The *Icosahedral Nonhydrostatic Weather and Climate Model (ICON)* is a complex modeling framework designed to capture all effects needed to accurately model the Earth. It is a software maintained by the community and led by a collaboration between the German Weather Service (DWD) and the Max Planck Institute for Meteorology and has hundreds of users and contributors aiming to become a unified global numerical weather and climate model. One of the main goals for the collaboration is to develop an accurate model code that scales to massively parallel supercomputers to achieve kilometer-scale resolution for global and regional forecasting [3].

As a *climate and weather modeling framework*, ICON supports a wide range of models, such as ocean, atmosphere, land, and so on, that can be *composed into configurations*. For example, numerically predicting the regional weather will not need to model oceans like a climate simulation model but may require modeling different physical effects (e.g., pollen).

Thus, the large number of components in ICON can be *configured into a runnable model, like Lego building blocks* that can be combined to model both a plane or a car.

We design a methodology to quickly derive performance models that capture the requirements as well as execution performance properties of specific ICON configurations. While these models differ for each configuration at hand, we follow ICON's philosophy and timer infrastructure to develop an easy-to-use performance modeling framework for all conceivable ICON configurations.

This framework enables us to conduct *back-of-the-envelope* calculations for a large-scale *30-year climate simulation run at high (1.23 km) resolution with ICON*. We show that this run (in the current implementation and configuration we study) *requires about 11 Zflop*. If we assume an optimistic hypothetical floating-point efficiency of 1% on an *exaflop/s system, we would require about 13 days of the full system to generate one simulation trajectory* (at about 2.4 simulated years per day [SYPD] throughput). Running with 2^{14} ($\approx$ 16k) Message Passing Interface (MPI) processes, the total communication volume at each process would be 3.66 PiB, making an average communication bandwidth of 3.25 GiB/s per process. Assuming we output seven 3D variables at 70 layers in 16-bit precision every six hours of simulated time, we *would require 14.4 PiB of storage*! This would equal to an *average I/O bandwidth of 12.8 GiB/s* to a file system. We see a huge potential to compress the output before writing [4, 5]. Assuming we run the job with 16k MPI processes, our model predicts a *problematic memory requirement per process of 95.7 GiB*. We suspect a memory scalability bug in the MPI communication parts of the code.

This is just one simple example of how the models can be used to derive a system design with specific network and file system bandwidths and floating-point performance numbers. More advanced uses of the model enable programmers to focus on which components become important at scale. One major insight is that *the relative importance of the dynamical core quickly grows relative to the physical parameterization due to the finer time stepping*. Thus, optimizations for large-scale runs should focus on the dynamical core.

10.1. Toward Machine Learning Acceleration

Artificial intelligence-based techniques will soon play an important role to improve climate simulations in speed and accuracy. Data-driven statistical machine learning predictions can replace pieces of a simulation ("ML inside"), replace full simulations, or postprocessing and analyses ("ML on top") [6, 7]. While this article does not directly consider these techniques, it addresses the most important gap toward enabling them: data to learn from. Today, *the lack of high-resolution data to train machine learning models is the biggest impediment to having accurate machine learning models*. Many models train at a coarse resolution of 0.25° (27.8 km at the equator), the resolution of the ERA-5 dataset [8]. Unfortunately, 0.25° resolution is not sufficient to model many important cloud phenomena [6]. In this work, we outline the computational requirements for producing high-resolution data that is needed to train high-precision climate machine learning models. We also address storage requirements while we note that the data could be streamed through a learning model without being stored, or it could be compressed significantly.

Furthermore, our performance models of a realistic production-level weather and climate code will enable researchers and practitioners to focus their attention to the most promising pieces for supplementation by artificial intelligence modules. Furthermore, the ICON-specific model can easily be generalized to other applications using a similar methodology. Thus, **our performance modeling work forms an important first step in the long journey toward high-resolution machine learning predictions in weather and climate sciences**.

10.2. ICON Grids

ICON discretizes the simulated domain using an icosahedral grid that can tile the spherical Earth relatively uniformly. Each ICON run requires a grid to model the two surface (horizontal) dimensions of the simulation that can be generated with the tool icongridgen. Icosahedral grids in ICON are created recursively by starting from a convex regular icosahedron with 20 faces and dividing the edges into n parts followed by k iterative edge bisections—the resulting grid is called RnBk.

Source: ICON Tutorial 2023

The figure on the right [3] illustrates the construction of a R2B1 grid: the original icosahedron is in red; the single edge division is shown in dotted black lines; and the final single bisection is shown with solid red lines. The number of grid points for an ICON mesh is thus $N = 20n^2 4^k$ and the grid resolution is approximately $\Delta x \approx 5050/(n \cdot 2^k)km$. The resulting grid is largely regular: by construction, each newly created point has six neighbors; however, the 12 points of the original icosahedron have only five neighbors and are often called "pentagon points." It is stored following the recursive cuts (k) first and then the "levels" resulting from the original edge bisections. Thus, the storage approximates a space-filling curve locally. The choice of n and k can be arbitrary when generating a grid at a specific resolution.

The number of neighboring grid cells around a central cell at cell-distance r is: $N_{N(r)} = 12\sum_{i=1}^{r} 6r(r+1)$. For example, $N_{N(1)} = 12$, $N_{N(2)} = 36$, $N_{N(3)} = 72$. This does not apply if pentagon points are within the neighborhood.

The actual ICON grid is a result of an optimization process that aims to reduce the impact of the irregularity at the pentagon points by "stretching" the grid to an ideal sphere with two pentagon points placed exactly at the North and South Poles, respectively. This procedure slightly deforms the grid cells but does not change their number of neighborhood relations and is thus not relevant for performance directly. Yet, the changed numeric properties may lead to a higher required resolution to resolve certain processes.

The grid is then instantiated into the third dimension by adding height coordinates on each cell, extending it into a vertical column. Since clouds are moving in nonhydrostatic models, the pressure is not simply a function of the height but depends on the mass of the air column above, which is computed based on the atmospheric state. This is illustrated in the figure on the right. Thus, ICON uses height-based coordinates that follow the terrain. The total number of levels is, like the horizontal grid configuration, a system parameter, called num_lev.

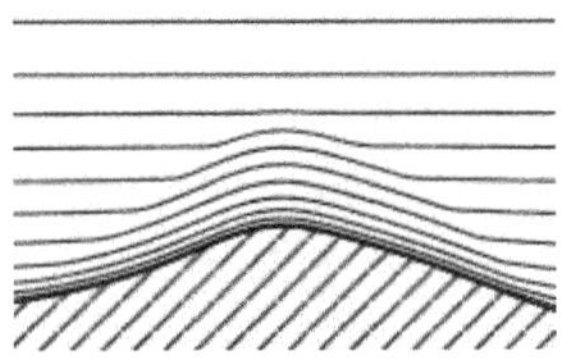

Source: ICON Tutorial 2023

10.3. ICON Time and Space Discretization

ICON simulates discrete time steps to advance the state of the grid. To solve the Euler equation, an approximation of the Navier Stokes equations, the dynamical core uses an explicit predictor–corrector solver for each time step. In space, all operations are explicit except for the vertical discretization, which is implicit and is solved using the Thomas algorithm. The vertical integration runs on each column independently.

With the explicit time-stepping scheme and the Courant–Friedrichs–Lewy (CFL) condition, the time step must be small enough such that the fastest waves in the system (i.e., sound waves) do not cross over adjacent grid points to produce correct results. However, not all physical equations are bound to sound waves like the air fluid solver. For example, transport processes can be solved on slower timescales given wind speeds and air densities. Thus, ICON runs the dynamical core with smaller time steps than the tracer (usually 5×).

ICON generally fixes the transport process as the default time step δt and defines all other time steps relative. For example, the dynamical core time step is then $\delta\tau = 5$ and is defined as the frequency increase relative to δt. Some physical process parametrizations (e.g., radiation, convection, gravity wave drag) can live on even longer timescales and reduce the frequency with respect to δt. Those can be chosen individually for each physical process model; for example, the expensive radiative transfer is often updated only every 30 min. There are some constraints; for example, it is recommended that radiation and convection are called at the same steps.

As a rule of thumb, the maximum time step δt allowed depends on the resolution: $\delta t < 9\,\delta x$ s/km [3] (assuming $\delta\tau = 5$). Furthermore, it is recommended to choose δt always smaller than thousands for numerical stability. δt is set by the configuration variable time.

10.4. ICON Components

ICON contains multiple models, but the basic structure is always divided into three major components: dynamical core, numerical advection or tracer transport, and physical parameterization. The dynamical core solves the governing equations for fluid motion forward in time, the advection aka tracer transport scheme moves entities (e.g., humidity and clouds) according to the fluid motion, and the physics emulate processes that are happening on scales too small for the grid (e.g., cloud formation). We separate the transport from the dynamical core due to its slower time stepping.

The tracer transport works on a number of tracers, where each models a different physical entity. Tracers are essentially three-dimensional fields (arrays) that track certain entities (e.g., dust, hail, etc.). The number and type of tracers is configured by the user. ICON offers different horizontal and vertical tracer implementations, and some may require smaller time steps for numerical stability, called "sub-cycling." We model all tracers (specific to a physics process configuration) as a single entity.

The physics processes are called at each time step after the grid has been updated by the dynamical core, horizontal diffusion, and tracer transport. ICON differentiates between fast and slow physics. Each fast physics process is called at each (tracer) time step, updates the variables, and passes the updated grid to the next fast physics process. Slow physics processes (e.g., cloud cover, radiation, gravity wave drags) are stepped forward in time independently as specified by the user. All physical processes are generally limited to one column and do not interact with neighboring columns.

ICON output data can be generated on different grids and supports restarting from a checkpoint. The user can specify an output time interval to determine the output frequency.

The components for any given configuration may be different and thus, the performance model will be specific to the configuration. Here, we provide a method to identify the different components such that they can be modeled independently to determine whether they become bottlenecks or not. While the dynamical core and the tracer are part of every configuration, the physical parameterizations are specific to each configuration. Below, we utilize two "aquaplanet" setups, one using the Atmosphere Earth System (AES) physics we received from the Max Planck Institute for Meteorology (MPI-M) and the German Climate Research Centre (DKRZ), as well as the Numerical Weather Prediction (NWP) physics we received from the EXCLAIM team at ETH Zurich and MeteoSwiss.

We first relate the overview structure above to the detailed timers in the code; we name the timers in brackets (timer). We identify kernels of interest and assign short names in square brackets [name]. The dynamical core consists of three main components: the nonhydrostatic solver (nh_solve), the nonhydrostatic diffusion operator (nh_diff), and the tracer (transport). We model the dynamical core with two phases [solv] for the substepped solver and [tran] for the diffusion and transport operators. The physics differs between the AES and NWP configurations.

The AES physical parameterization combines many different schemes. It also uses its own data representation and thus explicitly copies data from the dynamical core to the physics representation (dyn2phy, including boundary condition preparation [aes_bcs]) and back (phy2dyn) [pini]. In our current configuration, we use six physics parameterization schemes: (1) cloud cover (interface_aes_cov) [pcov], (2) radiation (interface_aes_rad) [prad], (3) radiative heating (interface_aes_rht) [prht], (4) vertical diffusion and surface (interface_aes_vdf) [pvdf], (5) (microphysics) graupel scheme (interface_cloud_mig) [pmig], and (6) WMO tropopause height (interface_aes_wmo) [ptro].

The call-sequence (and time tree) in the AES configuration is

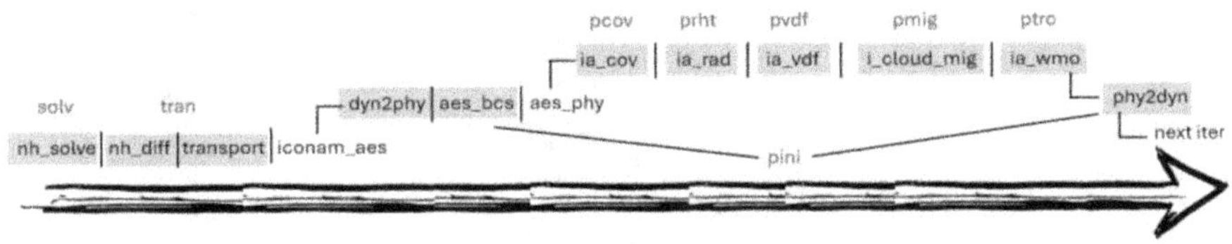

It shows one iteration of the time step loop, the associated icon timers, and our assigned phase names (in red—related to the gray-shaded timers). Vertical levels are call depth; for example, iconam_aes invokes dyn2phy.

The NWP physical parameterization uses several different schemes as well. The call-tree in the NWP configuration is

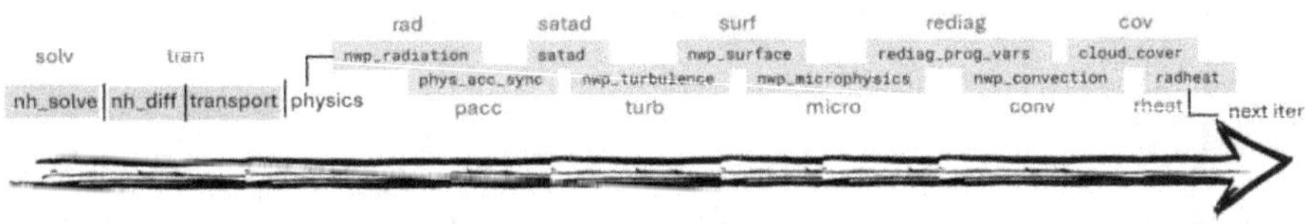

It shows one iteration of the time step loop, the associated icon timers, and our assigned phase names (in red—related to the gray-shaded timers). Here, we differentiate 10 physics kernels.

We currently do not model the static grid refinement in ICON because this is largely used in regional setups. Furthermore, we do not explicitly consider physics parameterizations that are not part of our setup. We also do not explicitly model physics executed on different grids; for example, a reduced radiation grid to reduce radiation computation overhead up to 2×. Those reduced grids may be part of a configuration but are not parametrized in the model. All those are simple to model with our following proposed methodology.

10.5. ICON Structure and Optimizations

The horizontal icosahedral grid does not have an obvious ordering and is stored in a one-dimensional (1D) array with an index for each cell that locally approximates a space-filling curve. Most arrays represent centers of the triangular grid cells, but some represent edges or vertices. To store three-dimensional variables, the 1D array is extended with a second dimension representing the vertical level. The 1D array representing the horizontal dimensions is split into chunks of configurable size nproma such that this 1D array is stored in two dimensions and the overall array is stored in the order (horizontal index in block, vertical level, index of the block) as illustrated in the figure [3]. This storage allows passing a full block, including the vertical levels, into a subroutine. Loops that iterate over grid cells, edges, or vertices are blocked in jb and jc for cache efficiency. The code uses indirect addressing to determine neighborhood relationships.

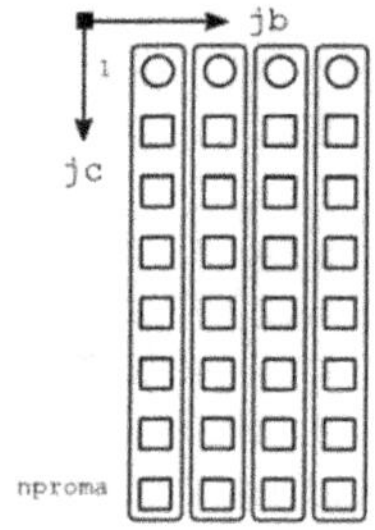

Source: ICON Tutorial 2023

ICON uses double precision per default and can be compiled to use mixed single and double precision calculations. Many local arrays in the dynamical core and some in tracer transport are then stored and computed as single precision variables.

10.6. ICON Parallelism

ICON offers OpenMP, OpenACC, and MPI parallelisms. We first describe the MPI parallelization.

ICON can use limited functional parallelism to decouple logical steps: worker ranks advance the simulation, I/O ranks write the output data, restart ranks write the asynchronous restart data, and prefetch ranks read the boundary data asynchronously. We will focus on a setup where we only use worker ranks and the simulation progress is halted during writing of the output data. The computational grid domain is distributed across the worker ranks.

The distribution is performed by cutting only the horizontal grid, that is, each process owns all vertical levels of any triangular cell it owns. ICON uses a balanced recursive latitude–longitude bisection to determine which process owns which cell: given the whole (potentially partially refined or regional) grid, it cuts it first into two balanced longitude halves. Then, it proceeds to cut those halves each into two balanced latitude halves (for uneven process counts, assign the odd process to an arbitrary partition). The procedure is applied recursively until the number of processes is exhausted. Mapping grid cells to processes is flexible, and one can think of other decompositions also, including the vertical grid. Here, we describe what is used in the configurations we analyzed.

The per-process grid is stored in the same arrays as in a sequential run. It distinguishes between inner cells and halo cells that are needed by neighboring processes. All inner cells are stored first in the array, and the halo cells are stored last.

10.7. Input Problem—Aquaplanet

While a configuration defines how to combine the available modules into a simulation, the input problem determines the scale of the simulation (e.g., the resolution in space and time). An input problem defines the parameters of the performance model. We are interested in scalability with increased grid resolution as well as an increased number of MPI processes. The main critical performance parameters [9] that are influenced by scaling these two entities are

Symbol	Description (name in configuration file)	Unit
δt	the main (transport) time step ("modelTimeStep")	s
δrad	radiation time step ("aes_phy_config(1)%dt_rad")	s
δvdf	vertical diffusion time step ("aes_phy_config(1)%dt_vdf")	s
δmig	graupel scheme time step ("aes_phy_config(1)%dt_mig")	s
δx	the effective resolution—specified by the grid refinement "RnBk," where $\delta x \approx 5050/(n \cdot 2^k)$ with the number of grid points $N = 20n^2 4^k$	km
T	overall simulated time	s
P	number of worker ranks in the MPI job	-

When varying δx, we use the nine preconfigured grids[a] with the following δt parameters:

δx [km]	n	k	n	Max δt [s]	Actual δt
315.63	2	3	5,120	2,840	1800
157.81	2	4	20,480	1,420	900
78.91	2	5	81,920	710	450
39.45	2	6	327,680	355	225
19.73	2	7	1,310,720	177	150
9.86	2	8	5,242,880	88	75
4.93	2	9	20,971,520	44	25
2.47	2	10	83,886,080	22	20
1.23	2	11	335,544,320	11	10

We use δrad = 1,800 s (30 mins), $\delta vdf = \delta t$, $\delta mig = \delta t$ (same as fast stepping), and nlev = 70 for all runs and adjust the used δt to be smaller than the maximum suggested and divide the physics time steps.

[a]From http://icon-downloads.mpimet.mpg.de/mpim_grids.xml

After some simple manipulation of the equations for N and δx, we find $N = 20 \cdot 5050^2 / \delta x^2$.

We model the requirements of each invocation of each phase in isolation as $R_{phase}(\delta x, P = 1) = a_{phase}/(\delta x^2 P) + b_{phase}$, where a_{phase} and b_{phase} are phase-specific constants to express its requirements per process. For sequential models, the optional parameter P is set to 1 and can be omitted. For example, for AES, $phase = \{solv, tran, pini, pcov, prht, pvdf, pmig, ptro\}$.

Now, for AES, we can then compute the overall requirements of an ICON run for a time interval T as:

$$\begin{aligned} R(\delta x,\ T, P = 1) = T/\delta t \cdot (&5R_{solv}(\delta x, P) + R_{tran}(\delta x, P) + R_{pini}(\delta x, P) + R_{pcov}(\delta x, P) \\ &+ \delta t/\delta rad \cdot R_{prad}(\delta x, P) + R_{prht}(\delta x, P) + \delta t/\delta vdf \cdot R_{pvdf}(\delta x, P) \\ &+ \delta t/\delta mig \cdot R_{pmig}(\delta x, P) + R_{ptro}(\delta x, P)) \end{aligned}$$

with $\delta t < 9\delta x$.

For the NWP configuration, we use the same δt and δx steps, but we vary the physical parameterization frequencies in step with δt: $\delta rad = 4 \cdot \delta t$, $\delta cov = 2 \cdot \delta t$, and $\delta conv = 2 \cdot \delta t$. For both the AES and NWP configurations, we halve T every time we decrease δt thus ensuring we are always simulating the same number of time steps:

$$\begin{aligned} R(\delta x, T, P = 1) = T/\delta t \cdot (&5\, R_{solv}(\delta x, P) + R_{tran}(\delta x, P) + \delta t/\delta conv\, R_{conv}(\delta x, P) \\ &+ \delta t/\delta cov\, R_{cov}(\delta x, P) + \delta t/\delta rad \cdot R_{rad}(\delta x, P) + 2R_{turb}(\delta x, P) \\ &+ R_{micro}(\delta x, P) + R_{satad}(\delta x, P) + R_{surf}(\delta x, P) + R_{rediag}(\delta x, P) \\ &+ R_{radheat}(\delta x, P) + R_{accum}(\delta x, P)) \end{aligned}$$

with $\delta t < 9\delta x$.

Thus, instantiating the rates in the general equation above, the requirements equation becomes:

$$\begin{aligned} R(\delta x,\ T,\ P = 1) = T/\delta t \cdot (&5\, R_{solv}(\delta x,\ P) + R_{tran}(\delta x,\ P) \\ &+ 0.5\, R_{conv}(\delta x,\ P) + 0.5\, R_{cov}(\delta x,\ P) + 0.25 \cdot R_{rad}(\delta x,\ P) \\ &+ 2R_{turb}(\delta x,\ P) + R_{micro}(\delta x,\ P) + R_{satad}(\delta x,\ P) + R_{surf}(\delta x,\ P) \\ &+ R_{rediag}(\delta x,\ P) + R_{radheat}(\delta x,\ P) + R_{accum}(\delta x,\ P)) \end{aligned}$$

with $\delta t < 9\delta x$.

We note that when using NWP, some physics components are also called once during initialization; therefore, an additional initialization requirement exists:

$$\begin{aligned} R_{init}(\delta x, P = 1) = &R_{conv}(\delta x, P) + R_{cov}(\delta x, P) + R_{rad}(\delta x, P) \\ &+ R_{satad}(\delta x, P) + R_{turb}(\delta x, P) \\ &+ R_{radheat}(\delta x, P) + R_{accum}(\delta x, P) \end{aligned}$$

For long enough simulation times, R_{init} should become negligible.

10.8. Requirements Modeling

Our first models will determine the requirements of the phases of ICON. Most of those are independent of the specific architecture. For example, the number of required floating point operations, the required memory, or the communication volume solely depends on the configuration, input problem, and the domain decomposition. Others, such as cache misses, depend on the architecture (cache size).

In the following, we will utilize hardware counters to *count the machine-independent requirements* for several executions with varying critical parameters. For this, we compile ICON version rc2.6.7 with the GNU compiler suite version 10.2.0 with the optimization flag "–O2."

10.8.1. *Required operation counts (sequential work)*

To collect performance counters, we extend ICON's timer infrastructure with LibLSB [10] with a small patch (<50 lines of code). We then count the total operations and parametrize the model: ${R^{op}}_{phase}(\delta x,\ P) = {a^{op}}_{phase}/(\delta x^2\, P)$ and we also count the floating point operations and parametrize the model: ${R^{fp}}_{phase}(\delta x,\ P) = {a^{fp}}_{phase}/(\delta x^2\, P)$.

When compiled in mixed precision, only the dyc phase uses fp32. In that case, 14% to 15% of the dyc flops are fp32, all others are fp64. The actual coefficients for a^{fp} and a^{op} for AES are shown in the following table:

Phase	a^{fp} [Tflop]	a^{op} [Top]	Flop/op ratio
solv	19.23	811.37	2.37%
tran	58.00	1,444.53	4.02%
pini	8.43	255.73	3.30%
pcov	0.12	5.78	2.03%
prad	1,491.12	18,301.39	8.15%
prht	0.37	14.63	2.55%
pvdf	34.13	828.85	4.12%
pmig	5.94	96.11	6.18%
ptro	3.50	14.98	23.37%

For NWP, the coefficients are

Phase	a^{fp} [Tflop]	a^{op} [Top]	Flop/op ratio
solv	16.64	804.36	2.07%
tran	43.14	986.63	4.37%

(Continued)

Phase	a^{fp} [Tflop]	a^{op} [Top]	Flop/op ratio
cov	5.09	44.89	11.34%
rad	705.40	9,691.36	7.28%
conv	11.17	171.78	6.50%
micro	7.42	60.81	12.20%
satad	2.77	57.71	4.80%
turb	10.51	185.31	5.67%
phys_acc_sync	2.42	66.32	3.65%
surface	0.01	0.23	6.46%
rediag	3.13	37.12	8.43%
radheat	3.41	24.36	14.00%

The quality of all fits is with an R^2 of >0.998 and thus very accurate. The table also shows the ratio of total operations to floating-point operations for the different phases. Note that the floating-point operations are likely to be bound to the algorithm, while the total operations depend on the target architecture as well as the compiler.

The cost of the radiation schemes in AES and NWP differs by more than a factor of two, which is largely due to the differences in the schemes and different implementations. The slight difference in the cost of the solver (dynamical core) is likely due to the difference in the way the Rayleigh damping near the model top is used. The AES configuration has a larger number of vertical levels in the damping layer, thereby adding to the extra cost.

This model is already useful to understand the compute requirements for various configurations. For example, let us model the requirements for a run for 30 years (946 Msec) with a 1.2-km resolution and our aquaplanet configuration from above. We choose $\delta t =$ 10 s, which makes 94.6 M transport time steps and 437 M dycore time steps. So we can parametrize the total flop required equation to

$$
\begin{aligned}
R(1.2,\ 946M) = 94.6M \cdot (5\, R_{dyn}(\delta x) + R_{tran}(\delta x) + R_{pini}(\delta x) + R_{pcov}(\delta x) \\
+ 1/180 \cdot R_{prad}(\delta x) + R_{prht}(\delta x) + 1/90 \cdot R_{pvdf}(\delta x) \\
+ 1/90 \cdot R_{pmig}(\delta x) + R_{ptro}(\delta x)).
\end{aligned}
$$

The resulting requirements for AES are listed in the following table (in Zettaops, i.e., 1e21 ops):

Phase	Zflop	Zop	Share of total
solv	5.9857	252.4956	54.85%
tran	3.6100	89.9067	33.08%
pini	0.5246	15.9166	4.81%

pcov	0.0073	0.3597	0.07%
prad	0.5156	6.3281	4.73%
prht	0.0232	0.9105	0.21%
pvdf	0.0236	0.5732	0.22%
pmig	0.0041	0.0665	0.04%
ptro	0.2178	0.9322	2.00%
sum	**10.9119**	**367.4891**	**100.00%**

For NWP, we get

Phase	Zflop	Zop	Share of total
solv	5.1774	250.3140	48.76%
tran	2.6852	61.4073	25.29%
cov	0.0035	0.0310	0.03%
rad	0.2439	3.3510	2.30%
conv	0.0077	0.1188	0.07%
micro	0.4619	3.7845	4.35%
satad	0.1724	3.5920	1.62%
turb	1.3084	23.0668	12.32%
phys_acc_sync	0.1508	4.1275	1.42%
surface	0.0009	0.0140	0.01%
rediag	0.1947	2.3106	1.83%
radheat	0.2123	1.5162	2.00%
sum	**10.6191**	**353.6338**	**100.00%**

10.8.2. *Communication characteristics*

For communication, we consider three increasingly complex aspects: (1) the communication pattern, (2) the total communication volume per phase, and (3) the message count and size distribution. We collect the data using liballprof (a part of the LogGOPSim toolchain [11]) to profile each call to any MPI function during parallel program runs and postprocess those using bespoke Python scripts.

We first illustrate the decomposition and messaging on an idealized square domain with periodic boundary conditions in both dimensions (the triangular grid will be similar).

For a $\sqrt{N}x\sqrt{N}$ square domain, we see that for the special case with two processes, there is only one message of size $2\sqrt{N}$ (left and right boundary) exchanged. Beginning with four processes, each process exchanges the top and bottom as well as the left and right boundaries with four other processes; the size of each exchange is $\sqrt{N}/2$. For eight processes, each process exchanges two messages of size $\sqrt{N}/2$ for top and bottom, and two messages of size $\sqrt{N}/4$ for left and right. For 16 processes, each process exchanges messages of size $\sqrt{N/4}$ with four neighbors.

We only consider powers-of-two process-counts beginning from four processes in our modeling. If P is a power of four, each process sends four messages of size $\sqrt{N}/\sqrt{P}$ to each of the neighbors. If P is a power of two but not a power of four, then each process sends two messages of size $\sqrt{N}/\sqrt{2P}$ and two messages of size $2\sqrt{N}/\sqrt{2P}$ to four neighbors.

Thus, each process has exactly four faces for $P \geq 16$ due to the decomposition symmetry. The actual number of communication partners varies between four and 10 across different ranks. This is due to the details of the distributed halo zones and the icosahedral grid, where most elements have six neighbors, but some elements have five neighbors. Shown in Fig.10.1.

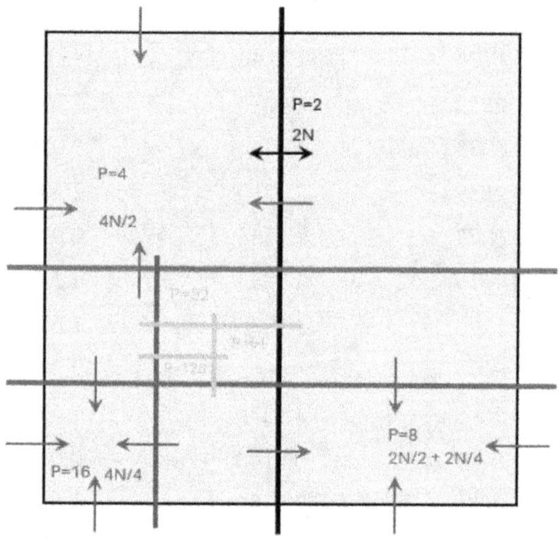

P	C
2	$2\sqrt{N}$
4	$\frac{4\sqrt{N}}{2}$
8	$\frac{2\sqrt{N}}{2}+\frac{2\sqrt{N}}{4}$
16	$\frac{4\sqrt{N}}{4}$
32	$\frac{2\sqrt{N}}{4}+\frac{2\sqrt{N}}{8}$
64	$\frac{4\sqrt{N}}{8}$
128	$\frac{2\sqrt{N}}{16}+\frac{2\sqrt{N}}{8}$
256	$\frac{4\sqrt{N}}{16}$

Fig. 10.1 Neighborhood relationship in parallel domain decomposition

Since N depends on δx, we model the communication volume per process per phase as: $C_{phase}(\delta x,\ P) = a^{com}{}_{phase}/(\delta x \cdot \sqrt{P}) + b^{com}{}_{phase} \cdot \sqrt{P}$ for P being a power of four, where $a^{com}{}_{phase}$, $b^{com}{}_{phase}$ are phase-specific constants to express its requirements per process.

In NWP, only the solv, tran, and one physics parameterization phase (phys_acc_sync) communicate. We model the communication volume for those and provide the coefficients in the table below:

Phase	a^{com} [MB]	b^{com} [KB]
solv	757.20	0.2918
tran	1375.77	0.4176
phys	949.77	0.2803

Here again, the R^2 is bigger than 0.998 indicating an excellent fit. For the 30-year simulation with a resolution of 1.23 km, the following communication volumes would be expected:

Phase	a^{com} [PB]	b^{com} [TB]	Share of total
solv	2.27	3.53	61.84%
tran	0.82	5.06	22.58%
phys	0.57	3.39	15.58%
sum	**3.66**	**11.98**	**100.00%**

The message size distribution is more complex, and we will model only bounds and show distributions empirically. We show examples for a fixed grid and varying numbers of processes (strong scaling) as well as a varying grid and fixed number of processes.

We first vary the grid size, while keeping the number of processes constant (P = 8). The results shown in Fig. 10.2, in order, R2B3 (top left), R2B4 (top right), R2B5 (bottom left), R2B6 (bottom right). We notice that the distribution remains similar, but the size of messages being exchanged roughly doubles with each increase in grid size.

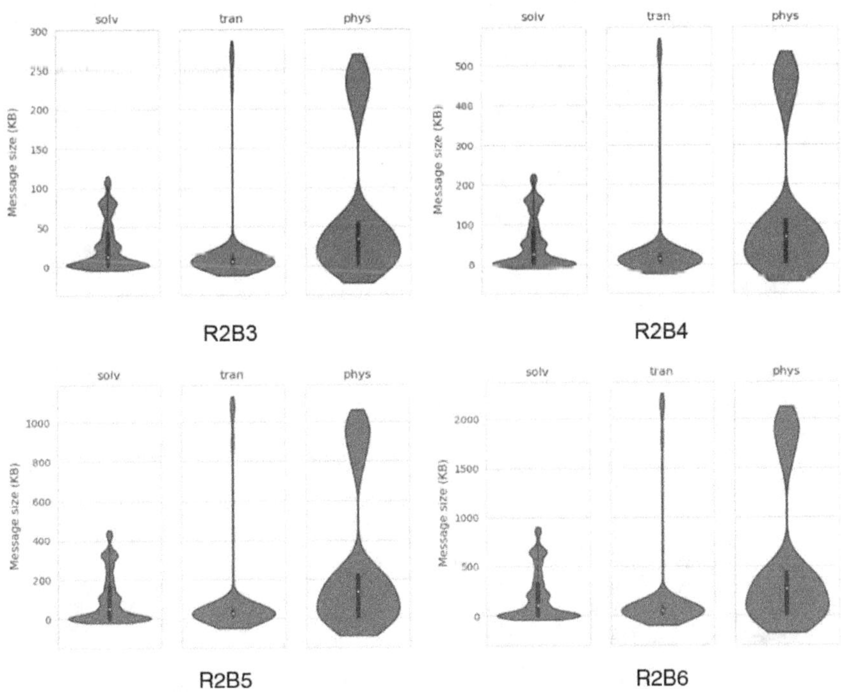

Fig. 10.2 Message size distributions for different domain sizes on eight processes

The same cannot be said about the variation of MPI processes, which has a more complex impact on the distribution of message sizes and their counts and cannot be easily fit into an analytical expression. This is also a result of the icosahedral (triangle) decomposition in which the neighborhood relations differ across processes. Fig. 10.3 shows a constant grid size for varying numbers of MPI processes. The results show, in order, two processes (top left), four processes (top right), eight processes (middle right), 16 processes (middle left), 32 processes (bottom left), and 1,024 processes (bottom right):

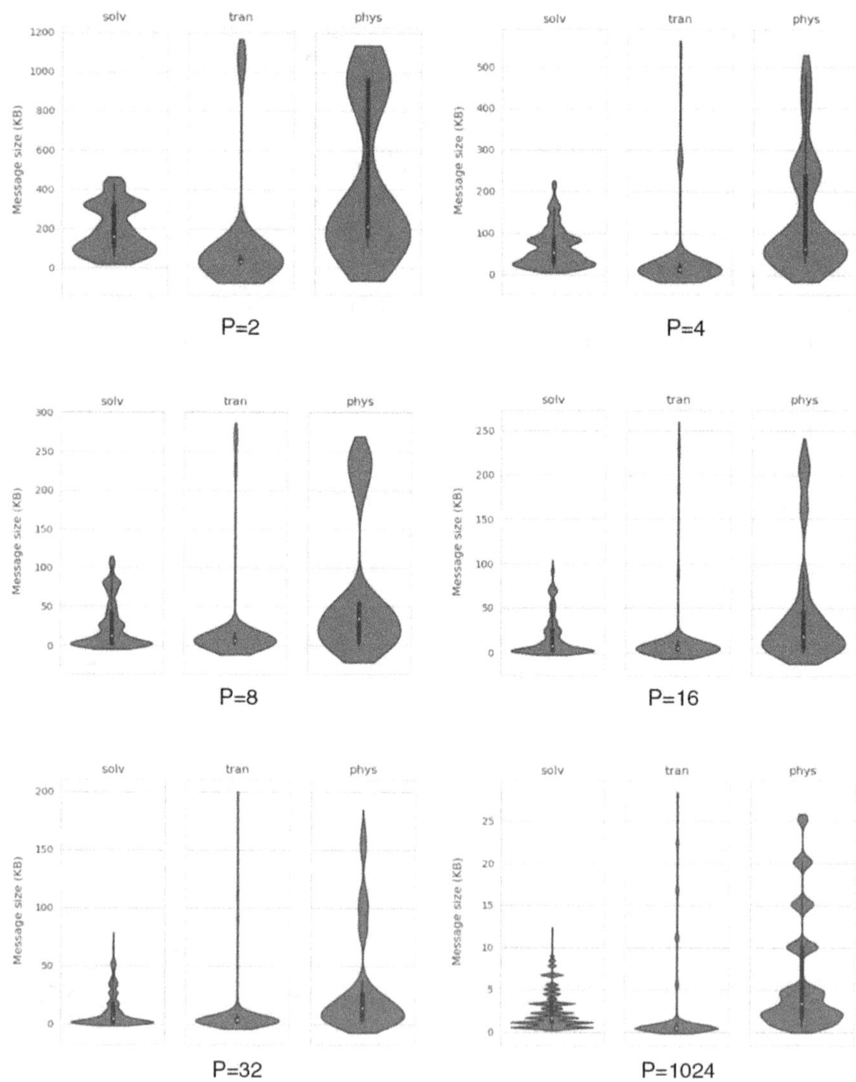

Fig. 10.3 Message size distributions for different numbers of processes on R2B3 domain

10.8.3. *File I/O volume*

ICON can write the simulation data in multiple formats to disk. For the output, one defines a variable list and output intervals for each variable. The output size is simply the number of written elements per step E times the number of output time steps per variable T_o. The number of points per level is $N = 20 \cdot 5050^2 / \delta x^2$ and $E = N \cdot nlev$.

For example, for a 30-year simulation at approximately 1-km resolution with an output time step of 15 min and values in FP16, the amount of storage needed per 2D variable is 705 TiB and per 3D variable with 70 levels would be 49 PiB. Usually, different variables are written at different intervals. For example, wind speed requires high-frequency output, while temperature or humidity can often be recorded at lower frequencies.

10.8.4. *Memory requirements*

We also consider maximum memory requirements as a machine to execute ICON must have at least this amount of memory available for a run. For this, we measured the maximum memory consumption (VmPeak in Linux) through various run configurations depending on N (δx) and P.

As expected, the memory consumption per MPI rank grows with the grid and decreases with an increasing number of MPI ranks (modeled by a). We also observe a term in the memory consumption that grows with the number of MPI ranks (modeled by b), explained by the local data structures required by each MPI process that depend on the total number of processes as well as a sizable constant memory requirement (modeled by c). The memory requirement M can therefore be expressed as follows: $M(\delta x,\ P) = a_M/(\delta x^2\, P) + b_M \cdot P + c_M$. In our configuration, we found the following concrete values: $M(\delta x,\ P) = 20 \cdot 5050^2 \cdot 1.01/(\delta x^2\, P) + 4.6 \cdot P + 915.6$ [MiB].

10.9. Summary and Conclusions

Our performance model enables scientists to fully assess requirements for climate simulations with the ICON code. It not only counts the number of required floating point operations accurately, but it also counts messaging volume and I/O volumes. The relative magnitude of these requirements will allow application users to configure each simulation run to a particular system, and it will also allow system designers to optimize future supercomputers to the ICON weather and climate workloads.

Specifically, our model allows scientists to reason about the computational requirements for the next step in global kilometer-scale climate simulations.

Acknowledgments

We thank W. Sawyer, T. Jahns, F. Prill, and B. Stevens for useful discussions that improved the manuscript.

References

1. N. Gruber, P. W. Boyd, T. L. Frölicher, et al. Biogeochemical extremes and compound events in the ocean. *Nature*. **600**, 395–407 (2021). https://doi.org/10.1038/s41586-021-03981-7.
2. P. Forster, T. Storelvmo, K. Armour, et al. The Earth's energy budget, climate feedbacks, and climate sensitivity. The Physical Science Basis. Contribution of Working Group I to the Sixth Assessment Report of the Intergovernmental Panel on Climate Change (2021).
3. F. Prill, D. Reinert, D. Rieger, and G. Zängl. Working with the ICON Model. (Mar, 2023). https://doi.org/10.5676/DWD_pub/nwv/icon_tutorial2023.
4. L. Huang and T. Hoefler. Compressing multidimensional weather and climate data into neural networks. In *The Eleventh International Conference on Learning Representations* (May, 2023).
5. M. Kloewer, M. Razinger, J. J. Dominguez, P. D. Düben, and T. N. Palmer, Compressing atmospheric data into its real information content, *Nat. Comput. Sci.* **1**, 713–724 (2021). https://doi.org/10.1038/s43588-021-00156-2.
6. T. Hoefler, B. Stevens, A. F. Prein, et al. Earth virtualization engines: A technical perspective, *Comput. Sci. Eng.* **25**(3), 50–59 (May–June, 2023). https://doi.org/10.1109/MCSE.2023.3311148.
7. P. Bauer, P. D. Dueben, M. Chantry, et al. Bjorn Stevens: Deep learning and a changing economy in weather and climate prediction, *Nat. Rev. Earth Environ.* **4**(1), 507–509 (Aug, 2023).
8. H. Hersbach, B. Bell, P. Berrisford, and S. Hirahara, The ERA5 global reanalysis. *Q. J. R. Meteorol. Soc.* **146**, 1999–2049 (2020).
9. G. Bauer, S. Gottlieb, and T. Hoefler. Performance modeling and comparative analysis of the MILC lattice QCD application su3 rmd. In *Proc. 2012 12th IEEE/ACM Int. Symposium on Cluster, Cloud and Grid Computing (ccgrid 2012)*, pp. 652–659, Ottawa, Canada, (May, 2012). IEEE Computer Society, ISBN: 978-0-7695-4691-9.
10. T. Hoefler and R. Belli. Scientific benchmarking of parallel computing systems. In *Proc. Int. Conference for High Performance Computing, Networking, Storage and Analysis (SC15)*, pp. 73:1–73:12, ACM, Austin, TX, USA (Nov, 2015). ISBN: 978-1-4503-3723-6.
11. T. Hoefler, T. Schneider, and A. Lumsdaine. LogGOPSim: Simulating large-scale applications in the LogGOPS model. In *Proc. 19th ACM Int. Symposium on High Performance Distributed Computing*, pp. 597–604, ACM, Chicago, Illinois (Jun, 2010). ISBN: 978-1-60558-942-8.
12. P. Forster, T. Storelvmo, K. Armour, et al. *The Earth's Energy Budget, Climate Feedbacks, and Climate Sensitivity*. In eds. V. Masson-Delmotte, P. Zhai, A. Pirani, et al. *Climate Change 2021: The Physical Science Basis. Contribution of Working Group I to the Sixth Assessment Report of the Intergovernmental Panel on Climate Change*, pp. 923–1054, Cambridge, New York (2021).
13. N. Gruber, P. W. Boyd, T. L. Frölicher, and M. Vogt, Biogeochemical extremes and compound events in the ocean, *Nature*. **600**, 395–407 (2021). https://doi.org/10.1038/s41586-021-03981-7.
14. T. Hoefler and R. Belli. Scientific benchmarking of parallel computing systems. In *Proc. Int. Conference for High Performance Computing, Networking, Storage and Analysis (SC15)*, pp. 73:1–73:12, ACM, USA, (Nov, 2015). ISBN: 978-1-4503-3723-6.
15. L. Huang and T. Hoefler. Compressing multidimensional weather and climate data into neural networks. In *Eleventh Int. Conference on Learning Representations*, p. 12538, Cornell University, New York (May, 2023). https://doi.org/10.48550/arXiv.2210.12538.

https://doi.org/10.1142/9789819813049_0011

CHAPTER 11

Dimension Walks on Generalized Spaces

Ana Paula Peron[1,2,*] and Emilio Porcu[2,3,†]

[1]*Department of Mathematics, University of São Paulo, São Carlos, Brazil*
[2]*Department of Mathematics, Khalifa University, Abu Dhabi, UAE*
[3]*ADIA Lab, Abu Dhabi, UAE*
[*]*Corresponding author. E-mail: apperon@icmc.usp.br;* [†]*Contributing authors: emilio.porcu@ku.ac.ae*
This paper is dedicated to Daryl J. Daley and Robert Schaback. Such beautiful minds.

There has been an increasing interest in stochastic processes that are defined over product spaces in many branches of applied sciences, including climate modeling, atmospheric sciences, geophysical science, and even finance. Our work provides the mathematical foundations for certain classes of stochastic processes that are defined over special classes of product spaces. Specifically, let $\boldsymbol{d}, \boldsymbol{k}$ be positive integers. We call generalized spaces the Cartesian product of the $\boldsymbol{d}$-dimensional sphere, $\mathbb{S}^{\boldsymbol{d}}$, with the $\boldsymbol{k}$-dimensional Euclidean space, $\mathbb{R}^{k}$. We consider the class $\mathcal{P}\left(\mathbb{S}^{d} \times \mathbb{R}^{k}\right)$ of continuous functions $\varphi : [-\mathbf{1}, \mathbf{1}] \times [\mathbf{0}, \infty) \to \mathbb{R}$ such that the mapping $C : \left(\mathbb{S}^{d} \times \mathbb{R}^{k}\right)^{2} \to \mathbb{R}$, defined as $C\left((x, y), (x', y')\right) = \varphi\left(\cos\theta\left(x, x'\right), \|y - y'\|\right), (x, y),\ (x', y') \in \mathbb{S}^{d} \times \mathbb{R}^{k}$, is positive definite. We propose linear operators that allow for walks through dimensions within generalized spaces while preserving positive definiteness.

Keywords: Positive Definite Functions, Montée Operators, Descente Operators, Spheres, Euclidean Spaces, Generalized Product.

11.1. Introduction

11.1.1. *Context*

The paper deals with positive definite functions over what we term *generalized spaces*, that is, product spaces that involve manifolds of different natures. In fact, those are defined here as the Cartesian product of the k-dimensional Euclidean space with a d-dimensional unit sphere. Albeit this work is of clear mathematical essence, it provides the foundations of stochastic processes over product spaces as certified by the increasing interest in several branches of applied sciences. Some motivations to consider the present framework are listed below.

(a) There has been an increasing interest from several branches of statistics, machine learning, and finance, for positive definite functions defined over these product spaces, and the reader is referred to the recent review by Porcu et al. [1]. The applications to real cases are ubiquitous, ranging from climate and atmospheric sciences to deep learning on manifolds.

As far as finance is concerned, Gaussian processes play a central role in financial modeling. The field of econometrics has devoted much effort to the modeling of financial time series [2]. The Brownian motion is essential to the pricing of financial derivatives [3]. The Ornstein–Uhlenbeck process is often used to develop investment and trading strategies [4]. Gaussian processes are one-dimensional applications of the general concept of Gaussian random field (GRF). We motivate some of the uses of GRFs in finance. A key feature of financial datasets is time and spatial dependence. Coetaneous observations from variables in close proximity tend to be more similar. For example, returns from US stocks last month are more similar to returns from US stocks this month than returns from US stocks 1 year ago or returns from Chinese stocks last month. Willinger et al. [5] noted that a Brownian motion with drift does not replicate the time dependence observed in asset returns. Not surprisingly, GRFs have attracted considerable interest among researchers interested in modeling the joint time-space dynamics of financial processes. To cite a few examples, Refs. [6] and [7] modeled the term structure of interest rates as a two-dimensional random field. In their models, time increments are independent, while the correlation structure between bond yields of different maturities can be modeled with great flexibility. Kimmel [8] enhanced this approach by adding a state-dependent volatility. Albeverio et al. [9] introduced Lévy fields to the modeling of yield curves. Özkan and Schmidt [10] applied random fields to incorporate credit risk into the modeling of yield curves. As important as the term structure of interest rates is, it is not the only financial application of Gaussian fields. At least two further applications stand out: option pricing and actuarial modeling. For example, Hainaut [11] proposes an alternative model for asset prices with sub-exponential, exponential, and hyper-exponential autocovariance structures. Hainaut sees price processes as conditional Gaussian fields indexed by time. Under this framework, option prices can be computed using the technique of the change of numeraire. Biffis and Millossovich [12] applied random fields to modeling the intensity of mortality in an attempt to incorporate cross-generation effects. Biagini et al. [13] built on that work to price and hedge life insurance liabilities.

(b) Several branches of spatial statistics and computer sciences are interested in the simulation of random processes defined over generalized spaces, and we refer the reader to Ref. [14]. It turns out that the use of these operators becomes crucial when associated with turning band techniques [15], which allow for simulation of a given random process from projections on lower dimensional spaces.

(c) Projection operators for radial positive definite functions allowed to build positive definite functions that are compactly supported over balls embedded in k-dimensional Euclidean spaces. This inspired a fertile literature from spatial statistics with the goal of achieving accurate estimates while allowing for computational scalability. For instance, the tapering approach [16] is substantially based on this idea.

(d) There is a fertile literature from projection operators for symmetric (or radially symmetric) distributions, where radial symmetry is intended with respect to the composition of a given candidate function with the classical α-norms [17].

11.1.2. *Literature review*

Let $\mathbb{R}^k$ denote the k-dimensional Euclidean space, and let $\mathbb{S}^d$ be the d-dimensional unit sphere embedded in $\mathbb{R}^{d+1}$. Let $\|\cdot\|$ denote Euclidean distance and $\theta(x,y) := \arccos(\langle x,y\rangle)$ denote the geodesic distance in $\mathbb{S}^d$, with $\langle .,.\rangle$ denoting the dot product in $\mathbb{R}^{d+1}$. A continuous function $C : \mathbb{R}^k \to \mathbb{R}$ is called radially symmetric if there exists a continuous function $f : [0,\infty) \to \mathbb{R}$ such that $C(x) = f \circ \|x\|, x \in \mathbb{R}^k$, with $\circ$ denoting composition. The function f is called the radial part of C. Radial symmetry is known as *isotropy* in spatial statistics [18]. A function $C : \mathbb{S}^d \times \mathbb{S}^d \to \mathbb{R}$ is called geodesically isotropic if $C(x,y) = g \circ \theta(x,y)$ for some continuos function $g : [0,\pi] \to \mathbb{R}$.

Positive definite functions that are radially symmetric over k-dimensional Euclidean spaces have a long history that can be traced back to Ref. [19]. Projection operators that map a positive definite radial mapping from $\mathbb{R}^k$ into $\mathbb{R}^{k\pm h}$, for h a positive integer, have been considered in Matheron's clavier spherique [15, 20]. Matheron coined the terms *descente* and *montée* to define special operators that will be described throughout. The terms originate from an appealing physical interpretation in a mining context. These projection operators have then been investigated by Ref. [21], and subsequently by Refs. [22–24] in the context of positive definite radial functions that are additionally compactly supported on balls embedded in $\mathbb{R}^k$ with given radii. The work by Daley and Porcu [18] provides a general perspective of such operators, in concert with some generalizations of the previously mentioned works. These linear operators have turned out to be very useful to establish criteria of the Pólya type for radially symmetric positive definite functions [25], as well as in the definition of multiradial positive definite functions [26]. In probability theory, similar projection operators turned useful in the seminal paper by Ref. [17] and in Ref. [27].

Positive definite functions that are geodesically isotropic on d-dimensional spheres have been characterized in Ref. [28]. Projection operators for this class of functions have been studied to a limited extent only, and we refer to the recent papers by Ref. [29] and more recently to the same authors [30, 31]. Properties of these operators have then been inspected in Ref. [32].

11.1.3. *The problem and our contribution*

The characterization of projection operators on product spaces of the type $\mathbb{S}^d \times \mathbb{R}^k$ has been elusive so far. The only exception is Ref. [33], who consider the product space $\mathbb{S}^d \times \mathbb{R}$, and projections that are defined marginally for the sphere only.

Our paper contributes to the literature as follows. In Section 11.2, we provide the notations and basic literature. In Section 11.3, we define the Descente and Montée operators on the generalized space $\mathbb{S}^d \times \mathbb{R}^k$. The main results are statement in Section 11.4, and their proofs are in Appendix A.

11.2. Notations and Background

Let X, Y be nonempty sets. A function $C : (X \times Y)^2 \to \mathbb{R}$ is called positive definite if, for any finite system $\{a_k\}_{k=1}^N \subset \mathbb{R}$ and points $\{(x_k, y_k)\}_{k=1}^N \subset X \times Y$, the following inequality is preserved:

$$\sum_{k=1}^{N} \sum_{h=1}^{N} a_k C\left((x_k, y_k), (x_h, y_h)\right) a_h \geq 0.$$

We deal with the case $X = \mathbb{S}^d$ and $Y = \mathbb{R}^k$, for d and k being positive integers. Additionally, we suppose C to be continuous and that there exists a continuous function $\varphi : [-1, 1] \times [0, \infty) \to \mathbb{R}$ such that

$$C\left((x, y), (x', y')\right) = \varphi\left(\cos\theta\left(x, x'\right), \|y - y'\|\right), (x, y), (x', y') \in \mathbb{S}^d \times \mathbb{R}^k. \tag{11.1}$$

We call $\mathcal{P}\left(\mathbb{S}^d \times \mathbb{R}^k\right)$ the class of such functions, φ. Analogously, we call $\mathcal{P}\left(\mathbb{S}^d\right)$ the class of continuous functions $\psi : [-1, 1] \to \mathbb{R}$ such that for the function C in Eq. (11.1) it is true that, for $y = y'$, $C\left((x, y), (x', y)\right) = \varphi\left(\cos\theta\left(x, x'\right), 0\right) = \psi\left(\cos\theta\left(x, x'\right)\right)$. The class $\mathcal{P}\left(\mathbb{R}^k\right)$ is defined analogously. The classes $\mathcal{P}\left(\mathbb{R}^k\right)$ and $\mathcal{P}\left(\mathbb{S}^d\right)$ have been characterized by Refs. [19] and [28], respectively. The class $\mathcal{P}\left(\mathbb{S}^d \times \mathbb{R}^k\right)$ has been characterized by Ref. [34] through a uniquely determined expansion of the type

$$\varphi(x, t) = \sum_{n=0}^{\infty} f_n^d(t) C_n^{(d-1)/2}(x), (x, t) \in [-1, 1] \times [0, \infty),$$

where the functions f_n^d belong to $\mathcal{P}\left(\mathbb{R}^k\right)$, $n \in \mathbb{Z}_+$, and

$$\sum_{n=0}^{\infty} f_n^d(0)\, C_n^{(d-1)/2}(1) < \infty. \tag{11.2}$$

The expansion above is uniformly convergent on $[-1, 1] \times [0, \infty)$. The coefficients functions f_n^d are called d-Schoenberg functions of φ. The functions $C_n^{(d-1)/2}$ are the Gegenbauer polynomials of degree n associated with the index $(d - 1)/2$ [35].

Proposition 3.8 in Ref. [34] shows that if φ belongs to the class $\mathcal{P}\left(\mathbb{S}^d \times \mathbb{R}^k\right)$, then it is continuously differentiable with respect to the first variable.

It is also important to note that a continuous function $x \in [-1, 1] \mapsto \varphi(x, t)$ has an Abel summable expansion for each $t \in [0, \infty)$ in the form [see the proof of Theorem 3.3 in Ref. [34]

$$\varphi(x, t) \sim \sum_{n=0}^{\infty} f_n^d(t)\, C_n^{(d-1)/2}(x), \tag{11.3}$$

where

$$f_n^d(t) = \varsigma_n^d \int_{-1}^{1} \varphi(x, t)\, C_n^{(d-1)/2}(x)(1 - x^2)^{d/2-1}\, dx, \tag{11.4}$$

and ς_n^d are positive constants.

11.2.1. *Some useful facts*

Arguments in Ref. [19] prove that, for every $n = 0, 1, \ldots$, each function $f_n^d \in \mathcal{P}\left(\mathbb{R}^k\right)$ in Eq. (11.2) admits a uniquely determined Riemann–Stieltjes integral representation of the form

$$f_n^d(t) = \int_0^\infty \Omega_k(tr)\, dF_n(r), \quad t \in [0, \infty), \tag{11.5}$$

where F_n is a non-negative bounded measure on $[0, \infty)$. The function $\Omega_k : [0, \infty) \to \mathbb{R}$ is given by

$$\Omega_k(t) = \Gamma\left(\frac{k}{2}\right)\left(\frac{2}{t}\right)^{(k-2)/2} J_{(k-2)/2}(t), \tag{11.6}$$

where J_ν is the Bessel function of the first kind of order ν given by

$$J_\nu(t) = \left(\frac{t}{2}\right)^\nu \sum_{m=0}^\infty \frac{(-1)^m}{m!\Gamma(m+\nu+1)}\left(\frac{t}{2}\right)^{2m}.$$

We follow Ref. [18], and we call F_n the k-Schoenberg measure of f_n^d. We also note that we are abusing notation when writing F_n instead of F_n^d. This last notation will not be used unless explicitly needed.

Some technicalities will be exposed here to allow for a neater exposition. The derivative function of the function Ω_k is uniformly bounded, and it is given by (see Refs. [18, 24, 26]).

$$\frac{d\Omega_k}{dt}(t) = \Omega_k'(t) = -\frac{1}{k}t\Omega_{k+2}(t), \quad t \geq 0. \tag{11.7}$$

Also,

$$|\Omega_k(t)| < 1 = \Omega_k(0), \quad t > 0. \tag{11.8}$$

Since $\lim_{t\to\infty}\Omega_k(t) = 0$ for $k > 0$ (see Ref. [18]), we have

$$\int_t^\infty u\Omega_k(u)\, du = (k-2)\,\Omega_{k-2}(t), \quad t \geq 0. \tag{11.9}$$

Some properties of Gegenbauer polynomials will turn out to be useful throughout. For instance, we can invoke 4.7.14 in Ref. [35] to infer that

$$\frac{dC_n^\lambda}{dx}(x) = \left(C_n^\lambda\right)'(x) = \delta_\lambda C_{n-1}^{\lambda+1}(x), \quad -1 \leq x \leq 1, \tag{11.10}$$

and, as a consequence

$$\int_{-1}^x C_n^\lambda(x)\, dx = \frac{1}{\delta_\lambda}\left(C_{n+1}^{\lambda-1}(x) - C_{n+1}^{\lambda-1}(-1)\right), \tag{11.11}$$

where

$$\delta_\lambda = \begin{cases} 2\lambda, & \lambda > -1/2 (\lambda \neq 0), \\ 2, & \lambda = 0. \end{cases} \tag{11.12}$$

Theorem 7.32.1 and Equation 4.7.3 in Ref. [35] show that, for $\lambda > -1/2$,

$$\left|C_n^{\lambda}(x)\right| \leq C_n^{\lambda}(1) = \frac{\Gamma(n+2\lambda)}{\Gamma(n+1)\Gamma(2\lambda)}, \quad x \in [-1,1]. \tag{11.13}$$

Also, it is true that

$$\frac{C_{n+j}^{\lambda-k}(1)}{C_n^{\lambda}(1)} \leq \frac{\Gamma(2\lambda)}{\Gamma(2\lambda-2k)} := \varrho_{\lambda,k}, \quad \forall n \in \mathbb{Z}_+. \tag{11.14}$$

The following inequality (see Ref. [36]) will be repeatedly used in the manuscript:

$$|f(t)| \leq f(0), \quad t \in [0,\infty), \quad f \in \mathcal{P}\left(\mathbb{R}^k\right).$$

We will also make use of the following fact: if $\varphi : [-1,1] \times \mathbb{R} \to \mathbb{R}$ has a derivative φ_x with respect to the first variable for each $t \in [0,\infty)$ and if both functions have Gegenbauer expansions of the form

$$\varphi_x(x,t) \sim \sum_{n=0}^{\infty} f_n^{\lambda}(t)\, C_n^{\lambda}(x), \quad \varphi_x(x,t) \sim \sum_{n=0}^{\infty} \tilde{f}_n^{\lambda+1}(t)\, C_n^{\lambda+1}(x), \tag{11.15}$$

$(x,t) \in [-1,1] \times [0,\infty)$, then

$$\tilde{f}_{n-1}^{\lambda+1}(t) = \delta_{\lambda} f_n^{\lambda}(t), \qquad n \in \mathbb{Z}_+^*, \quad \lambda > 0. \tag{11.16}$$

The proof is very similar to the Proof of Lemma 2.4 in Ref. [30] and we omit it for the sake of brevity.

11.3. An Historical Account on *Montée* and *Descente* Operators

Beatson and zu Castell [31] defined the Descente and Montée operators for the class $\mathcal{P}\left(\mathbb{S}^d\right)$. Specifically, the Descente $\mathcal{D}$ is defined as

$$(\mathcal{D}f)(x) = \frac{d}{dx}f(x) = f'(x), \quad x \in [-1,1],$$

provided such a derivative exists. The Montée $\mathcal{I}$ is instead defined as

$$(\mathcal{I}f)(x) = \int_{-1}^{x} f(u)\,du, \quad x \in [-1,1].$$

Beatson and zu Castell [31] has shown that $f \in \mathcal{P}\left(\mathbb{S}^{d+2}\right)$ implies that there exists a constant, κ, such that $\kappa + \mathcal{I}f \in \mathcal{P}\left(\mathbb{S}^d\right)$. Also, $f \in \mathcal{P}\left(\mathbb{S}^d\right)$ implies $\mathcal{D}f \in \mathcal{P}\left(\mathbb{S}^{d+2}\right)$. The implications in terms of differentiability at $x = 1$ are nicely summarized therein.

The *tour de force* by Ref. [31] has then been generalized by Ref. [33]: let $d \in \mathbb{N}$ and $\varphi : [-1,1] \times \mathbb{R} \to \mathbb{R}$ be continuous functions. The Montée $\mathcal{I}$ and Descente $\mathcal{D}$ operators are defined, respectively, by

$$\mathcal{I}(\varphi)(x,t) := \int_{-1}^{x} \varphi(u,t)\,du, \quad (x,t) \in [-1,1] \times [0,\infty), \tag{11.17}$$

when f is integrable with respect to the first variable, and

$$\mathcal{D}(\varphi)(x,t) := \frac{\partial \varphi}{\partial x}(x,t), \quad (x,t) \in [-1,1] \times [0,\infty). \tag{11.18}$$

They prove that if $\varphi \in \mathcal{P}\left(\mathbb{S}^d \times \mathbb{R}\right)$, then $\mathcal{D}\varphi \in \mathcal{P}\left(\mathbb{S}^{d+2} \times \mathbb{R}\right)$, and in their correction of Theorem 2.1, they provided conditions under $\varphi \in \mathcal{P}\left(\mathbb{S}^{d+2} \times \mathbb{R}\right)$ such that $\mathcal{I}\varphi \in \mathcal{P}\left(\mathbb{S}^d \times \mathbb{R}\right)$.

Montée and Descente operators with the class $\mathcal{P}\left(\mathbb{R}^k\right)$ have been defined much earlier, and we follow Ref. [24] to summarize them here. The Descente and Montée operators are respectively defined as

$$\mathcal{D}\varphi(t) = \begin{cases} 1, & t = 0 \\ \dfrac{\varphi'(t)}{t\varphi''(0)}, & t > 0, \end{cases} \tag{11.19}$$

where $\varphi''(0)$ denotes the second derivative of φ evaluated at $t = 0$, and

$$\widetilde{\mathcal{I}}\varphi(t) = \int_t^\infty u\varphi(u)\,du \left(\int_0^\infty u\varphi(u)\,du\right)^{-1}. \tag{11.20}$$

Gneiting [24] proved that if $\varphi \in \mathcal{P}\left(\mathbb{R}^k\right), k \geq 3$, and $u\varphi(u)$ is integrable over $[0,\infty)$, then $\widetilde{\mathcal{I}}\varphi \in \mathcal{P}\left(\mathbb{R}^{k-2}\right)$. Invoking standard properties of Bessel functions in concert with direct inspection, Ref. [24] proved that, if $\varphi \in \mathcal{P}\left(\mathbb{R}^k\right)$ and $\varphi''(0)$ exists, then $\mathcal{D}\varphi \in \mathcal{P}\left(\mathbb{R}^{k+2}\right)$. Under mild regularity conditions, the operators $\mathcal{D}$ and $\widetilde{\mathcal{I}}$ are inverse operators:

$$\widetilde{\mathcal{I}}\left(\mathcal{D}\varphi\right) = \mathcal{D}\left(\widetilde{\mathcal{I}}\varphi\right) = \varphi.$$

11.3.1. *Descente and Montée operators on generalized spaces*

We start by defining the following Descente and Montée operators. The first is actually taken from Ref. [33]: we define the derivate operator D_1 by

$$D_1\varphi(x,t) := \varphi_x(x,t) = \frac{\partial \varphi}{\partial x}(x,t), \quad (x,t) \in [-1,1] \times [0,\infty). \tag{11.21}$$

The integral operator I_1 is given by

$$I_1\varphi(x,t) := \int_{-1}^x \varphi(u,t)\,du, \quad (x,t) \in [-1,1] \times [0,\infty), \tag{11.22}$$

when $\varphi(u,t)$ is integrable over $[-1,1]$ for each $t \in [0,\infty)$.

We define

$$D_2\varphi(x,t) := \begin{cases} 1, & (x,t) = (1,0) \\ \dfrac{\varphi_t(x,t)}{t\varphi_{tt}(1,0)}, & (x,t) \in [-1,1) \times (0,\infty) \end{cases} \tag{11.23}$$

whenever $\varphi_{tt}(1,0) := \frac{\partial^2\varphi}{\partial t^2}(1,0)$ exists, and

$$I_2\varphi(x,t) := \frac{\int_t^\infty v\varphi(x,v)\,dv}{\int_0^\infty v\varphi(1,v)\,dv}, \quad (x,t) \in [-1,1]\times[0,\infty), \tag{11.24}$$

when $v\varphi(1,v)$ is integrable over $[0,\infty)$ and provided the denominator is not identically equal to zero.

The composition between the operators defined in Refs. [33] and [24] provides a new operator, which we define here as

$$I_3\varphi(x,t) := \int_t^\infty \int_{-1}^x v\varphi(u,v)\,dudv, \qquad (x,t) \in [-1,1]\times[0,\infty), \tag{11.25}$$

when $v\varphi(u,v)$ is integrable over $[-1,1]\times[0,\infty)$.

Given $\kappa \in \mathbb{Z}_+$, we define the operator I_j^κ by recurrence as:

$$I_j^0\varphi := \varphi, \quad I_j^1\varphi := I_j\varphi, \quad \text{and} \quad I_j^\kappa\varphi := I_j\left(I_j^{\kappa-1}\varphi\right), \quad j = 1,2,3.$$

11.4. Dimension Walks within the Class $\mathcal{P}\left(\mathbb{S}^d \times \mathbb{R}^k\right)$

This section contains our original findings. Proofs are deferred to the Appendix.

11.4.1. *Descente operators*

We start with a simple result, which is an extension of Theorem 2.3 in Ref. [30]. In Appendix A, we provide a quick sketch of the main steps.

Theorem 11.4.1. *If $\varphi : [-1,1]\times[0,\infty) \to \mathbb{R}$ belongs to $\mathcal{P}\left(\mathbb{S}^d \times \mathbb{R}^k\right)$, then $D_1\varphi$ belongs to $\mathcal{P}\left(\mathbb{S}^{d+2} \times \mathbb{R}^k\right)$.*

The next result requires instead a lengthy proof and relates about the operator D_2.

Theorem 11.4.2. *Let $d,k \in \mathbb{Z}_+^*, \varphi : [-1,1]\times[0,\infty) \to \mathbb{R}$ be a function in $\mathcal{P}\left(\mathbb{S}^d \times \mathbb{R}^k\right)$ and let F_n be the k-Schoenberg measures associated with the d-Schoenberg functions of φ. If*

(1) $\int_0^\infty r^2 dF_n(r) < \infty$, *for all $n \in \mathbb{Z}_+$;*

(2) $0 < \frac{\partial^2\varphi}{\partial t^2}(1,0) = \sum_{n=0}^\infty \int_0^\infty r^2 dF_n(r) < \infty$,

then $D_2\varphi$ belongs to $\mathcal{P}\left(\mathbb{S}^{d+2} \times \mathbb{R}^k\right)$.

11.4.2. *Montée operators*

In this section we consider functions $\varphi : [-1,1]\times[0,\infty) \to \mathbb{R}$ belonging to $\mathcal{P}\left(\mathbb{S}^d \times \mathbb{R}^k\right)$ as in Eq. (11.2) such that

$$\int_0^\infty (1/r^{2\kappa})dF_n(r) < \infty \quad \left(\kappa \in \mathbb{Z}_+^*\right). \tag{11.26}$$

Thus, the functions defined by

$$g_n^\kappa(t) := \int_0^\infty \Omega_{k-2\kappa}(tr)\frac{1}{r^{2\kappa}}dF_n(r), \quad t\in[-1,1], \quad n,\kappa \in \mathbb{Z}_+, \tag{11.27}$$

belong to the class $\mathcal{P}\left(\mathbb{R}^{k-2\kappa}\right)$.

The first finding relates to the operator I_1. Again, the proof is deferred to the Appendix.

Theorem 11.4.3. *Let $k,\kappa \in \mathbb{Z}_+^*$ and d be an integer such that $d > 2\kappa$. If $\varphi : [-1,1]\times[0,\infty) \to \mathbb{R}$ is a function in $\mathcal{P}\left(\mathbb{S}^d \times \mathbb{R}^k\right)$ such that $u \mapsto I_1^{\kappa-1}\varphi(u,t)$ is integrable over $[-1,1]$ for each $t \in [0,\infty)$. Then, the function $I_1^\kappa\varphi$ has a representation in the form of a Gegenbauer series:*

$$I_1^\kappa(x,t) = \sum_{n=0}^\infty \tilde{f}_n^{d,\kappa}(t)\, C_n^{(d-2\kappa-1)/2}(x), \quad (x,t)\in[-1,1]\times[0,\infty), \tag{11.28}$$

where

$$\tilde{f}_n^{d,\kappa}(t) := \begin{cases} \tau^{d,\kappa}\sum\limits_{i=0}^\infty (-1)^i \chi_i^{n,d,\kappa} f_i^d(t), & n = 0,1,\ldots,\kappa-1, \\ \tau^{d,\kappa} f_{n-\kappa}^d(t), & n \geq \kappa. \end{cases} \tag{11.29}$$

The functions f_n^d are the d-Schoenberg functions of φ as in Eq. (11.2), the positive constant $\tau^{d,\kappa} := \left(\prod_{j=1}^\kappa \delta_{(d-2j+1)/2}\right)^{-1}$ and the coefficients

$$\begin{cases} \chi_i^{0,d,\kappa} := \sum\limits_{j=1}^{\kappa-1} (-1)^{j+1}\chi_i^{j-1,d,\kappa-1} C_j^{(d-2\kappa-1)/2}(1) - (-1)^{\kappa+1} C_{i+\kappa}^{(d-2\kappa-1)/2}(1), \\ \chi_i^{n,d,\kappa} := \chi_i^{n-1,d,\kappa-1}, \quad n = 1,2,\ldots,\kappa-1, \end{cases} \tag{11.30}$$

satisfy

$$\left|\chi_i^{n,d,\kappa}\right| \leq \Upsilon^{n,d,\kappa} C_i^{(d-1)/2}(1), \quad n = 0,1,\ldots,\kappa-1, \quad i \in \mathbb{Z}_+, \tag{11.31}$$

where, for each $n = 0,1,\ldots,\kappa-1$ and $\kappa \in \mathbb{Z}_+^*$, $\Upsilon^{n,d,\kappa}$ is a positive constant that depends only on d. Moreover, $\sum_{n=0}^\infty \tilde{f}_n^{d,\kappa}(0)C_n^{(d-2\kappa-1)/2}(1) < \infty$.

Corollary 11.4.4. *Under the conditions of Theorem 11.4.3, there exists a bounded function H^κ on $[-1,1]\times[0,\infty)$ such that $H^\kappa + I_1^\kappa\varphi$ belongs to $\mathcal{P}\left(\mathbb{S}^{d-2\kappa}\times\mathbb{R}^k\right)$.*

Remark 11.4.5. Direct inspection shows that $\chi_i^{0,d,\varkappa} \geq 0$, for $\varkappa = 1, 2$. Therefore, $\chi_i^{1,d,\varkappa}, \chi_i^{2,d,\varkappa} \ldots, \chi_i^{\varkappa-1,d,\varkappa} \geq 0$ for all $\varkappa \geq 2$ and $i \in \mathbb{Z}_+$.

Remark 11.4.6. By Remark 11.4.5, if $f_{2n+1}^d \equiv 0$ for all n, then $I_1^\varkappa \varphi$, for $\varkappa = 1,2$, belongs to the class $\mathcal{P}\left(\mathbb{S}^{d-2\varkappa} \times \mathbb{R}^k\right)$. Therefore, our result generalizes the corrected version of Theorem 11.2.1 in Ref. [33].

We can modify the functions $\tilde{f}_n^{d,\varkappa}, n = 0, 1, \ldots, \varkappa - 1$, in Eq. (11.28) so that the new *quasi* Montée operator belongs to $\mathcal{P}\left(\mathbb{S}^{d-2\varkappa} \times \mathbb{R}^k\right)$. Theorem 11.4.7 sheds some light in this direction.

Theorem 11.4.7. *Let the functions $\tilde{f}_n^{d,\varkappa} \in \mathcal{P}\left(\mathbb{R}^k\right), n \geq \varkappa$, and $h_{1,n}^\varkappa, h_{2,n}^\varkappa \in \mathcal{P}\left(\mathbb{R}^k\right)$ be as, respectively, defined at Eqs. (11.29) and (A.5).*

Let $k, \varkappa \in \mathbb{Z}_+^*$ and let d be an integer such that $d > 2\varkappa$. Let $\varphi : [-1, 1] \times [0, \infty) \to \mathbb{R}$ be a function in $\mathcal{P}\left(\mathbb{S}^d \times \mathbb{R}^k\right)$ such that $u \mapsto I_1^{\varkappa-1}\varphi(u, t)$ is integrable over $[-1, 1]$ for each $t \in [0, \infty)$. If

(1) $\sum_{n=0}^{\infty} C_n^{(d-1)/2}(1) \int_0^{\infty} dF_n(r) < \infty;$

(2) *There exists a constant $K > 0$ such that $\sum_{n=0}^{\infty} C_n^{(d-1)/2}(1) dF_n(r) \leq K, 0 \leq r < \infty$, then there exist $2\varkappa$ constants A^n and $B^n, n = 0, \ldots, \varkappa - 1$, such that*

$$\begin{aligned} I_1^{\varkappa, A^0..A^{\varkappa-1}, B^0..B^{\varkappa-1}} \varphi(x, t) := & \sum_{n=0}^{\varkappa-1} (A^n h_{1,n}^\varkappa(t) - B^n h_{2,n}^\varkappa(t)) C_n^{(d-2\varkappa-1)/2}(x) \\ & + \sum_{n=\varkappa}^{\infty} \tilde{f}_n^{d,\varkappa}(t) C_n^{(d-2k-1)/2}(x), \end{aligned} \tag{11.32}$$

belongs to $\mathcal{P}\left(\mathbb{S}^{d-2\varkappa} \times \mathbb{R}^k\right)$.

Remark 11.4.8. For any $A^n \geq 0, n = 1, \ldots, \varkappa - 1$ the function $I_1^{\varkappa, 0A^1..A^{\varkappa-1}, 0..0}\varphi$ belongs to $\mathcal{P}\left(\mathbb{S}^{d-2\varkappa} \times \mathbb{R}^k\right)$. This also can be seen as a generalization of the correction of Theorem 2.1 in Ref. [33] (to appear).

The next result is related to the operator I_2.

Theorem 11.4.9. *Let $d, \varkappa \in \mathbb{Z}_+^*$ and k be an integer such that $k > 2\varkappa$. If $\varphi : [-1, 1] \times [0, \infty) \to \mathbb{R}$ is a function in $\mathcal{P}\left(\mathbb{S}^d \times \mathbb{R}^k\right)$ such that*

(1) $g_n^\nu(0) = \int_0^{\infty} (1/r^{2\nu})\, dF_n(r) < \infty$, *for all $n \in \mathbb{Z}_+$ and $\nu \in \{1, 2, \ldots, \varkappa\}$.*

(2) $0 \neq \sum_{n=0}^{\infty} g_n^{(\nu)}(0) C_n^{(d-1)/2}(1) < \infty$, *for $\nu \in \{1, 2, \ldots, \varkappa\}$,* *then the function $I_2^\kappa \varphi$ has a representation in Gegenbauer series in the form*

$$I_2^\kappa \varphi (x,t) = \frac{1}{\sum_{n=0}^{\infty} g_n^\kappa (0)\, C_n^{(d-1)/2}(1)} \sum_{n=0}^{\infty} g_n^\kappa (t)\, C_n^{(d-1)/2}(x). \tag{11.33}$$

The functions g_n^κ are defined in Eq. (11.27), and F_n are the k-Schoenberg measures of the d-Schoenberg functions of φ.

Moreover, $I_2^\kappa \varphi$ belongs to $\mathcal{P}\left(\mathbb{S}^d \times \mathbb{R}^{k-2\kappa}\right)$.

We finish this part with the Montée operator I_3.

Theorem 11.4.10. *Let $\kappa \in \mathbb{Z}_+^*$, d, and k be integers such that $d, k > 2\kappa$. If $\varphi : [-1,1] \times [0,\infty) \to \mathbb{R}$ is a function in $\mathcal{P}\left(\mathbb{S}^d \times \mathbb{R}^k\right)$ such that*

(1) $g_n^\nu(0) = \int_0^\infty \frac{1}{r^{2\nu}} dF_n(r) < \infty$ *for all $n \in \mathbb{Z}_+$ and $\nu \in \{1,2,\ldots,\kappa\}$;*

(2) $\sum_{n=0}^{\infty} g_n^\nu(0) = \sum_{n=0}^{\infty} \int_0^\infty \frac{1}{r^{2\nu}} dF_n(r) < \infty$, *for and $\nu \in \{1,2,\ldots,\kappa\}$,*

(3) $\sum_{n=0}^{\infty} g_n^\nu(0) C_{n+\nu}^{(d-2\nu-1)/2}(1) < \infty$, *for and $\nu \in \{1,2,\ldots,\kappa\}$,*

then the function $I_3^\kappa \varphi$ has a representation in Gegenbauer series in the form

$$I_3^\kappa \varphi (x,t) = \sum_{n=0}^{\infty} h_n^\kappa (t)\, C_n^{(d-2\kappa-1)/2}(x), \quad (x,t) \in [-1,1] \times [0,\infty], \tag{11.34}$$

where

$$h_n^\kappa (t) := \begin{cases} \gamma^{d,k,\kappa} \sum_{i=0}^{\infty} (-1)^i \chi_i^{n,d,\kappa} g_i^\kappa(t), & n = 0,1,\ldots,\kappa-1, \\ \gamma^{d,k,\kappa} g_{n-\kappa}^\kappa(t), & n \geq \kappa, \end{cases} \tag{11.35}$$

with $\gamma^{d,k,\kappa} := \prod_{j=1}^{\kappa} \frac{k-2j}{\delta_{(d-2j+1)/2}} > 0$ and $\sum_{n=0}^{\infty} h_n^\kappa(0) C_n^{(d-2\kappa-1)/2}(1) < \infty$. The functions g_n^κ are defined in Eq. (11.27) and belong to the class $\mathcal{P}\left(\mathbb{R}^k\right)$ and $\chi_i^{n,d,\kappa}$ are given in Eq. (11.30).

Remark 11.4.11. By Remark 11.4.5, if $g_{2n+1}^\kappa \equiv 0$ for all n, then $I_3^\kappa \varphi$, for $\kappa = 1,2$, belongs to the class $\mathcal{P}\left(\mathbb{S}^{d-2\kappa} \times \mathbb{R}^{k-2\kappa}\right)$.

Corollary 11.4.12. *Under the conditions of Theorem 11.4.10, there exists a bounded function H^κ on $[-1,1] \times [0,\infty)$ such that $H^\kappa + I_3^\kappa \varphi$ belongs to $\mathcal{P}\left(\mathbb{S}^{d-2\kappa} \times \mathbb{R}^{k-2\kappa}\right)$.*

As previously mentioned, we can replace the functions $h_n^\kappa, n = 0,1,\ldots,\kappa-1$, with others such that the new *quasi* Montée operator belongs to $\mathcal{P}\left(\mathbb{S}^{d-2\kappa} \times \mathbb{R}^{k-2\kappa}\right)$. Theorem 11.4.13 provides a construction in this sense.

Theorem 11.4.13. *Let $\varkappa \in \mathbb{Z}_+^*$, d, and k be integers such that $d, k > 2\varkappa$. Let $\varphi : [-1,1] \times [0,\infty) \to \mathbb{R}$ be a function that belongs to the class $\mathcal{P}\left(\mathbb{S}^d \times \mathbb{R}^k\right)$ satisfying the hypotheses of Theorem 11.4.10. If additionally, the k-Schoenberg measures F_n of the d-Schoenberg functions of φ satisfy*

(1) $\sum_{n=0}^{\infty} g_n^{\nu}(0) C_n^{(d-1)/2}(1) = \sum_{n=0}^{\infty} C_n^{(d-1)/2}(1) \int_0^{\infty} \frac{1}{r^{2\nu}} dF_n(r) < \infty$, *for and* $\nu \in \{1, 2, \ldots, \varkappa\}$,

(2) *There exists a constant* $K > 0$ *such that* $\sum_{n=0}^{\infty} C_n^{(d-1)/2}(1) dF_n(r) \leq K, 0 \leq r < \infty$;

then there exist $2\varkappa$ *constants* A^n *and* $B^n, n = 0, \ldots, \varkappa - 1$, *such that*

$$
\begin{aligned}
I_3^{\varkappa, A^0..A^{\varkappa-1}, B^0..B^{\varkappa-1}} \varphi(x,t) := & \sum_{n=0}^{\varkappa-1} (A^n \tilde{h}_{1,n}^{\varkappa}(t) - B^n \tilde{h}_{2,n}^{\varkappa}(t)) C_n^{(d-2\varkappa-1)/2}(x) \\
& + \sum_{n=\varkappa}^{\infty} \tilde{h}_n^{\varkappa}(t) C_n^{(d-2\varkappa-1)/2}(x).
\end{aligned}
\tag{11.36}
$$

The functions $h_n^{\varkappa} \in \mathcal{P}\left(\mathbb{R}^k\right), n \geq \varkappa$ *and* $\tilde{h}_{1,n}^{\varkappa}, \tilde{h}_{2,n}^{\varkappa} \in \mathcal{P}\left(\mathbb{R}^k\right)$ *are defined, respectively, in Eqs. (11.35) and (A.10).*

Remark 11.4.14. For any $A^n \geq 0, n = 1, \ldots, \varkappa - 1$, the function $I_3^{\varkappa, 0A^1..A^{\varkappa-1}, 0..0} \varphi$ belongs to $\mathcal{P}\left(\mathbb{S}^{d-2\varkappa} \times \mathbb{R}^{k-2\varkappa}\right)$.

Acknowledgments

Ana Paula Peron was partially supported by Fundação de Amparo à Pesquisa do Estado de São Paulo—FAPESP, Brazil, # 2021/04269-0. The authors are indebted to Marcos López de Prado for the insightful discussions and the careful checking of our proofs.

Declarations

- Conflict of interest: There were no competing interests to declare that arose during the preparation or publication process of this article.
- Ethics approval: Not applicable.
- Consent to participate: All authors consent to participate.
- Consent for publication: All authors agree with the publication.
- Availability of data and materials: Not applicable.
- Code availability: Not applicable.
- Authors' contributions: All authors contributed equally to this work.

APPENDIX A

Proof of Theorem 11.4.1. Since φ belongs to $\mathcal{P}\left(\mathbb{S}^d \times \mathbb{R}^k\right)$, then φ is continuously differentiable with respect to the first variable (see Ref. [34, Proposition 3.8]) and has a Gegenbauer expansion as Eq. (11.3). Also φ_x has a Gegenbauer expansion in the form

$$\varphi_x(x,t) \sim \sum_{n=0}^{\infty} \tilde{f}_n^{d+1}(t) C_n^{(d+1)/2}(x).$$

Using Eqs. (11.15)–(11.16), the remainder of the proof follows as in Ref. [30, Theorem 11.2.3]. ■

Proof of Theorem 11.4.2. Let φ be a function as in Eq. (11.2). By Eq. (11.7),

$$\frac{df_n^d}{dt}(t) = \int_0^\infty -\frac{1}{k} tr^2 \Omega_{k+2}(tr)\, dF_n(r).$$

Deriving term by term, we obtain

$$\begin{aligned}\frac{\partial \varphi}{\partial t}(x,t) &= \sum_{n=0}^{\infty} \frac{df_n^d}{dt}(t) C_n^{(d-1)/2}(x) \\ &= -\frac{1}{k} \sum_{n=0}^{\infty} \left(\int_0^\infty \Omega_{k+2}(tr) r^2 dF_n(r) \right) C_n^{(d-1)/2}(x).\end{aligned} \tag{A.1}$$

By Lemma 3 in Ref. [37], we have

$$\frac{d^2 f_n^d}{dt^2}(0) = -\frac{1}{k} \int_0^\infty r^2 dF_n(r).$$

Thus,

$$\frac{\partial^2 \varphi}{\partial t^2}(x,0) = -\frac{1}{k} \sum_{n=0}^{\infty} \left(\int_0^\infty r^2 dF_n(r) \right) C_n^{(d-1)/2}(x), \quad x \in [-1,1]. \tag{A.2}$$

In particular,

$$\frac{\partial^2 \varphi}{\partial t^2}(1,0) = -\frac{1}{k} \sum_{n=0}^{\infty} \left(\int_0^\infty r^2 dF_n(r) \right) C_n^{(d-1)/2}(1). \tag{A.3}$$

Thus, by Eqs. (A.1) and (A.3), for $x \in [-1, 1\,)$ and $t > 0$, we have

$$D_2\varphi(x,t) = \frac{\varphi_t(x,t)}{t\varphi_{tt}(1,0)} = \frac{1}{\sum_{n=0}^{\infty} \int_0^\infty r^2 dF_n(r)} \sum_{n=0}^{\infty} g_n^d(t)\, C_n^{(d-1)/2}(x), \tag{A.4}$$

where the functions $g_n^d(t) : [0,\infty) \to \mathbb{R}$ are defined by

$$g_n^d(t) := \int_0^\infty \Omega_{k+2}(tr)\, r^2 dF_n(r).$$

We invoke Hypothesis (1) to imply that $g_n^d \in \mathcal{P}\left(\mathbb{R}^{k+2}\right)$. Thus, the series in Eq. (A.4) converges absolutely and uniformly on $[-1, 1] \times [0, \infty)$. Hence, letting $x = 1$ and $t = 0$ in the expression of the series in Eq. (A.4) provides

$$\frac{1}{\sum_{n=0}^{\infty} \int_0^{\infty} r^2 dF_n(r)} \sum_{n=0}^{\infty} g_n^d(0)\, C_n^{(d-1)/2}(1) = 1 = D_2\varphi(1,0).$$

Therefore, $D_2\varphi$ is a continuous function on $[-1, 1] \times [0, \infty)$ having a representation series as in Eq. (11.2) with d-Schoenberg functions $g_n^d \in \mathcal{P}\left(\mathbb{R}^{k+2}\right)$. Since, by (2),

$$\sum_{n=0}^{\infty} g_n^d(0) = \sum_{n=0}^{\infty} \int_0^{\infty} r^2 dF_n(r) < \infty,$$

we can conclude that $D_2\varphi$ belongs to $\mathcal{P}\left(S^d \times \mathbb{R}^{k+2}\right)$. ∎

Proof of Theorem 11.4.3. We prove the statement by induction on $\varkappa \in \mathbb{Z}_+^*$.
Step $\varkappa = 1$: We have

$$I_1^1\varphi(x,t) = I_1\varphi(x,t) = \int_{-1}^{x} \varphi(u,t)du.$$

By Eqs. (11.2) and (11.11), integrating term by term, we obtain

$$I_1^1\varphi(x,t) = \sum_{n=0}^{\infty} f_n^d(t) \frac{1}{\delta_{(d-1)/2}} \left(C_{n+1}^{(d-3)/2}(x) - C_{n+1}^{(d-3)/2}(-1) \right).$$

Since $C_{n+1}^{(d-3)/2}(-1) = (-1)^{n+1} C_{n+1}^{(d-3)/2}(1)$, we have

$$I_1^1\varphi(x,t) = \sum_{n=0}^{\infty} \tilde{f}_n^{d,1}(t) C_n^{(d-3)/2}(x)$$

where

$$\tilde{f}_n^{d,1}(t) := \begin{cases} \dfrac{1}{\delta_{(d-1)/2}} \displaystyle\sum_{i=0}^{\infty} (-1)^i \chi_i^{n,d,1} f_i^d(t), & n = 0 \\ \dfrac{1}{\delta_{(d-1)/2}} f_{n-1}^d(t), & n \geq 1, \end{cases}$$

where $\chi_i^{0,d,1} = C_{i+1}^{(d-3)/2}(1)$ and, by Eq. (11.14),

$$0 \leq \chi_i^{0,d,1} = \left| C_i^{(d-1)/2}(1) \frac{C_{i+1}^{(d-3)/2}(1)}{C_i^{(d-1)/2}(1)} \right| \leq \underbrace{\varrho_{(d-1)/2,1}}_{\Upsilon^{0,d,1}} C_i^{(d-1)/2}(1),$$

which implies

$$\left|(-1)^i \chi_i^{0,d,1} f_i^d(t)\right| \leq \Upsilon^{0,d,1} f_i(0) C_i^{(d-1)/2}(1)$$

and by Eq. (11.2), the series in the definition of $\widetilde{f}_n^{d,1}$ is uniformly convergent on $[0,\infty)$. Again by Eq. (11.14), for $n \geq 1$,

$$\left|\widetilde{f}_n^{d,1}(0)C_n^{(d-3)/2}(1)\right| \leq \frac{1}{\delta_{(d-1)/2}}\Upsilon^{0,d,1}f_{n-1}^{d}(0)C_{n-1}^{(d-1)/2}(1).$$

Thus, $\sum_{n=0}^{\infty}\widetilde{f}_n^{d,1}(0)C_n^{(d-3)/2}(1) < \infty$.

Step $\varkappa = 2$: By algebraic manipulation we have

$$I_1^2\varphi(x,t) = \sum_{n=0}^{\infty}\widetilde{f}_n^{d,2}(t)C_n^{(d-5)/2}(x)$$

where

$$\widetilde{f}_n^{d,2}(t) := \begin{cases} \tau^{d,2}\sum_{i=0}^{\infty}(-1)^i\chi_i^{n,d,2}f_i^d(t), & n = 0, 1, \\ \tau^{d,2}f_{n-\varkappa}^{d}(t), & n \geq 2, \end{cases}$$

with $\tau^{d,2} = \left(\delta_{(d-1)/2}\delta_{(d-3)/2}\right)^{-1}$ and

$$\chi_i^{0,d,2} := C_{i+1}^{(d-3)/2}(1)C_1^{(d-5)/2}(1) - C_{i+2}^{(d-5)/2}(1),$$

$$\chi_i^{1,d,2} := C_{i+1}^{(d-3)/2}(1) = \chi_i^{0,d,1}.$$

It is clear that $0 \leq \chi_i^{1,d,2} \leq \Upsilon^{1,d,2}C_i^{(d-1)/2}(1)$, with $\Upsilon^{1,d,2} = \Upsilon^{0,d,1}$. It is not difficult to see that

$$\chi_i^{0,d,2} = \frac{(d-5)\Gamma(i+d-1)(i+1)}{\Gamma(d-3)(i+d-3)\Gamma(i+3)} \geq 0$$

and, by Eq. (11.14),

$$\begin{aligned} \left|\chi_i^{0,d,2}\right| &\leq \left(\left|\frac{C_{i+1}^{(d-3)/2}(1)}{C_i^{(d-1)/2}(1)}C_1^{(d-5)/2}(1)\right| + \left|\frac{C_{i+2}^{(d-5)/2}(1)}{C_i^{(d-1)/2}(1)}\right|\right)C_i^{(d-1)/2}(1) \\ &\leq \left(\varrho_{(d-1)/2,1}\frac{\Gamma(1+d-5)}{\Gamma(2)\Gamma(d-5)} + \varrho_{(d-1)/2,2}\right)C_i^{(d-1)/2}(1) \\ &= \underbrace{\left(\varrho_{(d-1)/2,1}(d-5) + \varrho_{(d-1)/2,2}\right)}_{\Upsilon^{0,d,2}}C_i^{(d-1)/2}(1) \end{aligned}$$

By the same argument of the step $\varkappa = 1$, we can conclude that the series in the definition of $\tilde{f}_n^{d,2}$ for $n = 0, 1$ is uniformly convergent on $[0, \infty)$ and also $\sum_{n=0}^{\infty} \tilde{f}_n^{d,2}(0) C_n^{(d-5)/2}(1) < \infty$.

Induction step: Let us assume that the expression in Eq. (11.28) of $I_1^{\varkappa}\varphi$ holds up to $\varkappa$, and let us prove it holds for $I_1^{\varkappa+1}\varphi$. We have

$$I_1^{\varkappa+1}\varphi\,(x,t) = I_1\left(I_1^{\varkappa}\varphi\right)(x,t) = \int_{-1}^{x} I_1^{\varkappa}\varphi\,(u,t)\,du.$$

Using the induction hypothesis and integrating term by term, for $(x, t) \in [-1, 1] \times [0, \infty)$, we obtain

$$\begin{aligned} I_1^{\varkappa+1}\varphi(x,t) &= \sum_{n=0}^{\varkappa-1} \tilde{f}_n^{d,\varkappa}(t) \int_{-1}^{x} C_n^{(d-2\varkappa-1)/2}(u)du + \sum_{n=\varkappa}^{\infty} \tilde{f}_n^{d,\varkappa}(t) \int_{-1}^{x} C_n^{(d-2\varkappa-1)/2}(u)du \\ &= \sum_{n=0}^{\varkappa-1} \tau^{d,\varkappa} \sum_{i=0}^{\infty} (-1)^i \chi_i^{n,d,\varkappa} f_i^d(t) \frac{1}{\delta_{(d-2\varkappa-1)/2}} \left(C_{n+1}^{(d-2\varkappa-3)/2}(x) - C_{n+1}^{(d-2\varkappa-3)/2}(-1)\right) \\ &\quad + \sum_{n=\varkappa}^{\infty} \tau^{d,\varkappa} f_{n-\varkappa}^d(t) \frac{1}{\delta_{(d-2\varkappa-1)/2}} \left(C_{n+1}^{(d-2\varkappa-3)/2}(x) - C_{n+1}^{(d-2\varkappa-3)/2}(-1)\right). \end{aligned}$$

Thus,

$$\begin{aligned} I_1^{\varkappa+1}\varphi\,(x,t) &= \tau^{d,\varkappa+1} \sum_{n=0}^{\varkappa-1} \sum_{i=0}^{\infty} (-1)^i \chi_i^{n,d,\varkappa} f_i^d(t) \left(C_{n+1}^{(d-2\varkappa-3)/2}(x) - C_{n+1}^{(d-2\varkappa-3)/2}(-1)\right) \\ &\quad + \tau^{d,\varkappa+1} \sum_{n=\varkappa}^{\infty} f_{n-\varkappa}^d(t) \left(C_{n+1}^{(d-2\varkappa-3)/2}(x) - C_{n+1}^{(d-2\varkappa-3)/2}(-1)\right). \end{aligned}$$

After some algebraic manipulation,

$$I_1^{\varkappa+1}\varphi\,(x,t) = \sum_{n=0}^{\infty} \tilde{f}_n^{d,\varkappa+1}(t)\, C_n^{(d-2(k+1)-1)/2}(x),$$

where

$$\tilde{f}_n^{d,\varkappa+1}(t) = \begin{cases} \tau^{d,\varkappa+1} \sum_{i=0}^{\infty} (-1)^i \chi_i^{n,d,\varkappa+1} f_i^d(t), & n = 0, 1, \ldots, \varkappa, \\ \tau^{d,\varkappa+1} f_{n-(\varkappa+1)}^d(t), & n \geq \varkappa + 1, \end{cases}$$

with

$$\chi_i^{0,d,\varkappa+1} := \sum_{j=1}^{\varkappa} (-1)^{j+1} \chi_i^{j-1,d,\varkappa} C_j^{(d-2(\varkappa+1)-1)/2}(1) - (-1)^{\varkappa+1} C_{i+\varkappa+1}^{(d-2(\varkappa+1)-1)/2}(1)$$

and

$$\chi_i^{n,d,\varkappa+1} := \chi_i^{n-1,d,\varkappa},\ n = 1, 2, \ldots, \varkappa.$$

It is clear that $\left|\chi_i^{n,d,\varkappa+1}\right| \le \Upsilon^{n,d,\varkappa+1} C_i^{(d-1)/2}(1)$, with $\Upsilon^{n,d,\varkappa+1} = \Upsilon^{n-1,d,\varkappa}$.
Now, by Eq. (11.14),

$$\left|\chi_i^{0,d,\varkappa+1}\right| \le \left(\sum_{j=1}^{\varkappa} \frac{\left|\chi_i^{j-1,d,\varkappa}\right|}{C_i^{(d-1)/2}(1)} C_j^{(d-2\varkappa-3)/2}(1) + \frac{C_{i+\varkappa+1}^{(d-2\varkappa-3)/2}(1)}{C_i^{(d-1)/2}(1)} \right) C_i^{(d-1)/2}(1).$$

By induction hypothesis (11.31) and by Eq. (11.14) we obtain

$$\left|\chi_i^{0,d,\varkappa+1}\right| \le \underbrace{\left(\sum_{j=1}^{\varkappa} \Upsilon^{j-1,d,\varkappa} (d-2\varkappa-3) + \varrho_{(d-1)/2, 2(\varkappa+1)} \right)}_{\Upsilon^{0,d,\varkappa+1}} C_i^{(d-1)/2}(1).$$

The convergence of the series in the definition of $\tilde{f}_n^{d,\varkappa+1}$ for $n = 0, 1, \ldots, \varkappa$ and $\sum_{n=0}^{\infty} \tilde{f}_n^{d,\varkappa+1}(0) C_n^{(d-2(\varkappa+1)-1)/2}(1)$ follows as in the previous steps. ■

Proof of Corollary 11.4.4. Note that, for $n = 0, 1, \ldots, \varkappa - 1$, we can rewrite $\tilde{f}_n^{d,\varkappa}$ as

$$\tilde{f}_n^{d,\varkappa}(t) = h_{1,n}^{\varkappa}(t) - h_{2,n}^{\varkappa}(t),$$

where

$$h_{1,n}^{\varkappa}(t) := \tau^{d,\varkappa} \sum_{\iota=0}^{\infty} \chi_{2\iota}^{n,d,\varkappa} f_{2\iota}^{d}(t), \quad \text{and} \tag{A.5}$$

$$h_{2,n}^{\varkappa}(t) := \tau^{d,\varkappa} \sum_{i=0}^{\infty} \chi_{2i+1}^{n,d,\varkappa} f_{2i+1}^{d}(t) \tag{A.6}$$

Define the function $H^{\varkappa}$ on $[-1, 1] \times [0, \infty)$ by

$$H^{\varkappa}(x, t) := \sum_{n=0}^{\varkappa-1} h_{2,n}^{\varkappa}(t) C_n^{(d-2\varkappa-1)/2}(x) - h_{1,0}^{\varkappa}(t) C_0^{(d-2\varkappa-1)/2}(x)$$

which is bounded on $[-1, 1] \times [0, \infty)$ because, by Eqs. (11.13), (11.31), and (11.2),

$$\left|H^{\varkappa}(x,t)\right| \le \tau^{d,\varkappa} \sum_{n=0}^{\varkappa-1} \Upsilon^{n,d,\varkappa} \left(\sum_{i=0}^{\infty} f_{2i+1}^{d}(0) C_{2i+1}^{(d-1)/2}(1) \right) C_n^{(d-1)/2}(1)$$

$$+\tau^{d,\varkappa} \Upsilon^{0,d,\varkappa} \left(\sum_{i=0}^{\infty} f_{2i}^{d}(0)\, C_{2i}^{(d-1/2)}(1) \right) C_0^{(d-2\varkappa-1/2)}(1) < \infty,$$

for all $(x, t) \in [-1, 1] \times [0, \infty)$.

By Remark 11.4.5, it is clear that $h^{\kappa}_{1,n} \in \mathcal{P}\left(\mathbb{R}^k\right), n = 1, 2, \ldots, \kappa - 1$, and also $\tilde{f}^{d,\kappa}_n \in \mathcal{P}\left(\mathbb{R}^k\right)$ for $n \geq \kappa$. Therefore,

$$H^{\kappa}(x,t) + I^{\kappa}_1\varphi(x,t) = \sum_{n=1}^{\kappa-1} h^{\kappa}_{1,n}(t)C_n^{(d-2\kappa-1)/2}(x) + \tau^{d,\kappa}\sum_{n=\kappa}^{\infty} \tilde{f}^{d,\kappa}_n(t)C_n^{(d-2\kappa-1)/2}(x)$$

has an expansion uniformly convergent as (11.2) due to Theorem 11.4.3. By Theorem 11.3.3 of Ref. [34] (see Eq. (11.2)), we can conclude that the function $H^{\kappa} + I^{\kappa}_1\varphi$ belongs to the class $\mathcal{P}\left(\mathbb{S}^{d-2\kappa} \times \mathbb{R}^k\right)$. ∎

We observe that the function H^{κ} is not unique and that the construction presented allows us to highlight the properties of the coefficient functions and consider the maximum of the non-zero d-Schoenberg functions of φ.

Proof of Theorem 11.4.7. By Eq. (11.5), for any constants A and B,

$$Ah^{\kappa}_{1,n}(t) - Bh^{\kappa}_{2,n}(t) = \tau^{d,\kappa}\sum_{i=0}^{\infty}\int_0^{\infty} \Omega_k(tr)\left(A\chi^{n,d,\kappa}_{2i}dF_{2i}(r) - B\chi^{n,d,\kappa}_{2i+1}dF_{2i+1}(r)\right). \quad (A.7)$$

Since, by Eq. (11.31),

$$\int_0^{\infty} A\left|\chi^{n,d,\kappa}_i\right| dF_i(r) \leq A\Upsilon^{n,d,\kappa}C_i^{(d-1)/2}(1)\int_0^{\infty} dF_i(r),$$

we have

$$\int_0^{\infty}\left(A\chi^{n,d,\kappa}_{2i}dF_{2i}(r) - B\chi^{n,d,\kappa}_{2i+1}dF_{2i+1}(r)\right) < \infty.$$

By Eq. (11.31) and (1) the series in Eq. (A.7) converges absolutely and uniformly on $[0, \infty)$.
Thus,

$$Ah^{\kappa}_{1,n}(t) - Bh^{\kappa}_{2,n}(t) = \tau^{d,\kappa}\int_0^{\infty}\Omega_k(tr)d\left(\sum_{i=0}^{\infty}A\chi^{n,d,\kappa}_{2i}F_{2i}(r) - B\chi^{n,d,\kappa}_{2i+1}F_{2i+1}(r)\right).$$

By Eq. (11.31) and (2), the series $\sum_{i=0}^{\infty}\chi^{n,d,\kappa}_{2i}F_{2i}$ and $\sum_{i=0}^{\infty}\chi^{n,d,\kappa}_{2i+1}F_{2i+1}$ are uniformly bounded on $[0, \infty)$. Then we can choose A^n, B^n such that the series $\sum_{i=0}^{\infty}A^n\chi^{n,d,\kappa}_{2i}F_{2i} - B^n\chi^{n,d,\kappa}_{2i+1}F_{2i+1}$ is non-negative, which allows us to conclude that $A^n h^{\kappa}_{1,n} - B^n h^{\kappa}_{2,n} \in \mathcal{P}\left(\mathbb{R}^k\right)$. The convergence uniform of the series (11.32) follows by Theorem 4.3 and the result by Theorem 3.3 of Ref. [34] (see Eq. (11.2)). ∎

Proof of Theorem 11.4.9. We will prove Eq. (11.33) by mathematical induction on κ.
Step $\kappa = 1$: We have

$$I_2\varphi(x,t) = \frac{1}{\int_0^{\infty} v\varphi(1,v)\,dv}\int_t^{\infty} v\varphi(x,v)\,dv.$$

By Eq. (11.2), integrating term by term, we obtain

$$\int_t^\infty v\varphi(x,v)\,dv = \sum_{n=0}^\infty \left(\int_t^\infty v \int_0^\infty \Omega_k(vr)\,dF_n(r)\,dv\right) C_n^{(d-1)/2}(x).$$

Using Fubini Theorem, we have

$$\int_t^\infty v\varphi(x,v)\,dv = \sum_{n=0}^\infty \left[\int_0^\infty \left(\int_{tr}^\infty \frac{w}{r^2}\Omega_k(w)\,dw\right) dF_n(r)\right] C_n^{(d-1)/2}(x).$$

By Eq. (11.9), for $(x,t) \in [-1,1]\times[0,\infty)$,

$$\int_{tr}^\infty \frac{w}{r^2}\Omega_k(w)\,dw = \frac{(k-2)}{r^2}\Omega_{k-2}(tr).$$

Hence, for $(x,t) \in [-1,1]\times[0,\infty)$,

$$\int_t^\infty v\varphi(x,v)\,dv = (k-2)\sum_{n=0}^\infty g_n^1(t)\, C_n^{(d-1)/2}(x), \tag{A.8}$$

where g_n^1 is defined in Eq. (11.27). In particular,

$$\int_0^\infty v\varphi(1,v)\,dv = (k-2)\sum_{n=0}^\infty g_n^1(0)\, C_n^{(d-1)/2}(1), \tag{A.9}$$

which is nonzero and finite. By Eqs. (A.8) and (A.9), $I_2\varphi$ has the representation given in Eq. (11.33).

Induction step: Let us assume the expression in Eq. (11.33) of $I_2^\kappa\varphi$ holds up to κ, and let us prove it holds for $I_2^{\kappa+1}\varphi$.

We have

$$I_2^{\kappa+1}\varphi(x,t) = I_2\left(I_2^\kappa\varphi\right)(x,t) = \frac{1}{\int_0^\infty vI_2^\kappa\varphi(1,v)\,dv}\int_t^\infty vI_2^\kappa\varphi(x,v)\,dv.$$

Note that the Hypothesis (1) guarantees that $g_n^\kappa \in \mathcal{P}\left(\mathbb{R}^{k-2\kappa}\right)$ and consequently the series in (11.33) converges absolutely and uniformly.

Using the induction hypothesis, integrating term by term, using the Fubini theorem and Eq. (11.9), for $(x,t) \in [-1,1]\times[0,\infty)$, we obtain:

$$\begin{aligned}\int_t^\infty vI_2^\kappa\varphi(x,v)dv &= \sum_{n=0}^\infty \left[\int_0^\infty \left(\int_t^\infty v\Omega_{k-2\kappa}(vr)dv\right)\frac{1}{r^{2\kappa}}dF_n(r)\right] C_n^{(d-1)/2}(x)\\ &= (k-2\kappa-2)\sum_{n=0}^\infty \left[\int_0^\infty \Omega_{k-2(\kappa+1)}(tr)\frac{1}{r^{2(\kappa+1)}}dF_n(r)\right] C_n^{(d-1)/2}(x)\\ &= (k-2\kappa-2)\sum_{n=0}^\infty g_n^{\kappa+1}(t)C_n^{(d-1)/2}(x).\end{aligned}$$

In particular,

$$\int_0^\infty vI_2^\kappa\varphi(1,v)\,dv = (k-2\kappa-2)\sum_{n=0}^\infty g_n^{\kappa+1}(0)\,C_n^{(d-1)/2}(1),$$

which is nonzero and finite by (2). Therefore,

$$I_2^{\kappa+1}\varphi(x,t) = \frac{1}{\sum_{n=0}^\infty g_n^{\kappa+1}(0)C_n^{(d-1)/2}(1)}\sum_{n=0}^\infty g_n^{\kappa+1}(t)C_n^{(d-1)/2}(x)$$

and Eq. (11.33) is proved.

Finally, given $\kappa \in \mathbb{Z}_+^*$, by (1) the d-Schoenberg functions g_n^κ of $I_2^\kappa\varphi$ belong to the class $\mathcal{P}\left(\mathbb{R}^{k-2\kappa}\right)$ and together with (2) we can conclude $0 < \sum_{n=0}^\infty g_n^\kappa(0)C_n^{(d-1)/2}(1) < \infty$. Therefore, Theorem 3.3 of Ref. [34] (see Eq. (11.2)) allows us to infer that $I_2^\kappa\varphi$ belongs to $\mathcal{P}\left(\mathbb{S}^d \times \mathbb{R}^{k-2\kappa}\right)$. ∎

Proof of Theorem 11.4.10. We will prove Eq. (11.34) by mathematical induction on κ.

Step $\kappa = 1$: For each $(x,t) \in [-1,1]\times[0,\infty)$,

$$I_3^1\varphi(x,t) = \int_t^\infty \int_{-1}^x v\varphi(u,v)\,dudv.$$

Using Eqs. (11.2) and (11.5),

$$\int_t^\infty \int_{-1}^x v\varphi(u,v)\,dudv = \int_t^\infty \int_{-1}^x v\sum_{n=0}^\infty\left(\int_0^\infty \Omega_k(vr)\,dF_n(r)\right)C_n^{(d-1)/2}(u)\,dudv.$$

Integrating term by term and by the Fubini theorem, we have

$$\int_t^\infty \int_{-1}^x v\varphi(u,v)dudv = \sum_{n=0}^\infty\left[\int_0^\infty\left(\int_t^\infty v\Omega_k(vr)dv\right)dF_n(r)\right]\left[\int_{-1}^x C_n^{(d-1)/2}(u)du\right].$$

By Eqs. (11.9) and (11.11), we obtain

$$\int_t^\infty \int_{-1}^x v\varphi(u,v)dudv = \sum_{n=0}^\infty\left[\int_0^\infty \frac{(k-2)}{r^2}\Omega_{k-2}(tr)dF_n(r)\right]\times \times\left[\frac{1}{\delta_{(d-1)/2}}\left(C_{n+1}^{(d-3)/2}(x) - C_{n+1}^{(d-3)/2}(-1)\right)\right]$$

Since $C_{n+1}^{(d-3)/2}(-1) = (-1)^{n+1}C_{n+1}^{(d-3)/2}(1)$,

$$\int_t^\infty \int_{-1}^x v\varphi(u,v)dudv = \frac{(k-2)}{\delta_{(d-1)/2}}\left[\left(\sum_{n=0}^\infty (-1)^n C_{n+1}^{(d-3)/2}(1)g_n^1(t)\right)C_0^{(d-3)/2}(x) + \sum_{n=0}^\infty g_n^1(t)C_{n+1}^{(d-3)/2}(x)\right],$$

where g_n^1 is given in Eq. (11.27).

Therefore,

$$I_3^1\varphi(x,t) = \sum_{n=0}^{\infty} h_n^1(t)C_n^{(d-3)/2}(x),$$

where

$$h_n^1(t) = \begin{cases} \gamma^{d,k,1}\sum_{i=0}^{\infty}(-1)^i\chi_i^{0,d,1}g_i^1(t), & n=0 \\ \gamma^{d,k,1}g_{n-1}^1(t), & n\geq 1, \end{cases}$$

where $\gamma^{d,k,1} = \frac{(k-2)}{\delta_{(d-1)/2}} > 0$. Moreover $\sum_{n=0}^{\infty} h_n^1(0)C_n^{(d-3)/2}(1) < \infty$ because, by Eq. (11.31) and (2)–(3), we have

$$\sum_{n=0}^{\infty}\left|h_n^1(0)C_n^{(d-3)/2}(1)\right| \leq \Upsilon^{0,d,1}C_0^{(d-3)/2}(1)\sum_{i=0}^{\infty}g_i^1(0) + \sum_{n=1}^{\infty}g_{n-1}^1(0)C_n^{(d-3)/2}(1) < \infty$$

Induction step: Let us assume the expression in Eq. (11.34) of $I_3^\kappa\varphi$ holds up to κ, and let us prove it holds for $I_3^{\kappa+1}\varphi$.

We have

$$I_3^{\kappa+1}\varphi\,(x,t) = I_3\left(I_3^\kappa\varphi\right)(x,t) = \int_t^\infty\int_{-1}^x vI_3^\kappa\varphi\,(u,v)\,dudv.$$

Using the induction hypothesis, integrating term by term, using the Fubini theorem, and Eqs. (11.27), (11.9), (11.11), and making algebraic manipulations similar to the previous ones, for $(x,t)\in[-1,1]\times[0,\infty)$, we obtain

$$\begin{aligned}
\int_t^\infty\int_{-1}^x vI_3^\kappa\varphi(u,v)dudv &= \gamma^{d,k,\kappa}\sum_{n=0}^{\kappa-1}\sum_{i=0}^{\infty}(-1)^i\chi_i^{n,d,\kappa}\int_t^\infty vg_i^\kappa\,(v)\,dv\int_{-1}^x C_n^{(d-2\kappa-1)/2}(u)du \\
&\quad+\gamma^{d,k,\kappa}\sum_{n=\kappa}^{\infty}\int_t^\infty vg_{n-\kappa}^\kappa\,(v)\,dv\int_{-1}^x C_n^{(d-2\kappa-1)/2}(u)du \\
&= \gamma^{d,k,\kappa}\frac{(k-2\kappa-2)}{\delta_{(d-2\kappa-1)/2}}\times \\
&\quad\left[\sum_{n=0}^{\kappa-1}\sum_{i=0}^{\infty}(-1)^i\chi_i^{n,d,\kappa}g_i^{\kappa+1}(t)\left(C_{n+1}^{(d-2\kappa-3)/2}(x)-C_{n+1}^{(d-2\kappa-3)/2}(-1)\right)\right. \\
&\quad\left.+\sum_{n=\kappa}^{\infty}g_{n-\kappa}^{\kappa+1}(t)\left(C_{n+1}^{(d-2\kappa-3)/2}(x)-C_{n+1}^{(d-2\kappa-3)/2}(-1)\right)\right]
\end{aligned}$$

Thus, as in the Proof of Theorem 11.4.3,

$$I_3^{\kappa+1}\varphi(x,t) = \gamma^{d,k,\kappa+1}\sum_{n=0}^{\infty}h_n^{\kappa+1}(t)C_n^{(d-2(\kappa+1)-1)/2}(x),$$

where

$$h_n^{\varkappa+1}(t) := \begin{cases} \gamma^{d,k,\varkappa+1} \sum_{i=0}^{\infty} (-1)^i \chi_i^{n,d,\varkappa+1} g_i^{\varkappa+1}(t), & n = 0, 1, \ldots, \varkappa \\ \gamma^{d,k,\varkappa+1} g_{n-(\varkappa+1)}^{\varkappa+1}(t), & n \geq \varkappa + 1 \end{cases}$$

with $\gamma^{d,k,\varkappa+1} > 0$, By (11.31) and (2)–(3), $\sum_{n=0}^{\infty} h_n^{\varkappa+1}(0) C_n^{(d-2(\varkappa+1)-1)/2}(1) < \infty$ ■

Proof of Corollary 11.4.12. We can proceed as in the Proof of Corollary 11.4.4 and rewrite $h_n^{\varkappa}, n = 0, 1, \ldots, \varkappa - 1$, as

$$h_n^{\varkappa}(t) = \tilde{h}_{1,n}^{\varkappa}(t) - \tilde{h}_{2,n}^{\varkappa}(t),$$

where

$$\tilde{h}_{1,n}^{\varkappa}(t) := \gamma^{d,k,\varkappa} \sum_{i=0}^{\infty} \chi_{2i}^{n,d,\varkappa} g_{2i}^{\varkappa}(t), \text{ and}$$

$$\tilde{h}_{2,n}^{\varkappa}(t) := \gamma^{d,k,\varkappa} \sum_{i=0}^{\infty} \chi_{2i+1}^{n,d,\varkappa} g_{2i+1}^{\varkappa}(t). \tag{A.10}$$

Define the bounded function $H^{\varkappa}$ on $[-1, 1] \times [0, \infty)$ by

$$H^{\varkappa}(x, t) := \sum_{n=0}^{\varkappa-1} \tilde{h}_{2,n}^{\varkappa}(t) C_n^{(d-2\varkappa-1)/2}(x) - \tilde{h}_{1,0}^{\varkappa}(t) C_0^{(d-2\varkappa-1)/2}(x)$$

By Remark 11.4.5, it is clear that $\tilde{h}_{1,n}^{\varkappa} \in \mathcal{P}\left(\mathbb{R}^k\right), n = 1, 2, \ldots, \varkappa - 1$, and also $h_n^{\varkappa} \in \mathcal{P}\left(\mathbb{R}^k\right)$ for $n \geq \varkappa$. Therefore,

$$H^{\varkappa}(x, t) + I_3^{\varkappa}\varphi(x, t) = \sum_{n=1}^{\varkappa-1} \tilde{h}_{1,n}^{\varkappa}(t) C_n^{(d-2\varkappa-1)/2}(x) + \sum_{n=\varkappa}^{\infty} h_n^{\varkappa}(t) C_n^{(d-2\varkappa-1)/2}(x)$$

has an expansion as Eq. (11.2) with the series uniformly convergent on $[-1, 1] \times [0, \infty)$ due to Theorem 11.4.10. By Theorem 11.3.3 of Ref. [34] (see Eq. (11.2)), we can conclude that the function $H^{\varkappa} + I_1^{\varkappa}\varphi$ belongs to the class $\mathcal{P}\left(\mathbb{S}^{d-2\varkappa} \times \mathbb{R}^k\right)$. ■

Proof of Theorem 11.4.13. As in the Proof of Theorem 11.4.7, for any constants A and B, by Eq. (11.27),

$$\begin{aligned} &A\tilde{h}_{1,n}^{k}(t) - B\tilde{h}_{2,n}^{k}(t) \\ &= \sum_{i=0}^{\infty} \int_0^{\infty} \Omega_{k-2\varkappa}(tr) \left(A\chi_{2i}^{n,d,\varkappa} \frac{1}{r^{2\varkappa}} dF_{2i}(r) - B\chi_{2i+1}^{n,d,\varkappa} \frac{1}{r^{2\varkappa}} dF_{2i+1}(r) \right). \end{aligned} \tag{A.11}$$

Since, by Eq. (11.31),

$$\int_0^{\infty} A \left| \chi_i^{n,d,\varkappa} \right| \frac{1}{r^{2\varkappa}} dF_i(r) \leq A \Upsilon^{n,d,\varkappa} C_i^{(d-1)/2}(1) \int_0^{\infty} \frac{1}{r^{2\varkappa}} dF_i(r),$$

we have

$$\int_0^\infty \left(A\chi_{2i}^{n,d,\kappa}\frac{1}{r^{2\kappa}}dF_{2i}(r) - B\chi_{2i+1}^{n,d,\kappa}\frac{1}{r^{2\kappa}}dF_{2i+1}(r)\right) < \infty$$

and by Hypothesis (1) the series in (A.11) converges absolutely and uniformly on $[0,\infty)$.

Thus,

$$A\tilde{h}_{1,n}^{k}(t) - B\tilde{h}_{2,n}^{k}(t) = \int_0^\infty \Omega_k(tr)d\left(\sum_{i=0}^{\infty} A\chi_{2i}^{n,d,\kappa}\frac{1}{r^{2\kappa}}F_{2i}(r) - B\chi_{2i+1}^{n,d,\kappa}\frac{1}{r^{2\kappa}}F_{2i+1}(r)\right).$$

By (2), the series $\sum_{i=0}^{\infty}\chi_{2i}^{n,d,\kappa}\frac{1}{r^{2\kappa}}F_{2i}$ and $\sum_{i=0}^{\infty}\chi_{2i+1}^{n,d,\kappa}\frac{1}{r^{2\kappa}}F_{2i+1}$ are uniformly bounded on $[0,\infty)$. Then we can choose A^n, B^n such that $\sum_{i=0}^{\infty} A^n\chi_{2i}^{n,d,\kappa}\frac{1}{r^{2\kappa}}F_{2i} - B^n\chi_{2i+1}^{n,d,\kappa}\frac{1}{r^{2\kappa}}F_{2i+1}$ is non-negative, which allows us to conclude that $A^n\tilde{h}_{1,n}^{\kappa} - B^n\tilde{h}_{2,n}^{\kappa} \in \mathcal{P}\left(\mathbb{R}^k\right)$. The uniform convergence of the series (11.36) follows by Theorem 11.4.10 and the result by Theorem 11.3.3 of Ref. [34] (see Eq. (11.2)). ∎

References

1. E. Porcu, R. Furrer, and D. Nychka, 30 years of space-time covariance functions, *Wiley Interdiscip. Rev. Comput. Stat.* e1512 (2020).
2. J. D. Hamilton, *Time Series Analysis*. Princeton University Press (1994).
3. J. C. Hull, *Options, Futures, and Other Derivatives*. Pearson Education India (2003).
4. A. Lipton and M. López de Prado, A closed-form solution for optimal Ornstein–Uhlenbeck driven trading strategies, *Int. J. Theor. Appl. Finance.* **23**(08), 1–34 (2020).
5. W. Willinger, M. S. Taqqu, and V. Teverovsky, Stock market prices and long-range dependence, *Finance Stoch.* **3**(1), 1–13 (1999).
6. D. P. Kennedy, The term structure of interest rates as a Gaussian random field, *Math. Finance.* **4**(3), 247–258 (1994).
7. R. S. Goldstein, The term structure of interest rates as a random field, *Rev. Financ. Stud.* **13**(2), 365–384 (2000).
8. R. L. Kimmel, Modeling the term structure of interest rates: A new approach, *J. Financ. Econ.* **72**(1), 143–183 (2004).
9. S. Albeverio, E. Lytvynov, and A. Mahnig, A model of the term structure of interest rates based on Lévy fields, *Stoch. Process. Their Appl.* **114**(2), 251–263 (2004).
10. F. Özkan and T. Schmidt, *Credit Risk with Infinite Dimensional Lévy Processes* (2005).
11. D. Hainaut, Continuous mixed-Laplace jump diffusion models for stocks and commodities, *Quant. Finance Econ.* **1**(2), 145–173 (2017).
12. E. Biffis and P. Millossovich, A bidimensional approach to mortality risk, *Decis. Econ. Finance.* **29**(2), 71–94 (2006).
13. F. Biagini, C. Botero, and I. Schreiber, Risk-minimization for life insurance liabilities with dependent mortality risk, *Math. Finance.* **27**(2), 505–533 (2017).
14. X. Emery, A turning bands program for conditional co-simulation of cross-correlated Gaussian random fields, *Comput. Geosci.* **34**(12), 1850–1862 (2008).

15. G. Matheron, The intrinsic random functions and their applications, *Adv. Appl. Probab.* **5**(3), 439–468 (1973).

16. R. Furrer, M. G. Genton, and D. Nychka, Covariance tapering for interpolation of large spatial datasets, *J. Comput. Graph. Stat.* **15**(3), 502–523 (2006).

17. S. Cambanis, R. Keener, and G. Simons, On α-symmetric multivariate distributions, *J. Multivariate Anal.* **13**(2), 213–233 (1983).

18. D. J. Daley and E. Porcu, Dimension walks and Schoenberg spectral measures, *Proc. Amer. Math. Soc.* **142**(5), 1813–1824 (2014).

19. I. J. Schoenberg, Metric spaces and completely monotone functions, *Ann. Math.* **39**(4), 811–841 (1938).

20. G. Matheron, Random functions and their application in geology, In *Geostatistics*, pp. 79–87, Springer (1970).

21. M. L. Eaton, On the projections of isotropic distributions, *Ann. Statist.* **9**(2), 391–400 (1981).

22. H. Wendland, Piecewise polynomial, positive definite and compactly supported radial functions of minimal degree, *Adv. Comput. Math.* **4**(1), 389–396 (1995).

23. R. Schaback and Z.-M. Wu, Operators on radial functions, *J. Comput. Appl. Math.* **73**(1–2), 257–270 (1996).

24. T. Gneiting, Compactly supported correlation functions, *J. Multivariate Anal.* **83**(2), 493–508 (2002).

25. T. Gneiting, Criteria of Pólya type for radial positive definite functions, *Proc. Amer. Math. Soc.* **129**(8), 2309–2318 (2001).

26. E. Porcu, P. Gregori, and J. Mateu, La descente et la montée étendues: The spatially d-anisotropic and the spatio-temporal case, *Stoch. Environ. Res. Risk Assess.* **21**(6), 683–693 (2007).

27. K. W. Fang, *Symmetric Multivariate and Related Distributions*. CRC Press (2018).

28. I. J. Schoenberg, Positive definite functions on spheres, *Duke Math. J.* **9**(1), 96–108 (1942).

29. R. K. Beatson, W. zu Castell, and Y. Xu, A Pólya criterion for (strict) positive-definiteness on the sphere, *IMA J. Numer. Anal.* **34**(2), 550–568 (2014).

30. R. K. Beatson and W. zu Castell, One-step recurrences for stationary random fields on the sphere, *SIGMA Symmetry Integrability Geom. Methods Appl.* **12**, 043 (2016).

31. R. K. Beatson and W. zu Castell, Dimension hopping and families of strictly positive definite zonal basis functions on spheres, *J. Approx. Theory.* **221**, 22–37 (2017).

32. M. Trübner and J. Ziegel, Derivatives of isotropic positive definite functions on spheres, *Proc. Amer. Math. Soc.* **145**(7), 3017–3031 (2017).

33. N. H. Bingham and T. L. Symons, Dimension walks on $S^d \times R$. *Statist. Probab. Lett.* **147**, 12–17 (2019).

34. C. Berg and E. Porcu, From Schoenberg coefficients to Schoenberg functions, *Constr. Approx.* **45**(2), 217–241 (2017).

35. G. Szegö, *Orthogonal Polynomials*. American Mathematical Society Colloquium Publications, Vol. 23, Revised ed., American Mathematical Society, Providence, R.I. (1959).

36. C. Berg, J. P. R. Christensen, and P. Ressel, *Harmonic Analysis on Semigroups*, vol. 100, Graduate Texts in Mathematics, Springer-Verlag, New York (1984).

37. T. Gneiting, On the derivatives of radial positive definite functions, *J. Math. Anal. Appl.* **236**(1), 86–93 (1999).

SECTION

4

Trustworthy Artificial Intelligence

https://doi.org/10.1142/9789819813049_0012

CHAPTER 12 Trustworthy Artificial Intelligence: Nature, Requirements, Regulation, and Emerging Discussions

Francisco Herrera[1,5,*], Andres Herrera[1], Javier Del Ser[2,3], Enrique Herrera-Viedma[1], and Marcos López de Prado[4,5,6]

[1] *Department of Computer Science and Artificial Intelligence, DaSCI Andalusian Institute in Data Science and Computational Intelligence, University of Granada, Granada, Spain*
[2] *TECNALIA, Basque Research and Technology Alliance (BRTA), Derio, Spain*
[3] *Department of Mathematics, University of the Basque Country (UPV/EHU), Bilbao, Spain*
[4] *School of Engineering, Cornell University, Ithaca, NY, USA*
[5] *ADIA Lab, Al Maryah Island, Abu Dhabi, UAE*
[6] *Department of Mathematics, Khalifa University of Science and Technology, Abu Dhabi, UAE*
[*] *Corresponding author. E-mail: herrera@decsai.ugr.es*

Trustworthy artificial intelligence (TAI) is a framework and critical goal for developing and practically deploying reliable and ethical AI systems, properties essential for user confidence, societal acceptance, and responsible use. In this chapter, we explore TAI from three perspectives: (1) the importance of TAI and why it is essential; (2) a brief analysis of TAI requirements and characteristics as proposed by the high-level expert group on artificial intelligence commissioned by the European Commission and the American National Institute of Standards and Technology, preceded by a short discussion on trust in AI; and (3) an analysis of TAI's role within emerging discussions on AI regulation and governance. We also review contributions from the literature, offering reflections that complement this chapter's holistic vision of TAI, from theory to practice. TAI is expected to play a crucial role in the development of responsible AI systems, ensuring auditability and accountability throughout the design, development, and utilization phases, thereby creating ethical, reliable, and safe AI systems from a technological perspective.

12.1. Introduction

Artificial intelligence (AI) is rapidly transforming several aspects of our lives. With the emergence of generative AI, global debates have intensified over the past few years. In both the specialized press and scientific literature, we encounter increasing concerns, reflections, and inquiries that highlight AI's growing societal impact. Some of the critical questions include the following:

- How should AI be regulated?
- What risks does AI currently pose, and what risks may emerge in the future?
- How can we achieve responsible and safe AI?
- What AI advancements can we expect in the coming years?
- Is it possible to create an AI that operates at a human level (artificial general intelligence)?

Each of these questions requires extensive contemplation and discussion within the scientific community. In this contribution, we delve into the early stages of the debate surrounding ethical, responsible, reliable, and safe AI from a technological perspective. This debate began a few years ago, giving rise to an ethical guide for AI that, from a technological standpoint, has been known as trustworthy artificial intelligence (TAI). The paper introduces a brief history of the conceptualization of "trustworthy AI," which we will analyze later concerning the concept of "trust in AI" [1].

From a technological perspective, we turn our attention to the document published by the European Commission, entrusted to the high-level expert group (HLEG) on AI, titled *Ethics Guidelines for Trustworthy AI* [2]. This document, made public on April 8, 2019, outlines four ethical principles for AI systems: (1) respect for human autonomy, (2) prevention of harm, (3) trustworthiness, and (4) explainability. The document emphasizes that TAI is built on the following three key components, which must be maintained throughout the lifecycle of an AI-based system:

(1) Legality: AI systems must comply with all applicable laws and regulations.
(2) Ethics: AI systems must adhere to ethical principles and values.
(3) Robustness: AI systems must be reliable from both technical and social perspectives, preventing unintentional harm.

Although each of these components is necessary, none alone is sufficient for achieving TAI. These are further divided into seven technical requirements: human agency and oversight; technical robustness and safety; privacy and data governance; transparency; diversity, non-discrimination, and fairness; societal and environmental well-being; and accountability. A second document, published on July 17, 2020, "the assessment list for Trustworthy Artificial Intelligence (ALTAI) for self-assessment" [3], elaborates on these requirements. In January 2023, the American National Institute of Standards and Technology (NIST) released the AI Risk Management Framework (AIRMF) [4], including a similar set of TAI requirements, emphasizing concepts such as "secure and resilient," "explainable and interpretable," and "valid and reliable" AI systems. This framework also highlights that approaches that enhance AI trustworthiness can reduce negative AI risks.

Over the past 5 years, extensive debates in the literature have covered TAI at ethical, legal, and technical levels. Throughout these debates, one fundamental consideration remains: ensuring the trustworthiness of AI-based systems is critical for their successful adoption. A precise definition of TAI is provided as follows [5]:

Definition 12.1.1. *Trustworthy AI is an AI paradigm that encompasses all technical approaches and tools to develop, deploy, and use safe, legal, and ethical AI systems.*

Expanding on the three pillars mentioned earlier, TAI refers to design characteristics of AI systems that adhere to ethical, legal, and robust technical standards, ensuring the following:

(1) AI systems comply with legal requirements, including data protection laws, intellectual property rights, and other relevant legislation.
(2) AI systems align with ethical principles and societal norms, avoiding biases and unintended consequences while aligning with human values and needs.
(3) AI systems behave reliably, with robust technology to minimize harm, prevent unacceptable outcomes, and withstand attacks and unexpected conditions.

However, the practical implementation of TAI remains nascent [6, 7]. Conceptual models, such as the trustworthy artificial intelligence implementation (TAII) framework [8] and the Wasabi conceptual model [9], are still in their early stages and far from widespread adoption. A critical element in this context is the concept of a "responsible AI system" as defined below [10]:

Definition 12.1.2. *A responsible AI system is an AI system that ensures auditability and accountability during its design, development, and use, according to specifications and applicable regulations within its domain of practice.*

The implementation of "responsible AI systems" can help reduce bias, create more transparent AI systems, and increase end-user trust in those systems, supported by a governance approach throughout their lifecycle. In summary, as discussed by Díaz-Rodríguez et al. [10], achieving TAI requires a holistic approach, collaboration, and ongoing efforts to address challenges while building systems that benefit society under ethical, responsible, and safe behaviors.

In recent progress, 2023 and 2024 have seen intense advances and debates on AI regulation by governments and institutions such as the European Commission and the United Nations, among others. There is a growing demand for AI regulations that minimize risks to public safety and preserve human rights while fostering a flexible and innovative environment. These efforts must align with AI governance [11–13] to create a global framework for the secure implementation of AI in all applications where risks may arise. Within this regulatory and governance landscape, TAI plays an essential role.

This contribution aims to provide a transversal analysis of TAI, addressing the following four key points:

(1) An examination of the essential nature of TAI and its crucial role for ethical, legal, and practical reasons, fostering a positive and responsible AI ecosystem while addressing AI risks.

(2) An overview of TAI requirements and a brief discussion on human trust in AI, emphasizing how to understand trust in systems that rely on AI as their core technology.
(3) An analysis of recent developments in AI regulation and governance. AI governance is the legal framework and processes that ensure responsible AI systems are developed, including the required AI safety. These frameworks are crucial for guiding humanity through the ethical and responsible adoption of AI.
(4) A breakdown of the literature highlighting several contributions that offer insightful reflections, from theory to practice, complementing the holistic vision of TAI that this chapter aims to present to its readership.

We do not claim that the brief analysis of the literature in this manuscript is exhaustive. Our overarching goal is to highlight a selection of studies that provide a comprehensive vision of TAI from various authors' perspectives.

The rest of the chapter is organized as follows. Section 12.2 offers a brief analysis of the essential aspects supporting the importance and need for developing TAI. Section 12.3 explores the concept of trust in AI and introduces the ALTAI requirements and AIRMF characteristics. Section 12.4 briefly immerses the reader into the ongoing debate on regulation and expands on how TAI factors into this discussion. Section 12.5 presents a concise overview of the literature, highlighting six papers that collectively contribute to a global understanding of the current status of TAI and emerging discussions. Finally, Section 12.6 concludes with an outlook that encourages future research on this exciting topic.

12.2. Why Is Trustworthy Artificial Intelligence Essential?

This section provides a brief analysis of the key aspects that underscore the importance of developing TAI-based systems, referred to as responsible AI systems [10]. The analysis is twofold: (1) addressing the ethical, legal, and practical reasons for TAI and (2) examining AI risks and their interrelationship.

TAI is vital for ethical, legal, and practical reasons, fostering a positive and responsible AI ecosystem. Key considerations include the following:

(1) Ethical responsibility: TAI ensures that technology operates within ethical principles, preventing harm, unfair discrimination, and privacy violations.
(2) User confidence: Trustworthy AI systems inspire user confidence, leading to wider adoption and acceptance of AI applications.
(3) Legal compliance: TAI adheres to legal requirements, ensuring responsible use and reducing the risk of legal consequences.
(4) Mitigating bias: TAI actively addresses biases, promoting fairness and equity, and reducing the risk of legal consequences.
(5) Safety and security: TAI minimizes risks related to system failures, security breaches, and adversarial attacks.

(6) Explainability: A lack of transparency in AI models can lead to difficulties in understanding how AI uses data, potentially resulting in biased or unsafe decisions.
(7) Sustainable development: TAI contributes to sustainable development by considering long-term societal impact and environmental consequences.

From the AI risk perspective, as AI grows more sophisticated and widespread, concerns about its potential dangers become increasingly prominent. These risks include privacy violations, algorithmic bias due to poor data, socioeconomic inequality, job displacement through automation, deepfakes, market volatility, autonomous weapons, and the possibility of uncontrollable self-aware AI. Three key risk vectors summarize these concerns, highlighting the urgent need for regulation:

- The rise and amplification of misinformation (e.g., false and malicious content on social platforms).
- Biases that reinforce existing inequalities (e.g., gender and ethnic discrimination, the digital divide, social credit systems, etc.).
- The erosion of privacy through the collection of hidden data to fuel AI algorithms.

On a broader scale, global AI risks are also under discussion. Although we do not explore this in depth here, a concise summary is provided in the "Statement on AI Risk" by the Center for AI Safety: "Mitigating the risk of extinction from AI should be a global priority alongside other societal-scale risks such as pandemics and nuclear war" [11]. Two key papers offer comprehensive analyzes of AI risks: "A Taxonomy and Analysis of Societal-Scale Risks from AI" (TASRA) [12] and an overview of "Catastrophic AI Risks" [13]. Understanding and managing the risks associated with AI are crucial. In this context, TAI provides the path to building trust in AI systems.

12.3. Trustworthy Artificial Intelligence: European Commission and NIST

In this section, we briefly outline the requirements and characteristics of TAI proposed by the AI HLEG commissioned by the European Commission, as outlined in the ALTAI document (Section 12.3.2) and the AI Risk Management Framework (RMF) by NIST (Section 12.3.3). Before delving into these descriptions, we address the concept of human trust in AI, a controversial topic that remains central to ongoing discussions (Section 12.3.1).

12.3.1. *On human trust in AI*

With the publication of the *Ethics Guidelines for Trustworthy AI* in 2019 [2], the notions of trust and trustworthiness have become focal points in debates surrounding AI ethics, despite a general consensus that AI should indeed be trustworthy. Much discourse has arisen around the term "trustworthy" (e.g., whether it is the appropriate term compared to "reliable") and the limits of using human trust to assess machine reliability. We can infer that this debate hinges on the conceptual relationship between humans and AI systems. As humans tend to view AI systems as social actors and attribute human-like qualities such as competence, integrity, and benevolence to them, it is reasonable to suggest that humans do, or will, *trust* or *distrust* AI systems, even though these systems are not human.

The debate over human trust in AI has intensified over the years. Here, we introduce four key papers that provide insights into this complex issue, offering a broad overview of various perspectives. These papers are presented sequentially by publication date, reflecting the evolution of the discourse.

Glikson and Woolley provide a comprehensive review of empirical research on human trust in AI conducted across multiple disciplines over the past 20 years [14]. They identify the form of AI representation (e.g., robot, virtual, and embedded) and the level of machine intelligence (i.e., its capabilities) as key antecedents to trust development, proposing a framework to address the elements that shape users' cognitive and emotional trust. The authors also reveal the importance of AI's tangibility, transparency, reliability, and immediacy behaviors in developing cognitive trust and the role of AI's anthropomorphism specifically for emotional trust. They also note several limitations in the current evidence base, such as the diversity of trust measures and overreliance on short-term, small sample, and experimental studies, where trust development is likely to be different from in longer-term, higher-stakes field environments. Based on their review, they suggest the most promising directions for future research.

Jacobi et al. explore the nature of trust in AI and propose a model inspired by sociology's interpersonal trust, which hinges on two key properties: the user's vulnerability and the ability to anticipate the impact of the AI model's decisions [15]. They also formalize "contractual trust" and "trustworthiness," identifying intrinsic reasoning and extrinsic behavior as potential causes of warranted trust. The connection between trust and explainable AI (XAI) is examined through their formalization, with particular attention to how current evaluation methods in XAI address the vulnerability central to trust in AI.

Stix provides an overview of the concept of trustworthy AI, explaining that in recent years, the term "has been used to describe AI systems that are reliable, transparent, and ethical" [1]. The paper discusses the origins of the term and its adoption in government policies and highlights its potential pitfalls. The widespread adoption of the term "trustworthy AI" risks diluting its meaning to the point of losing both the original intent and the core substance it was meant to convey, potentially undermining serious policy efforts. It is important to note that "trustworthy AI" conflates at least five distinct meanings: trust in the proper functioning and safety of the technology; the technology being worthy of the trust of those using or encountering it; users or others experiencing the technology as trustworthy; and the technology being universally worthy of trust.

Reinhardt argues for an approach informed by research on trust from other fields, such as social sciences and humanities, particularly practical philosophy [16]. The paper offers a detailed overview of the concept of trust used in AI ethics guidelines to date and assesses their overlaps and omissions from a practical philosophical perspective. Four key questions regarding the divergence of trust in AI are particularly noteworthy:

(1) Why is trust important or valuable?
(2) Who or what are the envisioned trustors and trustees?
(3) What does trustworthiness entail?
(4) How should trustworthiness be implemented technically?

Further clarification is necessary on all four points, and that philosophy can help conceptualize trust and trustworthiness. At the same time, Reinhardt cautions against turning TAI into an "intellectual land of plenty," an umbrella term encompassing every desirable technical and ethical attribute for AI systems. Further, we need to discuss potential conflicts between the principles of trustworthiness and warns of the ambivalences and dangers of trust, suggesting that future research might reveal the need for institutionalized distrust, rather than more trust in AI.

As a short conclusion, achieving a high level of trust in AI requires an analysis that extends beyond the concept of trust itself. It involves aligning TAI requirements with trustworthiness, considering the scope of application, and understanding how AI users approach trust in specific contexts. Although this paper does not aim to delve deeply into the ethical and philosophical dilemmas of human trust in AI, we have briefly touched on the topic due to its relevance and the richness of the literature, as a precursor to the assessment lists for TAI that follow.

12.3.2. *Assessment list for TAI*

The assessment list for TAI (ALTAI) developed by AI HLEG, is designed for self-assessment purposes. It provides an initial framework for evaluating TAI systems [3], based on the *Ethics Guidelines for Trustworthy AI*. Developed over 2 years, the list incorporates valuable feedback from experts and industry stakeholders. It outlines seven key requirements to ensure ethical and trustworthy AI systems. The following is an exploration of these requirements, accompanied by supporting elements (see Fig. 12.1 for a visual summary of the assessment list), including the general requirement name, subareas, and a brief analysis of the supporting elements:

(1) Human Agency and Oversight (human agency and autonomy and human oversight):
  (a) AI systems should empower humans, allowing them to make informed decisions.
  (b) AI systems should ensure that humans remain in control and can intervene when necessary.
(2) Technical Robustness and Safety (resilience to attack and security, general safety, accuracy, reliability, fallback plans, and reproducibility):
  (a) AI systems should be technically reliable and safe.
  (b) AI systems should mitigate risks, avoid unintended consequences, and prevent harm.

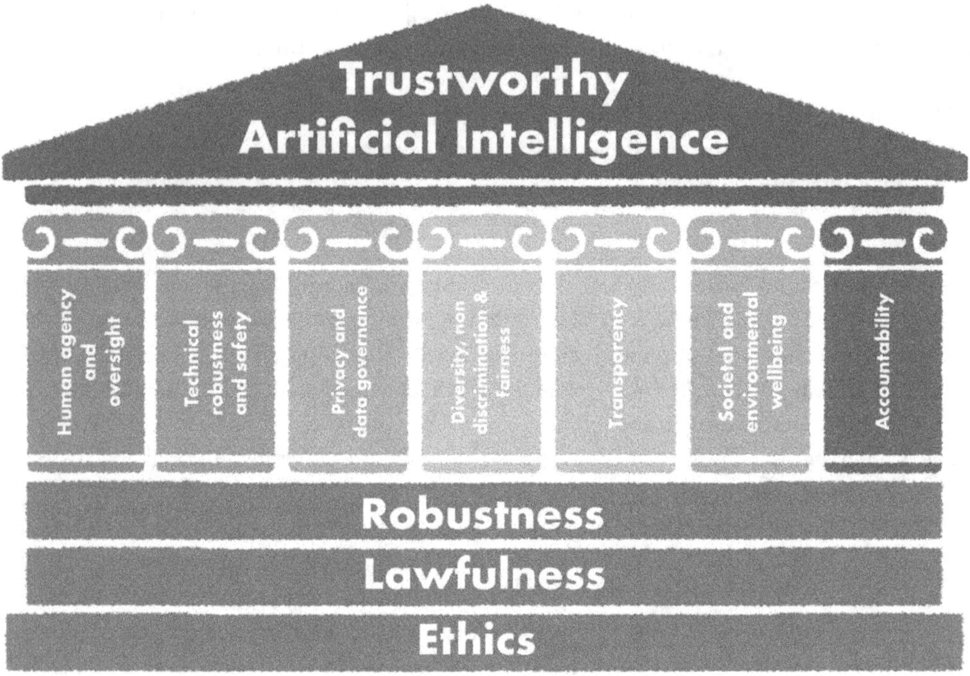

Fig. 12.1 ALTAI (inspired from Ref. [10]).

(3) Privacy and Data Governance:
   (a) AI systems should protect user privacy and handle data responsibly, implementing privacy-enhancing techniques.
   (b) They should adhere to data governance principles, applying policies and standards that promote data availability, quality, and security.

(4) Transparency (traceability, explainability, and communication):
   (a) Humans must be able to understand how to interact with an AI system, including its internal functioning, the data used, the algorithms applied, and the decision-making process.
   (b) AI processes and decisions should be explainable.
   (c) Clear insights must be provided into how AI reaches its conclusions.

(5) Diversity, Non-discrimination, and Fairness (avoidance of unfair bias, accessibility and universal design, and stakeholder participation):
   (a) Biases should be avoided, ensuring fairness across all user groups.
   (b) Discriminatory outcomes should be addressed proactively.

(6) Societal and Environmental Well-Being (stakeholder participation, impact on work and skills, and impact on society at large or democracy):
   (a) AI systems should consider their broader societal and environmental impact.
   (b) Efforts should be made to minimize negative effects and maximize positive contributions.

(7) Accountability (auditability and risk management):
   (a) Developers, operators, and organizations must be held accountable for AI outcomes.
   (b) Mechanisms for redress and responsibility should be established.

These requirements collectively contribute to building trustworthy and ethical AI systems.

12.3.3. *AI risk and trustworthiness: AIRM from NIST*

The NIST has introduced a framework that outlines the characteristics of TAI [4]. These characteristics are foundational for ensuring AI systems are reliable, ethical, and transparent, underscoring that approaches enhancing TAI can mitigate the negative risks associated with AI.

We proceed analogously to the previous section by exploring these characteristics (Fig. 12.2) along with a short list of supporting elements.

(1) Validity and Reliability
   (a) Validation refers to the "confirmation, through objective evidence, that the requirements for a specific intended use or application have been fulfilled."
   (b) Reliability is defined as the "ability of an item to perform as required, without failure, for a given time interval, under given conditions."
   (c) AI systems must deliver accurate and dependable outcomes.
   (d) Ensuring the data used for training and inference is valid and reliable is essential.
   (e) AI systems should be able to perform as required, without failure, for a defined period under given conditions.

(2) Safety
   (a) AI systems should not, under defined conditions, lead to a state in which human life, health, property, or the environment is endangered.
   (b) Prioritizing user safety and preventing harm is critical.
   (c) Identifying and mitigating risks associated with AI deployment is necessary.

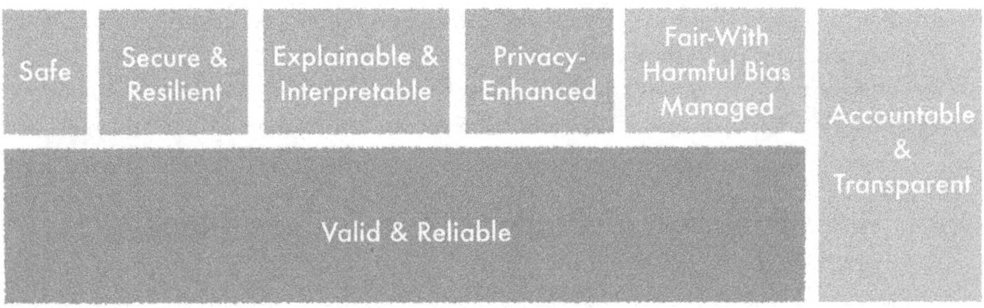

Fig. 12.2 AI risk and trustworthiness assessment list (inspired by AI_RMF).

(3) Security and Resiliency
  (a) Security and resilience, though related, are distinct. Resilience refers to the ability to return and also encompasses protocols to prevent, protect, respond to, and recover from attacks. Resilience involves robustness and addresses unexpected or adversarial use of the model or data.
  (b) Safeguarding AI systems from malicious attacks and ensuring resilience against challenges is essential.
  (c) Protecting AI systems from vulnerabilities and unauthorized access is crucial.

(4) Accountability and Transparency
  (a) TAI relies on accountability, which in turn requires transparency. *Transparency* reflects the extent to which an AI system's information and its outputs are available to users.
  (b) Transparency is often necessary for actionable redress in cases of incorrect or harmful AI outputs.
  (c) Human–AI interaction must be considered in ensuring transparency.
  (d) Developers and operators should be held accountable for AI outcomes.
  (e) Measures to enhance transparency and accountability should also weigh the impact on the implementing entity, including resource requirements and the need to safeguard proprietary information.

(5) Explainability and Interpretability
  (a) Explainability refers to representing the mechanisms underlying AI operations, whereas interpretability refers to the meaning of AI outputs in the context of their designed purposes.
  (b) Providing insights into how AI makes decisions is essential.
  (c) Humans should be able to understand and interpret AI models.

(6) Privacy Enhancement
  (a) Privacy relates to norms and practices that safeguard human autonomy, identity, and dignity.
  (b) Protecting user privacy and sensitive information is vital.
  (c) AI systems should implement privacy-preserving techniques.

(7) Fairness and Mitigation of Harmful Bias
  (a) Fairness in AI addresses concerns of equality and equity, particularly in managing harmful bias and discrimination.
  (b) Biases in AI algorithms should be addressed to prevent discriminatory outcomes.
  (c) Ensuring fairness across different user groups and managing harmful biases is essential.

12.4. Regulation and Institutional Approaches Aligned with TAI

As mentioned earlier, 2023 and 2024 have seen intense advances and debates on AI regulation by governments and institutions. This section highlights five key initiatives from 2023 and 2024 that are set to shape international efforts over the long term. These initiatives are closely tied to TAI. The governance and regulation of AI are based on principles of trustworthiness, risk mitigation, and the development of technologies to ensure the reliability of AI-based systems, particularly through trustworthy AI tools.

12.4.1. *US executive order on safe and trustworthy AI*

On October 30, 2023, the President of the United States signed an executive order regulating the development of AI, titled the "Executive Order on the Safe, Secure, and Trustworthy Development and Use of Artificial Intelligence" (EO14110) [17]. The order outlines eight guiding principles and priorities to govern and advance the practical use of AI:

(1) AI must be safe and secure.
(2) Promoting responsible innovation, competition, and collaboration will allow the United States to lead in AI and unlock the technology's potential to solve some of society's most challenging problems.
(3) The responsible development and use of AI must prioritize supporting American workers.
(4) AI policies should align with the administration's commitment to advancing equity and civil rights.
(5) The interests of Americans who increasingly use, interact with, or purchase AI and AI-enabled products in their daily lives must be safeguarded.
(6) As AI continues to advance, Americans' privacy and civil liberties must be protected.
(7) It is crucial to manage the risks associated with the Federal Government's use of AI and strengthen its capacity to regulate, govern, and support responsible AI use to deliver better outcomes for Americans.
(8) The Federal Government should lead global societal, economic, and technological progress, as it has during previous eras of disruptive innovation.

12.4.2. *AI Safety Summit and the Bletchley Declaration*

The AI Safety Summit, held in the UK from November 1 to 2, 2023, brought together representatives from 30 countries, including China and the United States. The summit focused on assessing the risks of AI, particularly at the frontier of development, and exploring how these risks can be mitigated through coordinated international action. The policy paper, "The Bletchley Declaration by Countries Attending" [18], was published during the summit. Noteworthy actions outlined in the declaration include:

- identifying AI safety risks of shared concern, building a shared scientific, evidence-based understanding of these risks, and maintaining that understanding as AI capabilities continue to increase. This will be part of a broader global approach to understanding AI's impact on society.

- building risk-based policies across participating countries to ensure safety, while recognizing that approaches may vary based on national circumstances and legal frameworks. This effort includes greater transparency from private entities developing frontier AI capabilities, appropriate evaluation metrics, safety testing tools, and enhancing public sector capabilities and scientific research.

12.4.3. *United Nations AI Advisory Body: Governing AI for Humanity Interim Report*

The United Nations has established an AI Advisory Body with a mandate to develop a final document on AI governance by mid-2024. The interim report, titled "Governing AI for Humanity. Interim Report" [19] (December 2023), outlines key guiding principles and institutional functions. The guiding principles are

- Guiding principle 1: AI should be governed inclusively, by and for the benefit of all.
- Guiding principle 2: AI must be governed in the public interest.
- Guiding principle 3: AI governance should be aligned with data governance and the promotion of data commons.
- Guiding principle 4: AI governance must be universal, networked, and rooted in adaptive, multistakeholder collaboration.
- Guiding principle 5: AI governance should be anchored in the UN Charter, International Human Rights Law, and other international commitments, including the Sustainable Development Goals.

The advisory body has also identified several key institutional functions for AI governance. These include regularly assessing the state of AI and its trajectory, enhancing interoperability, harmonizing standards, safety, and RMFs, facilitating deployment, fostering international multistakeholder collaboration to empower the Global South, monitoring risks, coordinating emergency response, and developing binding accountability norms (Fig. 12.3). Each function requires international cooperation among all stakeholders involved.

Fig. 12.4 presents a simplified schema of the AI governance landscape (both existing and emerging) that the advisory body will further develop in its next phase of work. This simplified schema is intended to promote interoperability between different efforts surrounding AI governance.

In September 2024, the Final Report "Governing AI for Humanity" [20] was published, presenting an executive summary reaffirming the imperative of global governance. It emphasizes the need for dialog among countries, pointing out that although there are divergences across countries and sectors, but also a strong desire for dialogue. Engaging diverse experts, policymakers, businesspeople, researchers, and advocates—across regions, genders, and disciplines—has shown that diversity need not lead to discord, and dialog can

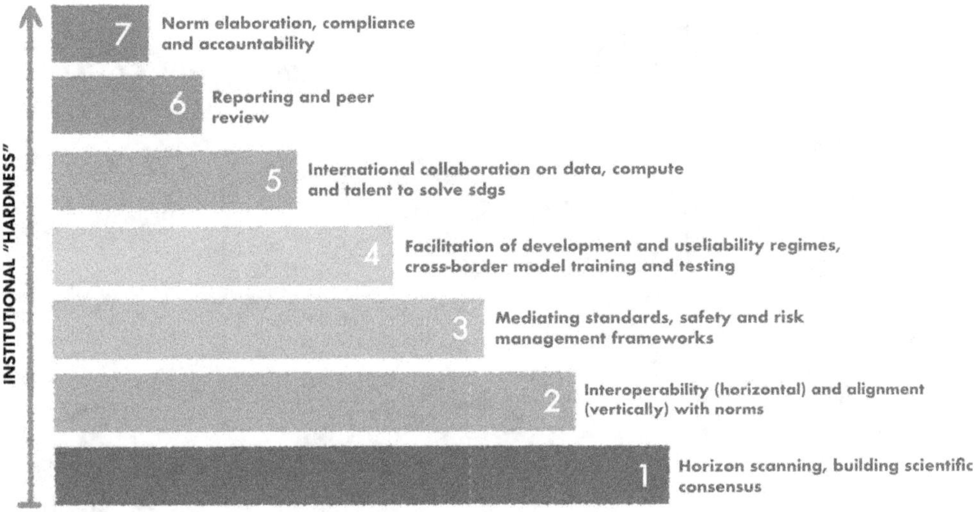

Fig. 12.3 AI governance functions (inspired from https://www.un.org/en/ai-advisory-body).

lead to common ground and collaboration. We highlight point 218, page 78, the penultimate reflection by authors, in section "Conclusion: a call to action." It reflects the spirit and initiative of this second and final report:

> *"The implementation of the recommendations in the present report may also encourage new ways of thinking: a collaborative and learning mindset, multistakeholder engagement and broad-based public engagement. The United Nations can be the vehicle for a new social contract for AI that ensures global buy-in for a governance regime that protects and empowers us all. Such a contract will ensure that opportunities are fairly accessed and distributed, and the risks are not loaded onto the most vulnerable – or passed on to future generations, as we have seen tragically with climate change."*

12.4.4. *Artificial Intelligence Act*

The European Parliament and the Council of Europe have reached a consensus to approve the AI Act [2] in 2024, published on June 13, 2024. This regulatory framework, based on risk levels, aims to ensure that AI systems deployed and used in the EU are safe and uphold fundamental rights and European values. For high-risk AI systems, the regulations mandate risk-mitigation systems, comprehensive documentation, clear user information, high-quality datasets, activity logging, human oversight, and robust measures to ensure accuracy and cybersecurity.

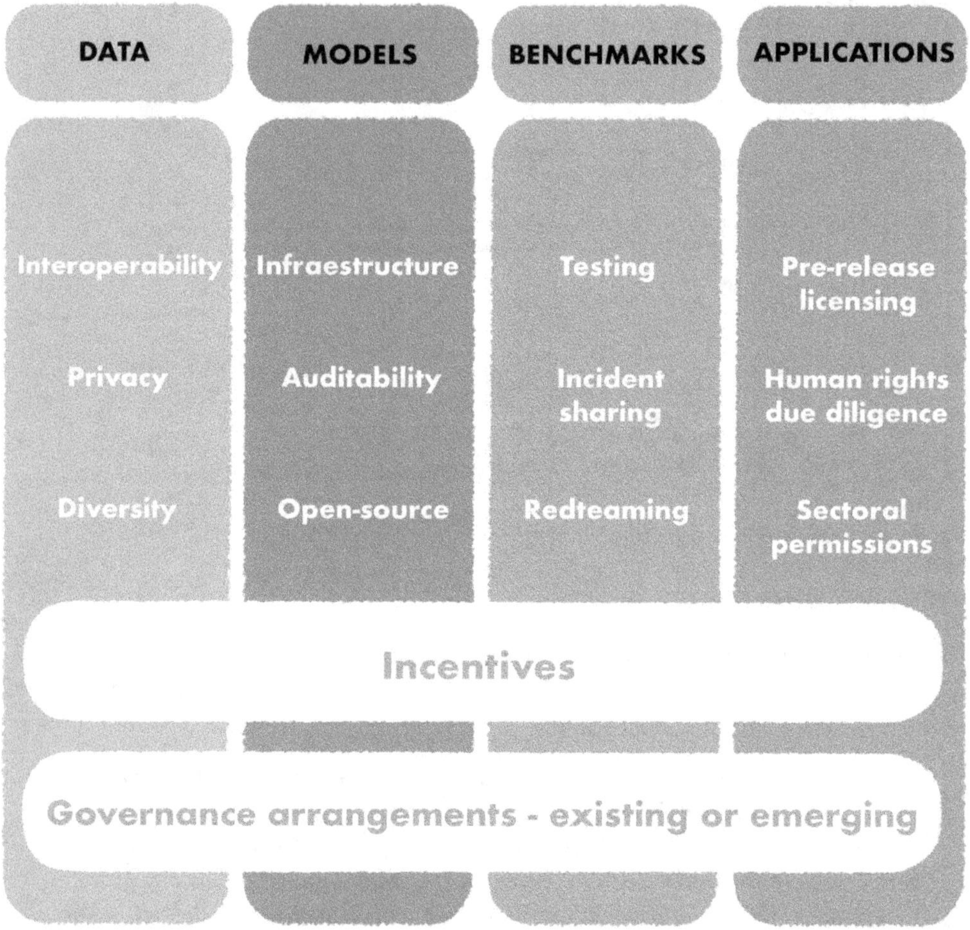

Fig. 12.4 presents A simplified schema for considering interoperability across different AI governance efforts [16].

The European regulation classifies AI systems into four risk levels (Fig. 12.5), where auditability is essential for systems in level 2, those identified as high-risk. The details of these risk levels are elaborated below:

- **Level 3 and 4**. The majority of AI systems fall under minimal risk. These include applications like AI-driven recommendation systems and spam filters, which will generally have no obligations. Companies may, however, choose to adopt voluntary codes of conduct for these AI systems.
- **Level 2**. High-risk AI systems fall under this category. They will be subject to the discussed regulatory requirements and must undergo an auditing process.

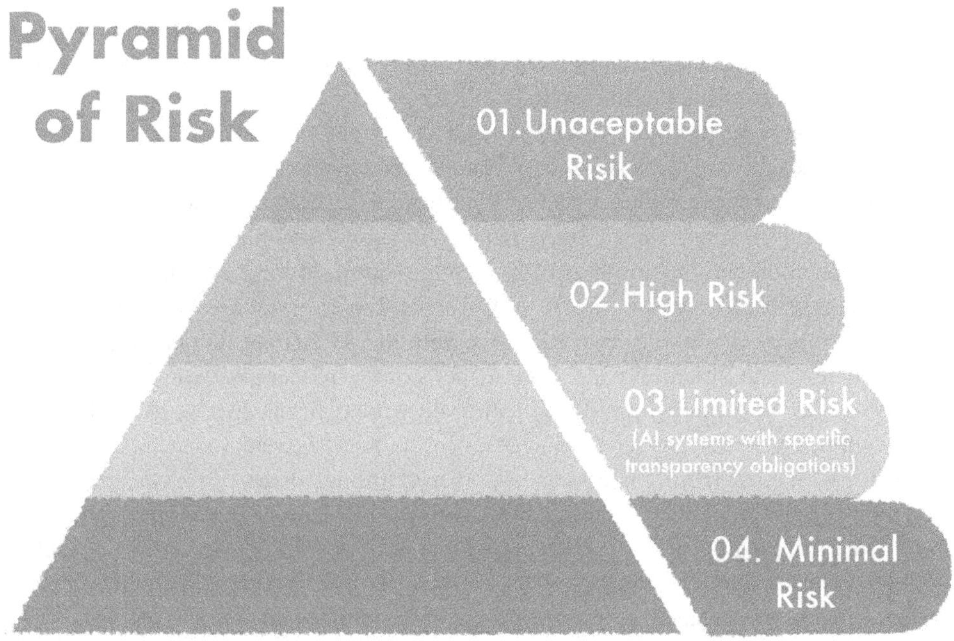

Fig. 12.5 Pyramid of risk levels.

- **Level 1**. AI systems deemed to present an unacceptable risk will be banned. These include systems that pose a clear threat to safety, livelihoods, and rights, such as government social scoring and toys that use voice assistance to encourage dangerous behaviors.

The regulation seeks to establish a flexible framework that accommodates the incorporation of new AI systems as technology continues to evolve. Key aspects of the regulation include:

Regarding the subject matter, the compromise text of Article 1(1) includes a high-level statement that one of the purposes of the AI Act is to ensure a high level of protection for health, safety, and fundamental rights, as enshrined in the Charter, which includes democracy, the rule of law, and environmental protection. However, all subsequent references in the Regulation focus solely on risks related to health, safety, and fundamental rights, in accordance with the Council's mandate.

One key aspect is the explicit restriction on the use of biometric identification systems (BIS). BIS use in public spaces for police purposes must be subject to prior judicial authorization and limited to a list of crimes. These systems may also be used for the selective search of individuals convicted or suspected of committing serious crimes. "Real-time BIS must meet strict conditions, and its use will be limited in time and place for purposes such as specific searches for victims (e.g., kidnapping, trafficking, sexual exploitation), prevention of a specific and current terrorist threat, or locating or identifying individuals suspected of crimes such as terrorism, human trafficking, sexual exploitation, murder, kidnapping,. rape, armed robbery, participation in a criminal organization or against the environment," according to a release from the European Parliament.

Regarding general-purpose AI systems (GPAIS or GPAI models), the compromise agreement defines them as AI systems based on models capable of serving a variety of purposes. Article 52 introduces new provisions regarding GPAI models. These new rules introduce horizontal obligations for all GPAI models, including maintaining up-to-date technical documentation and making it available, upon request, to the AI Office and national competent authorities. They also require providing certain information and documentation to downstream providers to ensure compliance with the AI Act. Additional requirements apply to models with systemic risks, such as performing model evaluations, conducting risk assessments, implementing risk mitigation measures, ensuring adequate cybersecurity protection, and reporting serious incidents to the AI Office and national authorities. Compliance with these requirements can be achieved through codes of practice developed by the industry and participants, with the involvement of Member States (through the AI Board) and facilitated by the AI Office. The process of drafting these codes of practice should be open, inviting participation from all interested stakeholders, including companies, civil society, and academia. The AI Office will evaluate and formally approve these codes of practice or, if found inadequate, may common rules for implementing the obligations through an implementing act. The compromise agreement also allows for future compliance through established standards.

The penalties for violating various aspects of the AI Act include a sanctioning regime for non-compliant companies, which may face fines ranging from 35 million euros or 7% of global turnover to 7.5 million euros or 1.5% of turnover, depending on the violation and the company's size.

The compromise agreement allows for 24 months for most parts of the regulation, to come into effect, with shorter deadlines for specific elements: 6 months for prohibitions, 12 months for provisions related to notifying authorities and notified bodies, governance, general-purpose AI models, confidentiality, and penalties, and a slightly longer deadline of 36 months for high-risk AI systems.

High-risk scenarios include the following:

(1) Critical infrastructures (e.g., transport) that could endanger the life and health of citizens.
(2) Educational or vocational training systems that may determine access to educational and professional opportunities (e.g., scoring of exams).
(3) Safety components of products (e.g., AI application in robot-assisted surgery).
(4) Employment, worker management, and access to self-employment (e.g., CV-sorting software for recruitment procedures).
(5) Essential private and public services (e.g., credit scoring that could deny loans).
(6) Law enforcement applications that may affect people's fundamental rights (e.g., assessing the reliability of evidence).

(7) Migration, asylum, and border control management (e.g., verifying the authenticity of travel documents).
(8) Administration of justice and democratic processes (e.g., applying law to specific facts).

As mentioned, all AI systems classified as level 2 risk will be subject to an auditing process. In this context, auditability is defined as:

> *How a government or a third party can verify that an AI system is responsible. Grading schemes adapted to the specific use case are needed to validate intelligent systems.*

Auditability will become increasingly important as TAI technical requirements are transformed into practical tools and algorithms. For example, when an AI system interact with a user, grading schemes specific to the use case are required to validate the system. The auditability of a "responsible AI system" may not necessarily cover all requirements but will focus on those mandated by ethics, regulation, specifications, and protocol testing adapted to the application sector (i.e., vertical regulation).

The European regulation requires compliance with the AI Act through the fulfillment of the following seven requirements (AI Act, Title III, Chapter 2):

(1) Adequate risk assessment and mitigation systems (Art. 9—Risk management system).
(2) High-quality datasets to minimize risks and discriminatory outcomes (Art. 10—Data and data governance; Art. 9—Risk management system).
(3) Logging of activity to ensure traceability of results (Art. 12—Record-keeping; Art. 20—Automatically generated logs).
(4) Detailed documentation providing all necessary information about the system and its purpose, enabling authorities to assess compliance (Art. 11—Technical documentation; Art. 12—Record-keeping).
(5) Clear and adequate information for the user (Art. 13—Transparency).
(6) Appropriate human oversight measures to minimize risk (Art. 14—Human oversight).
(7) High level of robustness, security, and accuracy (Art. 15—Accuracy, robustness, and cybersecurity).

Of course, the level of involvement of these elements will vary depending on the scenario in which the AI system is applied. In summary, two main points can be made about the auditability of *responsible AI systems*:

- They must be auditable to ensure they adapt to the problem context and meet ethical and legal requirements.
- They must include governance elements that ensure their robustness and security throughout their lifecycle, including AI inspection and monitoring approaches.

Responsible AI systems will only reach their full potential when trust is established at every stage of their lifecycle, from design to development, deployment, and use. As previously discussed in Section 12.3.1, analyzing the full potential of these systems requires a thorough examination by type of risk problem, context, or technology. Auditing language models is not the same as auditing image processing models in dimensions like explainability, safety, and so on.

Finally, two fundamental aspects of this framework can be highlighted, according to the Commission:

- "The AI Act transposes European values into a new era. By focusing regulation on identifiable risks, today's agreement will foster responsible innovation in Europe."
- "By guaranteeing the safety and fundamental rights of people and businesses, it will support the development, deployment, and take-up of trustworthy AI in the EU. Our AI Act will make a substantial contribution to the development of global rules and principles for human-centric AI."

12.4.5. *AI Seoul Summit: The Seoul Declaration Summit*

The AI Seoul Summit, held on May 21, 2024, followed the AI Safety Summit in Bletchley and reaffirmed the commitment to international cooperation and dialog on AI. The summit emphasized the importance of AI governance discussions to promote safety, innovation, and inclusivity, aiming to shape a global strategy on AI governance. The policy paper, "The Seoul Declaration for safe, innovative and inclusive AI by participants attending the Leaders' Sessions" [21], focused the attention on the mentioned critical priorities for countries and industry leaders.

(1) *Safety:* Reaffirm commitment to AI safety and further develop a roadmap to ensure AI safety.
(2) *Innovation:* Emphasizing the importance of promoting innovation in the development of AI
(3) *Inclusivity:* Advocating for equitable sharing of opportunities and benefits of AI.

The event concluded with a strong commitment to continued dialog and concerted action toward responsible AI development.

12.5. Two Core Tasks of Agreement: Governance and Safety

Among the aforementioned five institutional initiatives, governance and safety emerge as the fundamental core of agreement.

- AI governance is critical for guiding regulation, managing the legal framework, and ensuring that TAI technologies are developed to help humanity navigate the adoption and use of responsible AI systems in a safe, ethical, and responsible manner.

- AI safety is crucial for the future as AI systems become more integrated into our lives. Ensuring these systems operate reliably and ethically is essential to prevent unintended consequences and potential harm. Prioritizing safety will help harness AI's benefits while mitigating risks.

AI governance refers to the legal framework and processes that ensure responsible AI systems are developed with appropriate goals [22]. From a holistic point of view, AI governance 360° regulates and manages the AI lifecycle, comprising the well-known stages and processes (see Fig. 12.6):

(1) Data collection and preprocessing along with enabling data quality processes.
(2) Model training together with validating performance processes.
(3) Model deployment together with AI safety inspection and continuous monitoring of AI systems.

Over the past 5 years, extensive debates in the literature have covered TAI at ethical, legal, and technical levels. Throughout these debates, one fundamental consideration remains: ensuring the trustworthiness of AI-based systems is critical for their successful adoption. A precise definition of TAI is provided as follows [5]:

AI safety is an interdisciplinary field focused on preventing accidents, misuse, or other harmful consequences that may arise from AI systems [23, 24]. AI safety encompasses:

- *Machine ethics.* It is a part of the ethics of AI concerned with adding or ensuring moral behaviors of man-made machines that use AI. It is also called machine morality.
- *AI alignment.* Its research aims to steer AI systems toward humans' intended goals, preferences, or ethical principles. An AI system is considered aligned if it advances the intended objectives. A misaligned AI system pursues some objectives, but not the intended ones. Misaligned AI systems can malfunction or cause harm.
- *Robustness*, which refers to an AI system's ability to maintain performance against various perturbations and adversarial inputs along the AI lifecycle.
- *Monitoring systems* in AI. It includes tools designed to continuously observe and evaluate AI models' performance, ensuring they operate reliably and adhere to predefined standards.
- External safety, also systemic safety or AI security, addressing broader contextual risks in how AI systems are managed. Cybersecurity and decision-making play decisive roles in whether AI systems fail or are misdirected.

Following the auditability of AI systems, the next step involves certification to demonstrate that a responsible AI system and organizational practices meet the requirements of established AI regulations, laws, best practices, specifications, and standards. This includes evaluating responsible AI systems and organizational maturity.

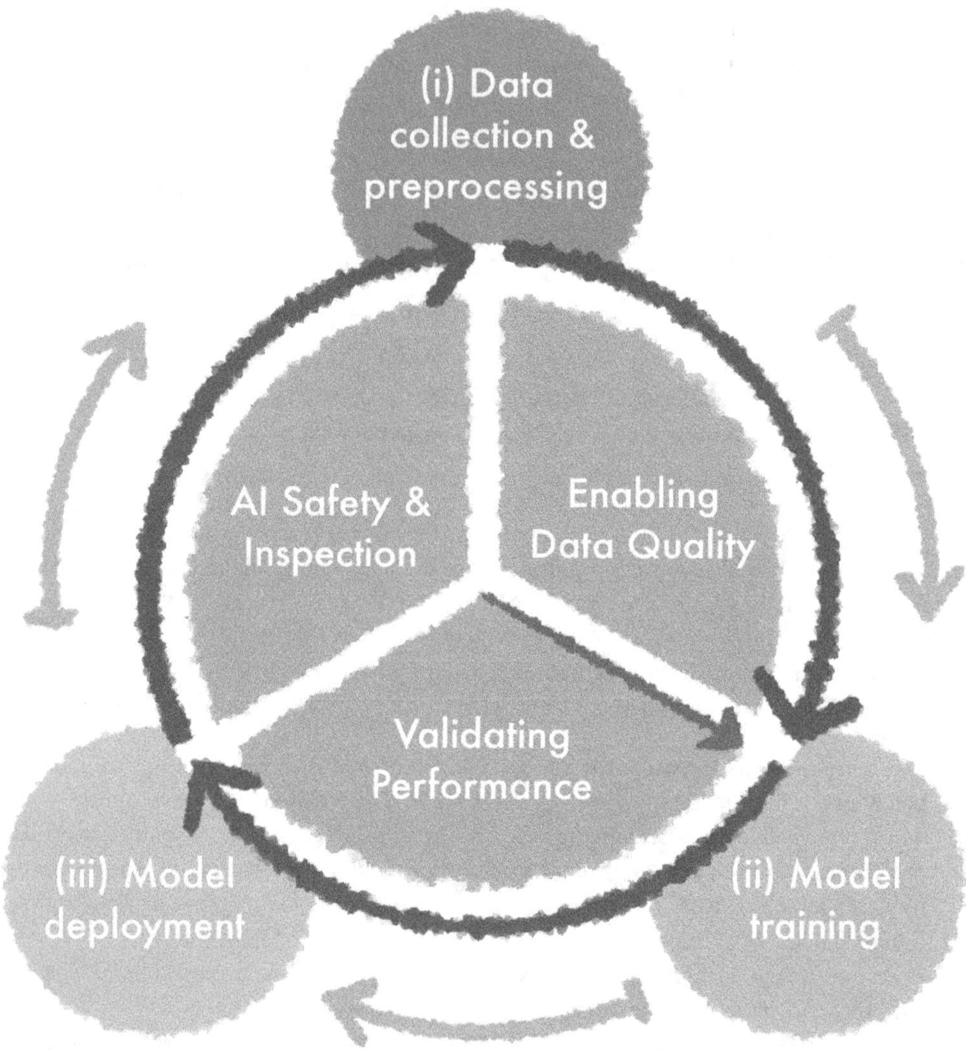

Fig. 12.6 AI lifecycle for AI governance design.

In summary, AI governance and safety are important to understanding and managing the risks presented by AI development and adoption. They also help build a consensus on acceptable risk levels for the use of AI technologies in society and business.

12.6. Breaking Down the Literature for TAI: Six Key Reflections

There is a wealth of literature on TAI, making it difficult to select articles that present in-depth approaches, analyzes, and visions on the subject. While selecting just a few papers risks overlooking many other valuable works, we have highlighted six published journal manuscripts that offer a broad perspective on the current state of discussions around TAI.

These emerging discussions, presented from various viewpoints, take place in a dynamic context with rapid developments in different areas such as regulation, governance, or safety. Among the topics discussed in these selected manuscripts, the following are particularly insightful:

(1) Foundational principles of TAI, including beneficence, non-maleficence, autonomy, justice, and explicability, along with discussions on the "exemplary tension between data and TAI principles" [25].
(2) Analysis of different approaches to mitigating AI risks and increasing trust and acceptance, particularly highlighting the Human-Centered Approach to Making AI Trustworthy, based on human control points throughout the AI lifecycle—from planning to oversight [26].
(3) Consideration of the computational aspects of building trustworthy AI systems, debate around the interactions—both accordant and conflicting—among different TAI dimensions, such as explainability, accountability and auditability, environmental well-being, privacy, non-discrimination and fairness, and safety and robustness [27].
(4) The necessity of ensuring that trustworthiness is consistently upheld throughout the AI lifecycle, from principles to practice, covering data acquisition, model development, system development and deployment, and continuous monitoring and governance [7].
(5) The multidisciplinary perspective on TAI, including principles for ethical AI development, philosophical takes on AI ethics, risk-based approaches to EU AI regulation, definitions of responsible AI systems, and the role of regulatory sandboxes as a pathway from theory to practice and regulation [10].
(6) An opening debate on TAI, particularly the challenging conflation of "trustworthiness" with the "acceptability of risks" in the AI Act, and how requirements could be extended or revised to converge on "acceptable" AI [28].

Subsequently, the titles of the six papers and references are provided, ordered by year, including a brief description of their content and a highlight of their novel aspects and points of reflection:

- **"Trustworthy Artificial Intelligence" [25].** The authors discuss how trust is essential for realizing the full potential of AI. This perspective considers trust in AI development, deployment, and use. It covers the foundational principles of TAI, including beneficence, non-maleficence, autonomy, justice, and explicability, offering a unique TAI vision. It also proposes a data-driven research framework for TAI and explores future research avenues, particularly regarding distributed ledger technology-based realization of TAI. Figure 12.2 (p. 456) is notable for its vision of data as the key resource of AI-based systems, or Data-Centric AI, and its concept of the "exemplary tension between data at the different stages of the AI."

- **"Trustworthy Artificial Intelligence: A Review" [26].** This overview analyzes TAI requirements through a literature-based lens. It provides an overview of various approaches to mitigating AI risks and increasing trust and acceptance of AI systems by engaging users and society. Another key point is the discussion of existing strategies for validating and verifying these systems, along with the current standardization efforts for trustworthiness. The human-centered approach to make AI trustworthy is highlighted, focusing on human control points along the AI lifecycle, with different levels of human involvement and control for enhanced controllability. The paper concludes with an analysis of current methods to verify and validate AI systems.
- **"Trustworthy AI: A Computational Perspective" [27].** This survey explores TAI from a computational viewpoint, helping readers understand the latest technologies for achieving trustworthy AI. It delves into the computational aspects of building trustworthy AI systems, discussing the interactions—both accordant and conflicting—among different dimensions (explainability, accountability and auditability, environmental well-being, privacy, non-discrimination and fairness, and safety and robustness). The paper also identifies future areas of research, highlighting dimensions such as human agency and oversight, creditability, and interactions among these various dimensions.
- **"Trustworthy AI: From Principles to Practices" [7].** This paper provides a comprehensive guide to building TAI systems. It covers aspects such as robustness, generalization, explainability, transparency, fairness, privacy preservation, and accountability, organizing them across the entire lifecycle of AI systems—from data acquisition to model development, system development and deployment, and continuous monitoring and governance. It includes perspectives on data preparation, algorithm design, software engineering, and management and governance. The authors prescribe concrete action items for practitioners and societal stakeholders to improve AI trustworthiness and stress that AI trustworthiness is a long-term research goal to benefit society while minimizing new risks. Raising end-user awareness about AI trustworthiness is identified as a key driver.
- **"Connecting the Dots in Trustworthy Artificial Intelligence: From AI Principles, Ethics, and Key Requirements to Responsible AI Systems and Regulation" [10].** This paper presents a multidisciplinary perspective on TAI, considering four essential axes: global principles for the ethical use and development of AI-based systems, a philosophical approach to AI ethics, a risk-based approach to EU AI regulation, and key pillars and requirements. It defines responsible AI systems and highlights the role of regulatory sandboxes as a path from theory to practice and regulation. The paper emphasizes the importance of regulation for achieving consensus and notes that TAI and responsible AI systems are crucial for high-risk scenarios. These systems will contribute to the convergence between technology and regulation, scientific advancement, economic prosperity, and the good of humanity, all while adhering to legal and ethical principles.
- **"Trustworthy Artificial Intelligence and the European Union AI Act: On the Conflation of Trustworthiness and Acceptability of Risk" [28].** In this paper, the authors

critically examine the EU's conceptualization of trust in the context of AI regulation. According to the summary, the paper makes four key contributions. First, it reconstructs the conflation of "trustworthiness" with the "acceptability of risks" in the EU's AI policy. Second, considering the extreme heterogeneity of trust research, it develops a prescriptive set of variables for reviewing trust research in the context of AI. Third, it uses these variables to structure a narrative review of prior research on trust and trustworthiness in AI in the public sector. Fourth, the paper relates the review's findings to the EU's AI policy, highlighting the uncertain prospects for the AI Act to successfully engineer citizens' trust. There remains a risk of misalignment between actual levels of trust and the trustworthiness of applied AI. The authors argue that the conflation of "trustworthiness" with "acceptability of risks" in the AI Act is inadequate. These factual obstacles to citizen assessments of trustworthiness indicate that "trustworthy" AI should not be equated with "acceptable" AI as judged by experts. This opens a debate on TAI and how to extend or modify requirements to converge toward "acceptable" AI.

This is not an exhaustive selection of articles on TAI, there is a large literature on the subject and many interesting analyses. As we mentioned, our overarching goal is to highlight a selection of studies that provide a comprehensive vision of TAI from various authors' perspectives.

12.7. Conclusions

In recent years, guidelines and regulatory white papers have been published to present mechanisms for ensuring responsibility and accountability in AI-based systems and their outcomes, as well as auditing methodologies to assess algorithms, data, and design processes. When considered as a whole, this body of literature provides a framework for ensuring that AI systems are developed and deployed responsibly and ethically. In this mission, TAI is a crucial paradigm for the development and deployment of responsible AI systems, ensuring that they are reliable, responsible, safe, secure, and include mechanisms for mitigation of harmful bias.

This chapter has performed a global analysis of TAI aspects, highlighting the importance and need for technologies aligned with TAI's core principles and requirements. We have also briefly touched on the current regulation debate and the necessary governance. The six highlighted studies complement the holistic vision of TAI presented in this study.

Building trustworthy AI is a collective effort involving researchers, policymakers, developers, and users. We draw three major conclusions as a reflection on this multistakeholder nature of TAI:

- Trustworthy AI is a holistic approach that must consider technical, ethical, societal, and environmental aspects. It is not just about model performance but also about the broader impact in all these dimensions.

- Trustworthiness is an ongoing process requiring continuous improvement, including regular revisitation of requirements, adaptation to changing contexts, and learning from mistakes.
- AI governance frameworks must go beyond the purely legal requirements and also consider the associated processes throughout the entire AI lifecycle. TAI technologies should be developed to ensure responsible AI systems are designed to help humanity navigate the adoption and use of AI systems in ethical, safe, and responsible ways.

We advocate for further reflections in this direction, to improve our understanding and practices on TAI, and to create AI systems that benefit society in a responsible manner.

Acknowledgments

The figures in this work have been designed by the artist and illustrator Pablo García Moral. The authors would like to thank Enago (www.enago.com) for the English language review.

F. Herrera and E. Herrera—Viedma acknowledge funding support by Grant "Convenio de Colaboración entre la Universidad de Granada y la S.M.E Instituto Nacional de Ciberseguridad de España M.P., S.A. para la Promoción de Proyectos Estratégicos de Ciberseguridad en España," funded by S.M.E. Instituto Nacional de Ciberseguridad de España M.P. S.A. ("INCIBE") and European Union—NextGenerationEU. J. Del Ser receives support from the Basque Government through the ELKARTEK program and the consolidated group MATHMODE (IT1456-22).

References

1. C. Stix, Artificial intelligence by any other name: A brief history of the conceptualization of "trustworthy artificial intelligence," *Discov. Artif. Intell.* **2**(1), 26 (2022).

2. High-Level Expert Group on AI. Ethics Guidelines for Trustworthy Artificial Intelligence (2019). Available at: https://digital-strategy.ec.europa.eu/en/library/ethics-guidelines-trustworthy-ai (accessed December 23, 2024).

3. The Assessment List for Trustworthy Artificial Intelligence (ALTAI) for self-assessment. High-Level Expert Group on Artificial Intelligence (2024). Available at: https://ec.europa.eu/newsroom/dae/document.cfm?doc_id=68342 (accessed December 23, 2024).

4. National Institute of Standards and Technology (NIST). Artificial Intelligence Risk Management Framework (AI RMF 1.0) (2024). Available at: https://airc.nist.gov/AI_RMF_Knowledge_Base/AI_RMF (accessed December 23, 2024).

5. A. Herrera-Poyatos, J. Del Ser, M. López de Prado, et al. Responsible artificial intelligence systems: A roadmap to society's trust through trustworthy AI, auditability, accountability, and governance, *Int. Rep.* (2025). (submitted).

6. D. Fernández-Llorca and E. Gómez, Trustworthy artificial intelligence requirements in the autonomous driving domain. *Computer*. **56**(2), 29–39 (2023).

7. B. Li, P. Qi, B. Liu, et al. Trustworthy AI: From principles to practices, *ACM Comput. Surv.* **55**(9), 1–46 (2023).

8. J. Baker-Brunnbauer, TAII framework for trustworthy AI systems. *ROBONOMICS*. **2**, 17 (2021). Available at SSRN: https://ssrn.com/abstract=3914105 (accessed December 23, 2024).

9. A. M. Singh and M. P. Singh, Wasabi: A conceptual model for trustworthy artificial intelligence, *Computer*. **56**(2), 20–28 (2023).

10. N. Díaz-Rodríguez, J. Del Ser, and M. Coeckelbergh, et al. Connecting the dots in trustworthy artificial intelligence: From AI principles, ethics, and key requirements to responsible AI systems and regulation, *Inform. Fusion*. **99**, 101896 (2023).

11. Center for Safety. Statement on AI risk (2024). Available at: https://www.safe.ai/statement-on-ai-risk (accessed December 23, 2024).

12. A. Critch and S. Russell, TASRA: A taxonomy and analysis of societal-scale risks from AI (2023). arXiv 2306.06924 (version v2).

13. D. Hendrycks, M. Mazeika, and T. Woodside, An overview of catastrophic AI risks (2023). arXiv:2306.12001 (Version v2).

14. E. Glikson and A. Woolley, Human trust in artificial intelligence: Review of empirical research, *Acad. Manag. Ann.* **14**(2), 627–660 (2020).

15. A. Jacovi, A. Marasović, T. Miller, and Y. Goldberg, Formalizing trust in artificial intelligence: Prerequisites, causes and goals of human trust in AI, In *ACM Conference on Fairness, Accountability, and Transparency*, pp. 624–635 (2021).

16. K. Reinhardt, Trust and trustworthiness in AI ethics, *AI and Ethics*. **3**(3), 735–744 (2023).

17. The White House. Executive Order on the Safe, Secure, and Trustworthy Development and Use of Artificial Intelligence (2023). Available at: https://www.whitehouse.gov/briefing-room/presidential-actions/2023/10/30/executive-order-on-the-safe-secure-and-trustworthy-development-and-use-of-artificial-intelligence/ (accessed December 23, 2024).

18. Policy paper. The Bletchley Declaration by Countries Attending the AI Safety Summit, 1-2 November 2023 (2023). Available at: https://www.gov.uk/government/publications/ai-safety-summit-2023-the-bletchley-declaration/the-bletchley-declaration-by-countries-attending-the-ai-safety-summit-1-2-november-2023 (accessed December 23, 2024).

19. AI Advisory Body of United Nations. Interim Report: Governing AI for Humanity (Dec, 2023). Available at: https://www.un.org/sites/un2.un.org/files/ai_advisory_body_interim_report.pdf (accessed December 23, 2024).

20. AI Advisory Body of United Nations. Governing AI for Humanity (Sep, 2024). Final Report. Available at: https://www.un.org/sites/un2.un.org/files/governing_ai_for_humanity_final_report_en.pdf (accessed December 23, 2024).

21. Policy paper. The Seoul Declaration for Safe, Innovative and Inclusive AI by Participants Attending the Leaders' Session: AI Seoul Summit, 21 May 2024 (May 21, 2024). Available at: https://www.gov.uk/government/publications/seoul-declaration-for-safe-innovative-and-inclusive-ai-ai-seoul-summit-2024/seoul-declaration-for-safe-innovative-and-inclusive-ai-by-participants-attending-the-leaders-session-ai-seoul-summit-21-may-2024 (accessed December 23, 2024).

22. V. Almeida, L. S. Mendes, and D. Doneda, On the development of AI governance frameworks, *IEEE Internet Comput.* **27**(1), 70–74 (2023).

23. D. Hendrycks, N. Carlini, J. Schulman, and J. Steinhardt, Unsolved problems in ML safety (2022). arXiv preprint arXiv:2109.13916 (Version v5).

24. D. Hendrycks, *Introduction to AI Safety, Ethics, and Society*, Taylor & Francis (2025).

25. S. Thiebes, S. Lins, and A. Sunyaev, Trustworthy artificial intelligence. *Electron. Mark.* **31**, 447–464 (2021).

26. D. Kaur, S. Uslu, K. J. Rittichier, and A. Durresi, Trustworthy artificial intelligence: A review, *ACM Comput. Surv. (CSUR)*. **55**(2), 1–38 (2022).

27. H. Liu, Y. Wang, W. Fan, et al. Trustworthy AI: A computational perspective, *ACM Trans. Intel. Syst. Tech.* **14**(1), 1–59 (2023).

28. J. Laux, S. Wachter, and B. Mittelstadt, Trustworthy artificial intelligence and the European Union AI Act: On the conflation of trustworthiness and the acceptability of risk, *Regul. Gov.* **18**(1), 3–32 (2024).

https://doi.org/10.1142/9789819813049_0013

CHAPTER 13 Getting More for Less: Better A/B Testing via Causal Regularization†

Kevin Webster[1] and Nicholas Westray[2,*]

[1] *Imperial College London, South Kensington Campus, London SW7 2AZ, UK*
[2] *Financial Machine Learning Researcher, Courant Institute of Mathematics Sciences, NYU, NY, USA*
[*] *Corresponding author. E-mail: nicholas.westray@nyu.edu*

Causal regularization solves several practical problems in live trading applications: estimating price impact when alpha is unknown and estimating alpha when price impact is unknown. In addition, causal regularization increases the value of small A/B tests: one draws more robust conclusions from smaller live trading experiments than traditional econometric methods. Requiring less A/B test data, trading teams can run more live trading experiments and improve the performance of more trading algorithms. Using a realistic order simulator, we quantify these benefits for a canonical A/B trading experiment.

Keywords: Algorithmic Trading, A/B Testing, Best Execution, Optimal Execution, Trading, Transaction Cost Analysis.

13.1. Introduction

The interplay of information and trading is critical to trade execution. Practitioners refer to price moves caused by their trading as *price impact* and price moves independent of their trading as *alpha*. As noted by Ref. [2]

> "Large scale trading will often occur in the presence of market drift (alpha) and the realized execution cost is a combination of alpha and the price impact" (p. 313, [2]).

An essential corollary is that trading causes price moves that otherwise would not have happened. Successful investment strategies across all asset classes trade to minimize the price impact and maximize the alpha during trading.

† Another version of this chapter appeared in Risk Magazine [1]. Both the authors thank Mauro Cesa and the team at Risk for allowing it to be reprinted.

The vast literature on modeling market impact proposes functional forms and describes statistical challenges for modeling price impact, including (among many others)

- Lillo et al. [3], Bouchaud et al. [4], and Cont et al. [5] use public trading data to fit price impact models in both US and non-US equities.
- Almgren et al. [6] and Bershova and Rhakhlin [7], who leverage proprietary orders from Citigroup US equity trading desks and AllianceBernstein to apply price impact models to transaction cost analysis (TCA).
- Donier and Bonart [8] and Tomas et al. [9, 10] who estimate standard price impact models on bitcoin, fixed income, and derivatives products.

The literature highlights a crucial challenge when estimating impact: alpha signals cause trades:

> "The larger the volume Q of a metaorder, the more likely it is to originate from a stronger prediction signal." ([11] p. 238)

Bouchaud et al. [11] refer to this bias as "Prediction bias" (p. 238). In Section 13.2, we provide a detailed instance of this bias and how it leads to suboptimal trading and lower P&L.

The industry standard for addressing this bias is through controlled live trading experiments, such as A/B tests that randomize decisions. For example, Bouchaud [12] leverages a year-long live trading experiment to identify price impact without bias. A/B tests address trading biases but present three downsides: First, one discards the bulk of their trading data. Second, there are far fewer trades without alpha than with alpha, making it challenging to estimate high-dimensional models using machine learning. Finally, the submission of alpha-less trades leads to additional trading costs.

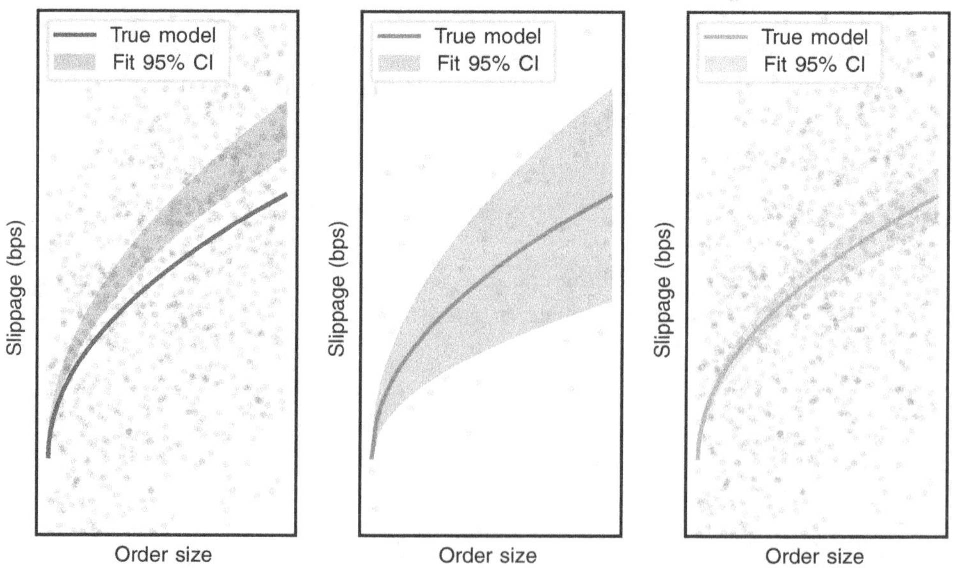

Fig. 13.1 Illustration of the bias and variance trade-off between data with alpha (blue) and data without alpha (red). The last panel combines both data through *causal regularization.*

The present article uses causal regularization, introduced by Janzing [13], to address these shortcomings. This method improves upon traditional A/B testing by analyzing *both* the unbiased A/B testing and biased trading data. Fig. 13.1 demonstrates this: in the left-hand panel, one uses the considerable trading data to fit an impact model leading to a biased estimation with small uncertainty. In the middle panel, one only uses unbiased data, which naturally gives an unbiased estimate but with large uncertainty. Finally, in the right-hand panel, causal inference blends both data, providing an unbiased estimate with small uncertainty, giving the *best of both*.

Five further sections structure the article. Section 13.2 provides our motivating example, Section 13.3 introduces causal regularization, Section 13.4 describes the simulations and experiments, Section 13.5 contains the results, and Section 13.6 concludes. Finally, Appendix A outlines the application of causal regularization to alpha research.

13.2. A Motivating Example

As a stylized example, consider a trading strategy on the Russell 3000 universe. Each day the strategy uses an alpha model to predict future returns across a subset of $N < 3{,}000$ stocks, leading to a distribution $\alpha_i \sim N(\mu, \sigma_\alpha^2)$ of alpha signals. The trading strategy applies a portfolio optimization model. The optimization considers alpha signals α_i to submit orders of size x_i. The equation

$$x_i = \gamma\alpha_i + \nu_i \tag{13.1}$$

models the order sizes, with $\nu_i \sim N(0, \sigma_\nu^2)$ and $\gamma > 0$.

The strategy trades orders of size x_i over the day, for example, with a VWAP algorithm, and the realized returns r_i take the form

$$r_i = \alpha_i + \sigma \operatorname{sign}(x_i)\sqrt{|x_i|} + \varepsilon_i, \tag{13.2}$$

where $\varepsilon_i \sim N(0, \sigma_\varepsilon^2)$, and the square root term represents the market impact of trading an order of size x_i.

The above structural model describes how alpha causes trades and how both alpha and trades cause price moves, in line with Bouchaud's definition of prediction bias. In the language of causal inference, this is a causal model, which we illustrate in Fig. 13.2.[a]

Two researchers now study the trading strategy from opposing angles.

(a) An execution researcher, charged with estimating the price impact of trading an order of size x, runs the following regression without intercept

$$r_i * \operatorname{sign}(x_i) \sim \sqrt{|x_i|}.$$

[a]See Section 2.2 "the causal discovery framework" (p. 43) of Pearl [20], for mathematical definitions of causal structures and models.

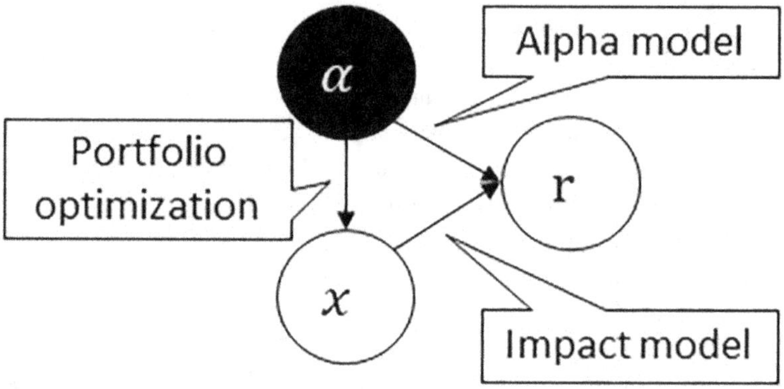

Fig. 13.2 Causal structure for trading involving an alpha α causing an order of size x. Both α and x affect the returns r.

The regression follows the industry practice of fitting realized signed returns against the square root of the absolute order size. However, the alpha biases the regression coefficient upwards due to its correlation with the order's size. This bias leads the execution researcher to slow down trading and capture less P&L for the strategy.

(b) An alpha researcher, charged with estimating the actual value of their alpha signals, runs the regression without intercept

$$r_i \sim \alpha_i.$$

Price impact biases the regression coefficient on α upward, leading the alpha researcher to oversize their order and capture less P&L for the strategy.

The problem faced by the execution researcher is due to a *causal bias*: the hidden alpha α confounds the estimation of price impact, as it both causes trades and price moves. This bias is only present because the execution researcher knows the alpha exists but does not observe it.[b] Mitigating this causal bias in estimating price impact is the main application of our causal regularization method. Appendix A describes the problem the alpha researcher faces.

13.3. A/B Testing and Causal Regularization

Live trading experiments tackle trading biases, such as the prediction bias from Section 13.2. For example, Bouchaud [12] leverages randomized trades to estimate price impact without bias.

[b]If the researcher observed the alpha, they could co-fit alpha and impact, leading to a bias-free estimate of both. However, the execution researcher's client is unlikely to share the trade's alpha.

> "We have actually shown that the short term impact of CFM's trades is indistinguishable [. . .] from purely random trades that were studied at CFM during a specifically designed experimental campaign in 2010–2011." (p. 4)

The scale and length of CFM's live trading experiment are impressive: submitting randomized trades is costly, and maintaining a controlled experiment for a whole year requires patience. Sotiropoulos and Battle [14] observe that for electronic brokers, such as Deutsche Bank, A/B experiments are small to allow for "routine changes" (p. 5) and to control the live trading experiment's cost.

In a recent article, Janzing [13] observes a correspondence between formulas for a finite-sample bias and a causal bias in a linear regression framework. Janzing shows that regularization addresses more than finite-sample biases. Indeed, regularization does not require specific assumptions on the bias, simply that the testing data does not have the same bias as the training data. Janzing's insight [13] is that regularization reduces the regression coefficient's norm, mitigating causal bias in our model. Moreover, the regularization parameter is commonly one-dimensional: one requires significantly fewer data to calibrate it. Regularization leads to the *best of both* methods defined in Algorithm 13.3.1.

Algorithm 13.3.1. Causal Regularization

Inputs:
(a) Observational Data: (y_O, X_O)
(b) Interventional Data: (y_I, X_I)
(c) Model w/parameter $\beta : \mathscr{M}(\beta)$
(d) Fitting method with regularization parameter λ

Steps:
(1) Use the fitting method to train β_λ for all values of λ on the observational data (y_O, X_O).
(2) Use the interventional data (y_I, X_I) as a testing set to tune the optimal $\ddot{\lambda}$.
(3) Use $\mathscr{M}\left(\cdot, \beta_{\hat{\lambda}}\right)$ for predictions.

With our causal model and regularization algorithm in hand, we restate the conclusions of Fig. 13.1 using the terminology of causal machine learning. Observational data refers to alpha-driven trades, and interventional data refers to alpha-less trades, so that:

(a) The large observational data (blue data points) gives a *biased estimator with small variance* (first panel).
(b) The smaller interventional data (red data points) gives an *unbiased estimator with large variance* (second panel).
(c) Using causal regularization to train on the observational data and tune the regularization parameter on the interventional data gives the best outcome: an *unbiased estimator with small variance* (third panel).

The assumption here is that, while the interventional data may not be large enough to fit a high-dimensional model, it is large enough to *de-bias* the model trained on observational data.[c] The researcher establishes the model's shape via the training data, and the testing data removes the last degree of freedom, λ. This approach blends the practical advantages of both observational and interventional data. Notably, in trading applications, observational data is plentiful but biased, and interventional data is scarce but bias-free.

To illustrate the success of our method, we perform a simulation study using Kolm and Westray's order simulator [15]. Our large-scale simulation study shows how even tiny interventions effectively control the bias and variance of causal parameters, hence our use of *more for less*. Finally, one can run more experiments in parallel as an additional practical benefit of small interventions.

13.4. Experiment Description

Sotiropoulos and Battle [14] show that live trading experiments are small. Consider again a situation where a firm has a trading universe of the Russell 3000 index and suppose that they trade 1,000 symbols daily, leading to 250K orders annually. A starting point that may seem statistically reasonable uses 10% of the order flow for A/B testing, yielding 25K orders in interventional data over a year. However, while the data's size is attractive, this corresponds to over a month's worth of unprofitable trades and requires traders to maintain the same live trading experiment for a year. Such a design is not realistic, so controlled live trading experiments are significantly more modest in size and duration. For example, one may more realistically allocate 3% of the orders over two months to the experiment, leading to interventional data of 1.25K orders or 0.5% of the observational data's size.

To rigorously assess our method, we need sizeable interventions to use as proper out-of-sample data and to try various sizes for the live trading experiment. Using such sizeable interventional data, we can measure our method's reduction in bias and variance across proposed experiment sizes. Unfortunately, only a simulation can realistically achieve an intervention of that size. Therefore, we leverage Kolm and Westray's simulator framework [15], which we briefly describe in Section 13.4.1.

13.4.1. *Order simulator*

When attempting to simulate orders, they must resemble real-life trades: we reproduce specific distributional properties and stylized facts.

[c]Rothenhäusler et al. [21] provide a method for dealing with the case where bias-free data is unavailable for testing: regularization is achievable if the researcher collects sufficient heterogeneous data through past experiments. Therefore, with causal regularization, a large history of heterogenous trading experiments *may* avoid the cost of implementing a dedicated experiment for a new problem.

(1) Order size as an Average Daily Volume (ADV) percentage positively correlates with participation rate as a volume percentage.
(2) Order size negatively correlates with market capitalization.
(3) The distribution of realized trading rates follows a power law.

Kolm and Westray's idea [15] is that, due to the prevalence of the Markowitz approach to portfolio management and mean-variance optimization, one simulates realistic orders by first taking a set of alphas α and solving the following portfolio optimization problem

$$\max_x \; \alpha^\top(w+x) - \lambda(w+x)^\top\Sigma(w+x)$$
$$w + x \in \mathscr{C}_1, x \in \mathscr{C}_2,$$

where w are the input portfolio weights, α the input alphas, Σ the stock covariance matrix, and λ the risk aversion parameter. The sets $\mathscr{C}_1 \& \mathscr{C}_2$ represent the constraints.[d] The resulting x are the required trades as a percentage of the portfolio notional. Looping over days and inserting new alphas generates a series of trades/orders. In addition, we can create additional orders by re-running the period with different alphas. As discussed above, this allows us to generate arbitrary interventions and assess our results as interventional data grows. Indeed, replicating this bootstrap would be prohibitively expensive using live trading data only.

To construct the alphas, we use the idea of *bootstrap alphas*. For a given day, for each stock indexed by i, we generate the vector of alphas

$$\alpha_i = \rho r_i + \sqrt{1-\rho^2} Z_i, \quad Z_i \sim N\left(0, \sigma_i^2\right),$$

where r_i and σ_i^2 are the stock's return and variance. We take the variance from the Northfield risk model. Choosing $\rho = 0$ provides alpha-less trades, and, more generally, ρ controls the strategy's profitability. We choose ρ such that the strategy's realized IC is around 5%. We choose the constituents of IWV, the iShares Russell 3000 ETF, as our trading universe to have the widest cross-section of stocks for our results.[e]

Because they are a mixture of actual returns and noise, the synthetic alphas have lower autocorrelation than in real life. In addition, the objective does not consider transaction costs: this simulation over-trades compared to an actual portfolio. However, the vital observation is that, for the study of price impact, we are not interested in precise portfolio characteristics, only resulting trades. Kolm and Westray [15] show that the simulated trades follow all essential stylized facts, and this property is all our study requires to assess price impact estimators.

13.4.2. *Methodology*

In this section, we describe three fitting methods, illustrated on the example from Section 13.2, using the simulated data from Section 13.4.

[d]We use a 5× leverage constraint and force the portfolio to be sector and delta neutral.
[e]The reader finds full details, including constituents, at iShares Russell 3000 ETF.

Using the order simulator, we generate:

(O) An extensive set of 2.5 million orders *with* alpha.
(I) Smaller sets of interventional alpha-less orders. Each interventional data emulates a live A/B-test limited in size and duration: they range from $n = 250$, representing 0.01% of the observational data size, to $n = 12{,}500$, representing 0.5% of the observational data size.[f]
(V) An extensive set of 2.5 million alpha-less orders as validation data.

Data (O) emulates a deep history of observational data that a trading team may have built up over years of trading. Unfortunately, (O) contains an unknown bias due to the orders' alpha. Finally, data (V) does not have a cost-effective counterpart in real life and simply serves as a simulation of the true out-of-sample for the price impact model.

For each order, we simulate price impact using three models from the literature: the original model proposed by Almgren et al. [6], the power-law model from Zarinelli et al. [16], and the square-root model from Bucci et al. [17]. Given a sample for (O), (I), and (V), a price impact model I, and a set of historical returns $\tilde{r}_i$, we construct synthetic returns r_i that contain the impact of the simulated orders via the formula

$$r_i = I(x_i) + \tilde{r}_i. \tag{13.3}$$

We define the linear regression model

$$r_i = \beta I(x_i) + \varepsilon_i. \tag{13.4}$$

When the fitted model perfectly recovers the impact parameter $\beta = 1$, the residuals ϵ_i match the historical returns $\tilde{r}_i$ from which we constructed our synthetic returns.[g]

We fit the model in three ways.

(1) We fit *using observational data*: a least-square regression runs on (O).
(2) We fit *using interventional data*: a least-square regression runs on (I).
(3) We fit *using causal regularization*: a ridge regression runs on the *observational* data (O), and the ridge meta-parameter maximizes the R^2 on the *interventional* data (I).

Remark 13.4.1 (Precision vs. Accuracy). *The regression with observational data only is the most precise, given the orders of magnitude more data it has available. For example, the confidence interval for the observational data (O) is* $\sqrt{200} \approx 14$ *times tighter than for the interventional data (I) of size* $n = 12500$, *assuming the Central Limit Theorem applies.*

[f]For example, while the trading team can leverage years of past (observational) trading data, A/B tests typically are only launched *after* proposing an experiment: therefore, their histories are short. The data is also limited in size by cost considerations: a well-designed controlled experiment randomizes key trading variables, leading to additional trading costs or opportunity losses.
[g]In a real-life setting, the residuals ϵ_i correspond to the impact-adjusted returns the alpha model predicts.

Due to the interventional data being bias-free, the regression on (I) is significantly less precise but more accurate. We show that causal regularization is both *precise and accurate, even for tiny sizes of the interventional data (I).*

Repeating the procedure with independent samples generates many parameter estimates and bootstraps the parameter distribution for each method. Finally, to assess the three fitting techniques, we introduce three performance metrics.

(1) *The bias* of the parameter estimate. Given that we know the actual value of the price impact parameter, we can quantify the bias of the parameter estimate for each method. The bias measures the model's *inaccuracy*.

(2) *The t*-stat of the parameter estimate. We compute the t-stat for each method from the bootstrapped distribution. The t-stat measures the model's *precision*.

(3) *The validation* R^2 of the model. Evaluating the models on data (I) unfairly biases the method based on interventional data only and produces a noisy evaluation. Instead, we leverage the validation data (V), which has the same size as the observational data and is bias-free, to compute each model's validation R^2.

One can only realistically estimate the above performance metrics in simulation: the bootstrap methodology and the validation data require an impractical number of interventions for a team to replicate in live trading. Therefore, the simulation environment from Section 13.4 plays a crucial role in assessing experimental designs and statistical methods.

13.5. Results

We first describe the simulated orders. Table 13.1 summarizes the distribution of the order size (ADV%), stock market capitalization, and order speed (Participation of Volume, PoV%). Fig. 13.3 highlights the correlation between the three essential variables in the order set. Fig. 13.4 provides the sampling distributions of the sizes and PoVs used for the calculations. First, the mean-variance optimization's constraints bound the order size and speed. Second, order size and speed correlate: the larger the order, the faster the execution to attain the desired position promptly. Finally, the traded stocks' market capitalization presents a heavy tail and a negative correlation with order size: the mean-variance optimization problem submits smaller orders on more liquid names.

The reader finds the results of the three estimation methods in Fig. 13.5 and Table 13.2. The figure shows the distribution of empirical β as we evaluate different interventional data (I) and estimation techniques. In addition, the table provides the bias and t-stat of the fitted β and the R^2 on the validation data (V).

As expected, the observational data provides a precise but biased estimate of β. For small experiments, using interventional data provides a noisy but unbiased estimator. The method becomes precise once the intervention size reaches 12,500 randomized trades. Fig. 13.5 illustrates how causal regularization achieves a tighter distribution of empirical β for a given experiment size. The results are robust across all three impact models.

Table 13.1 Summary statistics of the simulated orders. Each column represents the average of a metric over a given quantile. The first column of each row specifies the quantile.

Quantile	ADV(%)	Mkt Cap(bil)	PoV (%)
0.0–0.2 (ADV%)	0.1	25.7	4.1
0.2–0.4 (ADV%)	0.4	14.8	4.2
0.4–0.6 (ADV%)	1.0	9.3	4.6
0.6–0.8 (ADV%)	1.8	6.2	5.2
0.8–1.0 (ADV%)	3.2	4.2	6.7
0.0–0.2 (Mkt Cap)	1.0	0.3	4.7
0.2–0.4 (Mkt Cap)	1.4	0.9	5.0
0.4–0.6 (Mkt Cap)	1.6	2.1	5.2
0.6–0.8 (Mkt Cap)	1.5	5.3	5.2
0.8–1.0 (Mkt Cap)	1.0	51.7	4.7
0.0–0.2 (PoV%)	0.9	16.6	2.2
0.2–0.4 (PoV%)	1.0	13.0	2.8
0.4–0.6 (PoV%)	1.2	11.1	3.8
0.6–0.8 (PoV%)	1.5	10.1	5.7
0.8–1.0 (PoV%)	1.9	9.5	10.2

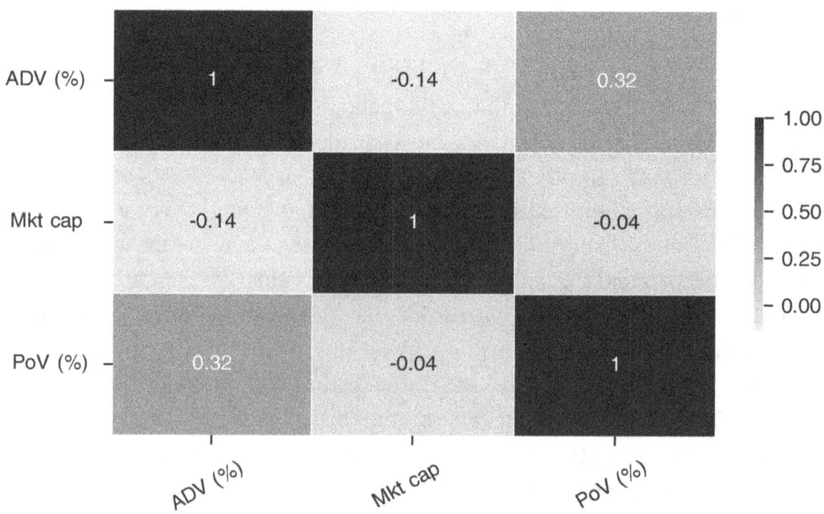

Fig. 13.3 Correlations between variables in our simulated orders.

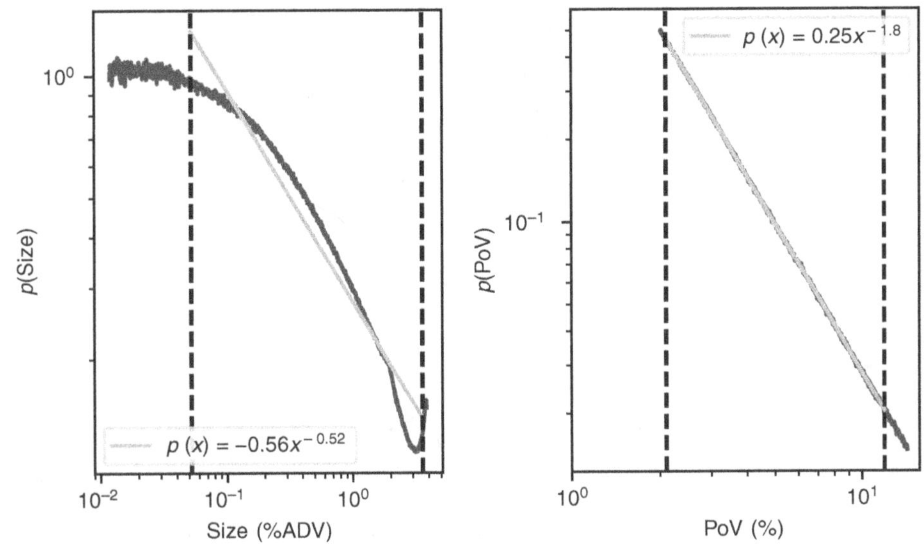

Fig. 13.4 Distribution functions of the order sizes and PoVs used for the simulation.

Causal regularization achieves unbiased, precise measurements using an order of magnitude less randomized trades. For example, the causal regularization estimator with $n = 250$ randomized trades outperforms the naive estimator with $n = 1{,}250$ randomized trades.

13.6. Conclusion

This article revisits A/B testing in a trading context. When designing live trading experiments, the critical trade-off is best described using the language of causal inference: observational data is plentiful but biased, while interventional data is bias-free but scarce. The authors find causal machine learning particularly well-suited for trading applications and hope that quantitative finance follows the technology industry in applying these methods to real-life problems. The Microsoft Research Summit of 2021 [18] had over a dozen talks within its causal machine learning track, one of its seven science tracks.

> "This track focuses on emerging causal machine learning technologies and the opportunities for practical impact at the intersection of academia and industry, with contributions from researchers at Microsoft and the broader academic and industrial research communities."

Causal inference is not only well-suited to describe the trade-off inherent to A/B testing: causal machine learning methods also significantly outperform traditional econometric

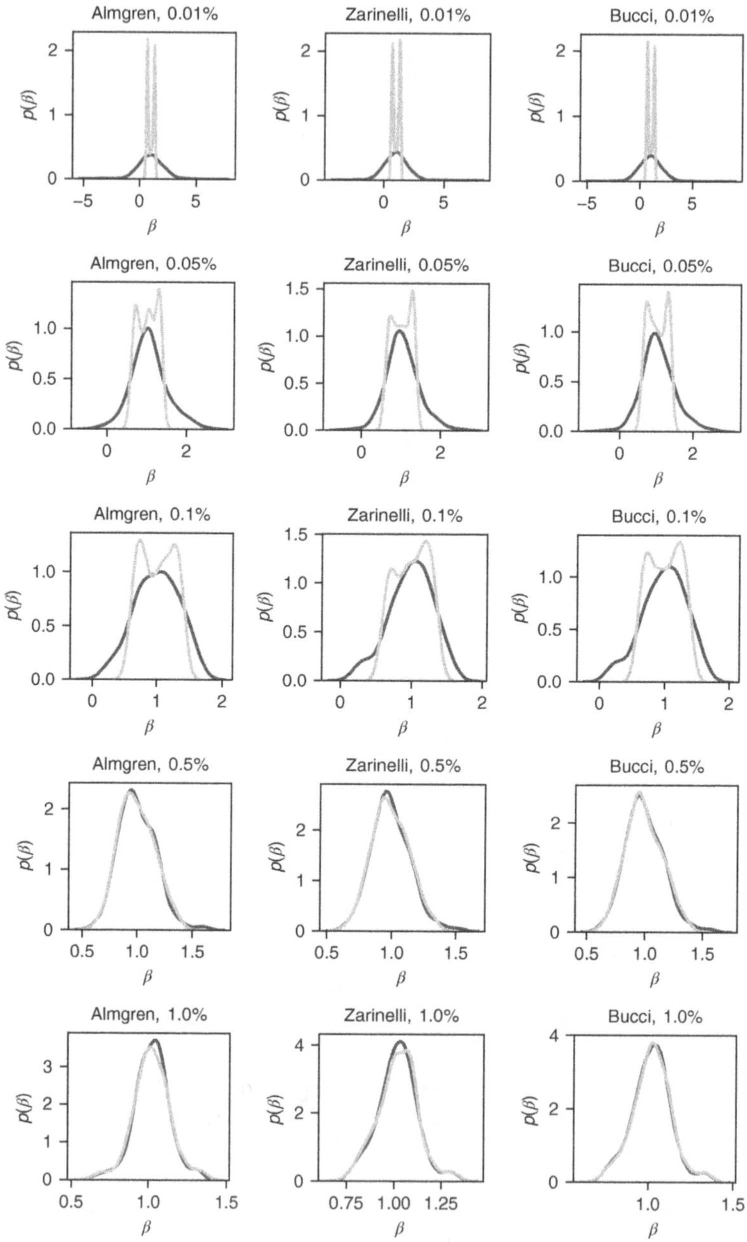

Fig. 13.5 KDE plots of the simulated regression betas: the columns represent different price impact models. The rows represent assorted intervention sizes. The actual value is $\beta = 1$. Betas from fits on the interventional data alone are in blue and from the causal regularization approach in green.

Table 13.2 Statistical results across fitting methods and with intervention sizes ranging across 0.01% (n = 250 randomized trades), 0.05% (n = 12,500 randomized trades), and 0.5% (n = 12,500 randomized trades) of the observational data.

Intervention size	Fitting method	Bias	t-stat	$R^2(V)$
0%	Observational data only	0.319	30.2	70 bps
0.01%	Interventional data only	−0.010	0.92	−10 bps
0.01%	Causal regularization	−0.010	3.32	70 bps
0.05%	Interventional data only	0.05	2.40	63 bps
0.05%	Causal regularization	0.01	4.12	72 bps
0.5%	Interventional data only	−0.002	6.38	75 bps
0.5%	Causal regularization	−0.005	6.66	75 bps

techniques in the data regime most common in trading. We illustrate this via a rigorous and extensive simulation experiment for trading. We show that a trading experiment with only 250 randomized trades using our causal regularization method outperforms a standard A/B test with 1,250 randomized trades.

In a well-controlled simulation environment, the paper presents a concrete, robust analysis of causal regularization's benefits to the bias-free estimation of price impact. The range of applications is significantly broader; see, for instance, Appendix A on alpha research, and is likely to increase with continued demand for A/B testing in a trading and best execution context.

Acknowledgments

We are grateful to Northfield for providing their risk model and Dan diBartolomeo and Steve Gaudette, in particular, for answering our data questions. In addition, the authors thank Petter Kolm and Johannes Muhle-Karbe for comments which helped improve this article.

APPENDIX A. A SECOND USE CASE

In this appendix, we revisit the motivating example in Section 13.2 from an alpha researcher's point of view. Recall that the returns follow the model.

$$r_i = \alpha_i + \sigma \text{ sign}(x_i)\sqrt{|x_i|} + \varepsilon_i \tag{13.5}$$

where r are the observed returns, α the alpha researcher's signal, and σ sign$(x)\sqrt{|x|}$ the price impact of the strategy's historical orders.

Imagine a scenario where an alpha researcher does not collect their own trading data but relies on a third party, for example, a broker, to capture their trading data and estimate its price impact. The alpha researcher knows that the historical regression

$$r_i \sim \alpha_i.$$

is biased due to the presence of price impact. Waelbroeck et al. [19] propose a method to remove this bias *under a given choice of price impact model*:

> "the system may estimate corrected market prices that would have been observed had price impact not existed" ([19] p. 11)

In Waelbroeck's solution, the alpha researcher takes the price impact model from their broker at face value and, for our square root impact model, runs the regression

$$r_i - \beta\sigma \text{ sign}(x_i)\sqrt{|x_i|} \sim \alpha_i.$$

An alpha researcher can implement Algorithm A13.1 by Waelbroeck et al. [19].

Algorithm A13.1. Waelbroeck's price impact adjustment algorithm

Inputs:
(a) Alphas α_i
(b) Observed returns r_i
(c) Price impact quoted by third-party I_i

Steps:
(1) Compute corrected market returns $\tilde{r}_i = r_i - I_i$
(2) Regress $\tilde{r}_i \sim \alpha_i$.

But what if the alpha researcher wants to fit their alpha free of a particular price impact model? An alpha researcher using causal regularization Algorithm A13.2 can fit their alphas without depending on a third party's price impact model.

Algorithm A13.2. Causal regularization for alpha research

Inputs:
(a) Alphas α_i
(b) Observed returns r_i
(c) A randomized set $\mathscr{I}$ of *unsubmitted* trades i

Steps:
(1) Define $\mathscr{I}$ as the interventional data and its complement $\mathscr{O}$ as the observational data.
(2) Apply the causal regularization Algorithm 13.3.1 to the linear regression $r_i \sim \alpha_i$.

To use Algorithm A13.2, an alpha researcher randomly sets aside a small set of names and disables their trading strategy on those names. The alpha researcher then monitors the returns of these *unsubmitted trades* to tune their regularization penalty. The causal regularization algorithm, Algorithm A13.2, calibrates the correct ridge parameter for the researcher's alpha model based on this bias-free data. In conclusion, the algorithm considers the confounding effect of price impact *in a model-free way*, reducing the researcher's reliance on broker data and models.

The researcher cannot practically implement this approach without causal regularization: the opportunity cost of *not* submitting profitable trades is prohibitively high. Unfortunately, standard econometric techniques demand enormous interventional data. But *causal regularization gets more for less* and adjusts alpha for price impact in a model free way with minimal opportunity costs.

References

1. K. Webster and N. Westray. Getting more for less—better a/b testing via causal regularization. *Risk Magazine* (2023). https://www.risk.net/cutting-edge/7957700/getting-more-for-less-better-a-b-testing-via-causal-regularisation.
2. R. Velu, M. Hardy, and D. Nehren. *Algorithmic Trading and Quantitative Strategies*. CRC Press (2020).
3. F. Lillo, J. D. Farmer, and R. N. Mantegna. Econophysics: Master curve for price-impact function. *Nature*. **421**, 129–130 (2003).
4. J. P. Bouchaud, Y. Gefen, M. Potters, and M. Wyart. Fluctuations and response in financial markets: The subtle nature of random price changes. *Quant. Finance*. **4**(2), 176–190 (2004).
5. R. Cont, A. Kukanov, and S. Stoikov. The price impact of order book events. *J. Financ. Econom.* **12**(1), 47–88 (2013).
6. R. Almgren et al. Direct estimation of equity market impact. *Risk*. **18**, 58–62 (2005).
7. N. Bershova and D. Rakhlin. The non-linear market impact of large trades: Evidence from buy-side order flow. *Quant. Finance*. **13**(11), 1759–1778 (2013).
8. J. Donier and J. Bonart. A million metaorder analysis of market impact on the bitcoin. *Mark. Microstruct. Liquidity*. **1**(2), 1550008 (2015).
9. M. Tomas, I. Mastromatteo, and M. Benzaquen. How to build a cross-impact model from first principles: Theoretical requirements and empirical results. *Quant. Finance*. **22**(6), 1017–1036 (2021).

10. M. Tomas, I. Mastromatteo, and M. Benzaquen. Cross impact in derivative markets. *Preprint*, 2022. https://arxiv.org/abs/2102.02834.

11. J. P. Bouchaud, J. Bonart, J. Donier, and M. Gould. *Trades, Quotes and Prices*. Cambridge University Press (2018).

12. J. P. Bouchaud. The inelastic market hypothesis: A microstructural interpretation. *Preprint*, 2021. https://arxiv.org/abs/2108.00242.

13. D. Janzing. Causal regularization. *Advances in Neural Information Processing Systems*, 2019.

14. M. Sotiropoulos and A. Battle. *Extended Transaction Cost Analysis (TCA)*. Deutsche Bank (2017).

15. P. Kolm and N. Westray. Mean-variance optimization for simulation of order flow. *J. Portf. Manag*. 2022.

16. E. Zarinelli, M. Treccani, J. D. Farmer, and F. Lillo. Beyond the square root: Evidence for logarithmic dependence of market impact on size and participation rate. *Mark. Microstruct. Liquidity.* **1**, 1550004 (2015).

17. F. Bucci, M. Benzaquen, F. Lillo, J.-P. Bouchaud. Slow decay of impact in equity markets: Insights from the ANcerno database. *Mark. Microstruct. Liquidity.* **4**, 1950006 (2018).

18. Microsoft Research. *Microsoft Research Summit 2021*. (2021). https://www.microsoft.com/en-us/research/event/microsoft-research-summit-2021/.

19. H. Waelbroeck, A. M. Waelbroeck, C. Gomes, and N. Bershova. Methods and systems related to securities trading, US Patent 8,301,548 (2012).

20. J. Pearl. *Causality*. Cambridge University Press (2009).

21. D. Rothenhäusler, N. Meinshausen, P. Bühlmann, and J. Peters. Anchor regression: heterogeneous data meet causality. *Preprint*, 2020. https://arxiv.org/abs/1801.06229.

https://doi.org/10.1142/9789819813049_0014

CHAPTER 14 Toward Automating Causal Discovery in Financial Markets and Beyond

Alik Sokolov[1,*], Fabrizzio Sabelli[2], Behzad Azadie Faraz[3], Wuding Li[4], and Luis Seco[5]

[1]*Managing Director of Machine Learning at RiskLab;*
University of Toronto and CEO at Responsibli; CEO of Sibli, Toronto, Canada
[2]*Masters student in Mathematics at Université de Montréal;*
Quantitative Researcher at RiskLab, University of Toronto, Montreal, Canada
[3]*Ph.D. student of Financial Mathematics at Sharif University of Technology;*
Quantitative Researcher at RiskLab, University of Toronto, Tehran, Iran
[4]*Ph.D. student in Mathematics, Department of Mathematics and Statistics, University of Montreal;*
and a Quantitative Researcher at RiskLab, University of Toronto, Montreal, Canada
[5]*Professor of Financial Mathematics, University of Toronto; Director of RiskLab, University of Toronto;*
Director of the Master's of Mathematical Finance Program, University of Toronto, Toronto, Canada
[*]*Corresponding author. E-mail: sokolovo@mail.utoronto.ca*

This paper introduces a novel machine learning (ML) framework for causal discovery based on recent advances in large language models (LLMs) and discusses the applications of these causal discovery techniques to investment management. Unlike typical data-driven methods for data discovery, the framework using the implicit "world knowledge" in state-of-the-art LLMs to automate the expert judgment approach to causal discovery. A key application that is explored in detail is end-to-end causal factor analysis, where the authors demonstrate the utility of our method in specifying and analyzing detailed causal models for financial markets. This paper also conducts a comparative analysis, juxtaposing the new approach with conventional methods, to underscore the enhanced capability of the framework in revealing intricate causal dynamics in financial data.

Key Takeaways:

(1) The authors propose and implement an end-to-end method for causal modeling with applications to financial markets, from causal discovery to causal scenario modeling.
(2) The authors demonstrate the application of the end-to-end framework to factor investing and how the framework can be applied to different sets of input features.
(3) The authors show that large language models have taken a significant step forward toward automating causal discovery in finance and potentially across many more diverse business domains.

14.1. Introduction

In recent years, the intersection of machine learning (ML) and causal inference has emerged as a vital research area, promising to unveil deeper insights into the causal structures within complex datasets. Traditional approaches to causal discovery often struggle with the intricacies and nonlinear relationships present in real-world data. In addition, ML techniques have historically lacked a "world model," which meant an over-reliance on statistical modeling and observed effects and difficulty in overlaying priors regarding causal relationships in an automated fashion. To address these challenges, the authors introduce a novel ML framework for causal discovery, designed to be versatile and applicable across a spectrum of domains, by leveraging recent advances in large language models (LLMs).

Factor investing, which involves identifying and leveraging specific factors or drivers behind asset returns, serves as a robust testbed to showcase the efficacy of the framework. The finance industry, characterized by its complex and dynamic data, demands robust methods for causal analysis to enhance investment strategies and risk management. Unlike conventional correlation-based analyses, this paper looks at creating alternate systematic approaches for selecting factors for constructing factor models.

The paper outlines the process of employing this ML-driven framework for causal discovery in factor investing. The authors begin with the formulation of causal models and applications of LLMs to their formulation (causal discovery). This is followed by an end-to-end experiment for how an LLM-assisted causal discovery approach can aid in creating causal factor models, as well as a demonstration of how the framework can be easily applied to different feature sets.

A key aspect of the end-to-end application is the analysis of factor betas, their stability, and their significance in the causal framework. The authors utilize do-calculus for conducting simulations that assess the causal impact of various factors on asset returns. As with traditional causal investing frameworks, these simulations provide insights into the potential effects of market shifts or strategic interventions.

The structure of the paper is as follows: Section 14.2 provides the theoretical background and reviews related work, Section 14.3 details the methodology, and Section 14.5 presents the application in factor investing with results. Section 14.6 concludes the paper and provides potential directions of future work.

14.2. Literature Review

14.2.1. *Causal modeling in finance*

The field of causal modeling is becoming of greater importance in finance and investment management, addressing the need for formulating robust economic theories to counteract the ease with which financial strategies that perform well on a backtest but may not generalize well into the future can be found. The advent of ML and big data has accelerated the trend of false investment theories being identified in research as shown in de Prado [1], and causal methods in finance have been proposed as a general methodology for making the search of investment strategies more robust as seen in Prado [2].

In classical approaches to factor investing, such as Fama and French [3] and Fama and French [4], the authors theorize that simple models of several *factors* can explain components of equity returns. These methods are predicated on hidden hypothesis of causal relationships between the factors used and returns. On the other hand, the betas that are computed in practice using supervised techniques such as ordinary least squares (OLS) are based on correlation and represent an associational rather than causal relationship, and so most of the time it is an unstable estimated value that can result in "spurious" findings in econometrics and finance. As in Prado [2], causal frameworks for factor investing have been proposed in which an explicit causal relationship between factors and returns of assets, formulated as a *directed acyclic graph (DAG)*, is the starting point. These frameworks make the pre-assumed hypotheses of causality falsifiable by causal discovery algorithms or experts' opinions.

Classical approaches to this problem include data-driven methodologies as seen in Zhang et al. [5], where the authors claim that classical feature selection algorithms in quantitative finance like stepwise regression analysis (SRA), principal component analysis (PCA), decision tree (DT), and information gain are based on correlation, and so they cannot represent the causal direct influence of features on assets' returns. They propose the causal feature selection (CFS) algorithm, and they show that their CFS method improves feature selection in both accuracy-based and investment metrics.

14.2.2. *Causal discovery in finance*

Causal discovery is a core aspect of causal modeling approaches, and causal discovery in finance holds a particularly important role due to the lack of consensus around causal relationships in economics and the widespread use of novel datasets and factors.

In Polakow et al. [6], the authors take a philosophical view toward the rising number of applications of causal inference in quantitative finance. They argue that these applications may be limited due to the complexity and reflexivity of the financial markets. First, causal graphs can be verified ex-post and models being used ex-ante for prediction need calibration. Second, as financial markets are not a closed system, the causal mechanism in the market may change over time. Also, due to the reflexivity of the market and different models that financial activists use, the arrow of causation may change in different periods. This increases the need for more automated and dynamic approaches for causal discovery and combinations of "first-principles" and data-driven causal discovery methods; the framework shows an end-to-end automation for both.

In Hao et al. [7], the authors explain the limitations of data-based causal discovery algorithms in high-dimension data sets, which is the case in finance, due to the reduction of accuracy and increase of computation complexity. They mention two main approaches of causal discovery algorithms: Structure learning approaches and direction learning approaches. They classify the structure learning approaches into two main groups: *constraint-based methods* like PC and FCI and *search & score methods* like Bayesian information criterion (BIC). The problem with these methods is that they only identify the DAG up to the Markov equivalence class. The conditional independence (IC) test that these methods are based on, in high-dimensional data, becomes extremely difficult, and searching space of the DAG becomes super-exponential in the number of variables. For the directional learning approaches, that are based on additive noise models (ANM), they mention two *LINGAM* and *Information-Geometric Causal Inference* (IGCI) algorithms that decrease the time complexity of causal discovery but work only on low-dimensional data sets. To overcome the curse of dimension in the causal discovery method, they introduce a three-step algorithm, the *causal discovery in high dimension* (CDHL).

In a more recent attempt for causal discovery in a high-dimensional data set, in Hasan and Gani [8], the authors remind the necessity of causal structure in causal ML for simulating the data generation process. They also mention the difficulty of the causal discovery task for high-dimensional data. As a solution, they propose imposing a prior on the structure of the DAG from prior knowledge, expert opinion, or other information sources. To use this prior knowledge for causal discovery from data, they introduce a reinforcement algorithm that penalizes the causal discovery algorithm for deviating from priors. Thus, they offer a systematic way to impose priors on the DAG.

14.2.3. *Large language models for causal discovery*

LLMs have recently begun seeing widespread use for causal discovery. In Lampinen et al. [9], the authors deal with the question of whether a passive learner can learn causal intervention strategies that it can use in the test data to uncover its underlying causal structure. They designed a two-stage agent that in the first stage (*experimentation strategy*), intervenes in the data generation process and learns the causal structure, and in the second stage (*exploitation strategy*), it uses its causal knowledge to intervene in the remaining of the episode to achieve a goal g. To learn the experimentation part, they use a large language model (a 70 billion parameter Chinchilla) and train it by the next word prediction task. They deduce that despite confounding variables in the training data set and passive learning, the passive learner agent can come up with causal discovery tasks in the test data, though an active RL learner with human feedback on on-policy data may improve the results.

In Zhang et al. [10], authors mention three types of causal inference that one may expect from a LLM. Type I is to identify the causal relationship between two subjects using domain knowledge. Type II is causal inference from a data set, and for example, deciding which variable is the cause of the other. Type III is the quantitative estimation of the effect of a cause variable on a dependent variable. This paper shows several practical improvements for prompt engineering strategies to determine Type I causal relationships, as well as combining LLMs for causal discovery with existing methodoloigies to create an end-to-end system that can combine all three forms of causal inference.

In Jin et al. [11], authors construct a verbalized task of inferring causation from correlations, CORR2CAUS, using conventional causal discovery methods like Peter–Clark (PC), which consists of 400K data points. By prompting this task to 17 main LLMs, they deduce that the outputs are almost random for all language models, and none of them are able to infer causality from correlation structure. By fine-tuning these models with this task, the results improve slightly but still not significantly. This paper shows that the usage of current state-of-the-art LLMs (GPT-4) combined with robust prompt engineering strategies can generate causal inferences that are of practical use.

In Kıcıman et al. [12], the authors take a positive attitude toward causal discovery and causal reasoning by LLMs. They divide causal discovery from two points of view. The first angle is *covariance vs. logic-based causality*. Covariance causality is the causal discovery using statistical methods and numerical evidence to discover the existence and strength of a causal relationship between two variables. While in a logic-based approach, it uses logical reasoning and domain expertise to discover a causal relationship. The other view is *type vs. actual causality*. In type causality, it tries to perform a causality inference such as causal discovery or causal effect estimation between two variables. While actual causality probes for causal reasons for a special event. The authors also consider various causal tasks, including *causal discovery*, *effect inference* and *attribution*. Using GPT-3.5 and GPT-4, the authors claim that they could achieve a higher accuracy in various causality tasks. They've achieved 97% accuracy for pairwise causal discovery, 92% accuracy in logic-based (or counterfactual) reasoning tasks, and 86% accuracy in actual causality tasks, which improve the current causal discovery algorithms by more than 10%. Despite these improvements, LLMs make some trivial mistakes that open new doors for further research and developments in the field of causal reasoning by LLMs.

In Naik et al. [13], the authors use LLMs to draw causal edges between 18 medical features related to lung cancer. The authors mention the lack of use of domain experts in usual score-based or constraint-based causal discovery methods that can be filled by using LLMs for achieving DAGs. They compare the DAGs generated by LLMs in both edge-by-edge prompting or prompting for the whole graph at once, and they achieve higher accuracy with respect to usual methods of causal discovery when compared based on the Bdeu score. They also mention that the accuracy might even increase if the LLM was trained over a specialized database. The framework presented within this paper allows for DAG generation that is more robust and scalable to hundreds of input features, as detailed in Section 14.3.

In Long et al. [14], the authors mention that usual causal discovery methods have the limitation that they only find the DAG up to *Markov equivalence class (MEC)*. And then an expert can choose the right DAG from the MEC. For cases when experts can make mistakes, they formalize the question of finding the true DAG among MEC by an *imperfect expert* as minimizing the size of the MEC chosen by the usual causal discovery method while the probability of inclusion of the true DAG is controlled and superior to a constant. Then they use an LLM as an imperfect expert that mitigates the performance. They suggest using a Bayesian causal discovery approach and replacing the MEC-based prior with a learned posterior distribution over graphs. This paper uses similar ideas by splitting the DAG generation task into sub-graphs, as detailed in Section 14.3.2.

While the articles just mentioned use LLMs as domain experts to deduce causal relationships between variables, in Ban et al. [15], the authors combine the classical score-based causal structural learning (CSL) methods with LLMs for obtaining the DAG for a data set. They query various LLMs, including GPT-4, for causal relationships between pairs of variables, giving a short description of the variables. Then they use the LLMs response as a prior for score-based CSL algorithms in two hard and soft settings. In the hard setting, they enforce the causal ancestry relations proposed by the LLM to be completely satisfied by the set of Bayesian networks they search in. In the soft setting, they consider a penalty for deviating from the prior conditions but let some of the LLMs suggestions be violated. The authors report that they have achieved a higher accuracy for the causal discovery task and drawing the true DAG, when using the LLMs as a prior for CSL algorithms compared to the case that they run the CSL algorithms directly on the data without LLMs suggestions as a prior.

In Hollmann et al. [16], the authors propose using LLMs for *Context-Aware Automated Feature Engineering (CAAFE)*. They mention that the most time-consuming tasks of a data scientist are data cleaning and feature engineering, and most data engineering algorithms come up with disintuitive features. So they propose CAAFE as a pipeline for automatic feature engineering empowered by vast knowledge of LLMs. They describe the task and the data set by a prompt to an LLM. The LLM generates a Python code that transforms the initial raw data into processed features that an AutoML system can use as input data. It also describes the features that are extracted in terms of natural language that increases the interpretability of the AutoML pipeline. Although they increase the ROC AUC by this method, LLMs' hallucinations are still pitfalls of this automated feature engineering method. This paper utilizes some similar ideas for constructing different features to represent graph edges in the causal DAGs, as detailed in Section 14.4.2.

Overall, there has been a significant uptick in research for LLMs for causal discovery and modeling, but this paper provides perhaps the most complete overview to date of an end-to-end causal discovery and modeling framework applicable in the finance and investment management domains.

14.2.4. *Large language models for quantitative finance*

The field of finance has been influenced by the introduction of *the natural language processing* (NLP) method by sentiment analysis and nowcasting. With the introduction of LLMs, finance has been considered one of the first fields to benefit from, and the rising number of articles related to the applications of LLMs in quantitative finance in recent years just shows this. However, using LLMs that are trained on general databases and even Fin-LLMs that are trained on financial data in financial tasks may lead to challenges reviewed in this section, including availability, output volatility, and hallucinations.

In Liu et al. [17], the authors propose the problems of using LLMs trained on general text data for applications in finance. The difficulty might be in the different meanings or sentiments of words in general and financial contexts or the dilution of financial data in a general database. There have been some efforts, like BloombergGPT to train LLM models on financial data that have overcome general LLMs in financial tasks. But lack of access to their database and API's to the public makes it difficult to use them for research and development purposes and making contributions. In addition, training their model is expensive, and for real applications in finance, we'd need to fine-tune the model on new and live data. So the authors propose *Financial generative pre-trained transformer* (Fin-GPT) as a solution for democratizing financial LLMs. They provide financial data from 34 different data sources regularly updated through API. They also introduce reinforcement learning with stock prices as a method for fine-tuning LLMs with market data. They show empirically the effectiveness of their method in various financial tasks.

In Yu [18], the author studies the effect of uncertainty in the LLMs and its impact on decision-making in finance. The uncertainty in the output of an LLM might be due to the temperature setting or the ambiguity of or change in the query. For example, in the task of sentiment classification, the sentence might not have a clear positive or negative sentiment. In this article, the author proposes a way to quantify the uncertainty and volatility of an LLM in an investment strategy without direct access to intermediate layers of the LLM in an LLM-based trading strategy. This quantification can be used to enhance the uncertainty effects in the financial decision-making or trading strategy.

In Kang and Liu [19], the authors study the hallucination as a deficiency in financial LLMs (FinLLMs). Hallucination is a main issue in financial tasks due to the intricate nature of financial concepts. They empirically measure the performance of FinLLMs in learning and memorizing financial concepts. They also measure the performance of LLMs for a basic financial task, say querying price data. They also investigate four methods to enhance LLMs' hallucination in finance, say *Few Shot Prompting*, *Decoding by Contrasting Layers* (DoLa), *the Retrieval Augmentation Generation method* (RAG), and *the prompt-based tool learning method*. However, they remind the necessity for more research on LLMs' hallucination issues in finance.

14.3. Methodology

The initial phase of the causal discovery framework involves the construction of a DAG, $\mathcal{G} = (\mathcal{V}, \mathcal{E})$, to represent the presumed causal relationships among the variables. In this context, each node in $\mathcal{G}$ symbolizes a distinct variable, such as stock returns, economic indicators, or company fundamentals. The directed edges in $\mathcal{E}$ indicate the hypothesized causal directions. For instance, if variable X (e.g., a company's earnings) is conjectured to causally influence variable Y (e.g., stock returns), this relationship is depicted with a directed edge from X to Y in the DAG.

Upon establishing the DAG, the subsequent step entails utilizing observational data to deduce the strengths or weights of the defined causal relationships. This process typically employs statistical methodologies like regression analysis. For a simple scenario where Y is causally impacted by X, the regression model can be formalized as:

$$Y = \beta_0 + \beta_1 X + \epsilon,$$

where β_0 represents the intercept, β_1 is the coefficient indicating the causal effect of X on Y, and ϵ denotes the error term. The primary objective is to accurately estimate β_1, thereby quantifying the causal impact of X on Y. In essence, the DAG functions as a pre-modeling feature selection mechanism, guiding the formulation of the regression model.

The concept of interventions, operationalized through the *do operation*, is pivotal in simulating the influence of external manipulations on the variables. For example, to explore the effect on stock returns (Y) following a hypothetical increase in a company's earnings (X), the *do operation*, denoted as $\text{do}(X = x)$, is applied. This operation effectively severs any incoming causal links to X in the DAG, rendering X independent of its usual precursors. The distribution of Y under this intervention is denoted as $P(Y \mid \text{do}(X = x))$, representing the distribution of Y when X is externally set to a particular value x.

In the context of a simple causal relationship where X directly influences Y without confounders, $P(Y \mid \text{do}(X = x))$ can be directly inferred from the regression model by substituting x for X. In more intricate scenarios involving confounders or indirect causal paths, additional adjustments and analytical steps are necessitated to accurately compute $P(Y \mid \text{do}(X = x))$ using do-calculus rules, assuming a correctly specified causal model.

14.3.1. *LLMs for causal discovery*

The authors propose the following general framework for automated causal DAG construction based on any arbitrary set of features for a supervised learning task with the single constraint being each feature must have a valid name and definition.

Though recent advances in LLMs have greatly increased the length of the input context window, the longest context-length models are in practice not always the most performant for highly complex tasks. Due to the complexity of causal discovery and the nondeterministic behavior of LLMs, the authors have observed the following current limiting factors in causal DAG generation:

(1) Current state of the art LLMs have limited bandwidth relating to the quantity of features that can be evaluated simultaneously. Indeed, the authors have observed a drop in causal inference quality when the input context contained upward of 30 features for experiments with GPT-4.

(2) The set of causal relationships generated for each LLM inference is not unique.

In order to tackle these limitations, the authors split the causal discovery method into two distinct phases: Feature clustering and causal discovery. The overall process is described below:

14.3.2. *LLMs for feature clustering*

The initial step in the proposed causal discovery process is splitting the input features F into distinct groups of at most n_{feat} features and generating a causal DAG for each group. This is a solution to the drop off in causal inference quality seen with inputting large numbers of features into a single forward pass for an LLM call. For the experiments in this paper, the authors set $n_{feat} = 30$ as that was the threshold after which the quality and consistency of causal relationships generated was observed to drop off significantly.

The authors propose as an alternative to classical correlation clustering algorithms using LLMs to cluster the input features into mutually exclusive groups. This process proceeds in three steps, implemented as three distinct styles of prompt. This approach helps greatly scale the number of input features F that a DAG can be constructed for. This approach can be generalized to work in a loop (applying Prompt 1 iteratively until the subgroups are small enough to apply Prompt 2) to scale up the number of input features even further.

Prompt 1—pre-clustering. The input features F are grouped into an initial grouping denoted as G_1. Each group g in G_1 contains a subset of features in F, such that $g \subset F$ and $G_1 = \{g_1, g_2, ..., g_n\}$, where n is the number of initial groups.

Prompt 2—creates sub-groups: For each group g in G_1, a set of subgroups is created. Denote the set of subgroups created from group g as S_g, where $S_g = \{s_{g1}, s_{g2}, ..., s_{gm}\}$ and m is the number of subgroups for group g. Each subgroup s is a subset of the parent group g, such that $s \subset g$.

Prompt 3—final clustering: Each subgroup s in each S_g is then used as the element in another clustering process. The result of this clustering process is the final grouping, denoted as G_f. Each group in G_f is formed by clustering the subgroups S_g from the initial groups G_1.

The final clustering is exhaustive and mutually exclusive. Now each group in G_f has an LLM-generated name and description. Thus, if necessary, one can combine groups together very easily to obtain a desired number of clusters. One can always also recluster groups in G_f if he wants more granular clusters. This technique thus provides a lot of liberty to the user.

The authors first construct a prompt that utilizes the names and definitions of each feature in F to separate them into n distinct groups or clusters $\{g_1, ..., g_n\}$.

Using the names and definitions of each feature, they construct a prompt to return another clustering of the initial groups $G_1 = \{g_1, ..., g_n\}$ into distinct sub-groups $S_g = \{s_{g1}, s_{g2}, ..., s_{gm}\} \forall g \in G_1$ of at most n_{feat} features each based on the definitions provided for each feature.

The authors compare the results obtained using a classical clustering algorithm versus the proposed method in the Applications section. Depending on the number of features and the average length of the feature names and definitions, it may be needed initially to partition the set of features into random distinct groups in order to fit the context length of the LLM. If the initial separation is needed, the intermediate groups S_g regrouped them all using the final prompt (Prompt 3). The authors also include a sample Prompt 4, which could be used to combine clusters using their names and definitions if G_f is considered too granular.

14.4. DAG Generation—LLM for Causal Discovery

Having generated the final set of groupings G_f, the authors now focus on the generation of the causal DAG modeling the intra-causal and inter-causal relationships between these groups.

In order to generate a valid final DAG, using the names and descriptions of the set of features, all possible causal relationships in each group of features are iteratively generated and modeled as DAGs. Subsequent prompts are then used to validate and refine each of the sub-graph DAGs obtained in this step, similar to the chain-of-thought technique seen in Wei et al. [20].

To model the inter-group causal relationships, the authors start by generating descriptions for each group based on the definitions of the features belonging to each cluster in G_f. Using these descriptions, they generate the inter-group causal DAGs. Finally, the causal relationships present in this inter-group DAG are used to link together each of the features belonging to each group. A visualization explaining this last step can be seen in Fig. 14.1.

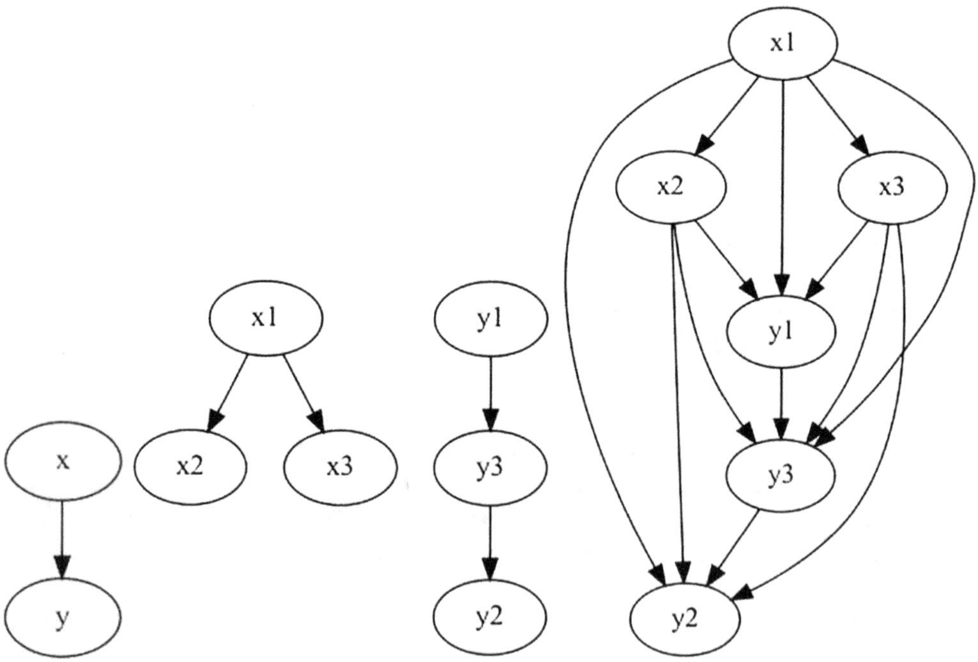

Fig. 14.1 A visualization of the last step combining all the groups into one unified graph. In this example, there are categories of features x and y. Each group is composed of three features. The DAG on the left models the inter-group causal relationships, the DAG in the middle models the intra-group causal relationships, and the DAG on the right is the final graph combining both results.

In this step, the inter-group causal relationships are fully connected, that is, if it is determined that $g_j \rightarrow g_k$ for some $g_j, g_k \in G_f$, it is not initially known which nodes (features) in g_j drive which nodes (features) in g_k. Thus, in order to not miss out on valid relationships, the authors elect to over-connect groups and filter out the irrelevant relationships in a step described in the Causal Validation section. Of course, an alternative approach here is to once again use an LLM to validate these emergent nodes, but the authors elect to go with an empirical causal validation approach for performance reasons.

In all the prompts, the authors include templates of the expected output format and describe the structure of the list of features in the input as these are best practices used to improve the quality of responses of GPT-4 [21]. The authors will omit mentioning this step for the rest of the paper.

Now, here is a detailed description of the necessary steps to generate a valid causal DAG for each group of features. These steps are also used to generate the final causal DAG used to link each group together; the sample prompts for this process can be seen in Appendix B:

(1) Generate the set of all possible valid causal relationships for a group of features using GPT-4 and model this as an undirected graph.
(2) Generate a causal DAG from the set of causal relationships obtained in the previous step by determining the directions of all the causal relationships using GPT-4.
(3) Verify the validity of all the causal relationships and correct any mistakes made during the initial generation of the DAG using GPT-4.
(4) Verify the corrections made were valid and verify if there are any remaining mistakes in the DAG using GPT-4.
(5) If there were any final mistakes, correct these mistakes and return the final version of the causal DAG.

The authors describe this process in three distinct phases: Causal Exploration, Causal Inference, and Causal Validation.

14.4.1. *Causal exploration*

During causal exploration, the causal DAGs are repeatedly generated over the same group of features in order to generate the set of all possible causal relationships for the given group. The DAGs were generated 10 times per group for the experiments described in this paper. This step is necessary to reduce the impact of the non-deterministic behavior of LLMs.

For each iteration of causal DAG generation, the authors provide the following definition of a causal relationship: *A causal relationship between two features means that a change in one feature causes a change in the other feature*. The authors also use general chain-of-thought instructions to instruct GPT-4 [20] to include the feature's definitions and the definition of causal relationship in its reasoning. The authors use in-context learning and justifications by example and thought processes as part of the prompt engineering process to generate high-quality outputs.

Sample prompts for these steps can be seen in Appendix Section C.1.

14.4.2. *Causal inference*

During causal inference, the authors include the set of edges in the prompt used to form the initial undirected graph generated during the causal exploration phase. These are outputted as a string that can be parsed into a list of tuples. Finally, the authors use the same techniques as in the previous phase and also include the definitions of a DAG and a causal relationship in the prompts.

Now for the set of edges, the authors prompt the LLM to generate a causal DAG. GPT-4 performs perhaps surprisingly well for this prompt and the prompt above, which in combination return a DAG based on definitions of the input features F forming the nodes in the graph. The LLM is also prompted to return a justification for each decision it makes when constructing the graph. Thus, the LLM returns a justification for the direction of each edge; the authors observe that including the justification also generates higher-quality outputs, similar to the approach seen in Wei et al. [20].

Sample prompts for these steps can be seen in Appendix Section C.2.

14.4.3. *Causal validation*

During the causal validation phase, the goal is to correct any mistakes the LLM makes have made during its initial DAG generation. The authors therefore use all the same techniques mentioned in the previous two phases in order to improve performance.

The authors also include the outputs of previous prompts in order to provide context and generated justification connected to the previous outputs. This history starts at the causal inference phase. Thus, before performing validation, the prompt includes the initial undirected graph representation, the features names and definitions, the initial DAG generation, and the justifications for each edges direction in the DAG. An example of this final validation prompt can be seen in Appendix Section C.3.

Now there are three main types of mistakes an LLM can make during graph generation:

(1) False negative/missing causal relationship.
(2) False positive causal relationship (i.e., produce a nonexistent/ illogical relationship).
(3) Produce a correct causal relationship with an incorrect causal direction.

The authors include this in the verification prompt and prompt the LLM to analyze the whole causal DAG generation process and attempt to remedy any mistakes made in this process. If so, the LLM returns a list of the invalid edges and a list of the corrections, both accompanied with justifications for their inclusions. The DAG is then corrected using the parsed responses before starting the final verification step.

During this final verification step, the authors also add to the concatenation of previous correction prompts (i.e., the "chat history") if any corrections needed to be made. The LLM is prompted to "verify its thought process" iteratively (in a loop) and apply corrections where necessary until the stopping criteria pre-specified within the prompt itself is hit.

Given the validity of the causal DAG, the authors use the do-calculus from observation data to further validate the causal relationship non-parametrically. Do-calculus provides a statistical significant value for each edge. Edges that are not statistically significant are removed from the DAG. In addition, a cross-validation is performed on a subset of the observation data to confirm the statistical significance of the edge. This final step is called the refutation step. The following definition captures the requirement that a causal query Q within the factors be estimable from the factor exposure:

Definition 14.4.1 *A causal query Q(M) is identifiable from a graph* $\mathcal{G}$, *given a set of assumptions A and the set of observed factors V, if for any pair of models* M_1 *and* M_2 *that satisfy A, we have*

$$P_{M_1}(v) = P_{M_2}(v) \Rightarrow Q(M_1) = Q(M_2).$$

When a query Q is given in the form of a *do*-expression, for instance, $Q = P(y|do(x), z)$, its identifiability can be decided systematically using an axiomatic system known as the *do*-calculus [22]. The axiomatic system replaces probability formulas containing the *do*-operator with ordinary conditional probabilities in three axiom schemes.

Let X, Y, Z, and W be arbitrary disjoint sets of nodes in a casual DAG $\mathcal{G}$. Denoting $\mathcal{G}_{\overline{\mathcal{X}}}$ the graph obtained from $\mathcal{G}$ by deleting all arrows pointing to nodes in X, $\mathcal{G}_{\underline{\mathcal{X}}}$ the graph obtained from $\mathcal{G}$ by removing all arrows emerging from nodes in X. The following three rules are valid for every interventional distribution compatible with $\mathcal{G}$.

Rule 1 (Insertion/deletion of observations):

$$P(y|do(x), z, w) = P(y|do(x), w) \;\text{ if } (Y \perp\!\!\!\perp Z|X, W)_{\mathcal{G}_{\overline{X}}}$$

Rule 2 (Action/observation exchange):

$$P(y|do(x), do(z), w) = P(y|do(x), z, w) \;\text{ if } (Y \perp\!\!\!\perp Z|X, W)_{\mathcal{G}_{\overline{X}\underline{Z}}}$$

Rule 3 (Insertion/deletion of actions):

$$P(y|do(x), do(z), w) = P(y|do(x), w) \;\text{ if } (Y \perp\!\!\!\perp Z|X, W)_{\overline{XZ(W)}}$$

where $Z(W)$ is the set of Z-nodes that are not ancestors of any W-node in $\mathcal{G}_{\overline{X}}$.

Note that in cases where the set X is empty, Rule 1 corresponds to the application of d-separation principles to interventional distributions, and Rule 2 becomes analogous to the backdoor adjustment criterion.

To establish identifiability of a query Q of factors, the rules of *do*-calculus are repeatedly applied to Q, until the final expression no longer contains a *do*-operator. The final *do*-free expression can serve as an estimator of Q. The do calculus was proven to be complete to the identifiability of causal effect [23, 24]. As such, the causality relationship generated by LLM is endorsed by observation data.

The authors also utilize L_1 regularization (Lasso Regression) when fitting the final models as a final causal validation/feature selection step, reducing the number of features used in the final model and reducing the multicollinearity of the final feature set. Since the Lasso model is fit on each training fold in a backtest, the final feature selection/causal validation step is dynamic for each period.

14.4.4. *LLMs for feature engineering*

In order to represent the relationships between the different features (edges) in the DAG as actual features, LLMs can also be used to select the most logical transformation of the two features composing each edge to create a new feature.

A simple approach for this is to provide a set of "primitives" or standard transformations and query an LLM to select one of the definitions of the features and the direction of the causal relationship between the two features.

This step could possibly be improved by using deep learning/LLM-based feature engineering frameworks or the newly proposed CAAFE framework cited in the literature review, as seen in Hollmann et al. [16].

14.5. Applications

The authors focus on two key applications of the framework outlined above: causal factor investing and the application of the DAG generation framework to other feature sets (using credit spread modeling as an example). In the following section, all the do-calculus computations on the DAG are done through the use of the following Python package: DoWhy [25]. The authors omit mentioning its use through the rest of the results section. The details of each are outlined below.

14.5.1. *Applications to causal factor analysis*

Factor investing is a financial theory aiming to explain the returns of stock as connected to risk *factors* that play a key role in risk management (where factor loads in a portfolio are carefully managed) and in investing strategies that aim to strategically load up on specific factors (e.g., "smart beta"). A researcher usually determines this set of factors by making causal assumptions and calculating factor exposures concerning the stock's returns using procedures inspired by Fama and French [3] and MacBeth [26] as mentioned in Prado [2].

Now even if these causal assumptions drive the subsequent modeling decisions the researcher will make in his analysis, they are rarely explicitly stated. Clearly stating these causal assumptions would require the researchers to provide empirical evidence to back their claims. Nevertheless, this opens up the opportunity to use the rules of do-calculus to de-bias their data and improve the explainability of the modeling structure, especially when using a large set of factors. Consequently, the proposed framework bridges this gap by automating this potentially incredibly laborious process.

The authors investigate the set of 153 factors presented in Jensen et al. [27]. Using the base definitions and names presented for each factor, the authors manually improve the definitions in order to make them more verbose and representative of their construction (another step that could potentially be automated/improved using LLMs). The time period analyzed is from November 30, 1971, to December 30, 2022. Each factor has an associated ETF modeling its daily returns over this period.

Now the authors compare the causal DAGs generated using their proposed LLMs clustering method to a classical correlation clustering algorithm (described in Section 14.3.2). They generate a first clustering using an LLM (GPT-4) and compare it to a baseline correlation clustering approach, as seen in, for example, Jensen et al. [27] using hierarchical agglomerative clustering. The authors in Jensen et al. [27] define the distance between factors in the second clustering as one minus their pairwise correlation and use Ward as the linkage criterion. The authors also define the correlation based on CAPM-residual returns of US factors signed as in the original paper by Hou et al. [28]. Figure 14.2 compares inter-cluster correlations of the two methods; although our proposed method naturally has lower inter-cluster correlations, the causal DAGs for each cluster are substantially more cohesive from an expert judgment perspective, as can be seen in this GitHub repository. Despite not using correlation or time-series data as an input, the LLM clusters produce average inter-cluster correlations of 0.292, compared to 0.543 for the correlation clustering approach, and intra-cluster correlations of 0.0527 compared to 0.0047. The clusters produced by the LLMs are also in some ways more orthogonal, having average absolute inter-cluster correlations of 0.086, compared to 0.1451 for the correlation clustering approach. The authors then generate a complete DAG for each set of clusters ("causal" LLM clusters or correlation clusters) as described in Section 14.3.

Now in order to confirm the causal DAGs using do-calculus, the ETF returns are used to construct proxies for the factors of each individual stock in the S&P 500 by computing the rolling beta exposures of each stock to the 153 factor ETFs. This generates a feature set X_t of 500 stocks and 153 features per stock per period, with each feature being a proxy for a factor exposure computed using an individual ETF. The authors then use these proxies for factor exposure to verify all the causal relationships in each causal DAGs generated by the LLM edge-wise. In other words, they use do-calculus to confirm the validity of edges in the causal DAGs. However, due to computational constraints, the authors did not run the do-calculus on the fully connected graph as in Figure 14.1. Indeed, they ran do-calculus separately on each DAG modeling the intra-group causal relationships.

In the case of the causal DAGs modeling the inter-group causal relationships, the authors executed the do-calculus using the first n principal components sufficient enough to explain at least 85% of the groups variance. If any of the components is proven invalid by the do-calculus computation, all associated edges are removed. Now, having validated all the causal DAGs, the authors add a new node, each of them representing the stock returns. An example visualization can be seen in Fig. 14.3. For each causal DAG representing the intra-group causal relationships, the authors then use do-calculus to analyze the causal relationships of each factor with respect to the S&P 500 constituents stock returns. The authors remove from the causal DAGs any causal relationship/edge to the stock returns that are not statistically significant with a p-value of 0.05. These statistically insignificant relationships represent factors that do not directly impact S&P 500 constituents stock returns. Nevertheless, their values may still impact the stock returns through their causal relationships with other features in the DAGs.

For an average period, there are a total of 103.4 factors left out of the initial 153 factors, combined with 184.6 features representing the edges in the DAG (from a total of 192 across all of the LLM-cluster DAGs).

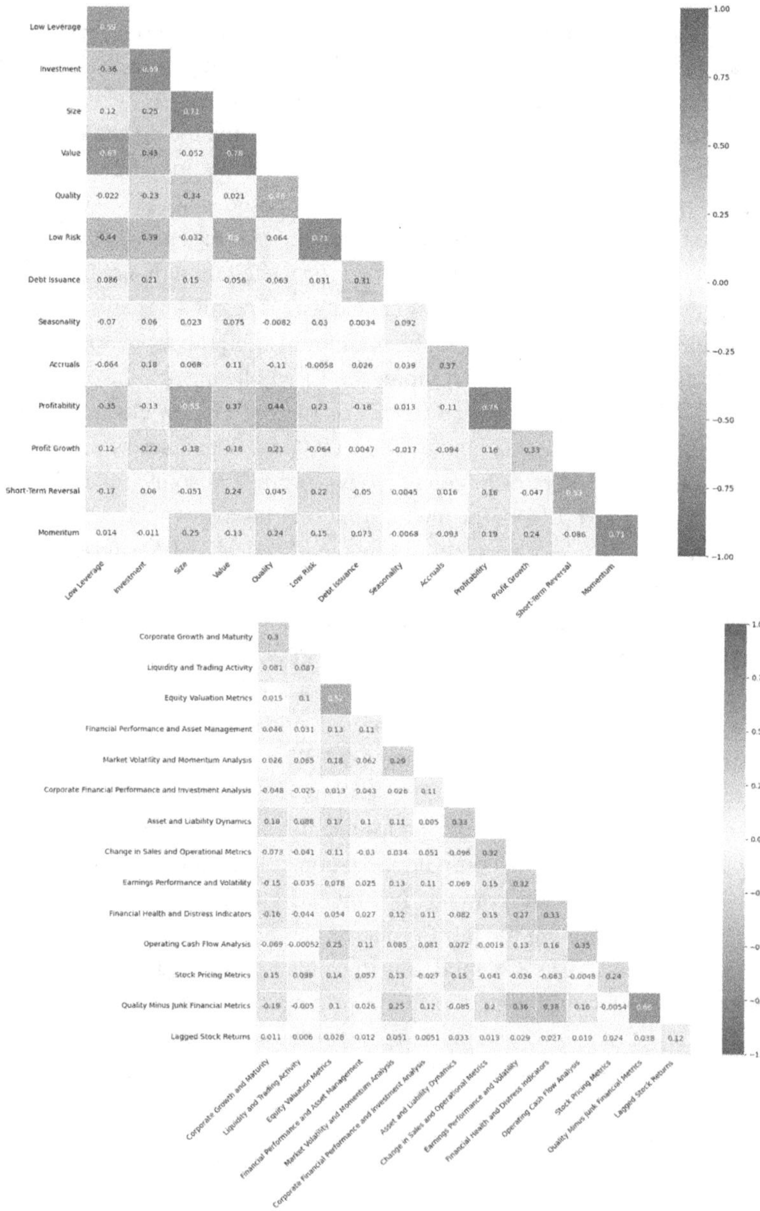

Fig. 14.2 This figure shows the average pairwise Pearson correlation between factors from different clusters and factors from the same clusters for hierarchical agglomerative clustering (left) and LLM clustering (right) using data on US stocks from 1971 to 2021. The figure on the left is inspired from Jensen et al. [27].

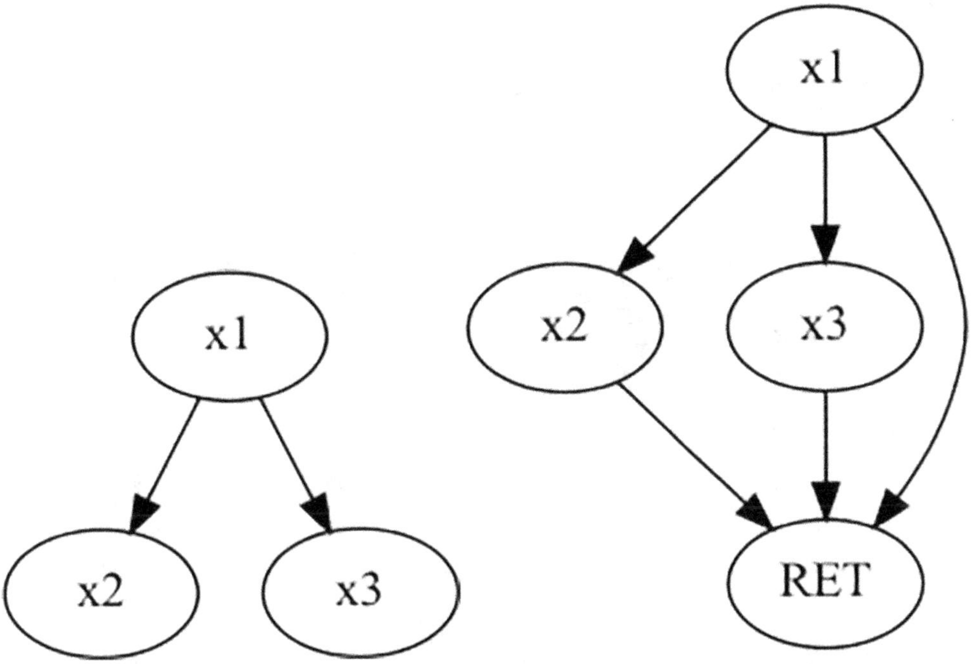

Fig. 14.3 This figure shows how the authors connect each feature to the Y node of interest. In the factor investing case, this Y node is represented by the stock returns RET.

A high-level comparison of the two clustering approaches can be Seen in Table 14.1. In addition, a more detailed analysis comparing the average performance per each of the hierarchical clusters as seen in Jensen et al. [27] is provided in Table 14.2, and of the LLM-clusters in Table 14.3. One can see that the LLM clusters provide a comparable level of predictive power for monthly returns, while providing a much less correlated and more interpretable feature set. The LLM clusters also utilize more edges per cluster, leading to a potentially richer representation of causal relationships. In addition, the percentage of the refuted nodes are much lower than in the combined dataset, given there is less redundancy within the individual clusters.

Table 14.1 A comparison of the DAGs generated using hierarchical and LLM-based clustering.

Clustering methodology	Average number of nodes	Average number of edges	Refuted nodes (%)	Refuted edges (%)
Correlation Clusters	10.93	13.71	3.64	31.29
LLM Clusters	11.77	11.54	3.15	32.43

Table 14.2 Summary statistics of in- and out-of-sample RMSE for each of the correlation clusters inspired by Jensen et al. [27].

	Avg RMSE (out-of-sample)	Avg R^2 (in sample)	Avg adjusted R^2 (in sample)	Avg number of nodes used	Total number of nodes on graph	Avg number of edges used	Total number of edges
Low leverage	0.0997	0.0496	0.0465	10.6818	11	13.9766	14
Debt issuance	0.0971	0.0290	0.0269	6.6703	7	10.9318	11
Profitability	0.1001	0.0468	0.0436	10.6993	11	14.9923	15
Short-term reversal	0.0972	0.0260	0.0247	5.6987	6	4.9538	5
Low risk	0.1006	0.0683	0.0641	17.6613	18	15.9772	16
Investment	0.1027	0.0645	0.0601	21.6206	22	17	17
Size	0.0958	0.0251	0.0241	4.7000	5	3.9856	4
Accruals	0.0967	0.0251	0.0235	5.7115	6	6.9643	7
Value	0.1012	0.0579	0.0540	17.6442	18	14.9987	15
Quality	0.0987	0.0571	0.0540	16.6799	17	10	10
Momentum	0.1044	0.0509	0.0474	7.6683	8	18.9626	19
Profit growth	0.0978	0.0419	0.0394	11.6651	12	9.9462	10
Seasonality	0.0973	0.0467	0.0446	11.6827	12	6.9011	7
Average	0.0992	0.0453	0.0425	11.4449	11.7692	11.5069	11.5385

Table 14.3 Summary statistics of in- and out-of-sample RMSE for each of the LLM clusters.

	Avg RMSE (out-of-sample)	Avg R^2 (in sample)	Avg adjusted R^2 (in sample)	Avg number of nodes used	Total number of nodes on graph	Avg number of edges used	Total number of edges
Corporate growth and maturity	0.0950	0.0122	0.0119	1.6827	2	0.9615	1
Quality minus junk financial metrics	0.0957	0.0205	0.0196	3.7452	4	3	3
Stock pricing metrics	0.0949	0.0121	0.0118	1.6731	2	1	1
Asset and liability dynamics	0.0999	0.0587	0.0546	18.6346	19	17.9647	18
Financial health and distress indicators	0.0977	0.0347	0.0329	4.7423	5	8.9744	9
Lagged stock returns	0.0993	0.0521	0.0490	9.7135	10	15.8894	16
Financial performance and asset management	0.1005	0.0599	0.0558	17.6528	18	16.9717	17
Change in sales and operational metrics	0.0957	0.0173	0.0161	3.6779	4	5.9135	6
Corporate financial performance and investment analysis	0.1010	0.0597	0.0549	15.6611	16	22.9791	23
Market volatility and momentum analysis	0.1181	0.0992	0.0900	26.6546	27	48.9714	49
Operating cash flow analysis	0.0965	0.0279	0.0265	5.6955	6	5.9744	6
Liquidity and trading activity	0.0999	0.0534	0.0507	11.6731	12	10.9773	11
Earnings performance and volatility	0.1002	0.0509	0.0473	11.6907	12	16.9604	17
Equity valuation metrics	0.1005	0.0547	0.0509	15.7212	16	14.9526	15
Average	0.0996	0.0438	0.0409	10.6156	10.9286	13.6779	13.7143

14.5.2. *Applications to causal modeling of credit spread drivers*

The drivers of changes in credit spread are a long-lasting argument. Early studies by Black and Scholes [29] and Merton [30] introduced a structural model to explain corporate default risk and inspired the search for company-level and macro variables; later, Collin-Dufresn et al. [31] stated the impact of market-related factors, and Chen et al. [32] identified the high correlation between the equity market performance and the spread. But is there any causality relationship between these discovered factors? If so, the redundant features can be removed using a causality approach.

To identify the causal relationship within the factors that might drive the credit spread, the authors utilize the dataset Gilchrist and Zakrajšek [33] and generate the DAG following the steps mentioned in the methodology. This numerical dataset consists of different macroeconomic factors and market-related factors. The data consists of monthly and quarterly data. Each edge in the DAG is validated using the rules of do-calculus. Table A14.1 presents the statistical significance of the rejection of causal relationships within the edges of the DAG.

In Table A14.1, each edge is associated with its effect (i.e., strength of the relationship), its p-value and its refutation p-value. The p-value represents the statistical significance of the edge and the refutation p-value represents the robustness of the p-value associated with the effect. Indeed, the refutation p-value is computed using K-Fold Stratification of the data to test the degree of randomness associated with the edge. The authors reject/remove any edge who's p-value is greater than 0.05 as shown in Figure A14.2. Any edge where the p-value is significant (i.e., smaller than 0.05), but whose refutation p-value is significant, is rejected as well. The authors will refer to the steps described as validating the causal DAG *edgewise*.

The authors reject 39 edges using do-calculus out of the 89 edges that GPT-4 returned. This is within the expectation as the LLM DAG generation approach focused mainly on recall and is expected to generate denser initial graphs. In addition, the dataset is much smaller than the dataset used in the previous section, leading to more frequent rejections.

Using the framework, the authors are able to identify the causality relationship within the drivers of credit spread; to a practitioner, this may be a good starting point for a feature set or a causal model, especially in situations where expert judgment in a given domain is not readily available in-house.

14.6. Limitations and Future Work

The authors leverage GPT-4 for all the analyses presented in this paper. In its current state, GPT-4 is a powerful language model that is able to produce causal relationships intuitive to human experts and those that align well with empirical observations.

Nevertheless, it has some key limitations researchers and practitioners should be aware of. One is in making unpredictable mistakes, which can be very costly in the causal DAG generation and similar use causes. Indeed, the authors of Kıcıman et al. [12] repeatedly mention this in their experiments on pair-wise causal discovery and full graph discovery that LLMs produce infrequent but unpredictable errors, making the process of automating causal discovery unfeasible for the moment. Thus, it is essential to have human supervision to correct the LLMs in the case they produce a hallucination (i.e., incoherent output). In order to make this process less laborious, an LLM can also be used to recursively correct its own mistakes (as can be seen in Appendix C). The authors of Kıcıman et al. [12] found that GPT-4 was the only model capable of verifying the consistency of its outputs (self-consistency), though the capabilities of LLMs are evolving rapidly, and it is possible other models can display similar capabilities with additional prompt engineering.

The authors also hope that the DAGs generated in the paper, which can be accessed on GitHub here, will spur further research into optimal representations for risk and factor models. This paper shows that causal approaches can now be scaled to provide a working alternative to correlation-based approaches for generating feature representations in cases where the universe of possible features is large and the signal-to-noise ratios are too low to find the optimal feature representations empirically.

These causal DAGs, similar to those demonstrated in this paper, can be leveraged to improve model robustness and out-of-sample performance, similar to the process of injecting expert judgment priors into predictive models. The authors are particularly interested in how these alternative feature representations can be used in constructing risk and factor models and how such models may compare with state-of-the-art models used by practitioners today.

It is also necessary to remember that the performance of the LLMs drastically relies on the prompt engineering process and the current state-of-the-art in foundational models. The authors believe that the end-to-end approach can be improved substantially both through injecting additional expert knowledge into the prompts and through the evolution of foundational models.

The authors believe that combining state-of-the-art LLMs and techniques that can be used to push their performance, as described in this paper, in combination with correlation-based methods as in Sharma and Kiciman [25], can be a fruitful area of research and a significant step toward automating end-to-end causal discovery in finance and beyond.

APPENDIX

A. Credit Spread Figures and Tables

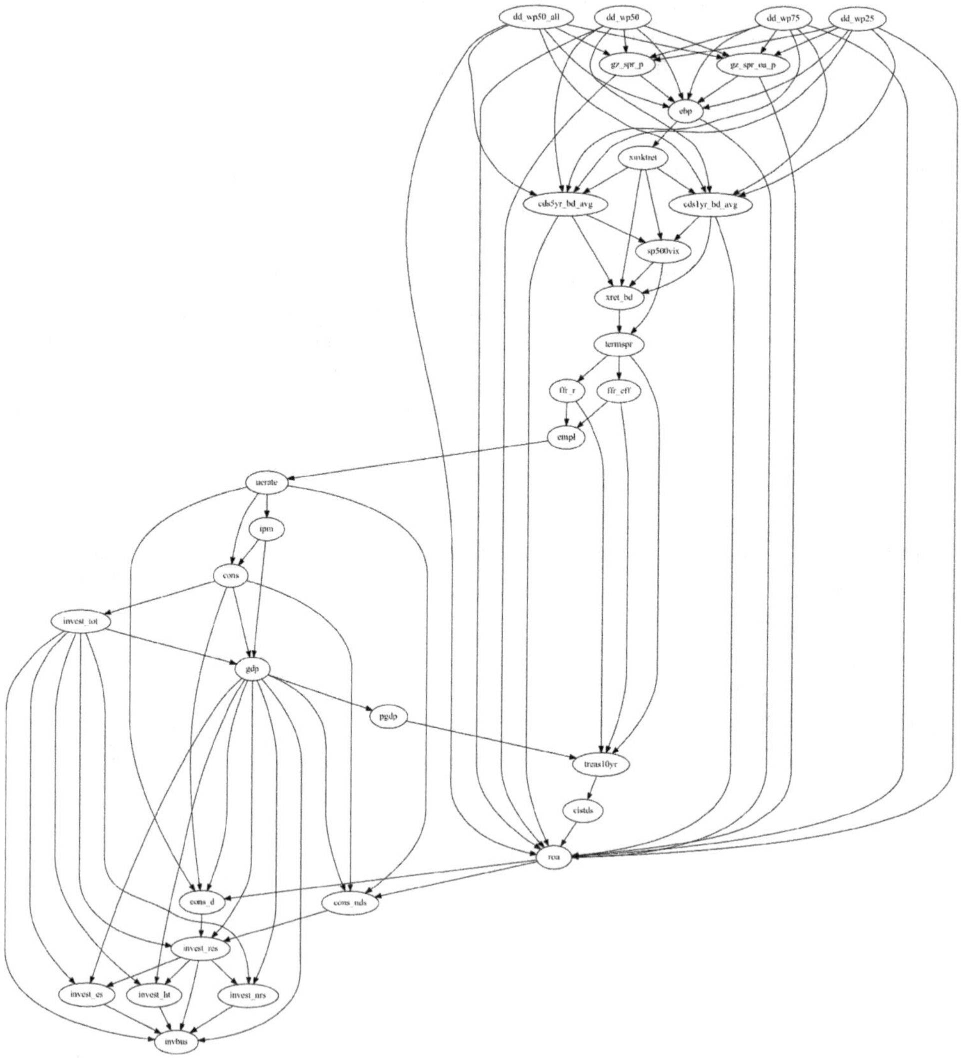

Fig. A14.1 This figure shows the credit spread DAG generated by the causal DAG generation framework before do-calculus.

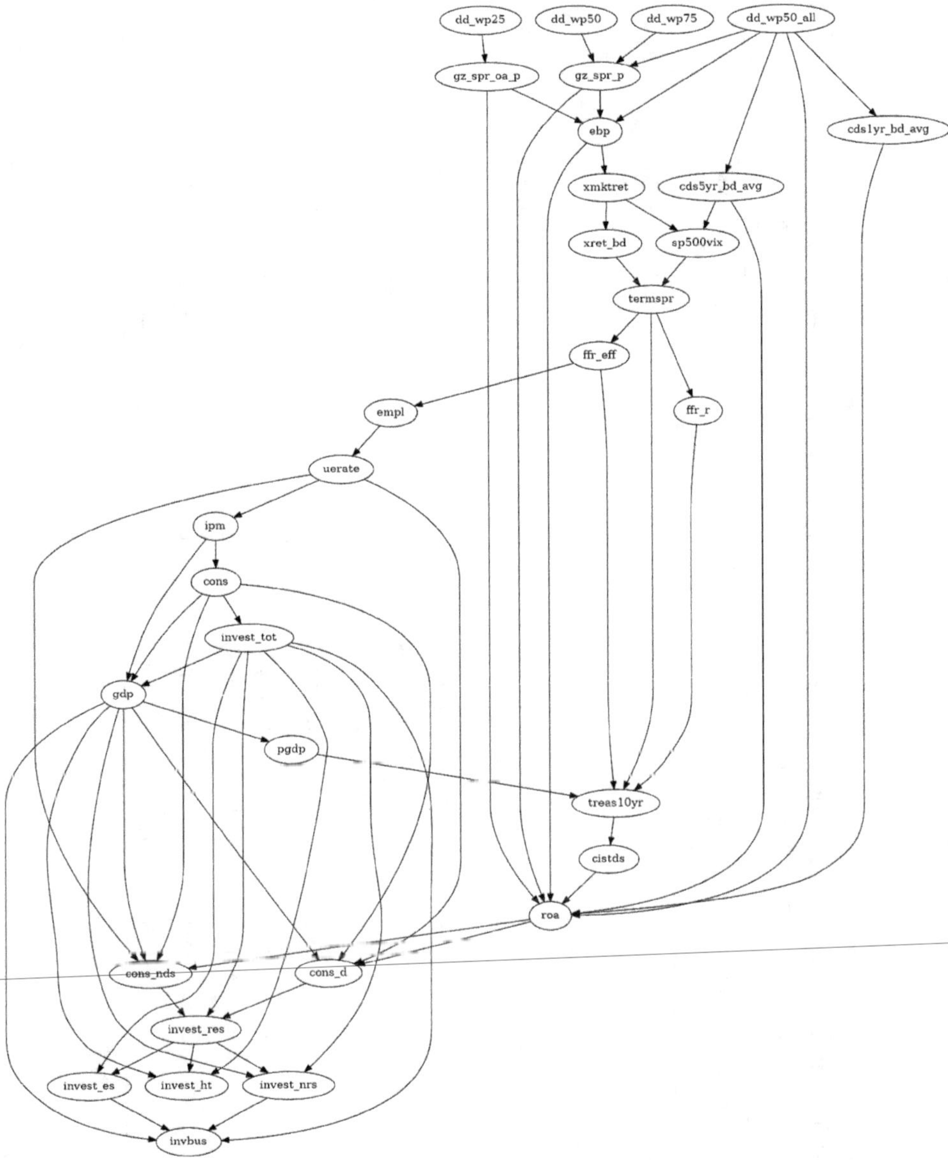

Fig. A14.2 The figure shows the process of how do-calculus removed the redundant edges within the LLM-generated causal DAG for credit spread. The original LLM-generated DAG can be found in Figure A14.1.

Table A14.1 Nonparametric causal estimation result for credit spread DAG. Each edge in the graph is designated by a start node and an end node. The effect consists of a measure of the strength of the causal relationship, the *p*-value signifies its level of significance, and the refutation *p*-value is a measure of how robust the *p*-value is by testing its significance through K-Fold stratification.

Start node	End node	Effect	*p*-value	Refutation *p*-value	Start node	End node	Effect	*p*-value	Refutation *p*-value
ebp	roa	–0.50	0.00	0.94	invest_res	invest_nrs	–0.15	0.00	0.84
ebp	xmktret	–2.20	0.00	1.00	dd_wp25	ebp	–0.29	0.16	0.96
xmktret	sp500vix	–0.36	0.00	1.00	dd_wp25	roa	0.19	0.55	0.70
xmktret	xret_bd	1.46	0.00	0.98	dd_wp25	gz_spr_p	–0.42	0.05	0.54
xmktret	cds1yr_bd_avg	0.02	0.05	0.84	dd_wp25	gz_spr_oa_p	–0.01	0.00	0.78
xmktret	cds5yr_bd_avg	0.01	0.19	0.94	dd_wp25	cds1yr_bd_avg	–0.18	0.64	0.72
sp500vix	xret_bd	–0.08	0.51	0.98	dd_wp25	cds5yr_bd_avg	–0.12	0.91	0.92
sp500vix	termspr	–0.09	0.00	0.96	dd_wp50	ebp	–0.26	0.13	0.98
xret_bd	termspr	–0.04	0.03	0.70	dd_wp50	roa	0.11	0.99	0.98
termspr	treas10yr	0.23	0.00	0.90	dd_wp50	gz_spr_p	–0.45	0.00	0.82
termspr	ffr_r	1.10	0.00	0.96	dd_wp50	gz_spr_oa_p	–0.06	0.62	0.94
termspr	ffr_eff	1.27	0.00	0.94	dd_wp50	cds1yr_bd_avg	–0.18	0.39	0.86
empl	uerate	0.00	0.00	0.96	dd_wp50	cds5yr_bd_avg	–0.09	0.93	0.94

uerate	ipm	−2.63	0.00	0.80	dd_wp75	ebp	−0.07	0.99	0.94
uerate	cons	40.35	0.05	1.00	dd_wp75	roa	0.00	0.51	0.96
uerate	cons_nds	233.01	0.00	0.96	dd_wp75	gz_spr_p	−0.29	0.01	0.78
uerate	cons_d	32.00	0.00	1.00	dd_wp75	gz_spr_oa_p	−0.08	0.09	0.90
ipm	gdp	135.04	0.00	0.92	dd_wp75	cds1yr_bd_avg	−0.06	0.93	0.80
ipm	cons	97.26	0.00	0.94	dd_wp75	cds5yr_bd_avg	−0.04	0.85	0.94
cons	gdp	1.25	0.00	0.86	dd_wp50_all	ebp	−0.47	0.00	0.86
cons	invest_tot	0.28	0.00	0.80	dd_wp50_all	roa	0.46	0.00	0.78
cons	cons_nds	0.87	0.00	0.92	dd_wp50_all	gz_spr_p	−0.54	0.00	0.56
cons	cons_d	0.11	0.00	0.90	dd_wp50_all	gz_spr_oa_p	−0.03	0.48	0.98
invest_tot	invest_res	1.02	0.00	0.86	dd_wp50_all	cds1yr_bd_avg	−0.41	0.00	0.90
invest_tot	gdp	0.63	0.00	0.90	dd_wp50_all	cds5yr_bd_avg	−0.35	0.00	0.98
invest_tot	invbus	0.44	0.00	0.88	gz_spr_p	roa	−0.84	0.00	0.98

(Continued)

Table A14.1 Nonparametric causal estimation result for credit spread DAG. Each edge in the graph is designated by a start node and an end node. The effect consists of a measure of the strength of the causal relationship, the *p*-value signifies its level of significance, and the refutation *p*-value is a measure of how robust the *p*-value is by testing its significance through K-Fold stratification. (*Continued*)

Start node	End node	Effect	*p*-value	Refutation *p*-value	Start node	End node	Effect	*p*-value	Refutation *p*-value
invest_tot	invest_es	0.76	0.00	0.80	gz_spr_p	ebp	0.08	0.00	0.74
invest_tot	invest_ht	–0.26	0.00	0.88	gz_spr_oa_p	roa	1.69	0.00	0.88
invest_tot	invest_nrs	0.39	0.00	0.88	gz_spr_oa_p	ebp	–2.46	0.00	0.88
gdp	invbus	–0.20	0.00	1.00	cds1yr_bd_avg	sp500vix	–4.53	0.22	1.00
gdp	invest_res	0.03	0.81	0.80	cds1yr_bd_avg	xret_bd	–1.23	0.51	0.98
gdp	pgdp	0.01	0.00	0.98	cds1yr_bd_avg	roa	–1.27	0.00	0.94
gdp	cons_nds	–0.08	0.03	0.98	cds5yr_bd_avg	sp500vix	16.35	0.00	0.94
gdp	cons_d	0.09	0.02	0.80	cds5yr_bd_avg	xret_bd	–1.77	0.37	0.94
gdp	invest_es	0.04	0.24	0.94	cds5yr_bd_avg	roa	–1.43	0.00	0.68
gdp	invest_ht	0.22	0.00	0.96	ffr_r	empl	691.27	0.06	0.98
gdp	invest_nrs	–0.21	0.00	0.76	ffr_r	treas10yr	0.44	0.00	0.96
pgdp	treas10yr	–0.14	0.00	1.00	ffr_eff	empl	3683.78	0.00	0.76
treas10yr	cistds	–21.59	0.00	0.94	ffr_eff	treas10yr	0.36	0.00	0.86
cistds	roa	–0.02	0.00	0.76	cons_nds	invest_res	–0.82	0.00	0.86
roa	cons_nds	36.22	0.00	0.78	cons_d	invest_res	2.11	0.00	0.96
roa	cons_d	35.81	0.00	0.86	invest_es	invbus	–0.76	0.00	0.90
invest_res	invbus	0.02	0.27	0.98	invest_ht	invbus	–2.60	0.47	0.98
invest_res	invest_es	0.31	0.00	0.98	invest_nrs	invbus	–0.96	0.00	0.96

B. LLM Clustering Prompts

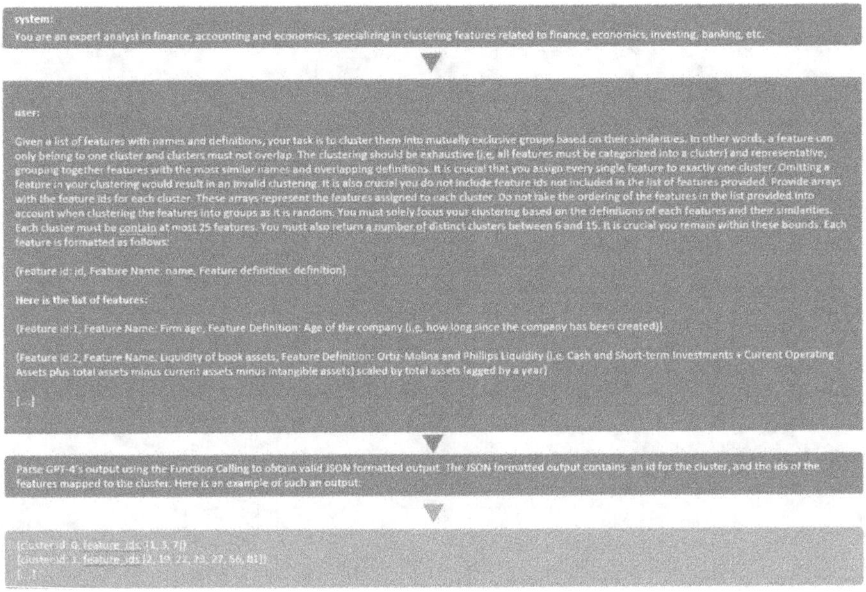

Fig. B14.1 Example of the first part of prompt 1 in the LLM clustering method. This prompts generates the initial clustering of features into mutually exclusive groups G_1.

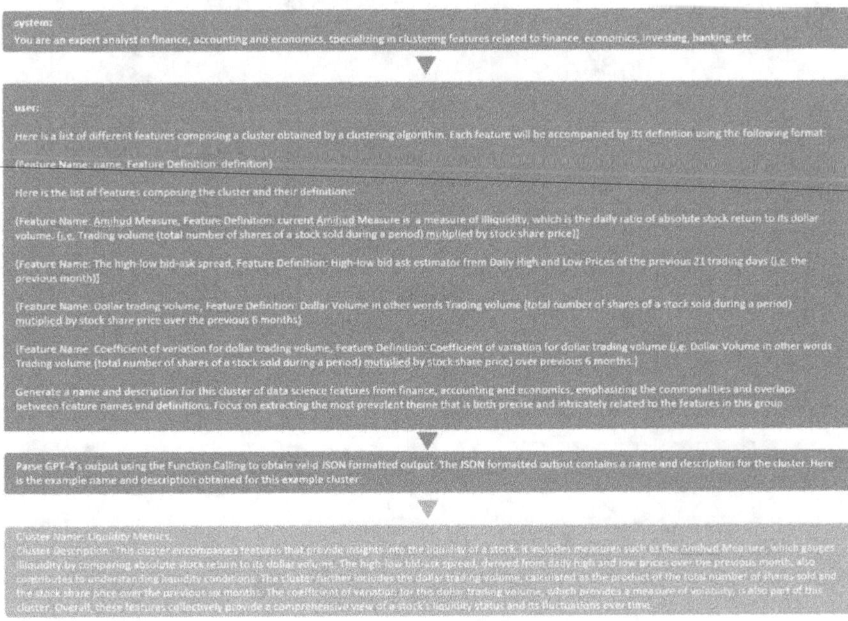

Fig. B14.2 This prompt generated names and descriptions for groups in G_1 for subsequent regrouping.

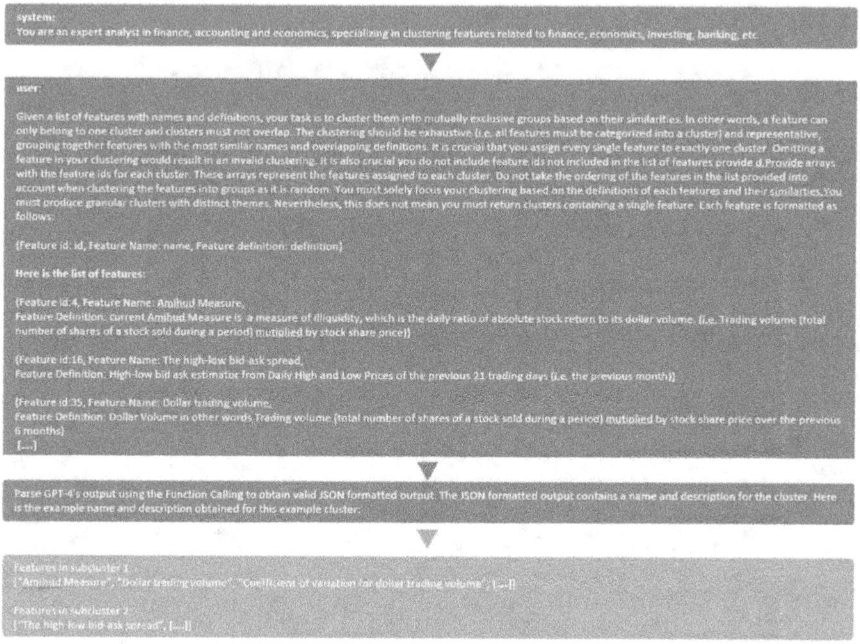

Fig. B14.3 This prompt sub-clusters each group $g \in G_1$ into a sub-grouping S_g.

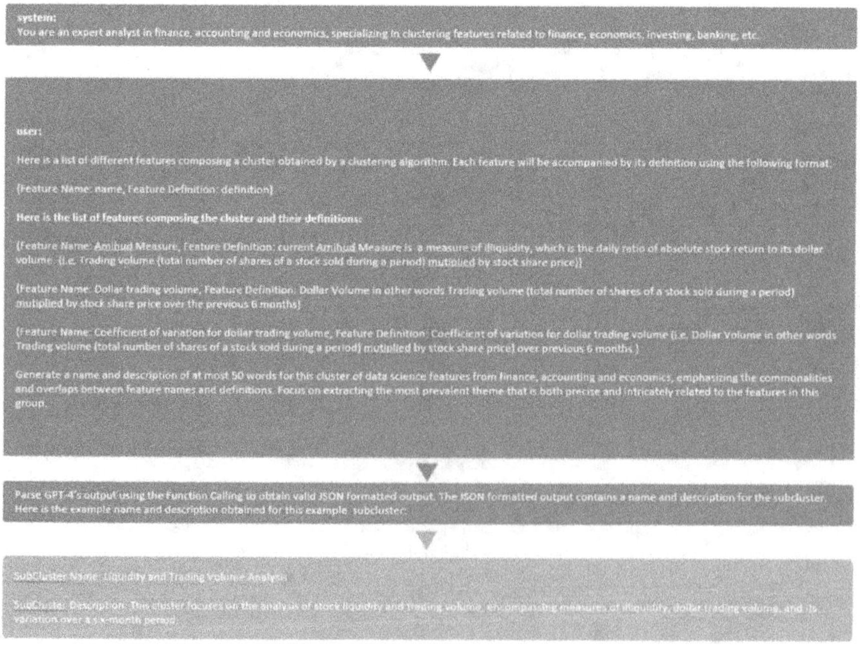

Fig. B14.4 The authors then generate names and description of the sub-groups S_g to allow for re-clustering of all sub-groups.

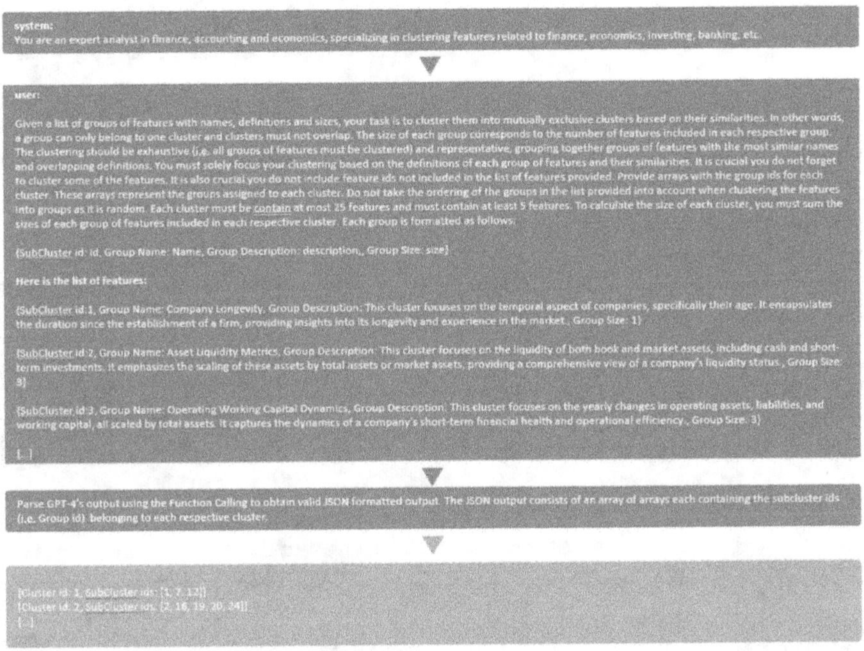

Fig. B14.5 This prompt generates the near-final grouping G_f by re-clustering all the sub-groups s, for each group g, into a brand new high-level grouping (now generated from sub-groups s rather than input features in F).

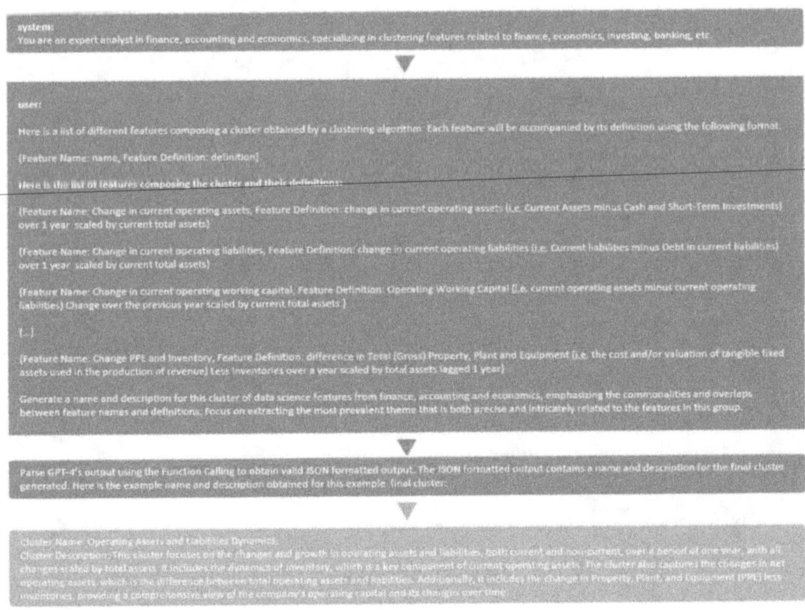

Fig. B14.6 Groups in G_f are also given names and detailed descriptions to enable final validation.

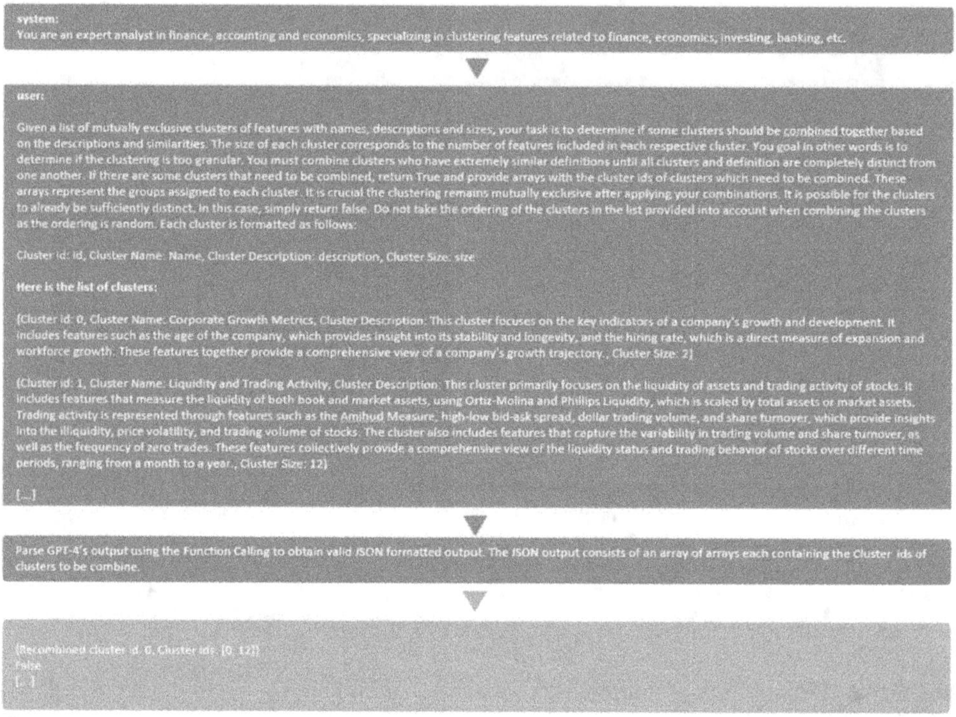

Fig. B14.7 The final grouping G_f is generated with a prompt aimed at identifying and remedying any "mistakes" in the final clustering by performing some additional merging of clusters in G_f.

C. DAG Generation Prompts

C.1. *Causal exploration prompts*

C.2. *Causal inference and causal validation prompts*

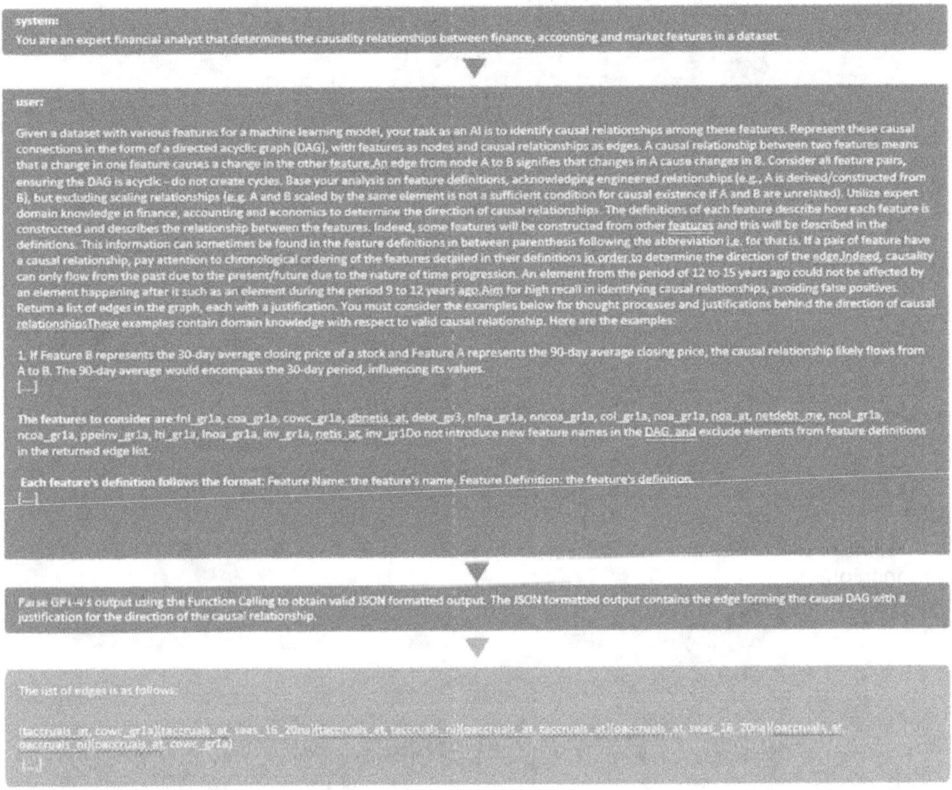

Fig. C14.1 This prompt produces candidate edges for each DAG G, by initially producing an undirected graph. It is applied once per cluster generated in the previous section.

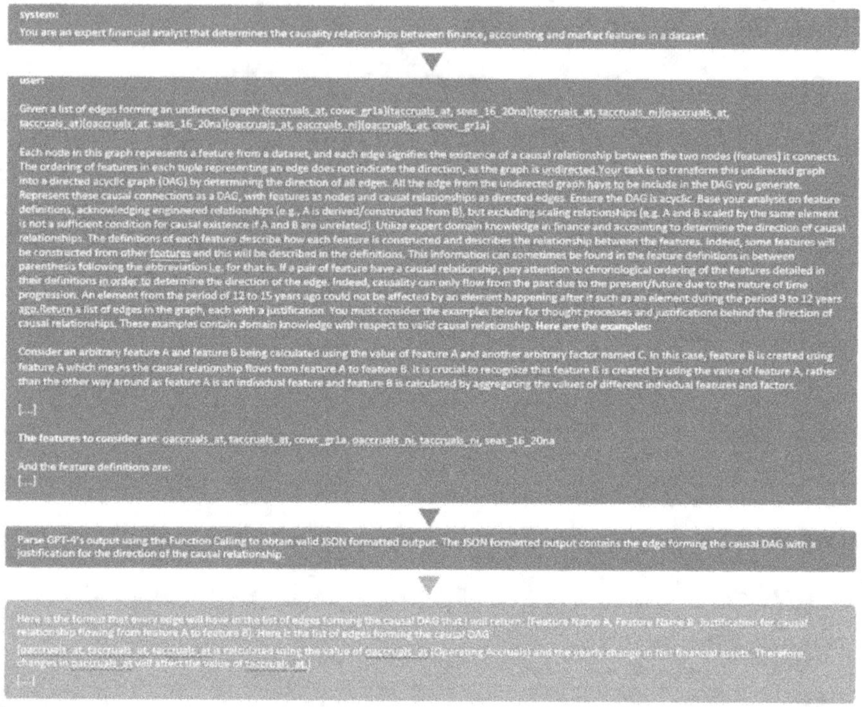

Fig. C14.2 This prompt refines the candidate edges, adding directionality to the relationships.

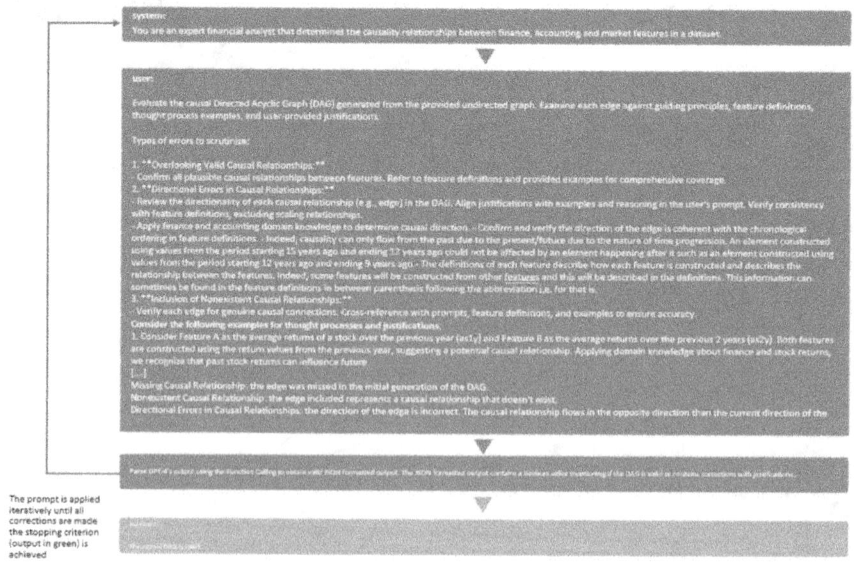

Fig. C14.3 This prompt is applied recursively to identify any logical errors in the initial DAG, running until the stopping criteria of the LLM not suggesting any more changes is reached.

References

1. M. L. de Prado, Clustered Feature Importance (Presentation Slides) (2020). Available at SSRN: https://ssrn.com/abstract=3517595.
2. M. L. de Prado, Causal Factor Investing: Can Factor Investing Become Scientific? In ed. R. Rebonato, *Elements in Quantitative Finance*. Cambridge University Press (2023). ISBN: 9781009397315. https://doi.org/10.1017/9781009397315.
3. E. F. Fama and K. R. French, Common risk factors in the returns on stocks and bonds, *J. Financ. Econ.* **33**(1), 3–56 (1993). https://doi.org/10.1016/0304-405X(93)90023-5. Available at ISSN: 0304-405X. https://www.sciencedirect.com/science/article/pii/0304405X93900235.
4. E. F. Fama and K. R. French, A five-factor asset pricing model, *J. Financ. Econ.* **116**, 1–12 (2015).
5. X. Zhang, Y. Hu, K. Xie, et al. A causal feature selection algorithm for stock prediction modeling, *Neurocomputing*. **142**(1), 48–59 (2014). https://doi.org/10.1016/j.neucom.2014.01.057.
6. D. Polakow, T. Gebbie, and E. Flint, Epistemic Limits of Empirical Finance: Causal Reductionism and Self-Reference (2023). https://arxiv.org/abs/2311.16570.
7. Z. Hao, H. Zhang, R. Cai, W. Wen, and Z. Li, Causal discovery on high dimensional data, *Appl. Intell.* **42**(3), 694–607 (2015). https://doi.org/10.1007/s10489-014-0607-0. Available at: https://dl.acm.org/doi/abs/10.1007/s10489-014-0607-0.
8. U. Hasan and M. O. Gani, KCRL: A prior knowledge based causal discovery framework with reinforcement learning. *Proc. 7th Mach. Learn. Healthc. Conf., PMLR*. **182**, 691–714 (2022).
9. A. K. Lampinen, S. C. Y. Chan, I. Dasgupta, A. J. Nam, and J. X. Wang, Passive Learning of Active Causal Strategies in Agents and Language Models (2023). https://doi.org/10.48550/arXiv.2305.16183.
10. C. Zhang, S. Bauer, P. Bennett, et al. Understanding Causality with Large Language Models: Feasibility and Opprotunities (2023). https://arxiv.org/abs/2304.05524.
11. Z. Jin, J. Liu, Z. Lyu, et al. Can Large Language Models Infer Causation from Correlation? (2023). https://arxiv.org/html/2306.05836v2.
12. E. Kıcıman, R. Ness, A. Sharma, and C. Tan, Causal Reasoning and Large Language Models: Opening a New Frontier for Causality (2023). https://doi.org/10.48550/arXiv.2305.00050.
13. N. Naik, A. Khandelwal, M. Joshi, et al. Applying Large Language Models for Causal Structure Learning in Non Small Cell Lung Cancer (2023). https://doi.org/10.48550/arXiv.2311.07191.
14. S. Long, A. Piché, V. Zantedeschi, T. Schuster, and A. Drouin, Causal Discovery with Language Models as Imperfect Experts (2023). https://doi.org/10.48550/arXiv.2307.02390.
15. T. Ban, L. Chen, X. Wang, and H. Chen, From Query Tools to Causal Architects: Harnessing Large Language Models for Advanced Causal Discovery from Data (2023). https://doi.org/10.48550/arXiv.2306.16902.
16. N. Hollmann, S. Müller, and F. Hutter, Large Language Models for Automated Data Science: Introducing CAAFE for Context-Aware Automated Feature Engineering (2023). https://doi.org/10.48550/arXiv.2305.03403.
17. X.-Y. Liu, G. Wang, H. Yang, and D. Zha, FinGPT: Democratizing Internet-scale Data for Financial Large Language Models (2023). https://arxiv.org/abs/2307.10485.
18. B. Yu, Benchmarking Large Language Model Volatility (2023). https://arxiv.org/abs/2311.15180.
19. H. Kang, and X.-Y. Liu, Deficiency of Large Language Models in Finance: An Empirical Examination of Hallucination (2023). https://arxiv.org/abs/2311.15548.

20. J. Wei, X. Wang, D. Schuurmans, et al. Chain-of-Thought Prompting Elicits Reasoning in Large Language Models, *arXiv: 2201.11903 [cs.CL].* (2023).

21. OpenAI. openai/openai-cookbook: Examples and guides for using the openai api (2023) Available at: https://github.com/openai/openai-cookbook (accessed October 30, 2023).

22. J. Pearl, Causal diagrams for empirical research, *Biometrika.* **82**(4), 669–710 (1995).

23. I. Shpitser and J. Pearl. Identification of joint interventional distributions in recursive semi-Markovian causal models. In *Proc. Twenty-First National Conference on Artificial Intelligence*, pp. 1219–1226, Menlo Park, CA: AAAI Press (2006).

24. Y. Huang and M. Valtorta, Pearl's calculus of intervention is complete. In eds. R. Dechter and T. Richardson. *Proceedings of the Twenty-Second Conference on Uncertainty in Artificial Intelligence*, pp. 217–224. Corvallis, OR: AUAI Press (2006).

25. A. Sharma and E. Kiciman, DoWhy: An End-to-End Library for Causal Inference, *arXiv preprint arXiv:2011.04216.* (2020).

26. E. F. Fama, and J. D. MacBeth, Risk, return, and equilibrium: Empirical tests, *J. Polit. Econ.* **81**(3), 607–636 (1973). Available at ISSN: 00223808, 1537534X http://www.jstor.org/stable/1831028 (accessed December 5, 2023).

27. T. I. Jensen, B. T. Kelly, and L. H. Pedersen, Is there a replication crisis in finance? *J. Finance.* **78**(5), 2465–2518 (2023). https://doi.org/10.1111/jofi.13249.

28. K. Hou, C. Xue, and L. Zhang, Replicating anomalies, *Rev. Financ. Stud.* **33**(5), 2019–2133 (Dec, 2018). https://doi.org/10.1093/rfs/hhy131. Available at ISSN: 0893–9454. eprint: https://academic.oup.com/rfs/article-pdf/33/5/2019/33710468/hhy131.pdf.

29. F. Black, and M. Scholes, The pricing of options and corporate liabilities, *J. Polit. Econ.* **81**(3), 637–654 (1973). https://doi.org/10.1086/260062.

30. R. C. Merton, On the pricing of corporate debt: The risk structure of interest rates, *J. Finance.* **29**(2), 449–470 (1974).

31. P. Collin-Dufresn, R. S. Goldstein, and J. Spencer Martin, The determinants of credit spread changes, *J. Finance.* **56**(6), 2177–2207 (2001).

32. L. Chen, P. Collin-Dufresne, and R. S. Goldstein, On the relation between the credit spread puzzle and the equity premium puzzle, *Rev. Financ. Stud.* **21**(6), 2205–2243 (2008). https://doi.org/10.2139/ssrn.687473.

33. S. Gilchrist and E. Zakrajšek, *Replication Data for: Credit Spreads and Business Cycle Fluctuations.* Nashville, TN: American Economic Association [publisher] (2012). Ann Arbor, MI: Inter-university Consortium for Political and Social Research [distributor], 2019-10-11. https://doi.org/10.3886/E112536V1.

www.ingramcontent.com/pod-product-compliance
Lightning Source LLC
LaVergne TN
LVHW011659200926
848484LV00004B/998
* 9 7 8 9 8 1 9 8 1 3 0 3 2 *